Edited by
RICHARD LAYMAN
DISCOVERING
THE MALTESE FALCON
AND SAM SPADE

The Evolution of Dashiell Hammett's
Masterpiece, Including John Huston's
Movie with Humphrey Bogart

**Kenneth Turan, *Los Angeles Times*:** "A treasure beyond price for fans of both the classic Hammett novel and the three (that's right, three) film versions of the doomed quest for a black bird. An incredible amalgam of photos, memos, letters, reviews, whatever, this will make fans of the book or the film gasp as one unexpected delight succeeds another. With this book, wonders really do never cease."

♠

**Christopher Metress, *Clues: A Journal of Detection*:** "A remarkable book, a handsome and comprehensive collection of hard-to-find material that is unlikely to be surpassed. … a visual delight as well as an intellectual pleasure."

♠

**Tom Nolan, *Los Angeles Times*:** "Amply and inventively illustrated, [it] holds a wealth of source material. There are too many other highlights in this marvelous reference work to list, let alone describe. [The novel and films are] superbly documented and appreciated by this unsurpassed reference tribute."

♠

**Michael Rogers, *Library Journal*:** (starred review) "This one-stop resource is a … dream. Highly recommended."

*Discovering The Maltese Falcon and Sam Spade* uncovers from institutional and private archives a wealth of surprises about Hammett's masterpiece, his detective Sam Spade, the three film versions of the novel, stage adaptations, Sam Spade short stories, radio presentations, and even comics.

Many of the discoveries here are previously unpublished. This book provides hundreds of rare documents and original source materials, including production notes for the three movie versions. It is illustrated with more than 200 photos, illustrations, and facsimiles. Contributors include Dashiell Hammett himself, plus Jo Hammett, Richard Layman, Mary Astor, Joseph Shaw, Dorothy Parker, John Huston, Hal Wallis, Darryl F. Zanuck, Joe Gores, William F. Nolan, and more than fifty additional writers.

THE ACE
PERFORMER
COLLECTION

"Hammett was the ace performer.
. . . He did over and over again what only
the best writers ever do at all."
*—Raymond Chandler*

THE ACE PERFORMER COLLECTION
is a series of books
by and about Dashiell Hammett

VOLUME 1:
*Lost Stories*
by Dashiell Hammett

VOLUME 2:
*Discovering* The Maltese Falcon *and Sam Spade*
edited by Richard Layman

VOLUME 3:
*Hammett's Moral Vision*
by George J. Thompson

FORTHCOMING:
*The Crime Wave: Collected Nonfiction*
by Dashiell Hammett

ADDITIONAL VOLUMES
TO BE ANNOUNCED

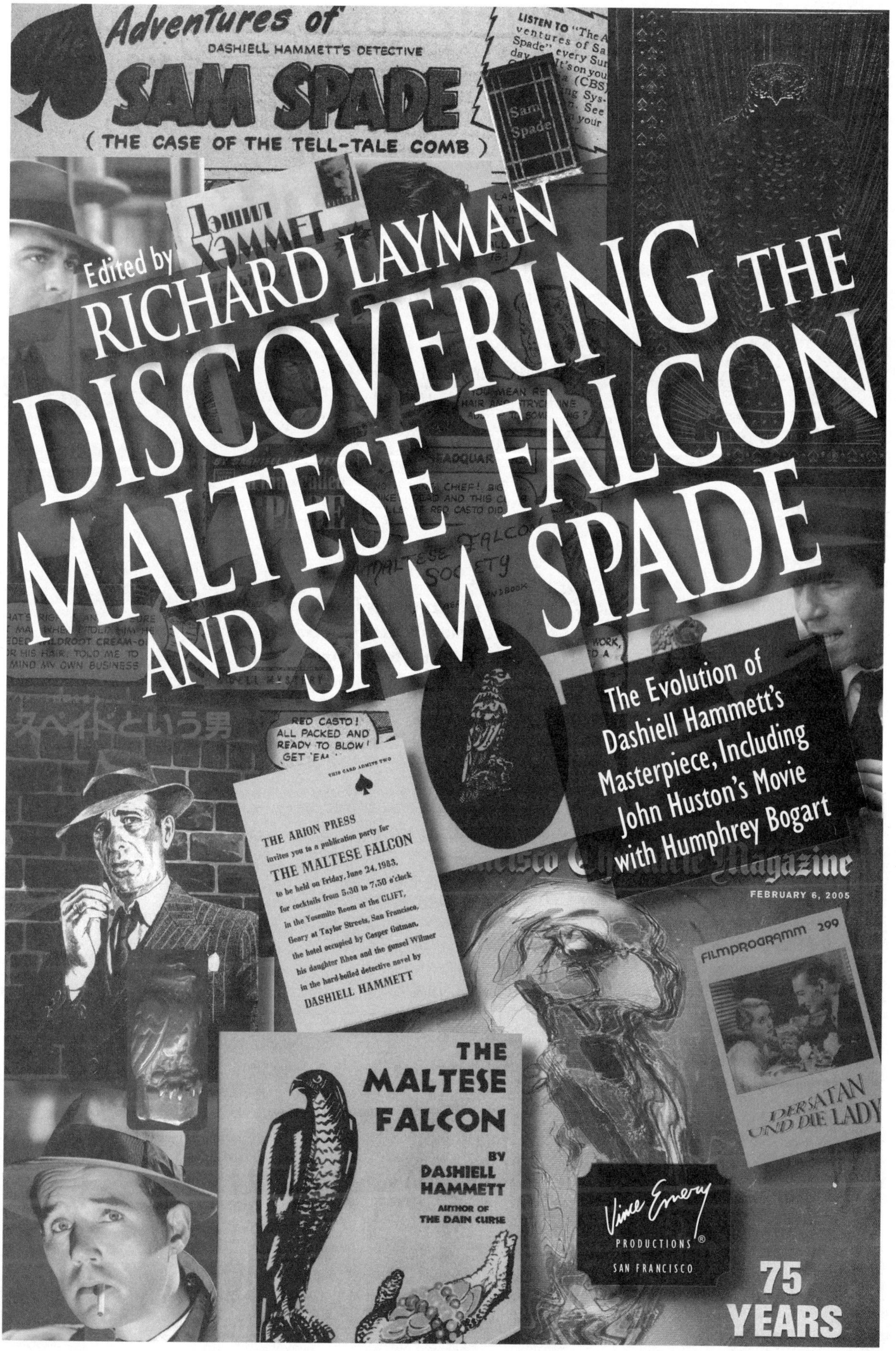
Edited by
RICHARD LAYMAN
DISCOVERING THE
MALTESE FALCON
AND SAM SPADE
The Evolution of Dashiell Hammett's Masterpiece, Including John Huston's Movie with Humphrey Bogart
Adventures of
DASHIELL HAMMETT'S DETECTIVE
SAM SPADE
( THE CASE OF THE TELL-TALE COMB )
RED CASTO! ALL PACKED AND READY TO BLOW! GET 'EM
THIS CARD ADMITS TWO
THE ARION PRESS
invites you to a publication party for
THE MALTESE FALCON
to be held on Friday, June 24, 1983,
for cocktails from 5:30 to 7:30 o'clock
in the Yosemite Room at the CLIFT,
Geary at Taylor Streets, San Francisco,
the hotel occupied by Casper Gutman,
his daughter Rhea and the gunsel Wilmer
in the hard-boiled detective novel by
DASHIELL HAMMETT
FEBRUARY 6, 2005
FILMPROGRAMM 299
DER SATAN UND DIE LADY
THE MALTESE FALCON
BY
DASHIELL HAMMETT
AUTHOR OF THE DAIN CURSE
Vince Emery
PRODUCTIONS®
SAN FRANCISCO
75 YEARS

*Discovering* The Maltese Falcon *and Sam Spade:*
*The Evolution of Dashiell Hammett's Masterpiece, Including John Huston's Movie with Humphrey Bogart*

Edited by Richard Layman

Published by Vince Emery Productions
P.O. Box 460279
San Francisco, California 94146 USA


www.emerybooks.com

**Vince Emery Productions produces books and videos
by and about established writers
to give readers a deeper, closer connection
with their favorite authors.**

Printed in USA

REVISED EDITION
Publication date: 7 September 2005

9 8 7 6 5 4 3 2 1

ISBN 0-9725898-6-4
EAN 9780972589864

# Permissions

Admits Plagiary of Novel," 26 September 1933; "British Bar Sale of Book," 28 September 1933; "Hammett's Rights Upheld in Britain," 14 October 1933; "At the Strand," 23 July 1936; Bosley Crowther, "'The Maltese Falcon,' a Fast Mystery-Thriller With Quality and Charm, at the Strand," 4 October 1941. Facsimiles of the following clippings: Announcement for the 1931 movie, 3 March 1931; "Mystery Galore," 29 May 1931.

*The New Yorker*
Reprinted by permission of Conde Nast: "Oh, Look–Two Good Books!" 25 April 1931; "Funny Coincidence Department," 13 July 1948.

William F. Nolan
"History of a Pulp: The Life and Times of *Black Mask*," in *The Black Mask Boys: Masters in the Hard-Boiled School of Detective Fiction.*

Publishers Enterprise Group
Joseph Attard, excerpts from *The Knights of Malta* (Malta: Publishers Enterprise Group, 1992).

Profiles in History (www.profilesinhistory.com)
Photos of falcon statuette on front and back outside covers, 2000.

Random House
Excerpts from *The Maltese Falcon* (New York: Knopf, 1930); excerpt from Mary Astor, *A Life on Film* (New York: Delacorte, 1971).

Harry Ransom Humanities Research Center,
      University of Texas at Austin
Facsimiles of the following Hammett manuscripts: "Seven Pages"; "The Secret Emperor"; and "The Boundaries of Science and Philosophy."

John M. Reilly
John M. Reilly, "Sam Spade Talking," *Clues,* Fall–Winter 1980.

San Francisco Historical Photograph Collection,
      San Francisco Public Library
Photographs of the following: Display case at Samuels Jewelers; Employees standing behind the counter at Samuels Jewelers; Geary Theater at Mason and Geary; Hunter-Dulin Building; Corner of Sutter and Montgomery; Main entrance to the Sir Francis Drake Hotel; Mural at Sir Francis Drake Hotel lounge by A. B. Heinsbergen; Mural depicting a Persian love legend in the lounge of the Sir Francis Drake Hotel; Bar of the Palace Hotel; Market St., east from Powell; Civic Center Plaza and City Hall, 1920s; View of downtown San Francisco from Stockton and California Streets; Intersection of Market, Ellis, and Stockton Streets; Pickwick Hotel; and Dashiell Hammett celebrating the birth of a comic-strip character, Secret Agent X-9, with acquaintances.

Milton Shaw
Milton Shaw, "Dashiell Hammett: One of the Early Masketeers." Joseph T. Shaw, introduction to *The Hard-Boiled Omnibus: Early Stories from Black Mask* (New York: Simon & Schuster, 1946). Facsimiles of the following: "An Interview with Joseph T. Shaw," *The Author and Composer,* August 1932; statements by Joseph T. Shaw in the January 1927, February 1927, 22 July 1927, October 1927, and June 1930 issues of *Black Mask;* an undated editorial in *Black Mask* responding to an attack on pulp fiction in *Vanity Fair;* a Shaw statement in *Writer's Digest,* October 1930; fan letters in Shaw scrapbook; and an affidavit of Joseph T. Shaw declaring the circumstances of his purchase rights to *The Maltese Falcon.*

*Variety*
Reviews of *The Maltese Falcon,* 2 June 1931; *Satan Meets a Lady,* 29 July 1936; and *The Maltese Falcon,* 1 October 1941.

Warner Bros. Archive, University of Southern California
Permission to reproduce the following facsimiles is granted courtesy of the USC Archives: Memo from production supervisor Darryl F. Zanuck, 2 April 1931; Manuscript of revised ending of the 1931 movie; Note from director Roy Del Ruth requesting script revisions in the 1931 movie; Final budget for the 1931 movie; Memo from Hal Wallis, 27 June 1934; Memo to Wallis from Henry Blanke, 27 May 1935; Memo from Joseph Breen, chief of the Production Code Administration, 4 June 1935; Memo from Breen, 27 November 1935; Memo in which Warner Bros.' obligation to Hammett is stipulated, 5 December 1935; Memo requesting bonus for office boy who came up with the title "Satan Met a Lady," 9 July 1936; Studio synopsis for *Satan Met a Lady,* 1 July 1936; List of possible cast choices for the 1941 movie, 19 May 1941; Memo from Breen, 27 May 1941; Final budget for the 1941 movie, 3 June 1941; Memo from John Huston to Wallis, 13 June 1941; Memo from Al Alleborn, 18 June 1941; Memo from Alleborn, 19 July 1941; First page of a contract between Hammett and Benjamin Glazer; Title page and staging note for Laurence Stallings's dramatization; and First page of the contract granting radio rights for the broadcast of the screenplay of *The Maltese Falcon,* 5 June 1946.

Western Illinois University
Christopher Metress, "Dashiell Hammett and the Challenge of the New Individualism: Rereading *Red Harvest* and *The Maltese Falcon*," and Jasmine Yong Hall, "Jameson, Genre, and Gumshoes: The Maltese Falcon as Inverted Romance," in *The Cunning Craft: Original Essays on Detective Fiction,* edited by Ronald G. Walker and June M. Frazer (Macomb: Western Illinois University, 1990).

Harry Winston, Inc.
Inside back cover photo of gold statuette, 1997.

*For Jo*

# DISCOVERING THE MALTESE FALCON AND SAM SPADE

## Table of Contents

# Introduction

Dashiell Hammett wrote *The Maltese Falcon* with the confidence of an artist. He announced his intention boldly to Blanche Knopf in a letter he wrote on 20 March 1928, when he was still planning his third novel: "I'm one of the few—if there are any more—people moderately literate who take the detective story seriously. I don't mean that I necessarily take my own or anybody else's seriously—but the detective story as a form. Some day somebody's going to make 'literature' of it (Ford's *Good Soldier* wouldn't have needed much altering to have been a detective story), and I'm selfish enough to have my hopes." His ambition was built on solid experience—as a detective, as a writer, and as a critic. Hammett's novel had many sources. It has become trite to point to his service as a Pinkerton's operative as a basis-in-fact for the novel; certainly the time he spent as a private investigator provided valuable material for him to mold, but life experience by itself is a relatively minor factor in creative expression. By the time he began *The Maltese Falcon*, Hammett had worked for six years writing short stories. He had forty-eight stories and two novels—*Red Harvest* and *The Dain Curse,* both published by Knopf in 1929—to his credit. He had experimented with characters, plot situations, and techniques that he would develop in *The Maltese Falcon;* he had carefully studied the work of other writers; and he had written about it, developing along the way his own literary aesthetic. He had read widely in science, in criminology, and especially in philosophy. He was an astute observer of his culture. All of that went into the making of *The Maltese Falcon,* along with Hammett's knowledge of criminal investigation.

*The Maltese Falcon* has endured because it rewards so many types of readers. It can be read and enjoyed as an entertaining story, or it can be reread to reveal its many complexities. It is a sophisticated detective story, a drama, a morality tale, a history lesson, and a study in cultural geography. It is a novel about honor, duty, professionalism, the philosophy of perception, the nature of authority, the power of lust, greed, betrayal, and the falsity of the American dream. The novel serves as a brilliant demonstration of literary technique—in its effective use of objective third-person narration, its memorably drawn characters, its precise dialogue, its exquisitely crafted dramatic scenes, and its unerring evocation of place. Because of its subject matter, critics have sometimes taken a narrow view, praising it as a masterful detective novel. As Sam Spade would point out, truth is what you choose to make it. *The Maltese Falcon* is a masterful detective novel, a masterful hardboiled novel; a masterful novel. It transcends facile classification.

The purpose of this volume is to provide researchers basic materials useful in studying *The Maltese Falcon.* The first chapter provides backgrounds—readings, photographs, and documents related to Hammett's life before he began writing. The second chapter presents material related to Hammett's writing life before he began work on *The Maltese Falcon,* including information about *Black Mask,* where he honed his literary skills. The third chapter is about the composition of the novel, suggesting sources in fact and in Hammett's own fiction for characters and scenes in the work. The chapter provides resources for studying the publication and reception of the novel, including reviews not previously collected. Of particular interest is the demonstration of the careful revision of the *Black Mask* text Hammett undertook in the fall of 1929 to prepare his novel for book publication. The fourth chapter is a sampling of critical response. The fifth chapter provides information about the three movies, the radio performances, and the various spin-offs from the novel. The sixth chapter lists known publications of *The Maltese Falcon* throughout to the world.

Many people deserve thanks for their assistance in the preparation of this volume, but none more than the Hammett family. Jo Hammett, her daughter Julie Rivett, and her son Evan Marshall have provided access to a wealth of material that otherwise would have been unobtainable. My debt to them is great. Milton Shaw, son of Joseph T. Shaw, has generously shared information about his father and *Black Mask*. A collector I have not had contact with in over twenty-five years, Nils Hardin, who edited the fanzine *Xenophile,* has contributed significantly to this work by providing a copy of Cap Shaw's scrapbook many years ago. The San Francisco Hammett aficionados—Vince Emery, chief among them—have done much of the legwork over the years that makes a compilation such as this possible: David Fechheimer and Joe Gores; Don Herron and Bill Arney; Mike Humbert. Keith Emmons has for the first time provided reliable information about the elusive Nell Martin.

Special collections safeguard literary treasures; they supply the lifeblood of literary study. Without the Harry Ransom Humanities Research Center at the University of Texas at Austin, the Warner Bros. Archive at the University of Southern California, the Historical Photograph Collection at the San Francisco Public Library, the Henry A. and Albert W. Berg Collection at New York Public Library, the Mills Music Library at the University of Wisconsin-Madison this book would not have been possible. Rare-book dealers have been important facilitators—not the speculators who treat books as commodities, but the dealers who know their field and see that good books make their way into the right hands. Private collectors who recognize the responsibility to share their collections contribute significantly as well. Thank you, Gary Milan. Primary materials are simply collectors' items unless they function as research tools. Matthew J. Bruccoli has done more than anyone in my generation to show us how to use them.

*—Richard Layman*

# Acknowledgments

This book was produced by Bruccoli Clark Layman, Inc. George Parker Anderson was the in-house editor.

Production manager is Philip B. Dematteis.

Administrative support was provided by Ann M. Cheschi and Carol A. Cheschi.

Accountant is Ann-Marie Holland.

Copyediting supervisor is Sally R. Evans. The copyediting staff includes Phyllis A. Avant, Caryl Brown, Leah M. Cutsinger, Melissa D. Hinton, Philip I. Jones, Rebecca Mayo, and Nancy E. Smith.

Editorial associates are Amelia B. Lacey, Michael S. Martin, Catherine M. Polit, and William Mathes Straney.

In-house prevetting is by Nicole A. La Rocque.

Permissions editor and database manager is Amber L. Coker.

Layout and graphics supervisor is Janet E. Hill. The graphics staff includes Zoe R. Cook and Sydney E. Hammock.

Office manager is Kathy Lawler Merlette.

Photography supervisor is Paul Talbot. Photography editor is Scott Nemzek.

Digital photographic copy work was performed by Joseph M. Bruccoli.

Systems manager is Donald Kevin Starling.

Typesetting supervisor is Kathleen M. Flanagan. The typesetting staff includes Patricia Marie Flanagan, Mark J. McEwan, and Pamela D. Norton. Freelance typesetter is Rebecca Mayo.

Walter W. Ross did library research. He was assisted by Jo Cottingham and the following librarians at the Thomas Cooper Library of the University of South Carolina: circulation department head Tucker Taylor; reference department head Virginia W. Weathers; reference department staff Brette Barron, Marilee Birchfield, Paul Cammarata, Gary Geer, Michael Macan, Tom Marcil, Rose Marshall, and Sharon Verba; interlibrary loan department head John Brunswick; and interlibrary loan staff Robert Arndt, Hayden Battle, Alex Byrne, Bill Fetty, Marna Hostetler, and Nelson Rivera.

# Publications by Dashiell Hammett

See also the Hammett entries in *DS 6: Hardboiled Mystery Writers: Raymond Chandler, Dashiell Hammett, Ross Macdonald; DLB Yearbooks: 1991, 1996,* and *2000;* and *DLB 226: American Hard-Boiled Crime Writers.*

BOOKS: *Red Harvest* (New York & London: Knopf, 1929);

*The Dain Curse* (New York: Knopf, 1929; New York & London: Knopf, 1930);

*The Maltese Falcon* (New York & London: Knopf, 1930; London & New York: Knopf, 1930);

*The Glass Key* (London: Knopf, 1931; New York: Knopf, 1931);

*The Thin Man* (New York: Knopf, 1934; London: Barker, 1934);

*Secret Agent X-9,* books 1 and 2 (Philadelphia: McKay, 1934);

*$106,000 Blood Money* (New York: Spivak, 1944); republished as *Blood Money* (Cleveland & New York: World, 1944); republished as *The Big Knock-Over* (New York: Spivak, 1948);

*The Battle of the Aleutians,* by Hammett and Robert Colodny (Adak, Alaska: U.S. Army Intelligence Section, Field Force Headquarters, Adak, 1944);

*The Adventures of Sam Spade* (New York: Spivak, 1944); republished as *They Can Only Hang You Once* (New York: The American Mercury/Spivak, 1949);

*The Continental Op* (New York: Spivak, 1945);

*The Return of the Continental Op* (New York: Spivak, 1945);

*Hammett Homicides,* edited by Ellery Queen (New York: Spivak, 1946);

*Dead Yellow Women,* edited by Queen (New York: Spivak, 1947);

*Nightmare Town,* edited by Queen (New York: Spivak, 1948);

*The Creeping Siamese,* edited by Queen (New York: Spivak, 1950);

*Woman in the Dark,* edited by Queen (New York: Spivak, 1951);

*A Man Named Thin,* edited by Queen (New York: Ferman, 1962);

*The Big Knockover,* edited by Lillian Hellman (New York: Random House, 1966); republished as *The Dashiell Hammett Story Omnibus* (London: Cassell, 1966);

*The Continental Op,* edited by Steven Marcus (New York: Random House, 1974);

*Woman in the Dark* (New York: Knopf, 1988);

*Nightmare Town,* edited by Kirby McCauley, Martin H. Greenberg, and Ed Gorman (New York: Knopf, 1999).

*Lost Stories* (San Francisco: Vince Emery, 2005);

**Collections:** *Complete Novels* (New York: Library of America, 1999);

*Hammett: Crime Stories and Other Writings* (New York: Library of America, 2001).

PRODUCED SCRIPTS: *City Streets,* motion picture, original screen story, Paramount, 1931;

*Mister Dynamite,* motion picture, original screen story, Universal, 1935;

*After the Thin Man,* motion picture, original screen story, M-G-M, 1936;

*Another Thin Man,* motion picture, original screen story, M-G-M, 1939;

*Watch on the Rhine,* motion picture, screenplay, Warner Bros., 1943.

OTHER: *Creeps by Night,* edited by Hammett (New York: Day, 1931; London: Gollancz, 1932);

*After the Thin Man,* in *Black Mask 5* and *Black Mask 6,* edited by Matthew J. Bruccoli and Richard Layman (San Diego, New York & London: Harvest, 1986).

**Magazine Publications:**

"The Parthian Shot," *The Smart Set* (October 1922), Anecdote;

"The Great Lovers," *The Smart Set* (November 1922), Article;

"Immortality," *10 Story Book* (November 1922), Story;

"The Barber and His Wife," *Brief Stories* (December 1922), Story;

"The Road Home," *The Black Mask* (December 1922), Story;

"The Master Mind," *The Smart Set* (January 1923), Article;

"The Sardonic Star of Tom Doody," *Brief Stories* (February 1923), Story;

"From the Memoirs of a Private Detective," *The Smart Set* (March 1923), Article;

"The Vicious Circle," *The Black Mask* (June 15, 1923), Story;

"The Joke on Eloise Morey," *Brief Stories* (June 1923), Story;

"Holiday," *New Pearsons* (July 1923), Story;

"The Crusader," *The Smart Set* (August 1923), Story;

"Arson Plus," *The Black Mask* (October 1, 1923), Story;

"The Dimple," *Saucy Stories* (October 15, 1923), Story;

"Crooked Souls," *The Black Mask* (October 15, 1923), Story;

"Slippery Fingers," *The Black Mask* (October 15, 1923), Story;

"The Green Elephant," *The Smart Set* (October 1923), Story;

"It," *The Black Mask* (November 1, 1923), Story;

"The Second-Story Angel," *The Black Mask* (November 15, 1923), Story;

"Laughing Masks," *Action Stories* (November 1923), Story;

"Bodies Piled Up," *The Black Mask* (December 1, 1923), Story;

"Itchy," *Brief Stories* (January 1924), Story;

"The Tenth Clew," *The Black Mask* (January 1, 1924), Story;

"The Man Who Killed Dan Odams," *The Black Mask* (January 15, 1924), Story;

"Night Shots," *The Black Mask* (February 1, 1924), Story;

"The New Racket," *The Black Mask* (February 15, 1924), Story;

"Esther Entertains," *Brief Stories* (February 1924), Story;

"Afraid of a Gun," *The Black Mask* (March 1, 1924), Story;

"Zigzags of Treachery," *The Black Mask* (March 1, 1924), Story;

"One Hour," *The Black Mask* (April 1, 1924), Story;

"The House in Turk Street," *The Black Mask* (April 15, 1924), Story;

"The Girl with the Silver Eyes," *The Black Mask* (June 1924), Story;

"In Defence of the Sex Story," *The Writer's Digest* (June 1924), Article;

"Our Own Short Story Course," *The Black Mask* (August 1924), Letter;

"Women, Politics and Murder," *The Black Mask* (September 1924), Story;

"Mr. Hergesheimer's Scenario," *The Forum* (November 1924), Book review;

"Who Killed Bob Teal?" *True Detective Mysteries* (November 1924), Story;

"The Golden Horseshoe," *The Black Mask* (November 1924), Story;

"Nightmare Town," *Argosy All-Story Weekly* (December 27, 1924), Story;

"Mike, Alec or Rufus," *The Black Mask* (January 1925), Story;

"Another Perfect Crime," *Experience* (February 1925), Story;

"The Whosis Kid," *The Black Mask* (March 1925), Story;

"Ber-Bulu," *Sunset Magazine* (March 1925), Story;

"Vamping Samson," *The Editor* (May 9, 1925), Article;

"The Scorched Face," *The Black Mask* (May 1925), Story;

"Genius Made Easy," *The Forum* (August 1925), Book review;

"Corkscrew," *The Black Mask* (September 1925), Story;

"Ruffian's Wife," *Sunset Magazine* (October 1925), Story;

"Caution to Travelers," *The Lariat* (November 1925), Poem;

"Dead Yellow Women," *The Black Mask* (November 1925), Story;

"The Gutting of Couffignal," *The Black Mask* (December 1925), Story;

"The Nails in Mr. Cayterer," *The Black Mask* (January 1926), Story;

"The Assistant Murderer," *The Black Mask* (February 1926), Story;

"The Creeping Siamese," *The Black Mask* (March 1926), Story;

"The Advertisement IS Literature," *Western Advertising* (October 1926), Article;

"The Cabell Epitome," *The Forum* (January 1927), Book Review;

"Poor Scotland Yard!" *The Saturday Review of Literature* (January 15, 1927), Book review;

"The Advertising Man Writes a Love Letter," *Judge* (February 26, 1927), Parody;

"The Big Knock-Over," *Black Mask* (February 1927), Story;

"Yes," *Stratford Magazine* (March 1927), Poem;

"$106,000 Blood Money," *Black Mask* (May 1927), Story;

"Goodbye to a Lady," *Stratford Magazine* (June 1927), Poem;

"The Main Death," *Black Mask* (June 1927), Story;

"Curse in the Old Manner," *The Bookman* (September 1927), Poem;

"How Samuels Campaign Developed," *Western Advertising* (October 1927), Article;

"The Cleansing of Poisonville," *Black Mask* (November 1927), Serialization of *Red Harvest*;

"Advertising Art Isn't ART–It's Advertising," *Western Advertising* (December 1927), Article;

"Crime Wanted–Male or Female," *Black Mask* (December 1927), Serialization of *Red Harvest;*

"Have You Tried Meiosis?" *Western Advertising* (January 1928), Article;

"This King Business," *Mystery Stories* (January 1928), Story;

"Dynamite," *Black Mask* (January 1928), Serialization of *Red Harvest;*

"The Literature of Advertising in 1927," *Western Advertising* (February 1928), Article;

"The 19th Murder," *Black Mask* (February 1928), Serialization of *Red Harvest;*

"The Editor Knows His Audience," *Western Advertising* (March 1928), Article;

"Black Lives," *Black Mask* (November 1928), Serialization of *The Dain Curse;*

"The Hollow Temple," *Black Mask* (December 1928), Serialization of *The Dain Curse;*

"Black Honeymoon," *Black Mask* (January 1929), Serialization of *The Dain Curse;*

"Black Riddle," *Black Mask* (February 1929), Serialization of *The Dain Curse;*

"Fly Paper," *Black Mask* (August 1929), Story;

"The Maltese Falcon," *Black Mask* (September 1929, October 1929, November 1929, December 1929, January 1930), Serialization of the novel;

"The Diamond Wager," *Detective Fiction Weekly* (October 19, 1929), Story;

"The Glass Key," *Black Mask* (March 1930), Serialization of *The Glass Key;*

"The Cyclone Shot," *Black Mask* (April 1930), Serialization of *The Glass Key;*

"Dagger Point," *Black Mask* (May 1930), Serialization of *The Glass Key;*

"The Shattered Key," *Black Mask* (June 1930), Serialization of *The Glass Key;*

"Behind the Black Mask," *Black Mask* (June 1930), Letter;

"Death and Company," *Black Mask* (November 1930), Story;

"On the Way," *Harper's Bazaar* (March 1932), Story;

"A Man Called Spade," *American Magazine* (July 1932), Story;

"Too Many Have Lived," *American Magazine* (October 1932), Story;

"They Can Only Hang You Once," *Collier's* (November 1932), Story;

"Woman in the Dark," *Liberty* (April 8, 1933; April 15, 1933; April 22, 1933), Story;

"Night Shade," *Mystery League Magazine* (October 1, 1933), Story;

"Albert Pastor at Home," *Esquire* (Autumn 1933), Story;

"The Thin Man," *Redbook* (December 1933), Bowdlerized version of the novel;

"Two Sharp Knives," *Collier's* (January 13, 1934), Story;

"His Brother's Keeper," *Collier's* (February 17, 1934), Story;

"This Little Pig," *Collier's* (March 24, 1934), Story;

"Committee on Election Rights," *The New Republic* (October 21, 1940), Letter;

"A Communication to All American Writers," *New Masses* (December 16, 1941), Public letter;

"The Thin Man and the Flack," *Click* (December 1941), Photo story;

"Help Them Now," *New Masses* (May 19, 1942), Public letter;

Letter advertisement, *Soviet Russia Today* (October 1947);

"A Man Named Thin," *Ellery Queen's Mystery Magazine* (March 1961), Story;

"The Thin Man," *City Magazine* (November 4, 1975), Fragment of unfinished novel.

Hammett also reviewed mystery fiction and true crime books for *The Saturday Review of Literature*. His reviews appear in the following issues: March 19, 1927, p. 668; April 16, 1927, p. 734; May 21, 1927, p. 846; June 11, 1927, p. 901; December 10, 1927, p. 349; February 11, 1928, p. 599; April 21, 1928, p. 810; October 13, 1928, p. 252; October 20, 1928, p. 282; October 27, 1928, p. 301; December 1, 1928, p. 440; December 8, 1928, pp. 492–493; December 22, 1928, p. 543; December 29, 1928, p. 559; January 5, 1929, pp. 576, 578; January 12, 1929, p. 591; January 26, 1929, p. 630; February 9, 1929, pp. 669–670; April 27, 1929, pp. 961–962; May 4, 1929, p. 983; September 7, 1929, p. 116; September 21, 1929, p. 164; October 5, 1929, p. 223; and October 12, 1929, p. 262.

**Newspaper Publication:**

Hammett was book reviewer for the *New York Evening Post* from April 5, 1930, to October 11, 1930. His reviews appeared in the Saturday book review section.

**The Following Stories Are Unlocated:**

"The Man Who Loved Ugly Women," *Experience* (probably before May 1925);

"A Tale of Two Women," *Saturday Home Magazine* (n.d.);

"A First Aide to Murder," *Saturday Home Magazine* (n.d.).

# Chronology

**1894**

27 May      Samuel Dashiell Hammett is born in Saint Mary's County, Maryland, to Richard and Annie Bond Hammett.

**1901**

After living less than a year in Philadelphia, the Hammetts move to 212 North Stricker Street in Baltimore, Maryland, and Dashiell enters Public School No. 72.

**1908**

September      Dashiell Hammett enters Baltimore Polytechnic Institute, where he studies for one semester before quitting school permanently to help his father run a small family business.

**1909–1915**

Hammett holds various odd jobs at such companies as the B&O Railroad and Poe and Davis Brokerage House.

**1915**

After his twenty-first birthday, Hammett becomes an operative for Pinkerton's National Detective Service.

**1918**

24 June      Hammett joins the U.S. Army, where he is a private in the Motor Ambulance Company at Camp Mead, Maryland.

6 October      Hammett suffers the first of a series of bronchial attacks, apparently related to the epidemic of Spanish influenza at the time.

**1919**

29 May      Hammett, now a sergeant, is discharged honorably from the army. He returns to his parents' house to live and works as an operative at Pinkerton's, probably part-time.

**1920**

May      Hammett moves to Spokane, Washington, where he works as a Pinkerton's operative.

6 November      Hammett is hospitalized, 100 percent disabled with pulmonary tuberculosis, at U.S. Public Health Service Hospital Number 59, also called Cushman Hospital, in Tacoma, Washington. While there he begins a romance with Josephine (Jose) Dolan, a nurse.

**1921**

21 February      Hammett leaves Cushman Hospital for USPHS Hospital Number 64 at Camp Kearney, near San Diego.

15 May      Hammett is discharged from the hospital and moves to Seattle.

June      Hammett moves to 120 Ellis Street in San Francisco.

7 July      Hammett marries Jose Dolan. He works as a Pinkerton's operative. They live at 620 Eddy Street.

16 October      The Hammetts' daughter Mary is born.

| | |
|---|---|
| 1 December | Hammett quits detective work for good. Some evidence suggests he may have continued work until February 1922. |
| **1922** | |
| February | Hammett begins a one-and-a-half-year course at the Munson School for business skills. |
| October | Hammett's first publication, "The Parthian Shot," appears in *The Smart Set,* and his work begins appearing regularly in pulp magazines, notably *Black Mask,* in December 1922. |
| December | Hammett's first appearance in *Black Mask.* In the next five years, before serialization of his first novel begins, Hammett publishes forty-three stories in pulps, most of them in *Black Mask.* |
| **1923** | |
| 1 October | "Arson Plus," Hammett's first Continental Op story, is published in *Black Mask.* |
| **1926** | |
| March | Hammett takes a job as advertising manager at Albert S. Samuels Company, Jewelers in San Francisco. After a dispute with *Black Mask* editor Philip Cody about money, Hammett quits writing for the magazine. |
| 24 May | The Hammetts' second daughter, Josephine, is born. |
| 20 July | Hammett resigns his full-time job at Samuels because of poor health, but he continues to work there part-time until late 1927. |
| October | Hammett is advised by doctors to move away from his young daughters to keep from infecting them with tuberculosis. Hammett moves first to 20 Monroe Street then to 891 Post Street, the model for Sam Spade's apartment in *The Maltese Falcon.* |
| November | Joseph Shaw becomes editor of *Black Mask.* He adopts an editorial policy promoting quality literature and encouraging a handful of favored writers to attempt longer works, including novels, which he serializes. He successfully invites Hammett to publish in *Black Mask* again and promotes his return enthusiastically. |
| **1927** | |
| 15 January | Hammett begins regularly reviewing mystery books for *The Saturday Review of Literature,* which he continues until 29 October 1929. |
| February | Hammett returns to *Black Mask* with the long story "The Big Knock-Over," which treats themes he refines in *The Maltese Falcon.* |
| **1928** | |
| 5–10 December | Time of the action in *The Maltese Falcon.* |
| **1929** | |
| 1 February | Hammett's first novel, *Red Harvest,* is published by Alfred A. Knopf. The novel had been serialized in four parts in *Black Mask* from November 1927 to February 1928. Hammett is widely reviewed and praised as an important young American writer. |
| 14 June | Hammett mails *The Maltese Falcon* to Knopf, with a request to his editor, Harry Block, that he "go a little easy on the editing." |
| 19 July | *The Dain Curse,* Hammett's second novel, is published by Alfred A. Knopf. It was serialized in *Black Mask* from November 1928 to February 1929. |
| September | The first installment of *The Maltese Falcon* is published in *Black Mask;* it is serialized in five parts through January 1930. |

| | |
|---|---|
| October | Hammett moves to New York, where he lives for a short time at 155 East Thirtieth Street, the address of his friend Nell Martin, to whom he dedicates his fourth novel. Josephine Hammett and their daughters move to Los Angeles. |

**1930**

| | |
|---|---|
| 14 February | *The Maltese Falcon* is published by Alfred A. Knopf. There are more than two thousand changes between the *Black Mask* version and the Knopf version, about two-thirds copy-editing changes, the rest rephrasing and minor rearranging of the text. The novel goes through seven printings in 1930. |
| March | The first of four parts of *The Glass Key,* Hammett's fourth novel, is published in *Black Mask*. |
| 5 April | Hammett begins a six-month stint as mystery book reviewer for the *New York Evening Post*. |
| 23 June | Hammett and Knopf sell motion-picture rights to Warner Bros. for *The Maltese Falcon*. |
| July | *The Maltese Falcon* is published by Alfred A. Knopf in England. |
| 1 August5 | Benjamin F. Glazer signs a contract with Hammett and Knopf to adapt *The Maltese Falcon* for the stage. The contract is voided on 19 December 1930. |
| 22 November | Hammett meets Lillian Hellman at a party given by Darryl F. Zanuck, then an executive at Warner Bros., with whom Hammett is negotiating a contract as a screenwriter and where Hellman works as a script reader. Hammett and Hellman commence a lifelong relationship comparable to marriage, though it is never formalized. Over the next nine years, Hammett works frequently as a movie scriptwriter. |

**1931**

| | |
|---|---|
| 3 January | Serialization of *The Maltese Falcon* begins in the *London Evening Standard*. |
| 20 January | *The Glass Key* is published by Knopf in London, three months before the first American book publication. |
| May | The first movie based on *The Maltese Falcon,* starring Ricardo Cortez as Sam Spade and Bebe Daniels as Ruth Wonderly (the Brigid O'Shaughnessy character), is released by Warner Bros. |

**1932**

| | |
|---|---|
| July | Hammett's short story "A Man Called Spade" is published in *American Magazine*. |
| October | Hammett's short story "Too Many Have Lived," featuring Sam Spade, is published in *American Magazine*. |
| November | Hammett's short story "They Can Only Hang You Once," featuring Sam Spade, is published by *Collier's*. |

**1933**

| | |
|---|---|
| 26 September | Twenty-one-year-old English author Cecil Henderson admits that his first novel is a plagiarism of *The Maltese Falcon*. |
| December | *The Thin Man,* Hammett's fifth and last published novel, appears in *Red Book*. |

**1934**

| | |
|---|---|
| January | *The Thin Man* is published by Knopf. |

**1936**

| | |
|---|---|
| July | The movie *Satan Met a Lady,* loosely based on *The Maltese Falcon,* is released by Warner Bros., starring Bette Davis as the femme fatale, Valerie Purvis, and Warren William as the detective, Ted Shayne. |

**1938**

9 October

*The Maltese Falcon* is syndicated by King Features Syndicate in the United States, appearing in *The Philadelphia Record,* among other newspapers.

**1941**

October

The movie *The Maltese Falcon,* directed by John Huston and starring Humphrey Bogart as Sam Spade and Mary Astor as Brigid O'Shaughnessy, is released by Warner Bros.

**1942**

17 September

Hammett rejoins the army as a private. Most of his duty is served in Adak, Alaska. He is discharged as a sergeant on 6 September 1945.

9 February

John Huston's movie *The Maltese Falcon* is nominated for three Academy Awards: best picture; best screenplay, by John Huston; and best supporting actor, Sydney Greenstreet.

**1943**

8 February

A radio dramatization of *The Maltese Falcon* is broadcast on the Lux Radio Theater.

**1944**

14 April

*The Adventures of Sam Spade,* including three Sam Spade stories and others by Hammett, is published by Laurence Spivak under his Bestseller Mysteries imprint. The collection is republished by Spivak in 1949 as *They Can Only Hang You Once.*

July

The first American mass-market paperback edition of *The Maltese Falcon* is published by Pocket Books.

**1945–1946**

Laurence Stallings writes a complete script for "Here's to Crime," a stage adaptation of *The Maltese Falcon.* On 7 February 1946 his agent voids the contract, claiming the adaptation was never completed.

**1946**

5 June

Hammett is elected president of the Civil Rights Congress of New York, a position he holds until the mid 1950s. During his term he works actively in support of the Communist Party and various causes the party advocates.

12 July

The radio serial *The Adventures of Sam Spade* premieres. It is broadcast on CBS until 1949 and on NBC from 1949 to 1951.
*The Maltese Falcon* comic book, Feature Book no. 48, is published by David McKay.

**1948**

28 May

The U.S. Court of Appeals affirms Hammett's literary rights to the characters in *The Maltese Falcon* in a suit brought by Warner Bros. claiming the radio serial based on the novel breached the rights granted them in their 1930 contract with Hammett.

9 June

Hammett files a petition in U.S. District Court to have his rights to the character Sam Spade affirmed.

**1951**

9 July

Hammett refuses to testify before a U.S. District Court judge about his activities on behalf of the Communist front organization the Civil Rights Congress of New York. He is sentenced to six months in jail for contempt of court. Radio serials based on his work are canceled immediately, and his books are withdrawn from publication in the United States.

9 December

Hammett is released from the Federal Correctional Institute in Ashland, Kentucky. The Internal Revenue Service (IRS) promptly attaches his income in lieu of payment of a debt for back taxes and penalties of $111,008.60. His health is failing and he is broke.

| 28 December | Warner Bros. sues the broadcaster, sponsor, producer, and director of the radio series "The Adventures of Sam Spade," claiming copyright infringement because Warner bought all broadcast rights in 1930. |

**1953**

| 26 March | Hammett testifies before Joseph McCarthy's Senate subcommittee investigating the purchase of books by Communists for State Department libraries abroad. |

**1961**

| 10 January | Hammett dies at Lenox Hill Hospital in New York City. |
| 13 January | Hammett is buried at Arlington National Cemetery. |

**1963**

| 18 November | Lillian Hellman and Arthur W. A. Cowan purchase Hammett's copyrights, which had been attached by the U.S. government for payment of federal taxes and penalties amounting at the time of his death to $163,286.46, free of all liens, for $5,000 at an auction arranged by her with the consent of the IRS. |

**1984**

| 30 June | Lillian Hellman dies. In her will she sets up the Literary Property Trust of Dashiell Hammett, with three trustees: Peter Feibleman, Richard Poirer, and William Abrahams. Though ostensibly for the benefit of Hammett's daughters, the trust stipulates that 40 percent of the gross receipts of Hammett's literary property go to the trustees, with no limit on expenses. After agents' fees of 15 percent of gross receipts and exorbitant accounting and legal fees deducted from the remaining money, little is left for Hammett's family. |

**1989**

The 1941 movie version of *The Maltese Falcon* is selected for inclusion in the National Film Registry at the Library of Congress.

**1995**

| March | In a compromise agreement, the trustees of the Literary Property Trust of Dashiell Hammett agree to cede all income from Hammett's novels to his heirs. |

**1998**

The 1941 version of *The Maltese Falcon* is named one of the 100 Greatest American Movies by the American Film Institute.

The editorial board of The Modern Library names *The Maltese Falcon* one of the 100 best novels in English of the 20th century.

**2003**

| February | Richard Poirer and Peter Feibleman, the two surviving trustees of the Literary Property Trust of Dashiell Hammett, agree to resign in favor of replacements designated by the Hammett family. |

**2005**

| 10 February | The United States Senate approves a resolution introduced by Senator Dianne Feinstein commemorating the 75th anniversary of *The Maltese Falcon* and recognizing it as a "great American crime novel." |

| 19 March | 891 Post Street, where Hammett lived when he wrote *The Maltese Falcon* and where he set Sam Spade's apartment, is designated a National Literary Landmark by Friends of Libraries USA. |

# Hammett's Detective Days

## Biographical Overview

**Dashiell Hammett, 1894–1930**
Richard Layman
*Selected Letters of Dashiell Hammett* (New York:
Counterpoint, 2001), pp. 3–7

Samuel Dashiell Hammett was born on May 27, 1894, in rural Saint Mary's County, Maryland. His father, Richard Hammett, was an opportunist who tried his hand at several occupations, none very successfully. His mother, Annie Bond Dashiell, was trained as a nurse, but respira- tory illness kept her at home most of the time—that and the demands of her three children, Dashiell, his older sister, Reba, and his younger brother, Richard, called Dick. At the time Dashiell was born, his family was living with his pater- nal grandfather on a plot of land the Hammetts called "Hopewell and Aim."

When Dashiell was six, his father failed in a bid for political office after an acrimonious campaign and felt com- pelled to leave the county. He took his family to Philadel- phia, where the prospects did not meet his expectations, and, after a year, they turned to Mrs. Hammett's mother for support, moving in with her in the house she rented in

*Annie Bond and Richard Hammett, with their children, Dashiell, Richard, and Reba, circa 1908
in Baltimore (courtesy of Judi Hammett)*

Baltimore. Richard Hammett was struggling to support the family and Dashiell dropped out of high school after one semester to help. He never returned to the classroom. His early education came from the streets, from his avid reading, and from a series of odd jobs he held during his teens. When he turned twenty-one, he began what he considered a career as an operative for Pinkerton's National Detective Agency. The job suited his intelligence, his sense of adventure, and his curiosity.

Hammett was still living with his parents in 1918 when he took leave from Pinkerton's to join the army during World War I. Though he did not travel more than about fifteen miles from his home during the war, the experience turned his life upside down. He was stationed at Camp Mead, Maryland, and assigned to a Motor Ambulance Company, transporting wounded soldiers returning from Europe. The worldwide Spanish Influenza epidemic was especially evident in the United States at military installations, where soldiers returning from foreign service spread the disease that killed more people during the war years than warfare did. In 1919, Hammett was struck, and he spent the rest of his military service recuperating.

"I have always had good health until I contracted influenza, complicated by bronchial pneumonia treatment," Hammett told a doctor during his pre-discharge medical exam on 24 May 1919. The army pronounced his tuberculosis "arrested," and he was able to resume his pre-war occupation as an operative for the Pinkerton's National Detective Service, working first in Baltimore, and then, after the beginning of 1920, in Spokane, Washington. Eighteen months after his discharge, however, his TB flared up again and he "broke down," in the words of a medical report. In November 1920 Hammett was among the first patients admitted to the newly opened Cushman Institute, a U.S. Public Health Service hospital in Tacoma, Washington.

Josephine Dolan, a pretty twenty-three-year-old from Anaconda, Montana, was among the staff of half a dozen nurses in the respiratory illnesses ward at Cushman. She and Hammett struck up a friendship that quickly became amorous. (She was never convinced that his tuberculosis was confirmed, despite the doctors' reports, and so discounted the possibility of becoming infected herself, a measure of how lovestruck she was.) Within a month they were dating; within two they were intimate. By the end of his third month, Hammett was among a group of tubercular patients transferred south to U.S.P.H.S. facilities in a warmer, drier climate. She stayed behind; he was admitted to the hospital at Camp Kearney near San Diego, and they

continued their courtship by mail. He was twenty-six years old when he began writing to Josephine Dolan in February 1921. They apparently did not know she was pregnant.

When Hammett was discharged from Camp Kearney in May 1921, he went first to see her in Spokane, stopping at Cushman to complain about his labored breathing. He then went to San Francisco, to search for an apartment where they could begin their married life. He and Josephine, whom he called Jose (pronounced "Joe's"), were married in the rectory at St. Mary's Cathedral in San Francisco on 7 July 1921. Their daughter Mary Jane was born on 16 October. Hammett returned to work as a private detective, but soon found he was not physically fit for the job. He stood six feet one and a half, weighed 135 pounds, and suffered from dizziness, shortness of breath, and chest pains on exertion. He told a U.S.P.H.S. nurse that he was employed as a detective "at intervals" in the fall of 1921, earning $21 per week when he worked, to supplement his disability income of $40 a month. By the end of December he was too sick to work at all. His disability rating was revised to 100 percent, but his pension, though increased to $80 a month, barely paid the rent. And he had a family to support.

Hammett began vocational rehabilitation at Munson's Business College in February 1922, training as a reporter. That fall, he began writing fiction on spec to supplement his income and soon after-

---

*Hammett provided this biographical statement in a letter to the editor.*

I was born in Maryland, between the Potomac and Patuxent rivers, on May 27, 1894, and was raised in Baltimore.

After a fraction of a year in high school—Baltimore Polytechnic Institute—I became the unsatisfactory and unsatisfied employee of various railroads, stock brokers, machine manufacturers, canners, and the like. Usually I was fired.

An enigmatic want-ad took me into the employ of Pinkerton's National Detective Agency, and I stuck at that until early in 1922, when I chucked it to see what I could do with fiction writing.

In between, I spent an uneventful while in the army during the war, becoming a sergeant; and acquired a wife and daughter.

For the rest, I am long and lean and grayheaded, and very lazy. I have no ambition at all in the usual sense of the word; like to live as nearly as possible in the center of large cities, and have no recreations or hobbies.

—*Black Mask* (November 1924): 128

ward reported to a visiting nurse that he was writing stories four hours a day. The pulp magazines were an easy market to crack, and though the pay was only a penny or two a word, an industrious writer could make thirty or forty dollars a month. Hammett had his experience as a private detective to mine for material, and he soon became a favorite of detective pulps readers for his tough stories that had the ring of truth. He churned them out at the rate of nearly one a month, and the paychecks bought groceries.

That was how he lived until 1926, when Jose became pregnant again. Now Hammett needed more money, and when he failed to get it from the editors at *Black Mask* magazine, his most reliable publisher, he decided to venture again into the workforce. This time, he determined to draw on his writing ability and the journalistic skills he learned in his vocational training course. He answered a want ad for an advertising copy writer/ad manager at Albert S. Samuels Jewelers. The pay was $350 a month–about four times the income from his writing and pension combined. The job seemed perfect for him. Samuels was a congenial boss, and the social aspects of the job were very attractive to a man who had been a virtual shut-in for most of the past six years. Hammett enjoyed the freedom of the workplace; he enjoyed it too much. He began drinking heavily, spending too many evenings in speakeasies with cronies. Within six months the pace caught up with him. He collapsed at his office in a pool of blood, suffering from hepatitis and a recurrence of tuberculosis. Once again he was unable to hold a full-time job. That was his situation in winter 1926–1927, when Joseph Shaw, the new editor at *Black Mask* magazine, wrote to Hammett with ambitious plans for revamping the magazine with a stable of star writers.

Shaw was a promoter with business savvy. He understood that the fortunes of his magazine were directly related to the success of his writers. He also recognized that readers respect novelists more than short-story writers, so he encouraged his stable to undertake longer works and to aspire to book publication. Meanwhile, he began promoting them as an elite group pioneering a new type of mystery fiction. Shaw bragged that Herbert Hoover, J. P. Morgan, and A. S. W. Rosenbach read *Black Mask* and that Hammett's contributions to the magazine were some of the best mystery fiction ever published. Soon Hammett had completed his first novel and submitted it unsolicited to Alfred A. Knopf, Publishers, who had just launched an imprint called Borzoi Mysteries. Within a year's time, Hammett

had emerged as the most celebrated young mystery novelist in America, and respected reviewers were declaring him as good if not better than Ernest Hemingway.

While Hammett's reputation soared, his personal life deteriorated. When his second daughter was born, health service nurses advised that Jose and the girls should not share quarters with the tubercular writer who was sometimes too ill to walk unassisted to the bathroom. They went to Montana to visit Jose's relatives in the fall of 1926, then took an apartment fifteen miles north of San Francisco, where Hammett visited them on weekends. Such conditions made married life difficult; soon even the pretense of a marriage was abandoned. Hammett loved and supported his family, but he looked elsewhere for companionship and found it easily. His brief experience with family life had proven what he had clearly suspected: that it was not for him, especially when so many opportunities were available. He had a career to develop that required all his energies.

Within two years after his collapse at the jewelry store, Hammett had written three novels. *Red Harvest* and *The Dain Curse* were among the most prominently reviewed books of 1929, and *The Maltese Falcon* was recognized as possessing, in the words of one reviewer, "the absolute distinction of real art." Hammett was not satisfied, though. He saw greater opportunities in the writing game.

In 1927, David O. Selznick introduced sound to motion pictures with *The Jazz Singer*. By Valentine's Day 1930, when *The Maltese Falcon* was published, studios had already abandoned silent films because they recognized the enormous audience for talkies. That, in turn, created an unprecedented need for writers to provide scripts. The money was huge, even during the Depression, and Hammett capitalized on the opportunity to turn his reputation as a writer into pure gold. He left San Francisco for New York in the fall of 1929 and kept steady company with writer-musician Nell Martin, to whom he dedicated *The Glass Key* in 1931. They both had interests in Hollywood. *Roadhouse Nights*, a movie adaptation of Hammett's *Red Harvest*, was released by Paramount in February 1930, and her novel *Lord Byron of Broadway* was released as a movie by M-G-M in March. That year Hammett claimed to be making $800 a week–twice as much each month as the average American worker made in a year. And he spent it all, on starlets and hotel suites and limousines and chauffeurs and bootleg liquor and speakeasy nights. When he had money left over, he gave handouts to his friends.

## Working as a Detective

*Pinkerton's National Detective Agency, founded in 1850, set the standard for criminal investigation in the United States in the days before there were well-organized local police forces and before there was a national police force of any description. Pinkerton's introduced the first national directory of criminals, was a pioneer in the use of fingerprints to identify criminals, and used wanted posters to enlist the aid of citizens in tracking lawbreakers. With the rise of municipal police forces and the institution of the U.S. Secret Service to help track criminals who traveled from one jurisdiction to the other, Pinkerton's agents assumed the role of private policemen hired by clients who could afford to buy supplemental police protection and investigation, often in high-profile cases in which they operated alongside of, if not in opposition to, local authorities. Particularly in the West, Pinkerton's was employed by industrial bosses to break strikes, often violently. In the East after the turn of the century Pinkerton's concentration was on felonies that required professional investigation. Hammett used Pinkerton's as the model for his Continental Detective Agency, drawing on such legendary Pinkerton's operatives as Charles Siringo and James McParland. The deliberate investigative procedure that characterizes Sam Spade was drawn from the Pinkerton's model.*

### Pinkerton's in the Twentieth Century

James D. Horan

*The Pinkertons: The Detective Dynasty That Made History*
(New York: Crown, 1967), pp. 490–502

As he wrote to his brother, Bob Pinkerton was determined to make the nation's racetracks free of crime. In 1906, with the ringers and the syndicate defeated, he ordered his operatives to concentrate on pickpockets, forgers, confidence men, and other petty criminals. During the Gravesend meets he was a familiar sight, dressed in a tweed suit and wearing his porkpie-style hat, making his way through the crowds, an operative close by, ready to pounce on a pickpocket lifting a wallet, a known counterfeiter "pushing the queer," or one of Ben Chilson's ringers, hoping he would miss "meeting the Eye." After a day's tour of the track, a feature writer reported:

> There is no place where the swell thieves go more constantly than the races, and probably in the great crowds there are thousands of crooks of one kind or another. Yet robberies are scarcely ever heard of. The reason is that Bob Pinkerton has established the most perfect of systems. Every professional thief knows that if he committed a robbery at the racetrack he would never be safe again. He would be pursued to the end, even his closest friends might betray him, while no pawn broker or other receiver would deal with him. He

*The Continental Trust Building, at the corner of Baltimore and Calvert Streets, headquarters of the Baltimore offices of the Pinkerton's National Detective Service when Hammett was an operative. The building is the source of the name for Hammett's fictional Continental Detective Agency.*

could commit burglary the night before but he could not rob at the track.[1]

Robert's drive to clean up the nation's racetracks prompted poetry, assassination attempts, and editorial criticism. The New York *Recorder* published a long jingle that their track expert reported was being sung in the grandstands:

> Sing High for the bountiful poolroom man
> Sing low for the politic poolroom man
> But oh, breathe not the name of the Pinkerton man
> In the sensitive ear of the poolroom man!

When the powerful *Sporting World* complained in an open letter to Bob Pinkerton that young hoodlums were annoying "young ladies" leaving the tracks, Pinkerton guards refused to admit them the following day.

14

But the New York *World* indignantly pointed out that the hoodlums should be readmitted "because they are all the sole support of their aged mothers."

When the Eastern Jockey Club, on the recommendation of Pinkerton, continued to pass stricter rules to drive the criminal element from the tracks, the battered New York syndicate decided that Robert had to be killed. A gunman was hired, and for days stalked the burly detective as he made his way through the crowds at the Gravesend track. In July, 1906, he was standing near the rail with a friend from Buffalo when he suddenly turned his head. His friend gave a sharp cry, and dropped, blood pouring from his forehead. Doctors later extracted a rifle slug from under the skin. The bullet, police surmised, had missed the huge Pinkerton as he turned, and glanced off the forehead of his smaller friend.

Every week underworld informants passed along information about a new murder plot against Robert, who shrugged them off. One track plunger he had driven from the Gravesend track was Steve L. Hommidieu, a quick-tempered Creole who swore to kill Pinkerton. During the New Orleans Fair Grounds meet, he followed Pinkerton into Lomothe's, a famous restaurant of its day. "You had me ruled off down east, didn't you?" he shouted as he followed the detective to a table.

Pinkerton took his seat, studied the menu for a moment, then looked up. "Yes, I did. I chased you away because you were corrupting jockeys and owners and I caught you with the goods."

The big Creole pulled a gun, but Pinkerton drove his fist into L'Hommidieu's stomach, knocked him over a table, and "delivered him to the local authorities."

Robert also expanded the Pinkerton's guard and security forces to cover international expositions and world's fairs, a practice that is carried on to this day. The Nashville, Tennessee, Centennial Fair in 1897, the Trans-Mississippi at Omaha in 1898, Pan American at Buffalo, Jamestown in 1907, San Francisco, San Diego, Chicago in 1892—all were protected by the Pinkertons.

Pinkerton operatives were also a part of the great days of circuses, both in the United States and in Europe, where the Pinkerton's identification card read:

G. V. Bird
De la
New York, EUA
Agent pour
Le Barnum & Bailey
Plus Grande Cirque de Monde

Attention was drawn to the card's autre côte, listing officers, divisions, and European branch

*One of the two gilded falcons over the north entrance to the Continental Trust Building in Baltimore. There are smaller falcons at the bottom edges of all the windows in the building.*

offices of the Agency and the important fact of "telephone connections."

The operative's duties, as outlined by Robert Pinkerton, were first to get in touch with the police officers in the places where the circus was to play, and establish friendly relations: "The detective usually rides on the first or third train . . . detective on the first [train] should watch for rubbernecks or local ruffians who will swarm into enclosure or horse tents." On European trips the operatives were warned to expect "very little help from the police who leave their posts and sneak into the tent to see the performance."

Criminal bands followed the circus, and the operative assigned usually maintained a string of informants along the route the wagons were using. The Wells Brothers, Ringling Brothers, Hagenbeck-Wallace—all the great circuses of the late nineteenth and early twentieth centuries before the mergers, as well as Buffalo Bill's Wild West Show—were protected by the Pinkertons. The "route book" of the operative attached to the Buffalo Bill

*Hammett in Baltimore, circa 1917, when he was working as a Pinkerton's detective (courtesy of Judi Hammett)*

had to cancel his act, while in Fort Wayne, at the peak of an immense business." Little Mary, a Sioux papoose, died and was buried in the local cemetery, with all hands attending. Impassive Sioux chiefs and warriors, canvasmen and strikers, and perhaps Buffalo Bill in his buckskins and shoulder-length hair crowded the rural cemetery to watch the tiny coffin being slowly lowered. It was a rough season, the operative reported to Robert, so rough that "William Baker, the boy giant," packed his bags, and left.

William and Robert heard from an old adversary in those years, Sophie Lyons, the Lady from Lyons, as the Sûreté called her, the faithful friend of Adam Worth, Baron Shinburn, and other masterful thieves of the Victorian Age. Although they arrested her with regularity, she never failed to call on Robert in New York or William in Chicago whenever she visited those cities. Five foot two, with the aloof air of a president of a DAR, Sophie joined the staff of the New York *World* in the winter of 1897 to become America's first society columnist. Sophie Lyons's total take from blackmailing, swindling, extorting, and shoplifting was about $1,000,000, the Pinkertons estimated.[3]

In 1907, two years before the Pinkertons severed relationship with the American Bankers Association, the Agency had 2,000 employees and safeguarded 4,000 banks in the United States through the association. The Houston *Post* had published the story of the two bank robbers who returned the $50,000 in negotiable bonds they had stolen rather than be pursued by the Pinkertons. The penciled notation to the bank president read:

"Put your ABA sign out where your customers can see it."[4]

Both Pinkertons loved to travel abroad, and in the 1890's and 1900's they frequently toured Europe and the Orient. In the winter of 1907, Robert began to complain about his health, "but usually with a joke," as his New York superintendent recalled. At the urging of William, he finally agreed to visit Germany's Nauheim baths. In August, accompanied by an old male crony, Florence Sullivan, former Washington correspondent for the Chicago *Call,* he left for Europe on the liner *Bremen*.

A few days later, a cablegram was delivered to William at Saratoga, notifying him that Robert had been found dead in his cabin. Two large scrapbooks testify to the news coverage of Pinkerton's death. Every large newspaper in the country and throughout Europe hailed Robert as one of the world's greatest detectives; columns recalled his exploits in

show, 1899, gives a fascinating picture of the pathos, difficulties, and humor of early American show business.[2] It covers the period from April 17th to October 14th, ending at Urbana, Ohio. There are log entries, mileage, railroad connections, and so on, and Buffalo Bill's famous "Order of Parade:" "Col. W. F. Cody and his outriders, Sioux Indians, German Garde-Kurassiers of his Majesty, Kaiser Wilhelm II; Electric Light Engine, No. 1, group of Riffian Arabs . . . famous Cowboy Band Mounted, Old Deadwood Stage Coach . . ."

In May, the operative recorded that in Richmond, Indiana, a howling twister came up suddenly to "make the lot very rough." Battling the billowing, soggy canvas, a man fell from a wagon top and was killed. Johnnie Baker, the famous sharpshooter, injured his hand in Chester, Pennsylvania, "and

*Pinkerton's badge from the era when Hammett was an operative (Collection of Richard Layman)*

such cases as the Northampton bank robbery, his capture of the giant Red Leary, and his fight to clean up the American racetracks.

At the services, held in Brooklyn's First Reformed Church, crowds overflowed into the streets. In Chicago five moving vans took the floral wreaths to Graceland Cemetery, and seven carriageloads of roses were distributed to the city hospitals at William's request.

Not only the famous but also the infamous were among his mourners. One newspaper reporter talked to an old bank robber Robert had befriended when the thief was down in his luck. His eulogy was, "He was a square one."[5]

After the death of Robert, his son, Allan II, succeeded to his father's interest in the Agency. Allan, young and energetic, but always overshadowed by his famous uncle, made many improvements in the sometimes creaky business methods of the Agency.

From the terse notes and memorandums that passed between them, one gets the impression that William glowered and grunted every time his nephew made an improvement, forgetting the days, forty years earlier, when William was sending similar letters to his father.

In 1911, Pinkerton heard from an old friend, Winston Churchill. In June, in response to a cablegram from Churchill, he went to London to assist Scotland Yard during the coronation of Edward VII. G. C. Thiel, Spokane superintendent, reported to New York:

> Extreme steps are being taken to keep out anarchists and dangerous criminals. All steamship landings are being closely watched. The Continental police are cooperating with the Pinkertons. Since his arrival today William Pinkerton has been in constant communication with the Home Office which has the responsibility for the King's safety.[6]

However, not all of the Pinkertons' activities were courageous and exemplary. The role they played in San Francisco's celebrated Tom Mooney bombing case was ugly and unfair. Their investigation of the rape-murder of fourteen-year-old Mary Phagan in Atlanta in April, 1913, was shoddy and at times despicable. Leo Frank, the factory owner who ironically had hired the Atlanta Pinkerton office to find the killer of his young employee, was himself indicted for the crime. William S. Burns was called into the case, uncovered new evidence, publicly named the killer, and was almost lynched by a mob.

Later the Georgia governor, risking his political life, commuted Frank's death sentence with the observation that the evidence uncovered by Burns was "powerful evidence" in behalf of the defendant.

But an anti-Semitic mob invaded the Milledgeville Prison Farm with no resistance from the guards, kidnapped Frank, and lynched him at Marietta.

In 1914, the French government retained the Pinkertons to investigate a ring of agents working in New Orleans for the Central Powers. An operative infiltrated the group to become acquainted with a German mechanic named Hans Helle, a saboteur of unusual skill and nerve. Like countless operatives before him, the Pinkerton man obtained rooms in Helle's boardinghouse, drank beer with Helle, and agreed with his violent pro-German arguments. One day, Helle confided to the operative that he had manufactured a bomb, set to detonate in six days, to be hidden on a French ship. At a conference with the district attorney the Pinkertons, in order to make a tight legal case, urged the prosecutor to let them accompany Helle to the ship and make the arrest as he was hiding the bomb. They were overruled on the grounds of public danger.

For several tense hours, the Pinkertons and the New Orleans police waited in Helle's darkened room. As the operative reported: "In the final wait, the size and power of the bomb was magnified in all our minds." One police officer warned the others: "If you grab this guy, lift him right off the ground, he'll be wired like a submarine." With them was a representative of a local explosives company. When he heard that Helle was carrying a bomb he announced that he was only a dynamite expert, and left. Helle finally entered the room, and was surrounded and handcuffed. While the police, frozen to the floor, watched, the operatives removed the clock and trigger of the bomb.

Helle was confined in the same prison where [Pinkerton operative Frank] Dimaio had been imprisoned [undercover] with the Mafia twenty-five years earlier. However, he was later released because of a technicality in the indictment.

After America's entry into the war, a Pinkerton operative who had worked on the New Orleans investigation spotted Helle on a Chicago street. He followed him to a wartime munitions factory where he discovered the German saboteur had recently been hired as a foreman. On the Pinkerton's information, Helle was arrested by the Secret Service and detained for the duration of the war.[7]

At the outbreak of the war, Allan Pinkerton, II, enlisted in the army, serving with distinction as a major. He was badly gassed, and invalided back to the States. William, now sole head of the Agency, was summoned to Washington to outline a series of proposals to halt sabotage, but, as he tersely recalled, he left after they failed to "accept my suggestions." It was a striking parallel to 1861, when his father left Washington after Lincoln had kept him waiting.

There are no letters from William explaining the puzzle of why the Pinkerton's, the world's most famous detective agency of its time, was not recruited by the government as it had been in 1861–1862. The answer assuredly lies in Pinkerton's address to the International Association of Police Chiefs in 1919. That speech, which had headlines across the country, revealed that inefficiency, incompetence, a lack of centralization, and jealousy between federal agencies had often "spoiled" important cases of espionage, and were no match for the experienced agents of the German spymasters, Von Bernstorff, Von Papen, Dr. Albert, and others. Although he did not say it in so many words, it had been a case of the amateurs disdaining the professionals or the professionals refusing to work with the amateurs. As he told the police officers:

> Persons selected to perform important Government secret service in the Army and Navy Intelligence Department were often selected from among doctors, bankers, merchants, architects, etc., and I am credibly informed that of these, less than one per cent, or one person in a hundred, had previous police or detective experience. This created separate forces of thousands without training for incredibly important work, which, at all times, requires training and experience to be of real service.
>
> The limited results achieved by these hastily organized Intelligence, or Secret Service Departments, are known to you through your almost helpless efforts to cooperate and assist these inexperienced forces. Their inexperience, zeal and jealousy frequently spoiled important clues of cases of major importance, that otherwise could have been successfully developed.

Pinkerton also denounced the issuance of a list of dangerous alien sympathizers by Army Intelligence:

> This list since its publication has been shown to be so inaccurate and so unjust to persons named therein, that the War Department had to take drastic steps to curb the zeal of the employees of the Intelligence Department and removed the names of the injured persons from this list.

The heart of Pinkerton's speech was his proposal for "a central government agency force of Federal detectives that will centralize, connect up and weave together data gathered by its representatives North, South, East and West.

"This would soon eradicate such elements [enemy agents] as require the attention of our courts."

This organization, he went on, would be beyond the reach of politicians, "and would never be used against labor or against capitalism; never become involved in their differences, an organization to which any suspicious coming to the notice of City, County or

## When a Man's Partner Is Killed, He's Supposed To Do Something about It

*One of the most famous cases involving Pinkerton's was its pursuit of the James-Younger Gang. The following excerpt describes the famous gunfight that took place near the small Missouri settlement of Roscoe, in which John Harrison Younger was killed. Of particular interest is the pseudonym of Pinkerton's detective John Boyle: James Wright. Hammett told Frederic Dannay that the Continental Op was based on Pinkerton's agent James Wright, who has not been otherwise identified.*

Allan's operatives had a brief but bloody encounter with the James gang in 1871 but financial constraints prevented the Agency resuming its campaign against these desperadoes until 1874. At the beginning of that year William Pinkerton sent a young agent named John W. Whicher to Missouri to infiltrate the gang. In March his hideously mutilated body was found at the roadside near Independence; he had been bound, then shot in the head and body, several times, at very close range. Allan was outraged at this brutal, cold-blooded murder and a few days later sent in two of his best men. Louis Lull had been a captain in the Chicago Police Department before joining the Agency. Now he travelled to Missouri under the name of W.J. Allen, uncannily close to Allan's own wartime alias. Lull was accompanied by John Boyle, a former St Louis policeman, using the alias of James Wright. At St Clair County they were joined by a deputy sheriff, Edwin B. Daniels. The three men, posing as cattle dealers, met John and Jim Younger on Chalk Hill Road on 16 March. The outlaws called them to halt and then opened fire. Wright galloped off as the gunslingers shot off his hat; but Daniels and Lull were stopped and disarmed. When Lull drew a hidden Smith and Wesson revolver and shot John Younger, brother Jim shot the detective several times. Lull was found the following day and rushed to a hotel in Roscoe where he died of his wounds after making a detailed statement. Allan wanted to hire a special train to bring Lull back to Chicago but the local doctor, D.C. McNeil, wired that Lull was too ill to be moved. Mrs Lull, accompanied by Robert Linden, assistant superintendent in the Philadelphia office, went to Roscoe to be with the wounded detective at the end.

After this débâcle Allan wrote bitterly to Bangs [head of the New York office] in New York:

I have no soldiers but all officers in my regiment—all are capital men to give orders, few will go forward unless someone goes ahead. I know that the James Youngers are desperate men, and that if we meet it (*sic*) it must be the death of one or both of us. They must repay . . . There is no use talking, they must die. Mr Warner [Frank Warner, superintendent of the Chicago office] and William refused to go with the men to Missouri, both declared they were not to be made a notch to be shot at . . . Consequently I made no talk but simply say I am going myself.

—James Mackay, *Allan Pinkerton: The First Private Eye* (New York: Dodd, Mead, 1963), p. 210

*Allan Pinkerton, founder of the Pinkerton's National Detective Agency in 1850. Pinkerton is credited with developing the first national investigatory organization that could track criminals without regard to jurisdictional boundaries. He died in 1884.*

State authorities could be reported . . . in other words a centralized clearing house of secret service data for the protection of the people. . . ."

Pinkerton also pointed out that had the United States had such an agency, its experienced operatives would have alerted Washington to the overthrow of the Kerensky government in Russia. War-ravaged Europe, Pinkerton warned, was a fertile ground for the spread of Communism. While the "Reds" were as yet no danger to this country, he predicted they would be in the years to come. The superagency of his dreams, he told the assembled officers, would surely take care of that threat. Pinkerton could have been discussing the Federal Bureau of Investigation.[8]

Pinkerton's strong feeling about the "radicals" of his day was a reflection of the decline, if not the end, of progressivism in the United States, when its leaders failed to unite after 1918. Among the reasons were the flowering of American enterprise under the impact of technical and financial developments and the economic and social status of the urban class, who had begun to realize they were building a new type of America based

*Robert Pinkerton, who, with his brother William, ran Pinkerton's National Detective Agency from 1884 until his death in 1907, the years of the agency's most extensive criminal investigations. In the late nineteenth century, Robert Pinkerton was involved in tracking the James gang, the Younger brothers, and the Wild Bunch.*

on mass production and consumption, shorter hours, increasing prosperity. Their country, comparatively untouched by the Great War, was healthier than ever. The middle class had little interest in rebellion or revolt against governments or establishments that might disturb the status quo. It was the age of Babbitt and the solid citizen who feared that bomb-and-whisker Bolsheviks were going to take over Washington. This fear had been heightened by a series of violent strikes that shook the nation shortly after the end of the war. In Pinkerton's time, most Americans were inclined to view them as Red-inspired.

The "Big Red Scare" of 1919–1920 resulted in a national crusade against left-wingers whose Americanism was suspect. More than six thousand were rounded up by Attorney General A. Mitchell Palmer. The nation's fear increased when Palmer's house was bombed in Washington. The fear verged on hysteria in September, 1920, when a bomb, still unexplained, exploded in front of J. P. Morgan's offices at 23 Wall Street, killing thirty-eight and wounding several hundred more.

In these turbulent years, old and familiar faces began to disappear from the Agency's roster. In May, 1918, William wrote to his nephew that he was "going to bury McParland" in Denver. After the funeral he told newspapermen that he "doubted [Pinkerton's Western Division manager, James] McParland could get convictions today as he did then. Times have changed."

In the postwar years, Pinkerton traveled across the country to campaign for the adoption of national fingerprinting. As he told a convention of law-enforcement officers: "No one who has a practical knowledge of both systems [fingerprinting against the Bertillon system] will for one minute question the superiority of the fingerprint system over the Bertillon system."

Pinkerton also held a series of conferences in London with Sir Edward William, who had introduced fingerprinting in England. In a report to the International Association of Police Chiefs, Pinkerton warned: "You will be behind the times if you do not introduce fingerprinting so that it becomes nationwide."

Fingerprinting had been first introduced in the United States at the World's Fair in 1904, but during World War I and the postwar years it was used only by the military and the Bureau of Immigration. Pinkerton's speeches, as well as the proddings of police chiefs, are credited with helping to bring about national fingerprinting, today one of the most vital parts of local and federal law enforcement.

In the early 1920's, William was a legendary figure on the American scene, a huge man, heavily jowled, with thick gray hair, and brooding black eyes under shaggy white brows. He usually wore an old-fashioned black cravat, a heavy gold watch chain stretched across his large stomach, and a western sombrero-type hat.

Although he often insisted that he didn't care for personal publicity, he never dodged a newspaperman. With young and impressionable female reporters, he played the role of the grim, silent lawman of old. As one wrote, "It is as hard to get him to talk about himself as it is to get him to smile." The more experienced big-city reporters who knew Pinkerton certainly smiled at such naïveté.

Usually the interviews or feature stories were mostly reminiscences of the Old West or the days of Adam Worth, Baron Shinburn, the Molly Maguires, and the colorful thieves of the past, but they also contained many succinct, shrewd observations of American life. When one reporter asked Pinkerton what was America's greatest deterrent against crime, he snapped, "Education and more education." He also suggested that the government, to instill interest in education in the nation's ghettos–"tenement districts" he called them–offer scholarships for the children of the poor, a proposal a half century before its time.

In 1920, when he was seventy-four, Pinkerton created a national stir when he publicly denounced Prohibition as the cause for the national crime wave. He also criticized Hollywood for its flood of "crime movies, a prime motivation for young criminals."[9] William told a Los Angeles *Times* reporter that the postwar years

have produced an entirely new type of criminal, difficult under our present methods to deal with and have produced conditions that have never before been so rotten in the history of our country.

Everyone is getting big prices for their products. Salaries are high but so are expenses. This new affluence, following the terrible strain we have been through during and since the war, has produced the new criminal element that is providing headaches for the nation's police.

As for Hollywood's lurid crime movies, he said:

We [the nation's police heads] have found that this is a prime motivation of the younger type of criminal. Please don't think I am condemning the movies, for there is no greater movie fan than myself. But there are certain types of pictures which I personally think should be suppressed. I mean those that illustrate and glorify crime and criminals. You and I may forget the pictures we have just seen but the young chap with criminal tendencies does not.

In several interviews Pinkerton pointed out that the whipping post in Delaware had cut down crime in that state. When a reporter challenged him to prove this, he told the story of a group of Broadway "mobsmen," as the racketeers were called in those days, who were caught burglarizing a banker's home in Wilmington. They were sentenced to ten years and forty lashes. Pinkerton said:

The years in the penitentiary were a joke to them. They knew they could eventually buy their way free, but the thought of the lashes horrified them. They hired the best attorneys but their sentences were upheld. They were all tied up in public and given forty lashes, then sent to the penitentiary. Word of their terrible humiliation went back to Broadway and it was a long time before any New York mobsmen paid Delaware a visit.

Brutal? Perhaps the Whipping Post Law is brutal, but it should also be pointed out that crimes, thousands of times more brutal than the post, are being committed in this country these days with the innocent usually the victim.

It was curious that Pinkerton's sixty or more years on the side of the law had not taught him that increases in crime often follow disturbances in human relations, and are caused by them. Thus, crime can almost be termed the "war after the war."

Pinkerton's proposal was followed by countless editorials praising or denouncing his ideas of a whipping post or crime-ridden states. Perhaps the most thoughtful was in the San Francisco *Call-Post,* which pointed out while Pinkerton was a necessary part of organized society, sorely needed to keep it from inner destruction, men of some future civilization would perhaps look back and remark that the police and the detectives and the armies of our time were expressions of weakness and not of strength.[10]

Survivors and echoes of famous cases continued to plague William Pinkerton in his last years. In 1920, ["reformed" murderer of former Idaho governor Frank Steunenberg] Harry Orchard, now a cheery, suntanned middle-aged man who walked about the prison yard wearing a farmer's straw hat, wrote to a friend in New Jersey, asking him to get the Pinkertons "to write up some kind of record forms" to help him gain a parole. In this letter Orchard revealed that former State Prosecutor James H. Hawley, who had tried Haywood, Pettibone, and Steve Adams, and former Governor Frank R. Gooding were recommending his release.[11]

Orchard recalled how McParland, who had died two years earlier, "used to tell me a great deal about the large cases he had been connected with and how they always recommended clemency for those who had helped them uncover crimes in various degrees."

Orchard's request was sent to William Pinkerton's Chicago office. At the time, Pinkerton was America's legendary detective, and there is little doubt his recommendation could have helped Orchard. But as he wrote to his general manager in New York: "I know that McParland always thought Orchard should have been released for testifying, but I still regard Orchard as a cold-blooded murderer who killed many innocent persons and who testified only to save his own skin."[12]

The Molly Maguires also refused to remain in the past. When A. Conan Doyle published his *Valley of Fear,* a novel based on McParland's famous adventures, William Pinkerton was furious, and sent an angry note to George D. Bangs, Jr., his New York superintendent. As his letter revealed, Doyle had been his shipmate on a transatlantic cruise. One night in the smoking lounge he told the famous English author the story of McParland's adventures

*William Pinkerton, who ran the Pinkerton's National Detective Agency from 1884 until his death in 1923, first in partnership with his brother Robert, then with Robert's son Allan Pinkerton II. William Pinkerton was particularly interested in bank robberies, racetrack fraud, and illegal activity among circus workers. Hammett was involved in cases of each type.*

in the Pennsylvania minefields. The late Ralph Dudley, Pinkerton's general manager, recalled:

> W. A. P. raised the roof when he saw the book. At first he talked of bringing a suit against Doyle but then dropped that after he had cooled off. What made him angry was the fact that even if Doyle was fictionizing the story, he didn't have the courtesy to ask his permission to use a confidential discussion for his work. They had been good friends before but from that day on their relationship was strained. Mr. Doyle sent several notes trying to soothe things over and while W. A. P. sent him courteous replies he never regarded Mr. Doyle with the same warmth.[13]

The story was typical of William, his father, and his brother: a wrong, fancied or real, was never forgotten.

Pinkerton continued to be an important news source for London reporters, who crowded about him in the ship's lounge, putting a multitude of questions ranging from America's gang wars to disarmament. Their favorite, which they never failed to ask, was his opinion of Sherlock Holmes, Old Sleuth, or other fictitious detectives of the day.

"Gum shoe detectives of fiction are usually just plain rot," he said in 1922. "Detective work is only using good common sense and nothing else." The *Express,* whose headline read, "The Sherlock Holmes of America Arrives Here," found Pinkerton that year to be "a quiet, gray-haired man full of vigor. He is the antithesis of the popular impression of the great detective. He might be mistaken for a prosperous banker."

On his trips to London, Scotland Yard never failed to give Pinkerton a banquet at the Savoy, with a prominent American as toastmaster or main speaker of the evening. On his 1922 visit, the Savoy's main ballroom was packed with Americans and Britons who listened to Ambassador George Harvey praise Pinkerton as one of the outstanding men of his time.

If anyone thought the old man was quietly dozing in the sun, and tried to trespass on his authority, they always drew back, bloodied. A prominent midwestern police official once claimed credit for the arrest of a gang of notorious criminals. A few days later, Pinkerton sent New York a blistering letter of what he intended to tell the official, "that hog that never fails to try and take credit for the work our Agency has done. . . . I shall not hesitate to tell him at the proper time my opinion regarding this matter."

His nephew, Allan, now back with the Agency as his uncle's partner, also felt the old man's sting. In the 1920's a New York State newspaper published a lengthy article quoting William's story of how a certain President had been swindled in a mine deal while in office. The President was not named, but the wire services picked up the story, which was given prominent space throughout the country. William was in London at the time, and the superintendent in New York wrote a brief note, and enclosed the clipping. Allan had scrawled a few angry lines on the bottom of the note, advising his uncle that he thought the story was "slush" and should never been told. Back came a cold, sharp letter from William saying that he "resented such comments and I don't want you to write me anything of that kind in the future. . . ." The story, he explained, had been given to the paper by an old friend to whom he had told it in confidence many years ago. "If I wanted publicity," he wrote, "God knows I could get all I wanted while I was in Europe."

At seventy-seven William had his own teeth, a thick thatch of iron-gray hair, a healthy appetite, and used old-fashioned rimmed spectacles only for reading. His memory was extraordinary; he could still identify photographs of criminals by a glance. He now enjoyed the theatre, and was an ardent first nighter. As a magazine of the period observed, he was "a patron of the arts." But William's favorite role was that of Principal of the world's greatest detective dynasty. Six months out of the year he toured the country, visiting branch offices, listening to complaints, untangling administrative difficulties, offering suggestions, and examining profits and losses. He could no more stop being a detective than he could breathing. Informers still gave him their tips, rather than talk to anyone else. He would stop on a street and slip a bill to a bedraggled-looking vagrant, explaining to his companion that it was an "old-timer down on his luck." The once great forgers, bank robbers, and confidence men, old, sick, and penniless, never failed to come away with a "loan." Perhaps to Pinkerton they represented an era, the most exciting and triumphant of his lifetime, which inexorable time had swallowed.

When Joe Killoran, a famous paroled bank robber of the 1880's whom the Pinkertons had sent away for a long term, appeared, frail, dying of TB, and with only one leg—the other had been amputated in prison—William gave the old thief a small loan. Judging from his correspondence, he spent many days arranging interviews between Killoran and the representative of a company selling pipe cleaners. Pinkerton bought two hundred of the cleaners to set Killoran up as a salesman. "Let him start out in this way, selling them," William wrote to his New York assistant general manager. "I always like to help these old fellows and put them on their feet."

When George Bliss White, one of the truly cultured bank robbers of the 1890's, who planned and executed the famous robbery of the Ocean Bank of New York in the 1870's, wrote to Pinkerton that he was sick and destitute, William sent an operative to his boardinghouse to confirm the story. When the operative returned with the news that White was seriously ill and broke, Pinkerton paid the bank robber's board bill and gave him a loan "to put him back on his feet to go straight." White, as his New York superintendent wryly reminded William, "had stolen more money than any other human being."

White later returned to thank Pinkerton, the old opponents sitting in the detective's sun-splashed office, reminiscing of men they had known on both sides of the law. White later wrote an autobiographical best seller, and became a popular lecturer. William, who had seen too much of life and men to be surprised by ingratitude, almost jovially told his New York superintendent that "he [White] never fails to put the heat on me or my brother" in his lectures.

William celebrated his seventy-seventh birthday in Hot Springs, and the nation's dailies reported how he had been given a surprise party in the ballroom of the local hotel. Judges, senators, congressmen, millionaire horsemen, old friends, associates, and industrialists jammed the room.

There were many speeches, and telegrams from famous persons, both in the United States and in Europe, were read. At the end, William rose and said simply: "Thank you. This is an evening I will never forget."

In the winter of 1923, he prepared for his annual national tour of the Agency's branch offices. He still spent a full day behind his desk either in New York or in Chicago, reading copies of every report and dictating notes of suggestions, praise, and criticism to his superintendents. Now, from where he sat in that Age of Wonderful Nonsense, he could look back up the long road of history he had traveled that stretched even beyond the Civil War. There was the bitter winter morning when he had helped his father escort the fanatical abolitionist John Brown and the weary slaves to the train that would take them the last miles to freedom in Canada. There was the front-line tent after Antietam where he had sat with his father and the handsome general, while all about them McClellan's army, badly mauled, wearily rested on its arms. And there was the day in the White House when Lincoln had put a hand on his shoulder and admonished his father for using his sons on dangerous missions behind the Confederate lines. There were also many great and grim mileposts along the road: the fires of Homestead, the rattle of six-shooters, and the thousands of miles on horseback, slogging after the outlaws of the Wild West; Victorian London and Adam Worth's dazzling nightclub in the Rue Scribe; gay Havana, where he had captured the Bidwell brothers who had robbed the Bank of England. He had known all the Presidents from Lincoln to Harding, as well as kings, dictators, and criminals of every class. He had experienced countless dangers, from the tangled wildwoods of the Ozarks and the Great Smokies to the mining camps of the West, and had fought for his life in the moonlight on the deck of a riverboat when Mark Twain had worked on the Mississippi.

At seventy-seven he could tell a young reporter: "I guess you can say I lived a full life."

In December, 1923, he arrived in Los Angeles to preside over a series of conferences. On the eleventh, he was stricken with a heart attack, and died in his hotel room.

The obituaries, numerous and lengthy, fill a huge scrapbook, and his funeral was one of the largest in the history of Chicago. He was buried beside his brother and father in Chicago's Graceland Cemetery.

A man and an era had been laid to rest.

## Notes

1. Newark *Call,* August 25, 1907.
2. Route Book for Buffalo Bill's circus, Monday, April 17, Baltimore, to Saturday, October 17, Urbana, Ohio, PA.
3. The New York *World,* December 3, 1897.
4. Houston *Post,* September 1, 1907.
5. Extensive obituaries on Robert Pinkerton were published in every large newspaper in the world, from the United States to the Orient. Among them were the New York *Times,* New York *Tribune,* New York *World,* Brooklyn *Eagle,* Chicago *Evening Post,* Denver *Post,* Philadelphia *Bulletin,* New York *Telegram,* all of August 17–19, 1907.
6. G. C. Thiele, Superintendent, Spokane office to George D. Bangs, Jr., June 17, 1911, PA.
7. Copy of Operative's Report, New Orleans office, on the arrest of Hans Helle, 1914, forwarded to the New York office, PA.
8. Address by William A. Pinkerton, Annual Convention, International Association of Chiefs of Police, New Orleans, April 15, 1919. The Federal Bureau of Investigation was originally created in 1908 as the Bureau of Investigation, with authority only to conduct investigations for the Department of Justice. After J. Edgar Hoover became director in 1924, Congress gradually added one duty after another until the bureau was reorganized in 1933 as the Division of Justice in the Department of Justice. In 1935, it was formally designated the Federal Bureau of Investigation.
9. *World Magazine,* April 25, 1920.
10. San Francisco *Call-Post,* March 28, 1921.
11. Albert E. Horsley (Orchard's real name) to C. P. Connelly, New Jersey, December 31, 1920, PA. Orchard died on the morning of April 13, 1954. Obituaries in the large city dailies briefly recalled his exploits. But the thunder of his bombs, the horror they inflicted, the turbulent times were now only faint, almost undistinguishable echoes.
12. William Pinkerton to George D. Bangs, Jr., January 3, 1921, PA.
13. An interview with the late Ralph Dudley, general manager, and the author, 1948.

---

*Regarded as the father of modern scientific criminal research, Hans Gross wrote* System der Kriminalistik *(1891), a landmark text emphasizing the importance of reconstructing the crime scene for investigative purposes. Hammett used the English adaptation of Gross's book,* Criminal Investigation: A Practical Textbook for Magistrates, Police Officers and Lawyers *(1924), as a reference in his writing. Excerpts from the first chapter of this work, in which the character and methods of the investigator are discussed, are published below.*

## The Investigating Officer
Hans Gross
*Criminal Investigation: A Practical Handbook*
    (London: Sweet & Maxwell, 1924), pp. 1–34

### Section i.–General Considerations.

Of all the duties that an official can be called upon to perform in the course of his service those of an Investigating Officer are certainly not the least important. That his services to the public are great and his labours full of interest will be generally admitted, but rarely, even among specialists, is full credit given to the difficulties of the position. An Investigating Officer should possess the vigour of youth, energy ever on the alert, robust health, and extensive acquaintance with all branches of the law. He ought to know men, proceed skilfully, and possess liveliness and vigilance. Tact is indispensable, true courage is required in many situations, and he must be always ready on emergency to risk his health and life; as when dangerous criminals are dealt with, fatiguing journeys undertaken, persons stricken with infectious diseases examined, or dangerous *post-mortems* attended. He has to solve problems relating to every branch of human knowledge; he ought to be acquainted with languages, he should know what the medical man can tell him and what to ask the medical man; he must be as conversant with the dodges of the poacher as with the wiles of the stock jobber, as well acquainted with the method of fabricating a will as with the cause of a railway accident; he must know the tricks of card-sharpers, why boilers explode, how a horse-coper can turn an old screw into a young hunter. He should be able to pick his way through account books, to understand slang, to read ciphers, and be familiar with the processes and tools of all classes of workmen.

But it is not on the day of his appointment alone that an Investigating Officer can learn all this or acquire the activity and perspicacity requisite for his work. It should therefore be a fundamental rule only to nominate as Investigating Officer those who, besides being mentally and bodily fit, possess a veritable encyclopædic culture, who know the world, have observed life, and have undergone many experiences; finally, who are ready to place at the service of society with all the energy of which they are capable the knowledge thus painfully acquired. Every criminalist knows that the Investigating Officer in the exercise of his functions may be compelled to draw on all, absolutely all, the varied knowledge he has amassed, and that he will feel at least once in his life a profound regret for his ignorance of what he has neglected to acquire.

If an Investigating Officer is wanting in such general information, the cause is lack of interest in the work; and in this case he will never make a good Investigating Officer. He will do well to seek without delay to utilise his legal knowledge, which may perhaps be of great value, in other branches of judicial work. As an Investigating Officer he will not only fail to play his rôle well but his life will be miserable; he will be definitely forced to busy himself with affairs that do not interest him and, being deficient in the necessary information, he will never secure good results. He will be obliged to confess, sooner or later, that he is not occupying a situation suitable to him; and nothing is more discouraging to a man than work under such conditions. He who would spare himself such disappointment ought to make sure of possessing the qualities indispensable to an Investigating Officer before entering on this thorny and difficult career.

But knowledge alone is not everything. The Investigating Officer must possess not only legal and other acquirements, a general training, special fitness, and ideas ever ready for development, but also such a complete devotion to his profession that even outside the exercise of his official functions he will be always seeking to learn something calculated to extend his knowledge. He who seeks to learn only when some notable crime turns up, will have great difficulty in learning anything at all. His knowledge should be acquired beforehand by constant application in his ordinary life. Every day, nay every moment, he must be picking up something in touch with his work. Thus the zealous Investigating Officer will note on his walks the footprints found on the dust of the highway; he will observe the tracks of animals, of the wheels of carriages, the marks of pressure on the grass where someone has sat or lain down, or perhaps deposited a burden. He will examine little pieces of paper that have been thrown away, marks or injuries on trees, displaced stones, broken glass or pottery, doors and windows open or shut in an unusual manner. Everything will afford an opportunity for drawing conclusions and explaining what must have previously taken place. For what we call "adducing proof" consists only in concluding from the knowledge of one fact the knowledge of other facts which must have followed or preceded it. And these lessons must be learned in advance in connection with matters of small importance and not waited for until some murder has to be investigated. Quite insignificant words uttered by passers-by, striking the ear by chance, or little suspicious acts accidentally

CRIMINAL INVESTIGATION

A PRACTICAL TEXTBOOK

FOR

MAGISTRATES, POLICE OFFICERS AND LAWYERS

ADAPTED FROM THE

SYSTEM DER KRIMINALISTIK

OF

DR. HANS GROSS

*Professor of Criminology in the University of Prague*

BY

J. COLLYER ADAM, BARRISTER-AT-LAW

*Public Prosecutor, Madras*

LONDON:

SWEET & MAXWELL, LIMITED,

3 CHANCERY LANE, W.C.2.

| TORONTO: | SYDNEY, MELBOURNE, BRISBANE: |
| THE CARSWELL COMPANY, LTD. | LAW BOOK CO. OF AUSTRALASIA, LTD. |

1924.

*(Printed in England.)*

*System der Kriminalistik (1891) by Professor Hans Gross is regarded as the pioneering work in modern criminal investigation, providing the earliest practical guide for detectives. It was first translated into English in this edition, which Hammett knew well and which he refers to in* The Thin Man *(Collection of Richard Layman).*

observed, may afford precious opportunities for putting two and two together. It is equally useful to get others to relate events, insignificant or important, at which they as well as oneself have been present. These recitals, supposing that those who make them really wish to speak the truth, are extremely interesting on account of their variations; and this is the simplest and indeed only way of learning how the depositions of witnesses should be appreciated.

Nor ought the budding Investigating Officer to neglect any opportunity of obtaining information concerning any profession, the work of an artisan, technical processes, etc., etc., nor, *last not least,* of learning to know men. For this every man with whom we come in contact may be taken as an object of study, and whoever takes the trouble can always learn something from the biggest fool.

## Section ii.–The Duties of the Investigating Officer.

If we now ask "How should the Investigating Officer set about his work?" we can come to but one conclusion "His whole heart must be set upon success." If not, he reduces his work to the mere dispatching of documents and firing off reports as fast as he can. If he would succeed in each inquiry his work will be by no means easy, smooth, or peaceful; on the contrary, he will have to devote himself completely and continually to his task, working with all his might and never pausing for rest.

Nervous people are useless as investigators. Success in a mission means the complete elucidation of the business in hand. No matter what may be his profession, a man must, if he be conscientious, bring his task to a successful termination. But here is not a task in which one can advance little by little, along a natural and clearly demarcated route, terminating when one has completed a certain amount of work mapped out in advance; there is always a new problem to unravel; the investigator whose work is half done has accomplished nothing. Either he has solved the problem and quite finished the work; that means success: or he has done nothing, absolutely nothing.

"Obtaining a result" must not be confused with "producing an effect." The work of the investigator ought to make neither noise nor sensation: suffice it that the culprit must be discovered at any price. To succeed in his mission the Investigating Officer must just commence his work at the start with the resolution of devoting to it every effort humanly possible and the determination not to pause till it is finished. The end has not been attained simply by the elucidation of the affair in an ordinary way. It is very easy and convenient to say, "It is impossible to go further." But if one says continually, "Another step forward must be taken," one finally advances several leagues. In every case that he has to solve the Investigating Officer has first to obtain facts, often not without worry and trouble. As adversaries he has the accused, and often the witnesses, circumstances, natural events, difficulties that crop up from time to time, and if he loses sight of the proverb, "If you don't allow yourself to be beaten to-day, you are saved a hundred times over," then on the first difficulty arising he will throw up the sponge. He will take a difficulty for an impossibility and say "Thus far and no farther."

## Section iii.–The Procedure of the Investigating Officer.

When he starts work, the most important thing for the Investigating Officer is to discover the exact moment when he can form a definite opinion. The importance of this cannot be too much insisted upon, for upon it success or failure often depends. If he should come to a definite conclusion too soon a preconceived opinion may be formed, to which he will always be attached with more or less tenacity till he is forced to abandon it entirely: by then his most precious moments will have passed away, the best clues will have been lost—often beyond the possibility of recovery. If on the other hand he misses the true moment for forming an opinion, the inquiry becomes a purposeless groping in the dark and a search devoid of aim. When will the Investigating Officer find this true moment, this psychological instant, of which we speak? It is impossible to lay down a general rule: all that can be said is, that the Investigating Officer will of necessity always find it if he set to work under the guidance of fixed and immutable principles, never losing sight of the fact that a "definite opinion" *on an affair as a whole* will not come to him all of a sudden; to arrive at it he must advance step by step while making use of such "definite opinions" as may be prudently formed about phenomena, facts, and isolated events *as they arise.*

The case must be taken up from the start with an open mind. The complaint or information received by the Investigating Officer ought to have no more value in his eyes than this statement, "It is said that such and such a crime has been committed at such and such a place." Even if details about the perpetrator, the injury, the motive, etc., are published, he should attach no more importance to them than if he had heard the remark, "It is said that the affair must have happened thus." Supposing that an important crime is involved and he repairs to the scene, certainly a great number of strong and lively impressions will bring themselves to bear upon him and the task of ordering them in his mind will be hard enough. In addition, he will receive communications from all quarters; officials, authorized and unauthorized, desire to make statements more or less important; he does not wish to dismiss them, for they may tell him something which he will be able to turn to account in forming at once, if he is so disposed, a definite opinion. His work at this important stage of the inquiry must enter into great detail; just as if he gathered up with a sponge one by one all the drops of water he sees, in order, when it is quite soaked, to squeeze into a basin all the drops that have been collected. No matter for the moment whether the drops are clear liquid or dirty slush, he gathers them all in. Little by little as the work advances, certain opinions and ideas become separate and fixed: such or such a witness makes a good impression and one begins to believe what he states; an idea is obtained of the way in which the criminal has reached the spot; account is taken of the instruments he has employed; or certain indications appear which restrict the period of time in which the deed must have been committed.

When a certain number of ideas on the incidents of the case, considered individually, seem at length determined, the Investigating Officer will seek to obtain a precise idea of the way in which everything has happened, even if only the most general view be possible. Perhaps the conclusion will be forced on him that the real facts are not what they appear on the surface and that a false complexion has been given to them; or on the other hand he may be enabled to say with certainty that a crime of such or such a nature has been committed. In short the Investigating Officer will be sufficiently advanced to erect a framework on which a provisional theory or scheme may be developed. To set out this scheme beforehand would be superfluous and dangerous; superfluous because it may have to be changed at any moment, dangerous because with a prematurely formed plan one can easily get off the track and proceed in a wrong direction. We do not imply that the Investigating Officer must not at the beginning establish a classification to be followed in his operations, for without that he would only grope about, finding nothing and advancing nowhither: but between a provisional classification to guide inquiry and a definite scheme of the crime there is a great difference.

But if it is difficult to construct the plan of campaign, it is still more difficult to conduct the inquiry according to that plan. A scheme of inquiry cannot be compared with a scheme devised in view of circumstances which can be brought into existence and modified at will. It is drawn up in view of circumstances which alter of themselves, which are often unknown, and which do not depend on the person applying the scheme. It resembles, not the design of a house to be built, but a plan of campaign. It is based upon data which the Investigating Officer possesses, or believes himself to possess, when he constructs it. It must be rigidly adhered to as long as these data are unchanged or have undergone only their natural development, but it must be modified in part or in whole as soon as these data are found to have changed or to be false. One would imagine that this could be done quite naturally and spontane-ously, but such is human nature that so simple a principle is rarely conformed to.

The greater difficulty there is in securing anything, the more one holds on to it; that is why fools are so obstinate. They never willingly abandon an idea, because they have had trouble in getting it into their heads. Now the scheme of an inquiry is difficult to follow out, and, when one has already worked in conformity therewith, it is not willingly abandoned; but still pursued unthinkingly and almost automatically. It happens at times that one perceives all of a sudden that one is following with exact minuteness a plan based upon data the falsity of which should have become apparent long ago, or which are so modified that the work constructed, if not built altogether in the air, is quite crooked. This advice may seem pedantic: yet, however unimportant an inquiry may be at each step (examination of witnesses, visits to localities, technical or expert reports, etc.), the information upon which a scheme has been based, must be verified anew, to ascertain if the data remain unchanged and, if not, in what way the scheme must be modified.

It will therefore be not only the easiest but usually also the best and safest way to construct the hypothesis in the simplest possible manner. Strange and extraordinary suppositions should be disregarded. And never forget the one great stupid fault which a criminal nearly always commits, especially in big crimes. It has happened hundreds of times that criminal investigators, already on the right track, have left it thinking: "The man who has committed this crime cannot have been so foolish as to do that," but innumerable cases prove that he *has* been so foolish; it matters not whether he was confused, suddenly frightened, has made a miscalculation, acted hastily, or what not. It is therefore always best for the Investigating Officer to take the simplest view at the outset.

*Pfister* in his "Curious Criminal Cases" rightly says:—"The greatest art of the Investigating Officer consists in conducting the inquiry in such a way that the initiated at once perceive that there has been 'a directing intelligence,' while the uninitiated imagine that everything has fallen into place of its own accord." But in order to perceive this "directing intelligence," the whole must rest upon a scheme continually verified and thoroughly carried out. How often do we not come across inquiries where the Investigating Officer has started on an excellent plan, but has adhered to it with desperate tenacity even when the data upon which it was based have long since changed. Thus to continue to follow a line the falsity of which has been demonstrated, may sometimes prove more fatal and more dangerous than to grope about with no plan at all: in the latter case it is still possible to hit the right clue, in the former it is impossible. The case for instance, where an inquiry runs the greatest risk of failure is when the scheme supposes a certain person to have been the author of the crime; and after having worked entirely with this idea, it suddenly becomes evident that that person is innocent.

When an almost incalculable amount of time has been lost on such a false scent, it may be concluded as a general rule that the inquiry will prove abortive. The Investigating Officer has expressed his ideas on the manner in which things have come about, he has utilised the elements of proof in view of a predetermined result, and, what is graver still, he has allowed time to slip away. And now his original supposition has been found to be false; he has first to combat his own discouragement and that of his assistants: if a new scheme is drawn up he cannot muster the same degree of interest, and the elements of proof seem neither so certain nor so useful. Many have disappeared and can no longer be found, and with each production of new proofs he will make the objection, or others will make it for him, that in the original scheme they would have borne another meaning and pointed to another conclusion. There is only one way to obviate such a danger, never to allow himself to be dominated exclusively by one idea and never to follow exclusively that sole idea.

. . . . . . . . . .

There is an old adage that the Investigating Officer can often remember to good purpose, namely, "*Cherchez la femme*," "Seek for the woman." Sounding rather like a phrase in a novel, every practitioner of experience will certify that it contains a large portion of truth. Mistakes however can be made in relying on it, either by believing that the crime, no matter what, has been instigated by a woman, or by declaring the explanation sufficient only because the name of some woman has been mentioned during the inquiry. In the first case one goes too far, in the second the goal has not yet been reached. The proper procedure is to endeavour, without any pedantic obstinacy, to look for a woman as having been an influencing factor in the crime. The suggestion of a crime does not always of necessity emanate from a woman, but one will frequently find that the most important deeds done before or after the crime itself have been done at the instigation of a woman or on account of a woman. This is assuredly not a minor point. We never feel sure of our case when we can assign no motive for some

*Hammett in the yard at his Baltimore home in 1918
(courtesy of Judi Hammett)*

important action revealed by the inquiry, and we are not disposed to believe that such an action has taken place so long as we do not know what the motive is. The Investigating Officer will therefore always do well to admit at the beginning that a woman may have something to do with the crime; it is not necessarily so, but inquiry in that direction is recommended. Take the simplest of facts; a farm servant steals wheat in order to buy a pair of shoes for his young woman; an honest woodcutter has turned poacher so as to be able to cut a dash in new buckskin breeches before his girl; or let us go further and take a great political trial, in which we see how an offended beauty stirs up partisans to carry out projects tending to the overthrow of the State; everywhere we find a woman.

Offences against property are committed for the purpose of getting married or spending the proceeds on prostitutes. At balls, dancing parties, and public assemblies of all kinds, brawls for the most part break out on account of women. The safest hiding-place for stolen objects is with a woman of apparent innocence. It is almost always with the aid of a woman that criminals succeed in escaping and concealing themselves. In frauds and coining on a large scale, women are almost always the agents for putting false goods into circulation. The worst gambling dens are invariably run by women, crimes of passion innumerable have been committed on account of women, and many men have turned criminal through associating with them. Every criminal expert almost without exception, having a certain amount of experience, is wont in criminal matters to go in search of the woman as a matter of course. Doubtless mistakes and errors may arise from that procedure, but for all that one must never forget the old adage.

---

## On Pathological Lying

*In the second chapter of* Criminal Investigation, *titled "Examination of Witnesses and Accused," Gross discusses the difficulty to the investigator posed by habitual liars, like Brigid O'Shaughnessy.*

This is not as a rule due to sickness or disease. But there must have been undoubtedly a train of circumstances causing the individual to be, at least temporarily, in an abnormal state of mind leading him to accept falsehood as truth. Such cases present great difficulties to the Investigating Officer, for while these lies are without motive, at least any apparent motive, yet the impression produced by such persons is absolutely normal, and their statements are always so cleverly and clearly presented that one would never, apart from extraneous circumstances, suspect their falsity. Such cases, which may be called "pathological," occur particularly among persons gifted with a lively imagination, among women and children, and pass through every grade from the small exaggeration to the complete invention of the whole story.

The Investigating Officer encounters his greatest difficulties when he has to deal with people whose character is what *Forel* calls *"Ethico-Idiotic,"* which renders them absolutely incapable of speaking the truth.

—p. 74

---

### Section iv.–Preconceived Theories.

The method of proceeding just described, that namely, in which parallel investigations are instituted, which to a certain extent mutually control each other, is the best, and one is tempted to say the only, way of avoiding the great dangers of a "preconceived theory"– the most deadly enemy of all inquiries. Preconceived theories are so much the more dangerous as it is precisely the most zealous Investigating Officer, the officer most interested in his work, who is the most exposed to them. The indifferent investigator who makes a routine of his work has as a rule no opinion at all and leaves the case to develop itself. When one delves into the case with enthusiasm one can easily find a point to rely on; but one may interpret it badly or attach an exaggerated importance to it. An opinion is formed which cannot be got rid of. In carefully examining our own minds (we can scarcely observe phenomena of a purely psychical character in others), we shall have many opportunities of studying how preconceived theories take root; we shall often be astonished to see how accidental statements of almost no significance and often purely hypothetical have been able to give birth to a theory of which we can no longer rid ourselves without difficulty, although we have for a long time recognised the rottenness of its foundation.

Nothing can be known if nothing has happened; and yet, while still awaiting the discovery of the criminal, while yet only on the way to the locality of the crime, one comes unconsciously to formulate a theory, doubtless not quite void of foundation but having only a superficial connection with the reality; you have already heard a similar story, perhaps you have formerly seen an analogous case; you have had an idea for a long time that things would turn out in such and such a way. This is enough: the details of the case are no longer studied with entire freedom of mind. Or a chance suggestion thrown out by another, a countenance which strikes one, a thousand other fortuitous incidents, above all losing sight of the association of ideas, end in a preconceived theory, which neither rests upon juridical reasoning nor is justified by actual facts.

Nor is this all: often a definite line is taken up, as for instance by postulating, "If circumstances M. and N. are verified then the affair must certainly be understood in such and such a way." This reasoning may be all very well, but meanwhile, for some cause or other, the proof of M. and N. is long in coming; still the same idea remains in the head and is fixed there so firmly that it sticks even after the verification of M. and N. has failed, and although the conditions laid down as necessary to its adoption as true have not been realised.

It also often happens that a preconceived theory is formed because the matter is examined from a false

*Hammett is fifth from the right in the back row. He had contracted Spanish influenza in October 1918.*
*This photo was taken a month before he was discharged, having temporarily recovered. His respiratory*
*illness recurred seventeen months after his discharge and caused him serious disability*
*throughout the 1920s (courtesy of Judi Hammett).*

point of view. Optically, objects may appear quite different from what they really are, according to the point of view from which they are looked at. Morally, the same phenomenon happens, the matter is seen from a false point of view which the observer refuses at all costs to change; and so he clings to his preconceived theory. In this situation the most insignificant ideas, if inexact, can prove very dangerous. Suppose a case of arson has been reported from a distant locality: immediately in spite of oneself the scene is imagined; for example, one pictures the house, which one has never seen, as being on the left-hand side of the road. As the information is received at headquarters the idea formed about the scene becomes precise and fixed. In imagination the whole scene and its secondary details are presented, but everything is always placed on the left of the road; this idea ends by taking such a hold on the mind that one is convinced that the house is on the left, and all questions are asked as if one had seen the house in that position. But suppose the house to be really on the right of the road and that by chance the error is never rectified; suppose further that the situation of the house

has some importance for the bringing out of the facts or in forming a theory of the crime, then this false idea may, in spite of its apparent insignificance, considerably confuse the investigation.

All this really proceeds from psychical imperfection to which every man is subject. Much more fatal are delusions resulting from efforts to draw from a case more than it can yield. Granted that no Investigating Officer would wish by the aid of the smallest fraud to attach to a case a character different from or more important than that which it really possesses, yet it is only in conformity with human nature to stop the more willingly at what is more interesting than at what belongs to everyday life. We like to discover romantic features where they do not exist and we even prefer the recital of monstrosities and horrors to that of common every-day facts. This is implanted in the nature of everyone, and though in some to a greater, in some to a lesser extent, still there it is. A hundred proofs, exemplified by what we read most, by what we listen to most willingly, by what sort of news spreads the fastest, show that the majority of men have received at birth a tendency to exaggeration. In itself this is no great evil; the penchant for exaggeration is often the penchant for beautifying our surroundings; and if there were no exaggeration we should lack the notions of beauty and poetry. But in the profession of the criminal expert everything bearing the least trace of exaggeration must be removed in the most energetic and conscientious manner; otherwise, the Investigating Officer will become an expert unworthy of his service and even dangerous to humanity. We cannot but insist that he should not let himself slip into exaggerations, that he should constantly with this object criticise his own work and that of others; and that he should examine it with extra care if he fail to find traces of exaggeration. These creep in in spite of us, and when they exist no one knows where they will stop. The only remedy is to watch oneself most carefully, always work with reflection, and prune out everything having the least suspicion of exaggeration. It is precisely because a certain hardihood and prompt initiative are demanded of Investigating Officers that one finds in the best of them a slight leaning towards the fictitious: one will perceive it in careful observation of oneself and get rid of it by submission to severe discipline.

*Krafft-Ebing,* a psychologist of repute, has stated that great artists, poets, and actors are "mostly neuropathic individuals." We are sure that in saying this he does not intend to suggest that the occupations connected with art, poetry and the stage are conducive to madness, but that a certain neuropathic nature leads those who follow them to become what they have become, *i.e.,* their nature is the cause and not the effect of their occupations. But not only those who are called poets, artists, and actors have this neuropathic nature; many other people in less poetic professions possess it. Though in an unpoetic profession, they may be so highly intellectual that they may be called (as *Krafft-Ebing* has called them) "neuropathic people." Their nerves, it may be said, are of such a nature that they are poetically inclined. Those gifted in this way are the greatest amongst us, but at the same time they have the heaviest responsibility in using such gifts.

A special variation of the preconceived opinion consists in holding to the characterization first given to a fact. This characterization is based on the first impression and may be entirely justified by that impression; but another consideration comes in, namely, to see if what has been noticed at the beginning continues to bear the same aspect throughout the inquiry. It is self-evident that details must be modified, but we do not here refer to these; we confine our attention to the nature of the crime.

The most important examples to be noticed here are those where the problem is whether a violent death is caused by suicide or by unknown causes. Too much attention cannot be given to cases of this kind; they will be treated of later, *e.g., Chapter XVI, Section* vi, "Poisoning"; *Section* iv, "Death by firearms"; *Section* v, "Death by strangulation." Above all a minute examination must be proceeded with where persons are believed to have been drowned, to have fallen from a height, to have been suffocated, or to have died of sudden illnesses (with vomitings, diarrhæa, cramp, etc.).

It is safe to affirm with certainty that an enormous proportion of such cases is due to the hand of another. Many other crimes are often in reality quite different from what one wanted to take them for. The Investigating Officer of experience will disregard at first sight quite a series of crimes and will inquire whether he does not find himself in the presence of something quite different; to this category belongs robbery with violence, or armed with deadly weapons. People often pretend to have been victims to this grave crime where they wish to cover up the loss of money. The Investigating Officer must therefore be on his guard when a person declares that a sum of money has been stolen from his custody, even the grave wounds which the victim of the theft will pretend to have received may be disregarded. Often a man who has gone wrong, lost at cards, dissipated or hidden money held in trust, will inflict such wounds upon himself. The author has met with two cases of this kind in which a peasant, having lost at play the money received for the sale of his cattle, made pretence of robbery merely to avoid the reproaches of his wife.

Rape, again, is often set up to hide the downfall of a young girl who wishes to avoid her shame, by turning the pity and sympathy of everyone towards her; girls often enough invent attacks by quite unknown persons or, graver still, they bring false accusations against persons named. In such cases the real seducer is hardly ever accused of the rape,—he is spared—and no charge is made until the fact of pregnancy is certain. Then the woman allows herself to be seduced by a second person and the latter only is accused of the rape. Unhappily in this case the proof of the falsity of the charge can often only be made later on, at the birth of the child; the date of this shows that conception must have occurred long before the pretended rape. In such a case, therefore, one must never neglect immediately after the birth to have the child examined by experts in order to know whether or not it has attained its full term, for, as we have supposed, at the time of the pretended rape the woman was already a long time enceinte.

It is not uncommon to find people who inflict wounds on themselves; such are, besides persons pretending to be the victims of assaults with deadly weapons, those who try to extort damages or blackmailers;

thus it often happens that after an insignificant scuffle, one of the combatants shows wounds which he pretends to have received. To this category also belong people who declare that certain named persons have recently caused them wounds which in reality date from a long time before: the profit made in such cases from dislocations, old sores on the eyes or ears, and above all from rupture, is well known. Ninety per cent. of affections of this kind, alleged to be the outcome of recent quarrels, bad treatment, etc., date from long before. Profit is also made from wounds received from machinery, etc.; they are exaggerated or fraudulently mixed up with old complaints: the cure is also purposely delayed. We are acquainted with not a few cases where, when the author of the wounds is rich, all sorts of means are employed to keep them open or aggravate them in order to obtain a bigger indemnity. Railway and insurance companies are particularly exposed to frauds of this description.

It is only too little known that many quacks follow the profession of helping people who require "an artificial sickness." In some countries in which conscription exists, these gentlemen drive a roaring trade in giving young men illnesses to free them from military service. They can confer heart disease, carbuncle, jaundice, boils, skin diseases and injuries of every kind.

Singular, but not so very rare, are cases where individuals castrate themselves and impute these mutilations to nomads, gypsies, tinkers, pedlars, &c., but always to unknown people. It is characteristic of these voluntary mutilations that most frequently those who perform them do not quite complete the operation, and that they are for the most part men who manifest excessive piety, or lead a solitary life, as shepherds, gamekeepers, &c.

Among wrongs to property, theft and arson are the most frequently simulated. In the first case, loss of fortune and breach of trust are most frequently sought to be accounted for by the pretence of theft; as a rule it is not very difficult to prove the falsity. The most important point is for the Investigating Officer to remind himself continually that the theft may have been a sham. In many cases the point must be elucidated; it is not necessary to make a noise about it straight away, but let him keep this idea ever before him and examine from this aspect each of the circumstances. After considering what any fact would signify if there had been a real theft, let him ask himself what the fact would signify if the theft were only concocted. The Investigating Officer ought never to permit himself to abstain from making this examination by the rank and situation of the supposed victim of the theft, by the cleverness of the *mise-en-scène,* or by any other consideration. Not only must the self-made victim be

exposed, but innocent people who may be suspected must be protected.

It often happens that people set fire to their own property in such a way as to arouse a suspicion that a fire has been started by others; their aim is often to obtain the amount for which they are insured, often to hide the bad state of their affairs, often to get rid of the traces of a murder or some other crime. In many cases the proof of these facts is not so difficult as it appears. The important point is always to remember that it is possible that they may have wished to hide something; this ought not to be from the start a suspicion amounting to strong probability, but only a door open to every explanation. In order to know exactly the attitude to be maintained towards what has passed, all the circumstances of the crime must be clearly taken into account and submitted to strict logical examination from their commencement to their last stage. If at a given moment something has not been explained, suspicion is justified and pause must be made at the point where the logical sequence is broken, for the purpose of examining if there is no better way of explaining the fact. If one is found the rest of the inquiry is easy.

### Section v.–Certain Qualities essential to an Investigating Officer.

It goes almost without saying that an Investigating Officer should be endowed with all those qualities which every man should desire to possess—indefatigable zeal and application, self-denial and perseverance, swiftness in reading men and a thorough knowledge of human nature, education and an agreeable manner, an iron constitution, and encyclopædic knowledge. Still there are some special qualities the importance of which is frequently overlooked, and to which attention may be peculiarly and forcibly directed.

First and above all an Investigating Officer must possess an abundant store of energy; nothing is more deplorable than a crawling, lazy, and sleepy Investigating Officer. Such a man is fit to be a gentleman-at-large. He who recognises that he is wanting in energy can but turn to something else for he will never make a good investigator. Again the Investigating Officer must be energetic not only in special circumstances, as when, for example, he finds himself face to face with a witness or an accused person who is hot-headed, refractory, and aggressive, or when the work takes him away from office and he proceeds to record a deposition or make an arrest without having his staff or office bell to aid him; but energy must always be displayed when he tackles a difficult, complicated, or obscure case. It is truly painful to examine a report which shows that the Investigating Officer has only fallen to his work with timidity, hesitation, and nervousness, just touching it,

*Photo from the Hammett family photo album. Hammett, standing in back and identified in his wife's hand, seems to be part of a western work crew, possibly Pinkerton's strikebreakers (courtesy of Josephine Hammett).*

so to speak, with the tips of his fingers; but there is satisfaction in observing that a case has been attacked energetically and grasped with animation and vigour. The want of special cleverness and long practice can often be compensated by getting a good grip of the case, but want of energy can be compensated by nothing. Those incomparable words of Goethe, true for all men, are above all true for the criminal expert,

> "Strike not thoughtlessly a nest of wasps,
> But if you strike, strike hard."

The Investigating Officer must have a high grade of real self-denying power. It is not enough for him to be a clever reckoner, a fine speculator, a careful weigher of facts, and to possess a good business head, he must also be self-denying, unostentatious and perfectly honest, resigning at the outset all thoughts of magnificent public successes. The happy-go-lucky apprehension of the policeman, the effective summing-up of the judge, the clever conduct of the case by counsel, all meet with acknowledgment, astonishment and admiration from the public but such triumphs are not for the Investigating Officer. If the latter be working well, those few people who have had an opportunity of really studying the case as it goes along will discover his unceasing and untiring

work from the documents on the record and will form some correct idea of the brain work, power of combination, and extensive knowledge which the Investigating Officer has employed. The Investigating Officer will be held responsible for the smallest and most pardonable mistake, while his care and his merits are seldom acknowledged. Let him be conscious of having done his duty in the only possible way. Beyond this we can only say, "Virtue is its own reward."

Another quality demanded at any price from the Investigating Officer is absolute accuracy. We do not mean by this that he must set out details in the official records exactly as they have been seen or said, for it goes without saying that this will be so done. The quality indicated consists in not being content with mere evidence of third parties or hearsay when it is possible for him to ascertain the truth with his own eyes or by more minute investigation. This is to say no more than that he should be accurate in his work, in the sense of being "exact," as that word is used in its highest scientific signification. Indeed the high degree of perfection to which all sciences have to-day attained is entirely due to "exact" work; and if we compare a recent scientific work, whatever the subject, with an analogous book written some decades ago, we shall notice a great difference between them arising almost wholly from the fact that the work of to-day is more exact than that of yesterday. Naturally in all inquiries a certain amount of imagination is necessary; but a comparison between two scientists of our time will always be to the advantage of the one whose work is most exact: the brilliant and fruitful ideas of the scientist which astonish the world being often far from sudden and happy inspirations but the outcome of exact research. In close observation of facts, in searching for their remotest causes, in making unwearied comparisons, in instituting disagreeable experiments, in short, in attempting to elucidate a problem, the Investigating Officer will observe it under so many aspects and passing through so many phases that the new ideas will spontaneously come to him which, if found to be accurate and skilfully utilised, will certainly give positive results. Since "exactness," or accuracy of work, is of so much importance in all branches of research, this accuracy must also be applied to the work of the Investigating Officer. But what is to be understood by accurate work? It consists in not trusting to others but attending to the business oneself, and even in mistrusting oneself—and going through the case again and again. By so proceeding, one will certainly bring about an accurate piece of work. A thousand mistakes of every description would be avoided if people did not base their conclusions upon premises furnished by others, take as established fact what is only possibility, or as a constantly recurring incident what has only been observed but once. True it is that in his work the Investigating Officer can see but a trifling portion of the facts nor can he repeat his observations. He is obliged largely to trust to what others tell him and it is just here that the difficulty and insufficiency of his work lie. But this inconvenience can to a certain extent be remedied; on the one hand by, wherever possible, making sure of things for himself instead of accepting what others tell him; and on the other hand by trying to give a more exact form to the statements of others, by comparison, experiment, and demonstration, for the purpose of testing the veracity of the deponent's observation and obtaining from him something exact, or at least more exact than before. In endeavouring to verify the facts for himself the Investigating Officer must personally examine localities, make measurements and comparisons, and so form his own opinion. If a small matter which can only be established by accurate observation is in question, not *data* furnished incidentally, but only ascertain facts and investigations specially carried out, must be relied upon.

. . . . . . . . . .

There is but one way to avoid this [building a case on false assumptions], to proceed "steadily," be it at a walk, at a trot, or at the charge; but in such inquiries a halt must from time to time be made and instead of going forward he must look back. He will then examine one by one the different points of the inquiry, taking them up in order from the beginning. He will analyse each acquired result even to the smallest factor of those apparently of the least importance, and when this analysis is carried to its furthest limits, will carefully verify each of these factors, from the point of view of its source, genuineness, and corroboration. If the accuracy of these elements be established, they may then be carefully placed one with another and the result obtained examined as if viewed for the first time. The case will then generally assume quite another complexion, for at the outset the sequence was not so well known; and if it has a different aspect from at first each time the matter is so revised, the question must be asked whether it is in proper adjustment with the whole argument which has been formulated and whether there is any mistake to rectify. If the whole result is defective, the Investigating Officer must have sufficient self-denial to confess, "my calculation is false, I must begin all over again."

### Section vi.–Knowledge of Men.

One of the requisites necessary to enable an Investigating Officer to work with accuracy is a profound knowledge of men, for after all he cannot advance a step without utilising the agency of men. The people who play a rôle in an inquiry are only useful to furnish proofs; they render just as much or just as little service to the Investigating Officer as he knows how to exact from them. The impression of a foot found on the scene of a crime is absolutely of no significance to an ignorant Investigating Officer, but it is a decisive proof if he knows how to make use of it. A witness will tell nothing or make but inaccurate and unimportant statements to an incompetent Investigating Officer, while the very same witness will make precise, true, and important statements to an Investigating Officer who can read him at a glance and knows how to handle him. And if an Investigating Officer who has no knowledge of men by chance discovers the truth, it is worthless to him. There are witnesses who really desire to tell the truth, but when witnesses do not wish to do so the result is truly lamentable. The record shows only how the Investigating Officer has let himself be duped by the witnesses and led by them just where they chose. A treatise on the knowledge of human character, teaching how really to know men, has never yet been written and probably never will be; we can but indicate certain methods available in particular cases, few though these unfortunately are.

When the accused is an old offender, a most important and really valuable means is the study of documents, if there be any, forming the record of his career. One can then start with more confidence. If the matter is of some importance, the old record must be studied as if bearing on the case in hand. It is not sufficient for example merely to read through the statements of the accused and to look up a few important registers,–the record must be studied in its entirety, the whole history must be gone through step by step and in its fullest development, in order to see how the accused has defended himself on previous occasions and compare that defence with his present one. It is astonishing how men stick to the same defence and justification of their conduct, even after a long space of time. This is not to say that an individual who pleads guilty once will do so always, or that if he has once endeavoured to vindicate himself by throwing suspicion upon the witnesses, that he will repeat the charge upon every occasion; nothing in life repeats itself with such servile accuracy; but the broad lines of the picture, the whole impression that the examination has produced, will be renewed as often as he is examined. Every Investigating Officer who, following the procedure indicated, studies at the outset the antecedent record of the accused will receive at the commencement of the new examination the impression that the accused is striking out a new line; but as the examination advances he will regain, little by little but very accurately, the impression as a whole and will be definitely convinced that his man has not changed. The process is indeed identical, only perhaps with the difference that the individual has in the meantime acquired more experience, has become more cunning and more circumspect, or on the other hand that he has become older and has fallen away somewhat in craftiness and address. The picture previously seen has become tarnished, but the broad lines stand out quite plainly. If one is in possession of the records in several cases relating to the accused, and if they have been carefully studied, one will know his man so well as to be able to say in advance how he will behave and what explanations he will give, on what points he may be believed, about what he will lie, and how he must be handled in order to extract the truth from him. The study of old records is very important not only in the case of the accused, but also as regards important witnesses who are themselves old offenders or who have given evidence in other cases. In this way one often discovers how easiest to handle the witness, what to say to him, how far to believe him, and the readiest method of proving him to be a liar.

Another guide to the knowledge of men consists in bringing to the examination the closest attention and in seeking all the time to read the very soul of the man.

If the Investigating Officer wishes to know men, every individual who enters his room must become an object worthy of study from the first moment. The manner in which he presents himself, looks around, allows himself to be questioned, replies, asks questions in return, in a word the way in which he behaves, ought never, even in the most insignificant affair, to be a matter of indifference to the conscientious Investigating Officer. He must always make himself form an idea as to whether the person has spoken the truth and the whole truth, or whether he has lied, or passed over something in silence. He must also look for the motives prompting the individual to act in the way in which he has done, how his statements fit in with the circumstances which have to be taken into account, the effect he has desired to produce, what was of importance to himself, and what means he has employed to make his testimony appear sincere and accurate. The Investigating Officer ought to remember, or better still note down, what he has thus observed or believes he has observed. This will be of use to him during the course of the inquiry. If in its course he finds a circumstance proving the accuracy or inaccuracy of the previous observations, he secures in the first case confirmation of the view taken and in the second will endeavour to find out why he has been deceived and discover where and how the error has taken birth.

Before finally leaving a case the Investigating Officer has a fresh opportunity at the time of the general revision, always necessary on other grounds, of going over all he has observed and comparing it with the results obtained; this work costs much time and trouble but great profit is obtained from it in the shape of valuable and interesting observations for future guidance. Above all, where the Investigating Officer has succeeded in completely elucidating an intricate case and has arrived at an unexpected result, then it is most useful to go again over the inquiry and verify all the depositions of the witnesses, noting how they accord with the now known course of events. He can then understand why such a witness spoke with so much hesitation or why another was so embarrassed, and he comprehends a mass of equivocal and uncertain statements. Many things which appeared to be quite contradictory now fit in together neatly: he can explain the tone of voice, the doubt, or the assurance, shown by the witnesses while giving evidence; for future cases this task is most valuable.

Yet it is not in the exercise of his duty that the Investigating Officer can best acquire this knowledge of men, but in his daily and ordinary life, in his relations with his fellows, and in the course of ordinary events. He does indeed learn while working and every case teaches him something new; but his necessary occupa-

*Hammett with other patients at the U.S. Public Health Service Cushman Hospital in Tacoma, Washington, winter 1920–1921 (courtesy of Josephine Hammett)*

tions give him so much to do and in so many ways that they are not precisely the best suited for imparting instruction. In following his profession he must always be in possession of pre-acquired knowledge; this may be perfected and increased, but the true time for studying is gone. The principal reason is that nothing can be properly learned without actual experience. "Practice is better than precept," rightly says a popular proverb. But experience can be very well gained in private life, while it is not always convenient to acquire it during the exercise of one's profession. To this end everything in life can be utilised. Every conversation, every concise statement, every word thrown out by chance, every action, every aspiration, every trait of character, every item of conduct, every look or gesture, observed in others, be it only for a moment or during a long course of years, and compared with events as they arise, ascertained facts, and realities. The Investigating Officer ought indeed to keep a balance sheet for every man with whom he comes into contact, noting down therein his observations upon his acts, his words, and physiognomy, balancing them with events, making comparisons, and controlling and verifying them. The best way to fill his diary, if he keeps one, will be to write down observations on himself and others. But many things can be learned without written notes. As a rule we find no difficulty in remembering the impression made upon us by the actions of others and do not easily forget the

discovery of the mistakes we have made as regards them. To him who goes through life with no desire to enlighten himself, these disillusionments only produce a painful impression; but he who wishes to profit by his experiences in life can obtain from them lessons of utility. "The best employed money," says a philosopher, "is that of which we have been defrauded, because with that money we have purchased the circumspection necessary to life."

The Investigating Officer can also profit by those painful experiences, which are the most numerous in life. They invariably arise from false ideas we have acquired and, when the mischief comes, we may yet derive great profit from it, if, instead of bewailing our loss, we look upon it as an "interesting problem" and try to find the cause. He will in such a case revive the idea first formed, attempt to discover how he formed it, and compare it with the experience just undergone; the mistake committed may then be recognised, he will not repeat it, and will be able to make use of the acquired results of experience in his profession.

Other experiences than those in which we ourselves take part may prove valuable. The smallest observation may some day be of decisive importance. We are told something and believe it and later we discover its inaccuracy; something is told us which we do not believe and afterwards find to be quite true. This sort of thing appears of little importance in life, but there is matter for instruction in it if we care to find out how we have allowed ourselves to fall into error, how the mistake arose—whether voluntarily or not,—how we might have been able to discover the truth at the time, and why we did not discover it. Perhaps subsequent events will even enable us to find out the exact reason why the truth was kept dark, how our mistake came about, and finally the truth itself. Let us place ourselves in our former position and consider what our conclusion would then have been. By acting frequently in this way we shall be the less liable to make mistakes when analogous cases crop up.

What is above all of importance in private life is to ferret out the motive for a lie. When a story about something has been related either to ourselves or to others, false in some particular which we only discover later on, we more often than not carry the matter no further, because it is of no importance in itself; but if we wish to gather a lesson therefrom we will try—by a direct method for preference, as by frankly and honestly asking the question—to discover why the lie has been told. Most often we shall find that the lie has been started out of human weakness rather than through real perversity. Throughout life we will find that lying is infinitely more common than is generally believed. We shall be much less disposed to be indignant about falsehoods if we recognise that the motives for them are most often perfectly childish and foolish. What an Investigating Officer has thus learned in private life can often be utilised in important cases. He will understand that a man is not necessarily in league with a thief because he has not spoken the truth, and that if he has told a falsehood it is often out of vanity or some other little human weakness.

## Section vii.—"Orientation"—Finding his Bearings.

The Investigating Officer is "*orienté,*" that is, "has found his bearings" (the metaphor is derived from the mariner's compass), when he knows his department, his district, his subordinates, his auxiliaries, the means at his disposal for facilitating his work, his possible difficulties, in short when he is acquainted with everything he may come across in his official career and what may be of service or disservice to him. He must not forget that every case of even ordinary complexity presents or may present so many difficulties that when he comes to attack it he has neither time nor opportunity for studying the means calculated to lighten his labour or solve his difficulties. All this ought to have been seen to beforehand.

Suppose that an Investigating Officer has just arrived at his post. His first duty is to make the acquaintance of his superiors and subordinates. It is self-evident that the most important person to him is his principal assistant—the magisterial clerk, or police sub-inspector, or station-house officer, as the case may be—for all depends on this man's intelligence, willing co-operation, and knowledge of the district and people. When he can be trusted, his information is most valuable, more especially if the assistant happens to have been for a long time in his post. The Investigating Officer will then try to obtain information about the other officials so as to know what to expect from them. Every official under Government, no matter what his duties, is bound to promote the general welfare and it is incumbent on him in important cases to lend assistance to officials in other services. But in order to command the help of other officials when needed, the Investigating Officer ought to be on good terms with them beforehand and in his own sphere to show himself as serviceable to them. This co-operation may be most varied and extend to every imaginable branch of information. As a rule the most important thing to know is, to what extent one can rely upon and trust people with whom one has business.

. . . . . . . . . .

The Investigating Officer ought to study as accurately as possible the local topography. From the moment an official becomes an Investigating Officer, he is no longer anything but an Investigating Officer. All that he does, observes, studies, or hears, ought to be subordinated to the single aim of knowing how he can make use in his work of what he has learned. He ought not exclusively to occupy himself with one side of things, his knowledge ought to be extensive,—as extensive as possible. Everything can be of service to him, and it is exactly for this reason that he ought to obtain information about everything—but always with the view of making use of it as an Investigating Officer. He will be indeed unable to "go for a walk," in the sense of strolling with mind at rest, enjoying peacefully the beauties of Nature. He cannot go to the band merely for the pleasure of listening to the music. In all the walks he makes, either for pleasure or duty, an ordnance or survey map should be in his hand so as to study thereon all the roads, hills, and watercourses, engraving their names upon his memory. He ought to know to whom the smallest hut belongs, to make note of every road traversed, to seek out known localities, and establish their relative situation, their distance apart, and the means of communication between them, to know what can be seen therefrom, and how far the view extends. When he sets out he should look at his watch and should afterwards mark on the back of his map the time it takes from point to point. A peasant can but give in measures of time the distance from his house to the church, the market, the nearest railway station, etc., etc., for he finds it inconvenient to arrive late at a religious ceremony, miss his train, etc. If he is questioned upon any other distance, he will no doubt always answer promptly but also invariably inaccurately; and this may often be the source of grave mistakes. It is not always possible when necessity arises to have the distance measured by an official and therefore a note of it should be taken in advance as opportunity presents.

There are localities which the Investigating Officer must examine in the light of future events—hotels and drinking-shops and brothels, because of brawls that may take place in them, mortuaries because of *post mortems* that may be carried out there, ponds and wells in villages on account of possible accidents by drowning, forests because of poaching and illicit felling, etc. He must try to become acquainted with the local police stations, the organisation of forest guards, the beats of the perambulating police force, customs circles, irrigation systems, the manner of closing doors, windows, stables, and outhouses. Within the distance of a league one often finds quite dissimilar practices.

Attention must also be paid to industrial works and technical installations, which vary greatly according to localities; because, when the case arises, one often finds very great difficulty in understanding them from the descriptions given of them, which are always more or less defective. A flour-mill, an oil-mill, a saw-mill, a blacksmith's forge, a stone quarry, a coke furnace, a brick and tile kiln, and many other industrial establishments, differ in appearance in different localities and cannot be pictured from mere description; to know what they are really like, they must have been seen. Everyone has found by experience that he can form but a very inexact idea of one of these places from a mere verbal description; on the other hand it is thoroughly comprehended if seen only once. A great many educated people have never entered a flour-mill or a saw-mill in their lives, and yet such establishments have considerable interest. This is all the more surprising as everyone must have passed, say an oil-mill, hundreds of times and could have inspected it without any inconvenience. The Investigating Officer should never let slip an opportunity of visiting an industrial establishment or factory, of having everything shown and explained to him in the most detailed manner; he will generally find the management ready to afford every information. Every man, especially the plain man, is pleased when interest is shown in his work and what he happens to be doing; when he can teach and explain anything, he always exhibits willingly and readily whatever there is to be seen. If one already knows something of what he is showing you, so much the better; he

will be the more disposed to speak. If one knows nothing, care must be taken in questioning him, for ordinary folk cannot imagine that educated people know nothing of such every-day things. He may become distrustful and circumspect, fancying that he is being played with. One must be contented in such a situation with examining, asking short questions and listening; on the next occasion things will work better.

If the Investigating Officer has some technical knowledge of this kind he can in many cases facilitate his work. Take for example a mill, not a very rare thing, and suppose that the Investigating Officer has never in his life set foot in one. An accident takes place in the mill, or a burglary, or a fraud or embezzlement by the staff, or a fire, etc. Each of these cases will have some connection with the technical construction of the mill. The accident has been brought about for instance by a fault of manufacture, or material, or want of supervision in some part of the building; the burglar will also have profited by some portion of the machinery; the staff could not have carried out the frauds without knowing the plan of the interior and the relative position of the various departments; as regards fire one cannot possibly find how it has taken place without knowing the complete fitting up of the mill. How can an Investigating Officer conduct the inquiry in such a case when he possesses not the slightest assured base for his investigations? Let it be again remarked that the recollection of places once seen is easily retained—most men find little difficulty in remembering places; even when the details have been forgotten, the memory is soon refreshed when a witness begins to speak about them.

Another important point is that of the means of communication in a district, main roads, ordinary roads, cart-tracks, footpaths, etc. It is not difficult to become acquainted with these. The Investigating Officer has only to find and mark on the map all the roads he has passed over and see whether they are correctly set down, which will probably be the case. As regards the principal arteries, corrections will mainly show where a main road has degenerated into a side-track through the making of a new main road, or where a second-class road has been promoted to the position of a main road. He will also note down any other changes that may have taken place, such as new buildings, houses abandoned, changes in the nature of the crops, alterations in watercourses, etc.; in short his map must always be kept up to date. Nor should ordinary footbridges newly made or disused be forgotten; nor wells, tanks, marshes, ponds, or other pieces of water be overlooked. To these latter special attention must be given. On a map the extent and direction of the water may be seen, but this is not enough. We must note the depth, nature of banks, change in the volume of water, sluices, fords and dams, in short all particulars in connection with the water. For water plays a rôle in many a criminal case, and it is not easy to do good work while unacquainted with its usual aspects.

Finally, attention must be paid to the interior of houses. When in the country the Investigating Officer has examined in full detail several peasants' houses, big and small, he knows practically all others, for they are constructed in accordance with a small number of types. But these several types must be known. The various parts of the houses and the uses they are put to must be noticed. Otherwise great difficulties would be encountered in the very first case of theft or burglary.

It is also of the greatest importance that the Investigating Officer should be thoroughly posted up about the experts that he will have at his command when the occasion arises. Naturally he ought to be perfectly well acquainted with the special talents, singularities, and weaknesses, of the most important aspects—the medical jurisprudents. But experts in other departments ought also to be known to him, such as experts in firearms, building, valuations, etc. All these should be known beforehand; he must learn what to expect from them and how they may be usefully employed. But for this it will not suffice merely to know their profession, this can be done by reading; their particular talents and singularities must be accurately ascertained.

. . . . . . . . . .

If in towns the police force and its auxiliaries are of great value to the Investigating Officer, the rural police are none the less so, for without them he could do little and often nothing at all. But the result obtained with the aid of the police will in fact depend on the Investigating Officer himself. If he is on good terms with the police force and knows how to make use of it he will obtain good results; otherwise the result will be negative; and in the latter case the Investigating Officer is always at fault and not the police. But a subordinate is not a machine; even a policeman, put into uniform and subjected to military discipline, preserves his individuality; you cannot kill it and must therefore submit to learn how to make use of it. This is why the Investigating Officer should possess the most accurate information as to the humour, character, and education of his assistants. One officer is distinguished for tact, another for energy, another for unusual physical strength; if in a difficult case one of these qualities is specially demanded, everything may be lost if the right man is not employed. If he knows his men he will have the right officer sent to him, explain the case, and give him his opinions and plans; he will listen also to the views of the other, he will take precautions against inci-

*Jose Dolan, Hammett, and a nurse chaperone, Cushman Hospital, winter 1920–1921. Hammett and Jose fell in love while he was a patient and she was a nurse in the respiratory unit. They were married the following summer (courtesy of Josephine Hammett).*

dents which may crop up, he will discuss with him the various ways of setting to work; in a word he will explain the whole matter as clearly as possible.

Thus posted up the officer will certainly do his best; his self-conceit, thus awakened, will prove a powerful stimulant. And if his work is well done, he should be congratulated on his success; a cordial word of encouragement and praise is so quickly given and goes so far. Think of the difficulty of a policeman's work: often heavily laden, often insufficiently protected from cold or heat, he has to tramp many miles to fulfil a mission for which he is solely responsible, strictly tied down by the innumerable ligaments of red tape, unable to take counsel with anyone. He must display the finest tact, indomitable courage, do neither too much nor too little, and finally reduce the whole to the limits of a complete and accurate report. If he has done all this without a mistake, his co-operation must prove most valuable; and it is only common justice on the part of his superior, whom he has saved so much trouble and work and whom he has provided with so useful a foundation for his further inquiries, to tender his devoted assistant a word of acknowledgment and thanks. He should also express his satisfaction in presence of the man's comrades and superiors; honour to whom honour is due. Well-earned praise is the best stimulant of zeal; nothing discourages a man so much as to find his superior always discontented, constantly finding fault, and never having a good word to say of anyone or anything; this must be kept in view in all our relations with subordinate officials.

### Section viii.–Jurymen.

It will be useful for the Investigating Officer to bear in mind that his work may at times be submitted to a body of men whose decisions often can be explained by no discoverable principles and whose intellectual and moral faculties work in mysterious ways. Considering also that his labours will be presented to this body by a third person, it is all the more incumbent on him to endeavour, before the case leaves his hands, to eliminate every possible cause of error discernible by the eye of ordinary human intelligence.

In this view, the Investigating Officer will endeavour to present the case to himself as it would appear to a person absolutely devoid of the experience he himself possesses. He possesses knowledge of legal theories, of substantive law, and of procedure. The juryman knows nothing of these things and the Investigating Officer should therefore never forget that his work may one day be placed before a jury of the uninitiated. These bestow great attention upon the mode in which an inquiry has been conducted, they are always trying to find out if the Investigating Officer is worthy of belief or not. As judges they are also incompetent; an inexact though absolutely unimportant piece of information, an insignificant contradiction, an unimportant gap, which a juryman has himself discovered in the inquiry, is sufficient motive for distrusting the whole case for the prosecution; it loses all value in their eyes; and the accused is acquitted in face of the most overwhelming proofs of his guilt. On the other hand a smart bit of procedure, the revelation of an accessory fact, or some other circumstance, will so please a jury that it will condemn the accused simply from confidence in the Public Prosecutor.

. . . . . . . . . .

The best method to adopt in every case that is to go before a jury is to arrange everything as if one were dealing with a child; stick to the truth, draw no conclusions, exclude everything that may appear contradictory, use the simplest words, and be absolutely clear. In this way failure may sometimes be avoided.

### Section ix.–The "Expeditious" Investigating Officer.

The struggle with crime is after all only a war for which the first necessity is plenty of money; money is the best aid for the conduct of criminal justice. But if the service is undermanned and the pecuniary allotment is insufficient, what is to be done? In answer to this query we have the invention of "the Expeditious Officer." Every inquiry may be closed extremely quickly if one wishes; if one considers it unnecessary to take the evidence of certain persons who have been named, there is no need to enter their names in the list of witnesses for the prosecution, and if they are not on the list, there is no necessity to question them; here is time gained at once! Let some ignorant persons be asked whether a visit to the spot will help to clear up the case and they will reply no; here then is sufficient excuse for not paying the visit and here again time is saved. A band of thieves is accused of having committed a dozen burglaries. There is quite enough evidence to get them convicted and one is not absolutely obliged to start the police upon investigations which may perhaps bring to light another dozen which the same band has committed; here again time is saved. Suppose there is a big cheating case, it is quite the thing to pick up certain "well established" facts and stop there; doubtless to do the thing well one ought to place the matter on a wide basis and to study and clear up in its entirety the procedure of the person who has committed the fraud and examine the whole business from the point of view of loyalty to one's employers: but is one under any obligation to do so? By not doing so more time is saved. Again what a lot of work there is to fix the real blame in an accident case. What endless consultations with experts, what repeated visits to the spot, what minute questionings, all taking up such an enormous amount of time; by fixing the responsibility upon the first workman who is found at fault, the whole case is ended like a shot. These examples might be multiplied without end; a little time saved in each inquiry ends in the gain of a considerable amount in the long run; the inquiries run on all right and when our artistic Investigating Officer is sufficiently skilled in suppressing the difficulties and obstacles that may

*Hammett in 1921. He was transferred from Cushman Hospital to Camp Kearney near San Diego, another U.S. Public Health Hospital, where he stayed until his discharge in May 1921. He moved to Seattle briefly before settling in San Francisco in June (courtesy of Josephine Hammett).*

prove troublesome in quick work, he will well deserve the title of "expeditious."

Let the Investigating Officer who has no qualms of conscience when gathering such laurels, act thus if he so desires. It would be useless to try to turn him from his course. Whether he will be able to look back without remorse upon his work even though his fame for being "expeditious" has brought him many substantial advantages, is another question. No one will suggest that inquiries should languish or be conducted slowly, that it is necessary to write or do what is absolutely superfluous, but in a serious inquiry we *must* seek out what may however indirectly furnish or corroborate proof of the guilt or innocence of an accused. The Investigating Officer who neglects this primary duty incurs a very great responsibility. The conduct of every inquiry costs much time and trouble; the smallest piece of forgetfulness or the most pardonable carelessness may have the gravest and worst consequences; to do good work and to be "expeditious," are two things which mutually exclude each other. Every Investi-

gating Officer should renounce the vain glory of being considered "expeditious."

### Section x.–Accuracy and Precision in Details.

We shall now notice certain details which, small in themselves, are of importance when taken together. It seems superfluous to state that the Investigating Officer should avoid all disorder, and yet it too often happens that an Investigating Officer who has not a natural instinct for order and neatness does not keep his eye close enough to many small matters, especially when he is much worried in his work.

Notes must be kept in most minute order, the most insignificant things must be written down at once, so as not to accumulate for a future date fully occupied with unexpected work. Mistrust the hourly expression, "I will not forget." It is just the more important things which one thinks will never be forgotten, and in consequence it is just the important things that are forgotten. . . .

*Hammett was an avid reader of true-crime stories, especially those told with authority. He was particularly fond of* Celebrated Criminal Cases of America. *Thomas S. Duke was Captain of Police in San Francisco in the early years of the twentieth century. His short descriptions of memorable cases are told in a straightforward style from the perspective of a professional law enforcement officer. The case reprinted here recounts a murder committed to gain possession of treasures that are not what they seem.*

### The Murder of George Hill
### for a Worthless Cluster of Imitation Diamonds
Thomas S. Duke
*Celebrated Criminal Cases of America*
(San Francisco: James H. Barry, 1910), pp. 63–65

In 1865 there resided in San Francisco a young man named George Hill, who had inherited a comfortable fortune, which he had almost entirely dissipated in the gambling games. He was a flashy dresser and constantly wore a scarf pin, said to contain a cluster of diamonds valued at $1,500.

Hill had a room in the Mansion House, on Dupont, near Sacramento street, and on February 15, 1865, he disappeared. Being of a somewhat wild and roving disposition, no significance was attached to this, either by his landlady or associates.

Some weeks after his disappearance, a gardener named Mr. McGloin was walking through the sand out near his home in San Souci Valley, which is now better designated as the vicinity of Fulton and Baker streets. A dog he had with him began pulling and tugging at a piece of hay rope, which appeared to be securely fastened to something buried under the sand.

Curiosity prompted Mr. McGloin to investigate, and to his horror he found that the rope was tied around the badly decomposed body of a man. He immediately informed the police of his discovery and the body was brought into town for identification. There was a hole in the side of the head made by some blunt instrument which had evidently caused his death. All valuables had been removed from the body.

Owing to the advanced state of decomposition, it was very difficult to identify the body and the authorities were about to bury the remains when a newspaper reporter who knew Hill well, identified the body.

The police then proceeded to Hill's room, and the landlady stated that the day after his disappearance, a young man whom she described accurately had come to her house and stated that Hill was about

# CELEBRATED
# CRIMINAL CASES
# OF AMERICA

BY
THOMAS S. DUKE
CAPTAIN OF POLICE, SAN FRANCISCO

PUBLISHED WITH APPROVAL OF THE HONORABLE BOARD OF
POLICE COMMISSIONERS OF SAN FRANCISCO

SAN FRANCISCO, CAL.
THE JAMES H. BARRY COMPANY
1910

*Title page from a true-crime book Hammett admired. Sam Spade keeps a copy of this book on his bedside table, and Nick Charles quotes a long passage from Duke in* The Thin Man *(Collection of Richard Layman).*

to go to Contra Costa County to procure some money, but that he had met with an accident.

The stranger produced a shirt which had some blood on it and stated that Hill had instructed him to exchange it for a clean one. He was admitted to Hill's room and, after putting the bloody shirt in the trunk and removing some other articles, he departed, but returned shortly afterward to regain possession of the shirt. The landlady's suspicions becoming aroused she refused to admit him to Hill's room.

One of the officers who heard the landlady describe this man recalled that a man then in custody on a charge of forgery answered that description perfectly. Upon being brought before the landlady he was positively identified as the man she referred to

*James McParland, the Pinkerton's operative called the greatest detective in the West by Clarence Darrow. McParland worked under cover to expose the Molly Maguires in Pennsylvania in 1866 and 1867 and investigated the murder of former governor of Idaho Frank Steunenberg in 1906 and 1907, implicating high-ranking members of the Western Federation of Miners, who were acquitted at trial. McParland was superintendent of Pinkerton's Denver office, known for its union-busting activities, and Western Division manager. He is regarded by some historians as a model for Hammett's Old Man of the Continental Detective Agency. He died in 1918.*

and it was learned that his name was Thomas Byrnes, a butcher by trade and the son of the keeper of a roadhouse near Calvary Cemetery.

Mr. McGloin, who discovered Hill's body, was a warm friend of the family of the murderer.

It was ascertained that on the evening of February 15, 1865, Hill procured a two-horse buggy from Wright & Roden's livery stable on Kearny street, near Pine, and in company with Byrnes started for the Cliff House.

About midnight the horses returned alone to the stable, causing the stable-keeper to conclude that there had been a runaway and that the horses had broken away from the vehicle. After a while Byrnes came in and stated that they had met with an acci-

dent and that his partner being injured, had sent him for another team.

Before starting away with his second rig, Byrnes asked for a shovel, stating that he wanted to dig the wheels of the other buggy out of the sand. It was observed by the stable man that Byrnes threw a piece of hay-rope into the buggy.

When Hill and Byrnes started the first time, Byrnes insisted on taking a monkey-wrench along, stating that it might be needed.

When they arrived at a spot near where the body was found, Byrnes crushed Hill's skull with the monkey-wrench, the end of which fitted into the wound perfectly. He then cut the harness and scared the horses away, to make it appear that Hill met his death in a runaway accident. He reconsidered, however, and decided that a runaway would not account for the loss of Hill's property, so the idea of burying the body came to his mind. The rope was used to drag it into the sand, and of course the shovel was used to dig the grave.

It was afterwards learned that Byrnes attempted to pawn Hill's jewelry and was greatly chagrined to learn that "diamonds" which he thought were worth nearly two thousand dollars, were in reality worth less than three dollars.

Byrnes was found guilty of murder and after a futile appeal to the Supreme Court was executed on September 3, 1866.

---

*Phil Haultain was located by San Francisco detective David Fechheimer in the course of research for his Hammett issue of* City of San Francisco *magazine in 1975. Haultain is the only Pinkerton to have been interviewed about his service with Hammett.*

### We Never Sleep
*City of San Francisco*, 9 (4 November 1975): 33–35

### Phil Haultain Looks Back

"I was 80 last week. I've got a big oak tree in my patio that is probably 150 or 200 years old and I always worry about it. It's the kind that loses its leaves in the winter. It's huge and it's old and there could be a loss in property value if it dies."

We were sitting across the desk from Mr. Haultain at his office in Emeryville (he's head of a company that makes conveyor belting). He had responded to an ad in the *Chronicle* seeking out old-time Pinkerton operatives. The correct pronunciation, he told us, is op-e-ra-tives, with a long *a*. This is what else he had to say:

CITY: *Are you a native San Franciscan?*

*The James Flood Building at the corner of Market and Powell Streets. The San Francisco Pinkerton's office was in suite 314. Albert Samuels Jewelers, where Hammett later worked as advertising manager, was less than one block east on Market Street (San Francisco Historical Photograph Collection).*

H: No, I was born in San Jose. In 1906 I was living in Muir Woods with my parents. We came over the day of the earthquake and watched the Palace Hotel burn down. That was quite a fire. You guys weren't around then.

CITY: *When did you become a Pinkerton?*

H: In 1921. My first day I went up to Calistoga with an Australian chap by the name of Robinson. This was on the Arbuckle case.

CITY: *Was Hammett with Pinkerton then?*

H: Yes. He was senior to me in the agency. He was on the Arbuckle case, too. We were working for Arbuckle's lawyers.

CITY: *What were you doing in Calistoga?*

H: Robinson and I were supposed to shadow the two witnesses that the district attorney's office had in tow—two young women. But you can't do a shadow job very well in Calistoga. Calistoga was a very small thing at that time. So it was decided that the best thing was to fraternize with 'em and we broke the ice by fraternizing with that female caretaker from the district attorney's office. That worked much better than trying to shadow them. The fraternizing might have been Hammett's idea. We were staying in touch with the San Francisco office for instructions.

CITY: *So what was the result?*

H: They finally got wise and the district attorney's office in San Francisco called them back. Robinson had his car and we tried to follow them down to the city but they sidetracked us.

CITY: *What happened next?*

H: I continued working on the case down in San Francisco partly with Hammett, partly with others . . . I

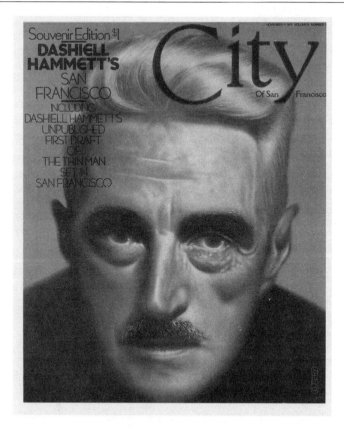

*Cover for the issue that features an interview with Phil Haultain, who worked with Hammett as a Pinkerton's agent (Collection of Richard Layman)*

told my wife today that Sam Hammett made me a good shadow man, even though I always wore a hat like this at that time. (Haultain pointed to his brown Stetson.) I remember going down Stockton Street, past what is now Macy's, with Hammett. I think we were shadowing a couple from Los Angeles. Not a married couple; they were witnesses for the prosecution. And Hammett taught me. We circled around them, and even with this hat, they still didn't get wise. He was a wonderful investigator.

CITY: *What was he like?*

H: He was tall, thin, smart as a steel trap. He knew his business. He wasn't a drinking man in those days, not that I know of. But he used to smoke like hell. Rolled his own cigarettes.

CITY: *What was his position at the agency?*

H: He rated at the very top with them. Very experienced. Yeah, he rated high.

CITY: *Who ran the San Francisco office?*

H: The superintendent was Phil Geaque (pronounced Gee-ack). Geaque at that time was probably around 40. Very smart investigator, smarter than hell. I think he came out of Pinkerton Chicago or somewhere back there. He was short. Bald-headed. Heavy cigarette smoker. (Philip Geaque went on to a career in the Secret Service, where he was FDR's bodyguard.)

CITY: *Did Hammett have a lot of respect for him?*

H: Yeah. He was an exciting guy to work for. He was sharp, and I think that's probably why he liked Hammett. Hammett was smart and Geaque was smart and that was a long time ago.

CITY: *How much money did you make as a Pinkerton?*

H: Six dollars a day, 24 hours a day, 365 days a year. I don't know how you guys work nowadays, but we'd be idle for some days and then we'd be on something right along. Bang bang bang.

CITY: *Did you carry guns?*

H: Oh yes, at times. I remember this one time, we were working on the hold-up of the California Street Cable Company on California and Hyde. And Sam Hammett said, "You'd better take a gun. No, you'd better take two." So I took two guns. But nothing happened.

CITY: *Did Hammett have a gun?*

H: Oh I think so. I'm sure he did.

CITY: *Do any cases stand out in your memory? Either with Hammett or without him?*

H: I remember I had a job over in Oakland at one time, to shadow a police officer that the chief of police suspected of skullduggery and I shadowed him down around 14th and Broadway and he carried a cane like I do. Though I only carry mine for protection against my wife. But he, this little cop, used it to beat up a woman on the street at 14th and Broadway, which of course was nice for the chief, who wanted to get something on him.

CITY: *When did you get out of detective work?*

H: After a few years. I went to work for an electrical appliance company.

CITY: *Did you ever do detective work again?*

H: No. But I'll tell you: it gets in your blood. You'll find it someday. It's hard to get out of. Yeah, even though you don't make any money at it.

CITY: *What else do you remember about Hammett?*

H: He lived up on Eddy Street and he had another place where I used to visit him up at 408 Turk on the northwest corner of Turk and Larkin. On the first floor.

CITY: *What was the apartment like?*

H: It was neat, and he had a lot of books lying around. And he was a great smoker.

CITY: *Was he writing in those days?*

H: He was writing potboilers, just to keep going. Then he came out eventually with *The Maltese Falcon*. That made him.

CITY: *Did you still know him when he published the* Falcon?

H: No, I had lost track of him entirely. But when *The Maltese Falcon* came out, it rang a lot of bells. (*At this point Haultain pointed to a black, jewel-encrusted object on his expansive desk. [. . .] "There's something over there," he said. "Take a look at it." The top came off and we were looking at two ivory hemispheres and what appeared to be a ceremonial spoon.*)

H: It's the skull of a very holy man. A lot of museums would like me to give it to them. But unless they have funds to buy it, I'll keep it as a family heirloom.

CITY: *Who was the holy man?*

H. A guy who had a good skull.

CITY: *What's the spoon and stuff for?*

H: I understood that it was used to sip blood from human sacrifices.

CITY: *When did you get it?*

H: About 50 years ago. More than 50. An uncle of mine who lived in Calcutta, India, sent it to me. It was taken as loot by a member of the British Younghusband Expedition to Lhasa, Tibet. The original owner might have put a curse on it.

CITY: *Did you ever show this to Hammett?*

H: I can't remember. But I'm pretty sure I had it back then.

CITY: *Do you remember anything else about Hammett?*

H: He was quite a character. But you guys weren't around then.

CITY: *What's the secret of your having stuck around so long, Mr. Haultain?*

H: I've led a pure life. I tell my wife that. I've hit two big Keno tickets at Harrah's in Reno. And now I'm heading for a third. If I can do it three times, that's a record.

# Hammett's Cases

*There is scant information about cases Hammett worked on as a Pinkerton's agent. The New York office, where his reports before his move to Spokane in May 1920 were likely filed, was destroyed by fire, and Pinkerton's claims all the case files were lost. From May to November 1920 Hammett worked in the Northwest, probably under the direction of James McParland, who ran the western regional office in Denver that was heavily involved in strikebreaking on railroads and in mines. In 1921 Hammett worked in San Francisco, almost certainly on a part-time basis because of his health. None of his case reports from either the Denver office or the San Francisco office has been located. He claimed he worked on the Gus Schaefer jewel robbery case, the SS Sonoma gold-specie robbery, and for the Fatty Arbuckle defense during his first trial. Pinkerton's agent Phil Haultain says he and Hammett worked together on the California Street Cable Car robbery and the Fatty Arbuckle cases. In interviews Hammett occasionally alluded to other cases, but the evidence for his involvement is anecdotal. Aside from these assignments, there are questionable accounts of his work on other cases—such as the Nicky Arnstein bond theft in 1921—and claims that are difficult to believe, such as Lillian Hellman's statement that Hammett was asked to assassinate labor leader Frank Little in 1917.*

## The Schaefer Jewel Robbery

*In 1934 when his syndicated comic strip "Secret Agent X-9" was published, King Features Syndicate promoted Hammett as a former detective who wrote from experience. To make the point, they ran accounts of the "Gloomy Gus" Schaefer jewel robbery, crediting Hammett with Schaefer's arrest. Contemporary accounts of the case vary from the 1934 version syndicated by King Features.*

## Hammett Traps Gem Holdup Suspects
*San Francisco Call-Bulletin,* 26 January 1934, p. 7

In December, 1921, three thugs rifled the Shapiro Jewelry Company of St. Paul and escaped with $130,000 in gems and silver.

Two months later bay region police received the flash that the suspects were thought to be hiding somewhere near San Francisco.

Dashiell Hammett, author of "Secret Agent X-9," detective picture strip, which begins Monday on The Call-Bulletin comic page, was at that time a Pinkerton operative. He was assigned the case along with other investigators.

## Hideout Near Vallejo

Weeks of searching revealed the gang headquarters at a roadhouse near Vallejo. Hammett, disguised as a wealthy business man in search of pleasure, frequented the hangout until he had his men well marked.

One night there was a meeting of the gang. To eavesdrop, Hammett went outside the house and climbed upon a side porch. Suddenly the porch, with a loud crash, gave way. Hammett, though badly bruised and shaken, managed to make a getaway before anyone could ask embarrassing questions.

The gang, convinced they were trailed, disappeared.

Hammett, after recovering, hopefully hung around Vallejo in various disguises. His efforts were soon rewarded. One day he saw "Gloomy Gus" Schaefer, one of the suspects.

## Schaefer Shadowed

Schaefer was shadowed for weeks, the detective trying to get some tangible evidence with which to hold him after the arrest. Eternal vigilance brought results. Schaefer's wife was nabbed opening a safe deposit box in one of the Oakland banks. In the box were some of the stolen Shapiro jewels.

The whole gang was soon rounded up and sent back to St. Paul to stand trial. "Gloomy Gus" was the only one convicted. He was sentenced, and a few years ago pardoned.

Schaefer is now on trial with the Touhy gang for the Jake Factor kidnaping. When through in Chicago, Schaefer will be brought to California to be tried for the Sacramento mail robbery pulled last year.

\* \* \*

### *Sonoma* Gold Specie Robbery
*It is reasonably certain that during his days as a private investigator in San Francisco Hammett worked on the Sonoma gold-specie robbery described in this and the following newspaper story. He claimed to have found the gold and thus to have cheated himself out of a trip to Australia, the ship's next ultimate destination. One of the working theories of the case was that the gold might have been hidden in Honolulu, a port on the way to San Francisco and the next port after the ship's departure for Australia.*

## $125,000 in Gold Coin Stolen on S. F. Liner
*San Francisco Examiner,* 23 November 1921, pp. 1, 2

One of the biggest midocean robberies in Pacific Ocean annals was revealed on the arrival of the liner Sonoma in this port yesterday when the vessel's specie tanks were opened and $125,000 in English gold coin, put aboard at Sydney, was found to have vanished.

The loot comprised five steel money chests of the fifteen chests that were shipped. Only ten chests remained in the strong room.

WHEN WRITER SOLVED GEM ROBBERY

PAY $241,000,000: U. S. TO ALLIES

THE SAN FRANCISCO CALL

5 CENTS

FINAL NIGHT EDITION

DRY AGENT SCORES CHIEFS

# TRAP U. S. THIEF RING

Dashiell Hammett (left), author of "Secret Agent X-9," detective picture strip which begins Monday in The Call-Bulletin, was at one time San Francisco operative for Pinkertons. He was instrumental in causing the arrest of "Gloomy Gus" Schaefer (right) and his pals, wanted for a St. Paul robbery. The headline is from The Call, March 10, 1922. Schaefer is now on trial for the Jake Factor kidnaping.

*Reprinted article from the* San Francisco Call *distributed by King Features Syndicate in January 1934 to promote* Secret Agent X-9, *the comic strip based on Hammett's character and for which he contributed continuity (Collection of Richard Layman)*

The gold was consigned by the commonwealth of Australia to the International Banking Corporation of this city.

Weighing about 400 pounds, including the metal boxes, the whereabouts of the stolen treasure and the manner of its disappearance, after an all day search by police and private detectives, remained an inscrutable mystery.

**Suspect "Inside Job."**

An "inside job" involving several members of the Sonoma's crew is suspected. So thoroughly did the robbers plan their work that not the slightest clew has been discovered.

Three locks secured the door of the specie tank. Three different officers of the ship hold the keys and none of them can unlock the tank without the presence of the other two.

It was found that one of these locks had been sawed from the staple by a saw capable of cutting sheer steel. Another false lock had been put in its place.

The other two had been unlocked, evidently with keys. The work showed the hand of a master cracksman.

Evidence that the job had been carefully planned even before the liner touched at Sydney was seen in the sawing and replacing of one of the locks. This lock, the key to which is held by Captain J. H. Trask, had been removed and replaced at Sydney by the captain's orders, in view of the fact that the ship was to bear away an unusually large amount of treasure.

**Had Keys Duplicated.**

It was thought that impressions of the other two locks had been secured by the robbers aboard the liner from the keys as they hung on the racks in the quarters of First Officer Thomas McManus and Purser A. G. Conquest. It is believed that an impression of Captain Trask's key was similarly obtained, but that its use was defeated when he had the lock altered.

The stolen money was in English sovereigns, each box containing sovereigns to the value of 5,000 pounds, or approximately $25,000. The total value of the treasure shipped on the Sonoma was $375,000, of which a third was stolen.

An international ring of specie robbers, including either members of the crew or persons who frequently travel on the liners across the Pacific, is thought responsible for the crime.

The robbery was discovered after the liner had been moored to Pier 35. Officials of the International Banking Corporation immediately visited the ship, accompanied by armed guards and trucks to take the treasure to the vaults.

First Officer McManus and Purser Conquest accompanied them to the tanks, McManus securing Captain Trask's key. After the first two locks had been readily opened, Captain Trask's key failed to fit.

McManus immediately detected signs that the lock had been tampered with. A saw was procured and the staple cut. In the presence of the bank officials the strong-boxes were counted and the amazing robbery revealed.

Guards were immediately placed on the pier and aboard the liner. All members of the crew were

*The* SS Sonoma. *In fall 1921 Hammett was one of the Pinkerton's operatives who investigated the theft of $125,000 in gold specie from the ship's hold. The* Sonoma *is the model for* La Paloma, *on which Captain Jacoby brings the faux Maltese falcon to San Francisco for Brigid O'Shaughnessy (courtesy of the Mike McGarvey Collection).*

searched before they had opportunity to land. Search of the large vessel was immediately begun by a special detail of customs officers, accompanied by police and detectives.

A careful study of the movements of the ship since the gold was taken aboard at Sydney was made by Captain Trask in an endeavor to ascertain precisely where the robbery had taken place.

It was thought likely that the crime had been consummated after the Sonoma left Honolulu and perhaps only a short time before arrival at this port. Captain Trask stated that he had regularly inspected the locks of the specie bank each day, and had seen nothing irregular.

Assuming that the plans of the robbers were temporarily frustrated by the substitution of a new lock at Sydney, it was argued that Honolulu was the first port at which a similar lock, for purposes of duplication, could have been secured.

Advices were immediately wired to Hawaii, requesting the island police to search for evidence that such a lock had been purchased and by whom.

By elimination two possibilities were left; namely, that the $125,000 in gold is still aboard the liner in some disguised form and will be found when the cargo is unloaded; or else that it was removed from the ship in some way in the two hours between entering the Heads and tying to pier 3. During a portion of this time the Sonoma was in quarantine.

Another theory entertained by the officials is that the gold was taken from the boxes, wrapped in small packages, and concealed in mailsacks in the hold. This, it was said, was a practicable means, as the mail is handled by machinery and the weight would not be noticed.

Fifteen years ago the liner Alameda was robbed of a single box of gold, through substitution of a box exactly similar. The last big specie robbery on the Pacific was that of the Nile, owned by the China Mall. In this crime $10,000 in bullion was taken, after the liner had left the port bound for the Orient.

\* \* \*

**Dream Bares Hiding Place on S. F. Liner**
*San Francisco Examiner,* 29 November 1921, p. 1

Hours of close questioning of the members of the crew of the liner Sonoma yesterday led to the recovery of $102,300 of the $125,000 loot stolen from the specie tanks of the vessel as it neared this port last Tuesday on her homeward voyage from

Sydney. Police officials and Pinkerton detectives are hopeful of finding the remainder of the gold coin.

Four members of the crew whom the police suspect as having figured in the sea robbery were taken to the Hall of Justice last night and further questioned as to their movements aboard the boat shortly before its arrival in port. No arrests have been made pending further investigation and the questioning of others of the crew who may have knowledge of the theft.

Seventy-five thousand dollars was recovered in three strongboxes found submerged in the bay by stout cords from the stern of the vessel as she lay moored at pier 35. Each box contained approximately 5,000 English pounds or $25,000 in gold.

Tucked away in a fire hose, which had been slipped down the ventilating pipe, running from the upper deck to the oil tanks, another small fortune in gold sovereigns was found estimated at more than $25,000.

With these disclosures at hand, detectives immediately instituted a rigid interrogation of the entire crew.

**Finds Hidden Cache.**

The discovery of the gold was made by First Assistant Engineer Carl Knudsen. He had been ordered to continue his search of the craft with the other officers of the ship. He explained that the hiding place of the gold had been revealed to him in a dream.

Down in the engine room, Knudsen noticed that the ventilating pipe to the oil tank had been tampered with by a wrench and that paint on the pipe had been marked by the tools. Reporting his find to F. S. Samuels, general manager of the Oceanic Steamship Company, he was ordered to open the pipe.

One of the joints was taken off, but nothing was found. Not satisfied, Knudsen began tapping the pipe with a hammer up between each deck, and shortly discovered that instead of a ring to his knocks he produced dull thuds.

Again unscrewing a joint, a fire hose was found suspended in the pipe. Assisted by detectives, Knudsen pulled the hose out and from it rolled $25,000 in gold coins.

**Submerged in Bay.**

News of the discovery spread quickly about the vessel and the clew was offered the officials to the hiding place of the three strong boxes submerged under the stern of the liner.

Grappling hooks were employed and with little effort the three weighty chests, each containing

5,000 pounds in English money, or nearly $75,000, were brought to the surface.

Officials of the International Banking Corporation to which institution the gold was consigned and who have been present at the ship since the robbery was first discovered, took charge of the gold as soon as it was found.

Under guard of detectives the specie was removed from the cabin of the liner where it was counted and deposited late yesterday in the vaults of the bank.

\* \* \*

*In the following article Petrie argues that Hammett was not involved in the recovery of the stolen treasure of the* Sonoma. *Petrie was born in San Francisco and first went to sea in 1918 with the merchant marine.*

**The Looting of the *Sonoma***
Glynn Petrie
*The Californians*
(November/December 1985): 40–44

The *Sonoma* had ended a slow passage. Captain Trask, her master of 15 years, was making a cautious approach, seeking the pilot vessel. A little after 7:30 on the foggy morning of November 22, 1921, with the pilot conning, the *Sonoma* was heading for the Golden Gate. Three hours later, after a short stay at quarantine anchorage, she eased into her berth in Oceanic Line's Pier 35 in a fog almost as impenetrable as the mystery that would soon enshroud her.

Anyone standing on that pier and seeing the brown-leafed bundles of bananas stowed between latticed frames on the poop deck would have guessed rightly that Honolulu had been the *Sonoma's* last port of call.

A hundred passengers were lining the rail as they had three weeks before in Sydney. A half hour prior to sailing, they had watched officials of the Commonwealth of Australia deliver 15 chests containing a treasure of 150,000 English gold sovereigns. The Australians stood by as the steel door of the vessel's strong room was closed and chief officer Thomas McManus snapped on his lock. A foot below, purser A. G. Conquest put on his lock. A slight delay occurred when Captain Trask presented a new lock, its steel shackle no stronger than his old one. The chief officer, accustomed to the quirks of ship masters, removed the old lock from its chain and snapped the new one in place a foot above his own. Satisfied, the Australian officials went ashore and kept watch as the gangway was lowered. In a few minutes, *Sonoma* was homeward bound.

And now the passengers were on Pier 35, greeting relatives and friends as their baggage and the mail came ashore. Discreetly, the officers of the International Banking Corporation of San Francisco waited two hours for the arrival hubbub to subside. After all, no need to hurry; 15 years had passed since Oceanic's liner *Alameda's* strong room had been broached, and a chest of gold pirated. True, only a while ago, the China Mail's *Nile* had $10,000 in gold stolen. But the *Sonoma*, sailing under union conditions despite the Seamen's strike of 1921, had a veteran crew of loyal seamen.

The bank's officers came with armored trucks and guards, and soon stood confidently before the strong room door. The *Sonoma's* chief officer McManus began removing the locks and stopped, cursing under his breath, when the key wouldn't turn in the new lock. A quick climb to the master's office, "No, you have the right key," and McManus was back, puffing slightly. Trying again, he gasped; the new lock's shackle was not steel, but brass!

The carpenter was called to saw off the brass shackle. The steel door groaned open, the light switched on, McManus made a fast count . . . and fell back, mouth agape. Slowly he recounted: only 10 chests. Five chests, each weighing 80 pounds with 10,000 gold sovereigns, were short: 50,000 gold coins worth $125,000 had vanished!

In hurried confusion guards were posted about the vessel. Burns and Pinkerton detectives swarmed over the vessel. One Pinkerton man, Dashiel Hammett, moseyed thoughtfully if unproductively about. The baggage still on the pier and the mail (which had been stowed adjacent to the strong room) was searched for the missing gold.

The first futile search concluded, Oceanic's general manager Frederick Samuels announced that the gold had been removed in Pago Pago or Honolulu. The police of those ports were alerted and asked to investigate. Six hours after the discovery of the looting, the San Francisco Police Department was informed, and Captain Duncan Matheson, chief of detectives, took charge. While in San Francisco crew members ate ashore and were not allowed to sleep aboard; their rooms and homes were searched. The job was declared to be "the work of a master cracksman."

The following day, the theory was advanced that the theft was "the work of an international gang of specie thieves with the assistance of one or more passengers or crew members." All passengers ("except those of unquestioned reputation") were queried. Captain Matheson stated, "No one but a master in crime could commit such a daring robbery

51

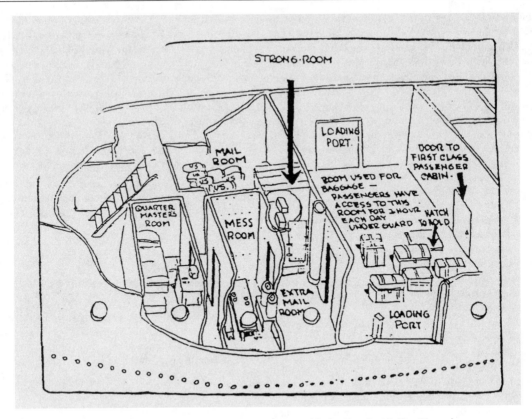

*Sketch of the area below deck on the* SS Sonoma *(courtesy of the San Francisco Maritime Museum)*

in such a workmanlike fashion without leaving a clue for the police to go by."

On Thursday, November 24, the vessel's radio log was checked for clues. Disagreeing with general manager Samuels' earlier statement that the gold had been removed "in Pago Pago or Honolulu," Captain Trask said *he* believed the theft took place between Honolulu and San Francisco. The Honolulu police were asked to check on the purchase of the replacement lock. Captain Matheson said, "We have every reason to believe we are dealing with master criminals."

On Saturday, November 26, after the vessel "had been searched in every nook and cranny," it was concluded that the gold "had been removed in Honolulu or San Francisco." It was also believed that the thieves had stolen the keys from the officers' rooms. By this time, San Francisco was enthralled by the confusion and the mystery of what was called "one of the most baffling, deftly plotted, and gigantic piracies ever perpetrated on the high seas." Four crew members were interrogated at the Hall of Justice. Along the Embarca-

dero, with other seamen, I watched the bewildered investigation flounder.

On Monday, November 28, the search continued. Carl Knudsen, first assistant engineer, decided to check the gas vent pipes from the fuel tanks. As he tapped, he listened to the sharp ring of his hammer. One pipe gave off a dull thud: Knudsen followed it to the boat deck. Finding the vent pipe blocked, he called detectives and, in their presence, hauled out a 20-foot fire hose, with the nozzle down. Out spilled $29,000-worth of gold sovereigns.

Word spread quickly. At noon, chief officer McManus went to quartermaster Ducrest who was standing gangway watch. "The s.o.b. that pulled this job," he growled, "better haul ass." Another quartermaster joined them to relieve Ducrest. "Going to chow?", he asked. "Guess I might as well," Ducrest said and, going down the gangway, threw his leg over a green motorcycle with a sidecar and took off.

Later that day, longshoremen reported oil tins floating under the vessel's stern without leaving with the tide. A boat was pressed into service. The tins had stout ropes attached. Three chests worth $75,000 were hauled from the bottom. Still missing was $21,000 in gold.

On Tuesday, November 29, it was revealed that "one passenger had made several voyages on the *Sonoma* and had been in close communication with crew members. He left the vessel with two trunks each weighing 180 pounds. He registered in the Palace Hotel, and later went to Sacramento, and is believed to be on his way East. He is a member of a prominent North West family that has been searching for him for three years."

Quartermaster Ducrest failed to report for his midnight watch Tuesday. On Wednesday, November 30, the police sought Ducrest for questioning. Divers searched the bottom around the vessel, but found nothing.

The hordes of searchers were making a mess of the *Sonoma*. Old Charlie, the Aussie bosun, growled through his white moustache as he roped off the promenade deck: it had to be covered with grey rubberized paint before sailing. He plugged the bottoms of the scuppers (drain pipes) from the boat deck. Charlie didn't want rain spoiling his deck.

A newspaper printed that Carl Knudsen had dreamed about the vent pipe with the gold but Knudsen scoffed, saying the find was the result of persistent work.

On Thursday, December 1, the paint was dry and Old Charlie set about removing the plugs from the scuppers. In one, he hit the jackpot. Down poured a shower of gold–$21,000-worth. (Well, almost. Two sovereigns were missing.)

On Friday, December 2, the police were calling it "a one-man job, with Quartermaster Ducrest the sole engineer and executor" and Judge Lazarus issued a warrant for the arrest of Joseph P. Ducrest. The police found the two gold sovereigns in a pawn shop. A man whose description fitted Ducrest had exchanged them for American money, a few cents less than five dollars– payoff for "the greatest modern act of piracies in the Pacific"!

On Thursday, December 6, the *Sonoma* sailed on schedule for the South Seas and excitement ashore subsided. Ducrest was never seen again. The case was closed, but several questions were left unanswered. How had Ducrest planned to get the loot ashore and disposed of? With the ship swarming with investigators, how had he poured the gold in the scupper? And finally, what had gone wrong with his plan?

The 1921 Seamen's Strike had failed and times were tough: the tide was out for thousands of seamen, including me. I had sailed quartermaster with Pacific Mail and Matson Lines. The *Sonoma* with her fine run and union conditions (50% better than other lines) attracted me and many other seamen. I was also intrigued by the looting mystery's unanswered questions.

Three voyages later, when the *Sonoma* tied up at Pier 35 another quartermaster left the vessel. On June 4, 1922 I shipped in his place. My watch mate, Haakon, was a handsome, black-haired Norwegian in his early 40s. The *Sonoma*'s old chief officer McManus had been replaced by a man named Drummond (dubbed "Bulldog" by the crew after a fictional detective of the time). The carpenter was a one-eyed man named Fischer who rose before dawn and, with a flashlight, scanned the decks for flying fish. He liked fresh fish for breakfast.

The crew was perplexed by 15-year-old Bob Frederick, deck boy, the lowest form of maritime life. Wearing a worn officer's cap squarely set over his sober young face, he was not properly awed by the crew's seamanship or his lack of it. He performed his lowly duties with poise and dignity. Mistaking his unusual confidence for hubris, we largely shunned him. Bob was unaffected by this, however. After the voyage, he intended finishing school at San Francisco's Lowell High, and then on to West Point. (In World War II, Bob would be the youngest American general commanding a division, and the most wounded–eight times, four in three days. He commanded the Devil's Brigade, and led his 45th "Thunderbolt" Division from France to the Rhine, in combat 511 days.)

As the *Sonoma* left Honolulu, a canvas swimming pool was set up on the foredeck. Before breakfast, Captain Trask, an admirable shipmaster, took a dip. Passengers had the pool for the rest of the day, but at 6pm it belonged to the crew. We would stand at the pool's edge, watching a few passengers paddling about. As four bells rang from the wheelhouse, we would dive in like porpoises and soon have the pool to ourselves.

Ashore, seamen talk ships, at sea they talk women; and, with all reticent because of the *Sonoma*'s blemished record, talk of the robbery was minimal. Haakon, my watch mate, was taciturn, seemingly brooding about somewhere beyond the horizon. Although we worked and ate together, he seldom spoke an unnecessary word. He was most sociable when I relieved him at the wheel. "Steering 2-30-2. Takes a little starboard helm. She's all yours, partner."

We had the graveyard watch, midnight to 4 am. Coming off duty, we would undress in our tiny fo'c'sle in the bow, a few feet from the strong room. Silently we would pull in our elbows to make room for each other, and I'd climb into my bunk above his. The last thing I'd see would be Haakon lying in his bunk, staring at nothing.

Many times I stood before the strong room door gazing at the heavy locks. And now we were homeward bound and I had learned nothing.

A four-hour stay at Pago Pago broke the monotony of the passage. An hour before sailing, a brass band of giant Samoans in colorful native dress stalked onto the pier, led by a diminutive American naval officer. The band filled the air with popular tunes as the passengers returned festooned with flower leis and laden with wooden curios. The naval officer raised his baton, and the band burst out with the hits of the day: "Stumbling All Around" and "Aloha Oe". As the *Sonoma* was warped from her berth and the last mooring line splashed into the water, symbolizing the breaking of their tie to the outside world, the band wailed into a tearful rendition of "We Never Will Forget You".

Coming off watch at 4am the next morning, I stopped for a cup of coffee. Leaving the messroom, the aroma of coffee in my nose, I held my breath against the stink of the green hides stowed in number one hold adjacent to our room. In one swift motion I opened the door and slipped in, hoping to keep the stench out. Haakon was not lying, staring wide-eyed in his bunk as usual. He was sitting and fingering a neatly-sewn canvas wallet. He shifted to his bunk leaving the chair to me.

"Partner," he said, "Ever read poetry?"

"Yeah, a little. *The Rubaiyatt, To His Coy Mistress, The Kasidah,* a few others."

Fishing in his wallet, he handed me a typewritten sheet. "Care to look at this?"

"This" was *Sonoma* by "Sheliah"–five verses, full of romance and nostalgia: the *Sonoma* swinging down the great circle through star-filled nights to the South Seas, the Southern Cross. Each verse ended with, "But whisper, Old Sonoma Girl, is Haakon at the wheel?"

I read it then looked back at Haakon. His dark eyes were pensive as he asked me, "What do you think?"

"That gal's surely took on you," I replied.

"She's in Sydney. About the poem?"

"I like it. She can handle words."

Apparently satisfied, Haakon put the wallet away and turned in.

A few mornings later, Haakon again broke his customary silence with, "You going to make the next voyage?" When I nodded he continued, "Did you really like the poem?"

"Yeah, I did. She must be quite a gal."

"She's a woman," he said with reverence. "Each voyage I bring her three pairs of silk stockings. If I give you the stockings would you call on her?"

"What the hell for? She's your gal."

"Was," he said. "I'll never see her again. That's finished. Will you?"

"What the hell would I want with her?"

"You could learn something."

"Oh yeah?"

"Yeah."

"But why don't you give them to her?"

"I won't be here. Leaving on sign off."

"What for? Hell, Haakon, as they say in the Matson Line, 'Baby, it's cold outside.'"

He regarded me for awhile. "You know, we're only a few feet from that strong room. Often we carry a shipment of gold sovereigns." His glance drifted to his narrow wooden bunk. "Four years I've lain in that bunk. Did more scheming and dreaming than sleeping. Enough gold to last a man a lifetime. I've wasted too much time at sea. Ninety bucks a month for being away from the world and everybody. Just a few feet from that gold. Think what that can do to a man."

"But what would you do with it?"

He leaned back and stared over my head. "I'd buy a little ketch and head for China."

I laughed. "Stow it, Haakon. I put a year on the China coast. In 1919 I was in a tanker in San Pedro. The *Silver Shell* loaded six million dollars worth of Mexican pesos, each peso worth 45 cents in Pedro. A month later in Shanghai each peso brought a Chinese dollar. With 80 cents Chinese, the company bought back an American dollar. China's on the silver standard. Aboard ship we'd sign for 10 American gold dollars, and they'd hand us eight Chinese." I shook my head. "You might have been dreaming four years, but you sure weren't scheming."

A slow acknowledging grin, and he said "Okay, you're right. I know a merchant in Chinatown. He'll give me 75 cents for a dollar of gold."

"It's been tried," I said. "Didn't pan out. Those three locks, how did Ducrest swipe the keys?"

"Didn't have to. Easy. Eight days alongside Sydney, two weeks in Frisco, the strong room's empty and open. The locks hang on chains. Replace them with look-alikes. Any locksmith can make keys. Put them back. In port with the room empty, who cares?"

"Okay," I said, "so the Old Man turns in every night at nine. By 10:30 the ship's a seagoing morgue. Between Hono and Frisco you lug them out. Each chest weighing 80 pounds. What then?"

Haakon lowered his voice and I wondered if he were talking to me or to someone in the past: "When we leave Hono, the poop will be stowed with bananas. Leaving enough space to work the mooring lines. That's where."

"So after tying up at Pier 35 Ducrest, if he was the one, went aft and tossed them into the water. What does that get you?"

"Not a damned thing," Haakon said ruefully. "The daylight arrival fouled up the plan. The rest was just an attempt to salvage something."

"So that's what went wrong . . ."

"The ship, see, usually arrives too late for quarantine. Has to anchor 'till dawn. It's a one-man job aboard. One ashore. The gold's in the bananas. A boat comes under the stern. You lower away. Talk about a mystery? Nobody would've known where the hell it went."

"So when Ducrest realized there'd be a daylight arrival, he couldn't return the chests. He'd sawed off the captain's lock. The five chests were in the bananas. He lugged one up to the boat deck and stowed the gold in the vent pipe. But later, with all the searchers, how did he load the scupper?"

"He did what he could. He knew that before sailing from Frisco, Old Charlie'd have to paint the promenade deck. Old Charlie always plugs the scuppers, case of rain. All Ducrest had to do the last night at sea was plug one scupper and load it."

"Well, he sure didn't panic," I said. "Have to give him that. Just set about methodically trying to save something." I shook my head in grudging admiration. "But Haakon, didn't you ever think another man might not only be scheming, but doing it? I mean, while you're in your bunk dreaming? Didn't you have some idea what Ducrest was up to?"

Haakon sat, lips slightly parted, and decided as to whether to go on. I waited awhile then asked, "Did the police question you?"

He compressed his lips for a moment then said, "Why should they? I wasn't aboard. Took that voyage off. Had to have some dental work done."

Taking off my shoes, I glanced sideways at his strong teeth, thinking that if there really had been a dentist he would have shined them a little. Haakon had been aboard, not at any dentist's office. All my questions were answered. When I was down to my shorts and ready to climb into my bunk, Haakon rose and stood with his back to me, swaying with the vessel's rolling.

"Living shoreside costs like hell," I said. "That voyage off must have set you back quite a bit."

Haakon didn't seem to be listening. His broad hand fanned over his bunk, smoothing a wrinkle. Then, more to himself than me, he said, "Yeah."

---

*One of Hammett's earliest publications was the following piece, which appeared in* The Smart Set. *This memoir is particularly interesting read in conjunction with the profile of William Pinkerton, who concentrated his efforts as an agency manager on cases of the type Hammett describes. This piece is notable for its straightforward, unembellished style, which Hammett developed over the next six years into the finely tuned hard-boiled narrative voice of* The Maltese Falcon.

**From the Memoirs of a Private Detective**
Dashiell Hammett
*The Smart Set,* 70 (March 1923): 87–90

### 1

WISHING to get some information from members of the W. C. T. U. in an Oregon city, I introduced myself as the secretary of the Butte Civic Purity League. One of them read me a long discourse on the erotic effects of cigarettes upon young girls. Subsequent experiments proved this trip worthless.

### 2

A man whom I was shadowing went out into the country for a walk one Sunday afternoon and lost his bearings completely. I had to direct him back to the city.

### 3

House burglary is probably the poorest paid trade in the world; I have never known anyone to make a living at it. But for that matter few criminals of any class are self-supporting unless they toil at something legitimate between times. Most of them, however, live on their women.

### 4

I know an operative who while looking for pick-pockets at the Havre de Grace race track had his wallet stolen. He later became an official in an Eastern detective agency.

### 5

Three times I have been mistaken for a Prohibition agent, but never had any trouble clearing myself.

### 6

Taking a prisoner from a ranch near Gilt Edge, Mont., to Lewistown one night, my machine broke down and we had to sit there until daylight. The prisoner, who stoutly affirmed his innocence, was clothed only in overalls and shirt. After shivering all night on the front seat his morale was low, and I had no difficulty in getting a complete confession from him while walking to the nearest ranch early the following morning.

Dashiell Hammett
20 Monroe Street
San Francisco
California

Seven Pages

By Dashiell Hammett

One

She was one of the rare red-haired women whose skins are
without blemish: she was marble, to the eye. I used to quote
truthfully to her, "Thou art all fair, my love; there is no
spot in thee." She was utterly unpractical. One otherwise
dreary afternoon she lay with her bright head on my knee while
I read Don Marquis' Sonnets to a Red-Haired Lady to her. When
I had finished she made a little purring noise and stared
dreamily distant-eyed past me. "Tell me about this Don Marquis,"
she said. "Do you know him?"

Two

I sat in the lobby of the Plaza, in San Francisco. It
was the day before the opening of the second absurd attempt to
convict Roscoe Arbuckle of something. He came into the lobby.
He looked at me and I at him. His eyes were the eyes of a
man who expected to be regarded as a monster but was not yet
inured to it. I made my gaze as contemptuous as I could. He
glared at me, went on to the elevator still glaring. It was
amusing. I was working for his attorneys at the time, gathering information for his defence.

*This typescript, one of at least two drafts, was prepared in fall 1926. In one of the vignettes, Hammett describes working for the defense during Fatty Arbuckle's December 1921 trial for the rape and murder of actress Virginia Rappe. Hammett sent another draft of this typescript to Peggy O'Toole, his co-worker at Samuels Jewelers (Harry Ransom Humanities Research Center, University of Texas at Austin).*

2

### Three

We would leave the buildings in early darkness, walk a
little way across the desert, and go down into a small canyon
where four trees grouped around a level spot. The night-
dampness settling on earth that had cooked since morning would
loose the fragrance of ground and plant around us. We would
lie there until late in the night, our nostrils full of world-
smell, the trees making irregular map-boundary division among
the stars. Our love seemed dependent on not being phrased. It
seemed if one of us had said, "I love you," the next instant
it would have been a lie. So we loved and cursed one another
merrily, ribaldly, she usually stopping her ears in the end
because I knew more words.

### Four

He came into the room in brown stocking-feet, blue policeman's pants and gray woolen undershirt. "Who the hell moved
that pi-ano? he demanded, and grunted and cursed while wheel-
ing it back into the inconvenient corner from which we had
dragged it. "It's my pi-ano, and it stays where I put it, see,"
he assured us before he went out again. His daughters were
quite embarrassed, since Jack and I had bought the whiskey that
was in him, so they didn't object when, just before we left,
we took all the pictures down from the walls and stacked them
behind the pi-ano. That was in the part of Baltimore called
Pig Town, a few blocks from another house where we had found
one night two in the company who would not drink alcohol. We
gave them root beer into which had been put liberal doses of
aromatic cascara.

3

## Five

I talked to her four times. Each time she complained of her husband. He was ruining her health, he was after her all the time, this supergoat, he simply would not let her alone. I supposed he was nearly, if not altogether, impotent.

## Six

The fat cook and I huddled to the fire that had thawed him out of his vomiting blue cold-sickness. Behind us the Couer d'Alene mountains rose toward Montana, down below us a handful of yellow lights marked a railway stop. Perhaps it was Murray: I've forgotten. "You're crazier than hell, that's what!" the fat cook said. "Any lousy bastard that says Cabell ain't a romantycist is crazier than hell!" "He's not," I insisted. "He's anti-romanticist: all he's ever done for romance is take off its clothes and laugh at it. He's a romanticist just like Mencken's a Tory, which is just like the wooden horse was a Trojan." The fat cook bunched his lips and spat brownly at the fire. "Grease us twice, Slim!" he complained. "If you ain't a son-of-a-gun for damn-fool arguments!"

## Seven

In Washington, D. C., I worked for a while in a freight depot. On my platform were two men who worked together, sweeping out cars, repairing broken crates, sealing doors. One of them was a man of fifty-something with close-clipped gray hair on a very round head. He was a small man but compact. He boasted of the hardness of his skull and told stories of butting duels, head-top crashed against head-top until blood came from noses, mouths, ears. His mate told me privately he thought

4

these combats degrading. "It's being no better than animals," he said. This mate of the butter was a younger man, a country-man, brown-skinned and awkward. He who boasted the hard gray head told me this countryman had a fly tattooed on his penis. Gray-head thought this disgusting. "I'd think it'd make his wife sick to her stomach," he said.

# Dashiell Hammett Confesses!

*Ace detective writer breaks down under third degree and bares secrets of his exciting 'Girl Hunt'*

He wrote "The Thin Man," which (l. to r.) William Powell, Maureen O'Sullivan and Myrna Loy made into a motion picture classic.

*Next week, in this magazine, Dashiell Hammett, above, will smash through with another thrilling story, "Girl Hunt."*

THERE'S as much jealousy between authors as between actresses and sopranos, but ask professional detective-story writers who their own favorite is, and they'll cast all their votes for Dashiell Hammett. Here one of Hammett's competitors as a crime novelist provides a vivid closeup of the author of "The Thin Man," "The Glass Key," "The Maltese Falcon" and "Girl Hunt," the mystery story beginning in this magazine next week.

**By JAMES H. S. MOYNAHAN,**
Author of "Blowoff," "The House That Death Built," "The Corpse of the Nude Girl."

HAMMETT—his full name is Samuel Dashiell Hammett—talks like "Continental Op No. 7," the character he has made as famous as Sherlock Holmes and who reappears in "Girl Hunt," beginning next week in this magazine.

When I arrived for this interview, I told him: "This will be practically painless."

"Dash," in coarse yellow lounging robe, nodded at the pantry: "Do yourself a drink, maybe it won't hurt you so much!"

I brought the brandy and soda out into a living room so filled with books that I had to move a couple of novels and the current London Mercury off the coffee table to set down my drink. These books are characteristic of the Hammett menage. A glance over these titles would tell Sam Spade, one of his famous detective characters, that here, undoubtedly, was the library of a college professor.

"How'd you come to write this yarn, 'Girl Hunt'?" I asked him when we were settled.

He bent his straight brows together and explained that there had been two famous cases of flypaper poisoning, and they had suggested a basic idea for a story. Just the idea, for as "Girl Hunt"

emerged from his typewriter it did not parallel the actual crimes in any detail.

I went on. "This McCloor, the big gangster in the 'Girl Hunt,' did he have a prototype in real life?"

I found that he did. The real Babe McCloor was a member of Jimmie the Riveter's mob—they were a bunch of boys that the Pinkertons, Mr. Hammett's former employers, ran down in the Winter of 1921-22. They'd been pulling stickups up and down the Pacific coast and knocking over various commercial enterprises until Jimmie was taken into custody coming out of the postoffice in Seattle. An army of deputies rushed the mob to the station in handcuffs. Just outside the station, the yegg who was McCloor's original made a dive, handcuffs and all, for a deputy's gun and shot it out right there in the street.

He knew another mobster as tough as Jimmie. "Once I was sitting with this Detroit mug when a fight started across the room. He tossed a .45 Colt into my lap. 'Will you hold that gun for me,' he asked, 'I wanna get into this fight.'"

In writing a story Hammett decides on his characters, he told me, and when he knows them thoroughly, and their relations to each other, he sits down and lets them work the story out for him. "If I don't like the way a character behaves," he told me, "I kill him off in the next paragraph." He spread his hands. "Why not? If somebody works for you and you don't like him you fire him, don't you?"

"Ever shot at yourself?" I asked.

"That's one thing you never get to like," he said. "It even gets worse every time." He didn't care much for the time he and other Pinkerton men went to a house to arrest a gang of negroes who had been stealing dynamite back during the war days. "Everybody thought it was the German," he explained, "and there was quite a scare. When I got inside this house men were being knocked around in fine shape. In the excitement I had a feeling something was wrong but I could

not figure out what it was till I happened to look down and saw this negro whittling away at my leg." He bears the scar to this day.

"How do you go about getting a confession?" I asked him, still on his years as a detective.

He laughed. "I'll tell you a hot one," he said. "I once knew a man who used to be an ace at that stuff and what do you think he used to do? He'd talk to these mugs about their mothers until he had them weeping. Then he'd get the confession and turn 'em in. He saw nothing inconsistent in it, either. But that's a funny thing—the way people confess. I used to think it'd be hard, but you'd be surprised how eager people seem to be to get put away.

"The best way, I've found, is to see their side. Why, we know you didn't mean any harm when you cut up these three gals in the bathtub, but if you start acting ashamed and secretive, the District Attorney may think there was something criminal about it. They go for it every time."

HAMMETT was born in St. Mary's County, Md., May 27, 1894, and was educated in public schools and the Polytechnic Institute of Baltimore. Successively clerk, stevedore and private detective, he turned to writing in 1922, while an invalid from war injuries he suffered in an ambulance corps.

His first stories appeared in Smart Set and Black Mask when those magazines were edited by Henry L. Mencken, Baltimore's other most distinguished citizen. He works on a typewriter and never rewrites; his first draft is his last; hence he produces slowly and laboriously the stories that established a new school of detective fiction and made him the most imitated writer of the time. His machine-gun style and sharp dialogue marked a new era in smartly-done thrillers.

He is married and has two daughters. He likes dogs, music and table tennis, and is a connoisseur of fine liqueurs. He reads endlessly of everything except detective stories. His favorite bedtime tale is Spengler's "Decline of the West."

Copyright, 1934, King Features Syndicate, Inc.

14

*1934 King Features Syndicate promotion for the newspaper reprint of one of Hammett's Continental Op stories. The interview-article provides one of the few instances when Hammett discussed his Pinkerton's cases in print (Collection of Richard Layman).*

**7**

Of all the men embezzling from their employers with whom I have had contact, I can't remember a dozen who smoked, drank, or had any of the vices in which bonding companies are so interested.

**8**

I was once falsely accused of perjury and had to perjure myself to escape arrest.

**9**

A detective agency official in San Francisco once substituted "truthful" for "voracious" in one of my reports on the grounds that the client might not understand the latter. A few days later in another report "simulate" became "quicken" for the same reason.

**10**

Of all the nationalities haled into the criminal courts, the Greek is the most difficult to convict. He simply denies everything, no matter how conclusive the proof may be; and nothing so impresses a jury as a bare statement of fact, regardless of the fact's inherent improbability or obvious absurdity in the face of overwhelming contrary evidence.

**11**

I know a man who will forge the impressions of any set of fingers in the world for $50.

**12**

I have never known a man capable of turning out first-rate work in a trade, a profession or an art, who was a professional criminal.

**13**

I know a detective who once attempted to disguise himself thoroughly. The first policeman he met took him into custody.

**14**

I know a deputy sheriff in Montana who, approaching the cabin of a homesteader for whose arrest he had a warrant, was confronted by the homesteader with a rifle in his hands. The deputy sheriff drew his revolver and tried to shoot over the homesteader's head to frighten him. The range was long and a strong wind was blowing. The bullet knocked the rifle from the homesteader's hands. As time went by the deputy sheriff came to accept as the truth the reputation for expertness that this incident gave him, and he not only let his friends enter him in a shooting contest, but wagered everything he owned upon his skill. When the contest was held he missed the target completely with all six shots.

**15**

Once in Seattle the wife of a fugitive swindler offered to sell me a photograph of her husband for $15. I knew where I could get one free, so I didn't buy it.

**16**

I was once engaged to discharge a woman's housekeeper.

**17**

The slang in use among criminals is for the most part a conscious, artificial growth, designed more to confuse outsiders than for any other purpose, but sometimes it is singularly expressive; for instance, *two-time loser*–one who has been convicted twice; and the older *gone to read and write*–found it advisable to go away for a while.

**18**

Pocket-picking is the easiest to master of all the criminal trades. Anyone who is not crippled can become an adept in a day.

**19**

In 1917, in Washington, D. C., I met a young woman who did not remark that my work must be very interesting.

**20**

Even where the criminal makes no attempt to efface the prints of his fingers, but leaves them all over the scene of the crime, the chances are about one in ten of finding a print that is sufficiently clear to be of any value.

**21**

The chief of police of a Southern city once gave me a description of a man, complete even to a mole on his neck, but neglected to mention that he had only one arm.

**22**

I know a forger who left his wife because she had learned to smoke cigarettes while he was serving a term in prison.

**23**

Second only to "Dr. Jekyll and Mr. Hyde" is "Raffles" in the affections of the daily press. The phrase "gentleman crook" is used on the slightest provocation. A composite portrait of the gentry upon whom the newspapers have bestowed this title would show a laudanum-drinker, with a large rhinestone horseshoe aglow in the soiled bosom of his shirt below a bow tie, leering at his victim, and saying: "Now don't get scared, lady, I ain't gonna crack you on the bean. I ain't a rough-neck!"

24

The cleverest and most uniformly successful detective I have ever known is extremely myopic.

25

Going from the larger cities out into the remote rural communities, one finds a steadily decreasing percentage of crimes that have to do with money and a proportionate increase in the frequency of sex as a criminal motive.

26

While trying to peer into the upper story of a roadhouse in northern California one night—and the man I was looking for was in Seattle at the time—part of the porch roof crumbled under me and I fell, spraining an ankle. The proprietor of the roadhouse gave me water to bathe it in.

27

The chief difference between the exceptionally knotty problem confronting the detective of fiction and that facing the real detective is that in the former there is usually a paucity of clues, and in the latter altogether too many.

28

I know a man who once stole a Ferris-wheel.

29

That the law-breaker is invariably soon or late apprehended is probably the least challenged of extant myths. And yet the files of every detective bureau bulge with the records of unsolved mysteries and uncaught criminals.

## Hammett's Twenty-Four Commandments

*Hammett worked as a mystery-book reviewer for the* New York Evening Post *from April to October 1930, passing judgment on eighty-five books in a column that appeared twice a month. He believed that a writer should know his subject, and in two successive columns he listed some suggestions for writers of mystery fiction.*

**Crime Wave**
Dashiell Hammett
*New York Evening Post,* 7 June 1930, p. 54

There is not much nourishment for adult readers in this group [of books to be reviewed]. The first part of the

Crawley work [*The Valley of Creeping Men*] is acceptable melodrama, but the rest of it deals with rather aimless doings in African jungles. The other members of our list are, from beginnings to endings, carelessly manufactured improbabilities having more than their share of those blunders which earn detective stories as a whole the sneers of the captious.

A fellow who takes detective stories seriously, I am annoyed by the stupid recurrence of these same blunders in book after book. It would be silly to insist that nobody who has not been a detective should write detective stories, but it is certainly not unreasonable to ask any one who is going to write a book of any sort to make some effort at least to learn something about his subject. Most writers do. Only detective story writers seem to be free from a sense of obligation in this direction, and, curiously, the more established and prolific detective story writers seem to be the worst offenders. Nearly all writers of Western tales at least get an occasional glimpse of their chosen territory from a car-window while en route to Hollywood; writers of sea stories have been seen on the waterfront; surely detective story writers could afford to speak to policemen now and then.

Meanwhile, a couple of months' labor in this arena has convinced me that the following suggestions might be of value to somebody:

(1) There was an automatic revolver, the Webley-Fosbery, made in England some years ago. The ordinary automatic pistol, however, is not a revolver. A pistol, to be a revolver, must have something on it that revolves.

(2) The Colt's .45 automatic pistol has no chambers. The cartridges are put in a magazine.

(3) A silencer may be attached to a revolver, but the effect will be altogether negligible. I have never seen a silencer used on an automatic pistol, but am told it would cause the pistol to jam. A silencer may be used on a single-shot target pistol or on a rifle, but both would still make quite a bit of noise. "Silencer" is a rather optimistic name for this device which has generally fallen into disuse.

(4) When a bullet from a Colt's .45, or any firearm of approximately the same size and power, hits you, even if not in a fatal spot, it usually knocks you over. It is quite upsetting at any reasonable range.

(5) A shot or stab wound is simply felt as a blow or push at first. It is some little time before any burning or other painful sensation begins.

(6) When you are knocked unconscious you do not feel the blow that does it.

(7) A wound made after the death of the wounded is usually recognizable as such.

(8) Finger-prints of any value to the police are seldom found on anybody's skin.

(9) The pupils of many drug-addicts' eyes are apparently normal.

(10) It is impossible to see anything by the flash of an ordinary gun, though it is easy to imagine you have seen things.

(11) Not nearly so much can be seen by moonlight as you imagine. This is especially true of colors.

(12) All Federal snoopers are not members of the Secret Service. That branch is chiefly occupied with pursuing counterfeiters and guarding Presidents and prominent visitors to our shores.

(13) A sheriff is a county officer who usually has no official connection with city, town or state police.

(14) Federal prisoners convicted in Washington, D.C., are usually sent to the Atlanta prison and not to Leavenworth.

(15) The California State prison at San Quentin is used for convicts serving first terms. Two-time losers are usually sent to Folsom.

(16) Ventriloquists do not actually "throw" their voices and such doubtful illusions as they manage depend on their gestures. Nothing at all could be done by a ventriloquist standing behind his audience.

(17) Even detectives who drop their final g's should not be made to say "anythin'"—an oddity that calls for vocal acrobatics.

(18) "Youse" is the plural of "you."

(19) A trained detective shadowing a subject does not ordinarily leap from doorway to doorway and does not hide behind trees and poles. He knows no harm is done if the subject sees him now and then.

\* \* \*

**Crime Wave**
Dashiell Hammett
*New York Evening Post*, 3 July 1930, p. 55

A few weeks ago, having no books on hand that I cared to talk much about, I listed in this column nineteen suggestions to detective story writers. Those suggestions having been received with extreme enthusiasm—to the extent of at least one publisher offering me a hundred dollars for a slightly more complete list—I, not needing that particular hundred dollars at the moment, herewith present a few more suggestions at the mere usual space rate:

(20) The current practice in most places in the United States is to make the coroner's inquest an empty formality in which nothing much is brought out except that somebody has died.

(21) Fingerprints are fragile affairs. Wrapping a pistol or other small object up in a handkerchief is much more likely to obliterate than to preserve any prints it may have.

(22) When an automatic pistol is fired the empty cartridge-shell flies out the right-hand side. The empty cartridge-case remains in a revolver until ejected by hand.

(23) A lawyer cannot impeach his own witness.

(24) The length of time a corpse has been a corpse can be approximated by an experienced physician, but only approximated, and the longer it has been a corpse, the less accurate the approximation is likely to be.

---

## San Francisco Years

*Josephine Hammett, the younger daughter of Dashiell Hammett, began making notes about her recollections of her father in the late 1990s in conjunction with the planned publication of his letters. The result was a personal biography that comes closer to capturing her father's energy, spirit, and character than any outsider could hope to. In this passage, she recounts her parents' early years in San Francisco.*

**Remembering Father**
Jo Hammett
*Dashiell Hammett: A Daughter Remembers*
(New York: Carroll & Graf, 2001), pp. 43–59

Mama took the train to San Francisco in July 1921 and stayed in the room Papa had booked for her at the Golden West Hotel. They were married on the seventh of that month in the rectory of Saint Mary's Cathedral. She was surprised to learn that he had been raised Catholic. I suppose the subject of religion hadn't come up much before then.

They moved into the Crawford Apartments at 620 Eddy Street. They were to stay at that address, in two different apartments at different times, longer than anywhere else in San Francisco. When Papa began writing, he worked nights in the kitchen and days, when he was well enough, at the public library. There was a flat roof that served as a playroom and setting for many of our early photos.

Papa had a small disability pension, but with a wife and baby on the way he needed more than that. He put up an "Employment Wanted" sign in a shoe repair store on Market Street. When that didn't pan out, he went back to work for Pinkerton's. But his lung problems came back with a vengeance, and in December 1921 he was out of work again.

Mary was born October 16 of that year. She came home from the hospital a long skinny baby, carrot-yellow with jaundice but grew into a pretty child with fine blonde hair—Papa called her the Tow Head—and Mother's clear blue eyes.

*Hammett in the mid 1920s in San Francisco (courtesy of Josephine Hammett)*

As is the case with most first-borns, Mary had lots of pictures taken of her. She is always well dressed and posed with impressive toys—stuffed animals, dolls, and a jumbo-sized elephant—too expensive to have been anything but gifts. In these early pictures she is sometimes smiling. She very rarely smiled in later ones.

You can usually tell who the photographer was. In Mother's shots heads are frequently cut off or lower limbs amputated. Papa's shots are well composed. Also he had a camera that let you write the subject and date on the negative. His printing is neat and accurate. Mother writes "Baby 9 months" on the back of her snapshots, leaving you to wonder what baby.

Papa began a course at Munson's Business College for newspaper reporters, dropped out, and then started writing advertising copy on a free-lance basis. He liked the writing and began to send out fiction pieces to magazines. In October 1922 *The Smart Set* published his first story, "The Parthian Shot." The pay was laughable, but he was on his way.

He put more and more of his time and energy into writing and sold to several different magazines. His style was gradually changing from the sort of pseudo-sophisticated stuff *The Smart Set* used to what it would

become: realistic and quietly ironic. He became a regular for the pulp magazine *Black Mask*. The first Continental Op story, "Arson Plus," appeared there in October 1923. He had found his niche.

Mary began school in San Francisco at Charing Cross kindergarten. A cab picked her up every morning, which must have been an expense. She learned to print in a neat boxy hand and practiced writing "Mary Jane Hammett" in crayon on any piece of paper she could find—on books and letters and on the last page of a *Dain Curse* galley proof. Papa played with her, drew little stick-figure pictures, and read to her. But he was strict, too. He returned the circus tickets he bought when she misbehaved. Mary wrote a note to Mother afterwards: "Mama i will be good a good girl. And the Baby to. And Papa will be a good boy. The End." Mama saved it along with Mary's embroidered baby shoes.

I was born in May 1926, three days before my father's thirty-second birthday. Papa had gone to work for Samuels Jewelers as advertising manager a few months before. It was his first well-paying job and gave him the kind of recognition he needed. But in July he fell ill again.

My mother said my father seldom drank in the San Francisco days. She blamed the sales meetings he had to attend when he was in advertising for getting him started. Mother was always one to shift blame away from the family when she could. But she saw, correctly, that he was a shy person and needed the confidence of the bottle for business and social occasions.

In the summer of 1926 my father was very sick. Alone in his apartment he waited to die. He was so weak that he arranged chairs across the living room so he could get to the kitchen and bath. My mother took us on a long visit to her Montana relatives. He didn't die, and we came back to San Francisco, but the Public Health Service nurses feared that we children would be infected, so they made us move apart. On my first birthday we were living across the bay in Fairfax. My father came over Sundays on the ferry and spent the day.

He kept a separate apartment even after we moved back into the city—people have suggested that he liked the freedom that gave him for poker parties or to entertain women. The latter is more likely, but I think that he just needed the peace and privacy to write and to be alone. My father was a man who always loved and needed solitude.

My mother came to accept the necessity of their living apart, but she never considered them to be "separated." From the tone of his letters at that time, I don't think he did either. Legal separation or divorce was a disgrace in my mother's eyes, and she bravely put up a front: Yes, they were temporarily living apart, but it was only because of his work, his special requirements.

It was a long gradual transition from that stance to admitting that their marriage was over. He had told her once that "she should take care of the children and he would take care of her." She held on to those words as long as she could, and he did too. His support checks might be late, but we never doubted they would come. Nor did we doubt that he loved us and thought of us as his family, even if living together as a family was not a possibility.

In pictures from the San Francisco days my mother looks thin and worn out. Her days were a rush to get us up and out to the park in the morning, home for lunch and naps at noon, and back to the park in the afternoon. Her social life was with the mothers and children she met at the park—visits to the beach, Fleischacker Zoo, donkey rides in Golden Gate Park. There was always worry about money and my father's health.

Papa helped as much as he could—sometimes made bread or lemon pies, stayed with us so Mother could go to Mass or the matinees she loved. He played with us—soaped the mirror and drew pictures on it, made shadow animals on the walls, crafted a little paste-up book for me of poems and pictures.

Both my sister and I disliked our given names, Mary with good reason, I thought. It would be hard to imagine one less suited to her after she grew up. The "Jane" was eventually dropped for just "Mary." But

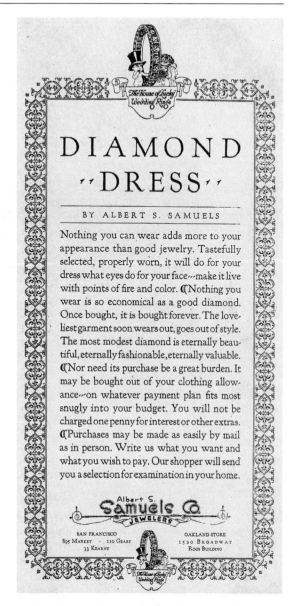

*Proof for one of the Samuels Jewelers advertisements Hammett wrote and sent to his wife (courtesy of Josephine Hammett)*

there was nothing more that could be done with that. When I complained of my unwieldy given names—"Josephine Rebecca" seemed an unnecessary burden on a child who struggled with penmanship and spelling—Papa disclaimed any responsibility. Mother was in charge of the name department he said, and she'd picked both of ours.

In time "Josephine" was shortened to "Jo" which had pleasant echoes of *Little Women*. But I still held some grievance against my father for not using his literary and

*Interior of Albert Samuels Jewelers, where Hammett worked as advertising manager in 1926 and was a part-time employee in the late 1920s (San Francisco Historical Photograph Collection, San Francisco Public Library)*

parental authority to give me a classier sounding name. If I had been asked I would have chosen "Margaret," the name of all my dolls and my maternal grandmother's name, though I didn't know it then. I can't imagine what he would have chosen.

Sometime in the forties my father mentioned wistfully to me that I was supposed to have been a boy. It's hard to believe with his health and their financial problems that I was really a planned baby, but clearly once I was on the way he hoped for a boy. I was offended to learn that I had been an instant disappointment and wondered for a moment if Papa would have been any happier with a son. No, I told myself; he would have been rebellious, ungrateful, and they would have fought a lot. Then I wouldn't think about it any more.

After his breakdown at Samuels, Papa entered a period of remarkable productivity. He turned out a rapid stream of *Black Mask* stories which, with the encouragement of editors Philip Cody and later Joseph Thompson Shaw, were longer and more fully developed. The Continental Op, an established favorite, became more human and three-dimensional. Characters emerged who would be used more subtly in his later work: The dangerous, and often red-headed woman; the pragmatic, dogged detective; the gullible thief, who could be turned against his pals. Key themes appeared: political and personal corruption; the problem of moral ambiguity.

*Dashiell Hammett and his daughter Mary on the rooftop of the Crawford Apartments, circa 1924, when he was writing* Continental Op *stories for* Black Mask *(courtesy of Josephine Hammett)*

Scene from Tillie's Punctured Romance, 1914. Charlie Chaplin, Marie Dressler, and Mabel Normand are in the forefront. Behind Normand (circled) is an uncredited extra identified as Nell Martin by her son-in-law (courtesy of the Margaret Herrick Library, Academy of Motion Picture Arts and Sciences). In October 1929 Hammett moved from San Francisco to live in the same building as Nell Martin in Manhattan. She married newspaper man Ashley Weed Dickinson on 16 December 1929.

Drawing of Nell Martin in the 1928 catalogue of new books by New York publisher Rae D. Henkle (Collection of Richard Layman)

Dust jacket for the book Martin dedicated to Hammett in 1933 (Collection of Richard Layman)

# EX-DETECTIVE HAMMETT

## *by Elizabeth Sanderson*

A CRITIC once said of Dashiell Hammett's work: "The writing is better than Hemingway, since it conceals not softness but hardness". If hardness consists of writing about criminals as though they were human, of looking on detectives with an unbiased eye and setting them down as less than paragons of shrewdness and integrity, of admitting corruption, human frailty and occasional pleasant qualities in both his man-hunters and their quarry, Dashiell Hammett's hardness is the main reason for his success. He writes of people he knows, people with whom he has worked professionally, and his characters, instead of being the stock marionettes of the usual detective story, are the flesh-and-blood figures of any good novel. As a consequence the usual detective story formulas are not enough to carry them, and Mr. Hammett disregards the old rules. The result is that he has written, in *Red Harvest, The Dain Curse, The Maltese Falcon* and *The Glass Key*, four of the best detective stories ever published. He is, in addition, a master of terse, abrupt prose, and he can tell more in one sentence of it than many an earlier mystery novel writer managed to convey in a chapter.

It was with a great deal of interest, then, that I set out to interview this man who had contributed a new form of fiction to contemporary literature.

Dashiell Hammett is tall, slim, sophisticated, with prematurely white hair above a young face. He was born in Maryland in 1894, and he holds that the only remarkable thing about his family is that there were, on his mother's side, sixteen army men of France who never saw a battle. The family name was De Chiel, and "Dashiell" is its Americanized version. (He will impress upon you that the accent falls on the second syllable.) He grew tired of school at the age of thirteen, and started on years of diverse jobs by working as a newsboy. Before the war broke out he had been a freight-clerk, a general worker around railroads, and a copy-writer for a small San Francisco jewel-

*The most significant early interview-article with Dashiell Hammett,* The Bookman, *January–February 1933 (Collection of Richard Layman)*

ler. The World War broke the De Chiel curse: Dashiell Hammett saw fighting, and when he left the army he left it with tuberculosis. During his recuperation he met and married a hospital nurse, who is now the mother of his two daughters, aged ten and five. The next job he found he held eight years: it was as a detective for the Pinkerton Detective Agency.

To Mr. Hammett being a detective was just another job; it was no fulfilment of a long-stifled boyish ambition born of reading Nick Carter. He admits that the first four years were full of interest and stimulation: he helped to send Nicky Arnstein to jail; he spent three months on a hospital cot trying to coax evidence from a suspect in the next bed; disguised as an ardent I.W.W. he was sent to Minnesota to follow another suspicious character; he worked on the Arbuckle case, which, he says, was a frame-up by some newspaper boys, who saw a big scoop in Arbuckle's guilt. (And politics in California, he asserts, are the most corrupt in the world.)

His Pinkerton career was interrupted for a time by another prolonged rest, and in his leisure he began to write. But he went back to Pinkerton's, and when I asked why he had finally left that profession he answered: "I suppose because they wouldn't let me go to Australia after some stolen gold. It sounded romantic. Later they found some of the gold in a San Francisco fire-hose". So Dashiell Hammett settled down to write for a living, and has written in some form or other—as often for the movies as for the bookstores—ever since.

Mr. Hammett says that the detective in *Red Harvest* and *The Dain Curse* was drawn from a real man. Spade, in *The Maltese Falcon*, is half real and half imaginary, and all the rest of Hammett's characters were made by combining the traits and experiences of

people he really knew as a detective. A detective is not actually a romantic figure, and few thieves or murderers are ever pure "criminal types". So Dashiell Hammett left the Philo Vances to Mr. Van Dine and wrote of what he had seen as a hard-working man among men of very little culture or nobility.

With all his experience to draw on, and in spite of the remarkable success that has come to him from his detective stories, Mr. Hammett does not want to go on writing them. He wants to write a play. Later he will write straight novels, but not until he has written his play.

He ought to be successful as a playwright. His dialogue is dramatic, accurate and economical. He can inject qualities into commonplace scenes that turn them into extraordinary situations. His characters are living persons, compounded of good and evil qualities. He can portray ruthlessness and greed

as well as William Faulkner. His characters are not pathological, as Faulkner's are, but Mr. Hammett d r a w s them just as pitilessly and far more directly. He knows the effective use of suspense. The prospects for a good p l a y look auspicious.

In the course of the i n t e r v i e w I gathered that Mr. Hammett has written s o m e v e r s e. T h a t he t h i n k s Robinson Jeffers the best story-teller he has ever read, and the cruellest. That he likes Hemingway, Faulkner and Hecht. He thinks Wilbur Daniel Steele is a competent magazine writer. He considers *The Dain Curse* a silly story, *The Maltese Falcon* "too manufactured", and *The Glass Key* not so bad—that the clews were nicely placed there, although nobody seemed to see them. (I told him that everyone hadn't been a detective.) He had Mickey Mouse's orchestra on top of

his bookcase, and on his desk were a lot of his own publicity photographs, of which he gave me the most flattering. W h e n h e works his enthusiasm carries h i m through thirty-six-hour p e r i o d s of steady w r i t i n g, which explains the evenness of his atmosphere.

At present Mr. Hammett is working on a story for Marlene Dietrich, and after it is finished he plans to go abroad. He wants to stay in Europe a year or two while he finishes his play and tries his hand at a straight novel. I suspect that despite what he says the Pinkerton days have left an ineradicable imprint; that notwithstanding the plans for the play, the novels and the scenarios, he will weaken from time to time and write other detective stories. I devoutly hope so. He is sufficiently versatile and talented to write excellently in all these forms.

# The Pulps and the Making of the Novel

## *Black Mask*

*There are several histories of pulps that include informa-tion about* Black Mask, *but the reliability varies. The best account of the development of the magazine and the hard-boiled detective story is this one, by one of Hammett's early biographers.*

**History of a Pulp: The Life and Times of *Black Mask***
William F. Nolan
*The Black Mask Boys: Masters in the Hard-Boiled
School of Detective Fiction*
(New York: Morrow, 1985), pp. 19–34

No grand vision inspired the creators of *The Black Mask*. In fact, litterateur H. L. Mencken and drama critic George Jean Nathan despised their brainchild and refused to allow their names to be included on its mast-head.

*Black Mask* was an economic necessity, created for the purpose of aiding another financially crippled publi-cation edited by Mencken and Nathan.

By 1918, *The Smart Set* was in trouble. This highly regarded, innovative magazine, which had launched the professional career of F. Scott Fitzgerald and which was designed for the sophisticated reader, had never been a moneymaker. Subtitled "A Magazine of Cleverness," *The Smart Set* was a bit *too* smart and clever to reach a mass audience.

In order to keep it solvent, Mencken and Nathan (who also shared in its ownership) had entered the more lucrative field of the pulps with *Parisienne* and *Saucy Stories*. Both titles proved successful.

Pulp magazines were then of a standard size—seven by ten inches, with gaudy, bright-colored covers (a reflection of their Dime Novel origins). They could be produced at a relatively low cost due to the use of paper made from ground wood. This "pulp" paper was short-fibered, fragile, and difficult to preserve, and clearly separated these publications from the "slick" magazines printed on smooth, higher-quality paper stock.

Even though Mencken and Nathan did well with *Parisienne* and *Saucy Stories*, their financial battle had not yet been won. Another mass-market pulp publication seemed the only solution.

According to historian Ron Goulart, the editor-publishers "turned down the opportunity to do an all-Negro pulp . . . [and] finally decided they'd try a mys-tery magazine."

Their decision was no doubt inspired by the suc-cess that Street & Smith had achieved with *Detective Story*. As the only ongoing crime pulp, it had steadily increased its circulation since its first appearance in October of 1915.

Early in 1919, writing to his friend Ernest Boyd about the problems at *Smart Set,* Mencken declared: "I am thinking of venturing into a new cheap magazine scheme . . . The opportunity is good and [we] need the money."

A line drawing of Satan, in a black mask, was fea-tured on each issue of *Smart Set* as part of its cover logo—which gave Mencken and Nathan the idea for their new title. The logo chosen for the new publication was a thin black pirate's mask with a dirk and a flint-lock pistol crossed behind it.

That first issue of *The Black Mask* was dated April 1920, priced at twenty cents. It contained a dozen sto-ries in its 128 pages and was subtitled: "An Illustrated Magazine of Detective, Mystery, Adventure, Romance and Spiritualism." (Through the years this subtitle was constantly revised as new genres of fiction were added or dropped.) Spiritualism as a cover subject was dis-carded after the first issue. Western fiction was eventu-ally added, becoming a *Black Mask* staple (into the 1930s), along with adventure tales set in exotic locales around the world.

In the second issue (May 1920), an editorial headed "Five Magazines in One!" attempted to show readers that the *Mask* was open to almost any type of story:

> What we propose to do is to publish in every issue the best stories obtainable . . . of Adventure, the best Mys-tery and Detective Stories, the best Romances, the best Love stories, and the best stories of the Occult.

# AS I WAS SAYING:—

THE following letter is typical of very many being received by *Black Mask* in almost every mail. Moreover, its inquiry forms such a happy introduction to our editorial purpose, that we cannot do better than reproduce it.

"The Editor,
BLACK MASK:

"I hope you do not think that your readers are tired of Race Williams, Ed Jenkins and the like characters. We are not; for they are supreme in their line.

"Where is Hammett's 'Continental Crook'? Where is 'Mac,' that other sleuth who was such a super-entertainer?

"You think it well, perhaps, to give us a change once in a while, but you must not let your old actors die, for they have won too firm a footing in the pages of *Black Mask*.

"I have become the bane of Los Angeles and 'Frisco booksellers, worrying them to get me all back numbers of *Black Mask* possible. My worldly troubles are many and varied but I forget them all when I take your excellent magazine in hand.

"E. W. J.........."

And here is our answer:

Not long since we had a roundup with all the old, dependable contributors to *Black Mask*—the early builders of the magazine. We conveyed to them our purpose and inspiration—to make *Black Mask* bigger and better—the best of all. We invited them to sit in with us, take off their coats and accomplish this very thing. We looked around very carefully and asked a few more to join in—men worthy to take their places with this select group.

And their reply?

One and all, from the Atlantic to the Pacific, from the far North to the luring tropics, have sent in the message, in the inspiring words of Stanley Gardner:— "LET'S GO!"

And it would seem that all at once the thing has started, with renewed life, with reawakened interest, with increased virility.

Carroll John Daly has commenced a brand new line for Race Williams, a great, ambitious work.

Erle Stanley Gardner has just sent us the first of a new Ed Jenkins series— a popular favorite in the most thrilling, gripping action we have seen in a long while.

J. Paul Suter, whose delightful style satisfies the most hardboiled critic, is preparing some stiff problems for the Reverend McGregor Daunt to crack.

Dashiell Hammett has called back the Continental detective from his long retirement and is setting him to work anew. Francis James is returning with a harder punch than ever. Tom Curry has injected new fire of life into the old reliable "Mac" and is broadening the scope of his activities. Raoul Fauconnier Whitfield is hitting on all eight cylinders in a new airplane series. Frederick L. Nebel is deep in startlingly realistic tales of the Underworld.

And this is but a mere suggestion of what the old favorites of *Black Mask* readers are at work upon.

Others, newcomers to our pages, are crowding forward and bringing no less enthusiasm than our old reliables who have taken the hunch.

There is much more that we could tell you, but now we will just say that neither E. W. J. nor any other of our reader-friends need seek for past numbers of *Black Mask*, although—and here's more than a promise—you may soon find it advisable to place your orders in advance with your newsdealer for the new ones.

For right now we can see the momentum of this new, concerted effort gathering force and volume.

Already we can add to Erle Stanley Gardner's rallying call, the assurance that—WE ARE ON THE WAY!

THE EDITOR.

107

*Editorial statement by Joseph Shaw in the January 1927 issue of* Black Mask, *three months after he began editing the magazine (facsimile; Collection of Richard Layman)*

Published under the subsidiary name of Pro-Distributors, out of Warner Publications in New York, the editor of *Mask* was listed as F. M. Osborne. A woman. Miss Osborne used only her initials to project a masculine image, since the new magazine was aimed primarily at male readers. The main editorial chores were handled by Osborne and Wyndham Martyn (both of whom were associate editors on *The Smart Set*), but Mencken was soon complaining to Ernest Boyd: ". . . the thing has burdened both Nathan and me with disagreeable work."

Mencken made no secret of the fact that he cordially detested the *Mask,* calling it "a lousy magazine," adding that "reading manuscripts for it is a fearful job." But he also admitted, "It has kept us alive during a very bad year."

In November of 1920, just eight months after its first issue, Mencken and Nathan sold the *Mask* to Eltinge F. "Pop" Warner and Eugene Crowe, owner-publishers of *The Smart Set*. Since they had invested only $500 in the project, the Mencken-Nathan profit margin was a tidy one (at a reputed sale price of $12,250). [Some reports have placed the sum at $100,000, but this is obviously an overinflated figure.] Warner took over as business manager, retaining Miss Osborne as editor.

Within a year the magazine reached a very healthy circulation level, demonstrating that readers were starved for mysteries. Certainly, the early *Mask* displayed no hint of originality or literary merit.

Its writers supplied pale imitations of the fiction being printed in *Detective Story*. Early *Black Mask* crime solvers were dull and pretentious fellows, reflecting the overbaked melodramatic elements of the silent screen. They included foppish Inspector Des Moines, prim and proper Desmond Okewood, of the British Secret Service, and solemnly pompous criminal investigator F. Jackson Melville-Smith. Bores one and all.

Shaking off the feeling of dread that had settled upon him like an incubus, Grimstead resolutely walked up the weed-encumbered walk that led to the front door, armed with a key that he had experienced no difficulty in securing from a cynical real-estate agent, who promptly offered to wager that he would not stay the night out, a wager that Grimstead as promptly accepted.

That is just *one* sentence of "Fingers From the Grave" by Edwin Carty Ranck in the September 1920 issue. Ranck indeed!

Dialogue could be truly incredible. Witness this exchange from a *Mask* story printed in October 1922:

"My dear Inspector," protested the Professor. "You surely cannot expect me to believe that a mere monkey—"

"That monkey threw Madame La Tourette into uncontrollable hysterics," Inspector Donaldson insisted. "Fifteen years ago, while on a hunting trip in Africa, her husband was crushed to death in the arms of a giant gorilla. Madame La Tourette is said to have recovered . . . yet, in her imagination, she could see reenacted the tragedy of her husband's terrible end—even seem to hear the echo of the crunching of his bones and his agonized cries as a hairy monster of the jungle had squeezed the breath from him years before."

The awkward, heavy-handed titles of these early stories were in keeping with their outrageous plots and characters: "The Deviltry of Dr. Waugh," "The Strange Case of Nathaniel Broome," "The Uncanny Voice," "The House of the Fiend Who Laughs," "The Scar of the Gibbering Imp."

In a retrospective review of a late-1921 issue of *Mask* (which was then subtitled "A Magazine of Mystery, Thrills and Surprise"), pulp historian Robert Sampson brands the fiction as "inept drivel":

It is sorry work to plod among the pages. Over all of the stories hangs the gray taint of inability. Not only are the authors [Bessie Dudley, J. Frederic Thorne, Ward Sterling, George Fayerweather, etc.] pretty condescending about mystery fiction, but they are unaware that they do not know how to write the stuff . . .

In its early form *The Black Mask* was sterile. It existed without direction, without self-respect . . . What ailed *Mask* was the baleful influence of *The Smart Set*. The lesser magazine aped the attitudes of the greater. . . . *Mask* disdained its own fiction, smirked at reader tastes, and [was] haughtily aloof from the field in which it would [within a decade] stand pre-eminent.

Advertising in these early issues was often more engaging than the fiction. In 1920 one might order a full "110-piece Dinner Set" for "$1.00 Down." Or, if you were feeling a bit under the weather, you could order a dozen "AK Tablets" for the relief of "Headaches, Neuralgias, Colds and La Grippe, Women's Ills, Rheumatic and Sciatic Pains." All for twenty-five cents a bottle. Or how about "Re-Mo-Vo," described as "the Daintily Perfumed Hair Remover." Or you could "Make People Like You" by sending five cents in stamps for a little booklet titled "Personal Power." If your nose was "ill shaped" you could send for "The Original [strap-on] Anita Nose-Adjuster." Or you could "Reduce Your Fat" by using "Cosi Obesity Cream."

By the October 1922 issue, the masthead listed a new editor, GeorgMale W. Sutton, Jr.—with Harry C. North assisting him.

# AS I WAS SAYING:—

W HAT'S IN A NAME?
We regret to observe a growing inclination on the part of some of our otherwise esteemed contemporaries and particularly among book publishers to purchase and offer stories, like other merchandise, largely on the NAME value.

It's generally believed that the name alone of a popular writer is enough to sell a book or magazine, without regard to the actual quality of the particular story. And it often is. For, more than ever before, people are now looking for diverting reading, and, without giving the matter much thought, are inclined to turn first to some well-known name.

And so it goes on and, in this heydey of getting what you can while the getting is good, nothing much is said about it and the practice has become an established fact which you can confirm as often as you care to take a chance.

But—we want to say right now and as plainly as we can put the statement in words, that this sort of thing does NOT go for BLACK MASK.

Perhaps we are missing a few good bets—for they come before us almost daily. As a matter of plain fact, we have just been offered a story by an author whose name is a household word from one end of the country to the other. We are perfectly aware that by merely printing the name of this particular author on the cover of the magazine would bring us for that issue thousands, probably tens of thousands of additional readers.

The story in question is under contract for book publication by one of the best known houses in this country. That house will owe a debt of apology to its readers—but we won't. And the reason is that the story, judged by ourselves purely on its merits, is not up to BLACK MASK standards of quality.

Why—even with our own writers—names that are favorites with you constant readers of BLACK MASK—we have sent back story after story on occasion, under the belief that an author, like the magazine, should show a consistent upward tendency in his successive works. And this may amaze you, but in every single instance we have received word of gratefulness and appreciation that we were so carefully guarding the author's reputation with his BLACK MASK following.

The point of this, as, of course, will be evident to you, is that we are keeping faith with our authors and are equally keeping faith with our readers; that we are working for a long, strong pull and a pull all together; that we are seeking to establish confidence in BLACK MASK, confidence that the NAME stands for only the best and most interesting reading, that each issue, from cover to cover, contains stories filled with life and action and swift movement of natural and plausible character—just the kind of reading you like best.

Now—if these are your principles as well, and you want to see such principles vindicated, just take hold a bit and work with us. Collectively you are a powerful, irresistible force. Just a little individual trouble by all will accomplish it.

If you believe in pushing along a good thing, an enterprise that is founded and built on faith, just tell some of your friends what a really good magazine BLACK MASK is.                                      The Editor.

B.M.—Feb.—7

97

*Statement by Joseph Shaw in the February 1927 issue of* Black Mask, *continuing his editorial in the previous issue (facsimile; Collection of Richard Layman)*

Sutton's first editorial was an odd one. Headed "How to Read Black Mask Stories," it implored readers "not to skip quickly over the pages" and warned them against a "jump to the end 'to see how it comes out.' . . . You cannot get the full force of these stories if you spoil your own pleasure by reading them the wrong end first."

Sutton immediately began to improve the *Mask*. In November he launched a series by ex-auto bandit Joe Taylor called "My Underworld," based on Taylor's life in crime. And in December of that year he printed the seminal work of two authors destined to reshape the genre, Carroll John Daly and Dashiell Hammett (then writing under the pseudonym of "Peter Collinson"). Daly's story, "The False Burton Combs," and Hammett's "The Road Home" were the forerunners of the *Black Mask* school of fiction.

That following year, 1923, provided the turning point, with the birth of the world's first tough private eye, Terry Mack, in Daly's "Three Gun Terry" in the May 15 issue. (In June, *Mask* featured the debut of Race Williams in "Knights of the Open Palm.") Hard on their heels, in the October 1 issue, Hammett's first Continental Op tale, "Arson Plus," was printed.

In publishing these stories, *The Black Mask* had made history; a revolution was under way, and the detective genre would never be the same.

Sutton, however, was not yet aware of what effect this new type of fiction would have, and in the same issue containing Hammett's first Op tale the editorial promised "stories of rugged Adventure, and real . . . Romance, rare Western yarns . . . weird, creepy mystery tales and the only convincing ghost stories to be found anywhere."

One thing *did* become clear to George Sutton—the value of issue-to-issue heroes. He began promoting series characters, including The Scarlet Fox (by Eustace Hale Ball) and detective T. McGuirk (by Ray Cummings). Soon, however, Sutton's passion for motorboating began to replace his editorial interests. By April of 1924 he had resigned, and Philip C. Cody (who had been director of circulation) took over the editor's chair. North stayed on as Cody's associate.

Erle Stanley Gardner, who had been selling fiction to the *Mask* since 1923, appreciated Harry North's "patience and sense of humor." Gardner credited North with helping him to write "better stories [with his] coaching on the margin of rejection slips and in short personal letters."

Phil Cody, who always thought of himself as "primarily a businessman," proved to be a strong-minded, extremely capable editor; he saw what Sutton had failed to see—that the Hammett-Daly brand of tough, hard-edged storytelling represented a bold new step

beyond the traditional deductive school of crime fiction. He began to feature Hammett's Op stories, and he also urged Daly to write more about Race Williams. (Cody recognized the fact that Daly's work was far inferior to Hammett's, but he was wise enough to know that content counted more than quality in establishing the popularity of this new brand of fiction.)

It was Cody who (in 1925) encouraged Gardner to develop his Ed Jenkins Phantom Crook series, and by the January 1926 issue, Cody felt confident enough to announce in an editorial that "*The Black Mask* has found its stride and is forging . . . to the front. Its circulation is increasing rapidly . . . [because] *The Black Mask* gives its readers more real, honest-to-Jasper, he-man stuff . . . than any other magazine . . ."

Cody also introduced (in 1925–1926) the work of four other highly influential writers: Nels Leroy Jorgensen, Tom Curry, Raoul Whitfield, and Frederick Nebel.

Jorgensen was a New Jersey motorcycle patrolman who moonlighted as a fictioneer. His straight-shooting gambler from the Southwest, Stuart "Black" Burton, quickly earned reader approval—and Jorgensen continued Burton's adventures into 1938.

Curry also won favor with a series of yarns about Mac, a hard-knuckled New York police detective. Curry had been a police reporter for a major New York paper and claimed that his stories were "right out of life." Whenever he needed fresh plot material, he'd seek out one of his "detective pals" who would fill him in on the latest criminal cases.

Whitfield, who loved flying, provided Cody with aviation thrillers featuring pilot-hero Bill Scott—while Erle Stanley Gardner helped fill Cody's western fiction needs with the wild adventures of sagebrush bandit Black Barr.

Fred Nebel wrote just one story under Cody's editorship; his potential had yet to be realized.

According to Erle Stanley Gardner, Cody never received due credit for his formative role in editing *Mask:* "[He] had a keen appreciation of literature," Gardner declared. "And he didn't cater merely to one style of fiction . . . Under his regime, the new action type of detective story took a long stride forward." Gardner also pointed out that "Phil Cody was the first . . . to appreciate the real genius of Dashiell Hammett."

Gardner related a bizarre anecdote concerning himself, Cody, and Hammett. Early in 1926 Hammett declared that he could not afford to continue writing for *Mask* unless he got a raise in his basic rate (which was probably three cents per word at that time).

Cody began sweating. He couldn't give Hammett a raise without doing the same for Daly and others. Yet

LOOK
FOR THIS
COVER

WESTERN, DETECTIVE & ADVENTURE STORIES

**BLACK MASK**

Fly
Paper
By
DASHIELL HAMMETT

The Other
Cameo
By EARL &
MARION SCOTT

ON THE
NEWSSTANDS
JULY 12th

# FLY PAPER

Dashiell Hammett sends the "Continental" detective on a thrilling man hunt. A tense action drama of the present time, where the underworld laps over the borders of society, told with that faithfulness to character, fact and sense of reality that makes Mr. Hammett's stories grip like action scenes from life itself.

# SPAWN OF THE NIGHT

Bob Larkin, who faces pistols and knives with his own unique weapon, gets into red-hot action in a little-known place on the Border.

# THE OTHER CAMEO

A swift adventure of Cameo Kirby, one time jewel thief, who, against the suspicions of the police, plays a square game, although it is a dangerous one.

# AND OTHER STORIES

that fill the magazine from cover to cover with thrill and action.

*30,000 more people are reading BLACK MASK regularly today than a year ago.* WHY?

*Promotion from the August 1927* Black Mask *for the forthcoming issue featuring a Hammett story. Hammett was the most popular* Black Mask *author, and Joseph Shaw made good on his promise to promote him enthusiastically (facsimile; Collection of Richard Layman).*

if Hammett left, the magazine might fold without him. Cody contacted Gardner with his problem, and Gardner proposed that a penny per word be deducted from *his* rate and applied to Hammett's rate. That way Hammett would stay with *Mask* and Gardner would continue to have a ready market for Ed Jenkins.

Cody brought this proposal to Eltinge Warner. The publisher declared that Gardner "must be nuts" and that "it was a cockeyed offer and no good businessman would have made it." Besides, he'd never liked Hammett's work.

When Hammett failed to get his raise, he quit. And, indeed, the magazine suffered as a result. By the summer of 1926, circulation had dropped to 66,000—and Warner felt that *Mask* needed a new editor.

This suited Cody. He was unhappy with his editorial duties and wanted to return to the business end of publishing, as vice-president and circulation director. (In the 1930s he was promoted, replacing A. W. Sutton as president of the company.)

Warner contacted mystery writer Joel Townsley Rogers, who was then an editor with *Century* magazine, and offered him the editing job at *Mask*. Rogers wanted to say yes but could not extricate himself from his contract with *Century*.

Enter Joseph Thompson Shaw.

Historically, Shaw's name is directly linked with *Black Mask* as the man who shaped and perfected the hard-boiled genre of detective fiction. W. T. Ballard (who began writing for the magazine in 1933) recounted the story of how Shaw became editor: "Writing was what he most wanted to do . . . [and] he had a manuscript that he took to Phil Cody at Warner Publications. Shaw did *not* sell the story, but he so impressed Phil that Cody hired him to edit *Black Mask* on the spot."

Joseph Shaw's background was diverse and colorful. Born in 1874, he was a descendant of Roger Shaw, a New England immigrant of the 1630s.

From boyhood, Joe Shaw loved boats and sailing. A writer friend reported that "he always had a flair for adventure—which he humorously ascribed to the marriage of a Crusading ancestor and a Saracen princess."

Shaw attended venerable Bowdoin College, in Brunswick, Maine, where he edited the campus paper and specialized in athletics.

Following his graduation, he obtained a job with a New York paper, then took over the editorship of a semitrade weekly. In 1904, working for the American Woolen Company, he wrote his first book, *From Wool to Cloth,* and felt that he was on his way to becoming "a literary man."

After a trip to Spain, in 1909, his second book was published: *Spain of Today: A Narrative Guide to the Country of the Dons.*

He continued his interest in athletics and became a master of the sword, winning the national championship in sabers and the president's medal for his skill with foil, epée, and saber.

During the First World War, Shaw was a bayonet instructor, leaving the service as an army captain. (During his days with *Black Mask,* he was widely known as "Cap" Shaw.)

Following the war, for a period of five years, he functioned as chief of the Hoover relief mission in Czechoslovakia and Greece. He returned to the U.S. in the early 1920s, determined to make his living as a full-time writer—but as Raymond Chandler later stated, "[Shaw's work was] about the deadest writing I ever saw on a supposedly professional level."

In truth, Joe Shaw was a superb editor and a dreadful writer. He did manage to get four of his mystery novels into print during the 1930s (*Derelict, Danger Ahead, Blood on the Curb,* and *It Happened at the Lake*), but they were hopelessly flat and banal, betraying no evidence of his outstanding skills as an editor.

In 1926, when Shaw walked into the Warner offices at 25 West Forty-fifth Street, he knew absolutely nothing about pulps or pulp writing and had never read a single issue of the magazine he was hired to edit. He spent a full week poring over back numbers—and decided that Hammett was the writer whose work pointed in the direction Shaw wanted *Black Mask* to go.

But Hammett had, by then, quit writing pulp fiction. Shaw determined to lure him back and sent a letter to Hammett, suggesting that it was time to revive the Continental Op in a "longer form," in which situation and character could be fully explored. Shaw's ideas excited Hammett, and he returned to the fold with two long Op novelettes, forming a superb short novel, *Blood Money.*

Cap Shaw was off and running.

The first Shaw-edited issue (November 1926, subtitled "Western, DETECTIVE, and Adventure Stories") contained fiction by Daly, Whitfield, Nebel, and Gardner. Shaw continued to feature the work of these four writers, along with Curry and Nels Jorgensen. But he was actively seeking new talent.

For the June 1927 issue (which featured the opening installment of the first Race Williams serial), Shaw penned an editorial, "The Aim of Black Mask," in which he claimed that the publication now had "a definite purpose and a definite aim . . . [to] establish itself as the only magazine of its kind in the . . . world:"

> . . . detective fiction, as we view it, has only commenced to be developed. . . . all other fields have been worked and overworked [but detective fiction] has been barely scratched.
>
> . . . However, to be convincing . . . [such fiction] must be real in motive, character and action . . . must be plausible . . . clear and understandable . . . Therefore, word has gone out to writers of our requirements of plausibility, of truthfulness in details, of realism in . . . the portrayal of action and emotion . . . Slowly, but surely, we are moulding the contents of this magazine along the lines of our purpose.

Shaw was getting results. Several major new writers were to be developed under his editorship.

The first was Horace McCoy, who made his bow in the December 1927 issue (now subtitled "The He-Man's Magazine").

By 1928, Shaw was printing the team of Earl and Marion Scott (who created the Phil Craleigh series about a drunken lawyer trying to reform). Also in 1928, Fred Nebel began his popular MacBride-Kennedy police series for Shaw. And that year's December issue featured the debut of a new series character, Tex of the Border Service. Surprise: Tex carried a purse! Shaw was taking a gamble in bringing Katherine Brocklebank's secret-service heroine into the tough pages of the *Mask.* Yet, readers liked Tex, and Miss Brocklebank brought her back in three more adventures over the next seven months. [At least thirty other women had fiction printed in *Black Mask,* but nearly all of their contributions fall into the magazine's early "Romance" category.]

Shaw also brought western writer Eugene Cunningham to the *Mask* and later helped him devise his series of Cleve Corby fighting-ranger shoot-em-ups. (It is not generally known that although Shaw emphasized detective fiction, he also strongly favored westerns—and *Mask* did not become an all-crime magazine until 1932. Many of its covers in the 1920s depicted gunslingers and outlaws. Eventually, by 1933, the magazine was subtitled "Gripping, Smashing Detective Stories," reflecting its specialized approach.)

In order to achieve greater impact and unity, Shaw used only *one* artist for all of the magazine's interior illustrations—Arthur Rodman Bowker. Boldly sketched and highly stylized, Bowker's work offered a perfect counterpart to *Mask*'s hard-hitting fiction.

Beginning in 1927, Shaw had also tightened the magazine's title: *The Black Mask* was now simply *Black Mask.*

To Joe Shaw, the editor's job became very personal. From the outset, he functioned as a potent, ever-helpful father figure to his authors. He offered them practical advice and wise counsel, encouraged their goals, cheered them in times of stress, and sought, constantly, to bolster their confidence, to draw out their best work.

Shaw's credo included "simplicity for the sake of clarity, plausibility, and belief." He wanted action, but he felt that "action is meaningless unless it involves recognizable human character in three-dimensional form."

He hated the word "pulp." To him, it smacked of cheapness and vulgarity. He always referred to *Mask* as "a rough-paper book" and felt that he and his authors were fighting a war for quality in a market glutted with hasty, hack writing. It was "Cap and his boys" against the competition.

Shaw's editorials reflected the special pride he felt in *Black Mask.* Late in 1929, he wrote of "the change in the character of [crime] stories . . ." commenting that "this magazine has . . . been the pioneer in the development of the new type of detective story."

Series characters continued to dominate the *Mask.* Once Shaw was convinced of an author's talent, he would ask that writer to come up with a character strong enough to support a series. The ongoing success of Race Williams and the Continental Op proved that readers became emotionally addicted to continuing characters and would eagerly buy issues featuring their favorites. (Akin, today, to viewer addiction for series characters appearing weekly on television.)

In 1929, Shaw launched the Jerry Frost, Flying Ranger series by McCoy—and, in 1930, arranged for Whitfield to begin his Jo Gar, Island Detective stories under the suitably exotic pseudonym of "Ramon Decolta."

*Mask* continued to feature Dashiell Hammett as the "prime innovator in this field." Shaw was responsible for Hammett's mature development as a novelist, and it was in *Black Mask* that such all-time Hammett classics as *Red Harvest, The Dain Curse,* and *The Maltese Falcon* initially appeared.

"Hammett was the leader in the thought that finally brought the magazine its distinctive form . . ." declared Shaw. "[He] set character before situation and led . . . others along that path."

The February 1930 issue announced the results of a reader poll: "The leaders . . . are Dashiell Hammett, Carroll John Daly, Erle Stanley Gardner, Frederick Nebel, Raoul Whitfield, and the Scotts." McCoy was next.

The *Mask* lost one of its editors that year. In a December 1930 letter to McCoy, Shaw reported the death of George Sutton.

After delivering *The Glass Key* and a few more Op stories, Hammett left *Mask* at the close of 1930 for greener financial pastures. This was a blow to Shaw, who felt the loss keenly. However, Daly, Nebel, Whitfield, and Gardner continued to supply him with material—Daly with Race Williams, Nebel with his new Donahue series, Whitfield with Hollywood eye Ben Jardinn, and Gardner with stalwart Ed Jenkins.

The icy, diamond-hard Kells series (forming the novel *Fast One*) began in 1932, from Paul Cain; and in 1934, Norbert Davis created private eye Ben Shaley for *Mask.*

Davis had been a law student at Stanford when he sold his first story to Shaw in 1932. He obtained a law degree two years later but never took his bar exam, deciding that fiction writing was his proper profession. Davis became a frequent contributor to the pulps, later breaking into *The Saturday Evening Post* with his often humorous, well-crafted stories. But there was ultimate tragedy behind his humor, and at the age of forty, in 1949, depressed over the slow progress of his career, he died of carbon monoxide poisoning. A Cape Cod suicide.

Shaw introduced Theodore A. Tinsley to his readers late in 1932 with series character Jerry Tracy, a troubleshooting news columnist.

The following year proved to be Shaw's finest as he brought five powerful new writers into the *Mask:* Thomas Walsh, Roger Torrey, H. H. Stinson, W. T. Ballard, and (at the close of 1933) Raymond Chandler.

Walsh was unique in *not* creating a series hero.

Torrey contributed Mal Prentice, a ruggedly tough police detective. The toughness was genuine;

Torrey had been an Oregon lumberjack in his younger days. He was a "heavy boozer," who worked evenings on his pulp fiction in a sleazy New York hotel room. Then, his work done, he would "drink the night away" in the bars of New Jersey (which remained open until 6:00 A.M.). When his doctor warned him that alcohol was destroying his liver, Torrey gave up drinking. For exactly one month.

Shaw liked Torrey's work; it represented precisely what he was after in editing *Mask*. From the September 1933 issue, a sample of tough Torrey:

> Bruner leaned over without warning and hit Prentice in the mouth, and Prentice tried to roll with the punch. . . . Locked to the bed frame, he jerked a foot up and kicked at Bruner, who stepped out of range and jeered: "Not even close." He knocked Prentice's guarding hand aside, stepped in and struck again.
>
> Prentice wiped blood from his face . . . "I'll remember that." . . . His eyes were hot. He was shaking so the cuff rattled where it was fastened to the bed.

H. H. Stinson's series hero was quick-fisted Ken O'Hara, of the *Los Angeles Tribune*. Again, a very tough cookie.

Tod Ballard began an extensive *Mask* series with Bill Lennox, a Hollywood trouble-chaser for Consolidated Films. The series grew out of Ballard's earlier screen experiences. He'd walked away from an electrical engineering career in Cleveland and had bummed his way west in the late 1920s to become a contract writer for Columbia Studios. For the Lennox stories, Columbia became Consolidated, with Ballard creating one of the first popular hard-boiled series characters based on the film industry. (At Shaw's suggestion, Ballard later devised another hit series for *Mask* concerning race-track detective Red Drake.)

Chandler wrote his first two stories for Shaw about a tough private eye named Mallory. He also turned out four series stories for Shaw about another "private dick" named Carmady. They were the same man. In truth, all of Chandler's knight-detectives, under whatever name he gave them, were prototypes for Philip Marlowe.

In 1933, Shaw presented his personal view of "the ideal *Black Mask* reader." In a blatantly melodramatic editorial he described this romanticized man of action:

> He is vigorous-minded . . . hating unfairness, trickery, injustice . . . responsive to the thrill of danger, the stirring exhilaration of clean, swift, hard action . . . [he is] a man who . . . knows the song of a bullet, the soft, slithering hiss of a swift-thrown knife, the feel of hard fists, the call of courage . . .

In the 1934–1935 period, Shaw brought three more star writers into the *Mask:* Dwight Babcock (with detective Maguire, and later G-man Chuck Thompson), John K. Butler (who wrote about hard-edged government agents), and George Harmon Coxe.

Coxe had been a newspaper reporter on the *Los Angeles Express,* and he had also worked for other papers in Florida and New York. Coxe wanted to utilize his newspaper background, but, as he declared, "there were already too many reporter-detectives in the pulps. So I came up with a guy who was a crime photographer. Called him 'Flashgun' Casey."

Casey worked out of Boston and became a big success for Coxe. Beyond the pages of *Black Mask,* Casey went on to star on radio, in novels, and in films and television.

Coxe's crime photographer mellowed considerably through the years, but there was nothing mild about his early adventures in *Mask*. From "Hot Delivery" (July 1934):

> Casey dropped behind the desk as the automatic roared. He scrambled around the side on hands and knees. Flip screamed in pain, fired again. Then Casey straightened, leaped forward. Flip was trying to get out of the chair. Blinded, he waved the gun wildly, one hand clasped to his blackened, charred face . . . He was nearly erect when Casey hit him.
>
> Flip went over backwards with the chair. Casey landed on top, his hand on the automatic. He wrenched it free, struck once, twice. Crushing, violent blows. Flip's body did not move after that, probably would never move.

Attempting to justify the violence in his magazine, Shaw bragged that *Mask* was being read by "clergymen, bankers, lawyers, doctors." Among his readership he also claimed judges, embassy officials, and "the heads of large businesses."

As a *Black Mask* writer of that period recalled: "It was important to Cap that the magazine be respected. He *needed* to believe that he was editing a publication of real importance, and he took his job very seriously."

However, by the middle 1930s, *Black Mask* was in trouble.

When Shaw had taken over in 1926, he had increased circulation from 66,000 to 80,000 in the first year. The climb continued, peaking in 1930 at 103,000—but by the close of 1935, as America was suffering through the Depression era, circulation slumped to 63,000.

Hammett had been out of *Mask* for five years. Now Whitfield was gone, along with Daly, McCoy, and Curry. Even a per-issue price reduction late in

JOSEPH T. SHAW
EDITOR

# BLACK MASK

TEL. BRYANT 4895

45 WEST 45TH STREET
NEW YORK

July 22 , 1927 .

Dear Mr. Hammett :

Just a line to accompany enclosed check in an
early mail .

I have nothing but praise for POISONVILLE . In
one of your recent letters you spoke of keeping your feet on the
ground ; the sense of reality which this tale gives is gripping .
You can see the place , the scenes , the action , the faces and
the character of the actors . Some of the parts are raw meat ;
but it is not thrown out in ragged chunks . It is served with a
skill that preserves the virile strength of it and obliterates
any suggestion of coarseness . I am going to say that I like
this and , anticipating that the balance will be moulded in the
same spirit , I believe it will be a series to conjure with .

I am well aware that this sounds like enthusiasm .
Reading your note that accompanied the story , I have been casting
through my impression from first xxxxxxx consideration , and I
really do not see any important element to shun . This , of course,
is the set-up . Naturally , as I wired , the following episodes
will swing into quicker action . I suppose this would be more
helpful if I should pick out one or two slants for constructive
criticism . I shall read it over again more carefully in a few
days and may then have something more to say . Just now I am
satisfied that it holds well to the middle of the road .

I shall hope to hear from you when you find
opportunity and inclination to write .

With very best wishes , I am ,

Sincerely yours ,

*Joseph T. Shaw*

Editor .

Mr. Dashiell Hammett .

*The only located letter from* Black Mask *editor Joseph Shaw to Hammett during the time Hammett
was contributing to the magazine (courtesy of Josephine Hammett)*

**THE NOVEMBER ISSUE OF BLACK MASK WILL CONTAIN THE MOST WONDERFUL READING TO BE FOUND BE-TWEEN THE COVERS OF ANY MAGAZINE—ACTION, MYSTERY, AND EXCITEMENT, OF THE KIND THAT YOU MOST THOROUGHLY ENJOY.**

POISONVILLE—A complete novelette. The first story in a new series by this great writer of detective fiction, so true to life, so realistic that you seem to live through the tense action as you read................Dashiell Hammett

THE WAX DRAGON—A complete novelette. Commencing a brand new Ed. Jenkins series of thrilling adventure. The fight of the Phantom Crook with the police and the Underworld......................Erle Stanley Gardner

GET BURTON—A complete novelette. Blazing guns, the clash of wits and a running fight mark the climax of Burton's adventures on the border of crookdom in New York.......................................Nels Leroy Jorgenson

THE RAIDERS. A detective's part in the clashing of rival gangs.......................................Tom Curry

RED PEARLS. An unusually strong story in the devious ways of crime..........................Raoul F. Whitfield

WITH BENEFIT OF LAW. The love of a girl for a prizefighter and the manner in which she meets crookedness......................................Frederick L. Nebel

THE RETURN OF GUN EAGEN. When a man decides to face the music of false accusations, a clean-up usually follows.................................John W. McCardell

THE CRIME CIRCLE. Like a person lost in the woods, a man often returns to the scene of wrongdoing......Harold C. Firanze

ONE BAD MAN. They said the sheriff was too old; but they found he was not easy to fool and that he still could shoot.................................Everett H. Tipton

Most dealers sell out of BLACK MASK in a few days
Get your copy early. On sale October 12th

*Promotion from the October 1927* Black Mask *for the first installment of Hammett's first novel, published in book form as* Red Harvest *(facsimile; Collection of Richard Layman)*

1934 (from twenty cents to fifteen cents) had not helped.

Eltinge Warner told Shaw that he might have to make some salary cuts in 1936. Shaw made it clear that he would not abide by this. The situation became tense.

Meanwhile, Shaw brought another star talent to the *Mask* when he printed two stories about a treasure-hunting boat owner named Oscar Sail. These were written by Lester Dent, based on his own treasure-hunting adventures off the coast of Florida.

Best known under the pseudonym of "Kenneth Robeson," Dent was grinding out a 60,000-word Doc Savage novel every month for Street & Smith. (Eventu-

ally, he wrote more than 150 of these.) He lived aboard a forty-foot schooner in Miami and sidelined in professional photography. Originally a Teletype operator from the Midwest, he'd been writing pulp fiction since 1929 and had sold work to dozens of editors, but Shaw was something special. Dent praised him as "the finest coachwhip I ever met in an editor's chair. *Mask*, in Cap Shaw's hands, was akin to a writer's shrine . . . When you went into his office and talked with Shaw, you felt you were doing fiction that was powerful. You had feelings of stature."

Dent was plotting a third Oscar Sail novelette in October of 1936 when he received a note from Shaw reporting a salary dispute. After ten years with the *Mask,* Joe Shaw had been relieved of his editorial duties.

A shock wave ran through the ranks of "Joe's boys" from New York to California. Dent quit the *Mask,* and Chandler switched to *Dime Detective.* Nebel also left, and Paul Cain did no more pulp writing.

Shaw's remarkable decade was over, but he had achieved his goal: He had shaped and guided dozens of writers toward a new form of objective realism within crime fiction.

His stable had included Ed Lybeck, Reuben Jennings Shay, J. J. des Ormeaux, Eric Taylor, Stewart Stirling, Donald Barr Chidsey, Norvell Page, Hugh Cave, and John Lawrence.

By the December 1936 issue, *Mask* had a new editor, listed on the masthead as F. Ellsworth. Another woman in disguise. As the guiding editor of *Ranch Romances* (also a Warner publication), Fanny Ellsworth seemed an odd choice to helm a hard-boiled detective magazine. Indeed, her ideas on crime fiction were much "softer" than Joe Shaw's; she intended to bring "a more humanistic" type of story into *Mask,* feeling that the strict hard-boiled approach was too limiting.

Ellsworth certainly made an impressive start at her new job. Within a space of just eight months, between January and September of 1937, she brought no less than nine impressive talents to the *Mask.* Among them: Cornell Woolrich, Max Brand, Frank Gruber, and Steve Fisher.

Woolrich (who also gained fame as "William Irish") was a prime example of the "softer, more nakedly-emotional approach" in crime writing favored by Ellsworth. His detectives were never hard-boiled; they were usually "little" men, trying to do a job within the dark, threatening universe of a big city.

Woolrich himself existed inside such a universe, living with his mother in a series of cramped, friendless New York hotels. Writing was his salvation; it kept him sane.

Frederick Faust (who wrote as "Max Brand") was also an emotionalist, who believed "in the prime essentials of truth and beauty." A Renaissance man who loved Italy, he lived for many years with his family and servants in a hillside villa near Florence, turning out more than a million words a year for the pulps. He contributed only two stories to *Mask,* but Max Brand's name on the cover meant an upsurge in sales.

Another prolific pulpster, Frank Gruber, now brought his quirky series hero, Oliver Quade, "the Human Encyclopedia," into *Mask.* Gruber recalled that he had made several attempts to sell his work to Shaw. "[He] was charming man . . . [who] encouraged revisions of revisions. When he rejected your story it was

always with great regret. [He] wore me out with kindness."

Frank Gruber's pal, Steve Fisher, made his first *Mask* appearance just two months after Gruber. He, too, had been rejected by Shaw. As Fisher later commented: "[My] subjective style, mood and approach to a story was the antithesis of [a] Roger Torrey who, like Hammett, wrote objectively, with crisp, cold precision."

With Ellsworth, *Mask* had been opened to the subjective approach. Other authors she brought to the magazine during that first year included Baynard Kendrick, Donald Wandrei, Wyatt Blassingame, Lawrence Treat, and Dale Clark. Among them all, Shaw might have approved most of Clark's Mike O'Hanna—a tough "house dick" at a resort hotel.

Gruber described Fanny Ellsworth as strong-minded. "She was an extremely erudite woman. You would have thought she'd be more at home with a magazine like *Vogue* or *Harper's* . . . [but] she knew what she wanted."

Ellsworth's tenure at the *Mask* lasted until the spring of 1940. Circulation had taken another severe drop. Warner and his associates felt that it was time to get out.

They sold *Mask* to Popular Publications, whose *Dime Detective,* under the editorship of Kenneth S. White, had been *Black Mask*'s chief competitor. During the 1930s, Ken White had deliberately edited *Dime* in the Shaw tradition, luring several of "Cap's boys" into his magazine with a guarantee of higher word rates.

Now, ironically, in the summer of 1940, Ken White became editor of *Black Mask.* Immediately, he began injecting new life and vigor into its pages, reestablishing the magazine's tougher, hard-edged image.

Before the close of the year, White had printed work by Cleve Adams, D. L. Champion, and Robert Reeves.

Adams wrote in the direct hard-boiled Chandler manner, and Champion's Rex Sackler was a tough ex-cop operating as a private eye. With his offbeat detective, Cellini Smith, Reeves brought elements of wry humor into the magazine.

A major change was taking place in popular culture. Three emerging forms of entertainment—comic books, paperback mass-market editions, and television—were destined to wipe out the pulps. By 1940, the death knell had been sounded, and the pulp magazines began their inexorable slide toward oblivion.

Ken White fought to keep *Black Mask* solvent, but it was a losing battle. He utilized tough, wisecracking titles—"You're the Crime in My Coffin," "My Body Lies Over the Ocean," "Blood, Sweat and Biers," "Murder Had a Little Lamb," "Once Upon a Crime"—and he commissioned gaudy, sensationalistic covers by

UNLESS a man has a definite purpose in life, he is bound to wander around aimlessly, becoming eventually the hit or miss type, usually with emphasis on the "miss."

So with a magazine.

Months ago BLACK MASK decided upon a definite aim. This aim has been to fill the magazine, from cover to cover, with stories that would grip you with tense action and swift movement and hold you to the end with the plausibility of the plot and every detail.

Some readers still like fairy tales; but the only kind of story that will make you feel you are living through the action instead of reading fiction is the story that is likely to happen.

That is our belief, and from innumerable letters of approval and from the steady increase in circulation of BLACK MASK from month to month, it is evident that our readers agree with us—that this is the sort of magazine they have been looking for.

That has been our aim and we have worked hard to accomplish it. Slowly at first, month by month, we have come nearer our goal. At first the right kind of story was not easy to find in sufficient numbers to fill the magazine from cover to cover.

Then our writers took hold with us; they came to understand that they were selling their stories, not to the editor, but to the readers themselves. They wanted to interest their readers, to get them to look forward to their stories with every new number.

And now we can place before you, month after month, a BLACK MASK that will hold you from the first word to the last.

BLACK MASK has arrived! It is here!

Every month it is filled from the first page to the last with the most interesting reading you can find anywhere at any price. As one reader, among many hundreds who are writing us, says: "Stories that are plausible and at the same time intense in their interest . . . This letter is just an outburst of pride in your magazine!"

We are proud of it, too. And we are especially proud of the November issue which will represent our greatest accomplishment to date.

### Don't miss that number!

## November BLACK MASK on sale October 12th

*Editorial statement in the October 1927 issue of* Black Mask *magazine*
*(facsimile; Collection of Richard Layman)*

Raphael De Soto which portrayed scantily clad young ladies being threatened by unsavory thugs. White also brought in such diverse talents as Leslie Charteris (with The Saint) and Curt Siodmak (with his now classic science-fiction-suspense tale, "Donovan's Brain").

In the January 1941 issue, he printed stories featuring five series characters and appealed to reader loyalty with a strong editorial:

If any one thing can be said to be the main factor in *Black Mask's* success down through the years it is unquestionably the great parade of series characters who have marched through its pages bringing readers back issue after issue to renew old friendships.

In the early 1940s, White ran "timely" stories of government agents, Nazi villains, and espionage—but these efforts did little to increase circulation.

Finally, in 1944, White utilized the expert services of Joe Shaw as an adviser to new writers.* [*Shaw had been functioning as a New York literary agent. In 1946 he edited his famous collection of *Black Mask* stories, *The Hard-Boiled Omnibus*. By late 1951 he had opened his own literary agency, where he died at his desk in August of the following year. Among the writers paying him tribute was W. T. Ballard, who sadly reflected on Shaw's frustrations as a writer: "He could point the way for [others], contribute much to helping work out their problems with sympathy and understanding—but he could not do the same for himself, though writing was what he most wanted to do."

Chandler recalled Shaw as "a warm editor [who] always seemed to have time to write at length and to argue with you. To some of us, I think he was indeed a genuine inspiration in that . . . we wrote better for him than we could have written for anybody else."] White also brought "Flashgun" Casey back to the *Mask* in book-length adventures by Coxe. He purchased new work from Carroll John Daly, and featured Gardner's popular Ed Jenkins. He also printed other *Black Mask* veterans—Ballard, Davis, and Torrey—along with an impressive roster of new names and characters: C. P. Donnel, Jr. (with Doc Rennie), Merle Constiner (with Luther McGavock), William Campbell Gault (with Mortimer Jones), and John D. MacDonald (with Sam Dermott).

Added to these were Fredric Brown, Bruno Fischer, and, in 1949 with a single story, Louis L'Amour.

But *Mask* now had dropped back to bimonthly publication; the overall page content had been cut; the magazine's size was also reduced and the cover price raised to twenty-five cents. Nothing worked; the downward plunge continued. By 1950, White had left the magazine, and *Mask* was under the emergency supervision of its publisher, Harry Steeger. Reprints began to be used to cut editorial costs and soon dominated the contents page.

The long battle ended in July of 1951. *Black Mask* printed its final issue that month after more than thirty-one years of publication.† [†In the 1970s there was an abortive attempt to revive the magazine. Published by Adrian Lopez and edited by Keith Deutsch, it was aimed at bimonthly publication. Using mainly reprint material, the new *Black Mask* never got beyond its pilot issue, dated August 1974.] The bare statistics are awesome. In its three decades, *Black Mask* printed some 2,500 stories by 640 authors. Total wordage for 340 issues: over 30 million.

*Black Mask* was dead, but its place in the history of modern detective literature was secure. It had pioneered and developed a vital new genre, and its "hard-boiled boys" had become the stuff of legend.

NOTE: Beyond the writers named in this history, there were others who also contributed their talents to the *Mask,* many of whom helped shape the magazine's unique image. Some appeared only once or twice in *Mask,* yet deserve to be listed. Each name is followed by the date of the author's first appearance in the magazine.

Robert Arthur (1940)
S. Omar Barker (1929)
William E. Barrett (1933)
Maurice Beam (1937)
H. Bedford-Jones (1932)
Hal Murray Bonnett (1938)
Charles G. Booth (1923)
Anthony Boucher (1945)
William Donald Bray (1927)
Walter C. Brown (1938)
Curtis Cluff (1948)
Francis Cockrell (1933)
Richard Connell (1923)
William R. Cox (1938)
Frederick C. Davis (1922)
Richard Deming (1948)
Robert C. Dennis (1946)
James Duncan (1934)
Allan Vaughan Elston (1946)
Dean Evans (1949)
Paul W. Fairman (1948)
G. T. Fleming-Roberts (1940)
J. S. Fletcher (1922)
Richard E. Glendinning (1950)
Jackson Gregory (1939)
Brett Halliday (1944)
Cutcliffe Hyne (1926)
Francis James (1922)
Norman Katkov (1946)
Day Keene (1943)
W. H. B. Kent (1927)
Philip Ketchum (1941)
Jim Kjelgaard (1940)
C. M. Kornbluth (1946)
Murray Leinster (1922)
Maurice Level (1920)
Julius Long (1943)
William Colt MacDonald (1926)
Carl L. Martin (1927)
Robert Martin (1946)
Raymond J. Moffatt (1934)
James P. Olsen (1930)
Peter Paige (1939)
Edgar Pangborn (1938)
Hugh Pentecost (1942)
Herman Petersen (1922)
Henry Wallace Phillips (1927)
Talmage Powell (1949)
E. Hoffman Price (1945)
William Rollins, Jr. (1923)
William Rough (1942)
Richard Sale (1942)
Hank Searls (1950)
Robert E. Sherwood (1922)
Bertrand W. Sinclair (1930)
Charles Somerville (1923)

\* \* \*

*Joseph T. Shaw edited* Black Mask *for one illustrious decade. His authors included Hammett, Erle Stanley Gardner, Horace McCoy, Raoul Whitfield, Raymond Chandler, and Paul Cain. He is responsible for establishing the respectability of the hard-boiled school and, through his promotional genius, for introducing a generation of realistic crime writers to a general readership. Ten years after he stepped down as editor of* Black Mask, *Shaw edited an anthology of the best stories from his days as editor. In his introduction he discusses the editorial rationale he developed after he took over* Black Mask *in November 1926.*

### Introduction to *The Hard-Boiled Omnibus*
Joseph T. Shaw
*The Hard-Boiled Omnibus: Early Stories from* Black Mask
(New York: Simon & Schuster, 1946), pp. v-ix

We had recently returned from a five-year sojourn abroad during and following the First World War. Happening upon a sporting magazine, to which we had haphazardly contributed in years past, we were curious enough to investigate the remarkable change that had taken place in its format and appearance. We found the miracle man to be Ray Holland, a six-foot stalwart who, in addition to his familiarity with the birds and beasts, knew also the vital difference between the functions of an editor who knows his stuff and that of a publisher not so gifted. Ray also had the personality to enforce recognition of his knowledge and to keep the breach open. Hence, the success of the magazine.

In friendly conversation we were asked to edit another magazine in the same group: *Black Mask,* a detective story magazine. Before that, we had never seen a copy, had never even heard of the magazine. We had not even a bowing acquaintance with the "pulps." Yet we always held that a good story is where you find it regardless of author-fame or medium of publication. It has been said that with proper materials available, a good mouse trap can be built anywhere.

We meditated on the possibility of creating a new type of detective story differing from that accredited to the Chaldeans and employed more recently by Gaborieau, Poe, Conan Doyle—in fact, universally by detective story writers; that is, the

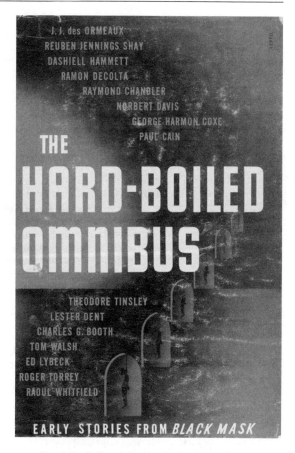

*Dust jacket for Joseph Shaw's collection of stories from the pulp magazine he edited from 1926 to 1936 (Collection of Richard Layman)*

deductive type, the cross-word puzzle sort, lacking—deliberately—all other human emotional values.

Obviously, the creation of a new pattern was a writer's rather than an editor's job. Consequently, search was made in the pages of the magazine for a writer with the requisite spark and originality, and we were amazingly encouraged by the promise evident in the work of one. Not that his pattern was different from that of others, but he told his stories with a new kind of compulsion and authenticity.

So we wrote to Dashiell Hammett. His response was immediate and most enthusiastic: *That is exactly what I've been thinking about and working toward. As I see it, the approach I have in mind has never been attempted. The field is unscratched and wide open.*

It was apparent that Mr. Hammett shared our hope for a medium in which he could achieve his aim while developing his talent into a highly skillful instrument. We pointed out that this particular medium—the magazine mystery story—was both constrained and restrained. We

# NOVEMBER BLACK MASK
*An issue of 100 per cent punch*

BLACK LIVES......................Dashiell Hammett
A complete novelette by the author of "The Cleansing of Poison-ville," and the first of a series of four adventures of the "Continental" detective. Mr. Hammett was formerly head of a large detective agency. He knows how a detective works and he tells it in this interesting story which leads to an unsuspected and terrific climax. Long a favorite with Black Mask readers, he is becoming generally recognized as the leader in an altogether new school of detective fiction.

THE LAW LAUGHS LAST...............Frederick L. Nebel
### A Complete Novelette
The third powerful story of The Crimes of Richmond City. A stirring tale of present conditions, of vice and graft linked with politics as an organized business and the methods used to flout the law and its honest representatives.

THE CURSE OF THE KILLERS..........Erle Stanley Gardner
### A Complete Novelette
An unusually swift tale of Black Barr, the fast-shooting wanderer of the Plains, whose fate leads him where the law of justice is un-known and is replaced by the law of the six-gun.

THE SKY-TRAP—A Complete Novelette.....Raoul F. Whitfield
A tense story of fighting and flying on the Border; the final duel between the Federal operative with Mac, the ex-flier, and the mur-derous gang of holdup men led by Antonio Flores, the flying bandit.

### THE SHORTER STORIES INCLUDE
DON'T CALL IT AIR-TIGHT, a swift yarn of Chink-running, by Lester Renard; BOULEVARD LOUIS, PATRON OF THE ARTS, the cleverness of a diamond thief, by Eric Taylor; LOTTERY TICKETS, a story of the Underworld, by Kennie MacDowd, and others.

## NOVEMBER ISSUE ON THE STANDS OCTOBER 12TH

*Promotion from the October 1928* Black Mask *for the forthcoming issue featuring the first installment of Hammett's second novel, retitled* The Dain Curse *for book publication ( facsimile; Collection of Richard Layman)*

felt obliged to stipulate our boundaries. We wanted sim-plicity for the sake of clarity, plausibility, and belief. We wanted action, but we held that action is meaningless unless it involves recognizable human character in three-dimensional form.

Dashiell Hammett had his own way of phrasing this: *If you kill a symbol, no crime is committed and no effect is produced. To constitute a murder, the victim must be a real human being of flesh and blood.*

Simple, logical, almost inevitable. Yet, amaz-ingly, this principle had been completely ignored by crime writers—and still is, in the deductive type of mystery story.

In physics, an explosion sends out sound waves. But if there are no ears within their range, there is no sound. If you read of a thousand aborigines wiped out by earth-quake or flood, you are abstractly interested, but you are not disturbed. But let a member of your own family be even remotely threatened and you are at once intensely concerned, emotionally aroused. This is true in real life. Why shouldn't it hold true in fiction, which must create the illusion of reality?

It was on this philosophic concept that we began to shape the magazine we wanted, the kind of story it would print.

The formula or pattern emphasizes character and the problems inherent in human behavior over crime solution. In other words, in this new pattern, character conflict is the main theme; the ensuing crime, or its threat, is incidental.

For a clear demonstration of this pattern, consider *The Thin Man* by Dashiell Hammett, and *The Big Sleep,* by Raymond Chandler. In approach and structure, both are singularly alike, since both adhere closely to the pattern. Otherwise they are as dissimilar as any two novels, which demonstrates the infinite variety attainable under this pattern. Neither can be tagged "just another detective story."

In both, characters, in full three dimensions, and character conflict are set up. The main crime and its victim are off-stage, and, while the solution of the crime is woven into the pattern of each story, it by no means constitutes the essence of the story. In fact, strip the crime from each book, and you still have a thrilling story, a test which the deductive type of mystery story could scarcely meet.

A London publisher wrote us that he recognized in our magazine a new school in writing, differing from anything else American, and unlike anything English. He accredited the *Black Mask* group of writers with its inception and accomplishment. We believe it was Mr. McKeogh, writing in the *New York World-Telegram,* who stated that all plots and props in detective stories had been used and abused, and there could be nothing new except treatment; and he, too, gave credit to the *Black Mask* writers for this innovation.

Such distinctive treatment comprises a hard, brittle style—which Raymond Chandler, one of its most brilliant exponents, declares belongs to everybody and to no one—a full employment of the functions of dialogue, and authenticity in characterization and action.

To this may be added a very fast tempo, attained in part by typical economy of expression which, probably, has had definite influence on writing in other fields. As Mrs. Harry Payne Burton said: "Hammett and his confrères have shown our authors how to attain the shortest distance between two points; and are we glad!"

The contributors of this brittle style were, notably, Hammett, Raymond Chandler, Raoul Whitfield, George Harmon Coxe, Roger Torrey, Forrest Rosaire, Paul Cain, Lester Dent, among others. It was rather extravagantly tagged as the "hard-boiled" school, and it was imitated throughout the "pulp" field. There is, however, this difference of distinction. While many *Black Mask* characters were admittedly "hard-boiled," the appellation belonged to the characters rather than to the school of writing. Style and treatment were something else again.

These writers observed the cardinal principle in creating the illusion of reality; they did not make their characters act and talk tough; they allowed them to. They gave the stories over to their characters, and kept themselves off the stage, as every writer of fiction should. Otherwise, as Raymond Chandler puts it, that most powerful factor, melodrama, becomes "used as a bludgeon and not as an art"—and loses ten-fold its effectiveness.

They did not themselves state that a situation was dangerous or exciting; they did not describe their characters as giants, dead-shots, or infallible men. They permitted the actors in the story to demonstrate all that to the extent of their particular and human capabilities. Moreover, as they attained their skill, they wrote with greater and greater restraint, careful of over-exaggeration in a word of their own where text demanded their descriptive contribution, adhering to the sound principle that whatever arouses the incredulity of a reader—no matter how true to life—has exactly the same effect as that which could not possibly happen. As a consequence, they wrote convincingly.

Long is the roster of the contributors to the magazine's individual type of crime fiction. Many who saw their first stories in print there have since risen to the heights in this and other fields of literature. It was often said, in that period, that their product, in its best examples, was several years ahead of its time. These writers were blazing new paths.

Most of the writers who together produced this magazine have since contributed the most skilled and successful crime novels written in the past decade, and have also contributed enormously to the best Hollywood has to offer in the mystery field. Hammett and Chandler are outstanding examples. There are a score of other writers who contributed their share to make the *Black Mask* group outstanding, writers who favored us with their first work and have since come into national recognition. We would like to mention them all individually, as we so clearly remember them. We would like to include in this volume examples of each one's work, but in both cases space forbids.

We make only one final point. We do not, and we cannot, claim credit either for the original work of these *Black Mask* writers or for their success. It is our conviction that no one person can bring forth successful writing from another. A discerning editor may help toward skill and craftsmanship, but application of that skill and the thought behind it are the sole properties of the writer himself. And so, without any further introduction from me, meet the artists who make *Black Mask* what it was, a unique magazine and a new influence in American literature.

\* \* \*

WESTERN, DETECTIVE & ADVENTURE STORIES

# BLACK MASK

## "Cap" Shaw
## and the
## Legacy of a Pulp

*Joseph T. Shaw, editor of* Black Mask

*Dashiell Hammett (standing, far right) at a 1936 dinner in Los Angeles for* Black Mask *writers. Others shown: (standing, left to right) R. J. Moffat (a guest), Raymond Chandler, Herbert Stinson, Dwight Babcock, Eric Taylor; (seated) Arthur Barnes, John K. Butler, W. T. Ballard, Horace McCoy, and Norbert Davis (UCLA).*

*Dr. Milton Shaw is the son of Joseph T. Shaw. This passage is an excerpt from his memoir-in-progress about his father.*

## Dashiell Hammett: One of the Early Masketeers
Milton Shaw

Some of these distinguishing qualities of character can be seen by examining the relationship between my father and Dashiell Hammett. Initially, it would seem that the personalities and life styles of the two men were about as alike as day and night. Hammett's love of the night life, his failure to constrain himself to traditional notions about the responsibilities of marriage and parenthood, his affinity for alcohol and womanizing, his fits of depression, and his sardonic tendencies were the antithesis of Dad's traits. For Dad, the marriage vows were inviolable, family was central to his life, and he did not indulge in self-destructive activities or fits of depression; on the contrary, he was very much the optimist and always bursting with enthusiasm and new ideas. He was not a teetotaler but I never knew him not to have alcohol consumption under control. Whereas Hammett seemed to do a lot of introspection, my father did not. Whereas Hammett had many career concerns, recognizing that his recurring illnesses often dictated which jobs he could or could not hold, Dad was not burdened by indecision. He put his hand into several different ventures, but he never hesitated to move on when he found something more challenging. More often than not, my father's activities kept leading him closer to the literary field, a field that, in spite of his love for the woods and water, inexorably became his primary calling. The disparity of these two men with regard to their formal education was amazing. Hammett gave up his schooling at age fourteen, my father graduated from prestigious Bowdoin College. Also there was a difference of twenty years to the month in their age. Dad being the elder could have been Hammett's father.

In spite of their differences, there were many similarities between these two men. Both had ancestral roots in Scotland, both were stubbornly independent non-conformists, both thrived on adventure and had a passion for books. Neither shied away from hard work; both had a deep sense of civic responsibility; both were unflagging patriots, Dad volunteering for service in World War I at age forty-four, Hammett volunteering for service in World War II at age forty-eight; both had an untouchable level of integrity; and both were gentle men. They were quite a pair.

Fortuitously, my father and Hammett were brought together through unique circumstances. An observation by W. Pronzini is revealing: "Two events made *Black Mask* the great, pioneering magazine it was in the detective field. One was the decision of Dashiell Hammett to submit the bulk of his early work for publication in its pages; the other was the hiring, in 1926, of Joseph T. 'Cap' Shaw as its new editor." Yes, this was the coming together of two great literary men, one an editor, one an author.

Upon his arrival at *Black Mask,* the first thing Dad did was to peruse previous issues of this magazine in an effort to understand what the magazine was all about so that he, in turn, could build on what Phil Cody had already established. Two areas he focused on were first the originality and authenticity of Dashiell Hammett's writing. Hammett alone seemed to realize the full potential of hard-boiled detective fiction beyond its gun-slinging appeal. As an ex-Pinkerton detective turned self-taught writer, Hammett was uniquely qualified to give his characters the three dimensions of which other writers of the tough detective story were incapable. My father's other observation was that Hammett was no longer submitting stories to the *Black Mask* magazine. The reason for Hammett's departure from *Black Mask* was related to three hundred dollars that he felt was owed to him by Phil Cody. Through correspondence with Hammett, Dad was able to develop the story format of what he would like to see in the magazine. "We wanted simplicity for the sake of clarity, plausibility and belief. We wanted action, but we held that action was meaningless unless it involves recognizable human character in three-dimensional form." Dad hit a responsive chord with Dashiell Hammett that enabled them to establish a pattern of story telling that emphasized character and the problems inherent in human behavior over crime solution. Hammett's response to Dad's recommendations was enthusiastic: " . . . the field is unscratched and wide open." The enthusiastic response was facilitated by a three hundred dollar payment to Hammett by *Black Mask.* Dad gave Hammett a free hand in creating this fiction, paid him premium rates for his work, and urged him to attempt longer more fully developed stories. Feeling that Continental Op in novel form could reach a large audience of book readers, my father suggested extending the Op's fictional range to allow greater depth and character expansion. In effect, Dad was laying the foundation for the novels that followed. In 1926 Hammett considered himself a retired fiction writer. Inability to provide the money for a second impending child prompted him to turn away from pulp writing and to enter the field of advertising. Hammett might never have produced *The Maltese Falcon* or any of his other novels had it not been for my father.

The relationship was being forged, one that centered around their common effort to produce stories calculated to expand *Black Mask* circulation, but there was also a warm personal relationship developing. Dashiell Hammett had been a guest at our home in Scarsdale, New York, on at least one occasion. At age two I retained nothing, but a picture dated 1929 does reveal his presence in Scarsdale. At another time, on a trip to the West Coast, my father personally gave a present to Dashiell Hammett's daughter Mary Jane. Dad wanted to know his authors at more than a professional level. Over a four-year period, he became something of a father figure to Hammett. He provided a ready market for Hammett's best fiction, extolled the strength of his stories in editorials, and raced to his defense when critics wrote demeaning appraisals of his work. He was a source of encouragement to Hammett and paved the way for him to write his full-length novel *Red Harvest*. It was indicative of their relationship that this first novel was dedicated to Joseph T. Shaw. On the other hand, my father didn't hesitate to exercise his editorial prerogatives of censorship, to make suggestions for changes in his stories, and to urge Hammett to set character before situation. With respect to censorship, sex and homosexual references were taboo as was the use of vulgarities and blasphemies in any story printed in *Black Mask*. Dad was a stickler on the implementation of this policy; however, this same policy subjected him to the antics of Dashiell Hammett, who once baited him with the terminology of "gooseberry lay" and "gunsel." A manuscript from Hammett contained both expressions. Dad thought the worst of "gooseberry lay" and had it expunged from the story. It also prompted a letter from my father to Hammett stating that *Black Mask* would never publish vulgarities of that sort. In truth "gooseberry lay" refers to a tramp who makes his living by stealing freshly laundered clothing from a clothes line and then selling it for a few pennies for food. On the other hand, "gunsel" is a mischievous word with homosexual connotations. Dad assumed that, because Hammett used the word so casually that it pertained to a hired gun, and allowed it to pass untouched. I don't know what Dad's reaction was to this duplicity of words but I cannot help but believe it was with a suppressed scowl.

It was a fruitful relationship, though it only lasted four years, Hammett did codify the model by which my father not only reshaped *Black Mask* but also established a whole new style of detective writing, namely, which became known as the "*Black Mask* School." *Red Harvest*, a "literary landmark" bound in hard covers, moved the hard-boiled school of detective fiction from the back room of the pulps into the bright lights of bookstores; the Conan Doyle prototype was displaced. This novel gave expression to Hammett's anger against injustice.

This anger was genuine, bitter and unrelenting. He projected a strong personalized viewpoint into a fictional framework thus enabling *Red Harvest* to be an expression of moral outrage exposing "the cancer of crime." What was encouraging about the utilization of a novel to share a personal predilection is that my father understood what Hammett was doing, respected it, and supported it. As Dad stated: "We knew he was great . . . but it took the *Black Mask* stories published in book form to wake up the country as to how great he really is." Unfortunately for *Black Mask* and its readers, Hammett stopped writing fiction for pulp magazines because he believed he could do better by concentrating on smooth paper magazines and developing novels. His last Continental Op story for Dad was published in the November 1930 issue, almost eight years to the month when his first *Black Mask* story appeared, and four years after Dad and Hammett started working together. My father realized the immense loss this was to the magazine and tried to entice him back but to no avail. Hammett saw greener fields beyond. It is interesting to note that, shortly after his departure, Hammett had three short stories about his protagonist Sam Spade published, two in *American Magazine,* and one for *Collier's*. These stories lacked intensity and the wry passion of the work he had done for *Black Mask*. This Spade was far inferior to the complex, richly textured Spade that Hammett had created in the *Maltese Falcon;* the new Spade was bland, all but invisible. Hammett had moved beyond the emotional environment of the series. In addition to the many individual articles published, four of his five novels were serialized in *Black Mask*. No other writer had made such an impact on *Black Mask* as did Hammett. With respect to my father, he, more than any of the other previous editors, defined the form of realistic detective fiction originated by Hammett; Dad is the man most closely associated with "the *Black Mask* School" of objective hard-boiled literature.

As Hammett moved off the scene, his place was taken by Raymond Chandler. Hammett and Chandler were the two *Black Mask* writers in particular who symbolized hard-boiled fiction. Their stories, with their harsh realism, violence, and terse dialogue, remain the best examples of a style of writing acknowledged to be the most important contribution the United States has made to the mystery genre. *Black Mask* had a secure place in American literary history because it stimulated a generation of genre writers who perceived a style of writing that would accurately reflect the modern world. With the exception of Hammett and Chandler, these writers are as important for their influence as for their writing–their influence was profound. Dad was the one who created the editorial environment within which individual growth could take place, and then pointed the way.

\* \* \*

*This letter from* Black Mask *contributor Lester Dent explains Shaw's editorial approach from an author's point of view. Philip Durham was an English professor at UCLA who was interested in the development of popular fiction. His research led him to study Shaw's* Black Mask.

La Plata, Missouri
October 27 1958

Mr. Philip Durham
Department of English, UC
Los Angeles, California

Dear Durham:

I don't foam easily, I'm pretty sure. But this chip of recognition you toss toward Cap Shaw and his Black Mask stirs my juices quite a bit.

Shaw was the finest coachwhip I ever met in an editors' chair. In my thirty-five years of free lancing fiction, no one stands out so. Hence I presume when you speak of Black Mask you speak of Joe Shaw.

Black Mask in Cap Shaw's hands was akin to a writer's shrine. I don't mean today, but in the Twenties and Thirties when Shaw presided. That was the brief wonderful time when American literature was endowed with the most effective training ground of all history--the pulp magazine. The writers whom Shaw published in Black Mask were sort of automatically endowed with a hair shirt that they wore with pride and some dubiousness, because where writers got together you were pointed out as a Black Mask man; not a Post writer, a Colliers writer, a Doc Savage writer or an Argosy writer, but as A Black Mask writer.

So Cap Shaw had recognition in his day.

His writers regarded Captain Shaw with---if any writer ever truly gave an editor such---reverence. At least I never heard a Black Mask writer be casual about Shaw.

My tenure with Cap was short. I sold him, I think, only three pieces. Then he gave up the helmsmanship of Black Mask over a policy dispute, which, I am convinced, is what kept me from becoming a fine writer. Had I been exposed to the man's cunning hand for another year or two, I could not have missed. Cap did try to work with me and guide me after he left Black Mask and became an agent. But in those days I was ficety and greedy, and also Joe no longer had the money-apple to dangle in front of me--a sale to Black Mask. Instead I wrote reams of saleable

crap which became my pattern, and gradually there slipped away the bit of power with words that Shaw had started awakening in me.

Cap was gentle with his writers. You went in to Black Mask and talked with him, you had feelings of stature, you felt you were doing fiction that was powerful. Cap gave this strength to his writers. He could, because he was so convinced it was the truth.

Cap himself was the personification of English culture. This was so sincere in him that it was almost a spiritual garment he wore. This facet struck me hard. I am a Missouri hillbilly, and I think I was at all times a bit skeptical of Cap Shaw's reality. For one thing he was an expert at fencing, and this was enough to make him incomprehensivle [*sic*] to me.

How did Shaw find and develop so many great writers? I wish I fully understood.

In my own case, I'd written a lot of published pulp, many millions of words of it, before I assembled enough guts to decide I might, just might, be able to do something near Cap's standard. So I telephoned him. Could I have a talk with him. I could. I went to the Black Mask office, expecting to get the customary puzzling generalities about what he wanted.

My first shock: Here was a cultured man editing a pulp. Second, here was an editor who thought his writers were truly great. I never did feel fully at ease that afternoon--three or four hours as I recall--because culture makes me itch, and an editor who didn't pretend his writers were crud-factories was unbelievable.

But here was a man who could breathe this pride of his into a writer. Cap didn't think I was a pulp hack. Joe felt I was a writer in step with the future. He thought that of all his writers. He had a way, with this device or some other device, of breathing power into his writers. I am sure all of Cap's writers---Hammet, [*sic*] Chandler, Gardner, the rest, probably felt this.

That day Shaw showed me a bit from a letter from Chandler, a piece so delicate and sensitive and perceptive that it forever moulded my view of Chandler, whom I have never met. The bit concerned some value Chandler was seeking, a thing that Shaw might congeal. Showing me the note from Chandler did exactly what Shaw probably wanted it to do--it sold me on the idea that I was not to sit down and do a hack hardboiled piece of pulp for Black Mask. I was to believe and feel I was doing a great piece.

Joe used his coach whip in strange gentle ways. He would start discussing his writers, their skill, and before you knew it you would find some Hammet or Chandler in your hands along with a blue pencil and Cap would be asking, "Would you cut that somewhere. Just cut a few words." The idea, of course, was that there was no wordage fat. You could not cut. Every word had to be there.

# From Shaw's Scrapbook

*In the late 1970s Nils Hardin, editor of the fanzine* Xenophile, *claimed to have the scrapbook Joseph Shaw kept when he edited* Black Mask, *from November 1926 to November 1936. The 11" x 17", sixty-four-page scrapbook is mostly made up of clippings about the magazine and its writers, and there are occasional handwritten comments or identifications. Mr. Hardin sent a photocopy to Richard Layman in about 1979, and the location of the original is not known. Facsimiles included in this chapter and following chapters are from that copy.*

WRITERS' DIGEST

October 1930

DEAR EDITOR:

It happens that I have just observed your excellent reference to the *Black Mask* market on page 57 of your September issue.

The only exception I can take to this well-written paragraph is the reference to the price we pay. Two cents a word up would come nearer the fact. A variation in rate has to do with the manner in which the particular story carries on and expresses our purpose.

We are always looking for new writers of promise, and gladly work with them to mutual advantage.

At the present time, the short story of say from 4000 to 8000 words has rather the better chance with us, although we are not apt to let a bang-up yarn of twice that length get away from us.

JOSEPH SHAW, Editor.
*Black Mask.*
578 Madison Ave., New York.

*Joseph Shaw's statement in* Writer's Digest, *October 1930, about pay rates and guidelines for* Black Mask *stories, from the Shaw scrapbook (facsimile; Collection of Richard Layman)*

# Among the New Books

## ARTS & DECORATION

DEVELOPING WRITERS

To Joseph T. Shaw, as editor of *Black Mask*, goes the honor of having discovered and developed the brilliant talent of Dashiell Hammett, a phenomenon among modern writers of detective stories. Hammett's hero, Sam Spade, the detective in "The Maltese Falcon" is one of the superb character creations in modern fiction.

Mr. Shaw writes me: "A few years ago we set ourselves the aim to produce in this magazine a new type of detective fiction in place of the old formula sort, with crime and solution as its chief and often only motivation." That was an inspired and magnanimous aim.

Hammett, who was formerly a Pinkerton operative, worked out his scheme of things in *Black Mask*, and, because he has a narrative gift that is trained down like a boxer to a taut springiness and precision, he has emerged as the most talked of contemporary writer of detective fiction. He has written four novels, and the best of these is "The Maltese Falcon" (Knopf).

Another writer Mr. Shaw has nurtured and developed in *Black Mask* is Raoul Whitfield and before the field gets too crowded with people congratulating Mr. Shaw on his discovery and shouting applause to Whitfield, I want to get in a yell for him. Take a look into his new novel, "Death in a Bowl" (Knopf). If you get that far, you will be glued to your chair until you finish reading it. So far Whitfield seems a notch below Hammett as a character creator and he is not as careful a writer as Hammett; but he is inventive and dramatic and his hard-boiled people are hard-boiled people.

*Undated article, circa 1931, from the Shaw scrapbook (facsimile; Collection of Richard Layman)*

## EL PASO TIMES.

### SUNDAY, MAY 24, 1931.

Well, we can't always be wrong! We have said and hereby and herewith reiterate, that Dashiell Hammett produced the finest detective novel in the English language, with "The Maltese Falcon."

A number of readers profess a hearty dislike for Hammett's writing. Investigation made in a spirit of scientific curiosity has shown, in some such cases, that the readers who dislike a Hammett book will point at other detective novels—books of the most cut-and-dried, hackneyed and stereotyped pattern—novels which could have interchangeable by-lines—so like is each of them to dozens and dozens of others—as representing their idea of the fine detective story.

Perhaps a reviewer's viewpoint cannot be entirely normal. A flood of detective fiction has swept over the reviewers' desks in the past couple of years. And when one reads a half dozen in a week, similarities, apings, are very apparent.

A letter received this morning from John F. Byrne, managing editor of the Fiction House Group of magazines, seems to prove that something about Hammett's work catches the eye and offers something new, to the jaded literary palate of an overworked editor, as to the book-saturated reviewer:

"I was glad to notice in The Times book page," Byrne writes, "that you thought so well of Dash Hammett's latest yarn. I am joining with you in any enthusiasm you write about his stories. About 50 detective yarns a month pass over my desk and I have to read big gobs of most of them. Ninety per cent of the detective stories published between board covers are nowhere near the standard we set for the tales published in our Detective Book Magazine and Detective Classics. So detective stories such as Hammett writes hit me all the harder."

\* \* \*

And . . . as this column goes to press . . . the reports from leading book stores spotted strategically from Maine to Florida and from Atlantic to Pacific, show that the latest Hammett book, "The Glass Key" (Knopf), is now the best selling mystery novel in every large city of the country. Critics and reviewers alike have greeted "The Glass Key" with praise of a kind rarely given to a detective or mystery story. The consensus is that Hammett's hard-boiled mystery novels are not only "thrillers" but literature.

## MAY 31, 1931

## THE EL PASO TIMES

### *The New School of Mystery Writing* ✔

Capt. Joseph T. Shaw, editor of Black Mask Magazine, rises up in pardonable pride, with publication of a recent article by Curtis Patterson in Town and Country.

I say "pardonable" because what Patterson terms a development of great importance in detective fiction —the growth of a brand-new type of detective story that is taking the place of the old-style, time-worn, formula story with its unreal, untrue-to-life characters and its super-clever detectives, that has the crime and the solution as its only kick—was the aim of Captain Shaw when he took the helm of Black Mask several years ago.

Hence the captain's "pardonable" elation when of the stories listed as exemplifying the new trend, all were first published in his magazine: Red Harvest—published by Shaw as Poisonville, The Dain Curse, The Maltese Falcon, Green Ice, Death in a Bowl, The Glass Key, Books by Raoul Whitfield, Carroll John Daly and Dashiell Hammett.

Captain Shaw remarks (with perfect truth) that others of the Black Mask writers are of equal importance, in this "growth of the new, realistic school of detective fiction": Erle Stanley Gardner—Ventura, California, lawyer; Fred Nebel; Nels Leroy Jorgensen; Horace McCoy; the Scotts.

"It is all very flattering," the captain writes. "And for the sake of the writers I am glad to see book-reviewers giving recognition to the effort of these men and women to bring stories and characters of three dimensions and throbbing with life to a field which has always been called the most hackneyed."

\* \* \*

*Clippings from the Shaw scrapbook ( facsimile; Collection of Richard Layman)*

93

*Statement by Joseph Shaw from the Shaw scrapbook*
*(facsimile; Collection of Richard Layman)*

You will hear it said Joseph Shaw told his writers what to write and how, demanded they do "Black Mask" style. This was not true. He demanded nothing of the sort. He did demand that every word mean something---he must be able to hardly touch your piece with a blue pencil. And he didn't rewrite himself---if there was one paragraph off, you got it back to re-do. That may be the secret of realism Shaw writers acquired. Anyway, when you did something lean and powerful, no excess wordage anywhere, then you had "Black Mask Style."

Cap had above all the power to impress you incredibly with the importance of the things he considered made a good story. This may have been partly the force of his dignity, his culture. As I wrote in the beginning, I have never met another like him. Possibly as a measure of my respect for him, I never troubled to submit another piece to the Black Mask market after he left, a thing I certainly did not discuss with him or with anyone but myself.

You ask about my own published material. It amounts to several hundred booklengths and shorts. My most recent, a short earlier in the year in the Saturday Evening post; a Wagon Train TV story; then in Colliers and other slicks, pocket books by Gold Medal and others, books by Doubleday, and for seventeen years and a bit more a book-length published yarn every month about a character called Doc Savage under Kenneth Robeson, a house name for Street and Smith. I think I did two hundred and eighty-seven Doc books.

I do hope you fellows grasp the idea that Black Mask was Joseph T. Shaw. He created its power.

My best to you,
Lester Dent
La Plata, Missouri

# THE AUTHOR and COMPOSER

## A DIGEST for

### Songwriters : Dramatists : Scenario Writers : Fictionists

EARLE I. STRICKLAND, Editor      PAUL CRUGER, Managing Editor      GRACE K. NORTON, Associate

Volume XIII      AUGUST, 1932      No. 8

# An Interview with Joseph T. Shaw

### Editor of Black Mask Magazine—by ED BODIN

THIS afternoon we have an enjoyable assignment. We are going to call upon one of the cleverest, friendliest and most popular editors in the all-fiction field—not only an editor and a gentleman, but an editor with a keen sense of humor—namely Joseph T. Shaw of Black Mask Magazine, whose new book, "Danger Ahead," released a few days ago has already found a fine reception.

We give the taxi-cab driver more than the usual tip as he fights his way through the tangled traffic of upper Fifth Avenue and shoots into Madison Avenue near 57th Street. We enter the Ley Building at 578 Madison, and an express elevator brings us quickly to the 11th floor.

The beautiful blonde receptionist of Black Mask and associated magazines, soon gets Mr. Shaw on the inter-office phone and nods her head as she says: "Mr. Shaw will see you at once—go right in."

As usual, the editor of Black Mask is up to his neck in manuscripts as he sits at his huge desk beside the wall where at least a hundred covers of Black Mask are framed and hanging in neat arrangement. They give off an atmosphere of virility and action.

Up comes Mr. Shaw's hand for a real handshake. No matter what he is ever doing, whether reading, dictating or talking to the President of the Writers' Union—he's never too busy to greet a guest with that uprising palm that bespeaks friendship and welcome. His grey-streaked hair and mustache add dignity to his middle-age appearance as he invites us to be seated.

"Mr. Shaw," we begin—"the readers of AUTHOR & COMPOSER have come for a short visit this afternoon for a personal chat and message to carry back home."

"Fine," he smiles. "I always knew that real people like Black Mask—that's why we intend to keep the reputation it has gained as the leading magazine in its field."

We answer quickly. "You don't have to tell us—we know that Black Mask's fiction whether it is an adventure, western or detective story, finds its place in homes from the White House to the mechanic's cottage."

Mr. Shaw interrupts at this point. "Yes," he says—"I've always wondered what a composite picture of the Black Mask readers would look like."

"A typical red-blooded virile American—fit he-man comrade for the many animated women who also enjoy the thrill of Black Mask fiction."

But we soon get to the point of the visit and we put the first query: "What chance has the unknown writer to click with Black Mask?"

"Best in the world," replies the editor, "if he carries the Black Mask standard of craftsmanship as well as the story. You see—Black Mask demands fine workmanship. The names in the author list of our magazine, are found in the Saturday Evening Post, Collier's, Liberty and the best magazines in the country; but names don't mean much unless the story is there too. That's why leading writers consider it a distinction to be on Black Mask's contents page."

Then Mr. Shaw makes this vital point: "Remember—when I read a story by a new author, I don't read it from the standpoint of that one story. I read it also as an example of that writer's workmanship. He might not click with that story—but if he writes Black Mask quality, he will know about it—for I am always looking for the fellow with the flair."

When asked to mention names of his writers he most preferred, Mr. Shaw replied quickly: "This wouldn't be fair to the many Black Mask writers—for one never knows when one of the authors who write Black Mask quality, will step ahead with a story that is exceptional. All my writers are fiction masksmen—that's why so many writers who get their first breaks in Black Mask, soon appear in the Post and others, along with their Black Mask appearances."

We interrupt at this point and ask: "The best way, therefore, to know Black Mask, is to read a copy?"

"Not exactly—but rather study the technique of the Black Mask writers—not one issue, but a dozen—and suddenly you will feel that fiction punch that tells why their stories were purchased. You'll find that expert swing and delivery in every story in Black Mask. Until you can sense it and duplicate it—you are not quite ready to click."

"Now as to the best lengths to try," we ask. "We presume the short would stand a better chance?"

"Yes, Black Mask doesn't like novelettes over 15,000 words—and, of course, seldom does the new fellow hit the bull's eye with that length. His best bet would be the 6,000-word story, or a little less."

—o—

Thus it is plain why Black Mask Magazine holds such a high reputation in the all-fiction field. The editor is not just a purchasing agent of virile, adventure, western, detective or border stories that are usually found in such magazines—but a Judge of the Supreme Court of two-fisted fiction who knows quality as well as story substance and considers them with the eyes of his readers. As a popular author himself he has both the author's and the editor's vision.

So don't send ordinary material to Joseph T. Shaw. While he wants to be friendly and helpful—his judgment cannot be fooled by inferior quality of workmanship or weak stories. When shooting at Black Mask, you are shooting at as fine a market as there is in the magazine field—and Mr. Shaw intends to maintain that reputation for Black Mask. Don't overburden him, or impose upon his good nature. He will meet you more than half-way—but you've got to show him that you have the flair.

*From the Shaw scrapbook ( facsimile; Collection of Richard Layman)*

## On Contemporary Detective Fiction

*From January 1927 to October 1929 Hammett was one of the mystery-fiction reviewers for* The Saturday Review of Literature, *edited by Henry Seidel Canby; and from April to October 1930 he reviewed mystery fiction for the* New York Evening Post. *He was a hard critic to please. This selection of his reviews is representative of his intolerance of sloppy writing and carelessness with facts. In his reviews Hammett expressed his literary standards, which he applied most successfully in* The Maltese Falcon. *The concluding selection for* The Saturday Review of Literature *is Professor Canby's advice to mystery writers, which is typical of the dismissive attitude of most critics before Hammett revolutionized the form.*

**Poor Scotland Yard!**
Dashiell Hammett
*The Saturday Review of Literature, 3*
(15 January 1927): 510

FALSE FACE. By SYDNEY HORLER. New York: George H. Doran Company. 1926. $2.
THE BENSON MURDER CASE. By. S. S. VAN DINE. New York: Charles Scribner's Sons. 1926. $2.
THE MALARET MYSTERY. By OLGA HARTLEY. Boston: Small, Maynard & Company. 1926. $2.
SEA FOG. By J. S. FLETCHER. New York: Alfred A. Knopf. 1926. $2.
THE MASSINGHAM BUTTERFLY. J. S. FLETCHER. Boston: Small, Maynard & Company. 1926. $2.

In some years of working for private detective agencies in various cities I came across only one fellow sleuth who would confess that he read detective stories. "I eat 'em up," this one said without shame. "When I'm through my day's gumshoeing I like to relax; I like to get my mind on something that's altogether different from the daily grind; so I read detective stories."

He would have liked "False Faces;" it is different from any imaginable sort of day's work. Scotland Yard promises to "safeguard the safety" (page 29, if you think I spoof) of an American inventive genius who has business with the British government. Arrayed against him and it is a medley of scoundrels–a "shuddersome" Communist with "a smile that revolted," a hyphenated "brute-beast" of a German, a Russian Baron who has "the air of a world cosmopolitan," and so on, including a nameless skeptic who doubts that a certain blueprint is an original drawing. Everybody moves around a good deal, using trains, motorcycles, automobiles, airplanes, submarines, secret passages, sewers, and suspended ropes. Most of the activity seems purposeless, but in the end dear old England is saved once more from the Bolshevists.

I don't think it will stay saved unless something is done to Scotland Yard. It is, if this evidence is to be believed, a scandalously rattle-brained organization: trivialities are carefully guarded while grave secrets are given out freely: no member ever knows what his coworkers are up to. But we aren't in a position to criticize our cousins: here in the same book is an American Secret Service operative occupied with stolen necklaces and red plots, when he should be home guarding presidents, or chasing counterfeiters, or performing some of the other duties of his department, and in "The Benson Murder Case" the New York police and district attorney are not a bit less haphazard.

Alvin Benson is found sitting in a wicker chair in his living room, a book still in his hand, his legs crossed, and his body comfortably relaxed in a lifelike position. He is dead. A bullet from an Army model Colt .45 automatic pistol, held some six feet away when the trigger was pulled, has passed completely through his head. That his position should have been so slightly disturbed by the impact of such a bullet at such a range is preposterous, but the phenomenon hasn't anything to do with the plot, so don't, as I did, waste time trying to figure it out. The murderer's identity becomes obvious quite early in the story. The authorities, no matter how stupid the author chose to make them, would have cleared up the mystery promptly if they had been allowed to follow the most rudimentary police routine. But then what would there have been for the gifted Vance to do?

This Philo Vance is in the Sherlock Holmes tradition and his conversational manner is that of a high-school girl who has been studying the foreign words and phrases in the back of her dictionary. He is a bore when he discusses art and philosophy, but when he switches to criminal psychology he is delightful. There is a theory that any one who talks enough on any subject must, if only by chance, finally say something not altogether incorrect. Vance disproves this theory: he manages always, and usually ridiculously, to be wrong. His exposition of the technique employed by a gentleman shooting another gentleman who sits six feet in front of him deserves a place in a *How to be a detective by mail* course.

To supply this genius with a field for his operations the author has to treat his policemen

TEN CENTS A COPY

# The Saturday Review

## of LITERATURE

### EDITED BY HENRY SEIDEL CANBY

VOLUME III     NEW YORK, SATURDAY, JANUARY 15, 1927     NUMBER 25

THOUSAND FEET. S. E. ELEVATION    WAD
*Scheme for a Mountain*

Where will our civic architecture stop?
Behold the office-buildings man erects!
Nay! "Own your own eyrie" on a mountain-top,—
I know an excellent firm of architects!

## The Age of Confession

THOSE inquisitive minds which like to expend their ingenuity in analyzing their times would do well to turn their attention to the outcropping of autobiographical writing in recent years. For here is a literature that in its diversity ranges from the tortured reflections of a philosophic mind to the stark sensationalism of a convicted murderer, that is sometimes sophisticated and sometimes crass, and that is now unrestrained through force of emotion and again frank by deliberate design. In either form it counts its readers in great numbers, in the one instance among the cultured and the reflective, and in the other among the vast commonalty which is interested in incident and passion rather than in character and temperament. But since in a democracy like ours that commonalty is so much in the ascendency, and mediocrity so much outbulks distinction, the memoir that engages attention is as apt to be that of the person who has attained a success which is comprehensible to the many as it is to be a chronicle of unique abilities.

All ages, of course, have had their uninhibited autobiographers, men who have made the world their confessional; but for our epoch alone has it been reserved to make a cult of self-revelation. Restraint has been cast to the winds, and from the movie actress who flaunts her "confessions" in a sensation-mongering magazine to the scholar who devotes a volume to displaying the tattered shreds of his domestic life, the whole gamut of society babbles its secrets to the world. Dignity, a decent respect for the opinions of mankind, a sense of the sanctity of human relationships, an appreciation of the unimportance of the individual in the general scheme of the cosmos, no one of these operates to prevent the outpouring of inconsequential nothings, indiscretions, and emotional vaporings that tarnish our contemporary writing. The improper study of mankind has become the vogue. There is a rage for personalities instead of personality, an appetite for the salacious rather than for the salty. Vulgarity and tawdriness stalk naked and unashamed. What has produced such a state of affairs? Something more, it would seem, must exist than a love of gossip and an inclination toward sensationalism to account for the interest in self-revelation that is so widespread today.

The tabloids and the cheap magazines that have so unashamedly catered to the worst in this passion for delving into the deepest intimacies of personal life have increased it but have not created it. They have merely been quick to seize upon an appetite which has grown with their indulgence of it, shrewd enough to recognize that in the romanticizing instinct of mankind lies a fertile field for exploitation. We say the romanticizing instinct, for it would appear that at bottom it is rather the yearning for the realization of a vision than lust of sensation that has given the "confession" its hold. Even the most unimaginative men in their secret souls treasure a dream—a dream of what they might have been or may still be. And here inscribed in these chronicles are the hopes and fears, the elation and the discouragement, that their own lives have known, described as merely the preamble or accompaniment to the success which they would make their own. What the average reader craves in the novel in which he demands a happy end is here as fact not fiction. In the main they are the successful who write, those most frequently who, not foreordained by wealth or position to fame, have achieved it, or at least notoriety, through happy chance or ardent persistence.

We are well aware that such an explanation is but partial, that love of sensation and an inclination to burrow into the secret recesses of the soul play their part in the popularity of the intimate autobiography. But in the main we believe that it is because these self-revelations furnish a springboard to the hopes of their readers that they have gained such currency. And it seems only fair to suppose that in more subtle fashion the increasing interest in autobiography of a higher type derives from the same impulse. In this day of standardization, when a complicated civilization has conferred upon conformity almost the sanction of obligation, the unventuresome soul finds comfort in vicariously living a life of divergence from the normal. The autobiographies the cultured man reads are not those which delight his less sophisticated fellows, but they, like the others, furnish him an escape from the monotony about him. In them his spirit finds the spur to imagination, and all that is pioneering in him finds satisfaction. Man cannot live by bread alone. And the moral? None, except the truism that literature must reck of man's dreams as well as of his deeds.

Freudianism and the development of interest in the psychology of the individual have of course had their part to play in this augmented interest in autobiography. Where formerly only the scientist or the layman of a scientific turn of mind took interest in the processes as well as the evidence of emotions, today the man in the street feels a vital concern in "complexes," or "reactions." He searches not only his neighbor's consciousness but his own,

(*Continued on next page*)

## Murder in Fiction

### By MRS. BELLOC LOWNDES
Author of "What Really Happened"

TO me it has always seemed an ironical turn of fate that the imaginative writer of today who is interested in the psychology of crime should be classed, as he or she almost always is, as a writer of "mystery stories." Although now and again there occurs in real life a murder which remains for a long time, sometimes for all time, a mystery, what surely must be the only point of paramount interest to every intelligent student of human nature is the part which motive and character play in what may be called, for want of a better phrase, intelligent murder.

Why is it that a human being, apparently with nothing in his appearance, manner, or nature differentiating him from his fellows, brings himself to commit the one dread act which has always been regarded from the beginning of the world and in every community, civilized and uncivilized, with peculiar horror? A modern sociological writer once wrote, "Murder is the one chink in the armor of a civilized community." And it remains true that murder is the one crime for which actually not one man or woman in a million is prepared, and which finds always its victim defenseless.

Few indeed are the great imaginative writers of the world who have not at some moment of their career been drawn to murder as a theme worthy of their finest art. Two of the greatest of Shakespeare's plays, "Macbeth" and "Hamlet," both have murder as central themes. Indeed it may be said with truth that the most outstanding murderess in fact or fiction remains Lady Macbeth.

Walter Scott, Dumas *père*, Victor Hugo, the three

This    Week

Scheme for a Mountain. Drawn by
*W. A. Dwiggins.*
Quatrain. By *William Rose Benét.*
Poor Scotland Yard. By *Dashiell Hammett.*
"Gilbert Stuart." Reviewed by
*Frank Jewett Mather, Jr.*
"The Secrets of a Showman" and
"After the Ball." Reviewed by
*Frank Tuttle.*
"Battleships in Action." Reviewed
by *Capt. Thomas G. Frothingham.*
"Turkey." Reviewed by *Hamilton Fish Armstrong.*
Qwertyuiop: A Shirtsleeves History.
"The Two Sisters." Reviewed by
*Robert K. Macdougall.*

### Next Week, or Later
The Plight of the Short Story. By
*Lloyd Morris.*

*Front cover of the first issue of* The Saturday Review of Literature *in which a Hammett review of mystery fiction was published. He was a regular reviewer for the next two years (Collection of Richard Layman).*

abominably. He doesn't let them ask any questions that aren't wholly irrelevant. They can't make inquiries of anyone who might know anything. They aren't permitted to take any steps toward learning whether the dead man was robbed. Their fingerprint experts are excluded from the scene of the crime. When information concerning a mysterious box of jewelry accidentally bobs up everybody resolutely ignores it, since it would have led to a solution before the three-hundredth page.

Mr. Van Dine doesn't deprive his officials of every liberty, however: he generously lets them compete with Vance now and then in the expression of idiocies. Thus Heath, a police detective-sergeant, says that any pistol of less than .44 calibre is too small to stop a man, and the district attorney, Markham, displays an amazed disinclination to admit that a confession could actually be false. This Markham is an outrageously naïve person: the most credible statement in the tale is to the effect that Markham served only one term in this office. The book is written in the little-did-he-realize style.

"The Malaret Mystery" has to do with a death in Morocco. The reader is kept in rural England and the clues are brought to him through two or three or more hands. The result is a tiresomely slow and rambling story altogether without suspense, but this method does keep the solution concealed until the very last from those readers who have forgotten the plot, which is an old friend in not very new clothes. The motivation, if you are interested in that sort of thing, is pretty dizzy.

"Sea Fog," in spite of its rather free use of happenstance, is by far the best of this group. To the coast of Sussex comes a boy bound for the sea. In a deserted mill he spies on Kest and his map, in the morning fog he sees Kest killed, in the days that follow he sees more dead men. If toward the end these dead men turn up with almost mechanical regularity, Mr. Fletcher's skill keeps it from being too monotonous a process. But even that skill doesn't quite suffice to make the forced ending plausible. Poor old Scotland Yard is put up to silly tricks again. However, "Sea Fog" offers more than two hundred decidedly interesting pages.

Most of the fifteen stories in "The Massingham Butterfly" deal with crime in its milder forms. They are all mild stories, some of them obviously written long ago. There is no especial reason for anyone's reading them.

\* \* \*

**Current Murders**
Dashiell Hammett
*The Saturday Review of Literature,*
3 (21 May 1927): 846

THE HOUSE OF SIN. By ALLEN UPWARD. Philadelphia: J. B. Lippincott Co. 1927. $2.
ALL AT SEA. By CAROLYN WELLS. The same.
THE GIRL IN BLACK. By VICTOR BRIDGES. The same.
THE TATTOO MYSTERY. By WILLIAM LEQUEUX. New York: The Macaulay Co. 1927. $2.
THE VICTORY MURDERS. By FOSTER JOHNS. New York: John Day Co. 1927. $2.

In "The House of Sin" the quick-acting poison is brought, for a change, from Nigeria instead of South America. Dr. Tarleton, medical adviser to the Criminal Investigation Department, is called to the residence of the Duke of Altringham to examine the body of a handsome young man who has been found dead—murdered, of course—in the Duke's conservatory. All hands lie to the doctor, very industriously. A great mound of trickery, intrigue, and the rest of it, is erected, with a fresh crime thrown on top every now and then. Tarleton, with his experience as physician and police official, should have hit on the truth fairly early in the story. The chances are you will find the solution—if not all its details—before the doctor does, but I recommend the experiment. "The House of Sin" is—except for the weakness mentioned—well and intelligently done.

The author of "All at Sea" has written something in the neighborhood of a couple of dozen detective stories, all conscientiously in accordance with the formula adopted as standard by the International Detective Story Writers' Convention at Geneva in 1904. One should expect that by now she would have learned to do the trick expertly. She hasn't. The present work is without skill in plot, incident, or wording. For instance, in setting the stage for the murder, the author puts Carmelita Valdon beside the man who is to be done in, and then, two paragraphs later, makes her go around another to get beside him. "One could distinguish them, most often, from their costumes, especially those of the women. . . . The speech grated on Ned Barron's taste. . . . Already the manager was planning to train the little chap up in the way he should go to become later a valuable clerk in the hotel": three hundred and some pages of that can annoy.

Garrett Folsom was knifed as he stood in a group of friends in the surf at a New Jersey resort, and the first detective immediately pronounced it "the most mysterious case I have ever heard of." You'll spot the murderer on sight. Any policeman would have had him or her (this

*Dashiell Hammett at Joseph Shaw's home in Scarsdale, New York, in fall 1929, after he moved to New York City (courtesy of Milton Shaw)*

been influenced by my dislike for the hero—a thoroughly stuffy young explorer with a *flair* for the limpest of wisecracks.

"The Tattoo Mystery" is another mimeographed affair. Lovely Lady Erica Thurston is held in horrible bondage by a most fearsome gang of international thieves, "The Money Spiders," who mark their victims with a terrible tattoo, the first warning of their doom. (If you think I composed that sentence with intent to sneer at the book, you're mistaken: I copied it from the jacket.) The lady talks like this: "I must be taken away from you by a cruel destiny," she said, interrupting me. "Have I not told you that we must never meet again, Mr. Remington? I mean what I say alas! even though it distresses me to repeat those words." People stand aghast and it's all very funny if you're in a mood for burlesque. If your desire is for excitement, pass on.

"The Victory Murders" doesn't redeem its jacket's promise of "a motive new in fiction," nor is there elsewhere much novelty in the tale's machinery. All its gadgets—including the quick-acting poison of which you may have heard previous mention—are second-hand, and as the story progresses it becomes unnecessarily complicated and not altogether plausible. Nevertheless it is far above the average prevalent in its field—an entertaining history of the deaths of charming ladies, of intrigue, deceit, and blithe violence in Marseilles, London, Paris, and New York, with a villain whose guilt is adequately concealed, and a couple of detectives who go sanely about the business of detecting. A deft handling of old materials, "The Victory Murders" deserves a reading.

\* \* \*

**Review of *Reminiscences of an Ex-Detective***
Dashiell Hammett
*The Saturday Review of Literature*,
    4 (10 December 1927): 439

REMINISCENCES OF AN EX-DETECTIVE. By FRANCIS CARLIN. Doran. 1927. $5.

The author of these reminiscences joined the Metropolitan Police in 1890 and was assigned to a Limehouse beat. In 1919 he became a C. I. D. Superintendent, one of the "Big Four." Last year he resigned and, as is the custom of Scotland Yard officials, wrote a book. In it he describes a dozen and a half of the crimes that gave him employment during his thirty-six years of policing. It is not likely that they were the most interesting dozen and a half, in either commission or detection. In Mr. Carlin's account of them can be found no sign of any considerable intelligence on either side of the law, of daring desperation, or any of the

vagueness is rather over-ethical in the circumstances) jailed within the hour. Suspicion is thrown at (not on, because you're credulous indeed if any of it fools you) this one and that one. The chief suspect puts himself to an enormous amount of trouble to endanger his neck. Toward the last Fleming Stone is brought in. He's as useless as the other detectives. On page 339 the murderer confesses, for no reason at all except that it's time to end the story. The final explanation is unduly preposterous.

"The Girl in Black" is about one of those beautiful and mysterious ladies who tote important documents, are pursued by scoundrels, and eventually clear the names of dear old fathers. I may be wrong. This one may be no worse than others of the same sort. It seemed pretty terrible to me, but I admit I may have more colorful emotions. Mr. Carlin's trade was the catching of criminals and the assembling of sufficient evidence to convict them. His success at his trade was largely due to his never bothering his head with anything beyond it. In these 265 pages you will find no hint of interest in—or even awareness of—motives, relationships, characteristics that are subtler, more intricate, than the multiplication table. Mr. Carlin's two twos always make four, never twenty-two. Two chapters devoted to "The Methods of the Scotland Yard Man" are neither thorough nor clearly informative. A chapter on "The Psychology of the Criminal" is intelligent, but adds nothing to what has been previously published on the subject. In "Comparative Murderers of Recent Years," Mr. Carlin sets out to portray the minds of Crippen, Armstrong, True, Mahon, and Thorne, decides that one was callous, one smug, one vain, and so on, and lets it go at that. The book is written with that smugness which, characteristic of famous detectives addressing lay audiences, reaches its finest development when the sleuth is British. It is not the most interesting book in its field, nor the least. It is a volume for the confirmed crime-history addict, not for him who can take his crimes or let them alone.

\* \* \*

**Review of *Mysteries of the Missing***
Dashiell Hammett
*The Saturday Review of Literature,*
4 (11 February 1928): 599

MYSTERIES OF THE MISSING. By EDWARD H. SMITH. Dial. 1927. $3.50

In writing this book Mr. Smith imposed on himself two handicaps. The first of these was in the selection of material: only famous disappearances were included. Unfortunately, those mysteries which attract the most attention are not always—nor, with such exceptions as the Charlie Ross affair, even usually—the most interesting. There have been, for instance, many disappearances far more puzzling, more fascinating, than either Ambrose Bierce's or Doctor André's. Bierce, no longer young, went to Mexico in 1913 for a final taste of war, either as correspondent or soldier, and was never heard of again. Doctor Andrée set out for the north pole in a balloon, in 1897, and was never heard of again. Well, "missing" by itself, is a word but feebly connotative of mystery in war and aviation: it is simply a hazard of the two trades.

The second of Mr. Smith's self-imposed handicaps is stated in his preface: "Neither have I attempted any technical exploration of the conduct and motives of vanishers and kidnappers. It must be sufficiently clear that a man unpursued who flees and hides is out of

tune with his environment, ill adjusted, nervously unwell. Nor need we accent again the fact that all criminals, kidnappers included, are creatures of disease or defect." Granting that a vanisher may have been out of step with his environment, and that a kidnapper may have been a creature of disease or defect, one still wonders how it is possible to write intelligibly about them without investigating their conduct and motives. The answer seems to be that it isn't possible. Dorothy Arnold and Ambrose Small apparently were voluntary vanishers. Mr. Smith gives each a chapter, but he will have nothing to do with any exploration of their conduct and motives, and so the chapters come to nothing.

This same lack of inquisitiveness allows the kidnapping chapters—one apiece is given to Charlie Ross, John Conway, Marion Clarke, Eddie Cudahy, Willie Whitla, Willie McCormick, and Joe Varotta—to take on a common character, to become merged in the reader's mind so that they can hardly be remembered apart. Superficially, kidnappings are pretty much all alike, or, at least, had many conspicuous features in common: the distinguishing features are usually, unfortunately for Mr. Smith, matters of conduct and motive.

Yet "Mysteries of the Missing" is an honest book: even when relating mysteries that are not mysteries it indulges in no sleight-of-hand, but sticks to the available facts and their accepted interpretations. A sprinkling of guesses would have made it a more exciting book.

\* \* \*

**Review of *Great Detectives and Their Methods***
Dashiell Hammett
*The Saturday Review of Literature,*
4 (21 April 1928): 810

GREAT DETECTIVES AND THEIR METHODS. By GEORGE DILNOT. Houghton Mifflin. 1928. $4.

"As a class detectives do not, as might be hastily assumed, become hardened and callous by their profession," Mr. Dilnot writes. No? Then neither do judges, bill collectors, reporters, dentists, loan-shop keepers, nor hangmen. One pities those who don't!

"Only two things are certain about the real detective. He is as unlike Sherlock Holmes as he is different from the square-toed clodhoppers displayed on the stage, on the screen, and in books." Thereafter Mr. Dilnot exhibits a flock of "real detectives" unlike anything except Horatio Alger heroes who had turned to thief-catching instead of commerce. Some of these gentlemen may actually have been as stodgy as herein shown, but all couldn't have been, not even all the British ones.

Mr. Dilnot's insistence that the storybooks are wrong, that life's detectives are more impossibly wooden than fiction's, ties together twenty-two chapters packed with anecdotes of detection, stories of crime and its solution. Not even the stuffed figures with which the author populates them can prevent their being interesting, their fulfilling the jacket's promise of "fascinating information and exciting stories."

* * *

## Throw Out the Detective
Henry Seidel Canby
*The Saturday Review of Literature,*
5 (1 December 1928): 421–422

Our slogan for 1929 is—fewer and better detective stories. In 1928, every novelist and short-story writer who knew how to spell "sleuth" wrote at least one detective story. Bookshops and circulating libraries were fetid with amateur crime. If you believe the newspapers, as soon as a treaty was signed, a president elected, or a "big deal" concluded, all hands called for detective stories as they used to call for grog. (There is an interesting relationship between Prohibition and the spread of the crime story which we won't go into now.) Nervous indigestion is the national disease, and reading detective stories seems to have become the national patent medicine for overwork and boredom. The baby calls for an all-day sucker and his parents for ten new detective stories.

Ten, you notice, not one. There is no safety in one.

If we could get a good detective story every time, the problem of what to do with our expanding leisure would be solved. As business grows honest, scientific, and dull, let literature deal more and more with the dishonest, the improbable, and the unexpected. Thus the balanced life would be kept on an even keel!

But the mystery story business needs an overhauling before everyone can have his pet crime just when and as he needs it. One detective story is about as useful today as a single match on a wet day. The chances are ten to one against ignition. Nine out of ten of the current product miss fire or go out at the first flicker. Hence detective stories are bought by the bunch (which may please the publishers), and read three or four at a sitting in the hope of finding one worth going through with. You send your friend a good book—or four detective stories.

The difficulty goes deeper than over-production. We have some very ingenious writers who would surely be more original if they had a fair chance. But the public will not let them. The public asks for mysteries, but it will not recognize a mystery as such unless there is a detective in it.

There must be a crime, a stupid detective, and a wise detective (or gifted amateur). Within such limits are 99 out of a 100 mystery stories worked out, and all the other mysteries and all the other detectors, who are not detectives, left longing for the creative imagination to make them into story.

The way out is to get rid of the detective. He is a stock figure, like the clown in a circus, and when Poe invented him in the nineteenth century had his great uses, and still is useful. When he appears, we thrill by habit, just as we laugh by habit when the clowns run on. But he is no more indispensable to mystery than folk lore is to literature. Are lost pearl necklaces, million dollar pictures, criminal influences, the only causes of mystery in modern experiences? No, but they, with others like them, are the only ones where a detective can function usefully. Cut out the detective and the number of mysteries suitable for good stories increases a hundred fold. The pursuit (for a mild example) of a wife's elusive personality by her loving but puzzled husband has a hundred variations, each of them exciting, but there is no job there for the detective. It is not the theft of a $100,000 from the bank which was its most interesting mystery, but some far more human complication for which the Board of Directors called in no professional expert in blood stains, cigar ashes, and deductive reasoning. List the really sensational, really mysterious happenings in your own experience, and ask how many of them involved the physical presence of a sleuth. When a writer calls in a detective he binds himself to the kind of story which fits a detective, and so ties his imagination fast to a symbol.

Throw out the detective. Can him, as we have canned the black-whiskered villain, the duenna, the confidante, the pious child, and other conventions of fiction; or better, save him for situations where he is indispensable. Let the mystery tale go free.

The difficulty is the audience. We are children when we read, and ask for symbols. Give up the craving (now merely a bad habit) for Inspector A, and Mr. Van B the eccentric connoisseur, and the red-faced blundering policeman X, and you will begin to get real stories—especially if you will stretch your imagination to take in the great mysteries that lie beyond murder and blackmail and theft. Mr. Bolitho has shown what can be done with only a partial release, in his "Murder for Profit," where he has kept crime but studied the mystery of motive not the means of detection. Mr. Priestley has written an excellent mystery story, "The Old Dark House," without a detective or a crime. That was the reason for its seeming freshness as one read. But there are a hundred roads for a mystery story to travel if it doesn't have to carry a detective on its back.

# The Crime Wave
## By Dashiell Hammett

### Mary Roberts Rinehart's
### *The Door*

It is very easy to find a lot of things wrong with the story. It is certainly too long, too wordy as well as too cluttered up with nowise important action put in merely to make it more confusing. The maintenance and complication of the mystery depend too largely on folks consistently missing each other by unpredictable inches in the dark and unpredictable seconds in the light. The final explanation is unnecessarily weak, implausible, and, what is worse, leaves several loose ends not accounted for though Mrs. Rinehart does not sin here in that respect so much as she did in her earlier "The Red Lamp." It is simply impossible to believe in the arch-criminal. The constant use of the ancient device for building up suspense—by hinting at dark deeds ahead—becomes annoying. And, to be picayune in the end, walking-sticks buried naked in earth that is stamped down over them are not dug up fairly covered with anybody's fingerprints, and there is undoubtedly something at least pitiable about the plight of characters condemned to run around with standard legal documents stuffed in their shoes.

When all this fault-finding has been done, however, there is this to be said for "The Door": nobody who begins it is at all likely, barring acts of God, to leave it unfinished. He may hoot at its soft spots, he may be irritated by its old-fashioned cast—Mrs. Rinehart is distinctly not a writer of this decade—but he will read it through. Well, readability is the standard by which books of this sort should be judged.

*—New York Evening Post,*
5 April 1930, p. M11

## Excerpts from Hammett's Reviews for the *New York Evening Post*

### Philip MacDonald's
### *The Noose*

This, you can see, is all familiar stuff, stuff that can be found in dozens of detective stories now stacked on bookshop shelves, but what lifts Mr. MacDonald's book above those dozens is the deftness of his carpentry. "The Noose" has the neatest plot I have seen in months. It is logical, it is simple, and it is baffling.

*—New York Evening Post,*
12 April 1930, p. M11

### Kay Cleaver Strahan's
### *Death Traps*

Ever since "The Desert Moon Mystery" there have been rumors that Mrs. Strahan writes what is sometimes called graceful English. I have not yet been able to verify these rumors. The outstanding characteristics of her style seem to be an assortment of rather acrobatic synonyms for "said" and a waiving of the difference between transitive and intransitive verbs.

*—New York Evening Post,*
26 April 1930, p. M11

## Edgar Wallace's
### *The Hand of Power*

It is Wallace at his best, at his least adult, at his most naively melodramatic: the Wallace who can juggle complete sets of false whiskers—with mustachios—trap-doors, the secret passages they lead to, and forged wills, birth certificates and whatnot with his left hand; an occult poison or two, the necessary hypodermic needles, stolen heritages and at least one impersonation with his right; while balancing a stack of cowled menaces, a kidnapping and as many murders as you like on his head and managing a typewriter—using the ribbon's red stratum—with his feet.

There has been only one man who could beat Wallace at this game and he, George Bronson Howard, has been dead some seven years and is completely forgotten. Herman Landon can sometimes hold the pace for a chapter or two, but seldom for longer than that. Sydney Horler's warehouses are well stocked with hocus-pocus but in action he is all thumbs. M. P. Shiel, mechanically Wallace's one undoubted superior in this dizzy field, is often enough—even in such essentially dull opera as "The Purple Cloud"—too authentic a magician to deserve a place among the masters of clap-trap.

*—New York Evening Post,*
3 July 1930, p. S5

## Basil King's
### *The Break of Day*

"The Break of Day" comes unluckily into my hands. In the first place, Mr. King always succeeds in annoying me before I am two chapters into him. His primness annoys me. The priggishness of his characters annoys me. His too obviously soldered plot-incidents annoy me. And most of all, his manner of always addressing himself to a spinster who has never in the sixty years of her life been out of Newton Abbot annoys me. In the second place, I tried to read this particular work during the middle of a July day between Albuquerque and Gallup, under a New Mexican sun that melted the tops of ginger ale bottles between the buffet car and my compartment. So it is not at all likely that Mr. King's book is any worse that it seemed to me, and it may be better.

*—New York Evening Post,*
19 July 1930, p. S5

## Paul Selver's
### *Private Life*

Mr. Selver has done very little with his splendid idea, and that little is by no means good. He is self-consciously literary. His sentences, like his thoughts, ramble along in no particular direction, toward no particular goal. The impression most of the book makes on one is that the author, having nothing to say, is merely covering the pages until he reaches one with a sufficiently high number to merit the denouement.

*—New York Evening Post,*
20 September 1930, p. 12

## Earl Derr Biggers's
### *Charlie Chan Carries On*

"Charlie Chan Carries On" has to do—or the nearly two hundred pages I read had to do—with the murders of a couple of members of an around-the-world tourist group and one of their wives in, respectively, England, France and Italy. Heretofore I have always blamed Charlie Chan's laborious quaintness for my inability ever to finish one of Mr. Biggers's products, but I was wrong. Charlie had not appeared when I put down this volume. To guess again, Mr. Biggers's works seem frivolous to me in the wrong manner; that is, too much attention is given to trivialities without compensating lightness and crime itself is treated too lightly without compensating humor. Anyway, something of that sort must be it, for I, who read much worse books—as these columns have borne witness—cannot finish these. Maybe you had better not pay any attention to me.

*—New York Evening Post,*
11 October 1930, p. D4

## Writing for the Pulps: Excerpts from the Stories

*As Hammett explained in his introduction to the Modern Library publication of* The Maltese Falcon, *some of his characters and plot situations were from life models. Others were products of his imagination and were refined from early stories for use in the novel. Characters, plot situations, and themes in* The Maltese Falcon *appear in rough forms beginning in stories that appeared early in Hammett's writing career. This section provides Hammett's remarks on his sources, as well as selections from Hammett's stories that introduce characters and plot situations appropriated for the novel.*

### Characters

*In 1934* The Maltese Falcon *was included in the prestigious Modern Library, which claimed to publish reprints of "the world's greatest books." It was the first detective novel so honored. Living authors were asked to provide a new introduction to the Modern Library publication explaining the circumstances of composition. This is Hammett's explanation of the sources for his novel.*

**Introduction to the Modern Library Edition**
Dashiell Hammett
*The Maltese Falcon*
(New York: Modern Library, 1934), pp. vii–ix

If this book had been written with the help of an outline or notes or even a clearly defined plot-idea in my head I might now be able to say how it came to be written and why it took the shape it did, but all I can remember about its invention is that somewhere I had read of the peculiar rental agreement between Charles V and the Order of the Hospital of St. John of Jerusalem, that in a short story called *The Whosis Kid* I had failed to make the most of a situation I liked, that in another called *The Gutting of Couffignal* I had been equally unfortunate with an equally promising dénouement, and that I thought I might have better luck with these two failures if I combined them with the Maltese lease in a longer story.

I can remember more clearly where I got most of my characters.

Wilmer, the boy gun-man, was picked up in Stockton, California, where I had gone hunting a window-smasher who had robbed a San Jose jewelry store. Wilmer's original was not my window-smasher, unfortunately, but he was a fair pick-up. He was a neat small smooth-faced quiet boy of perhaps twenty-one. He said he was only seventeen, but that was probably an attempt to draw a reform school instead of a penitentiary sentence. He also said his father was a lieutenant of police in New York, which may or may not have been true, and

he was serenely proud of the name the local newspapers gave him–The Midget Bandit. He had robbed a Stockton filling station the previous week. In Los Angeles a day or two later, reading a Stockton newspaper–there must be criminals who subscribe to clipping services–he had been annoyed by the description the filling-station proprietor had given of him and by the proprietor's statement of what he would do to that little runt if he ever laid eyes on him again. So The Midget Bandit had stolen an automobile and returned to Stockton to, in his words, stick that guy up again and see what he wanted to do about it.

Brigid O'Shaughnessy had two originals, one an artist, the other a woman who came to Pinkerton's San Francisco office to hire an operative to discharge her housekeeper, but neither of these women was a criminal.

Dundy's prototype I worked with in a North Carolina railroad yard; Cairo's I picked up on a forgery charge in Pasco, Washington, in 1920; Polhaus's was a former captain of detectives; I used to buy books from Iva's in Spokane; Effie's once asked me to go into the narcotic smuggling business with her in San Diego; Gutman's was suspected–foolishly, as most people were–of being a German secret agent in Washington, D.C., in the early days of the war, and I never remember shadowing a man who bored me as much.

*List of Spokane, Washington, booksellers from the 1920 city directory when Hammett lived there. In the introduction to the Modern Library edition of* The Maltese Falcon, *he says he used to buy books in Spokane from the model for Iva Archer (courtesy of Spokane Historical Society).*

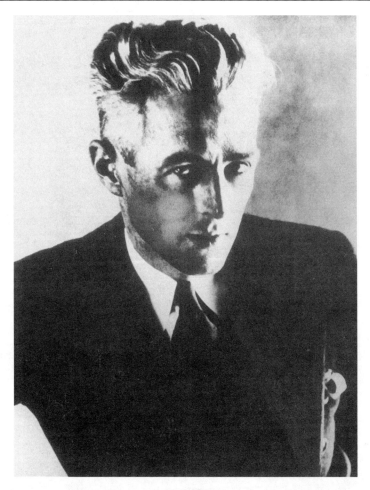

*Hammett, mid 1920s.* The Maltese Falcon *begins: "Samuel Spade's jaw was long and bony, his chin a jutting v under the more flexible v of his mouth. His nostrils curved back to make another, smaller, v. His yellow-grey eyes were horizontal. The v motif was picked up again by thickish brows rising outward from twin creases above a hooked nose, and his pale brown hair grew down—from high flat temples—in a point on his forehead. He looked rather pleasantly like a blond satan" (courtesy of Josephine Hammett).*

Spade had no original. He is a dream man in the sense that he is what most of the private detectives I worked with would like to have been and what quite a few of them in their cockier moments thought they approached. For your private detective does not—or did not ten years ago when he was my colleague—want to be an erudite solver of riddles in the Sherlock Holmes manner; he wants to be a hard and shifty fellow, able to take care of himself in any situation, able to get the best of anybody he comes in contact with, whether criminal, innocent by-stander or client.

\* \* \*

### Cairo

*In "The Main Death" Hammett introduced Bruno Gungen, a white-collar thief who combines the effeminate characteristics of Joel Cairo with the imperious manner and interest in collectibles of Caspar Gutman. Gungen's wife wears a distinctive perfume, one of the characteristics of Mrs. Gungen that Hammett gave Cairo in* The Maltese Falcon.

**The Main Death**
*Black Mask*, 10 (June 1927): 46–48

In the street I left the police sleuths and set out for Bruno Gungen's home in Westwood Park.

*Peggy O'Toole, one of Hammett's co-workers at Albert Samuels Jewelers, with whom Hammett had an affair before she was married. Albert Samuels said in an interview conducted late in his life that Hammett told him Miss O'Toole, whom Hammett called Margaret, was a model for Brigid O'Shaughnessy. In her inscribed copy of* Red Harvest, *Hammett suggested that she inspired the femme fatale Dinah Brand in that novel. O'Toole's inscribed copy of* The Maltese Falcon *was stolen from her bookshelf (courtesy of Susan Finn).*

The dealer in rare and antique jewelry was a little bit of a man and a fancy one. His dinner jacket was corset-tight around his waist, padded high and sharp at the shoulders. Hair, mustache and spade-shaped goatee were dyed black and greased until they were as shiny as his pointed pink finger-nails. I wouldn't bet a cent that the color in his fifty-year-old cheeks wasn't rouge.

He came out of the depths of a leather library chair to give me a soft, warm hand that was no larger than a child's, bowing and smiling at me with his head tilted to one side.

Then he introduced me to his wife, who bowed without getting up from her seat at the table. Apparently she was a little more than a third of his age. She couldn't have been a day over nineteen, and she looked more like sixteen. She was as small as he, with a dimpled olive-skinned face, round brown eyes, a plump painted mouth and the general air of an expensive doll in a toy-store window.

Bruno Gungen explained to her at some length that I was connected with the Continental Detective Agency, and that he had employed me to help the police find Jeffrey Main's murderers and recover the stolen twenty thousand dollars.

She murmured, "Oh, yes!" in a tone that said she was not the least bit interested, and stood up, saying, "then I'll leave you to—"

"No, no, my dear!" Her husband was waving his pink fingers at her. "I would have no secrets from you."

His ridiculous little face jerked around to me, cocked itself sidewise, and he asked, with a little giggle:

"Is not that so? That between husband and wife there should be no secrets?"

I pretended I agreed with him.

"You, I know, my dear," he addressed his wife, who had sat down again, "are as much interested in this as I, for did we not have an equal affection for dear Jeffrey? Is it not so?"

She repeated, "Oh, yes!" with the same lack of interest.

Her husband turned to me and said, "Now?" encouragingly.

"I've seen the police," I told him. "Is there anything you can add to their story? Anything new? Anything you didn't tell them?"

He whisked his face around toward his wife.

"Is there, Enid, dear?"

"I know of nothing," she replied.

He giggled and made a delighted face at me.

"That is it," he said. "We know of nothing."

"He came back to San Francisco eight o'clock Sunday night—three hours before he was killed and robbed—

with twenty thousand dollars in hundred-dollar bills. What was he doing with it?"

"It was the proceeds of a sale to a customer," Bruno Gungen explained. "Mr. Nathaniel Ogilvie, of Los Angeles."

"But why cash?"

The little man's painted face screwed itself up into a shrewd leer.

"A bit of hanky-panky," he confessed complacently, "a trick of the trade, as one says. You know the genus collector? Ah, there is a study for you! Observe. I obtain a golden tiara of early Grecian workmanship, or let me be correct—purporting to be of early Grecian workmanship, purporting also to have been found in Southern Russia, near Odessa. Whether there is any truth in either of these suppositions I do not know, but certainly the tiara is a thing of beauty."

He giggled.

"Now I have a client, a Mr. Nathaniel Ogilvie, of Los Angeles, who has an appetite for curios of the sort—a very devil of a *cacoethes carpendi*. The value of these items, you will comprehend, is exactly what one can get for them—no more, little less. This tiara—now ten thousand dollars is the least I could have expected for it, if sold as one sells an ordinary article of the sort. But can one call a golden cap made long ago for some forgotten Scythian king an ordinary article of any sort? No! No! So, swaddled in cotton, intricately packed, Jeffrey carries this tiara to Los Angeles to show our Mr. Ogilvie.

"In what manner the tiara came into our hands Jeffrey will not say. But he will hint at devious intrigues, smuggling, a little of violence and lawlessness here and there, the necessity for secrecy. For your true collector, there is the bait! Nothing is anything to him except as it is difficultly come by. Jeffrey will not lie. No! *Mon Dieu*, that would be dishonest, despicable! But he will suggest much, and he will refuse, oh, so emphatically! to take a check for the tiara. No check, my dear sir! Nothing which may be traced! Cash moneys!

"Hanky-panky, as you see. But where is the harm? Mr. Ogilvie is certainly going to buy the tiara, and our little deceit simply heightens his pleasure in his purchase. He will enjoy its possession so much the more. Besides, who is to say that this tiara is not authentic? If it is, then these things Jeffrey suggests are indubitably true. Mr. Ogilvie does buy it, for twenty thousand dollars, and that is why poor Jeffrey had in his possession so much cash money."

He flourished a pink hand at me, nodded his dyed head vigorously, and finished with:

"*Voilà!* That is it!"

"Did you hear from Main after he got back?" I asked.

The dealer smiled as if my question tickled him, turning his head so that the smile was directed at his wife.

The Secret Emperor

Elfinstone: 35, tall, gaunt, powerful flat muscles, copper hair and eyes, lean, bony mouth and chin, nose like a knife. The foremost intelligence man of his time, a detective who is above the ordinary detective as Napoleon was above a private. A record that covers several continents, including the World War. He is now engaged in organizing secret service in a Latin American country. He is a ruthless man, without manners, impatient of stupidity of people with whom he comes in contact, with little love for his fellows. Driven into work by some burning restlessness within him.

Sheth Gutman: 50, black-haired, ivory skin, no lines in his suavely strong face, hawk nose, smooth-shaven, broad sloping forehead, hair thick and curly, oval face with something suggesting an Egyptian drawing in it, fairly plump but in perfect shape, except perhaps a bit soft. Dark, large intelligent eyes. Low, musical voice, charming personality. Since, being a Jew, he may not be president, he decides to be secret emperor of the U. S. He does not depend on money. For fifteen years now he has been patiently collecting information about political mogule, so that he may make them his tools. He has a chain of private detective agencies, a scandal sheet, hirelings in banks, in hotels and apartments, most of these working for scandal sheet. This sheet, Capital Whispers, sometimes may be bought off, sometimes not, as in one case where it ruined a presidential aspirant who had millions to offer it. Gutman's usual way of getting hold of a politician, is to get something on his secretary or other intimate who will know secrets, and use that as wedge into those secrets. He has also employed adventuresses.

He is now preparing to seize country. He has jockeyed Senator Jarboe into position where he will be nominate for president by one party, and a man named Rushton by other. He has dope on Rushton to spring during campaign, beating him. Jarboe is honest but vulnerable. His vice-president will be man named Haldorn, who is both vulnerable and weak. The plan is to force Jarboe to resign, making the tool Haldorn president. Twice Gutman has laid similar plans, each time defeated, and if he fails this time he will try again, knowing the laws of averages will give him victory and power soon or late, and then he will have the country. Archives are in fortified house suburbs of Washn.

Tamar Gutman: 21, black-haired, milk-skinned, red-mouthed, black arched eyebrows, perfect teeth, as beautiful and artificial as an Egyptian princess. Gray-green eyes, oval face, throaty voice, voluptuous, hard, passionate, slenderly perfect in body. Womanly superior to man's business.

General Dolliard: past middle-age, medium height, square, heavy, very much in love with his wife, whom he married in Paris during the war. He learned afterward, with out her knowledge, that she was suspected traitor or spy and is on French list of war criminals to be shot. He sets about collecting evidence to clear her, not knowing she is guilty. Has collected just about enough to show her guilt, to lead to her deportation, since she had a French husband when she married him--and that will mean her death. Has these dangerous papers in Balto. bank under alias.

He has knowledge of Haldorn's crime, hates Haldorn, and will certainly expose him if he runs for vice-president, so Gutman has papers removed to be photographed so he can make Dolliard keep quiet.

Helene Dolliard, nee Mady Brefina: was Bohemian secret agent of Teutonics during war. Married a French officer, and then, when intelligence officers of Allies almost got her, she married Dolliard and eluded them. In Austria before that she had been cause of death of Don Dolliard, the general's brother, who was working with Elfinstone. Don died that Elfinstone might get out alive with their information. Elfinstone saw her twice there, but he was not in France at time she married Dolliard, and so had never seen her again until he meets her when Dolliard sends for him. He knows her, and knows that she also has an Austrian husband.

*Character descriptions and outline for Hammett's 1925 uncompleted work that suggests basic plot elements he used in* The Glass Key, *his fourth novel. Elfinstone, a name Hammett used for an alter ego, resembles Sam Spade. This is Hammett's first use of the name Gutman (Harry Ransom Humanities Research Center, University of Texas at Austin).*

```
                    The Secret Emperor
                    16 §§ (1250): 20,000

Elfinstone: 35, tall, gaunt, powerful flat muscles, red hair,
            lean bony jaw, clean hard mouth, deep-set narrow
            copperish eyes (red-brown), straight nose like a
            knife.

Sheth Gutman: 50, black-haired, ivory-skinned, no lines in
            his face, hawk-nosed, smooth-shaven, broad sloping
            brow, hair thick and curly, worn rather long,
            oval face, with the appearance of an Egyptian
            drawing, fairly plump but in perfect physical
            preservation, except perhaps a bit soft. Suave.

Tamar Gutman: 21, black-haired, milk-skinned, red-mouthed,
            black arcs of eyebrows, tall, slenderly perfect
            body, green-grey eyes, red mouth, perfect teeth,
            rather voluptuous, a savage woman, oval face,
            passionate temperament, throaty voice.

 1: Elfinstone is called to Washington by Talbert and told of
    the General's troubles.
 2: He sets out to solve them and runs into mystery, but seems
    to be making headway. Violence in Baltimore.
 3: He meets Tamar and loves her, perhaps she saves his life,
    or tends his injuries.
 4: General Talbert calls him off when success is ahead. He
    pretends agreement, but determines to investigate on his
    own account.
 5: He is warned, but persists. Loses his job, his money.
    Tamar seems involved. Talbert suicides.
 6: He carries on investigation. Arrested, Given 30 days.
 7: Out of jail, broke, he goes ahead with work. Seeing Tamar
    now and then. Learns her father is his meat, but does not
    know what for.
 8: Interview with Sheth. The challenge.
 9: Days in which he begs on street, runs errands, anything to
    earn money to carry on investigation.
10: Interview with Tamar in which he puts what is between them,
    curses her father to her.
11: Is arrested again, investigating Sheth, as lunatic. Fakes
    with matches, and escapes.
12: Roams the streets, mad, dyes his hair hideously, a crazy
    beggar actuatted by hate and love mixed.
13: Is hunted by Gutman's men.
14: Gets part of dope on Gutman.
```

*The holograph additions at the bottom of the page read "15: Interviews Gutman" "16: Conclusion"*

"Did we, Enid, darling?" he passed on the question.

She pouted and shrugged her shoulders indifferently.

"The first we knew he had returned," Gungen interpreted these gestures to me, "was Monday morning, when we heard of his death. Is it not so, my dove?"

His dove murmured, "Yes," and left her chair, saying, "You'll excuse me? I have a letter to write."

"Certainly, my dear," Gungen told her as he and I stood up.

She passed close to him on her way to the door. His small nose twitched over his dyed mustache and he rolled his eyes in a caricature of ecstasy.

"What a delightful scent, my precious!" he exclaimed. "What a heavenly odor! What a song to the nostrils! Has it a name, my love?"

"Yes," she said, pausing in the doorway, not looking back.

"And it is?"

"*Dèsir du Cœur,*" she replied over her shoulder as she left us.

Bruno Gungen looked at me and giggled.

I sat down again and asked him what he knew about Jeffrey Main.

"Everything, no less," he assured me. "For a dozen years, since he was a boy of eighteen he has been my right eye, my right hand."

"Well, what sort of man was he?"

Bruno Gungen showed me his pink palms side by side.

"What sort is any man?" he asked over them.

That didn't mean anything to me, so I kept quiet, waiting.

"I shall tell you," the little man began presently. "Jeffrey had the eye and the taste for this traffic of mine. No man living save myself alone has a judgment in these matters which I would prefer to Jeffrey's. And, honest, mind you! Let nothing I say mislead you on that point. Never a lock have I to which Jeffrey had not also the key, and might have it forever, if he had lived so long.

"But there is a but. In his private life, rascal is a word that only does him justice. He drank, he gambled, he loved, he spent—dear God, how he spent! He was, in this drinking and gaming and loving and spending, a most promiscuous fellow, beyond doubt. With moderation he had nothing to do. Of the moneys he got by inheritance, of the fifty thousand dollars or more his wife had when they were married, there is no remainder. Fortunately, he was well insured—else his wife would have been left penniless. Oh, he was a true Heliogabalus, that fellow!"

* * *

### Gutman

*Hammett used Caspar Gutman's name in the draft of "The Secret Emperor," apparently intended to be a novel. He introduced his character in 1925 in a story published in* Sunset Magazine. *Like Gutman, Leonidas Doucas is a fat man who has a distinctive pattern of speech and is an international trader in stolen jewels. As in "The Main Death," Hammett seems to have been experimenting with qualities of the villainous characters who foreshadowed Gutman and Cairo.*

### Ruffian's Wife
*Sunset Magazine,* 55 (October 1925): 20, 86–87

A fat man in black was on the point of leaving the kitchen.

Margaret cried out, catching the robe high to her throat with both hands.

Red and crystal glinted on the hand with which the fat man took off his black derby. Holding the doorknob, he turned to face Margaret. He turned slowly, with the smooth precision of a globe revolving on a fixed axis, and he managed his head with care, as if it balanced an invisible burden.

"You–are–Mrs.–Tharp."

Sighing puffs of breath spaced his words, cushioned them, gave them the semblance of gems nested separately in raw cotton. He was a man past forty, with opaquely glistening eyes whose blackness was repeated with variety of finish in mustache and hair, freshly ironed suit and enameled shoes.

The dark skin of his face—ball round over a tight stiff collar—was peculiarly coarse, firm-grained, as if it had been baked. Against this background his tie was half a foot of scarlet flame.

"Your—husband—is—not—home."

It was no more a question than his naming her had been, but he paused expectantly. Margaret, standing where she had stopped in passageway between stairs and kitchen, was still too startled not to say, "No."

"You're—expecting—him."

There was nothing immediately threatening in the attitude of this man who should not have been in her kitchen but who seemed nowise disconcerted by her finding him there. Margaret's words came almost easily.

"Not just—I expect him, yes, but I don't know exactly when he will come."

Black hat and black shoulders, moving together, achieved every appearance of a bow without disturbing round head's poise.

"You—will—so—kindly—tell—him—when—he—comes—I—am—waiting. I—await—him—at—the—hotel." The spacing puffs prolonged his sentences interminably, made of his phrases thin-spread word-groups whose meanings were elusive. "You—will—tell—him—Leonidas—Doucas—is—waiting. He—will—know. We—are—friends—, very—good—friends. You—will—not—forget—the—name—, Leonidas—Doucas."

"Certainly I shall tell him. But I really do not know when he will come."

The man who had called himself Leonidas Doucas nodded frugally beneath the unseen something his head supported. Darkness of mustache and skin exaggerated whiteness of teeth. His smile went away as stiffly as it came, with as little elasticity.

"You—may—expect—him. He—comes—now."

He revolved slowly away from her and went out of the kitchen, shutting the door behind him.

. . . . . . . . . .

She stood in her dark bedroom, clutching the foot of the bed with both hands, the trembling of her body making the bed tremble. Out of the night questions came to torment her: shadowy questions, tangling, knotting, raveling in too swiftly shifting a profusion for any to be clearly seen, but all having something to do with a pride that in eight years had become a very dear thing.

They had to do with pride in a man's courage and hardihood: courage and hardihood that could make of thefts, of murder, of crimes dimly guessed, wrongs no more reprehensible than a boy's apple-stealing. They had to do with the existence or non-existence of this gilding courage, without which a rover might be no more than a shoplifter on a geographically larger scale, a sneak-thief who crept into strangers' lands instead of houses, a furtive, skulking figure with an aptitude for glamorous autobiography. Then pride would be silliness.

Out of the floor came a murmur all that distance and intervening carpentry left of words that were being said down in her tan-papered dining-room. The murmur drew her toward the dining-room, drew her physically, as the questions drove her.

She left her slippers on the bedroom floor. Very softly stockinged feet carried her down the dark front stairs, tread by tread. Skirts held high and tight against rustling, she crept down the black stairs toward the room where two men—equally strangers for the time—sat trafficking.

Beneath the portiere, and from either side, yellow light came to lay a pale crooked U on the hall floor. Guy's voice came through.

". . . not there. We turned the island upside down from Dambulla all the way to the Kala-Wewa, and got nothing. I told you it was a bust. Catch those limeys leaving that much sugar lay round under their noses!"

"Dahl—said—it—was—there."

Doucas' voice was soft with the infinitely patient softness of one whose patience is nearly at end.

Creeping to the doorway, Margaret peeped round the curtain. The two men and the table between them came into the opening. Doucas' over-coated shoulder was to her. He sat straight up, hands inert on fat thighs, cooked profile inert. Guy's white-sleeved forearms were on the table. He leaned over them, veins showing in forehead and throat, smaller and more vivid round the blue-black of his eyes. The glass in front of him was empty; the one before Doucas still brimmed with dark liquor.

"I don't give a damn what Dahl says." Guy's voice was blunt, but somehow missed finality. "I'm telling you the stuff wasn't there."

Doucas smiled. His lips bared white teeth and covered them again in a cumbersome grimace that held as little of humor as of spontaneity.

"But—you—came—from—Ceylon—no—poorer—than—you—went."

## Scenes

*The excerpts that follow pair scenes that Hammett first wrote for stories with the passages they foreshadow in the novel.*

### "Bad Business"

*In 1924 "Who Killed Bob Teal?" was rejected by Black Mask. Hammett sent it to a competing pulp. The plot device in which a detective is hired so that his murder can be used to cover up another murder is central to* The Maltese Falcon. *In this scene from the story, the Continental Op is given the facts of the case by the supervisor of the office, the Old Man. In the passage from the novel that follows, Spade gets the facts of Miles Archer's murder from Tom Polhaus, a San Francisco Police Force detective.*

### Who Killed Bob Teal?
*True Detective Mysteries,* November 1924

The Old Man didn't look at me as he went on. He was talking to the open window at his elbow.

"He was shot with a thirty-two, twice, through the heart. He was shot behind a row of signboards on the vacant lot on the northwest corner of Hyde and Eddy Streets, at about ten last night. His body was found by a patrolman a little after eleven. The gun was found about fifteen feet away. I have seen him and I have gone over the ground myself. The rain last night wiped out any leads the ground may have held, but from the condition of Teal's clothing and the position in which he was found, I would say that there was no struggle, and that he was shot where he was found, and not carried there afterward. He was lying behind the signboards, about thirty feet from the sidewalk, and his hands were empty. The gun was held close enough to him to singe the breast of his coat. Apparently no one either saw or heard the shooting. The rain and wind would have kept pedestrians off the street, and would have deadened the reports of a thirty-two, which are not especially loud, anyway."

The Old Man's pencil began to tap the desk, its gentle clicking setting my nerves on edge. Presently it stopped, and the Old Man went on:

"Teal was shadowing a Herbert Whitacre—had been shadowing him for three days. Whitacre is one of the partners in the firm Ogburn and Whitacre, farm-development engineers. They have options on a large area of land in several of the new irrigation districts. Ogburn handles the sales end, while Whitacre looks after the rest of the business, including the bookkeeping.

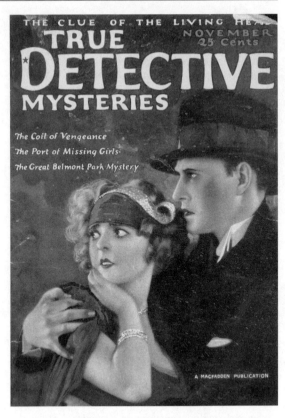

*Front cover of the pulp magazine that includes the story "Who Killed Bob Teal?" by "Dashiell Hammett of the Continental Detective Agency." After being criticized in print by Black Mask editor Phil Cody, who rejected this story, Hammett wrote a public apology in the magazine for "bringing [the Op] out and running him around whenever the landlord, or the butcher, or the grocer shows signs of weakness." Seven months later the story was published by a competing pulp (Collection of Richard Layman).*

"Last week Ogburn discovered that his partner had been making false entries. The books show certain payments made on the land, and Ogburn learned that these payments had not been made. He estimates that the amount of Whitacre's thefts may be anywhere from one hundred fifty to two hundred fifty thousand dollars. He came in to see me three days ago and told me all this, and wanted to have Whitacre shadowed in an endeavor to learn what he has done with the stolen money. Their firm is still a partnership, and a partner cannot be prosecuted for stealing from the partnership, of course. Thus, Ogburn could not have his partner arrested, but he hoped to find the money, and then recover it through civil action. Also he was afraid that Whitacre might disappear.

"I sent Teal out to shadow Whitacre, who supposedly didn't know that his partner suspected him. Now I am sending you out to find Whitacre. I'm determined to find him and convict him if I have to let all regular business go and put every man I have on this job for a year. You can get Teal's reports from the clerks. Keep in touch with me."

All that, from the Old Man, was more than an ordinary man's oath written in blood.

\* \* \*

*The Maltese Falcon*, pp. 14–19

Where Bush Street roofed Stockton before slipping downhill to Chinatown, Spade paid his fare and left the taxicab. San Francisco's night-fog, thin, clammy, and penetrant, blurred the street. A few yards from where Spade had dismissed the taxicab a small group of men stood looking up an alley. Two women stood with a man on the other side of Bush Street, looking at the alley. There were faces at windows.

Spade crossed the sidewalk between iron-railed hatchways that opened above bare ugly stairs, went to the parapet, and, resting his hands on the damp coping, looked down into Stockton Street.

An automobile popped out of the tunnel beneath him with a roaring swish, as if it had been blown out, and ran away. Not far from the tunnel's mouth a man was hunkered on his heels before a billboard that held advertisements of a moving picture and a gasoline across the front of a gap between two store-buildings. The hunkered man's head was bent almost to the sidewalk so he could look under the billboard. A hand flat on the paving, a hand clenched on the billboard's green frame, held him in this grotesque position. Two other men stood awkwardly together at one end of the billboard, peeping through the few inches of space between it and the building at that end. The building at the other end had a blank grey sidewall that looked down on the lot behind the billboard. Lights flickered on the sidewall, and the shadows of men moving among lights.

Spade turned from the parapet and walked up Bush Street to the alley where men were grouped. A uniformed policeman chewing gum under an enameled sign that said *Burritt St.* in white against dark blue put out an arm and asked:

"What do you want here?"

"I'm Sam Spade. Tom Polhaus phoned me."

"Sure you are." The policeman's arm went down. "I didn't know you at first. Well, they're back there." He jerked a thumb over his shoulder. "Bad business."

"Bad enough," Spade agreed, and went up the alley.

Half-way up it, not far from the entrance, a dark ambulance stood. Behind the ambulance, to the left, the alley was bounded by a waist-high fence, horizontal strips of rough boarding. From the fence dark ground fell away steeply to the billboard on Stockton Street below.

A ten-foot length of the fence's top rail had been torn from a post at one end and hung dangling from the other. Fifteen feet down the slope a flat boulder stuck out. In the notch between boulder and slope Miles Archer lay on his back. Two men stood over him. One of them held the beam of an electric torch on the dead man. Other men with lights moved up and down the slope.

One of them hailed Spade, "Hello, Sam," and clambered up to the alley, his shadow running up the slope before him. He was a barrel-bellied tall man with shrewd small eyes, a thick mouth, and carelessly shaven dark jowls. His shoes, knees, hands, and chin were daubed with brown loam.

"I figured you'd want to see it before we took him away," he said as he stepped over the broken fence.

"Thanks, Tom," Spade said. "What happened?" He put an elbow on a fence-post and looked down at the men below, nodding to those who nodded to him.

Tom Polhaus poked his own left breast with a dirty finger. "Got him right through the pump—with this." He took a fat revolver from his coat-pocket and held it out to Spade. Mud inlaid the depressions in the revolver's surface. "A Webley. English, ain't it?"

Spade took his elbow from the fence-post and leaned down to look at the weapon, but he did not touch it.

"Yes," he said, "Webley-Fosbery automatic revolver. That's it. Thirty-eight, eight shot. They don't make them any more. How many gone out of it?"

"One pill." Tom poked his breast again. "He must've been dead when he cracked the fence." He raised the muddy revolver. "Ever seen this before?"

Spade nodded. "I've seen Webley-Fosberys," he said without interest, and then spoke rapidly: "He was shot up here, huh? Standing where you are, with his back to the fence. The man that shot him stands here." He went around in front of Tom and raised a hand breast-high with leveled forefinger. "Let's him have it and Miles goes back, taking the top off the fence and going on through and down till the rock catches him. That it?"

"That's it," Tom replied slowly, working his brows together. "The blast burnt his coat."

"Who found him?"

"The man on the beat, Shilling. He was coming down Bush, and just as he got here a machine turning threw headlights up here, and he saw the top off the fence. So he came up to look at it, and found him."

"What about the machine that was turning around?"

"Not a damned thing about it, Sam. Shilling didn't pay any attention to it, not knowing anything was wrong then. He says nobody didn't come out of here while he was coming down from Powell or he'd've seen them. The only other way out would be under the billboard on Stockton. Nobody went that way. The fog's got the ground soggy, and the only marks are where Miles slid down and where this here gun rolled."

"Didn't anybody hear the shot?"

"For the love of God, Sam, we only just got here. Somebody must've heard it, when we find them." He turned and put a leg over the fence. "Coming down for a look at him before he's moved?"

Spade said: "No."

Tom halted astride the fence and looked back at Spade with surprised small eyes.

Spade said: "You've seen him. You'd see everything I could."

Tom, still looking at Spade, nodded doubtfully and withdrew his leg over the fence.

"His gun was tucked away on his hip," he said. "It hadn't been fired. His overcoat was buttoned. There's a hundred and sixty-some bucks in his clothes. Was he working, Sam?"

Spade, after a moment's hesitation, nodded.

Tom asked: "Well?"

"He was supposed to be tailing a fellow named Floyd Thursby," Spade said, and described Thursby as Miss Wonderly had described him.

"What for?"

Spade put his hands into his overcoat-pockets and blinked sleepy eyes at Tom.

Tom repeated impatiently: "What for?"

"He was an Englishman, maybe. I don't know what his game was, exactly. We were trying to find out where he lived." Spade grinned faintly and took a hand from his pocket to pat Tom's shoulder. "Don't crowd me." He put the hand in his pocket again. "I'm going out to break the news to Miles's wife." He turned away.

Tom, scowling, opened his mouth, closed it without having said anything, cleared his throat, put the scowl off his face, and spoke with a husky sort of gentleness:

"It's tough, him getting it like that. Miles had his faults same as the rest of us, but I guess he must've had some good points too."

"I guess so," Spade agreed in a tone that was utterly meaningless, and went out of the alley.

* * *

## "You know I'm not all bad, don't you?"

*"The Whosis Kid" is one of several Hammett stories that features a beautiful dangerous woman using her wiles to seduce a man whose protection she needs. This scene from the 1925 story was refined for use at the beginning of chapter 4 of the novel.*

### The Whosis Kid
*The Black Mask,* March 1925

She poured more brandy. By speaking quick I held my drink down to a size suitable for a man who has work to do. Hers was as large as before. We drank, and she offered me cigarettes in a lacquered box—slender cigarettes, hand-rolled in black paper.

I didn't stay with mine long. It tasted, smelt and scorched like gun-powder.

"You don't like my cigarettes?"

"I'm an old-fashioned man," I apologized, rubbing its fire out in a bronze dish, fishing in my pocket for my own deck. "Tobacco's as far as I've got. What's in these fireworks?"

She laughed. She had a pleasant laugh, with a sort of coo in it.

"I am so very sorry. So many people do not like them. I have a Hindu incense mixed with the tobacco."

I didn't say anything to that. It was what you would expect of a woman who would dye her dog purple.

The dog moved under its chair just then, scratching the floor with its nails.

The brown woman was in my arms, in my lap, her arms wrapped around my neck. Close-up, opened by terror, her eyes weren't dark at all. They were gray-green. The blackness was in the shadow from her heavy lashes.

"It's only the dog," I assured her, sliding her back on her own part of the bench. "It's only the dog wriggling around under the chair."

"Ah!" she blew her breath out with enormous relief.

Then we had to have another shot of brandy.

"You see, I am most awfully the coward," she said when the third dose of liquor was in her. "But, ah, I have had so much trouble. It is a wonder that I am not insane."

I could have told her she wasn't far enough from it to do much bragging, but I nodded with what was meant for sympathy.

She lit another cigarette to replace the one she had dropped in her excitement. Her eyes became normal black slits again.

"I do not think it is nice"—there was a suggestion of a dimple in her brown cheek when she smiled like that—"that I throw myself into the arms of a man even whose name I do not know, or anything of him."

"That's easy to fix. My name is Young," I lied; "and I can let you have a case of Scotch at a price that will aston-

B. M.

B. M.

# BLACK MASK

## NOT GUILTY

RECENTLY **Vanity Fair**, one of the white paper magazines, which caters to a very "select," "highbrow" audience of our "best people" published a long article about "woodpulps." By woodpulps it meant, of course, magazines printed on gray paper, as is **BLACK MASK**. It told all about how the woodpulps cater to people who don't know or care anything about real literature, and stated among other things that woodpulps are descendants of the old dime novel which youngsters used to read out behind the barn, that woodpulps have little to do with reality, but are pure romance of the thrilling, hair-raising kind, and that the authors who turn out this stuff do their work hurriedly, send in manuscripts that are extraordinarily bad, and generally know little or nothing of the people, places, and action about which they write.

The fact is that there are about seventy-five woodpulps differing as much in quality as in character of stories they publish. A further fact is that for many years past, the best fiction of its kind published in any magazine, slick or woodpulp, has appeared in **BLACK MASK**.

The article in **Vanity Fair** treats, without differentiation, of all woodpulps condescendingly, with amusement, as one would write about the antics and weird ideas of a lot of children, and since **Vanity Fair** has offhandedly included, by inference if not by name, **BLACK MASK**, in this wholesale group, we venture to assert that **Vanity Fair** itself would not find too favorable comparison between its regular fiction and article writers and those of **BLACK MASK**, such, for example, as Dashiell Hammett, Raoul Whitfield, Frederick Nebel, Erle Stanley Gardner, Carroll John Daly—to mention a few.

The absurdity of **Vanity Fair's** article, so far as **BLACK MASK** is concerned, is further borne out by the fact that since the works of the above-mentioned writers appeared in **BLACK MASK**, they have been sought by the highest rated of the fiction magazines, such as **The Saturday Evening Post**, by the best book publishers and by the movies.

Again, in comparison with **Vanity Fair**, we very much doubt if **Vanity Fair** pays on the average its fiction and article writers as much as **BLACK MASK** pays regularly for *its* stories.

Furthermore, without referring to the society matron who considers it smart to have on her table the so-called class magazine with its illustrations regardless of its text, but on the basis of real human enjoyment we doubt if **Vanity Fair** can show such reader appreciation of its quality and character as is given by letters in our files from men of the highest mental and moral caliber—lawyers, physicians, clergymen, bankers, writers and the like, telling us that they read **BLACK MASK** regularly and enjoy it immensely.

We are very well aware that **BLACK MASK** fans know that **BLACK MASK** is in a class by itself; that not one of the statements in the **Vanity Fair** article above quoted, truthfully applies to it; but we become a little weary when a careless member of the so-called class magazine fraternity parades its snootiness at the risk of rank misconception.

*The Editor*

5

*Joseph Shaw's editorial in* Black Mask *responding to a condescending article in* Vanity Fair *about pulp fiction, from the Shaw scrapbook ( facsimile; Collection of Richard Layman)*

ish you. I think maybe I could stand it if you call me Jerry. Most of the ladies I let sit in my lap do."

"Jerry Young," she repeated, as if to herself. "That is a nice name. And you are the bootlegger?"

"Not *the*," I corrected her, "just *a*. This is San Francisco."

The going got tough after that.

Everything else about this brown woman was all wrong, but her fright was real. She was scared stiff. And she didn't intend being left alone this night. She meant to keep me there—to massage any more chins that stuck themselves at her. Her idea—she being that sort—was that I would be most surely held with affection. So she must turn herself loose on me. She wasn't hampered by any pruderies or puritanisms at all.

I also have an idea. Mine is that when the last gong rings I'm going to be leading this baby and some of her playmates to the city prison. That is an excellent reason—among a dozen others I could think of—why I shouldn't get mushy with her.

I was willing enough to camp there with her until something happened. That apartment looked like the scene of the next action. But I had to cover up my own game. I couldn't let her know she was only a minor figure in it. I had to pretend there was nothing behind my willingness to stay but a desire to protect her. Another man might have got by with a chivalrous, knight-errant, protector-of-womanhood-without-personal-interest attitude. But I don't look, and can't easily act, like that kind of person. I had to hold her off without letting her guess that my interest wasn't personal. It was no cinch. She was too damned direct, and she had too much brandy in her.

I didn't kid myself that my beauty and personality were responsible for any of her warmth. I was a thick-armed male with big fists. She was in a jam. She spelled my name P-r-o-t-e-c-t-i-o-n. I was something to be put between her and trouble.

Another complication: I am neither young enough nor old enough to get feverish over every woman who doesn't make me think being blind isn't so bad. I'm at that middle point around forty where a man puts other feminine qualities—amiability, for one—above beauty on his list. This brown woman annoyed me. She was too sure of herself. Her work was rough. She was trying to handle me as if I were a farmer boy. But in spite of all this, I'm constructed mostly of human ingredients. This woman got more than a stand-off when faces and bodies were dealt. I didn't like her. I hoped to throw her in the can before I was through. But I'd be a liar if I didn't admit that she had me stirred up inside—between her cuddling against me, giving me the come-on, and the brandy I had drunk.

The going was tough—no fooling.

* * *

*The Maltese Falcon*, pp. 39–44, 46–49

MISS WONDERLY, in a belted green crêpe silk dress, opened the door of apartment 1001 at the Coronet. Her face was flushed. Her dark red hair, parted on the left side, swept back in loose waves over her right temple, was somewhat tousled.

Spade took off his hat and said: "Good morning."

His smile brought a fainter smile to her face. Her eyes, of blue that was almost violet, did not lose their troubled look. She lowered her head and said in a hushed, timid, voice: "Come in, Mr. Spade."

She led him past open kitchen-, bathroom-, and bedroom-doors into a cream and red living-room, apologizing for its confusion: "Everything is upside-down. I haven't even finished unpacking."

She laid his hat on a table and sat down on a walnut settee. He sat on a brocaded oval-backed chair facing her.

She looked at her fingers, working them together, and said: "Mr. Spade, I've a terrible, terrible confession to make."

Spade smiled a polite smile, which she did not lift her eyes to see, and said nothing.

"That—that story I told you yesterday was all—a story," she stammered, and looked up at him now with miserable frightened eyes.

"Oh, that," Spade said lightly. "We didn't exactly believe your story."

"Then–?" Perplexity was added to the misery and fright in her eyes.

"We believed your two hundred dollars."

"You mean–?" She seemed to not know what he meant.

"I mean that you paid us more than if you'd been telling the truth," he explained blandly, "and enough more to make it all right."

Her eyes suddenly lighted up. She lifted herself a few inches from the settee, settled down again, smoothed her skirt, leaned forward, and spoke eagerly: "And even now you'd be willing to–?"

Spade stopped her with a palm-up motion of one hand. The upper part of his face frowned. The lower part smiled. "That depends," he said. "The hell of it is, Miss—— Is your name Wonderly or Leblanc?"

She blushed and murmured: "It's really O'Shaughnessy—Brigid O'Shaughnessy."

"The hell of it is, Miss O'Shaughnessy, that a couple of murders"—she winced—"coming together like this get everybody stirred up, make the police think they can go the limit, make everybody hard to handle and expensive. It's not–"

He stopped talking because she had stopped listening and was waiting for him to finish.

"Mr. Spade, tell me the truth." Her voice quivered on the verge of hysteria. Her face had become haggard around desperate eyes. "Am I to blame for—for last night?"

Spade shook his head. "Not unless there are things I don't know about," he said. "You warned us that Thursby was dangerous. Of course you lied to us about your sister and all, but that doesn't count: we didn't believe you." He shrugged his sloping shoulders. "I wouldn't say it was your fault."

She said, "Thank you," very softly, and then moved her head from side to side. "But I'll always blame myself." She put a hand to her throat. "Mr. Archer was so–so alive yesterday afternoon, so solid and hearty and–"

"Stop it," Spade commanded. "He knew what he was doing. They're the chances we take."

"Was  was hc married?"

"Yes, with ten thousand insurance, no children, and a wife who didn't like him."

"Oh, please don't!" she whispered.

Spade shrugged again. "That's the way it was." He glanced at his watch and moved from his chair to the settee beside her. "There's no time for worrying about that now." His voice was pleasant but firm. "Out there a flock of policemen and assistant district attorneys and reporters are running around with their noses to the ground. What do you want to do?"

"I want you to save me from–from it all," she replied in a thin tremulous voice. She put a timid hand on his sleeve. "Mr. Spade, do they know about me?"

"Not yet. I wanted to see you first."

"What–what would they think if they knew about the way I came to you–with those lies?"

"It would make them suspicious. That's why I've been stalling them till I could see you. I thought maybe we wouldn't have to let them know all of it. We ought to be able to fake a story that will rock them to sleep, if necessary."

"You don't think I had anything to do with the–the murders–do you?"

Spade grinned at her and said: "I forgot to ask you that. Did you?"

"No."

"That's good. Now what are we going to tell the police?"

She squirmed on her end of the settee and her eyes wavered between heavy lashes, as if trying and failing to free their gaze from his. She seemed smaller, and very young and oppressed.

"Must they know about me at all?" she asked. "I think I'd rather die than that, Mr. Spade. I can't explain now, but can't you somehow manage so that you can shield me from them, so I won't have to answer their questions? I don't think I could stand being questioned now. I think I would rather die. Can't you, Mr. Spade?"

"Maybe," he said, "but I'll have to know what it's all about."

She went down on her knees at his knees. She held her face up to him. Her face was wan, taut, and fearful over tight-clasped hands.

*Advertisement from the Shaw scrapbook ( facsimile; Collection of Richard Layman)*

"I haven't lived a good life," she cried. "I've been bad–worse than you could know–but I'm not all bad. Look at me, Mr. Spade. You know I'm not all bad, don't you? You can see that, can't you? Then can't you trust me a little? Oh, I'm so alone and afraid, and I've got nobody to help me if you won't help me. I know I've no right to ask you to trust me if I won't trust you. I do trust you, but I can't tell you. I can't tell you now. Later I will, when I can. I'm afraid, Mr. Spade. I'm afraid of trusting you. I don't mean that. I do trust you, but–I trusted Floyd and–I've nobody else, nobody else, Mr. Spade. You can help me. You've said you can help me. If I hadn't believed you could save me I would have run away today instead of sending for you. If I thought anybody else could save me would I be down on my knees like this? I know this isn't fair of me. But be generous, Mr. Spade, don't ask me to be fair. You're strong, you're resourceful, you're brave. You can spare me some of that strength and resourcefulness and courage, surely. Help me, Mr. Spade. Help me because I need help so badly, and because if you don't where will I find anyone who can, no matter how willing? Help me. I've no right to ask you to help me blindly, but I do ask you. Be generous, Mr. Spade. You can help me. Help me."

Spade, who had held his breath through much of this speech, now emptied his lungs with a long sighing exhalation between pursed lips and said: "You won't need much of anybody's help. You're good. You're very good. It's chiefly your eyes, I think, and that throb you get into your voice when you say things like 'Be generous, Mr. Spade.'"

She jumped up on her feet. Her face crimsoned painfully, but she held her head erect and she looked Spade straight in the eyes.

"I deserve that," she said. "I deserve it, but—oh!—I did want your help so much. I do want it, and need it, so much. And the lie was in the way I said it, and not at all in what I said." She turned away, no longer holding herself erect. "It is my own fault that you can't believe me now."

Spade's face reddened and he looked down at the floor, muttering: "Now you are dangerous."

. . . . . . . . . .

"You picked a nice sort of playmate."

"Only that sort could have helped me," she said simply, "if he had been loyal."

"Yes, if." Spade pinched his lower lip between finger and thumb and looked gloomily at her. The vertical creases over his nose deepened, drawing his brows together. "How bad a hole are you actually in?"

"As bad," she said, "as could be."

"Physical danger?"

"I'm not heroic. I don't think there's anything worse than death."

"Then it's that?"

"It's that as surely as we're sitting here"—she shivered—"unless you help me."

He took his fingers away from his mouth and ran them through his hair. "I'm not Christ," he said irritably. "I can't work miracles out of thin air." He looked at his watch. "The day's going and you're giving me nothing to work with. Who killed Thursby?"

She put a crumpled handkerchief to her mouth and said, "I don't know," through it.

"Your enemies or his?"

"I don't know. His, I hope, but I'm afraid—I don't know."

"How was he supposed to be helping you? Why did you bring him here from Hongkong?"

She looked at him with frightened eyes and shook her head in silence. Her face was haggard and pitifully stubborn.

Spade stood up, thrust his hands into the pockets of his jacket, and scowled down at her. "This is hopeless," he said savagely. "I can't do anything for you. I don't know what you want done. I don't even know if you know what you want."

She hung her head and wept.

He made a growling animal noise in his throat and went to the table for his hat.

"You won't," she begged in a small choked voice, not looking up, "go to the police?"

"Go to them!" he exclaimed, his voice loud with rage. "They've been running me ragged since four o'clock this morning. I've made myself God knows how much trouble standing them off. For what? For some crazy notion that I could help you. I can't. I won't try." He put his hat on his head and pulled it down tight. "Go to them? All I've got to do is stand still and they'll be swarming all over me. Well, I'll tell them what I know and you'll have to take your chances."

She rose from the settee and held herself straight in front of him though her knees were trembling, and she held her white panic-stricken face up high though she couldn't hold the twitching muscles of mouth and chin still. She said: "You've been patient. You've tried to help me. It is hopeless, and useless, I suppose." She stretched out her right hand. "I thank you for what you have done. I–I'll have to take my chances."

Spade made the growling animal noise in his throat again and sat down on the settee. "How much money have you got?" he asked.

The question startled her. Then she pinched her lower lip between her teeth and answered reluctantly: "I've about five hundred dollars left."

"Give it to me."

She hesitated, looking timidly at him. He made angry gestures with mouth, eyebrows, hands, and shoulders. She went into her bedroom, returning almost immediately with a sheaf of paper money in one hand.

He took the money from her, counted it, and said: "There's only four hundred here."

"I had to keep some to live on," she explained meekly, putting a hand to her breast.

"Can't you get any more?"

"No."

"You must have something you can raise money on," he insisted.

"I've some rings, a little jewelry."

"You'll have to hock them," he said, and held out his hand. "The Remedial's the best place—Mission and Fifth."

She looked pleadingly at him. His yellow-grey eyes were hard and implacable. Slowly she put her hand inside the neck of her dress, brought out a slender roll of bills, and put them in his waiting hand.

He smoothed the bills out and counted them—four twenties, four tens, and a five. He returned two of the tens and the five to her. The others he put in his pocket. Then he stood up and said: "I'm going out and see what I can do for you. I'll be back as soon as I can with the best news I can manage. I'll ring four times—long, short, long, short—so you'll know it's me. You needn't go to the door with me. I can let myself out."

He left her standing in the center of the floor looking after him with dazed blue eyes.

\* \* \*

### Father Tells the Flitcraft Story

One beautiful summer day in the forties, my father and I were out on the lawn in the backyard of my mother's house in West L.A. There was a blanket on the grass and cards spread out. My father had been playing solitaire. He was in a good mood, leaning back against the lawn chair, wearing trunks and the sandals he'd asked me to find in Westwood. And out of nowhere particular he told me the Flitcraft story.

I admit that I hadn't read *The Maltese Falcon* since I was in grade school, and the story seemed unconnected. But he told it as a story he had just heard or read, not as if he had used it as a set-piece in a book. He told it with such delight and enjoyment, like a funny story you want to share while it's still fresh in your mind. It was both old to him and new. He told it as if it was sweet to him, a thing he had savored and relished that he wanted me to share.

Papa plunged into the story without any explanation. The words he used were identical with those Sam Spade uses. In Tacoma one midday a local businessman left his office to go out to lunch. On his way to the restaurant, passing an office building under construction, a beam came crashing down to the street barely missing him. He wasn't really hurt except for a scrape on his cheek, but he was badly shaken, more shocked than scared. He felt as if someone had taken the lid off life and let him look inside.

He had been leading a nice, orderly, reasonable life, with a wife, two sons, and a successful business. He'd been content because he'd believed that the world was a nice, orderly, reasonable place. Now he saw that that was an illusion. The world was chaotic. People lived and died by pure chance. It was a random universe, and by living in an orderly way, he had gotten out of sync with it. He left the city that day, left his business, his wife and children, and never went back. It seemed to him that by acting in a random way he could get back in step with the universe.

Years later he was found living in Spokane, with a business, two children, and a wife, who was more like his first than not. He wasn't sorry for what he'd done. It didn't seem strange to him that he had gone back to living the same kind of orderly life he'd led in Tacoma. And this was the part Papa liked best: That he'd gotten used to beams falling, then when they didn't fall, he got used to that, too.

What I remember is his delight in the story—as if it were a gift he had received that was just right. As a boy he had wanted to find the Ultimate Truth—how the world operated. And here it was. There was no system except blind chance. Beams falling.

–Jo Hammett, *Dashiell Hammett: A Daughter Remembers*, pp. 98, 100–101

*Hammett and his younger daughter, Jo, in the backyard of the house he bought his wife on Purdue Street in Los Angeles, circa 1946 (courtesy of Josephine Hammett)*

Dashiell Hammett
891 Post Street
San Francisco
California

750 words

Offered at
usual rates.

### THE BOUNDARIES OF SCIENCE AND PHILOSOPHY

By Dashiell Hammett

Science is concerned with percepts.  A percept is a defined, that
is a limited, difference.  The scientific datum that white occurs means
that white is the difference between a certain perceptual field and the
rest of the perceiver.  If you look at an unbroken expanse of white you
perceive white because your perception of it is limited to your visual
field: the surrounding, contrasting, extra-visual area of non-white gives
you your percept of white.  These are not scientific definitions.  They
cannot be.  Science cannot define, cannot limit, itself.  Definitions of
science must be philosophical definitions.  Science cannot know what it
cannot know.  Science cannot know that there is anything it does not
know.  (All scientists, it is to be hoped, know that there are things
science does not know, but only when they have stepped out of their scientific
roles: that knowledge is not a part of science.)  Science deals with percepts,
and not with non-percepts.  Thus, Einstein's theory of relativity, that the
phenomena of nature will be the same (that is, not different) to two observers
who move with any uniform velocity whatever relative to one another, is a
philosophical, and not a scientific, hypothesis.  That is why it produces a
theory of continuous intervening medium, while the study of atoms along purely

*Hammett had an interest in philosophy from his school days in Baltimore, and he was well-read on the subject. His familiarity with the pragmatists, particularly their theories about the nature of truth, is evident in* The Maltese Falcon. *In the Flitcraft story in chapter VII, Flitcraft takes the pseudonym Charles Pierce after he disappears, an allusion to the nineteenth-century philosopher Charles Peirce, whose philosophy included attempts to account for all actions, including random occurrences. This previously unpublished essay demonstrating Hammett's interests was written at about the same time as* The Maltese Falcon *(Harry Ransom Humanities Research Center, University of Texas at Austin).*

scientific lines leads always to discontinuities.

Philosophy, like science, cannot define, cannot limit, itself.
Definitions of philosophy must be made from a viewpoint that will bear
somewhat the same relation to philosophy that the philosophical viewpoint
bears to science. These definitions may be called metaphysical, and the
viewpoint that of metaphysics. Looking at philosophy from this height,
then, we may say that it involves the same attitude toward science that
science involves toward our perceptual white. Philosophy involves a sort
of scientific examination of science, and is subject to the same rules of
the game as science. Philosophy cannot know what philosophy cannot know.
Philosophy cannot know that there is anything it does not know. (All
philosophers, it is to be hoped, know that there are things philosophy
does not know, but only when they have stepped out of their philosophical
roles: that knowledge is not a part of philosophy.)

The practical difference between science and philosophy is that
science's datum is what philosophy calls the percept, and all science's
inferences must be made from that datum; and that philosophy's datum is
what metaphysics calls the perception, and all philosophy's inferences
must be made from that datum.

Science says, "White occurs." Philosophy can deal only with those
things that are not science's, or it becomes science and not philosophy.
Philosophy can have nothing to do with white, cannot know white, because
white is a percept---that is, the limited difference between parts of a
perceiver---and percepts are scientific data.

Philosophy's business is with the perception. Philosophy, to avoid

becoming science, must remove what is perceived, the percept, from the act
of perceiving. What is perceived is a limited difference between parts of
the perceiver. When that is removed from the act of perceiving, what remains
to philosophy is a residual uniformity of parts of the perceiver. This
uniform residue is philosophy's datum, and, since philosophy cannot know
that anything is not known to it, then all that science did not discover,
all that was not in the percept, must be uniform and must exist for the
philosopher.

Metaphysically then, the situation is this: Science can know only
the difference between the part of the perceiver that is sensitive to white
and the part that is not. That difference is science's datum, what science
calls an occurence or event, in this case white. Philosophy can know only
the difference ~~xxxxxxxxxxxx~~ between science's datum (which is itself the
difference between the sensitive and insensitive parts of the perceiver) and
the insensitive part of the perceiver. That second difference is philosophy's
datum, what philosophy calls uniform residue, primitive stuff, ether, or
matter.

Philosophy can no more know anything that science knows than science
can know anything that philosophy knows. The validity of science and philosophy
depends on this difference between them, just as the validity of scientific
and philosophical data depends on differences. Science can neither assert nor
deny that ~~xxxxxxx~~ any thing is white. Philosophy can neither assert nor
deny that anything is white. Thing belongs to philosophy, white to science,
and neither has an equivalent in the world of the other. You must put
science and philosophy together to get that entity, the white thing.

## "But I've got the falcon"

*In "The House in Turk Street" Hammett introduced the plot device of the detective-held-captive bargaining for his freedom with stolen goods he has hidden. This scene can be compared with the opening of "The Fall-Guy," chapter XVIII of the novel.*

### The House in Turk Street
*The Black Mask,* 15 April 1924

As she wheeled savagely toward me, he stuck the muzzle of an automatic in her side—a smart jab that checked the angry words she was hurling at me.

"I'll take your guns, Elvira," he said, and took them.

There was a purring deadliness in his voice that made her surrender them without a word.

"Where are the bonds now?" he asked me.

I grinned.

"I'm not with you, Tai. I'm against you."

He studied me with his little eyes that were like black seeds for a while, and I studied him; and I hope that his studying was as fruitless as mine.

"I don't like violence," he said slowly, "and I believe you are a sensible person. Let us traffic, my friend."

"You name it," I suggested.

"Gladly! As a basis for our bargaining, we will stipulate that you have hidden the bonds where they cannot be found by anyone else; and that I have you completely in my power, as the shilling shockers used to have it."

"Reasonable enough," I said, "go on."

"The situation, then, is what gamblers call a standoff. Neither of us has the advantage. As a detective, you want us; but we have you. As thieves, we want the bonds; but you have them. I offer you the girl in exchange for the bonds, and that seems to me an equitable offer. It will give me the bonds and a chance to get away. It will give you no small degree of success in your task as a detective. Hook is dead. You will have the girl. All that will remain is to find me and the bonds again—by no means a hopeless task. You will have turned a defeat into more than half of a victory, with an excellent chance to make it complete one."

"How do I know that you'll give me the girl?"

He shrugged.

"Naturally, there can be no guarantee. But, knowing that she planned to desert me for the swine who lies dead below, you can't imagine that my feelings for her are the most friendly. Too, if I take her with me, she will want a share in the loot."

---

### A Dislike for Murder

*One of the triumphs of* The Maltese Falcon *is diction. In this scene from "The House in Turk Street" Hammett gives his Gutman-like villain Tai an awkward speech. In a similar scene at the beginning of chapter 18, Hammett is more graceful. When he is accosted by Wilmer, Spade says, "Ask your boss if he wants me shot up before we talk." Gutman says, "Never mind Wilmer," and to Spade, "You certainly are a most headstrong individual."*

"If I hadn't a dislike for murder, and if I didn't think that you will perhaps be of some value to Elvira and me in effecting our departure, I should certainly relieve us of the handicap of your stupidity now. But I'll give you one more chance. I would suggest, however, that you think carefully before you give way to any more of your violent impulses." He turned to the girl. "Have you been putting foolish ideas in our Hook's head?"

–"The House in Turk Street"

---

I turned the lay-out over in my mind, and looked at it from this side and that and the other.

"This is the way it looks to me," I told him at last. "You aren't a killer. I'll come through alive no matter what happens. All right; why should I swap? You and the girl will be easier to find again than the bonds, and they are the most important part of the job anyway. I'll hold on to them, and take my chances on finding you folks again. Yes, I'm playing it safe."

And I meant it, for the time being, at least.

"No, I'm not a killer," he said, very softly; and he smiled the first smile I had seen on his face. It wasn't a pleasant smile: and there was something in it that made you want to shudder. "But I am other things, perhaps, of which you haven't thought. But this talking is to no purpose. Elvira!"

The girl, who had been standing a little to one side, watching us, came obediently forward.

"You will find sheets in one of the bureau drawers," he told her. "Tear one or two of them into strips strong enough to tie up your friend securely."

The girl went to the bureau. I wrinkled my head, trying to find a not too disagreeable answer to the question in my mind. The answer that came first wasn't nice: *torture.*

\* \* \*

*The Maltese Falcon,* pp. 212–213

The envelope, though not bulky, was heavy enough to fly true. It struck the lower part of Spade's chest and dropped down on his thighs. He picked it up deliberately and opened it deliberately, using both hands, having taken his left arm from around the girl. The contents of the envelope were thousand-dollar bills, smooth and stiff and new. Spade took them out and counted them. There were ten of them. Spade looked up smiling. He said mildly: "We were talking about more money than this."

"Yes, sir, we were," Gutman agreed, "but we were talking then. This is actual money, genuine coin of the realm, sir. With a dollar of this you can buy more than with ten dollars of talk." Silent laughter shook his bulbs. When their commotion stopped he said more seriously, yet not altogether seriously: "There are more of us to be taken care of now." He moved his twinkling eyes and his fat head to indicate Cairo. "And—well, sir, in short—the situation has changed."

While Gutman talked Spade had tapped the edges of the ten bills into alignment and had returned them to their envelope, tucking the flap in over them. Now, with forearms on knees, he sat hunched forward, dangling the envelope from a corner held lightly by finger and thumb down between his legs. His reply to the fat man was careless: "Sure. You're together now, but I've got the falcon."

Joel Cairo spoke. Ugly hands grasping the arms of his chair, he leaned forward and said primly in his high-pitched thin voice: "I shouldn't think it would be necessary to remind you, Mr. Spade, that though you may have the falcon yet we certainly have you."

Spade grinned. "I'm trying to not let that worry me," he said.

\* \* \*

### "You needed another protector"

*Sam Spade is defined by his ability to make a hard decision about Brigid O'Shaughnessy: to see her for what she is, and, more significantly, to turn her in to the authorities despite his attraction to her. Hammett had tried such scenes in his earlier work, as in this excerpt from "Who Killed Bob Teal?" more artfully executed in the last chapter of* The Maltese Falcon.

### Who Killed Bob Teal?

*True Detective Mysteries,* November 1924

"Now spill it!" he burst out. "How come all the startling developments, as the newspaper boys call 'em?"

"Well, first-off, I knew that the question 'Who killed Bob Teal?' could have only one answer. Bob wasn't a boob! He might possibly have let a man he was trailing lure him behind a row of billboards on a dark night, but he would have gone prepared for trouble. He wouldn't have died with empty hands, from a gun that was close enough to scorch his coat. The murderer had to be somebody Bob trusted, so it couldn't be Whitacre. Now Bob was a conscientious sort of lad, and he wouldn't have stopped shadowing Whitacre to go over and talk with some friend. There was only one man who could have persuaded him to drop Whitacre for a while, and that one man was the one he was working for—Ogburn.

"If I hadn't known Bob, I might have thought he had hidden behind the billboards to watch Whitacre; but Bob wasn't an amateur. He knew better than to pull any of that spectacular gumshoe stuff. So there was nothing to it but Ogburn!

"With all that to go on, the rest was duck soup. All the stuff Mae Landis gave us—identifying the gun as Whitacre's, and giving Ogburn an alibi by saying she had talked to him on the phone at ten o'clock—only convinced me that she and Ogburn were working together. When the landlady described 'Quirk' for us, I was fairly certain of it. Her description would fit either Whitacre or Ogburn, but there was no sense to Whitacre's having the apartment on Greenwich Street, while if Ogburn and the Landis woman were thick, they'd need a meeting-place of some sort. The rest of the box of cartridges there helped some too.

"Then to-night I put on a little act in Ogburn's apartment, chasing a nickel along the floor and finding traces of dried mud that had escaped the cleaning-up he no doubt gave the carpet and clothes after he came home from walking through the lot in the rain. We'll let the experts decide whether it could be mud from the lot on which Bob was killed, and the jury can decide whether it is.

"There are a few more odds and ends—like the gun. The Landis woman said Whitacre had had it for more than a year, but in spite of being muddy it looks fairly new to me. We'll send the serial number to the factory, and find when it was turned out.

"For motive, just now all I'm sure of is the woman, which should be enough. But I think that when Ogburn and Whitacre's books are audited, and their finances sifted, we'll find something there. What I'm banking on strong is that Whitacre will come in, now that he is cleared of the murder charge."

And that is exactly what happened.

\* \* \*

*A Webley-Fosbery automatic revolver, the gun used to murder Miles Archer. Between 1901 and 1915 Webley-Fosbery made six-shot .45 caliber automatic revolvers and, from the same design, rarer eight-shot .38s. In Hammett's novel, the gun is a "Thirty-eight, eight shot." Thinking to correct an error, John Huston introduced one by changing the gun to an eight-shot .45 in the 1941 movie (William Chipcase Dowell,* The Webley Story *[Kirkland, Wash.: Commonwealth Heritage Foundation, 1987]).*

The Maltese Falcon, pp. 255–259

"That's a lie," Spade said. "You had Thursby hooked and you knew it. He was a sucker for women. His record shows that—the only falls he took were over women. And once a chump, always a chump. Maybe you didn't know his record, but you'd know you had him safe."

She blushed and looked timidly at him.

He said: "You wanted to get him out of the way before Jacobi came with the loot. What was your scheme?"

"I—I knew he'd left the States with a gambler after some trouble. I didn't know what it was, but I thought that if it was anything serious and he saw a detective watching him he'd think it was on account of the old trouble, and would be frightened into going away. I didn't think—"

"You told him he was being shadowed," Spade said confidently. "Miles hadn't many brains, but he wasn't clumsy enough to be spotted the first night."

"I told him, yes. When we went out for a walk that night I pretended to discover Mr. Archer following us and pointed him out to Floyd." She sobbed. "But please believe, Sam, that I wouldn't have done it if I had thought Floyd would kill him. I thought he'd be frightened into leaving the city. I didn't for a minute think he'd shoot him like that."

Spade smiled wolfishly with his lips, but not at all with his eyes. He said: "If you thought he wouldn't you were right, angel."

The girl's upraised face held utter astonishment.

Spade said: "Thursby didn't shoot him."

Incredulity joined astonishment in the girl's face.

Spade said: "Miles hadn't many brains, but, Christ! he had too many years' experience as a detective to be caught like that by the man he was shadowing. Up a blind alley with his gun tucked away on his hip and his overcoat buttoned? Not a chance. He was as dumb as any man ought to be, but he wasn't quite that dumb. The only two ways out of the alley could be watched from the edge of Bush Street over the tunnel. You'd told us Thursby was a bad actor. He couldn't have tricked Miles into the alley like that, and he couldn't have driven him in. He was dumb, but not dumb enough for that."

125

He ran his tongue over the inside of his lips and smiled affectionately at the girl. He said: "But he'd've gone up there with you, angel, if he was sure nobody else was up there. You were his client, so he would have had no reason for not dropping the shadow on your say-so, and if you caught up with him and asked him to go up there he'd've gone. He was just dumb enough for that. He'd've looked you up and down and licked his lips and gone grinning from ear to ear–and then you could've stood as close to him as you liked in the dark and put a hole through him with the gun you had got from Thursby that evening."

Brigid O'Shaughnessy shrank back from him until the edge of the table stopped her. She looked at him with terrified eyes and cried: "Don't–don't talk to me like that, Sam! You know I didn't! You know–"

"Stop it." He looked at the watch on his wrist. "The police will be blowing in any minute now and we're sitting on dynamite. Talk!"

She put the back of a hand on her forehead. "Oh, why do you accuse me of such a terrible–?"

"Will you stop it?" he demanded in a low impatient voice. "This isn't the spot for the schoolgirl-act. Listen to me. The pair of us are sitting under the gallows." He took hold of her wrists and made her stand up straight in front of him. "Talk!"

"I–I–How did you know he–he licked his lips and looked–?"

Spade laughed harshly. "I knew Miles. But never mind that. Why did you shoot him?"

She twisted her wrists out of Spade's fingers and put her hands up around the back of his neck, pulling his head down until his mouth all but touched hers. Her body was flat against his from knees to chest. He put his arms around her, holding her tight to him. Her dark-lashed lids were half down over velvet eyes. Her voice was hushed, throbbing: "I didn't mean to, at first. I didn't, really. I meant what I told you, but when I saw Floyd couldn't be frightened I–"

Spade slapped her shoulder. He said: "That's a lie. You asked Miles and me to handle it ourselves. You wanted to be sure the shadower was somebody you knew and who knew you, so they'd go with you. You got the gun from Thursby that day–that night. You had already rented the apartment at the Coronet. You had trunks there and none at the hotel and when I looked the apartment over I found a rent-receipt dated five or six days before the time you told me you rented it."

She swallowed with difficulty and her voice was humble. "Yes, that's a lie, Sam. I did intend to if Floyd–I–I can't look at you and tell you this, Sam." She pulled his head farther down until her cheek was against his cheek, her mouth by his ear, and whispered: "I knew Floyd wouldn't be easily frightened, but I thought that if he knew somebody was shadowing him either he'd–Oh, I can't say it, Sam!" She clung to him, sobbing.

Spade said: "You thought Floyd would tackle him and one or the other of them would go down. If Thursby was the one then you were rid of him. If Miles was, then you could see that Floyd was caught and you'd be rid of him. That it?"

"S-something like that."

"And when you found that Thursby didn't mean to tackle him you borrowed the gun and did it yourself. Right?"

"Yes–though not exactly."

"But exact enough. And you had that plan up your sleeve from the first. You thought Floyd would be nailed for the killing."

"I–I thought they'd hold him at least until after Captain Jacobi had arrived with the falcon and–"

"And you didn't know then that Gutman was here hunting for you. You didn't suspect that or you wouldn't have shaken your gunman. You knew Gutman was here as soon as you heard Thursby had been shot. Then you knew you needed another protector, so you came back to me. Right?"

"Yes, but–oh, sweetheart!–it wasn't only that. I would have come back to you sooner or later. From the first instant I saw you I knew–"

Spade said tenderly: "You angel! Well, if you get a good break you'll be out of San Quentin in twenty years and you can come back to me then."

\* \* \*

## "I won't play the sap for you"

*Perhaps the most famous scene in hard-boiled detective fiction is the climax in the last chapter of* The Maltese Falcon *when Spade explains to Brigid why he is turning her in. Hammett had attempted the scene before, as early as 1924 in "The Girl with the Silver Eyes," and he alluded to what he regarded as a failed attempt at it again in his 1925 story "The Gutting of Couffignal." A comparison of Hammett's handling of this scene in these three instances demonstrates his development from a good pulp writer into a master prose stylist over the course of four years.*

### The Girl with the Silver Eyes
*The Black Mask,* June 1924

I've gone on record as saying that this girl was beautiful, and, standing there in the dazzling white of the headlights, she was more than that. She was a thing to start crazy thoughts even in the head of an unimaginative middle-aged thief-catcher. She was–

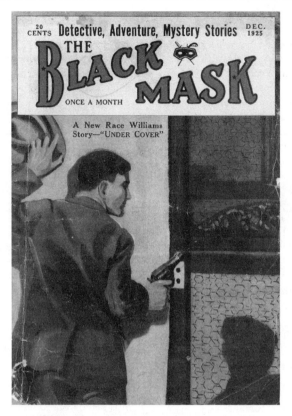

*Cover of the* Black Mask *that included "The Gutting of Couffignal," which concludes with one of Hammett's attempts at the scene he perfected in Spade's dramatic confrontation with Brigid O'Shaughnessy at the end of* The Maltese Falcon *(Collection of Richard Layman)*

Anyhow, I suppose that is why I scowled at her and said:

"Yes, poor Fag, and poor Hook, and poor Tai, and poor kind of a Los Angeles bank messenger, and poor Burke," calling the roll, so far as I knew it, of men who had died loving her.

She didn't flare up. Her big grey eyes lifted, and she looked at me with a gaze that I couldn't fathom, and her lovely oval face under the mass of brown hair—which I knew was phoney—was sad.

"I suppose you do think—" she began.

But I had had enough of this; I was uncomfortable along the spine.

"Come on," I said. "We'll leave Kilcourse and the roadster here for the present."

She said nothing, but went with me to Axford's big machine, and sat in silence while I laced my shoes. I found a robe on the back seat and gave it to her.

"Better wrap this around your shoulders. The windshield is gone. It'll be cool."

She followed my suggestion without a word, but when I had edged our vehicle around the rear of the roadster, and had straightened out in the road again, going east, she laid a hand on my arm.

"Aren't we going back to the White Shack?"

"No. Redwood City—the county jail."

A mile perhaps, during which, without looking at her, I knew she was studying my rather lumpy profile. Then her hand was on my forearm again and she was leaning toward me so that her breath was warm against my cheek.

"Will you stop for a minute? There's something—some things I want to tell you."

I brought the car to a halt in a cleared space of hard soil off to one side of the road, and screwed myself a little around in the seat to face her more directly.

"Before you start," I told her, "I want you to understand that we stay here for just so long as you talk about the Pangburn affair. When you get off on any other line—then we finish our trip to Redwood City."

"Aren't you even interested in the Los Angeles affair?"

"No. That's closed. You and Hook Riordan and Tai Choon Tau and the Quarres were equally responsible for the messenger's death, even if Hook did the actual killing. Hook and the Quarres passed out the night we had our party in Turk Street. Tai was hanged last month. Now I've got you. We had enough evidence to swing the Chinese, and we've even more against you. That is done–finished–completed. If you want to tell me anything about Pangburn's death, I'll listen. Otherwise–"

I reached for the self-starter.

A pressure of her fingers on my arm stopped me.

"I do want to tell you about it," she said earnestly. "I want you to know the truth about it. You'll take me to Redwood City, I know. Don't think that I expect– that I have any foolish hopes. But I'd like you to know the truth about this thing. I don't know why I should care especially what you think, but–"

Her voice dwindled off to nothing.

### XVII

Then she began to talk very rapidly–as people talk when they fear interruptions before their stories are told–and she sat leaning slightly forward, so that her beautiful oval face was very close to mine. . . .

### XVIII

Her voice died, and she shivered a little. The robe I had given her had fallen away from her white shoulders. Whether or not it was because she was so close against my shoulder, I shivered, too. And my fingers, fumbling in my pocket for a cigarette, brought it out twisted and mashed.

"That's all there is to the part you promised to listen to," she said softly, her face turned half away. "I wanted you to know. You're a hard man, but somehow I–"

I cleared my throat, and the hand that held the mangled cigarette was suddenly steady.

"Now don't be crude, sister," I said. "Your work has been too smooth so far to be spoiled by rough stuff now."

She laughed–a brief laugh that was bitter and reckless and just a little weary, and she thrust her face still closer to mine, and the grey eyes were soft and placid.

"Little fat detective whose name I don't know"– her voice had a tired huskiness in it, and a tired mockery–"you think I am playing a part, don't you? You think I am playing for liberty. Perhaps I am. I certainly would take it if it were offered me. But–Men have thought me beautiful, and I have played with them. Women are like that. Men have loved me and, doing what I liked with them, I have found men contemptible. And then comes this little fat detective whose name I don't know, and he acts as if I were a hag–an old squaw. Can I help then being piqued into some sort of feeling for him? Women are like that. Am I so homely that any man has a right to look at me without even interest? Am I ugly?"

I shook my head.

"You're quite pretty," I said, struggling to keep my voice as casual as the words.

"You beast!" she spat, and then her smile grew gentle again. "And yet it is because of that attitude that I sit here and turn myself inside out for you. If you were to take me in your arms and hold me close to the chest that I am already leaning against, and if you were to tell me that there is no jail ahead for me just now, I would be glad, of course. But, though for a while you might hold me, you would then be only one of the men with which I am familiar: men who love and are used and are succeeded by other men. But because you do none of these things, because you are a wooden block of a man, I find myself wanting you. Would I tell you this, little fat detective, if I were playing a game?"

I grunted noncommittally, and forcibly restrained my tongue from running out to moisten my dry lips.

"I'm going to this jail tonight if you are the same hard man who has goaded me into whining love into his uncaring ears, but before that, can't I have one whole-hearted assurance that you think me a little more than 'quite pretty'? Or at least a hint that if I were not a prisoner your pulse might beat a little faster when I touch you? I'm going to this jail for a long while–perhaps to the gallows. Can't I take my vanity there not quite in tatters to keep me company? Can't you do some slight thing to keep me from the afterthought of having bleated all this out to a man who was simply bored?"

Her lids had come down half over the silver-grey eyes; her head had tilted back so far that a little pulse showed throbbing in her white throat; her lips were motionless over slightly parted teeth, as the last word had left them. My fingers went deep into the soft white flesh of her shoulders. Her head went further back, her eyes closed, one hand came up to my shoulder.

"You're beautiful as all hell!" I shouted crazily into her face, and flung her against the door.

It seemed an hour that I fumbled with starter and gears before I had the car back in the road and thundering toward the San Mateo County jail. The girl had straightened herself up in the seat again, and sat huddled within the robe I had given her. I squinted straight ahead into the wind that tore at my hair and face, and the absence of the windshield took my thoughts back to Porky Grout.

Porky Grout, whose yellowness was notorious from Seattle to San Diego, standing rigidly in the path of a charging metal monster, with an inadequate pistol in each hand. She had done that to Porky Grout—this woman beside me! She had done that to Porky Grout, and he hadn't even been human! A slimy reptile whose highest thought had been a skinful of dope had gone grimly to death that she might get away—she—this woman whose shoulders I had gripped, whose mouth had been close under mine!

I let the car out another notch, holding the road somehow.

We went through a town: a scurrying of pedestrians for safety, surprised faces staring at us, street lights glistening on the moisture the wind had whipped from my eyes. I passed blindly by the road I wanted, circled back to it, and we were out in the country again.

### XIX

At the foot of a long, shallow hill I applied the brakes and we snapped to motionlessness.

I thrust my face close to the girl's.

"Furthermore, you are a liar!" I knew I was shouting foolishly, but I was powerless to lower my voice. "Pangburn never put Axford's name on that check. He never knew anything about it. You got in with him because you knew his brother-in-law was a millionaire. You pumped him, finding out everything he knew about his brother-in-law's account at the Golden Gate Trust. You stole Pangburn's bank book—it wasn't in his room when I searched it—and deposited the forged Axford check to his credit, knowing that under those circumstances the check wouldn't be questioned. The next day you took Pangburn into the bank, saying you were going to make a deposit. You took him in because with him standing beside you the check to which *his* signature had been forged wouldn't be questioned. You knew that, being a gentleman, he'd take pains not to see what you were depositing.

"Then you framed the Baltimore trip. He told the truth to me—the truth so far as he knew it. Then you met him Sunday night—maybe accidentally, maybe not. Anyway, you took him down to Joplin's, giving him some wild yarn that he would swallow and that would persuade him to stay there for a few days. That wasn't hard, since he didn't know anything about either of the twenty-thousand-dollar checks. You and your pal Kilcourse knew that if Pangburn disappeared nobody would ever know that he hadn't forged the Axford check, and nobody would ever suspect that the second

check was phoney. You'd have killed him quietly, but when Porky tipped you off that I was on my way down you had to move quick—so you shot him down. That's the truth of it!" I yelled.

All this while she had watched me with wide grey eyes that were calm and tender, but now they clouded a little and a pucker of pain drew her brows together.

I yanked my head away and got the car in motion.

Just before we swept into Redwood City one of her hands came up to my forearm, rested there for a second, patted the arm twice, and withdrew.

I didn't look at her, nor, I think, did she look at me, while she was being booked. She gave her name as Jeanne Delano, and refused to make any statement until she had seen an attorney. It all took a very few minutes.

As she was being led away, she stopped and asked if she might speak privately with me.

We went together to a far corner of the room.

She put her mouth close to my ear so that her breath was warm again on my cheek, as it had been in the car, and whispered the vilest epithet of which the English language is capable.

Then she walked out to her cell.

\* \* \*

### The Gutting of Couffignal
*The Black Mask,* December 1925

"You said a little while ago that you didn't care who I was," she began immediately. "But I want you to know. There are so many of us Russians who once were somebodies and who now are nobodies that I won't bore you with the repetition of a tale the world has grown tired of hearing. But you must remember that this weary tale is real to us who are its subjects. However, we fled from Russia with what we could carry of our property, which fortunately was enough to keep us in bearable comfort for a few years.

"In London we opened a Russian restaurant, but London was suddenly full of Russian restaurants, and ours became, instead of a means of livelihood, a source of loss. We tried teaching music and languages, and so on. In short, we hit on all the means of earning our living that other Russian exiles hit upon, and so always found ourselves in overcrowded, and thus unprofitable, fields. But what else did we know—could we do?

"I promised not to bore you. Well, always our capital shrank, and always the day approached on which we should be shabby and hungry, the day when we should become familiar to readers of your Sunday papers—charwomen who had been princesses, dukes who now were butlers. There was no place for us in the world. Outcasts easily become outlaws. Why not? Could it be said that we owed the world any fealty? Had not the world sat idly by and seen us despoiled of place and property and country?

"We planned it before we had heard of Couffignal. We could find a small settlement of the wealthy, sufficiently isolated, and, after establishing ourselves there, we would plunder it. Couffignal, when we found it, seemed to be the ideal place. We leased this house for six months, having just enough capital remaining to do that and to live properly here while our plans matured. Here we spent four months establishing ourselves, collecting our arms and our explosives, mapping our offensive, waiting for a favorable night. Last night seemed to be that night, and we had provided, we thought, against every eventuality. But we had not, of course, provided against your presence and your genius. They were simply others of the unforeseen misfortunes to which we seem eternally condemned."

She stopped, and fell to studying me with mournful large eyes that made me feel like fidgeting.

"It's no good calling me a genius," I objected. "The truth is you people botched your job from beginning to end. Your general would get a big laugh out of a man without military training who tried to lead an army. But here are you people with absolutely no criminal experience trying to swing a trick that needed the highest sort of criminal skill. Look at how you all played around with me! Amateur stuff! A professional crook with any intelligence would have either let me alone or knocked me off. No wonder you flopped! As for the rest of it—your troubles—I can't do anything about them."

"Why?" very softly. "Why can't you?"

"Why should I?" I made it blunt.

"No one else knows what you know." She bent forward to put a white hand on my knee. "There is wealth in that cellar beneath the garage. You may have whatever you ask."

I shook my head.

"You aren't a fool!" she protested. "You know—"

"Let me straighten this out for you," I interrupted. "We'll disregard whatever honesty I happen to have, sense of loyalty to employers, and so on. You might doubt them, so we'll throw them out. Now I'm a detective because I happen to like the work. It pays me a fair salary, but I could find other jobs that would pay more. Even a hundred dollars more a month would be twelve hundred a year. Say twenty-five or thirty thousand dollars in the years between now and my sixtieth birthday.

"Now I pass up that twenty-five or thirty thousand of honest gain because I like being a detective, like

the work. And liking work makes you want to do it as well as you can. Otherwise there'd be no sense to it. That's the fix I am in. I don't know anything else, don't enjoy anything else, don't want to know or enjoy anything else. You can't weigh that against any sum of money. Money is good stuff. I haven't anything against it. But in the past eighteen years I've been getting my fun out of chasing crooks and tackling puzzles, my satisfaction out of catching crooks and solving riddles. It's the only kind of sport I know anything about, and I can't imagine a pleasanter future than twenty-some years more of it. I'm not going to blow that up!"

She shook her head slowly, lowering it, so that now her dark eyes looked up at me under the thin arcs of her brows.

"You speak only of money," she said. "I said you may have whatever you ask."

That was out. I don't know where these women get their ideas.

"You're still all twisted up," I said brusquely, standing now and adjusting my borrowed crutch. "You think I'm a man and you're a woman. That's wrong. I'm a manhunter and you're something that has been running in front of me. There's nothing human about it. You might just as well expect a hound to play tiddly-winks with the fox he's caught. We're wasting time anyway. I've been thinking the police or Marines might come up here and save me a walk. You've been waiting for your mob to come back and grab me. I could have told you they were being arrested when I left them."

That shook her. She had stood up. Now she fell back a step, putting a hand behind her for steadiness, on her chair. An exclamation I didn't understand popped out of her mouth. Russian, I thought, but the next moment I knew it had been Italian.

* * *

*The Maltese Falcon,* pp. 260–265

Spade laughed. His yellow-white face was damp with sweat and though he held his smile he could not hold softness in his voice. He croaked: "Don't be silly. You're taking the fall. One of us has got to take it, after the talking those birds will do. They'd hang me sure. You're likely to get a better break. Well?"

"But—but, Sam, you can't! Not after what we've been to each other. You can't—"

"Like hell I can't."

She took a long trembling breath. "You've been playing with me? Only pretending you cared—to trap me like this? You didn't—care at all? You didn't—don't—l-love me?"

"I think I do," Spade said. "What of it?" The muscles holding his smile in place stood out like wales. "I'm not Thursby. I'm not Jacobi. I won't play the sap for you."

"That is not just," she cried. Tears came to her eyes. "It's unfair. It's contemptible of you. You know it was not that. You can't say that."

"Like hell I can't," Spade said. "You came into my bed to stop me asking questions. You led me out yesterday for Gutman with that phoney call for help. Last night you came here with them and waited outside for me and came in with me. You were in my arms when the trap was sprung–I couldn't have gone for a gun if I'd had one on me and couldn't have made a fight of it if I had wanted to. And if they didn't take you away with them it was only because Gutman's got too much sense to trust you except for short stretches when he has to and because he thought I'd play the sap for you and–not wanting to hurt you–wouldn't be able to hurt him."

Brigid O'Shaughnessy blinked her tears away. She took a step towards him and stood looking him in the eyes, straight and proud. "You called me a liar," she said. "Now you are lying. You're lying if you say you don't know down in your heart that, in spite of anything I've done, I love you."

Spade made a short abrupt bow. His eyes were becoming bloodshot, but there was no other change in his damp and yellowish fixedly smiling face. "Maybe I do," he said. "What of it? I should trust you? You who arranged that nice little trick for–for my predecessor, Thursby? You who knocked off Miles, a man you had nothing against, in cold blood, just like swatting a fly, for the sake of double-crossing Thursby? You who double-crossed Gutman, Cairo, Thursby–one, two, three? You who've never played square with me for half an hour at a stretch since I've known you? I should trust you? No, no, darling. I wouldn't do it even if I could. Why should I?"

Her eyes were steady under his and her hushed voice was steady when she replied: "Why should you? If you've been playing with me, if you do not love me, there is no answer to that. If you did, no answer would be needed."

Blood streaked Spade's eyeballs now and his long-held smile had become a frightful grimace. He cleared his throat huskily and said: "Making speeches is no damned good now." He put a hand on her shoulder. The hand shook and jerked. "I don't care who loves who. I'm not going to play the sap for you. I won't walk in Thursby's and Christ knows who else's footsteps. You killed Miles and you're going over for it. I could have helped you by letting the others go and standing off the police the best way I could. It's too late for that now. I can't help you now. And I wouldn't if I could."

She put a hand on his hand on her shoulder. "Don't help me then," she whispered, "but don't hurt me. Let me go away now."

"No," he said. "I'm sunk if I haven't got you to hand over to the police when they come. That's the only thing that can keep me from going down with the others."

"You won't do that for me?"

"I won't play the sap for you."

"Don't say that, please." She took his hand from her shoulder and held it to her face. "Why must you do this to me, Sam? Surely Mr. Archer wasn't as much to you as–"

"Miles," Spade said hoarsely, "was a son of a bitch. I found that out the first week we were in business together and I meant to kick him out as soon as the year was up. You didn't do me a damned bit of harm by killing him."

"Then what?"

Spade pulled his hand out of hers. He no longer either smiled or grimaced. His wet yellow face was set hard and deeply lined. His eyes burned madly. He said: "Listen. This isn't a damned bit of good. You'll never understand me, but I'll try once more and then we'll give it up. Listen. When a man's partner is killed he's supposed to do something about it. It doesn't make any difference what you thought of him. He was your partner and you're supposed to do something about it. Then it happens we were in the detective business. Well, when one of your organization get's killed it's bad business to let the killer get away with it. It's bad all around–bad for that one organization, bad for every detective everywhere. Third, I'm a detective and expecting me to run criminals down and then let them go free is like asking a dog to catch a rabbit and let it go. It can be done, all right, and sometimes it is done, but it's not the natural thing. The only way I could have let you go was by letting Gutman and Cairo and the kid go. That's–"

"You're not serious," she said. "You don't expect me to think that these things you're saying are sufficient reason for sending me to the–"

"Wait till I'm through and then you can talk. Fourth, no matter what I wanted to do now it would be absolutely impossible for me to let you go without having myself dragged to the gallows with the others. Next, I've no reason in God's world to think I can trust you and if I did this and got away with it you'd have something on me that you could use whenever you happened to want to. That's five of them. The sixth would be that, since I've also got something on you, I couldn't be sure you wouldn't decide to shoot a hole in *me* some day. Seventh, I don't even like the idea of thinking that there might be one chance in a hundred that you'd played me for a sucker. And eighth–but that's enough. All those on one side. Maybe some of them are unimportant. I won't argue about that. But look at the number of them. Now on the other side we've got what? All we've got is the fact that maybe you love me and maybe I love you."

"You know," she whispered, "whether you do or not."

"I don't. It's easy enough to be nuts about you." He looked hungrily from her hair to her feet and up to her eyes again. "But I don't know what that amounts to. Does anybody ever? But suppose I do? What of it? Maybe next month I won't. I've been through it before—when it lasted that long. Then what? Then I'll think I played the sap. And if I did it and got sent over then I'd be sure I was the sap. Well, if I send you over I'll be sorry as hell–I'll have some rotten nights–but that'll pass. Listen." He took her by the shoulders and bent her back, leaning over her. "If that doesn't mean anything to you forget it and we'll make it this: I won't because all of me wants to–wants to say to hell with the consequences and do it–and because–God damn you–you've counted on that with me the same as you counted on that with the others." He took his hands from her shoulders and let them fall to his sides.

She put her hands up to his cheeks and drew his face down again. "Look at me," she said, "and tell me the truth. Would you have done this to me if the falcon had been real and you had been paid your money?"

"What difference does that make now? Don't be too sure I'm as crooked as I'm supposed to be. That kind of reputation might be good business–bringing in high-priced jobs and making it easier to deal with the enemy."

She looked at him, saying nothing.

He moved his shoulders a little and said: "Well, a lot of money would have been at least one more item on the other side of the scales."

She put her face up his face. Her mouth was slightly open with lips a little thrust out. She whispered: "If you loved me you'd need nothing more on that side."

Spade set the edges of his teeth together and said through them: "I won't play the sap for you."

She put her mouth to his, slowly, her arms around him, and came into his arms. She was in his arms when the door-bell rang.

Spade, left arm around Brigid O'Shaughnessy, opened the corridor-door. Lieutenant Dundy, Detective-sergeant Tom Polhaus, and two other detectives were there.

Spade said: "Hello, Tom. Get them?"

Polhaus said: "Got them."

"Swell. Come in. Here's another one for you." Spade pressed the girl forward.

The Hunter-Dulin Building, 111 Sutter Street in San Francisco, where Spade's office was located. Built in 1926, the building was regarded as one of the finest in the financial district, an indication that Spade was a successful and prosperous detective (San Francisco Historical Photograph Collection, San Francisco Public Library).

## Sam Spade's San Francisco

*Novelist Joe Gores is among the best-informed sources on Hammett's San Francisco and, in particular,* The Maltese Falcon. *A detective turned novelist, Gores wrote* Hammett *as an homage to the modern father of realistic detective fiction. For the* City of San Francisco *magazine devoted to Hammett and edited by David Fechheimer, another detective with fine literary sensibilities, Gores wrote an article about the San Francisco setting of Hammett's fiction. The excerpt included here provides a reliable guide to the real places and the real models for the fictionalized settings in* The Maltese Falcon.

### A Foggy Night
Joe Gores
*City of San Francisco,* 9 (4 November 1975): 29–30

Sam Spade
    Probably no book has frustrated more San Franciscans than *The Maltese Falcon.* Its evocation of place is so strong that on a foggy night half the literate population of the city unconsciously expects to see Sydney

Greenstreet scuttling down a mist-swept sidestreet with a football-shaped bundle under one arm. But because Hammett liked to play name games, the novel frustrates hell out of anyone trying to retrace Spade's footprints through the city.

We hear him telling the fat man, for instance, "Maybe you could have got along without me if you'd kept clear of me. You can't now. Not in San Francisco," but we don't know where he says it. Hammett made up the Alexandria Hotel. He made up the St. Mark. He made up the Coronet where Brigid O'Shaughnessy poked the fire while making up lies to tell Spade. Even such basics as Spade's home and office addresses are hotly argued by aficionados.

If we take the three significant references to the location of Spade's apartment in *The Maltese Falcon* (none appear in the three Spade short stories) together with a fact from Hammett's own life, we can pinpoint not only the street, but the apartment house.

*Spade . . . crossed (Geary) street to board a westbound street-car . . . (he) left the car at Hyde Street and went up to his apartment . . .*

Does this suggest that Spade's apartment was on Geary Street near Hyde—an interpretation which seduced Fritz Leiber in his excellent "Stalking Sam Spade" (*California Living*, January 13, 1974)? If so, the "up" would obviously refer to going up to an apartment by either stair or elevator, as Leiber points out. But a second reference makes such an assumption suspect:

*He went out again, walked up to Sutter Street, and boarded a westbound car . . .*

Whoops. Why, if Spade lives on Geary Street with its own westbound streetcars, does he climb two arduous blocks up Hyde Street to catch a westbound Sutter car? Nobody has ever suggested that Spade loved to run up and down hills for the hell of it.

This would make that "up" in the first reference to going *up Hyde Street* toward his apartment. This might suggest that Spade lived on Hyde, except for the third reference, which shows that he lived on the street which lies *between* Geary and Sutter. This is when Spade volunteers to go outside and check, for a terrified Brigid, whether Wilmer Cook still has the apartment house under surveillance. I quote in full.

*Post Street was empty when Spade issued into it. He walked east a block, crossed the street, walked west two blocks on the other side, recrossed it, and returned to his building without having seen anyone except two mechanics working on a car in a garage.*

Lobby of the St. Francis Hotel on Union Square, the apparent model for the St. Mark, where Archer began shadowing O'Shaughnessy and Floyd Thursby the night of Archer's murder. The St. Mark combines the name of the San Francisco landmark hotel, the St. Francis, with that of the luxurious, newly built (in 1928) Mark Hopkins. The geography of the novel indicates that the St. Francis was Hammett's model (San Francisco Historical Photograph Collection, San Francisco Public Library).

Unequivocal. *Post Street* was empty when Spade issued into it. Post Street.

Is there any way to pinpoint the *exact* address? Yes. The *1928 Crocker-Langly San Francisco City Directory* lists Dashiell Hammett as residing at 891 Post St. This address, 891, is on the southeast corner of the Post-Hyde intersection. Since *The Maltese Falcon* existed in rough draft early in 1928 (correspondence between Hammett and his publisher establishes this), and since Hammett was living at 891 Post at the time, what more natural than to use his current apartment for Sam Spade's?

Spade's office address can be isolated in the same way, by a close textual analysis of the novel taken along with logical inferences from the San Francisco geography of the day.

*Spade walked up Sutter Street to Kearny (from his office) . . .*

This pins Spade's office into either the two blocks of Sutter between Market (where it starts) and Kearny, or

> *"Maybe you could have got along without me. You can't now. Not in San Francisco."*
>
> –Spade to Gutman

Hammett's apartment building at 891 Post Street; his apartment was in the upper right corner (Mary Spoerer, from Don Herron, The Dashiell Hammett Tour)

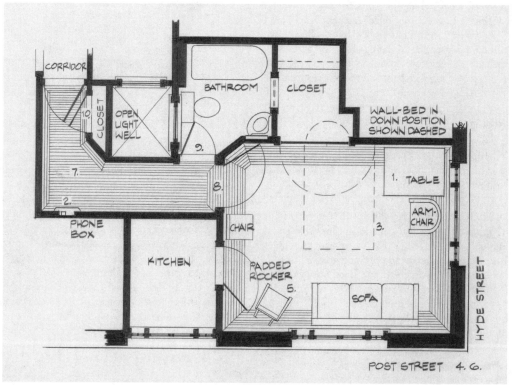

Architect's drawing of Hammett's apartment, the model for Spade's apartment in The Maltese Falcon
(courtesy of William Arney)

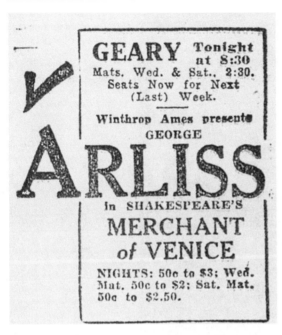

*Advertisement from* The San Francisco Call, *5 December 1928. Arliss played Shylock. Joel Cairo goes to see the play on Thursday night after visiting Spade's office (Collection of Richard Layman).*

*The Geary Theatre, at Mason and Geary near Union Square in San Francisco. Spade encounters Cairo in the lobby in chapter 6 of* The Maltese Falcon *(San Francisco Historical Photograph Collection, San Francisco Public Library).*

*The States Restaurant, 1937. Originally opened in 1927, the restaurant where Spade and Tom Polhaus have lunch in chapter XV changed its name to States Hof-Brau House late in 1928 and then reverted to its original name by 1931. The States, on Market Street at Fourth Street, is across from the Flood Building (upper right in this photo), where Hammett's office was when he worked for Pinkerton's and a block from Albert Samuels Jewelers, 895 Market, where Hammett worked in the mid 1920s (San Francisco Historical Photograph Collection, San Francisco Public Library).*

*Main entrance to the Sir Francis Drake Hotel at Sutter and Powell Streets, identified by Joe Gores as the likely model for Gutman's hotel. The luxurious hotel was built in 1928 (San Francisco Historical Photograph Collection San Francisco Public Library).*

to the only possible cross-streets, Sansome or Montgomery. And the next reference confirms Sutter as the street:

> *In the doorway of Spade's office-building he came face to face with the boy he had left at Gutman's. The boy put himself in Spade's path, blocking the entrance, and said: "Come on. He wants to see you." . . . They walked up Sutter Street side by side.*

From the office vestibule they start right up Sutter. No reference is made to turning into Sutter from either Sansome or Montgomery. And the next reference strongly suggests that it is in the 100-block of Sutter (bounded by Montgomery and Kearny) when we consider the fact that the Hotel Sutter is in this block, at Kearny Street.

> *Spade went into the Hotel Sutter and telephoned the Alexandria. Gutman was not in . . . Spade telephoned the Belvedere. Cairo was not in . . . Spade went to his office.*

Inescapable implication: that his office is near the Hotel Sutter. Logical conclusion: that it is in the same block. When we put our implication and our conclusion together with the next reference, which places the office building on a corner, we are very close to having it.

> *(Spade) went down to the night-lit street. An undersized youth . . . was standing idly on the corner below Spade's building.*

If any building had stood between Spade's and the corner, Hammett would have said so. But if we have reduced it to a corner building in the 100-block of Sutter, and not on the corner of Kearny because that's where the Hotel Sutter is, then it must be on the corner of Sutter and Montgomery. But is it the northwest or the southwest corner? A final reference settles that.

> *Carrying the parcel lightly under his arm, walking briskly . . . Spade went partly by way of an alley and a narrow court, from his office-building to Kearny and Post Streets, where he hailed a passing taxicab.*

Hammett is going *south* from Sutter to Post—and west from Montgomery to Kearny—by way of an alley and a narrow court. The only alley running south from Sutter to Post in this part of town is Lick Place. Obviously, since Spade is using the alley to get to Post Street because he fears the front of his building is under surveillance by Gutman's minions, his office cannot be on the north side of Sutter. He would have to cross Sutter openly to get to Lick Place.

*Two of a series of murals in the public rooms of the Sir Francis Drake Hotel illustrating passages from* The Arabian Nights. *The murals were painted under the direction of the Dutch artist Anthony B. Heinsbergen, who with his crew of 185 painters decorated more than 750 movie theaters and municipal buildings (San Francisco Historical Photograph Collection, San Francisco Public Library).*

But on the southwest corner of Sutter and Montgomery is the only building which lies between Montgomery and Lick Place: 111 Sutter. This is the building where Spade's office was located.

The next most frustrating address in *The Maltese Falcon* is the real location of Brigid O'Shaughnessy's fictional Coronet Apartments. Effie Perine tells Spade all—at first glance—it seems we shall ever know about it.

> "She's at the Coronet, on California Street, apartment one-thousand-and-one. You're to ask for Miss Leblanc."

No overt mention of a cross street—not here, and not anywhere else in the novel. Hammett gives his vital clues to the Coronet obliquely, but give them he does, and I am sure deliberately. The central directions are given when Spade wants to get to the Coronet without leading the murderous Wilmer there. He first boards a westbound Sutter car.

> Within half a dozen blocks of the Coronet, Spade left the car and went into the vestibule of a tall brown apartment-building. He pressed three bell-buttons together . . . and went down a long yellow-walled corridor (to) let himself out into a narrow court. The court led to a dark back street, up which Spade walked for two blocks. Then he crossed over to California Street and went to the Coronet.

Spade leaves the Sutter car "within half a dozen blocks of the Coronet" to enter an apartment house

137

Bar at the Palace Hotel, on Market Street at Montgomery. After his first meeting with Gutman, Spade eats lunch
at this hotel, at the beginning of chapter XII (San Francisco Historical
Photograph Collection, San Francisco Public Library).

Market Street, east from Powell. Samuels Jewelers is at 895 Market Street. At the corner in the upper left is the Pacific
Building, where the States Hof-Brau House was located. Spade and Polhaus have lunch there in chapter XV
(San Francisco Historical Photograph Collection, San Francisco Public Library).

which gives him access to an alley. Aha! Which alley might this be? We find immediately that there are only two alleys that could possibly fit: Hemlock, which parallels Sutter on the south for three blocks (from Larkin to Franklin); and Fern, which parallels it on the north for four blocks (between Larkin and Gough). Hemlock is obviously out, and for the same reason that the building on the northwest corner of Sutter and Montgomery was out for Spade's office. Spade would have to cross Sutter to get up to California. Too great a chance that Wilmer would spot him and pick up the trail again.

No, the apartment house Spade entered would have to be on the even-numbered, uphill side of Sutter. And since Fern runs for only four blocks altogether, and he walks west for two of those blocks before going north to California, the apartment house would have to be somewhere near either the Larkin or the Polk Street intersections.

And what do we find at 1114 Sutter, just one door away from Larkin Street? We find a tall brown apartment building with a suitable vestibule and a back door which opens on a court which once led to Fern alley, although now blocked by a building put in since World War II.

In 1928, the brown building at 1114 Sutter was known as the Yerba Buena Apartments. And in three of its ten apartments were women living alone (Dor-

*Civic Center Plaza and City Hall, 1920s, where Spade would have gone for his meeting with District Attorney Bryan in chapter XV (San Francisco Historical Photograph Collection, San Francisco Public Library)*

*Ferry Building at the foot of Market Street, 1927. In chapter XVI Spade learns that O'Shaughnessy had a cab take her there instead of to Effie Perrine's house. La Paloma was in dock behind the building (San Francisco Historical Photograph Collection, San Francisco Public Library).*

*View toward Market Street from the Cathedral Apartments on California Street, where O'Shaughnessy takes
her last apartment (San Francisco Historical Photograph Collection, San Francisco Public Library)*

othy MacFadden, Miss Ada Fray, and Viola Hawke) whose apartments Wilmer might well have ransacked in his search for Brigid. Spade tells her:

> *"That's where I shook him. That's why all three were women who lived alone. He tried the apartment that had women's names in the vestible-register, hunting for you under an alias."*

Spade, having shaken Wilmer, goes up to California Street and thence to the Coronet. This accounts for three of the six blocks between him and the Coronet that were referred to when he left the streetcar. If we assume he left the car at Larkin, three blocks west on California would put us at California and Franklin. In 1928, however, there were no likely apartment houses near this intersection, and it is very far from the tightly centered action of the novel.

But what if the devious Spade had ridden the streetcar *beyond* the Coronet, intending to backtrack? This is what I, and any other detective I know, would have done. But three blocks *east* on California from Larkin takes us to California and Jones. A

much more likely area for Brigid to take an apartment. And what do we find at California and Jones? At 1201 California, to be exact? The Cathedral Apartments. A big, fancy, imposing building in Hammett's day. And an apartment house which figures *by name* in the action of the original *Thin Man* fragment to be found elsewhere in this issue.

The Cathedral Apartments was the Coronet.

Hammett also plays games with the three hotels which figure prominently in the action of *The Maltese Falcon*. The Belvedere, where Joel Cairo stayed. The St. Mark, from which Miles Archer shadowed Brigid and Floyd Thursby to his death. And the Alexandria, where Casper Gutman doped Spade's drink. All three hotels are bogus.

Bogus, but discoverable. The Belvedere is almost surely the Bellevue. Cairo had tickets to an evening performance at the Geary Theater. The Geary was—and is—at 450 Geary, between Mason and Taylor. The Bellevue is in the next block, just beyond Taylor, at 505 Geary. What more probably than that Cairo, seeking entertainment, should get tickets for a theater half a block away?

*The intersection of Market, Stockton, and Ellis Streets, 1930s. John's Grill, where Spade eats chops in chapter XVII and where he has a car meet him for the ride to Burlingame, is just around the corner on Ellis Street, to the right of Roos Bros. (San Francisco Historical Photograph Collection, San Francisco Public Library).*

The St. Mark is obviously either the Mark Hopkins or the St. Francis. Both hotels are on Powell, one at the foot of Nob Hill, the other at the crest. How to choose? A fact outside the book gives us a first strong clue.

The Mark Hopkins was not opened to the public until December 4, 1926. Work on *The Maltese Falcon* was begun less than a year later. Yet in the novel the St. Mark is obviously a San Francisco landmark of long standing. In 1927–28 the St. Francis was; the Mark Hopkins had not yet become one.

Pinpointing the Alexandria is much messier, since the only two suggestions concerning the hotel's location are mutually contradictory.

*They walked up Sutter Street side by side . . . They went into the Alexandria, rode up to the twelfth floor . . .*

This tells us it is in Sutter Street. But the second reference suggests a quite different location:

*Spade rode down from Gutman's room in an elevator . . . He walked down Geary Street to the Palace Hotel, where he ate luncheon.*

The Palace (today the Sheraton-Palace, still at Market and New Montgomery) is real enough, at any rate; but what of the Alexandria? Is it in Sutter Street or Geary Street? Our facts are few and not too suggestive, but they will have to suffice. It is within easy walking distance of Spade's office. It is a first-class (on a par with the St. Mark) hotel. It is at least twelve stories high.

Still a toss-up. It would have to be either the Sir Francis Drake (Sutter and Powell) or the Clift (Geary and Taylor). My own preference is for the Drake, for a couple of reasons. The Clift, ten minutes by taxi from Spade's office, is not really within walking-distance— not easy walking distance. And would Cairo, with his fear of the fat man, really stay in a hotel which is directly across the street from Gutman's? I think not.

141

*The Pickwick Stage Terminal, where Spade checks the falcon at the parcel room in chapter XVII*
*(San Francisco Historical Photograph Collection, San Francisco Public Library)*

Restaurants Factual

If Hammett was remarkably inventive with his hotels in *The Maltese Falcon,* he was remarkably honest with his restaurants–beginning with the Palace Hotel Grill. When Spade meets Cairo at the Geary Theater, Wilmer is loitering "with other loiterers before Marguard's restaurant below." Marguard's, at Geary and Mason, in those days billed itself as "A Restaurant for Epicures." The States Hof Brau (in the Pacific Building at 821 Market) was obviously not for epicures, but good enough for Spade and Tom Polhause to share pickled pigs feet at one of big John's tables. The building survives; the States doesn't. Neither does Herbert's Grill (151 Powell St.) where Spade also breaks his fast.

Spade's hire-car driver picks him up at " *John's,* Ellis Street," which is then specified as *John's Grill,* today as then at 63 Ellis and proudly aware of its place in the legend of the jewel-encrusted falcon. Spade's menu at John's was chops, a baked potato, and sliced tomatoes.

Remedial Loan (where, Spade suggests, Brigid should hock her jewelry) is still at 932 Mission (Mission and Mint Alley), but the Pickwick Stage Terminal (for that read Bus Depot) around the corner in Fifth Street is no more. It survived for a decade or two as the Trailways Depot, but when that moved to the East Bay Terminal a few years ago, all trace of the check-room where Spade stashed the falcon disappeared. The terminal was between Jessie and Market; the name survives in the Pickwick Hotel, across the alley at 85 Fifth St.

Of course the most famous location in Sam Spade's San Francisco is the dead-end alley where Miles Archer met his unlamented end, Burritt Street, atop the Stockton tunnel. Just across Bush is 20 Monroe St., where Hammett lived during at least part of 1924. A brass plaque today marks the spot of Archer's demise, and two buildings added to the left (east) side of Burritt since 1928 would today prevent Archer's body from rolling down the dirt slope toward Stockton Street below (even if the dirt slope still existed). The billboard flanking Stockton today is part of an apartment house (the McAlpin). *Sic transit gloria mundi.*

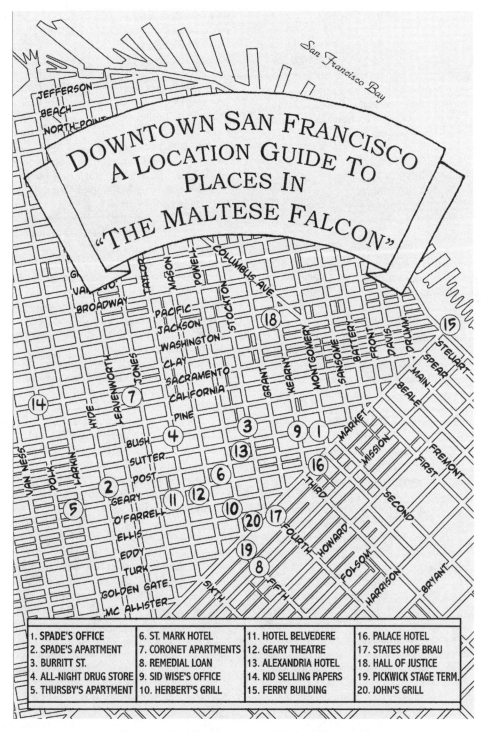

*Map prepared by Mike Humbert and published with his permission*

## History and the Falcon

*In "The Emperor's Gift," chapter XIII of* The Maltese Falcon, *Gutman tells Spade the history of the elusive statuette. The story of the falcon provides the central metaphor of the novel. Hammett paid careful attention to historical fact, although he took occasional license. The following history of the Templars provides background missing from Gutman's account and substantiates Gutman's claim that the templars promised to give Charles V of Spain a falcon each year as a symbol of their fealty to him.*

### In Palestine, Cyprus and Rhodes
Joseph Attard
*The Knights of Malta* (Malta: Publishers
   Enterprise Group, 1992), pp. 1–8

The land of Palestine where Jesus Christ had lived, died and arose from death, had never ceased to be considered as the Holy Land. For centuries after, it had become the pious practice for men and women from Europe and the West to make pilgrimages to the Lord's Sepulchre and the other Holy Places. Even when Jerusalem first fell into Moslem hands in the seventh century notwithstanding what difficulties were then arising, mostly because of sentiments of individual rulers, such pilgrimages continued to be allowed. Charles the Great, or better known as Charlemagne, who was one of the foremost Holy Roman Emperors, was able to open hospices in Jerusalem for the accommodation of such pilgrims. But with the approach of the eleventh century and the advent of new Moslem rulers the position changed. There began the harassing and ill-treatment of pilgrims, which was climaxed by the Fatimite Caliph Hakim, a fanatical and demented tyrant who in 1009 razed the Holy Sepulchre to the ground, and destroyed all Christian property.

Thirty years after Hakim's death, a number of charitable merchants from Amalfi (in Italy) managed to have hospices and the church of the Holy Sepulchre rebuilt. But even so, this did not remove the difficulties that continued to be encountered by pilgrims and christians in Palestine. It was a situation which raised much ferment in Europe, and instigated by the fiery sermons of an English preacher Peter the Hermit, and Pope Urbanus II, many of Europe's adventurous princes were enticed to embark on a Crusade in the way of a campaign to regain the Holy Places in Palestine from the Saracens. The first Crusade which materialised in 1096 came to grief, but there was another army to step into the breach and continue the fight

in 1097. This time the Crusade was successful and two years later Jerusalem fell to the Christians.

This successful turn of events encouraged the Amalfitan congregation by now engaged as hospitallers in a Benedictine hospital dedicated to St John the Baptist in Jerusalem to rally round their leader Brother Gerard de Saxo. He was a Patrician of Scala and a Benedictine, who was now all out to convert and expand the congregation into an Order of St John of Jerusalem. Grateful lords and princes who had been healed of their wounds in the hospital were soon bestowing portions of their estates on the newly founded Order enabling it not only to stand on its feet but also to establish its future 'Commanderies' and daughter homes in various places of Europe. In 1113 it was the turn of Pope Paschal II to take the Order under his protection and give Brother Gerard a new and more militant constitution in gratitude for services rendered. The original document concerning this important point in the history of the Order can still be found in the Malta Library. It reads that "Pope Paschal II grants to his venerable son, Gerard, founder and provost of the Hospital in Jerusalem, a charter of incorporation of the Order of the Hospital of St John of Jerusalem beyond or on this side of the sea, that is to say, in Asia or in Europe". Thus placing it as an exempt Order of the Church under the protection of the Apostolic See.

With the resumption of fighting with the Saracens some of the Knights of the Order had to become soldiers, and with new readily found recruits to the cause there was formed the element of Knights of the Temple or Templars. Even this Order soon gained much power and importance since its member knights were required to do the actual fighting with the Moslem infidels. The many remarkable forts and castles built by the Knight Templars in the course of their fighting years still crown strategic heights in Palestine, Syria and Jordan.

Nonetheless, another Crusade in 1147 was a complete failure, and it was only in 1180 that enough elements could be rallied for another. When this set forth it included amongst the leaders King Richard I of England who was largely responsible for what successes were obtained, and was soon being known as *Coeur de Lion*, the Lionheart. However, more than the lassitude that was now creeping in, the Order was plagued by quarrels between the leaders. The element of chivalry which had become the epitome of the Crusades began to be tarnished, and it was not long when King Richard was left to fight his battles alone. It was by his implacable certainty and singleness of purpose, as well as by his overwhelming energy

*Grotesque of a falcon on the outside wall of the palace of Charles V, in the Alhambra, Granada.*
*The palace was begun in 1533 and never completed (photograph by Tom Conelly).*

and self-sacrifice that he managed to win the battle for Acre. But that was the end, for he realised soon after that that alone as he was, his had become a lost cause. So he left Palestine and his departure might have marked the end of the Crusades.

With the movement of the Knight Templars to Cyprus in 1191 it befell to the rest of the Knights who had until then been more of a nursing brotherhood to take up arms when required to defend pilgrims whilst on their way to the Holy Land. This further emphasised a military role to the Order, now under its second head, and the first to be styled Master, Fra Raymond du Puy, which continued to grow in strength, influence and possessions. It was now that the Order acquired the additional character of an Order of Knighthood, with its member Knights being bound by the three monastic vows of Chastity, Obedience and Poverty. Even so, with their next spurt of activity in 1291, the Moslems occupied the last Christian strongholds, and the Order's position in Palestine became untenable, so it moved to Cyprus. This was only a Hobson's choice since the island did not pro-

vide the right environment for the scheme of reorganisation and perfection there was intended for the Order. Moreover, there was the unpleasant realisation that since their transfer to Cyprus one hundred years before, the Templars had succumbed to the temptations of power and were believed to have been drawn towards Freemasonry and other secret intrigues which certainly clashed with the ideals of the Order. And this brought even stronger pressure on the Knights to find a new home.

It took them nineteen years to do this, and in 1308 they found the ideal home in the Byzantine island of Rhodes thus acquiring also territorial sovereignty. A year after the Knights of St John had moved there, i.e. in 1309, the Templars had sunk so deep in their intrigues that their institution had to be suppressed. Five years later in 1314, their last Grand Master, Jacques de Molay, was to be burned at the stake in Paris. The Hospitaller Knights inherited a good part of their property. But there was the more important fact that the Order of St John was left with a clear field in which to attract

145

---

**Gutman Begins**

The fat man screwed up his eyes and asked: "What do you know, sir, about the Order of the Hospital of St. John of Jerusalem, later called the Knights of Rhodes and other things?"

Spade waved his cigar. "Not much—only what I remember from history in school—Crusaders or something."

*—The Maltese Falcon,* p. 148

---

the noble youth of Europe's aristocracy, and to go ahead with the reorganisation it badly needed and wanted to carry out.

Besides being one of the most beautiful islands in the Mediterranean, Rhodes was very fertile and fruitful. Another important factor was its geological structure which provided ample strong rock and sites for the Knights to build the fortifications they needed. With this point settled, the Grand Master at the time, Foulkes de Villaret who was one of the best, could carry on with the reorganisation so that the Order could evolve its characteristic form based on the same old vows of Chastity, Obedience and Poverty.

The Knights were divided into five groups. There were first the Military Knights of Justice who in a sense dominated the Order. These were all to be of noble birth from both parents for at least four generations, and in fact it can be said that all Military Knights were the sons of the greatest families in Europe. All requests to join the Order began to be carefully scrutinized, and no exceptions were made. Applicants that were accepted were conferred with the accolade of Knighthood with some pomp. Accompanied by the Grand Cross who would have just dubbed them, they would walk bareheaded in the armour and robes worn at the investiture. Their comrades would receive them in the hall of the Auberge, where they would be made to sit on a carpet laid on the ground, and be offered bread, salt and a glass of water. The Knight presiding at the ceremony however, would later on that day give a banquet to the new Knights and his friends, as if to make up for the sense of austerity conveyed by the ceremonial. The new aspirant Knights had then to undergo a novitiate of one year before they could join the Convent (as the central body of the Order was called) for military service, and with each year of such duty being termed a "caravan". Then after three such "caravans" a Knight would have to reside for at least two years in the Convent. After completing duties with the Order, Knights would be free to return to their home in Europe, but they would always be subject to recall by the Grand Master in case of need. Promotions to the

higher posts of Bailiff, Commander or Prior could be made from this group.

The second group in the Order was reserved for ecclesiastical service as Chaplains or Chaplains of Obedience. The encumbents who would have holy orders were normally to work in hospitals or conventual churches, but were still not exempted from duties in Caravans. They were eligible for promotion to Priors and even Bishops of the Order. The third group was made up of Serving Brothers who were only required to be respectable and not necessarily of noble birth. These were required to do military service. The fourth and fifth groups then were made up of Honorary Knights in the grades of Magisterial Knights and Knights of Grace as nominated by the Grand Master.

There was a further division made on the basis of nationality with the Knights being placed under one of eight Langues (Tongues). These were those of Aragon, Auverne, Castile, England (with Scotland and Ireland), France, Germany, Italy and Provence. Having three French langues was not incidental since the French had a numerical preponderance in the Order.

The command was vested in a Grand Master who was elected by his brother Knights on the basis of years of efficient services in the major positions. The Grand Master was also the President of the Supreme Council (Sacro Consiglio) which included also the Bishop, Priors, Conventual Bailiffs, Knights Grand Cross and Deans of the Langues. As for what one could call general administration procedures, there was the Chapter General to be normally convened every five years, sometimes even after ten. However, meetings were announced a year ahead so as to give chance to the various Langues and individual Knights to submit drafts for reforms. The symbol of the Order continued to be the eight pointed cross introduced by Grand Master Raymond du Puy, representing the Eight Beatitudes, with the four arms being also symbolical of the four virtues—Prudence, Temperance, Fortitude and Justice. The vows taken by the Knights were proof of the religious character of the Order. Newly proposed members embraced and kissed each other in token of friendship, peace and brotherly love. Hence they called each other *frater*.

With the taking of Rhodes from the Byzantines and the eventual ruling of the island, there commenced the recognition of the distinct Sovereignty of the Order. Thus all Christian Powers and Catholic nations began to look at the Order in its full descriptive title of the Sovereign Military Order of St John of Jerusalem. With its Grand Master also styled Prince of Rhodes it continued to grow into a more powerful and wealthy body of celibate nobles vowed to carry out the tasks of tending the poor, healing the sick, and waging a perpetual war on Islam in the Mediterranean. This last vow could not perhaps be rigidly adhered to since with Rhodes being an island, the Knights could not very well pursue military action on land. Nonetheless they had still to provide and maintain their weapons which included a coat of mail and plate armour both for the Knight and his horse. Each had to have three horses (a battle-charger, palfrey or courser, and a pack-horse). They had also to have and pay attendants to carry their shields and their banner. However, they were soon building more galleys and other ships which made it possible for them to mount more attacks on enemy shipping crossing from and to nearby Turkey. Indeed it was not long when the Knights added seamanship to their other attributes even to the extent of being eventually considered to have become Christian corsairs.

Although the spirit of the Crusades had long been dead and Christian states were often on friendly terms with Moslem–Mongol conquerors, the Order never lost sight of the danger which still threatened Christendom and persisted with its vow to fight Islam with or without assistance of others. The earliest naval action on record by the Knights from Rhodes concerned the Grand Master himself, Foulques de Villaret, who had previously been one of the Order's admirals, now with a small force destroyed twenty three Turkish coasting vessels in 1312. He was soon being emulated by the Grand Commander Albert of Schwarzbourg who supported by Genoese corsairs led a mixed fleet of twenty-four galleys and defeated fifty Ottomans out of Ephesus. Hardly had a year passed by when the same Albert Schwarzbourg with eight vessels of the Order and six Genoese galleys routed a fleet of eighty Turks.

In the year 1334 there was the Alliance of Avignon whereby the King of France, Venice, the Papal Navy and the King of Cyprus rallied under the standard of the Order in an attempt to fan the embers of the Crusades. Between them in a naval battle they destroyed an Ottoman fleet in the Gulf of Smyrna in Turkey, and then proceeded to capture the town. It seems that the fourteenth century was characterised by every nation on the side of Christendom wanting to have a fling at the Moslems as long as there was the Order to lead them or contribute ships for the action. It is however, certain that the Order was always ready to oblige as if considering their sense of mission as being touched by divine approval, and with the meek arrogance of the religious it might have even viewed opposition to its will as akin to apostasy. In an unpublished manuscript of *A Knight of St John,* Averil Mackenzie-Grieve had this to say about those times, "The galleys of St John were famous throughout Europe. In them the Knights made the swift, dauntless attacks which recognised no possibility of defeat. Their exploits were published in broad sheets in Naples, in Marseilles and in Venice. They became almost mythical. But strong men were needed for the Galleys. These were overcrowded with slave oarsmen, fighting men, and crew, cumbered with arms and provisions, so that often it was impossible to lie down to sleep. There was neither shade from the blazing sun nor shelter from rain and sea-water. Swept by sudden storms the food would become sodden and useless, the men sick or fever struck. After a successful encounter, the galleys would be still more overcrowded with captives and booty." The Order's exploits of those times elicit admiration even to-day when considering its limitations in size and strength to confront the mighty Islam. One wonders how in 1347, the Prince of Catalonia Fra Arnaldo de Peres Tortes managed to burn a hundred Turkish craft at Imbros. Ten years later it was the turn of the combined fleets of the Order and Venice under Raymond Berenger to destroy thirty-five Moslem ships. In 1361 Ferlino D'Airasca, one of the Order's admirals at the head of his own squadron and helped by Christian corsairs captured Adalia (or Satalia) but his bigger exploit came in 1365 when with only sixteen galleys he sacked Alexandria.

Not all the Order's naval actions were strictly of a military nature. There were occasions when the Knights played their part of Christian corsairs as they had indeed been dubbed. Because there were many occasions when they attacked and boarded Moslem ships as they returned to their nests with the plunder of spices, silks, gold and jewels. The loot would go to their coffers, and the crews to be taken as slaves for their galleys. In 1393 and again in 1399 galleys of the Order penetrated into the Black Sea and attacked the hornets' nests of corsairs long established there. In the first instance they did not do too well since they lost Grand Master d'Heredia who with many of his surviving Knights fell into the hands of the enemy. But they made up in the second occasion. Such were the risks of the game they were playing.

It was however no game at all. Whatever types of sallies were being made by the Order's ships were doing a lot of damage to the shipping of Islam, even more damage to their credit, but most of all to their pride. Something had to be done, and indeed throughout the fifteenth century the tide of Islam rose steadily about Rhodes.

The beginning of this turn of events came at Castelrosso, an isolated post of the Knights which fell to the Mamelukes of Egypt in 1440. Nineteen of the enemy ships also invested Rhodes itself, but the Knights under Grand Master Lastic repulsed the attack and pursued the Muslims right to Anatolia where they went ashore to fight the enemy killing 700 of his men at the cost of sixty Knights. In 1444 then, there was a further attempt to invest Rhodes which was again repulsed by the Knights. At this stage however there was the risk of the Ottoman Turks under Mahomet Fatih the "Conquerer" with his decision and oath to launch a determined attack upon Christendom. He started by capturing Constantinople in 1453, then four years later he also captured the islands of Cos, Lemnos and Lesbos in the Dodecanese group.

These Moslem successes were certainly not a flash in the pan and the Knights realised how these could well be tactical moves to surround Rhodes by potential outposts from where their island and headquarters could be eventually attacked. In 1462 the Order's Chapter General met specifically to consider the situation. The outcome was that considering that Rhodes was by that time already well fortified, as indeed it was, and with such fortifications that can be seen even now, there had to be made an effort to place the fleet in the highest level of efficiency. Two years later there was something else to worry the Knights when the Pope of that time tried to raise a combined fleet against the Moslems. However, because of internal dissension amongst them, all the Christian states stayed back. It seemed to the Order that henceforth it would have to face Islam alone.

There was respite for a few years after Mahomet Fateh died in 1481 and his sons began fighting each other. The Order now under Grand Master d'Aubusson was during this time wise enough to increase the efficiency of its forces as it had decided to do. And as if to prove that it had succeeded there was its Admiral Ludovicus di Scalenghe to capture a number of Turkish ships in 1502. As if to allay what doubts and fears there must have remained then, five years later the Order achieved its biggest victory after a merciless battle with a combined Muslim fleet off Alexandretta. But the Knights could not have known this was to be their last victory, and the beginning of the end of their stay in Rhodes of more than two centuries.

Suleiman the Magnificent, great-grandson of Mahomet Fateh, now the powerful Sultan of the Ottomans had not for one moment forgotten the Order of St John. He had always admired its growing prowess, and since acceding to the throne he had cultivated further a sense of chivalrous respect for the Knights and their new Grand Master Philippe Villiers de l'Isle Adam. Nonetheless, these feelings were still outweighed by his determination to honour the oath of his forefathers and throw the Order out of Rhodes. He bided his time until he could rally every vessel, every man and every engine of war under the flag of Islam. Then he launched his attack on Rhodes in 1522.

Much as the Order's fleet was in a state of preparedness, it was hopelessly outnumbered. So rather than wasting his vessels, l'Isle Adam disembarked his Knights to strengthen his garrison on the island. But Suleiman persisted with his pressure and besieged the defenders of Rhodes. After six months of siege, and betrayal by one of their own, d'Amaral, the decimated and half-starved Knights were forced to capitulate on Christmas Eve of that same year. Their heroic stand fired even further Suleiman's admiration and Grand Master l'Isle Adam together with his remaining Knights were not only allowed to leave Rhodes unmolested, but were also given a ceremonial guard of honour to see them off the island in their own galleys.

The Order was defeated, but not dishonoured. It retained its high prestige, and although in a state of disorder, it was given the chance to recoup and fight another day. Its only immediate problem was again in finding a new home.

\* \* \*

## The Knights in Malta
*The Knights of Malta*, pp. 9–17

Emperor Charles V of Spain wore the crown of the Holy Roman Empire. He had however also brought under his rule the dynasties of Castile, Aragon and Burgandy, as well as the Austrian possessions of the House of Habsburg, the Netherlands, Luxembourg, Sardinia, Sicily, the greater part of Italy and Spanish conquests in North Africa and the New World. Now he allowed the Order of St John to use Sicily as a *pied à terre* until it could find a new home.

The Knights rallied to the banner of l'Isle Adam in his temporary Convent at Syracuse. With them they carried all they could take out of Rhodes, including the galleys many of which were the Knights' own individual private property. Both the Order and the individual owner Knights used to have their large vessels built in various European shipyards, and it so happened that on 1st January, 1523 when they evacuated Rhodes, there was launched at Nice the carrack *St Anne* which had been constructed for the Order. This was eventually to be consigned to the Knights at Syracuse and join the remnants of their fleet there. But it would not be amiss to say something more about this carrack since besides epoch making she had to play more important parts in the history of the Order.

Carracks were heavy ships used for the carrying of stores and troops as well as anything else that could not be carried in galleys or smaller boats. They were not as mobile as the lighter vessels, and of course not so swift. But then they were more heavily armed and this made them valuable as auxiliaries to any fleet. The *St Anne* was one hundred and thirty two feet long and forty feet in the beam. Her super-structure rose 75 feet above the waterline. She could carry four thousand tons of stores or merchandise, and had stowage for six months' victuals. Moreover, she had a blacksmith's, shop, a bakery, luxurious saloons and cabins, as well as a chapel. Her armament consisted of fifty long range guns and a number of falconets and demi-cannon while her armoury held personal weapons for five hundred men. She had a crew of 300, but could also carry an additional 400 light infantry or cavalry. However, the most important feature in the *St Anne* was that it was sheathed in metal and was cannon proof. She was therefore the first ever armoured war vessel to be built and adapted to resist the projectiles of her own time. The Order had three other carracks, the *Santa Caterina, San Giovanni* and the *Santa Maria* which was captured from the Moslems.

It immediately became obvious that the Knights could not all be accommodated at the Convent of Syracuse so some of them began to be given other temporary homes. In the course of time there were such homes established in Candia, Messina, Civita Vecchia, Viterbo and also in nearby France at Villefranche and Nice. The periodical council meetings began to be held in Syracuse aboard the new carrack *St Anne*. It was to be expected that the subject most frequently discussed at such meetings would be the finding of a new home for the Order. But Grand Master l'Isle Adam was not in agreement. Rather than looking for a new place, he prefered to seek assistance to mount an attack and recapture Rhodes. It was with this aim in view that he set out from Syracuse to wander from one Court to another in Europe begging for help. Because of the preponderance of French Knights in the Order he went first to the King of France with his proposal, but Francis I was more concerned trying to obtain help from Suleiman against his enemy Emperor Charles V of Spain. Wherever l'Isle Adam went after this there was more or less always the same negative reply. It appeared as if however respected the Order might have been for its fighting prowess, it was no longer popular. This could have been because of the Knights' direct allegiance to the Pope and their vow to fight only the Infidel which therefore made them insusceptible and useless for national allegiances. The more so when at the time nationalism was becoming the dominant force in European affairs. One cannot of course rule out the possibility that because of its riches and influence the Order might have become suspect. On the other hand one cannot rule out the fear and apprehension that had crept amongst European nations of Suleiman the Magnificent who in the course of his Sultanate had not only conquered nations in the Persian Gulf and the shores of the Arabian Sea, but

had also reached Belgrade and Budapest in Europe with his armies and added them to his Ottoman Empire which was then at the peak of its glory.

It was only when l'Isle Adam went to King Henry VIII of England that he received a somewhat different reply. He didn't expect anything different from the others, and if anything he was prepared for the worst since the English monarch had by then already began his quarrelling with the Pope about his marital affairs, and was seeing the Order in England in a bad light. Yet he received l'Isle Adam with much respect at St James Palace and finished by giving him guns and armour to the value of 20,000 crowns. Much as these were appreciated they could be of very little help to the project. What the Grand Master wanted most was the support of galleys and troops. After the 19 guns given by the English monarch were taken to Malta via Syracuse by the Knight Sir John Sutton in January, 1530 they were eventually sent to be used in the defence of Tripoli. It was only recently that one of them was dug out from the bottom of Famagusta Harbour. It was identified by the badge of the Tudors it had on it, as well as the coat-of-arms of l'Isle Adam.

L'Isle Adam returned to Sicily a very disappointed man. He knew he would have to drop his plan for an attack on Rhodes, as he knew as well that spread out as they were and away from his watchful eyes the Knights were now going to be more susceptible to be touched by worldly aspirations and relax their monastic vows. There was also the question of idleness which could easily turn their formation into decay. This led him to the conclusion that unless a new home was found soon, the Order would very likely disintegrate.

His worries and disappointment also affected his Knights, as they also somehow reached Emperor Charles V who after the years the Order had been in Sicily without any sign of leaving made him also uneasy. Then someone prevailed on him to give Malta and her sister island of Gozo to the Order. The Emperor was inclined to agree. After all he knew those islands were mere barren rocks without vegetation and with scanty soil and water, and he had never made any use of them. But being the person he was he wanted something in return. He did not have money in mind, but something that would take off some heavy burden from his shoulders. Malta had already been a regular target for raids by corsairs which made her more of a useless possession. But what was causing him a bigger headache was Tripoli and he was very much stretched to maintain this dependency as a Christian enclave lost as it was amongst the Barbary States of North Africa. Why not hand it to the Knights to defend, and this as a condition to the transfer of Malta? The idea appealed to him and the offer was made to the Order.

L'Isle Adam was not taken in by the offer. He immediately realised where the snag was. But he could not

*Grand Master Philippe Villiers de l'Isle Adam being handed the keys to the ancient capital city Mdina in 1530, thus taking formal possession of Malta (from Joseph Attard,* The Knights of Malta; *Collection of Richard Layman)*

## Philippe Villiers de l'Isle-Adam

At the time of the cession of our islands to the Order of St John of Jerusalem, the grand master was Philippe Villiers de l'Isle-Adam, a Frenchman and perhaps the most remarkable head the Hospitallers ever had.

He reached Malta from Syracuse with his knights on the morning of 26 October 1530 and soon set his residence and the seat of the Convent at Birgu. On 13 November he proceeded a solemn procession to Mdina where he was met at its gate by the jurats and, after renewing his oath 'to observe and command the observance of all the privileges and all the graces granted to the island by the Invincible Kings of Aragon and Sicily', he received the keys of the city from the *capitaneo,* Paolo de Nassis, thus, putting him in possession of the island.

His first care was to fortify Birgu which he enclosed within a wall, flanked by a small bastion to secure it against any assault. He also built a palace which continued to be the residence of his successors until the time of La Valette.

He also set up a sound administration. He divided the island of Malta into two cantons: one comprising the city of Notabile and the parishes of Naxxar, Birkirkara, Siggiewi, and Żebbuġ, which he placed under the administration of the *Capitano della Verga;* and the other, including Birgu, the parishes of Żejtun, Żurrieq, Qormi, Gudja, and the adjoining districts, which were placed under the civil jurisdiction of a magistrate chosen by the grand master. The creation of this new official, who shared the administration of the island with the captain of the city, was the first assault upon the rights of the people. He, then, appropriated himself of the custom duties which the *universitas* had been authorized to impose by the king of Sicily and increased them.

The *universitas* of Malta and Gozo deeply resented this usurpation of their rights and privileges, and made remonstrances before the Council of the Order. But their complaints served no purpose. On 5 September 1533 l'Isle-Adam promulgated a body of laws which chiefly dealt with criminal matters under the title Statues and Ordinances.

He died at Rabat on 22 August 1534, and was buried in the chapel of Fort St Angelo.

—Pawlu Mizzi,
*The Grand Masters of Malta,* p. 5

refuse the offer outright. Time was running fast and even his stay in Sicily was only being tolerated at the pleasure of the Emperor. The least he could do was to ask for time until he could have a report made out about Malta. But when he received this from a commission he had quickly sent to the island, he was even more perturbed.

The island of Malta, the report said, was a rock of soft sandstone about seven leagues long and three or four wide. Its surface was barely covered with three or four feet of earth, mostly stoney and unfit for cultivation. Where this was possible the Maltese grew cotton and cumin which they exchanged for grain, as they also cultivated some fruit. With the exception of a few springs there was no running water, and the 12,000 inhabitants of Malta, and another 5,000 in the sister island of Gozo were largely poor farmers living in primitive villages. There was only one town which was the capital. In the way of defence then there were only two castles where the inhabitants took shelter during raids by corsairs. It was a dismal picture that was given, which only brightened a little when the report mentioned that the island of Malta had two spacious harbours capable of housing many galleys.

With the Order having become a powerful maritime power harbours would be useful and l'Isle Adam couldn't do without them anywhere he might have gone since the Order's coffers had always been filled to necessity by clean piracy. This needed ships, and these in turn needed harbours. And that was the only positive point that he registered in his deliberations. Nonetheless, under normal circumstances l'Isle Adam would not have accepted the Emperor's gift, but at the same time there were other things pressing on his tired mind. One and which was not the least amongst them was that some of the Knights, tired of waiting were already leaving the Convent to return to their by now impoverished Commanderies in Europe, and this might have flashed the first sign of the disintegration of the Order he feared. Indeed the situation had become one where beggars could not be the choosers. So l'Isle Adam accepted the offer.

The document in the form of a rescript by Charles V, still preserved in the National Malta Library, was despatched to l'Isle Adam, "bestowing on the Knights in order that they may perform in peace the duties of their Religion for the benefit of the Christian community and employ their forces and arms against the perfidious enemies of Holy Faith—the islands of Malta, Gozo and Comino in return for the yearly presentation, on All Saints Day, of a falcon to Charles, Viceroy of Sicily." And this was all conditioned, although not specifically mentioned, by the left-hand gift of Tripoli.

When the Maltese learned of this they were justifiably indignant as it was known how in 1428 King Alfonso V of Aragon had confirmed their ancient privileges and paid 30,000 gold florins which was the sum for which the

impecunious monarch had pawned the islands to Don Gonsalvo Monroy, and how on that day he had sworn on the four Gospels that they (the Maltese Islands) would never be transferred to another sovereignty. Ironically enough this Magna Carta of Maltese liberties is also still to this day preserved at the National Malta Library quite close to the other document by Charles V already mentioned. However the least the Maltese could do was to send an embassy of protest to the Viceroy of Sicily. But when the Maltese envoys arrived there, the galleys of the Order of St John were already in Syracuse, and Grand Master l'Isle Adam had already been invested with the sovereignty of Malta through his representative, the Bailiff of Monasca.

On the 26th October 1530, Grand Master l'Isle Adam and his Knights sailed into Grand Harbour at Malta, on the carrack *St Anne* to take possession of their new home.

It is a fact that the majority of the people of Malta at that time had gone through hard times. Their life had been one of continuous routine of backbreaking toil to make a living, with only the occasional interruption by attacks of the Moslem corsairs who would always take slaves. And in truth these people were past caring who would rule their country. But there was also the minority which included many noble families who had grown up as freemen and were quick to assume that the coming of the Knights could mean the loss of their political rights. So they began immediately to view them with

---

### The Tribute

"[The knights] persuaded the Emperor Charles V to give them"—Gutman held up three puffy fingers and counted them—"Malta, Gozo, and Tripoli."

"Yes?"

"Yes, sir, but with these conditions: they were to pay the Emperor each year the tribute of one"—he held up a finger—"falcon in acknowledgment that Malta was still under Spain, and if they ever left the island it was to revert to Spain. Understand? He was giving it to them, but not unless they used it, and they couldn't give or sell it to anybody else."

"Yes."

The fat man looked over his shoulders at the three closed doors, hunched his chair a few inches nearer Spade's, and reduced his voice to a husky whisper: "Have you any conception of the extreme, the immeasurable, wealth of the Order at that time?"

"If I remember," Spade said, "they were pretty well fixed."

—*The Maltese Falcon*, pp. 148–149

---

suspicion. It could have also been that such Maltese attitude was also sparked by what had been described by a Maltese historian as the haughty bearing of the Knights on arrival at Malta. It must be mentioned as well that rather than as one would have expected the Knights to arrive covered with the laurels of their many fine achievements, the word was soon going round of how many of them had by then lost their celibate and religious vows and were also inclined towards Freemasonry as had happened in the case of the Templars. This assumption or misconception particularly shocked the members of the clergy who in their own way were already apprehensive of new rulers who were under the immediate protection of the Holy See as were the Knights.

Besides their personal arms and belongings the Knights did not take much with them to Malta. They certainly took their sacred icon containing one of the hands of St John the Baptist, a silver processional cross (still to be seen at the Cathedral of Mdina) and some ecclesiastic vestments and treasures. The most important thing which they could not afford to leave behind, and which they carried with them was the set of their archives, which to-day is still preserved in Malta. This makes it obvious that it was their idea to start from scratch. And so they did.

For over 400 years the Maltese had regulated their internal affairs by means of an autonomous Commune also called *Università* made up of four executive members styled *Giurati* (Jurats) presided over by an official called the Captain of the Rod (della Verga). He was so called because of the rod or staff of office which was always carried behind him by a page, but was also known by the Arabic title of *Hakem*. Although elective and aristocratic this office was practically hereditary in the family of the Navas, Governors of Fort St Angelo. This body of men or parliament, as it could be called, ensured Maltese liberties, and the least the Maltese were hoping for was that these arrangements would not be stopped or changed.

Grand Master l'Isle Adam took formal possession of Malta at Mdina, a medieval town which was the island's capital.

The investure ceremonial was observed with all the pomp and formalities in which the important elements of Maltese society also participated. But the climax was reached when l'Isle Adam proceeded to the gate of the city beneath a baldachin borne by the Giurati, and then swore upon the great cross of the Cathedral and the cross of the Order of St John to observe the privileges and usages of the island as granted by the King of Aragon and Sicily. After this the Captain of the Rod knelt to kiss his hand and sur-

render the silver keys. It was then that the gate of the city was opened to allow the Grand Master to enter amidst salutes and the ringing of bells.

Mdina was then Malta's only town. Its name being the Arabic meaning for a walled town. But in 1428 after the Maltese had complained to their ruler King Alfonso V of Aragon and Sicily against the pawning of the island to his nobles when he was short of cash, the King had accepted their complaint and confirmed their ancient privileges. On that occasion he had referred to Mdina as "a notable and distinguished jewel of the royal crown." And the Maltese then began to refer to the town in official documents as Notabile. Although it remained Mdina in common parlance.

One would have expected the Knights to make this which was the only town in Malta their headquarters. But instead, they preferred to establish themselves in Birgu, a small village just in the entrance of what is now Grand Harbour, and lying in the shadow of Fort St Angelo. They probably made this choice because of their seafaring service, and at Birgu they could have their galleys at hand for whatever contingency that could crop up. But even so, the village of Birgu lacked the necessary amenities and accommodation to house them, which apparently did not affect them and they began immediately to attend to these needs. In the narrow streets of the village they began to build their Auberges, one for each Langue. Where more convenient, they leased premises for this purpose, as they had done in Rhodes. They also set forth to construct bastions to surround the place and fortify it against any eventual attack. Birgu was already endowed with a magnificent church dedicated to St Lawrence which was first erected in 1090 at the time of Count Roger the Norman and embellished throughout the years. The Knights now turned it into their Conventual Church.

L'Isle Adam, also conscious of the need of defensive fortifications began work to enlarge the defences of Fort St Angelo. This stronghold which dominated Grand Harbour as it still does now, had served its purpose during the times of Carthaginians, Romans, Byzantines, Normans, Angevines and Aragonese. It seems that the Grand Master could then perceive its eventual important use for the Order, and he started by establishing himself in the fort. He found a ready house there, built about a century before for the De Nava family then governors of St Angelo. These had also built a chapel at the same time dedicated to the "Mother of God". The Grand Master now enlarged this and rededicated it to St Anne. There was also work started on the walls of the town of Mdina with the same intentions of defence, and this was retained as the capital of the island.

It was a good beginning, no doubt watched and commented upon by the many islanders who were still not sure how the Order would fare in Malta. But after some time there was the expected beginning of a thaw and change. The first Order's coinage was struck with the principal coins being the scudo, the tari, the carlino and the grano or grain. With none knowing how these denominations were to persist in Malta's coinage five centuries later. But what might have helped to bring the Knights and Maltese closer was the Candlemas ceremony that was introduced. On this annual occasion, falling on 2nd February when the Church celebrates the Feast of the Purification of the Blessed Virgin, the Parish Priests of Malta and Gozo began to be asked to meet the Grand Master, and offer him a decorated wax candle. He would then address the assembly on the problems of the day, stressing the ways and means of how state and Church could cooperate for the benefit of the people. This function was to survive right to these very days. The construction works embarked upon created work for the Maltese, while each Langue now began to bring in its men-at-arms, serving brothers, clerics, artificers, sea-captains, seamen and military engineers. These newcomers to the island scene mingled with the people with the obvious results which introduced a new way of life to the islanders.

L'Isle Adam should have been happy since the transfer of the Order to Malta seemed to have been clicking successfully. But he wasn't. It seems that notwithstanding the faultless changeover he had still not effaced the memories of Rhodes and might have still been hoping he would one day recapture his former home. Had this been the case then his hopes might have been strengthened when his galleys had the first opportunity to strike at the Moslems from Malta, and took it. Five galleys of the Order under Admiral Bernardo Salviati, with two other Genoese vessels swooped on a Turkish fleet at Modon and destroyed it. Then they also sacked the city and returned to Malta with the loot and 800 Turkish slaves. Soon after, Salviati joined the great Genoese Admiral Andrea Doria in an attack on Coron.

These two naval actions should have lifted the spirits of l'Isle Adam since they signified the revival of the prowess of the Order which was so essential for its future in Malta. This might have appeared to be the case when he began to refurbish his quarters in Fort St Angelo, but what interest the old Grand Master tried to show was only skin deep, because by now he was having troubles of a different nature.

Following his debacle with the Pope, King Henry VIII of England had in 1532 declared himself Supreme Head of an English Church and began to raise difficulties to the further existence of the English branch of the Order. This was immediately reflected in Malta by the number of young nobles who began to be sent by the Grand Prior in England to join the Order in Malta. Members of the Tongue of England had to have been born within the territorial limits assigned to their Priories and Commanderies in England, Ireland and Scotland, as they had also to be of noble birth. It seems however that some of the first English arrivals in Malta at this time could not readily produce documented proof of this. L'Isle Adam gave them the benefit of the doubt and conditioned their joining the Order to the procurement of documented proof of their nobility within six months. As for aspirants and newcomers however the General Assembly or Chapter of the Knights enforced the immediate production of such proof. Also laying down that those failing to produce it, would be sent back, with all travelling expenses having to be paid by the Grand Prior himself.

However what harassed l'Isle Adam most was the insubordination of some of the younger Knights who not yet being schooled in the strict observance of the Order's rules were inclined to be out of hand. Some of them might have also exceeded in their follies of libertinism. And this seems to be confirmed by the addition of a disciplinary clause which the Chapter of the Order added to its statute. The clause read that "whosoever shall enter into the house of a citizen without being invited, and against the wish of the head of the family, or shall disturb the social gathering of the people during their festivals, dances, weddings or similar occasions, shall lose two years seniority without hope of pardon. Moreover, whosoever shall by day or night damage the doors and windows of the people, shall in addition suffer such rigid imprisonment as may be decreed by the Grand Master and Council." It had by now become difficult if not impossible to prevent duels amongst the hot-headed youths, especially the young novices, keenly alive to an affront, and ever ready to resent it. They regarded personal courage as the first of all human virtues.

There might have been some reprieve when besides aspirants for the Order there began to arrive in Malta fully fledged lords and Knights like Sir Nicholas Upton, Sir Philip Babington, Sir Henry Gerard, Sir Dunstan Newdgate, Sir David Gausson, Sir Nicholas Lambert and Sir Anthony Russell, just to mention a few. These brought colour and

## A Pirate's Booty

"All right, sir. Grand Master Villiers de l'Isle d'Adam had this foot-high jeweled bird made by Turkish slaves in the castle of St. Angelo and sent it to Charles, who was in Spain. He sent it in a galley commanded by a French knight named Cormier or Corvere, a member of the Order." His voice dropped to a whisper again. "It never reached Spain." He smiled with compressed lips and asked: "You know of Barbarossa, Redbeard, Khair-ed-Din? No? A famous admiral of buccaneers sailing out of Algiers then. Well, sir, he took the Knights' galley and he took the bird. The bird went to Algiers. That's a fact. That's a fact that the French historian Pierre Dan put in one of his letters from Algiers. He wrote that the bird had been there for more than a hundred years, until it was carried away by Sir Francis Verney, the English adventurer who was the Algerian buccaneers for a while. Maybe it wasn't, but Pierre Dan believed it was, and that's good enough for me.

"There's nothing said about the bird in Lady Frances Verney's *Memoirs of the Verney Family during the Seventeenth Century*, to be sure. I looked. And it's pretty certain that Sir Francis didn't have the bird when he died in a Messina hospital in 1615. He was stony broke."

—*The Maltese Falcon*, pp. 150–151

---

*In his recitation of the falcon's history, Gutman cites an impressive list of references to support his account. Among them is Lady Frances Verney's* Memoirs of the Verney Family During the Civil War. *The pertinent passage is reprinted below.*

**The Half Brothers, Sir Francis and Sir Edmund Verney**
Lady Frances Verney
*Memoirs of the Verney Family During the Civil War,*
    (London: Longmans, Green, 1892), volume 1,
    pp. 60–70

'A little more than kin, and less than kind.'—*Hamlet.*

The change in manners and modes of thought is very great when once we have buried the last Tudor and entered on the reigns of the Stuarts. We are almost beginning upon the spirit of modern politics, and the habits of modern life. The reign of James I. is still, however, a period of transition. Penetrated as he was with the old despotic spirit of gov-

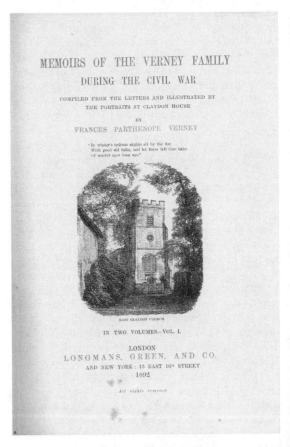

*Title page for the first volume of Lady Frances Verney's four-volume history of her family referred to by Gutman in chapter XIII of* The Maltese Falcon *(Collection of Richard Layman)*

---

strength to the Order, but they also brought more of the inevitable sense of pique in the English Langue.

Even with their lineage and high sense of snobbery such Knights were often causing trouble. It is recorded in the Order's archives how on 13th March 1534 Knights Oswald Massingberd and James Hussey came to blows with Knights William Tyrrel and Nicholas Upton. The Grand Master and Council placed all four of them under house arrest until their case could be investigated. When it transpired that Massingberd had indeed conspired against the life of the Grand Master he was first imprisoned in Gozo and then condemned to the loss of the habit. But when he came to be stripped in front of the Assembly of Knights gathered at the Conventual Church of St Lawrence in Birgu, Massingberd asked for mercy, and his sentence was changed to the forfeiture of the Commandery he held, and two years' loss of seniority.

This kind of behaviour of the Knights affected l'Isle Adam considerably, and the frail and tired Grand Master died on 21st August 1534.

\* \* \*

## Knights and Corsairs

For the first thirty years that the Knights were in Malta they inevitably found themselves in constant conflict with the corsairs of the Barbary coast, that whole area ranging from modern Libya, to Algiers and the strait of Gibraltar. The main founders of these groups of states, or semistates, were two remarkable brothers, Kheir-ed-Din and Aruj, 'Barbarossa' (or 'Red Beard' as they were known to the Christians). Although ardent Moslems, both brothers were the sons of a Christian Greek woman married to a Janissary who had been settled on the island of Lesbos by the Sultan as a reward for his service in its capture. It is unlikely that either of the brothers had any Turkish blood in their veins.

Operating principally out of Tunis they had made themselves the terror of the central Mediterranean shipping routes, and had often come into conflict with the ships and men of the Spanish monarch. The elder brother Aruj died quite early in 1518 in an action against the Spaniards in the neighbourhood of Oran. He was immediately succeeded as leader of the North African Moslems by his brother Kheir-ed-Din (Protector of the Faith), who was to prove himself as able politically as he was a commander at sea or ashore. Kheir-ed-Din, to whom the sobriquet of 'Barbarossa' was to be exclusively applied by Europeans, was an enemy of all Christians—and a worthy enemy at that.

So famous had Barbarossa become as a naval leader that he was summoned to Constantinople by the Sultan shortly after his brother's death, and was appointed High Admiral of the Turkish fleet by Suleiman himself. It was he who set in train the prodigious ship-building expansion of the Ottomans and he who, by introducing into the ranks of the Sultan's sea-captains a number of men of his own calibre, raised it to the point when it was, to all intents and purposes, the most efficient navy in the whole Mediterranean. Barbarossa soon secured Tunis and its surrounding area for the Sultan, and it was against this former pirate that the forces of the Spanish emperor were constantly engaged in warfare over the next decades.

Some idea of the conditions in the Mediterranean during the years when Barbarossa was supreme in North Africa, and the Knights were busy establishing themselves in Malta, can be gained from the account of Abbot Diego de Haedo in his *History of Algiers* (1612). Although written at a much later date, it was based on the Abbot's own experience of Algiers, and of his acquaintance with a number of Moslems who had known Kheir-ed-Din Barbarossa when they were young. The Mediterranean, it becomes immediately clear, had become a completely lawless sea, where no Christian ship or coastal town was safe—the Sea of the Corsairs. Over the centuries to come, the Order of St. John was to be constantly engaged in sweeping the sea-lanes and in doing their best to eradicate the menace of these pirates.

While the Christians with their galleys are at repose, [the Abbot writes] sounding their trumpets in the harbours, and very much at their ease regaling themselves, passing the day and night in banqueting, cards, and dice, the Corsairs at pleasure are traversing the east and west seas, without the least fear or apprehension, as free and absolute sovereigns thereof. Nay, they roam them up and down no otherwise than do such as go in chase of hares for their diversion. They here snap up a ship laden with gold and silver from India, and then gain another richly fraught from Flanders; now they make prize of a vessel from England, then of another from Portugal. Here they board and lead away one from Venice, then one from Sicily, and a little further on they swoop down upon others from Naples, Livorno, or Genoa, all of them abundantly crammed with great and wonderful riches. And at other times carrying with them as guides renegadoes (of which there are in Algiers vast numbers of all Christian nations, nay, the generality of the Corsairs are not other than renegadoes, and all of them exceedingly well acquainted with the coasts of Christendom, and even with the land), they very deliberately, even at noon-day, or just when they please, leap ashore, and walk on without the least dread, and advance into the country, ten, twelve, or fifteen leagues or more; and the poor Christians, thinking themselves secure, are surprised unawares; many towns, villages and farms sacked; and infinite numbers of souls, men, women, children, and infants at the breast dragged away into a wretched captivity. With these miserable ruined people, loaded with their own valuable substance, they retreat leisurely, with eyes full of laughter and content, to their vessels. In this manner, as is too well known, they have utterly ruined and destroyed Sardinia, Corsica, Sicily, Calabria, the neighbourhoods of Naples, Rome and Genoa, all the Balearic Islands, and the whole coast of Spain: in which last they feast it as they think fit, on account of the Moriscos who inhabit there; who being all more zealous Mohammedans than are the very Moors born in Barbary, they receive and caress the Corsairs, and give them notice of whatever they desire to be informed of. Insomuch that before these Corsairs have been absent from their abodes much longer than perhaps twenty or thirty days, they return home rich, with their vessels crowded with captives, and ready to sink with wealth; in one instant, and with scarce any trouble, reaping all the fruits that the avaricious Mexican and greedy Peruvian have been digging from the bowels of the earth with such toil and sweat, and the thirsty merchant has for so long been scraping together, and has been so many thousand leagues to fetch away, either from the east or west, with inexpressible danger and fatigue. Thus they have crammed most of the houses, the magazines, and all the shops of this Den of Thieves with gold, silver, pearls, amber, spices, drugs, silks, cloths, velvets &c., whereby they have rendered this city [Algiers] the most opulent in the world: insomuch that the Turks call it, not without reason, their India, their Mexico, their Peru.

—Ernle Bradford, *The Shield and the Sword:*
*The Knights of St. John,* pp. 131–133

ernment by divine right, yet he was soon made to feel that high-handed acts, which had been submitted to under Henry VIII. and his daughter, would not be endured from the wavering, garrulous, clever pedant who had succeeded the strong-minded Elizabeth, grasping firmly whatever power she could keep, and yielding in a politic and graceful way whenever she saw that resistance was useless.

Sir Francis Verney, eldest son of Sir Edmund, was only sixteen when his father died; he had lost his mother when he was but five years old, and seems never to have been under any control either from affection or education. His wild life was short and unhappy: in 1604, when not above twenty, he was living in St. Dunstan's-in-the-East, in the neighbourhood of Alsatia (showing the haunts he preferred), when one of his servants was slain, apparently in a drunken brawl, such as often disturbed that very unsavoury region. He seems to have quarrelled with his stepmother at the earliest possible moment after he came of age: his brother was too young to have aggrieved him, but he petitioned Parliament to set aside the settlement made by his father of part of his estates on Edmund and of Lady Verney's jointure, which the Act of Elizabeth's reign had confirmed. A Bill for this object was brought in, and Sir Randal Crewe (afterwards Parliamentarian Chief Justice) pleaded before the House on behalf of Sir Edmund's widow. Several members who had sat on the Committee to which the former Bill had been referred, gave evidence that 'Sir Edmund Verney the elder did follow the Bill himself, and laboured divers friends in it, and the repeal would overthrow many purchasers, sixty at least.' After 'much dispute and argument' the Bill was rejected. Sir Francis had claimed as eldest son under a former settlement by his uncle Edmund, which had been annulled in the Elizabethan Act, and his claim had a certain appearance of equity. There was said to be some hardship at least in being deprived by his father of his rights during his minority. This was probably urged on his stepmother, for she resigned her dower house at Quainton to him in 1606. The rejection of his Bill had, however, stung the young man to desperation; the dissensions and heart-burnings with his family, the keen sense of what he thought injustice, and probably the debts with which he was overwhelmed, at last determined him to sell everything and 'forsake the friends who had injured him, and the country which had refused him redress.'

Quainton was sold first: it consisted of about 800 acres with the advowson, and brought only 500*l.* Fleet Marston, where his ancestors had lived, went next; Penley,

where his father died, followed, and the furniture was sold with it, as if to show that the break-up was final.

At this time Francis seems to have taken a journey to the Holy Land, for a letter exists from George Carew, English ambassador at Paris, 'to my very good Lord the Earle of Salisbury, principal Secretary of Estate at Court,' telling how 'the bearer hereof, Sir Francis Verney, hath entreated me to accompany him with my letter, in which I can do no less than gratifie him, for his readinesse and respective offices used to me his Majesty's minister, whereof your L^{ppe} may be pleased to take notice. Since his retourne hither from Jherusalem, he hath frequented at my house and other where (as I understand) the exercises of our religion [at that time no English Protestant worship was allowed except at the embassy], which hath the rather moved me to give him this commendation to your Lordshippe. And so with my humble duty I have the same to the good protection of the Almighty.'

Lord Fermanagh's notes observe 'that this Francis was a great traveller and fought severall Duellos.'

He certainly was in England for some time in the summer and autumn of 1608, when he disposed of his other estates and of everything saleable, gave a general irrevocable authority to his uncle, Urian Verney, to act for him in all business concerned with the wreck of his property, and assigned his title deeds to another uncle, Ralph, described as 'of High Holborn, gentleman,' and then disappeared from all knowledge of his friends. His wife is not mentioned at this period, but as she was the daughter of his stepmother, and he had been married to her when only a boy, she was probably mixed up in his mind with the rest of his 'enemies.'

There is no doubt that he left England, and rumour and tradition declare that he went to Algiers, where it is reported that he 'turned Turk,' but this part of the story perhaps may be understood politically, not religiously (or irreligiously). A war of succession was going on in Morocco between the three sons of the Emperor Muley Hamet, who had lately died. One of these, Muley Sidan, obtained the services of a body of Englishmen, who were highly paid and well treated. They were under the command of Captain John Giffard, a near relation of Lettice, wife of Urian Verney, and daughter of Sir George Giffard who held the lease of Claydon. He was 'a gentleman of a worthy spirit, of the auncient stemme of the Giffards,' on whom 'Sidan bestowed a rich sword and a scarlet cloake, richly embrodered with pearle, sent to his father by our late sovereigne of famous memorie, Queene Elizabeth.' On one occasion the Moors during a battle ran shamefully away, and Muley Sidan sent to Captain Giffard and the other Englishmen to save themselves. 'The English returned word that they came not thither to run, but rather die an honourable death. . . . Giffard being charged by eight Abdelians, one behinde him shot him throw and so

*Sir Francis Verney, whom Gutman believed once possessed the Maltese falcon (Frances Parthenope Verney, Memoirs of the Verney Family During the Civil War; Collection of Richard Layman)*

was he slaine. Few of al the English nation were left alive.' As Francis Verney is known to have gone to Barbary, he probably joined these desperadoes for a time. It was an age of somewhat lawless adventure both by sea and land; during the war with Spain the English cruisers were employed as privateers with commissions from the queen herself. Sir Walter Ralegh's exploits were often little better than piracy, and the adventures of Elizabeth's famous Devonshire captains hovered perilously near to buccaneering. When James I. ascended the throne and made peace with Spain these commissions were recalled, but in the eyes of the public 'to spoil the Spaniard' continued to be considered good service, and they were 'slow to condemn such gallant fellows.' If the French and Venetians suffered also, it was no great harm in their opinion. When the English

ports were closed to them, the pirates took refuge on the coast of Barbary. The great tide of European commerce passed up the Mediterranean almost within sight of Tunis and Algiers, and here piracy was a recognised institution. Every man who could procure means to fit out a ship and collect a crew could, under the protection of the Dey, put out to sea and lie in wait for the richly freighted merchantmen. The prisoners were kept in slavery of the most cruel and hopeless description, and but few lived to be released on ransom like Cervantes, or to escape by the help of their captor's family like St. Vincent de Paul. It is clear that Sir Francis was in command of one of these ships and was the terror of even English merchant vessels, for in 1609 Cottington, attached to the embassy in Spain, writes word that 'Verney had taken three or four Poole shipps and one of Plymouth.' Another of the Giffards was also captain of the 'Fortune,' a buccaneering vessel, and the proceeds of successful piracy were such that it is said 'no English nobleman kept such state as Captain John Ward, who is called their chief, with whom were associated Sir Francis Verney, Granvile, and others.' In vain did King James endeavour to put them down. In one year nineteen of the pirates, some of them persons of note, were executed at Wapping. In another year a pardon for life and goods was offered upon their promise to give up freebooting, but 'the greater number still adhered to their wild and desperate life.' Above twenty sail were at one time plundering the commerce of the Mediterranean, and in return, whenever a Barbary vessel was taken, the captive Moors and Turks were made slaves, and were to be found serving in most great houses in Spain. 'The multitude of them was very great,' says Cottington.

Of Sir Francis' exploits we know nothing further, and the chroniclers admit that the pirates did not all turn Turks, though they 'submitted themselves under the protection of the Turks or Barbarians, . . . exercising all manner of despites, and speaking of blasphemy against God, their king, and country.' Above all, their greatest crime was that 'they taught the infidels the use of navigation, to the great hurt of Europe.'

There is an extremely fine portrait of Sir Francis at Claydon, called a Velasquez, but of too early a date for this to be probable, as the painter was only born in 1599. It is the very beau ideal of a gallant gentleman of the time: his tawny silk Spanish jerkin and trunk hose slashed and lined with dull red, his large loose boots of yellow Cordovan leather and gilt spurs, his embroidered gauntlet gloves and the plume of many-coloured ostrich feathers in the hat that lies on the table beside him, are all in the best taste of the best fashion of the period. He is immensely tall, and carries his fine clothes with the grace and dignity of a thorough gentleman; his face is handsome, with a small pointed beard, and set in a little quilted ruff which is very becoming. In his hand is a gilt cane, the two ends painted black, the original of which has been preserved and now hangs under the picture. He looks older than the twenty-three years which was his age when he left England for ever, yet it is difficult to imagine how it can have been done in Spain at any later period, after his life as a pirate captain had fairly begun. The expression is full of spirit and intelligence, without a trace in it of the desperate, wild manner of man which he afterwards became; and it makes one the more regret the sad fate of one evidently born for better things in life than to command a crew of Algerine desperadoes.

His reckless career went on for three or four more years of which we have no notice, till in 'the most delectable and true discours of an admirid and painful peregrination by William Lithgow,' published in 1623, we come on him once again. 'Here in Missina [in 1615] I found the sometime great English gallant, Sir Francis Verney, lying sick in a Hospital, whom six weeks before I had met at Palermo, who after many misfortunes, exhausting his large patrimony, abandoning his country and turning Turk in Tunisis, was taken at sea by the Sicilian galleys, in one of which he was two years a slave, whence he was redeemed by an English Jesuit upon a promise of conversion to the Christian faith. When set at liberty he turned common soldier, and here in the extremest calamity of extream miseries entreated death. Whose dead corps I charitably interred in the best manner time would afford me strength.' The chief authority of the great Hospital of St. Mary of Pity, Don Peter Garsia, 'pater magni Xenodochei,' certifies only that Sir Francis Verney, 'Anglum,' came to hospital sick, and that they took him in. Also that on September 6, 1615, he died there. This certificate was obtained for his family in England by John Watchin, an English merchant, and with it he sent home a turban, two fine silk pelisses, two pair of slippers, the cane, and a curious pilgrim's staff inlaid with mother-of-pearl crosses, belonging to Sir Francis, all still preserved; the last 'seems to show that he did not commit the unnecessary and improbable offence of becoming a renegade,' and also shows that he was not quite in such 'extream' poverty as Lithgow represents when he performed his 'pious offices.' A sadder story cannot be imagined; that in his misery he should never have applied for help to any of his friends at home—neither to his wife, the uncles in whom he trusted, nor to the brother who was too young when they parted to have had any real quarrel with, and who was now old enough to assist him—shows how desperate he must have considered his condition in the eyes of his country, and was probably also due to the wayward pride which had ruined his fair career in England. 'There, victor of his health, of fortune, friends, and fame,' ended poor Francis, aged thirty-one years only.

His widow, Ursula, married about four years after the son of Sir W. Clark, 'without his father's privity. . . .

Though there be no great inequality between them, either for wealth or years (he being four or five and forty, and she two or three and thirty), yet the old knight is so much offended that he threatens to disinherit him, and hath vowed they shall never come within his doors.' Parental authority was severe at that period and exercised unsparingly.

Ursula, Lady Verney, re-married a third time to John Chichely, Esq., and her long life continued until 1670, when her great-nephew Edmund writes to his brother John at Aleppo that 'old Aunt Ursula is deceased,' aged eighty-three.

The career of Sir Edmund Verney, who was now the head of the family, was in every respect, save that of courage, the greatest possible contrast to that of poor Francis—a high-minded, conscientious, chivalrous man, a most affectionate father and husband, devoted to his duties, 'both public and private, both of peace and war,' to fit a man for which Milton sums up as the ideal of education. After his father's death he lived in Drury Lane with his mother, who had no home in the country for some time when she had given up her house at Quainton to Francis. 'Dame Mary' received the rents of Claydon and Muresley during her son's minority for the purposes of his education, which was provided in the form then considered most becoming for a young man intended for the army and the Court. 'After some time spent with my Lord Goring to see the armies in the wars in the Low Countries, and some sallies out with my Lord Herbert and Sir Henry Wotton to see the Courts of France and Italy, he goeth with my Lord of Bristol into Spain,' says old Lloyd. On his return in 1616, 'an accomplished gentleman,' he was taken into the household of Prince Henry as chief sewer, where his Uncle Francis was one of the falconers, and Mr. Bruce remarks that it was evidently an additional recommendation to the prince, that he found sympathy in Sir Edmund's religious principles, which inclined to simplicity in worship and to the reformed Protestantism not in favour at James's Court, and beginning to be called Puritanism. In January 1611, he was knighted when just of age, and in the same year he visited Madrid, where Lord Digby was then the ambassador, apparently on some public business. It must have been shortly after his return to England that Prince Henry gave him his picture, a three-quarters, which hangs at Claydon; it represents a handsome, gentle, and somewhat sickly young man, sitting in a chair of state with a sort of sceptre in his hand. He and his brother 'were under the pedagogy of Mr. T. Murray, and Prince Charles was so studious that Prince Henry took Archbishop Abbot's cap one day, and clapt it on his head, saying that if he followed his book well he would make him Archbishop of Canterbury,' a better fate for Charles, and for which he was more fitted, than to be king of England.

# Magazine and Book Publication

AGREEMENT made this twenty-ninth day of March 1918, between Dashiell Hammett whose post-office address is 891 Post Street, San Francisco, California party of the first part hereinafter also referred to as the "Author"; and ALFRED A. KNOPF, INC., of 730 Fifth Avenue, Borough of Manhattan, New York City, party of the second part, hereinafter also termed the "Publisher."

WITNESSETH: WHEREAS the parties hereto are mutually desirous respectively of having published and of publishing a certain literary work:

NOW, THEREFORE, in consideration of the premises and the promises hereinafter set forth, and for valuable considerations by each to the other passed, receipt whereof is by both of them acknowledged, the said parties do hereby agree to and with each other as follows:

FIRST: THE AUTHOR AGREES:

(a) to grant and hereby does grant to the Publisher the sole and exclusive right to publish the work now entitled RED HARVEST (Tentative) in book form, in the United States of America, and all other countries and also grants to the Publisher such further rights as are set forth in paragraph Fourth hereof:

(b) to make timely application for the renewal of the copyright to be secured for the said work as hereinafter provided within one year before the expiration of the copyright therein; and to execute any further or other papers which may be necessary to extend the term of this agreement (if then in existence) so that the same shall be coincident with the term of the copyright in said work and the renewal thereof:

(c) to deliver to the Publisher not later than the day of a completed and legible typewritten copy of the manuscript or a copy in the form of corrected proof sheets, together with materials from which illustrations can be prepared without redrawing, should illustrations mutually be deemed necessary; and if the same shall not be delivered within said time, then upon request of the Publisher, if made within twenty (20) days after default in said delivery, to terminate this agreement;

(d) to grant and he/she hereby does grant to the Publisher no right, if the copyright be in the Author's name, to bring in the name of the Author as plaintiff or complainant any action or proceeding for the enjoining of any infringement of the copyright in the said work and for any damages resulting therefrom; and if in the Author's name, to hold the said copyright during the existence of this agreement subject to the rights in this agreement granted to the Publisher;

(e) to read when submitted and within fourteen days of the receipt thereof to return to the Publisher the galley and page proofs of the said work; and in the event of the failure by the Author to return the said proofs within the period aforesaid, then the Publisher shall have the right to publish the said work as submitted to the Publisher; and the Author shall pay or permit to have charged against royalties the amount of the expense incurred by the Publisher because of changes and/or additions other than correction of printer's errors made in and to the text made by the Author, in excess of fifteen per cent (15%) of the original cost of composition, provided an itemized statement of these charges be promptly forwarded to the Author, and the corrected proofs be presented for the inspection of the Author at the office of Publisher, upon the former's request therefor;

(f) in part consideration of the publication of the aforesaid work, to and hereby does grant to the Publisher the option to publish the next two novels/works of a mysterious or detective story type of more than 60,000 words in length to be written and/or offered for publication by the Author, the said novels/works to be published on the same terms as in this agreement set forth with regard to the novel/work first hereinbefore referred to, except that the option shall not apply to the said two succeeding novels/works; and the royalty shall be fixed as hereinafter set-forth; and said option is conditioned upon its being exercised within thirty (30) days after the submission of the manuscript thereof, and upon the Publisher in good faith fulfilling the terms and conditions of this agreement to be performed on its part; the publication of the succeeding novels/works shall be had in the corresponding season of the years immediately succeeding that set for publication of the first herein mentioned novel/work; and finally the said option shall not apply to the latter of the said succeeding novel/work if the same be not exercised by the Publisher as to the first of them;

*Knopf file copy of Hammett's contract for his first three books:* Red Harvest, The Dain Curse, *and* The Maltese Falcon *(courtesy of Alfred A. Knopf)*

(g) to and he/she hereby does represent and guarantee to the Publisher that he/she is the sole author of the said work, that he/she is the owner of all of the rights in this agreement granted to the Publisher, that the said work contains no libelous and/or unlawful matter; and that it in no wise infringes upon the copyright or violates any other right of any person or party whatsoever; and agrees to hold harmless the Publisher against any claim, demand or recovery finally sustained in any suit which may be brought against the Publisher by reason of any violation of proprietary right or copyright, or because of any libelous or unlawful matter contained in the said work; and to act promptly with regard to and defend any claim or demand which may be made and/or action which may be brought, based upon any assertions or allegations of infringement, violation, libel or unlawfulness, provided the Publisher shall notify the Author of any claim, demand or suit within three (3) days after the Publisher receives notice thereof or service therein and give to the Author such reasonable time as the exigencies of the situation will permit in which to undertake such defense; and if default shall be made by the Author in the respects aforesaid, then the Publisher is hereby granted the right to make such defense as it may be advised by counsel, and the costs and counsel fees thereof together with any recovery shall as aforesaid be charged to and paid by the Author; and the aforesaid representations and guarantees shall apply to the said subsequent works.

SECOND: THE PUBLISHER AGREES:

(a) to publish the said work at its own expense in book form in such style or styles as it deems best suited to the sale thereof at a catalog retail price of not less than $1.50 nor more than $3.00 per copy, regular trade edition; said publication to be made during the Spring season of 1929 provided the manuscript shall be delivered within the time hereinbefore stipulated; and if not so published (except on account of strikes, fires or other contingencies beyond the control of the Publisher or its suppliers, in which event publication shall be postponed until the next immediately succeeding spring or fall season), then the Author shall have the right to terminate this agreement and the rights herein granted shall revert to the Author, provided the Author shall forward notice of termination to the Publisher within twenty (20) days after the end of the season set for publication of said work; otherwise the publication shall be postponed to the next immediately succeeding season of spring or fall;

(b) to take all the steps required to secure copyright of the said work in the United States of America and such other countries as may be included in this agreement, except with regard to Canada, where the Publisher and Author shall cooperate in securing copyright. The said work shall be copyrighted either (1) in the name of the Author or (2) in the name of the Publisher; if in case (1), the Author shall hold the copyright as hereinbefore set forth in subdivision (d) of paragraph First hereof; and if in case (2), the Publisher shall either assign the copyright upon completion thereof to the Author, or hold all the rights comprised therein and not in this agreement granted to the Publisher for the benefit of the Author, and grant to the Author and his/her designees the right to bring any suit or proceeding necessary to protect the copyright against the infringement by the unauthorized use of any such rights for the Author, held in the name of Publisher as the record owner of the copyright, provided the Author or his/her designee shall properly secure the Publisher against the payment of any costs and expenses in connection with any such suit or proceeding;

(c) to pay to the Author a royalty of ten per cent on the catalog retail price of every copy of said work sold ~~up to~~ ~~thousand copies;~~ ~~per cent on every copy sold in excess of~~ ~~thousand~~ ~~and up to~~ ~~thousand; and~~ ~~per cent on all copies there~~ ~~after sold.~~ On copies sold for export at a reduced price the royalty shall be calculated on the price actually charged instead of the catalog retail price. Where copies are sold in quantities sufficient to justify special discounts of fifty per cent (50%) or more from the retail catalog price, i.e., in sales of more than copies to any individual purchaser, or in other specific instances especially arranged for in writing between the parties hereto the royalty shall be calculated on the price actually charged by the Publisher. If at the time of the publication of the ~~subsequent novel/work/works or either of them, any prior~~ ~~novel/work published under this agreement shall have attained sales in excess of~~ the number above stipulated at the minimum royalty, ~~then the royalties shall be advanced and the~~ minimum royalty for said ~~subsequent novel/work shall be that provided to be paid for the increased~~ ~~number of the prior novel/work to such time sold.~~

second book the first shall have sold ten thousand (10,000) copies then the royalty on the second book shall be fixed at fifteen (15) per cent on all copies sold; and if the second book earns a royalty of fifteen (15) per cent

No royalties shall be payable on copies furnished gratis, to the Author, or for review, advertising, sample or like purposes or copies destroyed by fire or water. No sales and deliveries of copies of this work shall be made dependent or conditioned upon the purchase of any other work published or to be published by the Publisher;

then the royalty on the third book shall be fixed at fifteen per cent (15) on all copies sold. But if the second book fails to earn a royalty of fifteen (15) per cent then the royalty on the third book shall be fifteen (15) per cent only if at the time of publication of the third book the second shall have sold ten thousand copies.

(d) to forward to the Author promptly upon completion thereof galley and page proofs with printer's corrections and to make no changes in the text or title of the said work without the written consent thereto of the Author;

(e) to render a semi-annual statement of account to the first day of January or the first day of July immediately succeeding the publication of the said work and to render similar semi-annual statements for all succeeding periods of six months during which copies of said work subject to royalty shall have been sold, and to forward such statements on or before the first day of February and the first day of August following to the address of the Author as the same appears at the beginning of this agreement, and to make payment in accordance with the said statements on the first day of May and the first day of November immediately following, and upon request of the Author to furnish him/her with duplicates of said statements and in instances where said accounts involve branch houses in countries without the United States of America and the Dominion of Canada or where payments are to be received semi-annually by the Publisher from foreign countries other than the Dominion of Canada such receipts shall be accounted for and payment of royalty on such sales and statements thereof shall be rendered yearly instead of semi-annually; and whenever the semi-annual sales fall below fifty (50) copies no accounting shall be made until after the sales aggregate fifty (50) copies; and such accounting shall be included in the semi-annual settlement immediately succeeding that in which the sales shall aggregate fifty (50) copies or more.

(f) to present to the Author        ten        free copies of the said work upon publication and to permit the Author to purchase further copies for his/her own use and not for resale at three-fifths of the catalog retail price thereof;

(g) in the event that after two years from the date of the first publication of said work, the same in the opinion of the Publisher is no longer merchantable or profitable, it shall give three months' notice to the Author of its desire and intention to discontinue publication; or in the event that the Publisher shall fail to keep the work in print and for sale and after written demand from the Author declines or neglects to reprint the same within six months and to offer it for sale, then in either of these events the Author shall have the right to terminate this agreement and upon notice to that affect by the Author to the Publisher, all rights granted under this agreement shall revert to the Author and any plates of the work, if such had been made and preserved with any plates of illustrations furnished by the Author and any remaining copies, shall be transferred to the Author; provided the Author shall pay    fifty    per cent of the actual manufacturing cost, including composition of such plates and the actual manufacturing cost of any remaining copies or sheets, the said right or rights to be exercised by the Author within three months after notice by the Author of termination; and in the event that the Author shall not exercise this option and shall not purchase the aforesaid plates or remainders then the Publisher shall have the right to melt any such plates and sell remaining copies or sheets at cost or less without payment of any royalty to the Author upon such copies; and the Author shall have the right to purchase the plates or the remainders on the basis aforesaid each without the purchase of the other;

(h) to and does grant to the Author the right upon his/her written request to examine or cause to be examined through certified public accountants the books of account of the Publisher insofar as the same relate to the said work; provided that if such examination shall not divulge errors of accounting (arising otherwise than from an interpretation of this contract) amounting to One Hundred Dollars ($100) or more to the Author's disadvantage, the cost of such examination shall be borne by the Author; otherwise it shall be borne by the Publisher.

THIRD: It is mutually agreed between the parties hereto as follows:

(a) that all notices which may be given and requests which may be made by either of the parties hereto to the other under this agreement shall be in writing and may be forwarded by one to the other by ordinary mail except notices of termination which shall be forwarded by registered mail, and all notices and/or requests shall be directed to the party designated at the address heretofore written unless notice of change shall be given in writing by either party to the other, and after receipt of such notice, the address therein stated shall be used in all further communications to said party;

(b) each of the parties hereto will execute for and forward to the other upon request therefor any further written instrument, document or certificate confirming or evidencing the grants in this agreement set forth;

(c) that regardless of the record holder of the copyright, the Publisher shall use or dispose of no right or rights comprised in the copyright to the said work other than those herein specifically granted to the Publisher and whether the said rights be now or may at any time hereafter be recognized as included in the copyright to the said work;

(d) that subsequent to the publication of the said work, the Publisher may publish under its own imprint a cheap edition of the said work or permit the same to be published by leasing the plates of the said work to a regular cheap edition publisher, and in the event that said cheap edition should be published under the imprint of the Publisher the Publisher shall pay to the Author ten per cent (10%) of the catalog retail price at which the Publisher shall sell same; and in the event the Publisher shall lease the use of the plates to the said work, then the Publisher shall pay to the Author one half of the amounts received from such lessee. Payments and accountings under this clause shall be subject to the provisions of Subdivision (e) of Paragraph Second of this agreement;

(e) that should the Publisher at any time after one year from the publication of the said work conclude that it is overstocked with copies on hand thereof and that it could not dispose of the same within a reasonable time, then the Publisher shall have the right to sell copies at the best price that it can obtain therefor and in the event that the sale of such copies shall be made at or below the actual cost thereof, then no royalty thereon shall be paid to the Author; and if the sales price shall exceed the said cost but be fifty per cent (50%) or less of the catalog retail price, then the Publisher shall pay to the Author a royalty of ten per cent (10%) on the actual price received and payments and accountings under this clause shall be subject to the provisions of Subdivision (e) in Paragraph Second of this agreement;

(f) that if the plates or type forms of the said work shall be destroyed or rendered valueless by fire or otherwise, then the Publisher shall have the option of reproducing the same or not and if it shall conclude not to reproduce them, then the rights herein granted by the Author to the Publisher shall revert to the Author except that the Publisher shall have the right to sell the remaining copies on hand subject to the provisions with regard to payments and accountings set forth in the immediately preceding subdivision of this agreement;

(g) in the event of the bankruptcy or the liquidation through any cause whatsoever of the Publisher, the Author shall have the right to buy back the rights in this agreement granted to the Publisher at the fair market value thereof, the same to be determined by the majority decision of three persons, one to be appointed by the Author, the other by the legal representative of the Publisher and the third by these two, and upon payment of the amount so fixed and the transfer of the rights, this agreement shall terminate except that the representative of the Publisher shall have the right to sell the reamining copies on hand, if the same are not purchased by the Author, at the best price he can obtain therefor, and without payment of any royalty thereon to the Author;

(h) in the event that the copyright of this work shall during the existence of this agreement be infringed, then upon notice thereof by either party to the other, the parties hereto shall meet and confer with regard thereto and if no arrangement mutually satisfactory shall be arrived at for their joint action in regard thereto, then either of the parties hereto shall have the right to bring an action for the enjoining of such infringement and/or damages. If they shall proceed mutually in the matter, the expenses and recoveries, if any, shall be shared equally; and if they shall not agree to proceed jointly in the matter and if one of them shall decline to do so on the basis aforesaid, then the other party hereto shall have the right to go forward with such proceeding and such party shall bear all the expenses thereof, and any recoveries had therein shall belong absolutely to such party; and if such party hereto shall not hold the record title of the copyright, then the other party hereto shall permit the action to be brought in his or its name as hereinbefore provided;

(i) that if this agreement shall be breached by the Publisher in any particular not hereinbefore specifically provided for, and if within thirty days after notice thereof by the Author to the Publisher, the breach complained of shall not have been remedied by the Publisher, then the rights herein granted shall revert to the Author. Upon the foregoing or any other reversion of the rights herein granted to the Author, the Publisher shall, if the copyright be of record in its name, transfer said copyright to the Author by due and proper legally executed and acknowledged assignment;

(j) that no waiver of any breach of any condition of this agreement shall be binding unless the same shall be in writing and signed by the party waiving the said breach, and no such waiver shall in any wise affect any other term or condition of this agreement or constitute a cause or excuse for a repetition of such or any other breach unless the waiver shall include the same;

(k) that this agreement regardless of the place of its physical execution shall be treated by the parties hereto as though executed within the State of New York and be interpreted within the purview of the laws and statutes of the State of New York and of the United States of America;

(l) this agreement shall be binding upon and inure to the benefit of the executors, administrators and assigns of the Author and upon and to the successors and assigns of the Publisher, but no assignment voluntary or by operation of law shall be binding upon either of the parties hereto without the written consent of the other party of this agreement, except as hereinbefore specifically provided.

FOURTH: It is hereby further agreed between the parties hereto as follows:

(a) that copyright to the said work referred to in subdivision (b) of paragraph "Second" shall be secured in the name of the        Publisher             and the proper copyright notice or notices necessary to protect copyright to and in the said work shall be printed on the reverse side of the title page in every copy thereof in the aforesaid name;

(b) that if any manuscript delivered to the Publisher under this agreement shall not be written in idiomatic or otherwise acceptable English and in the opinion of the Publisher properly prepared for the press, then the Publisher shall notify the Author of its dissatisfaction in these respects or any of them, and the Author shall have twenty (20) days after the receipt of such notice in which to make the necessary revision, and if not so made by the Author then the Publisher shall have the right to cause said revision to be made at the expense of and for the account of the Author and the Author shall pay for the same. It is however expressly agreed that this clause shall not be construed to grant to the Publisher the right to change the theme, plot, or any incident in any work by the Author without the written consent thereto of the Author, nor to change the text of the said work in any manner whatsoever except as may be necessary to conform the same to idiomatic or otherwise acceptable English and to style it for the press.

(c) that the additional rights included in subdivision (a) of paragraph "First" are: second serialization, selection, syndication, translation, dramatic, motion picture, radio broadcasting and all other rights excepting first serial. In the event of the sale of dramatic or motion picture rights, seventy-five per cent of the proceeds shall go to the Author and twenty-five per cent to the Publisher. The proceeds from the sale of all other rights shall be divided equally between Author and Publisher.

(d) in the event of the publication of the said work by the London house of the Publisher the royalty payable to the Author shall be ten (10) per cent of the English retail price on all copies sold; subject further to the provisions of clauses Second (e) and (g) except that should an edition be sold to Australasia as a special Colonial edition the royalty payable to the Author shall be threepence per copy.

(e) in the case of the sale of an edition in sheets to an English Publisher other than the London house of the Publisher at a price inclusive of royalty, the sum accruing over and above the actual manufacturing cost (not including overhead charges) shall be divided equally between Publisher and Author.

(f) in the case of the sale to an English publisher other than the London house of the Publisher for independent manufacture the proceeds are to be divided equally between Publisher and Author.

IN WITNESS WHEREOF, the Author has hereunto placed his hand and seal and the Publisher has caused this agreement to be executed by its ᵛⁱᶜᵉ President by authority of its Board of Directors and its seal to be hereunto affixed by like authority, all on the day and year first hereinbefore written.

In the presence of

———————————————————                    ———————————————————(L. S.)

                                        ALFRED A. KNOPF, INC.

*Frances McAnan*                        by *Blanche Knopf*

CONTRACT

with ——— Dashiell Hammett

for ——— RED HARVEST

dated ——— March 29, 1928

## The Editing of the Novel

*Editorial correspondence related to* The Maltese Falcon *is sparse, perhaps because Hammett was living in New York when the book was being prepared for publication, enabling him to meet face-to-face with Harry Block, his editor. More likely, pertinent correspondence and related materials, including records related to production and marketing of the book, were removed from the Knopf files at some point. These letters survive in the Knopf archive at the Harry Ransom Humanities Research Center, University of Texas at Austin. They are included in* Selected Letters of Dashiell Hammett, *edited by Richard Layman with Julie Rivett (Washington, D.C.: Counterpoint, 2001). The complete correspondence from Knopf to Hammett is published in "Knopf to Hammett: The Editorial Correspondence," edited by Richard Layman,* Dictionary of Literary Biography Yearbook: 2000.

16 June [1929], 891 Post St., San Francisco

Dear Mr. Block,

I started *The Maltese Falcon* on its way to you by express last Friday, the fourteenth. I'm fairly confident that it is by far the best thing I've done so far, and I hope you'll think so too.

Though I hadn't anything of the sort in mind while doing it, I think now that it could very easily be turned into a play. Will you let me know if you agree with me? I wouldn't take a chance on trying to adapt it myself, but will try to get the help of somebody who knows the theater.

Another thing: if you use *The Falcon* will you go a little easy on the editing? While I wouldn't go to the stake in defense of my system of punctuation, I do rather like it and I think it goes with my sort of sentence-structure. The first forty pages of *The Dain Curse* were edited to beat hell (hurriedly for the dummy?) and the rest hardly at all. The result was that, having amiably accepted most of your changes in the first part, I had my hands full carrying them out in the remainder, trying to make it look like all the work of the same writer.

Like most of the world most of the time I am just now rather desperately in need of all the money I can scrape up. If there is any truth in these rumors that one hears about advances against royalties, will you do the best you can for me? If my appreciation equals my need I can promise to quite overwhelm you with gratitude.

How soon will you want, or can you use, another book? I've quite a flock of them outlined or begun, and I've a couple of groups of connected stories that can be joined in a whole just as I did with *Red Harvest* and *The Dain Curse*. The best of them were written just before *Red Harvest,* a group that would make a book as exciting as *Red Harvest,* though less complicated, with *The Big Knock-Over* as title.

Also I've about two hundred and fifty thousand words of short stories in which the Continental Op appears. I know you're not likely to be wildly enthusiastic about the short-story idea; but don't you think that something profitable for both of us could be done with them by making a quite bulky collection of them—selling it by the pound, as it were? I don't know anything about the manufacturing costs—how far bulkiness could be carried at a fairly low price without eating up the profits. I'd want to rewrite the stories we included, of course, and there are possibly fifty or sixty thousand words of the quarter-million that I'd throw out as not worth bothering about. In the remainder there are some good stories, and altogether I think they'd give a more complete and true picture of a detective at work than has been given anywhere else. And I think *The Continental Op* would be a good title.

Also I've a horror-story I'd like to get to work on—a variant of the Frankenstein idea—tentatively entitled *AEAEA;* a pure plot detective story, *Two Two's Are Twenty-two;* a political murder mystery, *The Secret Emperor;* one something on the order of *The Maltese Falcon, That Night in Singapore;* and an underworld mystery, *Dead Man's Friday.* (All these titles are tentative, of course.)[1]

I had intended doing the story of a gunman next, but, according to Asbury, *Little Caesar* was *that.*[2] So, until I've read it I'm holding off. I'm a little afraid anyhow that gunmen and racketeers, as such, are going to be rather sour literary material by this time next year.

Sincerely,

Dashiell Hammett

**Notes**

1. Drafts for "AEAEA" and "Two Two's Are Twenty-Two" are at the Harry Ransom Center, University of Texas. The archive includes a character list, outline, and a fragment for "The Secret Emperor." "That Night in Singapore" and "Dead Man's Friday" are not located.
2. Herbert Asbury had enthusiastically reviewed W. R. Burnett's *Little Caesar* (1929). The classic movie made from this gangster novel was released in January 1931 by Warner Bros.

---

14 July 1929, 891 Post St., San Francisco

Dear Mr. Block,

I'm glad you like *The Maltese Falcon.* I'm sorry you think the to-bed and the homosexual parts of it should be changed. I should like to leave them as they are, especially since you say they "would be all right perhaps in an ordinary novel." It seems to me that the only thing that can be said against their use in a detective novel is that nobody has tried it yet. I'd like to try it.

Since writing you I've reread some of the short stories and novelettes I mentioned. I don't think I want to do anything with them. Most of them could be rewritten into fair shape, I think, but only fair shape, and I'd rather forget them. I've a title I like–*The Glass Key*–and at least part of a plot to go with it. I'll probably get going on it next week.

I like the *Dain Curse* jacket.

About the advance: I've no objections at all, of course, to drawing up a new contract for three more books, but I need more than a thousand dollars. As a matter of fact I'd like to have twenty-five hundred. This doesn't seem an at all unreasonable figure to me, since, after all, it would be actually, from my standpoint, an advance against six books.[1]

Sincerely,

Dashiell Hammett

**Note**

1. Hammett's first contract with Knopf was for three books and did not stipulate an advance against royalties. In July, before royalties had yet been paid on *Red Harvest,* which was published in January 1929, Block offered Hammett a $1,000 advance payable under a new contract for three more books, a total of six books under contract.

---

### A Matter of Pronunciation: Knopf, Inc., and the Title

*The first opinion from the publisher on the title "The Maltese Falcon" was a positive one, offered by Harry Block in a 6 August 1928 letter to Hammett:*

"the maltese falcon is a swell title and I am already very eager to read the book."

*Alfred A. Knopf, however, criticized the title after the novel was published, in a 16 June 1931 letter to the author:*

"What is wrong with THE MALTESE FALCON as a title is as plain as the nose on my face–and that if you recall it is very plain indeed. People don't know how to pronounce <u>falcon</u> and whenever people can't pronounce a title or an author's name, they are, more than you would think, too shy to go into a book store and try."

31 August 1929 [San Francisco]

Dear Mr. Block,

OK–go ahead and change them. I don't imagine a few words' difference will matter greatly, and, anyway, I'll soon be on hand to do in person whatever crying is necessary.

I won't try to express my gratitude for the *Times* page. It was, well . . . .

I've just finished reading *Monks Are Monks,* and liked its insolence a lot.

*The Glass Key* is going slowly, but I expect to have at least a third of it done before I go East, and I think perhaps it'll amount to something.

Sincerely yours,

Dashiell Hammett

---

*Covers of the* Black Mask *issues that included the five installments of* The Maltese Falcon
*(Collection of Richard Layman)*

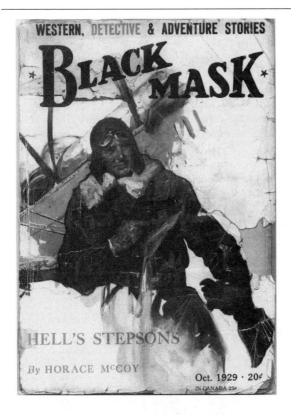

WESTERN, DETECTIVE & ADVENTURE STORIES

BLACK MASK

HELL'S STEPSONS

*By* HORACE McCOY

Oct. 1929 · 20¢

IN CANADA 25¢

WESTERN, DETECTIVE & ADVENTURE STORIES

BLACK MASK

HELL-SMOKE

*By* FREDERICK NEBEL

A CAPTAIN STEVE MacBRIDE YARN    NOV. 1929 · 20

IN CANADA 25¢

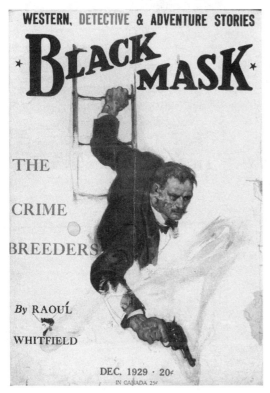

WESTERN, DETECTIVE & ADVENTURE STORIES

BLACK MASK

THE

CRIME

BREEDERS

*By* RAOUL

WHITFIELD

DEC. 1929 · 20¢

IN CANADA 25¢

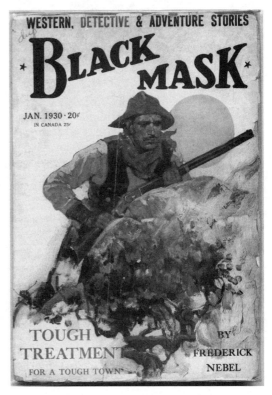

WESTERN, DETECTIVE & ADVENTURE STORIES

BLACK MASK

JAN. 1930 · 20¢

IN CANADA 25¢

TOUGH
TREATMENT

FOR A TOUGH TOWN

BY

FREDERICK
NEBEL

## From *Black Mask* to Book

There is no known pre-publication form of The Maltese Falcon. Hammett sent the novel to Knopf on 14 June 1929, at least two months before the Black Mask serialization began. Knopf published the novel on 14 February 1930. A comparison of the Black Mask and Knopf publications reveals that Hammett significantly revised the text for book publication. There are more than two thousand differences between the two texts. Some of the revisions were imposed by copyeditors at Knopf, but Hammett warned his editor that he felt they had been too intrusive in their handling of his first two novels and that he wanted them to go easy. On the following pages the Black Mask text is reproduced, with changes in the Knopf text indicated in the margins.

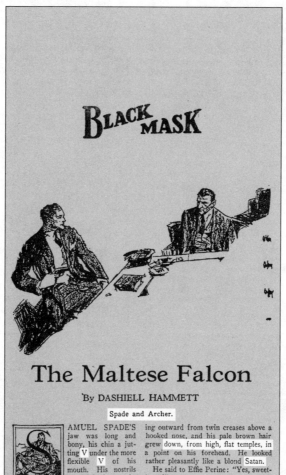

CHAPTER I
*Spade & Archer*

down—from high flat temples—in

satan

lanky sunburned

*Pages from the first serial installment, September 1929*

**8**        Black Mask

Her eyes were brown and playful in a shiny, boyish face.

She finished shutting the door behind her, leaned against it, and said:

"There's a girl wants to see you. Her name's Wonderly."

"A customer?"

"I guess so. You'll want to see her anyway; she's a knockout."

"Shoo her in, darling," said Spade. "Shoo her in."

Effie Perine opened the door again, following it back into the outer office, standing with a hand on the knob while saying:

"Will you come in, Miss Wonderly?"

A voice said, "Thank you," so softly that only the purest articulation made the words audible, and a young woman came through the doorway. She advanced slowly, with tentative steps, looking at Spade with cobalt-blue eyes that were both shy and probing.

She was tall. She was pliantly slender. Her erect, high-breasted body, her long legs, her narrow hands and feet, had nowhere any angularity. She wore two shades of blue that had been selected because of her eyes. The hair curling from under her blue hat was darkly red, her full lips more brightly red. White teeth glistened in the crescent her timid smile made.

Spade rose, bowing and indicating with a thick-fingered hand the oaken armchair beside his desk. He was quite six feet tall. The steep, rounded slope of his shoulders made his body seem almost conical, no broader than it was thick, and kept his freshly pressed gray coat from fitting very well.

Miss Wonderly murmured, "Thank you," softly as before, and sat down on the edge of the chair's wooden seat.

Spade sank into his swivel-chair, made a quarter turn to face her, and smiled politely. He smiled without separating his lips. All the V's in his face grew longer.

The tappity-tap-tap and the thin bell and muffled whir of Effie Perine's typewriting came through the closed door.

Somewhere in a neighboring office a power-driven machine vibrated dully. On Spade's desk a limp cigarette smoldered in a brass tray filled with the remains of limp cigarettes. Ragged gray flakes of cigarette ash dotted the yellow top of the desk and the green blotter and the papers that were there. A buff-curtained window, eight or ten inches open, let in from the court a current of air faintly scented with ammonia. The ashes on the desk twitched and crawled in the current.

Miss Wonderly watched the twitching and crawling gray flakes uneasily. She sat stiffly on the very edge of her chair, her feet flat on the floor, as if she were about to rise. Her hands in dark gloves clasped a flat, dark handbag in her lap.

Spade rocked back in his chair and asked:

"Now what can I do for you, Miss Wonderly?"

She caught her breath and looked at him. She swallowed and said hurriedly: "Could you—? I thought—I —that is—" Then she tortured her lower lip with glistening teeth and said nothing. Only her dark eyes spoke now, pleading.

Spade nodded and smiled as if he understood her, but pleasantly, as if nothing really serious were involved. The same assurance was in his voice when he spoke.

"Suppose you tell me all about it, and then we'll know what needs doing. Better begin as far back as you can, as near the beginning."

"That was in New York," she said.

"Yes," he said.

"I don't know where she met him. I mean I don't know where in New York. She's five years younger than I, only seventeen, and we didn't have the same friends. I don't suppose we were ever as close as sisters should be. Mama and Papa are in Europe. It would kill them. I've got to get her back before they come home."

"Yes."

---

**Left margin annotations:**

shiny boyish

no ¶

no ¶

anyway:

no ¶

intelligible,

She was tall and pliantly slender, without angularity anywhere. Her body was erect and high-breasted, her legs long, her hands and feet narrow.

rose bowing

steep rounded

conical–no

thick–and   grey

before and

quarter-turn to face her, smiled

v's

**Right margin annotations:**

grey
cigarette-ash

grey flakes twitch and crawl. Her eyes were uneasy. She sat on the very edge of the chair. Her feet were

flat dark

no ¶

smiled and nodded

nothing serious were involved. He said: "Suppose you tell me about it, from the beginning, and

can."

York."
"Yes."

I–only seventeen–and

we've ever been

"Yes," he said.

The Maltese Falcon    9

"They're returning the first of the month."

Spade's eyes brightened. "Then we've two whole weeks," he said.

"I didn't know what she had done until her letter came. I was frantic." Her lips trembled. Her hands mashed the dark handbag in her lap. "The fear that she had done something like this kept me from going to the police, and the fear that something had happened to her kept urging me to go. There wasn't anyone I could go to for advice. I didn't know what to do. What could I do?"

"Nothing, of course," Spade said amiably, "but then her letter came?"

"Yes, and I sent her a telegram asking her to come home. I sent it to General Delivery here. That was the only address she had given me. I waited a week, but no answer came, not a word from her. And Mama and Papa's return was drawing nearer and nearer. So I came to San Francisco to get her. I wrote her I was coming. I shouldn't have done that, should I?"

"Maybe not. It's not always easy to know what to do. Then you haven't found her?"

"I haven't found her. I wrote her that I would go to the St. Mark, and I begged her to come and let me talk to her even if she didn't intend going home with me. But she didn't come. I waited there three days, and Corinne didn't come, didn't even send me a message."

Spade nodded his blond Satan's head slowly, frowning sympathetically, his lips tightened together.

"It was horrible," she said, trying to smile. "I couldn't sit there like that and wait and wait, not knowing what had happened to her, what might be happening to her." She stopped trying to smile, and shuddered. "The only address I had was General Delivery. I wrote her another letter, and yesterday afternoon I went to the Post Office. I stayed there until dark, but I didn't see her. I went there again this morning, and still didn't see Corinne, but I saw Floyd Thursby."

Spade nodded again, but his frown had vanished. In its place was a look of sharp attentiveness.

"He wouldn't tell me where Corinne is," she went on, hopelessly. "He wouldn't tell me anything, except that she is well and happy. But how can I believe him? That is what he would tell me anyhow, isn't it?"

"Exactly," Spade agreed, "but it might be true."

"I hope it is. I do hope it is," she exclaimed. "But I can't go back home like this, without having seen her, without even having talked to her on the phone. He wouldn't take me to her. He said she didn't want to see me. I can't believe that. He promised to tell her he had seen me, and to bring her to see me if she would come—this evening at the hotel. He said he knew she wouldn't. He promised to come himself if she wouldn't. He—"

She broke off with a startled hand to her mouth as the office door opened.

THE man who had opened the door came in a step, said, "Oh, excuse me," hastily took his brown hat from his head, and backed out.

"It's all right, Miles," Spade told him. "Come in. Miss Wonderly, this is Mr. Archer, my partner."

Miles Archer came into the office again, shutting the door behind him, ducking his head and smiling at Miss Wonderly, making a vaguely polite gesture with the hat in his hand.

He was of medium height, solidly built, wide in the shoulders, thick in the neck, with a jovial, heavy-jawed red face and some gray in his close-trimmed hair. He was apparently as many years past forty as Spade was past thirty.

Spade said:

"Miss Wonderly's sister ran away from New York with a fellow named Floyd Thursby. They're here. Miss Wonderly has seen Thursby, and has a date with him tonight. Maybe he'll bring

---

*Left margin annotations:*

"They're coming home

two weeks,"

"I was too afraid she had done something like this to go

said,

she gave me. I waited a whole week, but no answer came, not another word

do. You

"No, I haven't."

intend to go

I waited three days, and she

message of any sort."
satan's head, frowned sympathetically, and tightened his lips together.

Miss Wonderly
that—waiting—not

smile. She shuddered.

until after dark,

*Right margin annotations:*

again. His frown went away. In its place came

was,"

was

that?

"Sure," Spade agreed. "But

me—if

the door

no ¶

me!"

no ¶

jovial heavy-jawed
grey

no ¶

Thursby and

50 Black Mask

to come to the office, and now I oughtn't come here. Do you mean I oughtn't chase after you? If that's what you mean why don't you say it right out?"

"Now, Iva, you've got no right to take that attitude."

"I know I haven't. I haven't any rights at all, it seems, where you're concerned. I thought I did. I thought your pretending to love me gave me some right, but—"

Spade said wearily:

"This is no time to be arguing about that, precious. What was it you wanted to see me about?"

"I can't talk to you here, Sam. Can't I come in?"

"Not now."

"Why can't I."

Spade said nothing.

She made a thin line of her mouth, squirmed around straight behind the wheel, and started the engine, staring angrily ahead.

When the sedan began to move Spade said, "Good night, Iva," closed the door, and stood at the curb with his hat in his hand until it had been driven away. Then he went indoors again.

Brigid O'Shaughnessy rose smiling cheerfully from the bench and they went up to his apartment.

CHAPTER VII

*G in the Air*

IN his bedroom that was a living-room now the wall bed was up, Spade took Brigid O'Shaughnessy's hat and coat, made her comfortable in a padded rocking chair, and, after looking up the number in the telephone directory, called the Hotel Belvedere. Cairo had not yet returned from the theater. Spade left his telephone number with the request that Cairo call him as soon as he came in.

Spade sat down in the arm chair beside the table and without any preliminaries, without any introductory remarks, began to tell the girl about a thing that had happened three years before in the Northwest. He talked in a steady matter-of-fact tone, devoid of emphasis or pauses, though now and then he repeated a sentence slightly rearranged, as if it were important to relate each detail exactly as it had happened. His eyes while he talked looked at memories over her shoulder.

At the beginning she listened with only partial attentiveness, obviously more surprised by the story than interested in it, her curiosity more engaged with his purpose in telling the story than with the story he told; but presently, as the story went on, it caught her more and more fully, and held her, and she became still and receptive.

A man named Flitcraft had left his real estate office, in Tacoma, to go to luncheon one day and had never returned. He did not keep an engagement to play golf after four that afternoon, though he had taken the initiative in making the engagement a bare half-hour before he went out to luncheon. His wife and children never saw him again. His wife and he were supposed to be on the best of terms. He had two children, boys, one five and one three. He owned his home in a Tacoma suburb, a new Packard car, already paid for, and the rest of the appurtenances of successful American living.

Flitcraft had inherited seventy thousand dollars from his father, and, with his success in real estate, was worth something in the neighborhood of two hundred thousand dollars at the time of his vanishing. His affairs were in order, though there were enough loose ends to indicate that he had not been setting his affairs in order preparatory to vanishing. A deal that would have brought him an attractive profit, for instance, was to have been completed the day after that on which he vanished. There was nothing to show that he had

Left margin:

- oughtn't to
- oughtn't to
- me–"
- no ¶
- sedan's engine
- shut
- wall-bed
- and telephoned
- not returned from the theatre.
- telephone-number

Right margin:

- armchair
- preliminary, without an introductory remark of any sort,
- some
- voice that was
- that each detail be related exactly as it had happened.
- Brigid O'Shaughnessy
- by his telling the story
- fully and
- real-estate-office
- less than half an hour
- the other
- house
- Packard, and
- he vanished.
- them
- concluded the day after the one on which he disappeared. There was nothing to suggest

*Pages from the second serial installment, October 1929*

The Maltese Falcon 51

more than fifty or sixty dollars in his immediate possession at the time of his going. His time for months past could be at least roughly accounted for too thoroughly to justify any suspicion of secret vices, or even of another woman, though of course either was possible.

"He went, like that," Spade said, "like a fist when you open your hand."

When he had reached this point in his story the telephone bell rang.

"Hello," he said into the instrument. "Mr. Cairo? This is Spade. Can you come up to my place, Post Street, now? Yes, I think it is." He looked at the girl, pursed his lips, and then said quickly: "Miss O'Shaughnessy is here and wants to see you."

She frowned a little and stirred in her chair, but said nothing.

Spade put down the telephone and told her:

"He'll be up in a few minutes. Well, that was in 1922. In 1927 I was with one of the national detective agencies in Seattle. Mrs. Flitcraft came in and told us somebody had seen a man who resembled her husband in Spokane. I went over there for her. It was Flitcraft, all right. He had been living in Spokane for a couple of years as Charles—that was his first name—Pierce. He had an automobile business that was netting him twenty or twenty-five thousand a year, a wife, a baby son, owned his home in a Spokane suburb, had all the trimmings that go with that kind of success, and usually got away to play golf after four in the afternoon during the season."

Spade hadn't been told very definitely what to do when he found Flitcraft. They talked in Spade's room at the Davenport. Flitcraft had no feeling of guilt. He had left his first family well provided for, and what he had done seemed to him perfectly reasonable. The only thing that bothered him was a doubt that he could make its reasonableness clear to Spade. He had never told anybody about it before, and thus had not had to attempt to make its reasonableness explicit. He tried now.

"I got it all right," Spade told Brigid O'Shaughnessy, "but Mrs. Flitcraft never did. She thought it was silly. Maybe it was. Anyway, it came out all right. She didn't want any scandal, and after the trick he had played on her, the way she looked at it, she didn't want him. So she divorced him on the quiet, and everything was swell all around.

"Here's what had happened to him. Going to lunch he had passed an office building—or the skeleton of one—that was being put up. A beam or something fell eight or ten stories to the sidewalk alongside him. It brushed close to him, but didn't touch him, though a piece of the sidewalk, a piece of brick or cement, was chipped off and flew up and struck him on the cheek. It only took a piece of skin off, but he still had the scar when I saw him. He rubbed it with his finger, thoughtfully, almost affectionately, while he told me about it.

"He was frightened, of course, he said, but he was more shocked than frightened. It was as if somebody had taken the lid off life and let him look at the works.

"He had been a good citizen, a good husband, and a good father, not by any outer compulsion, but simply because he was the sort of man who was most comfortable in step with his surroundings. He had been raised that way. The people he knew were like that. The life he knew was a clean, orderly, sane, responsible affair. Now a falling beam had shown him that life was fundamentally none of these things. He, the good citizen, could be wiped out between real estate office and restaurant by the accident of a falling beam. He knew then that men died at haphazard, like that, and lived only while blind chance spared them.

"It wasn't the injustice of it that disturbed him: he accepted that after the first shock. What disturbed him was the discovery that in sensibly ordering

---

*Left margin notes:*

habits

be accounted

woman in his life, though either was barely possible.

went like

telephone-bell

Spade

Cairo? . . . This place–Post Street–now? . . . Yes,

rapidly:

Brigid O'Shaughnessy frowned did not say anything. the telephone down

no ¶

big

in Spokane who looked a lot like her husband. I went over there.

automobile-business

suburb, and

had not

that

his story

*Right margin notes:*

and, after the trick he had played on her–the way she looked at it–she they were divorced on the quiet and

he passed an office-building that was being put up–just the skeleton.

stories down and smacked brushed pretty close

sidewalk was chipped off and flew up and hit his cheek.

finger–well, affectionately–when

no ¶ scared stiff

really frightened. He felt like

works."

Flitcraft had been a good citizen and a good husband and father,

a man

way.

clean orderly sane responsible

citizen-husband-father, could be wiped out between office

haphazard like

was not, primarily,

52               Black Mask

his affairs he had got out of step, and not into step, with life. He said he knew before he had gone twenty feet from the fallen beam that he would never again know peace until he had adjusted himself to this new glimpse of life. By the time he had finished his luncheon he had found his means of adjustment. Life could be ended for him at random by a falling beam; he would change his life at random simply by going off. He loved his family, he said, as much as he supposed was usual, but he knew he was leaving them provided for, and his love for them wasn't of the sort that would make absence from them painful.

"He went to Seattle that afternoon," Spade said, "and from there by boat to San Francisco. For two or three years he roamed around the country and then returned to the Northwest, settling in Spokane. Presently he married. His second wife didn't look like his first, and you could find more points of difference than of likeness between them; but both were the sort of women who play fair golf and bridge, take pains with their guest rooms, and welcome new salad recipes. He felt that what he had done was reasonable. He regretted none of it. I don't think that he was conscious of having stepped back naturally into the groove he had left in Tacoma. But that's the part of it that I like best. He had adjusted himself to the falling beam, and then no more beams had fallen, and he had adjusted himself to their not falling."

"How perfectly fascinating," Brigid O'Shaughnessy said. She left her chair and stood in front of him, close. Her eyes were wide and deep. "I don't have to tell you how utterly at a disadvantage you'll have me, with him here, if you choose."

Spade smiled slightly without separating his lips.

"No, you don't have to tell me that," he agreed.

"And you know I'd never have placed myself in this position if I hadn't trusted you completely?" Her thumb and finger twisted a black button on his blue coat.

Spade said, "That again," with mock resignation.

"But you know it's so," she insisted.

"No, I don't know it." He patted the hand that was twisting the button. "My asking for reasons why I should trust you brought us here. Don't let's get ourselves confused. You don't have to trust me, anyway, as long as you can persuade me to trust you."

She studied his face. Her nostrils quivered.

Spade laughed. He patted her hand again and said:

"Don't worry about that now. He'll be here in a moment. Get your business with him over, and then we'll see how we stand."

"And you'll let me go about it in my own way?"

"Of course."

She turned her hand under his so that her fingers pressed his. She said softly:

"You're a God-send."

Spade said: "Don't overdo it."

She looked reproachfully at him, though smiling, and returned to the padded rocker.

JOEL CAIRO was excited. His dark eyes seemed all irides, and his high-pitched thin-voiced words were tumbling out before Spade had got the door half open.

"That boy is out there watching the house, Mr. Spade, that boy you showed me, or to whom you showed me, in front of the theater. What am I to understand from that, Mr. Spade? I came here in good faith, with no thought of tricks or traps."

"You were asked in good faith." Spade frowned thoughtfully. "But I ought to've guessed that he might show up. He saw you come in?"

"Naturally. I could have gone on, but that seemed pointless, since you had already let him see us together."

The Maltese Falcon     51

*Left margin notes:*

no ¶   intend to if

him either

him and one or the other of them would go down.

one then

Floyd was caught and you'd be rid of him.

"S-something

him you

gun and

"Yes—though not exactly."
"But exact enough. And you had that plan up your sleeve from the first. You thought Floyd would be nailed for the killing."
"I—I thought they'd hold him at least until after Captain Jacobi had arrived with the falcon and—"
"And you didn't know then that Gutman was here hunting for you. You didn't suspect that or you wouldn't have shaken your gunman. You knew Gutman was here as soon as you heard Thursby had been shot."

but—oh, sweetheart!—it

no ¶   "You angel!

break you'll

years and

without comprehension at him

to Christ

*Main text:*

"Yes, that's a lie, Sam. I did mean to, if Floyd— I—I can't look at you and tell you this, Sam." She pulled his head farther down until her cheek was against his cheek, her mouth by his ear, and whispered: "I knew Floyd wouldn't be easily frightened, but I thought that if he knew somebody was shadowing him, either he'd— Oh, I can't say it, Sam!" She clung to him, sobbing.

Spade said: "You thought Floyd would tackle him, and one or the other would be killed. If Thursby was the one, then you were rid of him. If Miles was, then you could see that Thursby was caught, if he didn't go away then, and you'd be through with him. That it?"

"Something like that."

"And when you found that Thursby didn't mean to tackle him, you borrowed the gun from him and did it yourself. Right?"

"Y-yes."

"And then you thought Thursby would be nailed for the killing."

"Yes, and—and they'd hold him at least till after Jacobi had come and I'd had a chance to get the falcon."

"And you didn't know then—you didn't even suspect—that Gutman was here hunting for you; or you wouldn't have wanted to shake your gunman. You knew Gutman was here when you learned Thursby had been shot. Then you knew you needed another protector, so you came back to me. Right?"

"Yes, but, oh! sweetheart, it wasn't only that. I would have come back to you sooner or later. From the first instant I saw you I knew—"

Spade said tenderly:

"You're an angel. Well, if you get a good break, you'll be out of San Quentin in twenty years, and you can come back to me then."

She took her cheek away from his, drawing her head far back to stare up at him without comprehension.

He was pale. He said tenderly: "I hope to —— they don't hang you, pre-

cious, by that sweet neck." He slid his hands up to caress her throat.

In an instant she was out of his arms, back against the table, crouching, both hand spread over her throat. Her face was wild-eyed, haggard. Her dry mouth opened and closed. She said in a small parched voice: "You're not—" She could not get more words out.

Spade's face was yellow-white now. His mouth smiled and there were smile wrinkles around his glittering eyes. His voice was soft, gentle. He said:

"I'm going to send you over. The chances are you'll get off with life. That means you'll be out again in twenty years. You're an angel. I'll be waiting for you." He cleared his throat. "If they hang you I'll always remember you."

She dropped her hands and stood erect. Her face became smooth and untroubled except for the faintest of dubious glints in her eyes. She smiled back at him, gently.

"Don't, Sam, don't say that even in fun. Oh, you frightened me for a moment! I really thought you— You know you do such wild and unpredictable things that—" She broke off, thrust her face forward, and stared deep into his eyes. Her cheeks and the flesh around her mouth shivered, and fear came back in her eyes. "What—? Sam!" She put her hands to her throat again and lost her erectness.

Spade laughed. His yellow-white face was damp with sweat and, though he held his smile, he could not keep softness in his voice. He croaked:

"Don't be silly. You're taking the fall. One of us has got to take it—after the talking Gutman and Cairo will do. They'd hang me sure. You're likely to get a better break. Well?"

"But—but, Sam! You can't! After what we've been to each other you can't—"

"Like hell I can't."

She took a long, trembling breath. "You've been playing with me? Only pretending you cared? You didn't, at

*Right margin notes:*

hands

get no other

smile-wrinkles

no ¶

wait

no ¶

off. She thrust her face forward and

shivered and

into

and though
smile he could not hold

no ¶
it, after
those birds

Sam, you can't! Not after other. You

long trembling

cared—to trap me like this? You didn't—care

*Pages from the fifth serial installment, January 1930*

didn't–don't–l-love
came to
me asking
yesterday for Gutman
them and waited outside for me
sprung–I
me and
it if
And if
them it
stretches
to and
and–not wanting to hurt you–
wouldn't be able to hurt him."
towards
stood looking
no ¶ "You
you are
say you don't know down in your heart that, in spite of anything I've done, I love you."
short abrupt
yellowish fixedly
no ¶
double-crossing Thursby? You who double-crossed Gutman, Cairo, Thursby–one, two, three?

52 **Black Mask**

all? You didn't—you don't—l-love me?"

"I think I do," Spade said. "What of it?" The muscles holding his smile in place stood out like wales. "I'm not Thursby. I'm not Jacobi. I won't play the sap for you."

"That is not just," she cried. Tears glistened in her eyes. "It's unfair. It's contemptible of you. You know it was not that. You can't say that."

"Like hell I can't," Spade said. "You came into my bed to stop me from asking questions. You led me out for Gutman and Cairo yesterday with that phoney call for help. Last night you came here with them, and waited for me outside, and came in with me. You were in my arms when the trap was sprung, so that I couldn't have gone for a gun if I'd had one on me, and couldn't have made a fight of it until too late if I had wanted to. And, if they didn't take you away with them, it was only because Gutman's got too much sense to trust you except for short periods when he has to, and because he thought I'd play the sap for you and, not wanting to do anything to hurt you, I couldn't do anything to hurt him."

Brigid O'Shaughnessy blinked her tears away. She took a step toward him and stood there looking him in the eyes, straight and proud.

"You've called me a liar," she said. "Now you're lying. You're lying if you say that, in spite of anything I've done. down in your heart you don't know I love you."

Spade made a short, abrupt bow. His eyes were becoming bloodshot, but there was no other change in his damp and yellowish, fixedly smiling face.

"Maybe I do," he said. "What of it? I should trust you? You who arranged that nice little trick for—for my predecessor, Thursby? You who knocked off Miles, a man you had nothing against, in cold blood, just like swatting a fly, for the sake of ruining Thursby? You who've never played square with me for half an hour at a stretch since I've known you? I should trust you? No, no, darling. I wouldn't do it, even if I could. Why should I?"

Her eyes were steady under his, and her hushed voice was steady when she replied:

"Why should you? If you have been playing with me, if you do not love me, there is no answer to that. If you did, no answer would be needed."

Blood streaked Spade's eyeballs now, and his long-held smile had become a frightful grimace. He cleared his throat huskily and said:

"Making speeches is no damned good now." He put a hand on her shoulder. The hand trembled. "I don't care who loves who. I'm not going to play the sap for you. I won't walk in Thursby's and Jacobi's and God knows who else's footsteps. You killed Miles and you're going over for it. I could have helped you by letting the others go and standing off the police the best way I could. It's too late now. I can't help you, and —I wouldn't if I could."

She put a hand on his hand on her shoulder.

"Don't help me, then," she whispered. "But don't hurt me. Let me go away now."

"No," he said. "I'm sunk if I haven't got you to hand to the police when they come. That's the only thing that can keep me from being sunk with the others."

"You won't do that for me?"

"I won't play the sap for you."

"Don't say that, please." She took his hand from her shoulder and held it to her face. "Why must you do this, Sam? Surely Mr. Archer wasn't as much to you as—"

"Miles," Spade said hoarsely, "was a —— —— —— ——. I found that out the first week we were in business together, and I intended to kick him out as soon as the year was up. You didn't do me a damned bit of harm by murdering him."

"Then what?"

Spade pulled his hand out of hers. He

it even
his and
no ¶ you've
now and
no ¶
shook and jerked.
Christ
late for that now. I can't help you now. And I
no ¶ whispered, "but
hand over to
going down
this to me, Sam?
son of a bitch.
together and I meant
killing

no longer either smiled or grimaced. His wet yellow face was set hard and deeply lined. His eyes burned madly. He said:

"Listen. This isn't a damned bit of good. You'll never understand me, but I'll try once more, and then we'll give it up. In my part of the world when your partner's killed you're supposed to do something about it. It doesn't make any difference what you thought of him. He was your partner and you're supposed to do something about it. Then it happens that we were in the detective business. Well, when one of your employees, or a partner, or anybody connected with your detective business is killed, it's bad business to let the killer get away with it. It's bad all around, bad for that one agency, and bad for every detective—bad all around. Third, I'm a detective, and expecting me to run any criminal down and then let him go free is like asking a dog to catch a rabbit and then let it go. It can be done, all right, and sometimes it is done, but it's not the natural thing."

"But—"

"Wait till I'm through and then you can talk. Fourth, no matter what I wanted to do now, it would be absolutely impossible for me to let you go now without having myself dragged in with Gutman, Cairo and the kid. Next, I've no reason in God's world to think I can trust you, and if I did this, and got away with it, you'd have something on me that you could use if you ever happened to want to. That's five of them. The sixth would be that, since I'd also have something on you, I couldn't be sure you wouldn't decide to shoot holes in *me* some day. Seventh, I don't like the idea of even thinking that there might be one chance in a hundred that you'd played me for a sucker. And eighth—but that's enough. All those on one side. Maybe some of them seem unimportant, but look at the number of them. Now on the other side we've got what? All we've got is the fact that maybe you love me and maybe I love you?"

"You know," she whispered, "whether you do or not."

"I don't. It's easy enough for me to be nuts about you." He looked hungrily from her hair to her feet and up to her eyes again. "But I don't know what that amounts to. Does anybody ever? But suppose I do: what of it? Maybe next month I won't. I've been through it before—when it lasted that long. Then what? Then I'll remember you and I'll think I played the sap. And if I did it and got sent over, as I probably would, then I'd be sure I'd been the sap. Well, if I send you over I'll be sorry as hell—I'll have some rotten nights—but that'll pass."

She raised her hands to his cheeks and drew his face down.

"Look at me," she said, "and tell me the truth. Would you have done this if the falcon had been real, and you had been paid your money?"

"What difference does that make now? Don't be too sure that I'm as crooked as I'm supposed to be. That kind of a reputation might be good business, bringing in high-priced jobs and making dealings with the enemy easier."

She looked at him, saying nothing.

He moved his shoulders slightly and said: "Well, a lot of money would have been at least one more item on the other side of the scales."

She put her face up to his face. Her mouth was partly open, with lips thrust a little out. She whispered: "If you loved me you'd need nothing more on that side."

Spade set the edges of his teeth together and said through them: "I won't play the sap for you."

She put her mouth against his, slowly, her arms around him, and came into his arms.

She was in his arms when the doorbell rang.

SPADE, left arm around Brigid O'Shaughnessy, opened the corridor door. Lieutenant Dundy, Detective-Ser-

---

*Marginal annotations (left column):*

no ¶

more and

up. Listen. When a man's partner is killed he's

happens we

organization get's killed it's

around—bad for that one organization, bad for every detective everywhere.

detective and

criminals down and then let them

and let

thing. The only way I could have let you go was by letting Gutman and Cairo and the kid go. That's—

"You're not serious," she said. "You don't expect me to think that these things you're saying are sufficient reason for sending me to the—"

now it go without having myself dragged to the gallows with the others.

you and if I did this and it you'd whenever you

I've also got

a hole don't even like the idea of thinking

are unimportant. I won't argue about that. But

you."

*Marginal annotations (right column):*

enough to

do? What

I'll think

over then I'd be sure I was the sap.

pass. Listen." He took her by the shoulders and bent her back, leaning over her. "If that doesn't mean anything to you forget it and we'll make it this: I won't because all of me wants to—wants to say to hell with the consequences and do it—and because—God damn you—you've counted on that with me the same as you counted on that with the others." He took his hands from her shoulders and let them fall to his sides.

She put her hands up to his cheeks and drew his face down again.

no ¶ this to me if real and

sure of business—bringing it easier to deal with the enemy."

a little

slightly open with lips a little thrust out.

to

no ¶

corridor-door Detective-ser-

## BY DASHIELL HAMMETT

### RED HARVEST

"The liveliest detective story that has been published in a decade."—Herbert Asbury.

"When it is written by a man who plainly knows his underworld and can make it come alive for his readers, when the action is exciting, and the conversation racy and amusing—well, you'll want to read it. We recommend this one without reservation. We gave it A plus before we'd finished the first chapter."—The Outlook.

$2.00

### THE DAIN CURSE

"More than competently narrated by a cop with a picturesque lingo. Recommended for its weird characters and really astonishing speed."—Will Cuppy, in The New York Herald Tribune.

"We want to say right here that Mr. Hammett is our favorite detective story writer. . . . His knowledge of the ways of criminals and detectives, which has quite obviously not been gained by reading the detective stories of other writers. . . . We can think of only one story of the kind better than this second book of Mr. Hammett's and that is his first book."—Walter Brooks, in The Outlook.

$2.00

ALFRED A. KNOPF    PUBLISHER, N. Y.

---

## DASHIELL HAMMETT

writes a superior mystery novel because for many years he was a Pinkerton detective. He is probably the only "bull" who has ever turned his experience into the writing of crime stories. To Hammett, plot is not the main thing in the story. It is the behavior of the detective attacking a problem which intrigues him. The "op," as Hammett sees him, is "a little man going forward day after day through mud and blood and death and deceit—as callous and brutal and cynical as is necessary—towards a dim goal, with nothing to push or pull him towards it except that he's been hired to reach it."

The answer as to what originally turned Dashiell Hammett into a detective, in his own words, is this: "A firm of stock-brokers had fired me because I not only could seldom get the same approximate total out of any column of figures twice in succession, but still seldomer managed to get down early enough in the day to make any of my mistakes before noon. A week or so later, hunting for a job, I answered an enigmatic want-ad, and thus became a Pinkerton operative." Before that Hammett had numerous jobs: junior clerk in an advertising office, timekeeper in a machine shop, a stevedore, messenger for the B. and O. R.R. and when a boy in Philadelphia and Baltimore he sold papers. He was born thirty-six years ago in St. Mary's County, Maryland.

---

## THE MALTESE FALCON

### BY

### DASHIELL HAMMETT

$2.00 net

Sam Spade is a knock-out detective and yet, personally, he cares not a hoot for the law; so little so that constantly is he just on the verge of being pulled by the 'Frisco cops. When Spade goes out after anything neither lead slugs, women, nor the Old Nick himself can stop him from landing it. Here he sets himself to outwit three contending factions who all want the same thing which he also wants and it is only natural, therefore, that many murders strew his winding wake, that several persons suddenly fall doped and a great liner burns mysteriously to the water's edge.

*Joseph Shaw, Editor of Black Mask and an authority on mystery fiction, says: "We want to go on record as saying that this story is a marvelous piece of writing—the finest detective story it has ever been our privilege to read in book form, in any magazine of any kind, or in manuscript. Don't miss it."*

---

*Rear flap*                    *Front flap*

*Earliest jacket, with front cover and spine by F. H. Horvath for* The Maltese Falcon *(Kent State University)*

## By DASHIELL HAMMETT

### RED HARVEST

"*The liveliest detective story that has been published in a decade.*"—Herbert Asbury.

"*When it is written by a man who plainly knows his underworld and can make it come alive for his readers, when the action is exciting, and the conversation racy and amusing—well, you'll want to read it. We recommend this one without reservation. We gave it A plus before we'd finished the first chapter.*"—The Outlook.

$2.50

### THE DAIN CURSE

"*More than competently narrated by a cop with a picturesque lingo. Recommended for its weird characters and really astonishing speed.*"—Will Cuppy, in The New York Herald Tribune.

"*We want to say right here that Mr. Hammett is our favorite detective story writer. . . . His knowledge of the ways of criminals and detectives, which has quite obviously not been gained by reading the detective stories of other writers. . . . We can think of only one story of the kind better than this second book of Mr. Hammett's and that is his first book.*"—Walter Brooks, in The Outlook.

$2.50

ALFRED A. KNOPF — BORZOI BOOKS — PUBLISHER, N. Y.

---

## DASHIELL HAMMETT

writes a superior mystery novel because for many years he was a Pinkerton detective. He is probably the only "bull" who has ever turned his experience into the writing of crime stories. To Hammett, plot is not the main thing in the story. It is the behavior of the detective attacking a problem which intrigues him. The "op," as Hammett sees him, is "a little man going forward day after day through mud and blood and death and deceit—as callous and brutal and cynical as is necessary—towards a dim goal, with nothing to push or pull him towards it except that he's been hired to reach it."

The answer as to what originally turned Dashiell Hammett into a detective, in his own words, is this: "A firm of stock-brokers had fired me because I not only could seldom get the same approximate total out of any column of figures twice in succession, but still seldomer managed to get down early enough in the day to make any of my mistakes before noon. A week or so later, hunting for a job, I answered an enigmatic want-ad, and thus became a Pinkerton operative." Before that Hammett had numerous jobs: junior clerk in an advertising office, timekeeper in a machine shop, a stevedore, messenger for the B. and O. R.R. and when a boy in Philadelphia and Baltimore he sold papers. He was born thirty-six years ago in St. Mary's County, Maryland.

*Rear flap*

---

$2.50

## THE MALTESE FALCON

### BY

## DASHIELL HAMMETT

"The finest detective story it has ever been our privilege to read in book form, in any magazine of any kind or in manuscript. Don't miss it."—Joseph Shaw, Editor of *Black Mask.*

"It would not surprise us one whit if Mr. Hammett should turn out to be the Great American Mystery writer."—Will Cuppy, in *The New York Herald Tribune.*

"First and foremost among the new thrillers comes Dashiell Hammett's *The Maltese Falcon.* . . . This is not only probably the best detective story we have ever read, it is an exceedingly well written novel."—Walter R. Brooks, in *The Outlook.*

"It seems to me he is raising the detective story to that plane to which Alexandre Dumas raised the historical novel."—Carl Van Vechten.

"He stands alone as ace shocker. Hereafter even S. S. Van Dine must lower his monocle, cough up the encyclopedia and eat some humble pie. . . . It is everything you want. The writing is better than Hemingway; since it conceals not softness but hardness. It is the 'Broadway' of mysteries."—Ted Shane, in *Judge.*

"I can think of no one in the world who is his match. . . . I find it hard to figure out a way to tell you how good a book *The Maltese Falcon* is."— *The Cleveland Press.*

"For the first time in my knowledge, the American policeman and police detective have been adequately represented in fiction. . . . If you were to consider an amalgamation of Mr. Hemingway, the Mr. Burnett who wrote 'Little Caesar' and 'Iron Man,' that other disciple of Hemingway, Morley Callaghan, and Ring Lardner in his prize-fighting aspect, you would have a fair idea of the style and technique of Mr. Hammett."—*Town and Country.*

*Front flap*

---

*There are at least four printings of the first-edition jacket for* The Maltese Falcon. *The later printings have front-flap copy, as above, with either $2.50, $2.00, or no price. The same price is listed for the novels on the back as on the front flap. The book was published at $2.00 in February 1951; the price was changed to $2.50 in March and, late in the year, dropped back to $2.00 (Collection of Richard Layman).*

Other Books by
DASHIELL HAMMETT

## THE
## DAIN CURSE

'An extremely good detective story of the sensational type.'—*Sunday Express.*
'The ingredients of this mystery tale are varied and rich. There is dope in it. There is half a dozen murders. There is a bomb explosion. There is the middle-aged detective who tells the story : he is a mine of common sense and his speech is a mine for the student of slang. The mixture is the literary equivalent of a soul-slaying cocktail.'—*Irish Statesman.*

## THE
## GLASS KEY

'Easily one of the best detective stories we have read—extraordinarily realistic and fascinating. The characters live. The "Glass Key" reads like a page from real life; we could wish that all detective stories were as well written.'—*Aberdeen Journal.*
'A strong dose of cleverly arranged thrills. Characters which are thoroughly human.'—*Scots Pictorial.*

### 7/6
net each

*Rear flap*

## THE
## MALTESE
## FALCON
by
DASHIELL HAMMETT

Dashiell Hammett is an ex-Pinkerton detective whose experiences guarantee that his characters are men from real life. No other writer of detective stories shows so well the actual means by which criminals are run to earth, and he does it in a thrilling combination of racy dialogue and swift action as yet unmatched in his field. This story is concerned with a mysterious statuette of fabulous value, a beautiful girl who is a remorseless slayer, a desperate group of criminals, and with Samuel Spade, private detective, shyster, Don Juan, an all-round hard-boiled guy, whose quick wit, bravery, superb command of any situation, and complete lack of conscience make him the most formidable of those in pursuit of the falcon.

'This is an exciting book, a fresh sort of book, written by a man who knows how to write . . . and it should certainly be tried by all jaded readers of detective fiction.'—*Life and Letters.*

*Front flap*

*Second-printing dust jacket for the first British edition, initially published in London by Knopf in July 1930. On 17 April 1931 Knopf wrote Hammett to inform him that Knopf had sold his London imprint to Cassell, who rebound Knopf sheets and published them in a binding and dust jacket with the Cassell imprint in place of Knopf (Collection of Richard Layman).*

## The Contemporary Response

*The bracketed passages in the following review indicate those Hammett chose to include in excerpts he sent to his wife. See page 195.*

**New Hammett Book So Good it Stumps Critic:
"The Maltese Falcon" Is Best Detective Story
by Leader in Thriller Field**
Elrick B. Davis
*Cleveland Press,* 1 February 1930

[THERE are detective-story writers, and then there is Dashiell Hammett. I can think of no one in the world who is his match.] This for three very sound reasons: He can plot, and he can write, and he has been a detective. Those reasons are obvious. But his latest book is better than that.

He has been able to write for a long time. In the old smart set days, when he was still a Pinkerton operative, he was one of H. L. Mencken's discoveries. His history since then is romantic and well-known. I have recited it in this space; when his first detective story was published. That was "Red Harvest." After that came "The Dain Curse"—both last year. Both were better than ordinary detective stories because the detectives in them were real detectives.

But his new book, published this week, is as much better than the first two as they were much better than ordinary detective stories. The new book is called "The Maltese Falcon" (Knopf, $2.50). [I find it hard to figure out a way to tell you how good a book "The Maltese Falcon" is.]

To begin with it is a detective story and a mystery story and an uncommonly exciting one, so that [the blood of everyone I know who has read it has pounded in plunging jets thru every vein during all the reading.]

But for all that virtue it is a detective-mystery story in a sort of happily incidental fashion. That is, it is such a story because it is a book about a detective—a private operative in San Francisco.

He is retained by a mysterious and beautiful client, who turns out to be a crook.

Since Spade's client is a crook (and after awhile her crook-opponents are his clients, too, for he has one principle in life: Look out for No. 1), "The Maltese Falcon" turns out to be an underworld story, too.

[And what an underworld story! We've had a flood of them lately, between boards and in the magazines and in the movies, but nothing to touch this.] This book is, of course, frankly romantic—it is a story told to excite and amuse, and there isn't a real name in it—but [it is made of reality.] And the realist thing in it is also the most romantic thing in it. It is the hero, Sam Spade.

*Cover of the* Black Mask *issue that appeared the month after* The Maltese Falcon. *Joseph Shaw felt that the novel had been the most important publication of his career (Collection of Richard Layman).*

Spade

HE is a character, a definite contribution to the picaresque literature of the world. He is hard, he is canny, he is unscrupulous, he is able, he is shrewd. Women are his weakness, but he doesn't let even that interfere with the main chance. Within limits he himself is a crook and the limits are pretty broad. But they are definite. Under all, and after all, and above all, he is a manhunter. He is a craftsman, with that craft's philosophy. It is the philosophy of a "dick."

[The book is written with the snap and bite of a whiplash.] One of its greatest virtues is the fashion in which Hammett uses the jargon of the underworld.

But "The Maltese Falcon" [has a thousand virtues, of observation, of detail, of nuance, and of effect.]

\* \* \*

\* \* \*

## Mystery Yarns Assume More Literary Trend

### Basically Character Stories, Critic Says, Checking Recent Publications

THE SPECIAL tendency of mystery stories now, I gather from those lately on my desk, is to become more and more literary, so that their interest is the legitimate interest due a book rather than the pleasure to be found simply in a pell-mell rush or a puzzle.

At the same time the pell-mell style of mystery is becoming more and more just that; and the puzzler more and more a form of mathematics. Mystery stories that have not gone far in one of those three directions seem pretty old-fashioned now, even tho now and then one of them wins a prize somewhere.

I have remarked here before that Dashiell Hammett's swell detective story, "The Maltese Falcon" (Knopf, $2.50), is a mystery and adventure story in a sort of inevitably incidental fashion—packed with adventure and puzzling mystery tho it is—because what it really is is a glorious book about a detective. The basic interest is in character.

More good new mystery stories, even more literary, also are basically character stories.

–Elrick B. Davis, *Cleveland Press,* 6 March 1930
from Hammett's scrapbook

---

*There is a large, thirty-eight-page scrapbook, with Dashiell Hammett's name stamped on the front, in the Lillian Hellman Collection at the Harry Ransom Humanities Research Center, University of Texas at Austin. The scrapbook contains only news clippings, published primarily between 1926 and 1946. This scrapbook, compiled mainly from articles supplied by a clipping service, seems to have been kept by Hammett himself.*

*The following undated review is from Hammett's scrapbook. The bracketed passages indicate those Hammett chose to include in excerpts he sent to his wife. See page 195.*

### Mr. Hammett's Six-Foot Sam
### [Author of 'Red Harvest' Again Turns Out Mystery Tale That is Literature]
*Detroit News*

Mr. Hammett has abandoned his fat little operative of "Red Harvest" and "The Dain Curse," for Sam Spade, a lounging six-footer, and as single-minded a man as ever worked a case. Spade wades through blood, the blandishments of women, and the power of bribery to solve the mystery of a missing bird of fabulous value, and arrives at the end to discover that the object of his quest was only worthless lead.

No Philo Vance or Sherlock Holmes this man. As he puts it, he blunders along, just a little ahead of anyone else, sweeping from his path the obstacles that arise, finally arriving at his goal by a general policy of "muddling through."

[Again Mr. Hammett has written a fascinating story, thrilling from cover to cover, and amazing in its developments.] Spade is so close to the case that he himself is suspected of two slayings by the San Francisco police, and he extricates himself only by turning in the criminals himself. How he does it makes the story, and it is a bitter story from start to finish.

[Probably the chief pleasure of reading a Hammett novel is the author's evident knowledge of the people with whom he is dealing and his insight into their methods (if they can be called such) and their schemes.] People are shot to death; others fall suddenly doped or slugged and a great liner is burned to the water's edge. No matter—Sam Spade wins through, though at the cost of a heartache to himself and tragedy to others.

Dashiell Hammett writes what he knows, for he was for many years a Pinkerton "op" and gained firsthand experience for his stories. The illness which cost him his career in detection has proved the gain of the world that reads these stories, for he never would have turned to literature otherwise. [And grand literature it is, a racy American sort of writing, of hard, implacable people and desperate criminals and hardly less desperate detectives.]

---

### Taken for a Yokel

Dashiell Hammett, former Pinkerton operative and detective story writer, admits that someone tried to work the "stolen watch racket" on him the other day in New York. He was accosted on Times Square by an individual and offered a watch as a great bargain, the implication being that it was stolen. Hammett kidded the "racketeer" by telling him he had bought a watch just a couple of minutes before. As a successful detective and the author of "The Maltese Falcon," a shrewd detective story shortly to be published by Alfred A. Knopf, Hammett feels that it is very discouraging to be picked for a "yokel" by New York rogues.

–*Cincinnati Enquirer,* 8 February 1930
from Hammett's scrapbook

March 3, 1930

My dear Mr. Hammett:

I have just read THE MALTESE FALCON and I want to
thank you for giving me a lot of pleasure.  I am
ordering RED HARVEST and THE DAIN CURSE.

Cordially yours,

Bruce Barton
383 Madison Avenue
New York City


440 West 34th Street
New York City

February 3, 1930

Dear Hammett:

I have actually read "The Maltese Falcon" three times
since Knopf sent me down a copy, and the more I read it
the better I like it.  I think it is much better than
Red Harvest, and you may recall that I raved considerably over that.  But The "Falcon" is by all odds the
best detective story I have read in years; indeed, I
can't remember that I have ever read a better one.  Sam
Spade is perfect, and so is Brigid.  In every respect
the book is simply swell.  Helen, who is a bit critical
when it comes to detective stories, not only agrees
with me, but contends that she liked it even better
than I did.  Which, of course, is impossible.

Sincerely,

Herbert Asbury


Dear Mr. Hammett:

This is one of those letters that must  start "I have never
written to an author before."

I have never written to an author before.

I have just finished "The Maltese Falcon."  Again, and ever
more, I think you are great.  Thank you for writing; Lord,
what swell books.

Sincerely,

Dorothy Parker
Hotel New Weston
34 East 50th Street
New York City

*Fan letters retyped for Shaw scrapbook. Bruce Barton was a highly successful advertising agent and best-selling author of inspirational religious books. His ad agency, BBDO, created Betty Crocker and popularized the "Harvard Five-Foot Shelf" of classic literature. Dorothy Parker was a journalist, notably for* The New Yorker, *and short story writer. She was one of the wits of the Algonquin Round Table. Scott Cunningham was a book reviewer and friend of* Black Mask *(facsimile; Collection of Richard Layman).*

## A First Best Effort

*Hammett responds to a fan letter from Herbert Asbury, a journalist, book reviewer, and aspiring screenwriter whom he knew socially.*

6 February 1930, 155 E 30th St., New York City

Dear Mr. Asbury,

I can't tell you how pleased I am with your verdict on *The Maltese Falcon*. It's the first thing I've done that was—regardless of what faults it had—the best work I was capable of at the time I was doing it, and, well . . . . . .

*The Glass Key*, held back thus far by laziness, drunkenness, and illness, promises to get itself finished somehow by the latter part of next week. As soon as it's out of the mill I think we ought to get together and celebrate whatever there happens to be to celebrate.

My best to Helen.

Sincerely,
Dashiell Hammett

*—Selected Letters of Dashiell Hammett, 1921–1960, p. 53*

Dear Mr. Hammett:

I haven't - thank God - read every detective story ever published, but I think I've read every good one, and am conceited about my judgment. I've just finished The Maltese Falcon, and Joseph Shaw erred in his estimate only by omitting a few other adjectives that should properly have been used along with 'finest'. The book is swell and it ought to sell a mill on copies. Thank you very much for your letter. I hope you will be lenient with me, for I have taken the liberty of sending all three of the books to you, with the hope that you will inscribe them for me. I should be very genuinely grateful, if you will; and the bundle is wrapped with an eye towards easy disposal from your end. (I can't resist doing this, and realize quite well that I have no business at all further intruding upon your time.)

With felicitations;

Scott Cunningham

13 February 1930

Dashiell Hammett, Esq.

Dear Dashiell Hammett:

You can't do it again -- you know you can't. (I don't usually write in italics -- I tell you this so you will understand the pitch of enthusiasm I reached with the last word of THE MALTESE FALCON which I have just dropped on my desk.)

Leave Sam Spade, leave him, please, at the apogee of his development. I don't want to follow him down to the disappointing valleys and follow him I must if he returns.

With genuflections.

Imogene Stanley
137 E 57° St,
N Y C

Dear Mr. Hammett:

I consider myself something of an authority on mystery fiction although the recent innovations of "Crime of the Week" and "Detective of the Day" clubs have made my task rather hopeless. However when asked three days ago if I had ever read RED HARVEST, I was forced to confess that I had not and was gleefully told that it was the best ever. Well, cutting away a lot of unnecessary shrubbery, I read RED HARVEST Saturday night; THE DAIN CURSE Sunday night; and today bought THE MALTESE FALCON, and have just finished it. My only regret is that the list seems to have run out. When one thinks that Oppenheim has written reams of junk, Wallace has forgotten how many fictional atrocities that he has sired, and Van Dine turns out his ponderous messes on the heels of their predecessors it seems unjust that you have only given us three of your perfect yarns.

This is my first experience of writing testimonials, however worthy the cause, and I know that is probably gives you little joy to receive them but I had to express my appreciation of the fun that you have given me. I notice th t the current New Yorker magazine gives you a great big hand and I can only join in the cheering and hope that you write a lot more and the sooner the better.

I was high time that someone other than art critics and novelists wrote detective fiction. Also the heavy-handed and usually dull reminiscences of the retired sleuth did not fill the bill. Now we have the perfect combination of the erstwhile detective who knows how to write, writing about what he knows. Long may you wave, Mr. Hammett.

Yours,

Norman W. C. MacDonald

Monday, March 3, 1930

A-43 Hamilton Hall
Soldiers Field Station
Boston, Mass.

*Advertisement from Shaw scrapbook.* The Maltese Falcon *was published on Valentine's Day 1930, four and a half months after the stock market crash, at $2.00; in March it was advertised at $2.50, and later in the year the price was reduced back to $2.00 (facsimile; Collection of Richard Layman).*

Whether this story is the equal of its two predecessors is hard to say, but whether it is or not, it is a great tale and deserves great popularity.

\* \* \*

*The bracketed passages in the following review indicate those Hammett chose to include in excerpts he sent to his wife. See page 196.*

**Review of *The Maltese Falcon***
Will Cuppy
*New York Herald Tribune Books,* 23 February 1930, p. 17

[This department announces a new and pretty huge enthusiasm, to wit: Dashiell Hammett. Moreover, it would not surprise me one whit if Mr. Hammett should turn out to be the Great American Mystery Writer. (The fact is, he may be that right now, and this department is merely hopping aboard the Hammett bandwagon ere it be too late–Herbert Asbury, Walter Brooks and Joseph Shaw have already discovered him.)] The utterly convincing quality of Mr. Hammett's detective, Sam Spade, is the big news about "The Maltese Falcon"; Sam's 100 per cent authenticity is powerful enough to make one believe in the jeweled bird once presented by the Knights of Rhodes to the Emperor Charles V–a gadget which might turn up in almost any thriller. Add some most effective tricks of narrative and a satisfactory species of hard-boiled prose to his credit, too, not to mention a slick plot boasting of three murders incidental to a search for the rara avis in San Francisco. [The horsepower of Mr. Hammett's pen,] especially in his brutal and very "different" ending, [must be sampled to be believed]–of a mystery author. [In short, "The Maltese Falcon" is the best one,] outside the gay and polite classes, [in Lord knows when. Read it and see.]

\* \* \*

*Hammett excerpted the first sentence of this review for a letter to his wife. See page 196.*

## Review of *The Maltese Falcon*
*The New York Times,* 23 February 1930

[If the locution "hard-boiled" had not already been coined it would be necessary to coin it now to describe the characters of Dashiell Hammett's latest detective story.] All of the persons of the book are of that description, and the hardest boiled one of the lot is Sam Spade, the private detective, who gives the impression that he is on the side of the law only when it suits his book. If Spade had a weakness it would be women, but appreciative as he is of their charms, never, even in his most intimate relations with them, does he forget to look out for the interests of Samuel Spade. And it is as well that he does, for the criminals, men and women, with whom he comes in contact in this story are almost as hard-boiled as he. Mr. Hammett, we understand, was once a Pinkerton operative, and he probably knows that there is very little romance about the detective business. There is none of it in his book, but there is plenty of excitement.

\* \* \*

## Judging the Books
Ted Shane
*Judge* (1 March 1930)

Should you stumble on a frantic hundred-and-fifty pounder at Madison and Forty-eighth Street booing unheeding passersby; or if later in the day you should come on him pounding on bars, rudely accosting lady shoppers, insulting traffic cops and generally making himself painful around town, that would be us expressing ourself against him who hasn't read Dashiell Hammett. That twenty-minute hard-boiled boy has swept all the dilettante and drawing-room detecatiffs with their tiddledy-wink, card trick and cross-word puzzle mysteries out of Crime Hall and dragged in a free-for-all instead.

He writes with a lead-pipe and poisoned arrows as coups de grace. He stands alone as ace shocker. Hereafter even S. S. Van Dine must lower his monocle, cough up the encyclopedia and eat some humble pie.

We paeaned Hammett's "Red Harvest" till we went blue in the face and other publishers offered us bribes to lay off and give their tittivators a break. It was the pearl of underworld stories, and suggested the nice idea that the way to exterminate killers would be to let them slaughter themselves off. Then came "The Dain Curse," a love-cult mystery, overloaded with plot but 90 per cent pure bonanza. And now "The Maltese Falcon," a button-button-who's-got-the-falcon? of San Francisco.

---

### Some Mysteries And Grim Tales of Unusual Murders

Primarily a thriller, this is a tale of a hard-boiled private detective who deals with desperate characters. It is said that the author was once a Pinkerton detective, and he shows an expert knowledge of the game. With Samuel Spade, the fictional detective, detective work is a grim business. He likes the ladies, but when detective work comes in the door romance flies out the window for this sleuth. There is a neat detective mystery, and even the most sophisticated thrill-lovers will like it.

—*News* (Chattanooga, Tennessee), 1 March 1930
from Hammett's scrapbook

---

It is everything you want. The conventional ingredients of the typical guess-who are there but so handled as to bring on maximum blood pressure. The characters are hard, hatable and out of police headquarters family albums. Sam Spade, the private dick, is harder than Hammett himself. The writing is better than Hemingway; since it conceals not softness but hardness. It is the "Broadway" of mysteries and should have been chosen by a book club. Still unconvinced? Well, it's swell.

\* \* \*

## Not One Hoot for the Law
Donald Douglas
*The New Republic,* 62 (9 April 1930): 226

Let's get down to brass knuckles and argue that no one has any business reading detective stories because they're read by tired presidents, or because they teach coppers how to have and hold a crook. In real life, the important thing is to catch the murderer in the quickest round-up. In fiction, the important thing is *not* to catch the murderer for two hundred pages. And if in real life, our jaded presidents and unemployed wives find "escape" in detective fiction, then so do all readers of Norse myths and the Scotch ballads and the exploits of romantic cowboys. The real, right detective story *is* and should be a myth wherein the demigod (disguised as a superman) pursues the demon-crook through the tangled maze of heart-shuddering adventure. For "real" murders, you have the dullness of courtroom scenes and the dull evidence given by two-fisted dicks.

Until the coming of Mr. Dashiell Hammett in "Red Harvest" and now in "The Maltese Falcon," the memorable detectives were gentlemen. The ever-delightful M. Lecoq and his copy, Mr. Sherlock Holmes, are fair gods against the gnomes. Their only worthy successor, Father Brown, is a priest. Scratch every other detective and you'll

## A Knockout Detective

Sam Spade is a knockout detective, and yet, personally, he cares not a hoot for the law; so little so that constantly is he just on the verge of being pulled by the 'Frisco cops. When Spade goes out after anything neither lead slugs, women, nor the Old Nick himself can stop him from landing it. Here he sets himself to outwit three contending factions who all want the same thing which he also wants and it is only natural, therefore, that many murders strew his winding wake, that several persons suddenly fall doped and a great liner burns mysteriously to the water's edge.

Joseph Shaw, editor of Black Mask and an authority on mystery fiction, says: "We want to go on record as saying that this story is a marvelous piece of writing–the finest detective story it has ever been our privilege to read in book form, in any magazine of any kind, or in manuscript. Don't miss it."

–*News* (Oklahoma City), 7 March 1930
from Hammett's scrapbook

*Clipping in Shaw scrapbook (facsimile; Collection of Richard Layman)*

THE MALTESE FALCON. By Dashiell Hammett. (Alfred A. Knopf, New York.)

It seems a pity that this should be called a detective story. Yet that label is on it. Truly, it is a story about a detective, but it is so much about a detective that he becomes a character, and the sheer force of Hammett's hard, brittle writing lifts the book out of the general run of crime spasms and places it aloof and alone as a brave chronicle of a hard-boiled man, unscrupulous, conscienceless, unique.

The detective is Sam Spade. The book is Sam Spade. The courage is Mr. Hammett's. Courage because Mr. Hammett, writing, as he did, a detective story, subjected plot and all the gymnastic tricks of the usual uninspired detective story, to one clear-cut and memorable character. Yet this book should be read by all lovers of detective fiction. It moves rapidly. It has plot. The element of mystery begins without any preliminaries in the first chapter. Sudden death follows. Weird characters move throughout the book, yet each is delineated with such sure-handed skill that he becomes life-like. The book is entirely without tricks. There are no mysterious doors, no sliding panels, no clews the solution of which would try the patience of a saint. It is a new kind of detective story.

Mr. Hammett's prose is blunt, straightforward and packs a wallop. It is modern, but his sentences do not hang in the air. There is no studied awkwardness, no stilted striving for effect. The story moves on ball bearings and despite all the easy flow of words one suspects that the author tooled it with the conscientious effort of a good craftsman.

L. F. NEBEL

ST. LOUIS POST-DISPATCH 3/11/30

*Clipping in Shaw scrapbook. Frederick Nebel was a frequent contributor to* Black Mask *from March 1926 to August 1936 (facsimile; Collection of Richard Layman).*

More hooey from the press:

Gilbert Seldes in the New York Graphic last Monday—

"The detectives of fiction have been knocked into a cocked hat—
which is where most of them belong—by the appearance of Sam Spade in
a book called The Maltese Falcon. It is the work of Dashiell Hammett;
it is a novel and it is also a mystery story—the combination is so
rare that probably not half a dozen good examples exist between The
Moonstone and the present one.
"The central mystery is not an especial good one; three groups of
people are after an object of enormous value. But everything else,
characters, plot, and the general attitude of the author, are fresh and
novel and brilliant. Spade himself is hard-boiled, immoral, with a
free fist and a free tongue. After the high-minded detective heroes,
with their effeminate manners, their artistic leanings, and their
elaborate deductions, he is as startling as a real man in a show-window
of dummies. His actions and his language will shock old ladies.
"...the romance in the story is blown to bits by bitter realism.
"This book is far better written than most detective stories....
you read it with amazement and with wonder. Because this is the real
thing and everything else has been phony. The publishers quote someone
as saying that Mr. Hammett has done for the mystery story what Dumas did
for the historical romance. I consider that an enthusiastic, but not
unjustifiable, comparison."

Elrick B. Davis in the Cleveland Press:

"HAMMETT BOOK SO GOOD IT STUMPS CRITIC.
"THE MALTESE FALCON IS BEST DETECTIVE STORY BY LEADER IN
THRILLER FIELD.
"There are detective-story writers, and then there is Dashiell
Hammett. I can think of no one in the world who is his match....I
find it hard to figure out a way to tell you how good a book The Maltese
Falcon is....the blood of everyone I know who has read it has pounded
in plunging jets through every vain during all the reading....And what
an underworld story! We've had a flood of them lately, between boards and
in the magazines and in the movies, but nothing to touch this...it is
made of reality...The book is written with the snap and bite of a whiplash
....has a thousand virtues, of observation, of detail, of nuance, and
of effect."

Detroit News:

"AUTHOR OF RED HARVEST AGAIN TURNS OUT MYSTERY TALE THAT
IS LITERATURE.
"Again Mr. Hammett has written a fascinating story, thrilling from
cover to cover, and amazing in its developments....Perhaps the chief
pleasure in reading a Hammett novel is the author's evident knowledge
of the people with whom he is dealing and his insight into their methods
and schemes....And grand literature it is, a racy American sort of writing,
of hard, implacable people and desperate criminals and hardly less
desperate detectives."

*Excerpts from reviews Hammett typed and sent to his wife (courtesy of Josephine Hammett)*

Excerpts from early regiews of THE MALTESE FALCON:

"This department announces a new and pretty huge enthusiasm, to wit: Dashiell Hammett. Moreover, it would
not surprise us one whit if Mr. Hammett should turn out
to be the Great American Mystery Writer. (The fact is,
he may be that right now, and this department is merely
hopping aboard the Hammett band-wagon ere it be too late
----Herbert Asbury, Walter Brooks and Joseph Shaw have
already discovered him.)....The Horsepower of Mr. Hammett's
pen...must be sampled to be believed....In short, "The
Maltese Falcon" is the best one...in Lord knows when.  Read
it and see."  Will Cuppy in the Herald-Tribune.

"If the locution 'hard-boiled' had not already been coined
it would be necessary to coin it now to describe the
characters of Dashiell Hammett's latest detective story."
New York Times.

"First and foremost among the new thrillers comes Dashiell
Hammett's "The Maltese Falcon."  It stands out among the
rest like a .45 among a flock of cap pistols....The story
has plenty of action, a good plot, excellent characterization,
and a startling denouement.  Also, Mr. Hammett knows all
about detective work, and the authors who really know that
can be counted on the thumbs of one hand.  This is not only
probably the best detective story we have ever read, it is
an exceedingly well written novel.  There are few of Mr. Hammett's contemporaries who can write prose as clean-cut,
vivid and realistic."  Walter Brooks in Outlook.

"Until Mr. Hammett appeared, however, no American writer
has taken the detective novel seriously enough to do more
than ape the outstanding characteristics of the British school.
...If you were to consider an amalgamation of Mr. Hemingway,
the Mr. Burnet who wrote 'Little Caesar' and 'Iron Man,' that
other disciple of Hemingway, Morely Callaghan, and Ring Lardner
in his prize-fighting aspect, you would have a fair idea of the
style and technique of Mr. Hammett....There is less beating
about the bush, less mealy-mouthedness, more directness, more
staccato action, in the pages of 'Red Harvest' than in any
other one publication I remember recently....This is good
writing, it's vigorous writing, it is personal writing.  It
has character.  It has sincerity....I think Mr. Hammett has
something quite as definite to say, quite as decided an impetus
to give the course of newness in the development of the
American tongue, as any man now writing."  William Curtis in
Town & Country.

## Why Give Crook an Even Break?

### Ex-Cop, Turned Writer, Treats 'Em Rough.

"Nothing is more idiotic," says Dashiell Hammett, former detective, now one of the best detective story writers, "than giving a crook an even break. When I was with the Pinkertons a few years ago I was assigned to trail a jewelry salesman who was under suspicion. He changed trains twice a day. I stuck along. Finally we put up at the same hotel in New Orleans.

"'Haven't I seen you some place before?' he asked me. 'I think you have,' I told him. I said I was working for a national manufacturer and had been travelling about checking up on retailers.

### Warrant Arrives.

"The poor devil was lonely and needed a friend, and so he seized upon me. By that time the warrant for him had arrived. I took it to the police and gave them his room number.

"He was dumfounded when arrested. He pleaded for a few minutes to see a friend. The cops asked who the friend was, and when he told them they never batted an eye, but let him go to my room.

"The salesman pressed a number of letters into my hand and begged me to see they were delivered. I promised. Then he was led off to jail.

"The letters were to his wife and several sweethearts. They told where he hid jewelry he had stolen. I forwarded them to the Philadelphia prosecutor. The salesman went over the road.

"Taking advantage of him? Really, you can't take advantage of a crook."

### Master of Double-Cross.

Hammett's books are like that. His characters kick, bite and claw. His mysteries are solved by deduction–and a sock on the jaw. His detectives are masters of the double-cross.

Such is Spade, his detective in "The Maltese Falcon" (Knopf), his latest work, and of the same timber are his characters in "The Dain Curse" and "Red Harvest." He scorns the erudite dilettante detective and relies on actual detective methods to bring about his solutions.

One expects to find a big shouldered man, wearing a derby hat and talking out of the corner of his mouth. But Hammett is tall, lean and almost delicate in appearance. His face is thin, surmounted by a huge graying pompadour. His fingers are amazingly long. His voice is decisive but gentle. He reminds one of Philo Vance.

–Elmer Roessner,
*New York Telegram,* 4 April 1930
from Hammett's scrapbook

find a M. Lecoq. Now comes Mr. Hammett's tough guy in "Red Harvest" and his Sam Spade in "The Maltese Falcon," and you find the Pinkerton operative as a scoundrel without pity or remorse, taking his whiffs of drink and his casual amours between catching crooks, treating the police with a cynical contempt, always getting his crook by foul and fearless means, above the law like a satyr–and Mr. Hammett describing his deeds in a glistening and fascinating prose as "American" as Lardner's, and every bit as original in musical rhythm and bawdy humor.

There is nothing like these books in the whole range of detective fiction. The plots don't matter so much. The art does; and there is an absolute distinction of real art. It is (in its small way) like Wagner writing about the gnomes in "Rheingold." The gnomes have an eloquence of speech and a fascinating mystery of disclosure. Don't get me wrong, bo. It's not the tawdry gum-shoeing of the ten-cent magazine. It is the genuine presence of the myth. The *events* of "The Maltese Falcon" may have happened that way in "real" life. No one save Mr. Hammett could have woven them to such a silver-steely mesh.

\* \* \*

*Hammett's novel was published in London by Knopf in July 1930. It sold for 7s. 6d. in Great Britain.*

### Review of *The Maltese Falcon*
*The Times Literary Supplement,* 14 August 1930, p. 654

After the Knights of Rhodes had been expelled by Suleiman the Magnificent in 1523 they settled in Crete, by the grace of the Emperor Charles V., and persuaded him to give them Malta. But as a condition the Emperor demanded every year a falcon in acknowledgment that Malta was still under Spanish rule. The Knights hit upon the idea of sending Charles not an insignificant stuffed bird, but a falcon of chaste workmanship, made of gold and encrusted with jewels. For more than seventy years, so the story goes, the bird disappeared, until at length it was traced to an antique dealer in Paris, and later to the home of a Russian general in Constantinople. Here Mr. Gutman, a wealthy American, gets news of the bird, which has been covered with a coat of black enamel to hide its value from curious eyes. He hires two members of a gang, a beautiful, unscrupulous young woman and an overdressed Greek, to steal the bird for him. They succeed in doing so, but each is suspicious of the other, so the girl sneaks the bird on board a ship at Hong-kong, with instructions that it is to await her arrival in San Francisco. A detective is hired by other members of the gang to secure possession of the falcon–though when he finally does so, and presents it to Mr. Gutman, it is discovered that——. A good "thriller."

\* \* \*

# BEHIND THE MASK

YO-HO-HO . . . And a bottle of mucilage . . . And a pair of shears . . . We are busy . . . Cutting clippings . . . The papers are full of them . . . Also the mail . . . And here are a few . . . Will Cuppy says "He should turn out to be the great American mystery writer" . . . Carl Van Vechten says "He is raising the detective story to the plane Alexandre Dumas raised the historical novel" . . . Walter Brooks says "Probably the best detective story we have ever read" . . . Ted Shane says "Better than Hemingway. It is everything you want." . . . Eugene Cunningham says "The outstanding writer in the field of detective fiction." . . . Bruce Barton says "Thanks for the enjoyment you have given me." . . . There are lots more . . . But these are the best critics in America . . . Wait a moment . . . Perhaps we can get him over to the mike . . . Yes, here he comes . . . Ladies and gentlemen . . .

Dashiell  Hammett

*"Hello Folks . . . Glad to be with you . . . Will tell you a story of an Agency Op very soon . . . Thanks a lot . . ."*

119

*Editor's column in the June 1930 issue of* Black Mask *featuring Hammett*
*(Collection of Richard Layman)*

Yes, that was Mr. Hammett . . . Started writing in *Black Mask* . . . Still writing for us . . . We know him . . . And thought he would be great . . . But it took the *Black Mask* stories published in book form . . . To wake up the country . . . As to how great he really is . . . We get 'em in *Black Mask* first . . . And the critics wait for them in books . . . And then say how good they are . . . Fair enough . . .

HAPSBURG LIEBE who wrote RED DICE . . . In this issue . . . Tells us . . . "We have an honest-to-goodness cow country . . . Here in Florida . . . One outfit runs 200,000 . . . Head of cattle . . . A round-up is a 'cow-hunt' . . . Earmarks are considered . . . More important than brands . . . The Florida cowpoke uses a twenty-odd foot stock whip . . . With which he can cut a snake's head off . . . And take a cigarette out of your mouth . . . (Not mine, thank you kindly) . . . And never touch hide." . . .

GEORGE C. KERN of Buffalo writes . . . "I'd walk ten miles if necessary to get my copy of *Black Mask*" . . . Edward W. Jewell, of Vancouver, writes . . . "Mr. Gardner is a gifted writer . . . I hope he will soon get out Black Barr and dust him off" . . . L. B. Kohnen, of Mt. Healthy, O., writes . . . "I wish *Black Mask* was published weekly instead of monthly" . . . (He should have a heart!) . . . Upton Meriwether, Box 505, Clovis, N. M. . . . Boosts the idea of Behind the Mask and says . . . "I'd like to get acquainted with some of the other *Black Mask* readers" . . . Bruce Griss, of Jersey, Channel Islands, Great Britain, writes . . . "We have not a magazine in Europe to equal *Black Mask*" . . . Mrs. Susie Murphy, of Charleston, West Va., asks . . . "Why can't we have some more stories of the Rev. MacGregor Daunt?" . . . (Attention of J. Paul Suter) . . . Well—Here's the music . . . Write your own words . . .

J. T. S.

120

## An Appreciated Denial

Mayor Harding of New York *was published by Mohawk Press in New York in 1931. It was described by the publisher as a "novel by a world traveler who finally settled in New York and became active in its' [sic] political life."*

MOHAWK writes that they would appreciate the publication of a denial of the rumor that Dashiell Hammett is Stephen Endicott, author of "Mayor Harding of New York."

Even without consulting the author of "The Glass Key," we have a feeling that he, too, would appreciate the same denial.

*—New York Post*
from Hammett's scrapbook

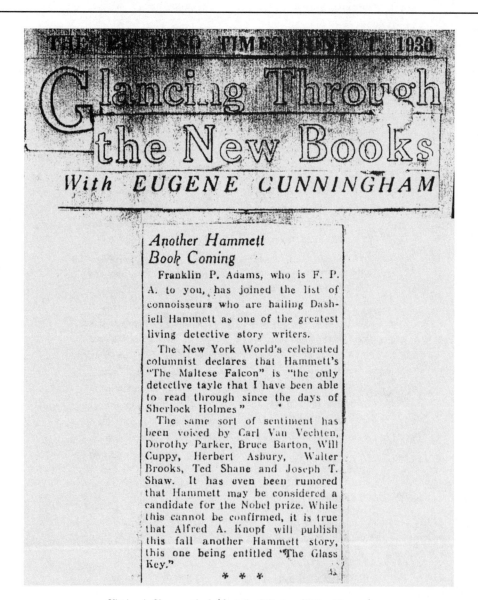

THE EL PASO TIMES, JUNE 1, 1930

# Glancing Through the New Books
## With EUGENE CUNNINGHAM

### Another Hammett Book Coming

Franklin P. Adams, who is F. P. A. to you, has joined the list of connoisseurs who are hailing Dashiell Hammett as one of the greatest living detective story writers.

The New York World's celebrated columnist declares that Hammett's "The Maltese Falcon" is "the only detective tayle that I have been able to read through since the days of Sherlock Holmes."

The same sort of sentiment has been voiced by Carl Van Vechten, Dorothy Parker, Bruce Barton, Will Cuppy, Herbert Asbury, Walter Brooks, Ted Shane and Joseph T. Shaw. It has even been rumored that Hammett may be considered a candidate for the Nobel prize. While this cannot be confirmed, it is true that Alfred A. Knopf will publish this fall another Hammett story, this one being entitled "The Glass Key."

\* \* \*

*Clippings in Shaw scrapbook (facsimile; Collection of Richard Layman)*

## Oh, Look–Two Good Books!

Dorothy Parker

*The New Yorker,* 7 (25 April 1931): 83–84

It seems to me that there is entirely too little screaming about the work of Dashiell Hammett. My own shrill yaps have been ascending ever since I first found "Red Harvest," and from that day the man has been, God help him, my hero; but I talked only yesterday, I forget why, with two of our leading booksy folk, and they had not heard of that volume, nor had they got around to reading its better, "The Maltese Falcon."

It is true that Mr. Hammett displays that touch of rare genius in his selection of undistinguished titles for his mystery stories–"The Maltese Falcon" and "The Glass Key," his new one, sound like something by Carolyn Wells. It is true that had the literary lads got past those names and cracked the pages, they would have found the plots to be so many nuisances; confusing to madness, as in "Red Harvest;" fanciful to nausea, as in "The Maltese Falcon;" or, as in the case of the newly-published "The Glass Key," so tired that even this reviewer, who in infancy was let drop by a nurse with the result that she has ever since been mystified by amateur coin-tricks, was able to guess the identity of the murderer from the middle of the book. It is true that he has all the mannerisms of Hemingway, with no inch of Hemingway's scope nor flicker of Hemingway's beauty. It is true that when he seeks to set down a swift, assured, well-bred young woman, he devises speeches for her such as are only equaled by the talk Mr. Theodore Dreiser compiled for his society flapper in "An American Tragedy." It is true that he is so hard-boiled you could roll him on the White House lawn. And it is also true that he is a good, hell-bent, cold-hearted writer, with a clear eye for the ways of hard women and a fine ear for the words of hard men, and his books are exciting and powerful and–if I may filch the word from the booksy ones–pulsing. It is difficult to conclude an outburst like this. All I can say is that anybody who doesn't read him misses much of modern America. And hot that sounds!

DASHIELL HAMMETT is as American as a sawed-off shotgun. He is as immediate as a special extra. Brutal he is, but his brutality, for what he must write, is clean and necessary, and there is in his work none of the smirking and swaggering savageries of a Hecht or a Bodenheim. He does his readers the infinite courtesy of allowing them to supply descriptions and analyses for themselves. He sets down only what his characters say, and what they do. It is not, I suppose, any too safe a recipe for those who cannot create characters, but Dashiell Hammett can and does and has and, I hope, will. On gentle ladies he is, in a word, rotten; but maybe sometime he will do a novel without a mystery plot, and so no doggy girls need come into it. But it is denied us who read to have everything, and it is little enough to let him have his ladies and his mysteries, if he

will give us such characters as Sam Spade, in "The Maltese Falcon," and such scenes as the beating-up of Ned Beaumont in "The Glass Key."

His new book, "The Glass Key," seems to me nowhere to touch its predecessor. Surely it is that Beaumont, the amateur detective of the later story, a man given perhaps a shade too much to stroking his moustache with a thumbnail, can in no way stack up against the magnificent Spade, with whom, after reading "The Maltese Falcon," I went mooning about in a daze of love such as I had not known for any character in literature since I encountered Sir Launcelot when I hit the age of nine. (Launcelot and Spade–ah well, they're pretty far apart, yet I played Elaine to both of them, and in that lies a life-story.) The new book, or, indeed, any new book, has no figure to stand near Sam Spade, but maybe all the matter is not there. For I thought that in "The Glass Key" Mr. Hammett seemed a little weary, a little short of spontaneous, a little dogged about his simplicity of style, a little determined to make startling the ordering of his brief sentences, a little concerned with having his conclusion approach the toughness of the superb last scene of "The Maltese Falcon." But all that is not to say that "The Glass Key" is not a good book and an enthralling one, and the best you have read since "The Maltese Falcon." And if you didn't read that, this is the swiftest book you've ever read in your life.

---

### A Boy's Choice

CHILDREN'S Book Week. Again we are assaulted with advice about good books for "children," as if children were like a row of carrots, all requiring the same chemical composition of the soil and the same weeding and harrowing. Again a host of parents and librarians report devoutly on "good children's books," meaning books they like, or, at most, books that their particular children like.

*Dumas and Mark Twain vs. Dashiell Hammett*

My own son, aged twelve, has been plowing through the works of Alexandre Dumas with somewhat the enthusiasm which I, at his age, gave to Cooper and Scott. He does not like Cooper or Scott. He adores Dumas and reveres Mark Twain. But when, the other evening, I interviewed the son of Harrison Smith, who is about the same age, he expressed a vague distaste for Dumas–I was not very sure that he had ever tried him; dismissed Mark Twain with the comment, "Well, he's O.K., but he overdoes things, and then he falls down badly"; and recommended earnestly the works of Dashiell Hammett. He had recently read a story by William Faulkner, and he did not like that either.

–Lewis Gannett, "Books and Things,"
*New York Herald Tribune,* 16 November 1931
from Hammett's scrapbook

# THE DETECTIVE'S STORY.

On another page to-day we print the first instalment of a very rare literary phenomenon—a detective story by a real detective. The history of Mr. Dashiell Hammett's life has been, in its way, as strange and unexpected as the histories he writes of other people's lives. A Pinkerton's man to begin with, he found his health so much injured by war service that his return to his old profession did not last long. But, fortunately for him and for great numbers of readers, he found at the same time that he could write, and that so well that very shortly it became apparent that there was no further need for him to trouble himself about anything else.

Now in real life the profession of a detective is not as a rule a romantic one, nor are detectives usually at all romantic persons. The tasks they have to carry out, necessary as they may be, are generally humdrum and often sordid. It is not a life which stimulates the imagination, and those who follow it are very infrequently imaginative persons. In this, at least, the old type of detective story, in which the amateur always outshone the professional, was right enough. Where it was wrong was in postulating the brilliant amateur. The hunting out of crime is almost always, in practice, the accumulation of a great heap of uninteresting details.

The professional detective who turns novelist has a tendency to bring the prosaic nature of his training even into what he intends to be his wildest flights of fancy. Further, the expert in any subject has always a tendency, whatever his desire may be, to write for other experts rather than for the public at large. Where anything in the way of entertainment is involved too much knowledge is a very dangerous thing indeed. The expert supposes that technical points which interest him and his colleagues must interest everyone else : he is afraid of leaving unexplained some trivial detail on which a fellow expert will seek to trip him up.

Now in this sort of fiction the public does not want scientific accuracy, but it does want movement, and these two things are often in conflict. That conflict Mr. Hammett has known how to avoid. He is not muscle-bound with too much knowledge. He moves as freely as though he were in the realm of fairyland and free imagination—and it is an assured fact that the best of all detective stories take place in fairylands of their own. But he provides an atmosphere of realism evidently drawn from his own experience. He really has made the best of both worlds, and that is a very remarkable and unusual performance.

On another page the readers of the "Evening Standard" will be able to follow the adventures of Sam Spade and his associates in pursuit of the Maltese Falcon. It is not in our province now to tell them what the adventures are going to be, and we are quite sure that th⋯ ⋯ ⋯ ⋯nk us for doing so. ⋯ ⋯ are sure also of another thing, that when they come to the end of them they will realise that they have been for a time in another world, which, whether it exists or not, certainly ought to exist, so strange and varied and exciting are the things that can happen in this world the ex-detective has created. We might not, perhaps, care to live in it in the flesh : it is a little too exciting for that—but we must be grateful for this vivid glimpse of it.

*Introduction and opening of the newspaper serialization of Hammett's novel in the* London Evening Standard, *clipped for the Shaw scrapbook ( facsimile; Collection of Richard Layman)*

Saturday, January 3, 1931. THE EVENING STANDARD.

**Something New in Detective Fiction.**

# THE MALTESE FALCON
### By Dashiell Hammett,

WHO TELLS OF

Samuel Spade, relentless sleuth : of medieval treasure of fabulous worth: of a beautiful and mysterious Irish girl : of a desperate gang of international criminals : of murder—of thrill after thrill.

*I Didn't Know:*

## A Case of Plagiarism

*The following undated article was clipped for Hammett's scrapbook.*

Book Stopped by a Publisher:
**Similarity Puzzle: Author's Statement**
*London Daily Express, 1933*

The discovery yesterday of an extraordinary similarity between two detective mystery "thrillers"—one by an American and the other by a young British writer—led to the decision last night to suspend one of them.

The two books are "The Maltese Falcon," by Dashiell Hammett, an American, which has been published both here and in the United States, and "Death in the Dark," by Cecil Henderson.

### First Publication

"The Maltese Falcon" appeared first in this country in August 1930. "Death in the Dark" was first published this year.

"The Maltese Falcon" was published by Messrs. Cassell, while the British author's work came from Messrs. Lincoln Williams and Co.

Following the discovery of the resemblance between the two books by the "Evening Standard," Mr. Williams last night informed a "Daily Express" representative that he had decided to suspend publication of his author's book.

"When I was told that there was this resemblance between the two books I communicated immediately with my solicitors," he said. "I have been advised by them of the course I should take.

"I have telephoned the author asking him to come and see me. Needless to say, my firm accepted 'Death in the Dark' in all good faith."

Mr. Newman Flower, managing director of Messrs. Cassell, said:

"Until our attention had been drawn to it we had not been aware of the resemblance.

"Our firm must take action immediately. Our solicitors will be instructed to investigate the matter."

### Author's "Model"

In an interview with a "Daily Express" representative last night Mr. Cecil Henderson said:—

"I have read 'The Maltese Falcon' several times.

"I was so much impressed with it that I decided to take it as a model for my literary work. I had no intention of doing anything that could be assumed to be wrong with Mr. Hammett's novel.

"I have another novel due to appear and I am quite willing to hand over the royalties from it to Mr. Hammett in compensation.

"It is my one hope that the book will be withdrawn immediately, for I have never done anything deceptive in my life, and I had no idea of causing any one any annoyance through my action."

\* \* \*

197

**Briton, 21, Admits Plagiary of Novel**
*The New York Times,* 26 September 1933

Says He 'Wrote Up' 'The Maltese Falcon,'
by an American, 'Just for Fun.'
BOOK POPULAR IN LONDON
Cecil Henderson Is Ready to Yield Royalties
to Author, Dashiell Hammett.
Special Cable to THE NEW YORK TIMES
LONDON, Tuesday, Sept. 26. —Cecil Henderson, 21-year-old amateur novelist, admitted tonight having plagiarized "The Maltese Falcon," a detective novel by an American, Dashiell Hammett. Henderson said he did it "just for fun."

"I am terribly sorry about the whole affair," said the young author after learning that the publication of his book, "Death in the Dark," had been suspended.

"I read 'The Maltese Falcon' many times," he said, "and was very much struck with it. I had often thought of writing a novel myself and frequently sketched out rough ideas. Then, simply for practice, I wrote up 'The Maltese Falcon.' Sometime later unthinkingly really.

I just submitted the manuscript to a publisher, who accepted it as an original work.

"I realize now how stupid I was. I would be willing to hand over any royalties to Mr. Hammett."

It is expected that Lincoln Williams, the hoaxed publisher, as well as the British publishers of "The Maltese Falcon" will take legal action against Henderson. His book was published last Friday and is selling well.

The similarity between the two books was revealed last night by The Evening Standard, which published in parallel columns identical paragraphs from the novels. The plots are almost identical, but "The Maltese Falcon" has two murders while Henderson's book had only one.

Henderson's publisher had another book from the young man, which was to have been published in a few weeks.

\* \* \*

**British Bar Sale of Book**
*The New York Times,* 28 September 1933, p. 26

Author and Publisher of Plagiaristic Novel
Are Enjoined.
Wireless to THE NEW YORK TIMES.
LONDON, Sept. 27.—A temporary injunction was granted today against Lincoln Williams, publisher, and Cecil Henderson, author of the thriller "Death in the Dark," an alleged plagiarism on "The Maltese Falcon," by the American writer, Dashiell Hammett.

The 21-year-old English author already has admitted he copied Mr. Hammett's best seller "just for fun." The injunction was applied for by Mr. Hammett's publishers, Cashell's, [sic] after the similarity was revealed by The Evening Standard.

\* \* \*

**Hammett's Rights Upheld in Britain**
*The New York Times,* 14 October 1933, p. 13

Injunction and Accounting Are
Fixed for Man Whose Book
Is Like 'Maltese Falcon.'
PUBLISHER ACCEPTS ORDER
Williams Agrees to Turn Over
Unsold Copies of Henderson's
'Death in the Dark.'
Wireless to THE NEW YORK TIMES
LONDON, Oct. 13.—The litigation over the similarity between two detective novels—"Maltese Falcon," by the American, Dashiell Hammett, and Cecil Henderson's "Death in the Dark"—was concluded in the courts today.

Mr. Henderson submitted to a perpetual injunction, an accounting for the profits and delivery of all unsold copies of the infringing book. He was ordered to pay the costs of the action. His publishers agreed to a similar order.

———

## Funny Coincidence Department

The city wasn't pretty . . . the smelters whose brick stacks stuck up tall against a gloomy mountain to the south had yellow-smoked everything into uniform dinginess. . . . The first policeman I saw needed a shave. The second had a couple of buttons off his shabby uniform. The third stood in the center of the city's main intersection–Broadway and Union Street–directing traffic with a cigar in one corner of his mouth.–*Dashiell Hammett in "Red Harvest," 1929.*

One look at Cranville was enough. . . . In the far distance I could see the high brick stacks of the smelters stuck up against the skyline. They belched black smoke that had, in the course of time, yellow-smoked everything into uniform dinginess. . . . The first policeman I saw needed a shave and two buttons from his uniform were missing. The second, directing traffic, had a cigar in his mouth.–*Raymond Marshall in "Blondes' Requiem," 1946.*

–*The New Yorker,* 13 July 1948
from Hammett's scrapbook

Dashiell Hammett, a former Pinkerton detective, wrote "The Maltese Falcon" in 1929. It was published by Alfred A. Knopf in 1930. In 1931, it was produced as a motion picture.

Last month, Cecil Henderson, 21-year-old amateur English novelist, wrote "Death in the Dark." He took the book to Lincoln Williams, a London publisher, who published it in good faith. A few days after its publication, when it had already become a big seller, The Evening Standard pointed out that it was almost identical with Mr. Hammett's "Maltese Falcon." The suit followed, being brought by Cashell's, [sic] Mr. Hammett's English publishers.

Mr. Henderson admitted, during the trial, that he had copied Mr. Hammett's book, said he did it "for practice," and declared himself willing to pay Mr. Hammett all royalties.

## Sales of *The Maltese Falcon*

*In 1948 Warner Bros. sued parties related to the radio series The Adventures of Sam Spade for copyright infringement. The suit was finally resolved in Hammett's favor on 28 December 1951, a decision upheld in U.S. District Court of Appeals on 9 November 1954. This affidavit was filed in connection with that suit.*

JOSEPH C. LESSER, being duly sworn, deposes and says:

That he is Treasurer of ALFRED A. KNOPF, INC., a New York corporation with its principal office at 501 Madison Avenue, New York 22, New York, which is named as a party plaintiff in this action. For convenience, said corporation will be hereinafter referred to as "Knopf".

The work entitled THE MALTESE FALCON by Dashiell Hammett was published by said corporation, under contract with the author, on February 14, 1930. The sales of said work from 1930 to 1934 were as follows:

| Year | Number of copies |
|---|---|
| 1930 | 9,006 |
| 1931 | 1,080 |
| 1932 | 45 |
| 1933 | 3 |
| 1934 | 75 |
| | Total - 10,209 |

In 1945, Knopf reissued THE MALTESE FALCON in The Black Widow Thriller series. Sales of said work in said series were as follows:

| Year ending | Number of copies |
|---|---|
| April 30, 1945 | 1,231 |
| "      " 1946 | 251 |
| "      " 1947 | 98 |
| "      " 1948 | 40 |
| "      " 1949 | 45 |
| "      " 1950 | 48 |
| 6 mos. ending October 31, 1950 | 28 |
| | Total - 1,741 |

Knopf also published a Hammett Omnibus volume which contained THE MALTESE FALCON, the sales of which were as follows:

| Year | Number of copies |
|---|---|
| 1935 | 2,808 |
| 1936 | 402 |
| 1937 | 221 |
| 1938 | 47 |
| 1939 | 48 |
| 1940 | 30 |
| January-April 1941 | 35 |
| Year ending April 30, 1942 | 146 |
| | Total - 3,737 |

In addition, Knopf published a "Complete Hammett", which likewise contained THE MALTESE FALCON, the sales of which were as follows:

| Year | Number of copies |
|---|---|
| 1943 | 6,280 |
| 1944 | 936 |
| Year ending April 30, 1945 | 8 |
| "        "        "    " 1946 | - |
| "        "        "    " 1947 | 195 |
| | 7,419 |

Knopf licensed reprint editions of THE MALTESE FALCON and omnibus volumes containing THE MALTESE FALCON, to the publishers hereinafter named, as follows:

## GROSSETT & DUNLAP:

1. Contract dated March 15, 1930, for an edition of THE MALTESE FALCON to retail at one dollar per copy, with royalties payable according to statements rendered semi-annually. Sales were reported to Knopf as follows, as of the dates indicated:

| Date | Number of copies |
|---|---|
| February 1931 | 7,500 |
| July 1931 | 4,252 |
| December 1931 | 4,138 |
| July 1932 | 1,025 |
| December 1932 | 460 |
| July 1933 | 334 |
| December 1933 | 359 |
| July 1934 | 1,585 |
| December 1934 | 1,458 |
| June 1935 | 668 |
| December 1935 | 578 |
| June 1936 | 373 |
| December 1936 | 344 |
| June 1937 | 313 |
| December 1937 | 288 |
| June 1938 | 184 |
| December 1939 | 208 |
| | Total - 24,067 |

2. Contract dated March 29, 1935, for a "Hammett Omnibus", which included THE MALTESE FALCON, to retail at one dollar per copy, with royalties in excess of the guarantee on 10,000 copies, payable according to statements rendered semi-annually. No statements were received by Knopf indicating sales in excess of the 10,000 copy guarantee.

3. Contract dated March 12, 1943, for a fifty cent edition, with royalties payable according to statements rendered semi-annually. Sales were reported to Knopf as follows, as of the dates indicated:

| Date | Number of copies |
|---|---|
| October 1943 | 15,047 |
| February 1945 | 3,199 |
| September 1945 | 5,002 |
| March 1946 | 1,222 |
| August 1946 | 411 |
| February 1947 | 9 |
| August 1947 | 6 |
| Total - 24,896 | |

## MODERN LIBRARY:

4. Contract dated November 1, 1933, for an edition to retail at the standard Modern Library price per copy, with royalties in excess of the guarantee on 5,000 copies, payable according to statements rendered semi-annually. Sales were reported to Knopf as follows, as of the dates indicated:

| Date | Number of copies |
|---|---|
| March 1934 | 5,000 |
| February 1936 | 584 |
| August 1936 | 508 |
| January 1937 | 504 |
| August 1937 | 647 |
| January 1938 | 452 |
| August 1938 | 351 |
| February 1939 | 397 |
| August 1939 | 422 |
| February 1940 | 350 |
| August 1940 | 347 |
| February 1941 | 284 |
| June 1941 | 587 |
| December 1941 | 943 |
| June 1942 | 2,553 |
| December 1942 | 1,818 |
| June 1943 | 2,389 |
| January 1944 | 3,047 |
| June 1944 | 3,405 |
| January 1945 | 1,371 |
| August 1945 | 4,100 |
| January 1946 | 2,172 |
| August 1946 | 2,979 |
| January 1947 | 1,762 |
| July 1947 | 1,122 |
| July 1948 | 254 |
| January 1949 | 174 |
| Total - 38,522 | |

*Dust jacket for the first Modern Library edition (Collection of Richard Layman)*

### THE WORLD PUBLISHING COMPANY

5. Contract dated February 14, 1944, for an Omnibus volume consisting of THE MALTESE FALCON and THE GLASS KEY, with royalties in excess of the minimum guarantee on 10,000 copies, payable according to statements rendered semi-annually. Sales were reported to Knopf as follows, as of the dates indicated:

| Date | Number of copies |
|------|------------------|
| August 1944 | 10,000 |
| February 1945 | 847 |
| August 1945 | 6,850 |
| February 1946 | 2,376 |
| August 1946 | 597 |
| May 1947 | 1,837 |
| September 1947 | 446 |
| April 1948 | 639 |
| | Total - 23,592 |

### READERS LEAGUE OF AMERICA:

6. Contract dated February 1, 1945, for a special edition - one printing only of 40,973 copies - for exclusive distribution to the American Red Cross. As the royalty was paid on completion of printing, no report of sales or distribution was made to Knopf.

### POCKET BOOKS, INC.:

7. Contract dated April 15, 1942, for a twenty-five cent paper bound edition, with royalties payable according to statements rendered semi-annually. Sales were reported to Knopf as follows, as of the dates indicated:

| Date | Number of copies |
|------|------------------|
| July 1945 | 319,185 |
| August 1945 | 176,842 |
| February 1946 | 153,532 |
| February 1950 | 35,397 |
| August 1950 | 9,004 |
| | Total - 693,960 |

## *Falcon* in the Modern Library

"Dashiell Hammett," once remarked Carl Van Doren in an outburst of enthusiasm, "has raised the detective story to that plane to which Alexandre Dumas raised the historical novel." This may sound a trifle odd, but it is simply Van Doren's way of saying that the crime stories written by this Pinkerton detective turned author are worth reading.

One of Hammett's crime stories has just been reprinted as the latest title in the Modern Library. It is "The Maltese Falcon," and it is the first detective story ever to be included in the Modern Library.

"The Maltese Falcon" is a hard-boiled crime story. It is to be read not so much for its mystery element, but rather for its grimly realistic depiction of the folkways of real detectives and criminals. Its verisimilitude, its rogues' gallery characters and atmosphere, is its outstanding feature.

The sleuth in this tale is Sam Spade, a private detective. No bookish character, but a real tough baby, hard, shifty, relentless. No Sherlock Holmes fiddling around with the various kinds of cigar ashes, no debonair Philo Vance drawling languidly about the best fragments of Menander, is this Sam Spade, but a hard-boiled sleuth whose counterpart you can find in any metropolitan police station.

In "The Maltese Falcon," Spade is mixed up with a lot of killing and general hell-raising over the jeweled statuette of a Maltese falcon, said to date from the early 16th century and to be of fabulous value. A gang of international crooks are after this bird, and when the pursuit reaches San Francisco, Spade is drawn into it.

His partner gets knocked off one night, and he gets in a bad jam with the cops, and he gets hold of the bird but it turns out to be a . . . but to find just what happens to this hard-boiled detective and just what he does, you will have to read this story yourself. It is decidedly different in tone and atmosphere and general management from the conventional detective story; it is far more life-like; and it is downright engrossing once you get well into it.

—*News* (Galveston, Texas), 1 April 1934

KING FEATURES SYNDICATE:

8. Contract dated January 31, 1945, for a paper bound "comic adaptation", to retail at 10 cents. Reports of sales received by Knopf were as follows: In March 1945, Knopf received a royalty payment based on 250,000 copies and in September 1946, Knopf received a royalty payment based on an additional 50,000 copies.

Sworn to before me this     [signed] __Joseph C. Lesser__
    day of January, 1951.

_____

    Notary Public

*New York: Spivak, 1942. Includes two Sam Spade short stories.*

*New York: Spivak, 1949. Retitled reprint.*

# Critical Views of *The Maltese Falcon*

The Maltese Falcon *has attracted a significant body of literary criticism. The best guide to scholarly works about the novel published before 1993 is* The Critical Response to Dashiell Hammett, *edited by Christopher Metress (Westport, Conn.: Greenwood Press, 1994). The* MLA Directory of Periodicals *lists fifty-five articles in professional journals about Hammett, not including important books about him, published in the decade after Metress's book. There are many more significant works in journals not catalogued by the Modern Language Association and a growing number of useful postings on the Internet. The articles included here have been selected to provide an indication of the approaches scholars have taken toward Hammett's work, not as recommendations about how to read the novel.*

## Sam Spade Talking
John M. Reilly
*Clues,* 1 (Fall–Winter 1980): 119–125

The exemplary image in the history of nineteenth century American literary prose is that of Samuel L. Clemens reading aloud to himself the fabulations of Mark Twain, adjusting written diction to the resonance of speech and adapting spoken language to the conventions of punctuation until the completed narrative achieved a synthesis of its vernacular origins and formal aims. Images to illustrate the further course of American prose in the twentieth century crowd upon us. There are Dreiser and Hemingway each in his own way employing the styles of newspaper writing, Faulkner extending the manner of Southern story-telling, Lardner heightening the humor of wise guys. But if we wish to observe in brief what becomes of the simulated American speech which Clemens refined as a literary instrument, we cannot do better than to attend to Dashiell Hammett's creation of Sam Spade talking.

One is tempted to say that Hammett exemplifies the twentieth century version of Clemens' project, because like his predecessor he made literature out of a popular story form, which is true, but equally true of many other authors. Nor can it be said, let alone urged, that Hammett's way of telling a story is in direct line of descent from Clemens'. No, Hammett signifies a relationship between nineteenth and twentieth century American fiction, because our imaginations are intrigued by the thought that Sam Spade is what Huck Finn would have become when he found the Territory, where he hoped to escape civilization, dotted with cities and when maturity converted his sense of complicity in events into a principle of behavior. Thus, to witness Hammett's representation of Sam Spade talking is to see the vernacular style Clemens refined for moral judgment amidst the evils of nineteenth century American social life adapted to the conditions of crime in modern, urban America.

Taking up *The Maltese Falcon,* we are struck at once by Hammett's severe restriction of the range of possibility for Spade's speech. Sam occupies the center of a narrative named not for him, but for the object serving as the nexus of relationships among thieves. The art of men fabricated the Maltese falcon as an emblem of power and subordination, and from the time of its creation it has, through the provocation of greed and conniving, confirmed a principle of alienation. Sam can direct events when he appears to have utility in securing the falcon for the conspirators. He cannot otherwise create relationships, however, for his will functions only in the context of other wills intersecting in relation to the falcon, and the entire pattern is determined by the authority of material wealth, to which the human inventions of moral significance are irrelevant. Appropriately, then, the adventures of Sam Spade are narrated in the third person, a point of view leaving Spade the possibility of appearing normative but denying his consciousness the power to preside over the narrative. Moreover, the authorial voice of the narrative sections unoccupied by Spade's talk has been similarly restricted. Purged of locutions and tone, the qualities it derives from standard American usage simply render it invisible as soon as it has accomplished its function of transmitting detail. Within the world Hammett posits by these stylistic choices regarding point of view the speech of character becomes intensely significant, for, with action compromised by necessity and narrative point of view necessarily reflecting that fact, there is only Sam Spade's talk on which to rely for guidance into the workings of the world.

The second chapter of *The Maltese Falcon*[1] opens as objective reporting. A telephone rings, one side of a

*Dashiell Hammett in 1934 at a celebration for the launch of the comic strip* Secret Agent X–9; *seated: Cliff Sterrett, Otto Soglow, Hammett, Alexander Raymond (the illustrator), Chic Young, and Lyman Young; standing: Bill Dwyer, H. H. Knerr, Darrell McClure, Ad Carter, and Rube Goldberg (San Francisco Historical Photograph Collection, San Francisco Public Library)*

conversation is heard: "Hello. . . . Yes, speaking. . . . Dead?. . . . Yes. . . . Fifteen minutes. Thanks" (p. 10). A light is turned on, and Sam Spade appears sitting on his bedside. Though the author is alone with his character, there is no subjective revelation. Instead we are given a purely physical description of Spade rolling a cigarette, dressing, and taking a taxi to the corner of San Francisco's Bush and Stockton Streets. The focus of description enlarges as the narrative voice presents the jumbled detail of the scene where Miles Archer's dead body lies, but nouns and verbs restrain the description within objectivity. When conversation occurs between Sam and the police officer Tom Polhaus, it, too, is matter-of-fact, limited at first to discussion of weapons. This is the conventionally tough style of description used in hard-boiled magazine fiction, some of it written by Hammett, except that the length of the passage presenting Sam's preparations to answer the telephoned request to come to the scene of the crime is excessive for *Black Mask*. Such a passage goes well beyond scenic utility and begins to make suggestions. Just what is being suggested emerges after Tom Polhaus asks Spade if he wants to look at Archer's body before it is moved. "No," says Spade, and when Tom, described as awkwardly stopped astraddle a fence by Sam's reply, looks at him questioningly, Spade explains the obvious: "You've seen him. You'd see everything I could" (p. 14). In the normal course of human exchange, however, it is not obvious that a person rejects participation in ritual. Tom has asked the predictable and always affirmatively answered question. Even tough men act out their emotion by viewing the body of their dead

companions, but for Sam toughness cannot be relaxed. Perhaps refusing to view Archer's remains seems to him an act of integrity, refusal to be hypocritical about a man he did not like, but since we have entry into Sam's consciousness throughout the novel only by our understanding of his speech, we can just speculate that his integrity might take this form. What is clear, though, is that Sam has momentarily enforced control over a situation through the simple refusal of ritual language. Denying linguistic convention, and the behavior it implies will follow, he banishes even the appearance of emotion from his scene, just as the author of the narrative has done in the earlier descriptive passages. And that is the point of both length, of physical description, and brevity, of Spade's speech. To have even limited control in the world of objective reality one must maintain the realization that events in the world are disconnected from our subjective feelings about them.

Control is not only a matter of refusing linguistic conventions that imply intimate connection between mind and matter. Sometimes indulgence in such conventional speech and action as Sam displays in his relationship with his faithful secretary Effie Perine works to maintain the distance one needs in order to cope with untoward events. The terms "sweetheart" and "darling" Sam always uses with Effie, as well as the air of physical mastery he conveys by the gestures he directs to Effie and the requests he makes of her, create a milieu of masculine dominance that is ironic in view of the power Iva Archer and Brigid O'Shaughnessy have to complicate his life, but the irony is certification of the necessity for Sam to try to assume the initiative in relationships with people. If the use of male chauvinist chat is an attempt to force behavior into predictable patterns, the unpredictable events that follow upon involvement with Iva and Brigid show the desirability of control, even if it must be achieved through such evidently anti-human ways as reducing people to the roles they perform and using reified language.

As his striving for dominance of acquaintances indicates, Sam is a manipulator. When, at the end of the novel, he accuses Brigid, who has become something much more than an acquaintance, of using sex and love for ulterior ends, she could rightly answer with the charge that he used her. Moreover, the narrative, centering as it does on Sam Spade, permits us to see how fully his actions jibe with his manipulative speech. After making love with Brigid he leaves her asleep while he goes to search her apartment, creating the appearance of a break-in to conceal his deed; and in the dramatic night watch near the end of the novel when Sam and the conspirators await delivery of the falcon, he humiliates Brigid by forcing her to strip naked to prove she is not concealing on her person the $1000 bill, which is just as likely and in fact is in Gutman's possession.

Stripping off Brigid's clothing near the end of the novel physically enacts the verbal stripping of her lies Sam accomplishes earlier. The man so laconic in emotional exchange, so mundane in his own use of the conventions of speech, appears intuitively sensitive to the false notes that creep into speech when a person is shamming. So Brigid's emotional confession to having deceived Sam during her first interview in his office and her asking for the protection his masculine manner had suggested was available he appraises as a very good acting job: "It's chiefly your eyes, I think, and that throb you get into your voice when you say things like 'Be generous, Mr. Spade'" (p. 32). Again, Sam brands her a liar when she first tells him of her connection with the falcon. Yet there is more to these dialogues between Sam and Brigid than the characterization of him as a person practiced in the uses of language. They also contain a proposition about the relations of language and the physical world. Brigid initially approaches Sam as if her words might gain autonomous reality. If she says something in a certain way, perhaps he will believe that in fact it is. Only when she uses the signals of physical seduction does he take what she offers at its intended value. Until the end of the novel Brigid does not see the distinction, while for his part Sam has demonstrated in his dialogues with Brigid that he uses or refuses the conventions of language because of the effect he estimates they will have within an immediate material context. For him language may be referential or instrumental, but never independent of context.

This is the reason Sam is as hard-boiled in his dealings with the police as with the crooks. For Sam there can be no abstract hierarchy of authority that might prohibit him from telling the police the patent lie that a fight between Brigid and Joel Cairo was contrived as a joke. Polhaus and Dundy know as well as Sam does that he is lying, but the regulations of police procedure, in this situation, demand that a citizen state a charge before they can intervene. It is a small victory, but it gains Sam some room for maneuver.

A much more serious denial of abstract structure is involved in Sam's assumption that there is no inviolable relationship to prevent his provocation of Gutman to present Wilmer to the police as responsible for the murders resulting from the struggle for possession of the falcon. Sam aims to break down the loyalty between Wilmer and Gutman and, thus, to increase his chances of gaining the initiative against a band of thieves otherwise linked only by greed. Does he, however, expect violation of the relationship, said by Gutman to be that of a father and son, to result as it does in murder? In defense of Sam one might recall that Gutman's willingness to use his daughter Rhea in the plot to secure the falcon shows no particular loyalty on his part to the principle of familial relationship, but such defense is morally implausible. In fact, no defense of Sam's behavior is possible on general moral grounds, for the world of *The Maltese Falcon* has suffered an epistemological break from the tradition of viewing reality in terms of moral constructions. Ironically "good faith" requires acknowledgement of alienation. Sam encourages the collapse of the artificial familial relationship between Gutman and Wilmer by verbally extending it to the conditions in which all relationships exist. It may be labeled a destructive and amoral act, just as some of his treatment of Brigid may be, but humanistic labels are foreign to Sam Spade's world where the conventional sense of individual responsibility is "bad faith." Individual will and, thus, one's personal style or code of behavior can be applied with some degree of certainty only in immediate situations. Ramifications of freely chosen actions can be conceived neither as a linkage of cause and effect nor even as concentric circles. Many patterns are possible, none definitely predictable. Literally, freedom, to control events and to accept responsibility for them, extends no further than the sound of one's voice.

Significantly these philosophical premises of *The Maltese Falcon* emerge by indirection. Neither the authorial voice nor the speeches of characters presume to erect verbal constructions where a foundation of abstract generality is impossible. Still, the impulse to apply the mind to making sense of life is hard to stifle. Sam Spade expresses such an impulse when he tells Brigid O'Shaughnessy the story of Flitcraft, the man

*Front cover; Hamburg, Paris & Bologna: Albatross, 1932 (Collection of Richard Layman)*

ence seemed reasonable to Flitcraft, says Sam, "I don't think he even knew he had settled back naturally into the same groove he had jumped out of in Tacoma. But that's the part of it I always liked. He adjusted himself to beams falling, and then no more of them fell, and he adjusted himself to them not falling" (p. 57).

Flitcraft was not sure anyone else would understand his story. Apparently, though, Sam understood the story even better than Flitcraft did. Flitcraft believed he had uncovered the principle of life as the beam fell and proceeded to conceive of his behavior in accordance with a theory of accident, even when his behavior was contradictory to the theory. The irony of the fact that Flitcraft had merely adjusted to events beyond his control while inventing explanations that portrayed his actions as freely chosen is what amuses Sam. Despite generalizations arising from the desire to explain experience, the premises of life remain within the immediate, material situations.

Significantly, in making this statement that amounts to an effort to give sense to life, Sam does so by a strategy of indirection. He narrates a tale which encapsulates meaning with the concreteness of a case he encountered on the job and conveys the theme of the tale not through his own generalization extracted from experience, but through ironic allusion to the misperceptions of Flitcraft. Moreover, the tale of Flitcraft is inserted as conversation into a scene in which Sam and Brigid are waiting for Joel Cairo, so that the tale is oblique to action, an example of speech used as transition between events. At one point a telephone call interrupts the tale, and throughout its telling Brigid is more interested in Sam's purpose in relating the story than in the story itself. He might as well be speaking to himself, which of course he is, except that readers overhear the story and find, as the novel continues to unfold, that the indirect strategy and curious subject of the Flitcraft tale blend perfectly to demonstrate how significant it is that we can only know Sam Spade through his speech.

If the tale of Flitcraft establishes the means by which Hammett renders character, and the scenes in which Spade manipulates linguistic conventions provide significance for behavior, then the novel's summation occurs in the passage where Sam attempts to explain to Brigid why he is turning her over to the police. There is no doubt of her guilt for participation in the crimes engendered by the quest for the falcon, and Sam knows also that she killed Miles Archer. Still there is more to the situation than that. For one thing, there is the evidence of Sam's behavior that gives no guarantee that he would feel obliged to enforce the consensus of criminal law. For another thing, there may well be love, unpredictably created during the times when Sam and Brigid dispensed with the mediation of

who had left his home and business in Tacoma one day never to return. Sam was employed by the detective agency Mrs. Flitcraft engaged to find her husband, but in time Sam found the missing husband living a way of life in Spokane that was identical to the one he had left in Tacoma. As Sam narrates the story of Flitcraft, he chooses to make the episode in which Flitcraft explained his actions the central one. While he was walking past a construction site, he told Sam, a beam had fallen within inches of him. The beam showed him that life is accidental rather than orderly, and that going about his affairs in a sensible orderly way had gotten him out of step with life. So he went off to live according to chance, and after a couple of years wandering he came back to the Northwest, settled in Spokane and married a woman like his first wife. The whole experi-

language and sought domination, one of the other, through the elemental appeals of sexuality. The conventions of physical love are less precise than those of verbal language, so control is even more difficult to exert and there might be love.

Sam's speech to Brigid first of all is an attempt to reassert control. "I'm going to send you over," he says in a soft, gentle voice. "The chances are you'll get off with life. That means you'll be out again in twenty years. You're an angel. I'll wait for you." Statement of irrevocable fact, masculine domination of sentiment, dismissal—these are the intentions of Sam's statement. But, of course, Brigid will not accept representation of her fate as beyond Sam's control. She pretends to pass off his remarks as a joke, then shows shock, the shock of lover and amoral colleague. He responds in tough guy manner. One of us has got to take the fall, he says, and you're likely to get a break. You can't, after all we've meant to each other, says Brigid. Calmness gone, distance closed, Sam retorts, "Like hell I can't" (p. 191).

As Brigid appeals to the fact that there is love and complicity between them, Sam attempts to diminish their connection. She has used him. What kind of love can that be? He won't play the sap for her. The need to justify is strong, but Sam has encountered an immediate experience he cannot control simply by manipulation of linguistic conventions. Among other things the tough approach to life means to keep emotion subordinate. Irony and cynicism—the manner of tough speech—depend upon the existence of some distance before they can effect detachment, but emotion will not leave sufficient distance.

All right, then, Sam will try again to justify. In a long speech that he refuses to allow Brigid to interrupt he assumes various roles to enunciate seven reasons for turning her over to the police. There are reasons he states in the role of businessman/detective. A person is supposed to avenge his partner's murder. The detective business has to maintain an image of power. A detective just naturally apprehends criminals. These are slight reasons, unlikely to be received as the absolute principles of a man as convinced of pragmatic immediacy as Sam is, so he seeks to objectify the action he will take by acknowledging it to be consistent with his own complicity in the episodes surrounding the falcon. If he lets her go, he is bound to become the fall guy for the police. She might blackmail him for letting her go, or she might kill him to prevent him from blackmailing her. Then there is the fact that he doesn't want to be played for a sucker. That's seven reasons, and he could go on to an eighth. That should be enough, though, because in numbers they outweigh the fact of emotional connection. So he says.

The apparent orderliness of Sam's adducing reasons to turn in Brigid cannot conceal their frailty. His speech is in the form of rhetorical communication, but actually its function is primarily interior. He must convince himself, reassert control over his own inclination to adapt to the immediacy of feeling for Brigid. Observing this function of Sam's speech at the end of the novel, we recall his earlier verbal manipulations and realize that throughout the course of the narrative he has been speaking as much to himself as to others, for his control depends upon placing speech between himself and circumstances. The defensive mediation of words sustains the distance he needs to feel in order to have the ability to be the subject of his actions.

Brigid intrudes upon Sam's interior speech by again appealing to love, closing with a breath the distance he sought to create. Conceding that his reasoning is ineffective, Sam confesses the pull of emotion: "all of me wants to say to hell with the consequences . . ." (p. 194). And he is back where he began with his argument. He won't play the sap for her. Only the arrival of the police at this point forestalls a further test of Sam's resolution.

Whether or not Sam Spade might have justified himself satisfactorily if the police were not on their way seems to be a provocative consideration, but to raise such a question would be to miss the logic of *The Maltese Falcon*. A change in circumstances, here the arrival of the police, is the only source of closure, and changed circumstances result not from actions taken upon principle but from the working out of possibilities that lie beyond humanistic direction. In his desperation before Brigid, Sam tries to employ the language used by those who believe in the capacity of words to organize experience. If someone else had done it, Sam would have heard the false notes. Also desperate, Brigid attacks his reasoning with an intuitive awareness of its inadequacy and forces him to confront the contradiction between his speech and feelings. All that Sam retains as a means of control then is fear of losing control, characteristically expressed in the tough guy slogan: "I won't play the sap for you."

In the naturalistic world conceived by Dashiell Hammett in *The Maltese Falcon* spoken language exists under great pressure. As its range of moral possibility has been reduced by hostile social conditions, the intensity of the significance it must convey through linguistic code has increased. It has become implausible to philosophize, because to the isolated American a fresh reality appears at every turn of events. Character is the only repository of sustained meaning, and character can be known, and know itself, only through speech in response to the world. In this respect the creation of Sam Spade talking is a proposition about modern real-

Philadelphia Record, *9 October 1938. This abridged version of the novel was published as a newspaper supplement (Collection of Richard Layman).*

*Meet This Week's Author*

Dashiell Hammett is one of the exceedingly few mystery story writers who have actually worked professionally at crime-detecting. Born in 1894 in St. Mary's County, Maryland, he was educated in Baltimore's public schools and the Polytechnic Institute of that city. After a juvenile career as newsboy, clerk and stevedore, he took up man-hunting with the Pinkerton Detective Agency. One of his most interesting cases was tracking down a man who had stolen a ferris wheel. His early writings appeared in the old Mencken-Nathan Smart Set, following a hitch as sergeant in the U. S. Army Motor Ambulance Corps during the great war. His first book, "Red Harvest" (1929), was full of blood and thunder; his most popular "The Thin Man," largely because of the superb motion picture version given it. Discerning students of crime-thrillers prefer "The Maltese Falcon," it having been called the "greatest American mystery story since Poe." Hammett for the last few years has been lending his talents to Hollywood scenarios. He is a voracious reader of philosophy, never reads other mystery stories, and champions civil liberty causes. He is married and has two daughters.

*Hammett identification included in the 9 October 1938 issue of the* Philadelphia Record
*(Collection of Richard Layman)*

ity. That is why it is so attractive to imagine Dashiell Hammett as a latter-day Samuel Clemens, carefully listening for the ways he might make the American language convey disillusion.

**Note**

1. Page citations in the text come from the Vintage Books edition of *The Maltese Falcon.*

\* \* \*

**Dashiell Hammett's Social Vision**
Robert Shulman
*Centennial Review*, 29 (Fall 1985): 400–413

Dashiell Hammett has suffered from a double stigma. He writes in a popular genre academics for the most part do not take seriously. And during the Cold War his politics were dangerous, and the most promising approach to his fiction was in disrepute. These conditions are changing. We are now in a position to develop the detailed criticism that intelligent evaluation of Hammett's work must be based on.

I

As Hammett knew, *genre* is more than a set of literary conventions, and the tough-guy detective novels he wrote are no exception. *Genre* also carries a concealed social message of its own, describes in fictional form the myths of a specific social system, and prescribes for its characters a set of interrelated dilemmas, all of which can be understood for Hammett as generated by the structures and values of his unstable, acquisitive America. In *Red Harvest, The Maltese Falcon,* and *The Glass Key* Hammett also brings alive the conflicting versions of individualism that society emphasizes. Particularly in *The Maltese Falcon,* Hammett is concerned with stories and storytelling, with a market society world that systematically demands improvisation, acting, and the manipulation of appearances, people, and feelings. In 1953 Hammett testified before a House investigating committee ostensibly concerned about "pro-Communist" books in the overseas libraries run by the State Department. Hammett refused to say whether he was a Communist but he did tell the committee he thought it "was impossible to write anything without taking some sort of social stand."[1] In at least three compelling and representative novels from some twenty years earlier, Hammett had elaborated in fictional form, in a version of the detective novel *genre,* a "social stand" which reveals a brilliant and penetrating analysis of a late capitalist acquisitive society.

*The Maltese Falcon* is his most precise and suggestive work but Hammett gives us a general outline of his characteristic world in his first novel, *Red Harvest* (1929). In it he exposes the violence and political corruption of Poisonville, a mess brought on when the town's upper class political boss had troops come in to break a striking union. The bad elements stayed to take over his control of the town. The Hammett detective, the Continental Op, is deeply involved in the underground, anarchic chaos and violence at the same time that he restores a kind of order. Hammett, who is fascinated with subterranean, anarchic energy, gives full expression to the individualistic violence and resourcefulness of the Continental Op. The order at the end is not in the name of the law or of official society but rather of the Op's desire to get the job done and his opposition to corrupt forces much like his own energies. His individualism differs from his opponents' in that he is not after political or economic power like those who make the allegorically named "Personville" into "Poisonville." Using as his vehicle the gangland warfare of the 1920's, through the Continental Op and his opponents Hammett thus develops a suggestively mixed view of the lawlessness, violence, and energy informing the surfaces and depths of an acquisitive, individualistic society. It is the America of Hobbes's war of each against all.[2]

In the best of the two books Hammett wrote immediately after *Red Harvest,* in his most famous novel, *The Maltese Falcon* (1930), Hammett also gives his social vision its fullest expression. As Ian Watt shows in *The Rise of the Novel,* Defoe bodied forth a myth appropriate to the individualistic society of his period. Hammett, in the tradition of *Robinson Crusoe,* does the same for the American version of that society 200 years later. In *The Maltese Falcon,* Gutman, Cairo, and Brigid O'Shaughnessy ruthlessly pursue their own self-interest as they try to obtain the jeweled black bird, a Satanic embodiment of fabulous wealth. The bird is fake but the quest continues. The characters are exotic but their motives are all too familiar and their destructive results constitute a judgment on the entire enterprise of single-mindedly pursuing wealth. Much more deeply and acutely than in his earlier work and in a different mode than in his subsequent fiction, Hammett brings to a suggestive focus his concern with American individualism.

Through the motives, the dark milieu, and the structure of relations in *The Maltese Falcon,* Hammett has created a myth of early twentieth-century capitalism, a world in which self-interested entrepreneurs fiercely compete for a property whose ownership is ambiguous.[3] On the capitalistic model, contracts and the pursuit of wealth hold society together. In the novel, characters give their word, form temporary alliances, talk extensively about "trust," and do what they feel they need to in order to obtain the treasure. The literal murders are less significant than the resulting pervasive killing of human ties and relations. Because of the human isolation, betrayals, and obsessive pursuit of false goals, the novel renders a hell-on-earth, a kind of vital death-in-life that brings the outside American world to the test and that finally brought Dashiell Hammett to an independent relation with the Communist Party. In *The Maltese Falcon* Hammett has thus refined, complicated, and made much more precise the world of individualistic, Hobbesian violence, warfare, and systematic absence of trust he had imagined in *Red Harvest* and the Continental Op stories.[4]

The creator of Sam Spade was deeply critical of an acquisitive society but his social stand was independent, not doctrinaire. Sam Spade represents a different style of individualism from the other characters in *The Maltese Falcon.* He is a "blond Satan" who functions in the dark underworld and who seeks the treasure, not, however, as property but for non-material reasons.[5] Spade has his professional curiosity and his code—"I'll bury my dead"—and he pursues his objective with all of the independence, cunning, and ruthlessness of those antagonists he partly resembles. And he suffers the same alienation, intensified by the fact that he probably loves a woman he cannot trust and must turn in. Spade, moreover, betrays Archer and Iva even as Brigid betrays him: "merry-go-round" appropriately characterizes more than Chapter Twelve. Like the Continental Op and Ned Beaumont, Spade is flawed but like them his individualism is a source of moral strength as well as of alienation. As his story about Flitcraft reveals, moreover, Spade has a poetic depth of awareness about the contingency of human mortality. Spade is an ambiguous hero, tainted, mixed, and finally admirable. Much of the social drama of the novel is generated because Spade's style of individualism intersects and opposes the Gutman-Cairo-Brigid version of competitive individualism.

In a world of competing individuals, ideally contracts and the legal system are the referees and constitute the social bonds tying together the atomistic competitors. In *The Maltese Falcon* the legal system and official society are represented by the detectives, Tom Polhaus and Dundy, and the D. A., Bryan. Spade is as much at odds with them as he is with Gutman, Cairo, and Brigid. Of course he has Effie Perine and Sam Wise on his side but basically Spade is an American

*Dust jacket; Stockholm: Continental Books/Zephyr, 1943*
*(Collection of Richard Layman)*

loner individualist, outside and opposed to both the official society and the underworld of the novel. Narrative tension results because Spade is under attack or suspicion from both sides and against powerful obstacles he must work things out for himself. Official society is almost as bad as the underworld and the law does not operate as a cohesive force, so that the sense of an atomized world is intensified.

Spade succinctly characterizes the official world and political system: "most things in San Francisco can be bought, or taken" (p. 48). Instead of examining the official world in any detail, Hammett simply takes its corruption for granted. His treatment of the underworld, however, illuminates official society, since Gutman, Cairo, and Brigid have the motives, rhetoric, and values of respectable entrepreneurs. To the extent we find these characters both more reprehensible and more fascinating than people in the "real" world, the negative judgment of the "real" world is intensified.

Joel Cairo says he heard Spade was "far too reasonable to allow other considerations to interfere with profitable business relations" (p. 44). "Reasonable" and "profitable" are key values in the world of competitive individualism, as are the "trust" and the "plain speaking and clear understanding" Gutman drinks to (p. 94). Even more important is Gutman's explicit statement of what is pervasive and implicit throughout the novel, namely, that the archetypal embodiment of property, the jeweled black bird, "is clearly the property of whoever can get ahold of it" (p. 114). The principle and its deadly results are at the heart of the system that produced the robber barons and the corporate warfare of early twentieth-century capitalism. Through Gutman and the others Hammett goes beneath the facade of capitalistic theory and exposes its predatory practices. The implicit corollary of Gutman's remark, moreover, is that the bird is valuable *because* so many people want to "get ahold of it." Thus it is "property" as "commodity." The bird is of no use to anyone (reinforced by the end of the novel where the actual object is revealed as black lead throughout), yet all the destructive energy of the novel's characters has its source in the exchange of the bird. Every time it changes hands, the value goes up.

Gutman, Cairo, and Brigid are the leading players in the serious game of exchange. They live in a world of trading, deception, expediency, risk-taking, and self-interest. These social qualities create a world that has no stability or certainty, so that the basis for uncertainty and instability is social and economic. As in *The Glass Key* the fog and darkness Spade must grope through are metaphors for a social and moral condition. By displacing his social probing, by doing it indirectly, Hammett thus creates a dark world that is vital, threatening, and deep. Through this mythic world he is able to get at conventional values and relations in a basic way, more suggestively than before or after *The Maltese Falcon*.

II

In Hammett's dark, unstable world, the most intimate ties between people are also necessarily unstable or corrupt. Hammett examines a series of love or family relations, and their characterization contributes powerfully to the novel's exposure of an acquisitive, individualistic world as a hell-on-earth or death-in-life. Immediately before he makes his most loyal associate the fall-guy, Gutman says "I feel towards Wilmer just exactly as if he were my own son" (p. 160). So much for the ties of friendship and loyalty or the affection between a father and son. In a quite different way Cairo, with his scented handkerchiefs and effeminate manners, is in love with Wilmer. In some ways it is the most genuine love in the book but Hammett presents it as in its very nature compromised or tainted. Like other loves in the novel, moreover, it is one-sided, not reciprocated. Although Spade continually baits Wilmer as a "gunsel" (underworld slang for "homosexual"), Wilmer is totally repelled by Cairo.

But it is through the central love relation in *The Maltese Falcon* that Hammett gives his most telling treatment of the death-in-life of his acquisitive society. Spade has his suspicions of Brigid early on, as he sees through her stories and pleas, but he is compelled by her nonetheless. A relation based on deception, pretense, and sex gradually deepens without ever losing the original duplicity and without Spade's ever encountering anything more or less genuine than Brigid's beauty, vitality, and consummate skill as an actress and inventive storyteller. He is compelled but not deluded by these qualities. At first we are taken in but Spade shows his superior insight by detecting almost immediately the false notes in her speech. "'You're good,'" he tells her, "'you're very good. It's chiefly your eyes, I think, and that throb you get into your voice when you say things like 'Be generous, Mr. Spade'" (p. 32).

"Be generous"; "trust me"–these appeals to the cohesive values of generosity, sympathy, and trust recur again and again in the scenes involving Brigid and Spade. The words always remind us of the human qualities that are missing from their relation, a void that cumulatively gives their love the aura of a dance of the damned. The social vision of the novel is tragic, partly because Spade loves a woman he cannot trust, someone whose duplicity is rooted in the acquisitive motives and values of the social order. This nightmarish combination of love without trust brings into the open the painful isolation and destruction of human ties ordinarily concealed in the everyday social world.

Brigid involves Spade because she needs protection but she is only vulnerable physically, not intellectually or emotionally. She uses her femininity, variously playing the role of a rich heiress in need of help or a seductress who distracts Spade from vital questions by going to bed with him. But she is a woman who plays brilliantly in a man's hard world for the same dark stakes as the other competitors. She is one of the few women characters in American literature who are endowed with the energy, motives, and capacities of the male characters, and not at the expense of her femininity. The social criticism in the novel gains tragic force because Brigid's rich possibilities are blighted by her involvement in the world of competitive individualism. That involvement is tragically intertwined with the very promise, qualities, and achievements which both elevate and undermine her. Brigid is the most tragic figure in the underworld because her death-in-life is inseparable from a saving vitality, so that her loss suggests the price of conventional success and constitutes a judgment on an entire value system and way of life.

The dilemma Henry Adams foresaw for the twentieth-century woman was that she could play the man's game in the world of power and become as restless, mechanical, and desexualized as the American male. Or she could remain powerless but fecund. Through Brigid's restless manipulation of her own and Spade's feelings and sexuality, Hammett confirms this tragic insight. Brigid's involvement in the acquisitive world is as fatal to her relation with Spade as it is to her own inner life. She is weary with herself and the perpetual lying, acting, and improvising she nonetheless continues with astonishing persistence and vitality. Her deceptiveness, manipulation, and fluidity of identity all have social sources: they answer to the demands of the market society. Because of her brilliant acting, we never know Brigid's true feelings. Brigid may well love only the pursuit of the black bird, although Spade's intelligence, force, and personal presence are not negligible. We do know, however, that a genuine union between Brigid and Spade constitutes the most promising force of human cohesion and renewal in the world of the novel. Through the course of the book this possibility is simultaneously suggested, brought to imaginative life, and destroyed. At the end, Brigid manipulates the central value of love and loses. She ends up imprisoned, separated from Spade and the world, and under the threat of the death penalty. For his part, at the end Spade is alone and shivering. Their situation epitomizes and judges what are for Hammett the divisive realities of the market society world he has transformed into the myth of *The Maltese Falcon*.

Central to the dark, unstable world of the novel is the need to act, to invent, and to deceive. Brigid in particular has facade beneath facade, story within story, lie on top of lie, and all compelling, as she is in her resourcefulness, beauty, and sexuality. She says her name is Brigid O'Shaughnessy but she also calls herself Miss Wonderly and Miss Leblanc. As Spade says, she has one name too many. In a fluid, unstable society, identities are also fluid. "'I'm not at all the person I pretend to be'" (p. 49), she tells Spade, and we can never be sure of the person she is. The unstable marketplace society of trading and deception is itself a world of appearances; in her rootlessness, lack of identity, and skill at manipulating appearances, Brigid is the perfect embodiment of that society.

On Hammett's vision this society demands acting and storytelling, the systematic manipulation of surfaces, feelings, and values. In her first story Brigid, a brilliant actress and storyteller, acts the part of a daughter deeply concerned about her parents and sister. In

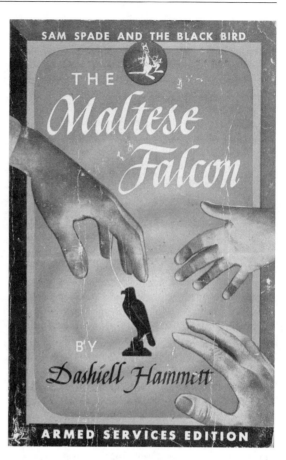

*Front covers; New York: Pocket Books, 1944, and New York: Readers' League of America. The book on the right, though designated an "Armed Services Edition," was not among the books distributed free to the military by the Council on Books in Wartime under the auspices of the U.S. War Department. It was distributed to servicemen through the American Red Cross (Collection of Richard Layman).*

the story she invents she wants to bring the family together again; in her version Thursby is the blocking force. Brigid's story plays on and subverts the cohesive value of family love, so that from the opening scene this central unifying value exists only to be exploited and thus degraded. The full consequences appear as Hammett develops the world Brigid lives in and embodies: deceptive, acquisitive, exciting, ruthless. In this hell-like version of the market society love exists to be manipulated, as Brigid manipulates Thursby and attempts to do with Spade. In her initial story the most direct irony is that Brigid presents Thursby as a dangerous seducer, as a person exploiting love for gain, although Thursby is loyal and she is the predatory seducer exploiting Thursby's love and the reader's desire to believe in family love and a concerned, upper-class daughter and sister in distress.

Hammett, however, does not allow us the ease of simple, direct inversions. In Brigid's world it is almost impossible to tell truth from falsehood. What we have instead is a constant process of invention, improvising, of making up stories. A convention of detective fiction, the motivation of "story," checking on a "story," seeing if a "story" fits the facts, becomes in Hammett a brilliant way of playing across different codes of explanation. Thus rather than explaining events, the social values of cohesion, loyalty, and trust are revealed as so many stories told for very different ends; the personal and psychological value of a stable identity likewise becomes an effect produced by the telling of stories rather than the origin of stories; and the epistemological ground of the "facts" dissolves into a seemingly endless chain of stories about stories about stories.

Spade is as good as Brigid at the process of inventing stories. To account to the police for the fight between Cairo and Brigid he improvises a story that includes a joke within a lie within the story. Spade always has a plausible explanation–for Iva, for Cairo, for Gutman. When Cairo challenges him about his facility he asks, "'what do you want me to do? Learn to stutter?'" (p. 86). Spade gives the impression of knowing but he is groping in the dark, trying to find the truth. He bluffs, he acts as if he knows more than he does to find out something so that he can continue the baffling, dangerous process of finding out more. Brigid, apparently his ally and lover, consistently withholds, distorts, interferes. When Gutman tells his story about the missing $1,000 and Brigid tells her version, Spade brings it to the test and finds out.

For the most part, however, empirical validation is either not possible or requires Spade to penetrate a labyrinth of deceptions and obstacles. Because of the socially generated network of stories, deception, and ruthlessness, Spade does not live in a neatly patterned world where empirical truth sits fixed and quiet for the observer to discover it. Instead he and the others live in a predatory world where in order to find the truth Spade must improvise, throw a monkey-wrench in the machinery, and get out of the way if he can as the parts fly. Spade lives in a world where beams fall at random but people systematically tell stories and use any means necessary to gain what they seek. In this ruthless, acquisitive world of stories and storytelling, what counts is not the truth but whether or not the story covers most of the facts in a way people will believe.

Spade's methodological scepticism is so deep that after he sends Iva to his lawyer he is simply neutral about the story she tells. He neither believes nor disbelieves it but he thinks it will work. Even Spade, however, must sometimes act on the stories he hears. As far as we can tell, he believes Rhea Gutman but in any case he goes on a wild goose chase as a result of her drugged act and story. The handling of point of view systematically avoids the inner processes of thought and feeling. As a result we can never be certain of what Spade or Brigid think or feel. Spade periodically voices his suspicions of Brigid but until the end we do not know what his feelings are. He acts as if he cares for her; she acts as if she cares for him. To an extent both are acting, telling stories to each other, but to an extent they may also be in love. This radical uncertainty about and manipulation of basic human feelings and ties is central to Hammett's commentary on the market society.

Brigid, in an especially touching confession, says "'Oh, I'm so tired, . . . so tired of it all, of myself, of lying and thinking up lies, and of not knowing what is a lie and what is the truth'" (p. 79). Like other great actresses and storytellers, she may well be telling part of the truth but she is also manipulating Spade and she immediately goes to bed with him to keep him from finding out what he is after. We have a deep need to believe Brigid, to have her confirm our sense that sys-tematic deception is destructive. We have a deep need to wake up from the nightmare of "not knowing what is a lie and what is the truth" because as human beings we crave the truth. Brigid is a significant modern character partly because Hammett endows her with a sensitivity to this human need and the ability simultaneously to violate it in the interests of her even deeper need to acquire the falcon. Brigid's ability is uniquely personal but her motives, her weariness about her identity, her self, and her related need to deceive, to invent stories, to manipulate people, feelings, and appearances—all these are rooted in the social order she emerges from and brilliantly embodies.

As Spade shows, to survive in this painfully uncertain world a person has to make up stories systematically. Survival also calls for a disciplined control over one's feelings, for an ability sometimes to disregard, sometimes to manipulate other people's feelings, and for a final ability to read other people's stories accurately and to deny even those feelings of love which momentarily redeem the darkness of deception and self-seeking.

In Hammett's hell-like version of the market society the cohesive values of love, trust, generosity, and honesty exist almost exclusively in stories people tell to gain advantage for themselves. As in Brigid's stories, these positive values are mixed with themes of betrayal, deception, theft, and killing. The events of the novel reinforce these grimmer themes. Even casual stories further this sense of betrayal and dishonesty, of people out for themselves. A movie-house owner tells Spade a story about a cashier he suspects of theft. Iva tells her story to bring the police down on Spade. Sometimes characters believe their own stories; sometimes the stories seem accurate and we believe them, as we do the movie owner or as we believe Tom Polhaus's story about Thursby.

Although not every story is a lie, the unstable, acquisitive society of the novel generates a ruthless world of stories and storytelling, of manipulation and deception, of truth mixed with guesses mixed with half-truths and lies. For Hammett this social condition has the metaphysical consequences he has Spade develop in his story about Flitcraft. Unlike the other characters, Flitcraft comes from the ordinary world of settled commercial life. Because he comes from the straight world, his realizations are especially telling. When for no reason at all he is nearly killed by a falling beam, Flitcraft is shaken into the awareness that he lives in a world where beams fall at random. "He felt like somebody had taken the lid off life and let him look at the works" (p. 56). He comes to see that beneath its placid suburban surfaces existence is conducted under the aspect of arbitrary, unmerited death. "He knew

THE Maltese Falcon

BY *Dashiell Hammett*

A BLACK WIDOW THRILLER

*Dust jacket; New York: Knopf, 1945*
*(Collection of Richard Layman)*

accurately as he can. Unlike Brigid, who has told her story so often her manner betrays her to Spade, Spade himself "repeated a sentence slightly rearranged, as if it were important that each detail be related exactly as it had happened" (p. 54). Honesty is the final test of a style for Whitehead. As a response to a metaphysical world where beams fall at random and a social world where people ruthlessly manipulate appearances to gain advantage, the morality of style is also important to Hammett. Telling the story precisely is one of the few redeeming possibilities in the dark social and metaphysical universe Hammett imagines for his characters. The Flitcraft story, moreover, is one of the few chances Hammett gives us to glimpse what goes on inside Spade and to sense Spade's view of what goes on in the depths of things.

Brigid's story about her family and Thursby, Spade's story about Flitcraft, and Gutman's story about the Maltese falcon are the most compelling of the countless stories that give the novel its characteristic texture. Like most of the stories that form the context for the Flitcraft story, in his story Gutman narrates a tale of theft and buccaneering, of predatory robber barons on the grand scale and more recent thieves on a smaller scale, of kidnapping and ransom, of concealment, intrigue, and deception. The evidence he presents is circumstantial but his manner is authoritative and he gives his account the authenticity of an encyclopedia article on an arcane subject. He claims an "oblique" reference in a French source—"oblique to be sure, but a reference still" (p. 111). Is this valid inference or the interpretation of a man with Sir Thomas Browne's quincunx in his head? The quincunx, Brown tells us, is a five-sided figure. Once you have it in your mind, you see five-sided figures everywhere.

Gutman also claims "a clear and unmistakable statement of the facts" in an unpublished source. Maybe yes, maybe no, although why would Gutman invest a fortune and seventeen years of his life if he at least did not believe it? An eighteenth-century source vouches for the existence of the bird as among the wedding presents of King Victor Armadeus II to his wife. That seems like solid evidence but what follows is more ambiguous and depends on the evidence of "a Greek dealer named Charilaos Konstantinides [who] found it in an obscure shop" (p. 112). Do we believe the story because even a wily Greek accepts it or do we dismiss the story as the invention of a wily Greek dealer? Effie Perine's uncle in the Berkeley History Department is excited over the possibility that the story could be true "and he hopes it is" (p. 124). Effie, though, is wrong about Brigid and Uncle Ted may or may not be just as wrong about the story. Spade maintains a wary scepticism: "'that's swell,'" he tells Effie about Uncle Ted,

then that men died at haphazard like that, and lived only while blind chance spared them" (p. 57). An intuitive existentialist, Flitcraft acts to get in step with existence, changes his life, and then in Spade's wry joke, Flitcraft resumes a routine identical to the one he had left. "He adjusted himself to beams falling, and then no more of them fell, and he adjusted himself to them not falling" (p. 57). Spade carefully tells a metaphysical parable that also recognizes the way ordinary people are.

Although we cannot be sure about Spade's motives in telling the story, they are probably mixed. Perhaps the story is a monkey wrench he throws in to find out how Brigid will respond. She ignores the suggestive power of the story and immediately returns to her story, to her act, trying to get Spade to trust her. She has her work cut out for her, since the man who has told the Flitcraft story has ideas about what goes on under the surfaces of things. Spade has narrated his view of existence as precisely as he can. Whatever his other motives, he wants to tell his story as clearly and

"'as long as he doesn't get too enthusiastic to see through it if it's phony'" (p. 124).

What we know for sure is that like Uncle Ted, we also hope the story is true. In the face of all the ambiguous evidence do we accept the story finally because this tale of deception and ruthlessness in pursuit of a fabulous treasure satisfies our sense of the way things are and appeals to our desire to believe? Are we, then, like Ratliff in *The Hamlet,* the victims of a socially generated myth of buried treasure, a story that exposes the grim practices of a predatory society and, through our acceptance of the story, our own involvement in that society? Maybe yes, maybe no. We do know for sure, however, that in the novel there is one object that is under its surface exactly what it appears to be: the lead falcon Gutman chips away at to reveal black lead right through to the center. This is as certain as the fact that for Hammett Gutman's ruthless, exciting quest is deadly and leads to his death, that Brigid and Spade are separated, and that at the end Spade is alone and shivering.

## Notes

1. Quoted in *Twentieth Century Authors, First Supplement,* ed. Stanley Kunitz (New York: Wilson, 1955), p. 408.
2. For this perception about Hobbes, see Steven Marcus, "Dashiell Hammett and the Continental Op," *Partisan Review,* 41 (1974): 373. More generally, see Frank M. Coleman, *Hobbes and America: Exploring the Constitutional Foundations* (Toronto: University of Toronto Press, 1977).
3. For narrative details on this phase of American capitalism, see Ida Tarbell, *The History of the Standard Oil Company,* 2 vols. (New York: McClure, Phillips, 1904); Gustave Myers, *History of the Great American Fortunes* (New York: Modern Library, 1910, 1936); and Theodore Dreiser's Cowperwood novels, *The Financier* (New York: Signet, 1912, 1967) and *The Titan* (New York, 1914, 1965). For analysis of the underlying principles, see C. B. Macpherson, *The Political Theory of Possessive Individualism: Hobbes to Locke* (New York: Oxford University Press, 1962).
4. Jacques Barzun and Wendell H. Taylor observe that "the tough guy story was born during the thirties and shows the Marxist coloring of its birth years," *A Catalogue of Crime* (New York: Harper, 1971), p. 11. Hammett, however, developed his social stand during the twenties. John Reilly sees *The Maltese Falcon* as embodying a populist, not a Marxist, view of society. "The Politics of Tough Guy Mysteries," *University of Dayton Review,* 10 (1973): 29, and Steven Marcus sees it as Hobbesian. These differences in terminology are not crucial. Hammett is rooted in the American grain and in the concerns of his period and he intuitively goes beneath conventional facades to what he sees as basic. Barzun and Taylor, Reilly, and Marcus seem to me more revealing about *The Maltese Falcon* than critics who stress the metaphysics or poetics of the novel. See, e.g., Robert I. Edenbaum, "The Poetics of the Private-Eye: The Novels of Dashiell Hammett" and Irving Malin, "Focus on *The Maltese Falcon,*" both in David Madden, ed. *Tough Guy Writers of the*

*Thirties* (Carbondale: Southern Illinois University Press, 1968), pp. 80–109.
5. Dashiell Hammett, *The Maltese Falcon* (New York: Vintage, 1930, 1972), p. 3. All other quotations will be cited in the text.

\* \* \*

## Dashiell Hammett and the Challenge of New Individualism: Rereading *Red Harvest* and *The Maltese Falcon*
Christopher Metress
*The Cunning Craft: Original Essays on Detective Fiction* (Macomb: Western Illinois University, 1990), pp. 89–108

In this present reconstructive era of American literary history, Dashiell Hammett's fiction has played an invaluable role in breaking down canonical barriers and empowering marginalized popular fictions with newly recognized importance. With the initial publication of his stories and novels in the 1920s, many influential critics praised Hammett's linguistic, structural, and thematic innovations, insisting, for example, that "Hammett has something quite as definite to say, quite as decided an impetus to give the course of newness in the American tongue, as any man now writing."[1] Along with this laudatory critical reception, Hammett captured wide readership as well. Thus, Hammett long remained on the threshold between what are often considered two antithetical positions in American letters—accepted literary artist and popular storyteller. When questions of canon formation and the politics of literary history became central to the focus of many critics, Hammett emerged as a seminal figure in the reconstruction of American literary studies. Today, his place in American literature is secure, and the critical accessibility of his art has for years now encouraged perceptive reevaluations of his literary progeny in both detective and hard-boiled fictions.

But security by no means suggests consensus, and Hammett's works have engendered diverse readings. Most often, Hammett is read in light of his contributions to the detective and hard-boiled genres. Even here, though commentators agree that Hammett fathered the American detective novel and laid the foundations for hard-boiled fiction, they disagree as to exactly what it is he fathered and whether or not his offspring misread him. Recently, however, critics have been willing to consider Hammett as more than simply a master of generic formulas and a constructor of heroic archetypes. Fortunately, critics have resisted Leonard Moss's 1968 plea that Hammett "cannot through any generosity be considered a complex author. It would be fatuous to search for profound ethical, sociological, or psychological implication."[2] Instead, critics have done exactly that; they have studied Hammett for the suggestive complexities which make his fiction, unlike so much else that has won popular approval, richly rewarding.

Perhaps the most misunderstood dimension of Hammett's work is his position on individualism. We expect Hammett to be an unabashed proponent of rugged individualism, for are not the descendants of Hammett's heroes such representative individualists as Chandler's Phillip Marlowe, Spillane's Mike Hammer, Ross Macdonald's Lew Archer, and John D. MacDonald's Travis McGee? Critics have noted how the hard-boiled detective of the twentieth century is merely an urban reincarnation of the nineteenth-century apotheosis of American individualism—the cowboy. Understanding the American detective hero as the distinct progeny of the American cowboy (in the words of Leslie Fiedler, the modern detective is "the cowboy adapted to life on the city streets"),[3] too many critics, however, thoughtlessly embrace the notion that writers of American detective fiction are unequivocal advocates of nineteenth-century-styled American individualism. As founder of this fiction, so the logic goes, Hammett too must be such an advocate: "If there is any Romantic element in Hammett's worldview," insists H. H. Morris, "it is the glorification of every individual, the passionate commitment to personal freedom that underlies the American myth of the frontier."[4] In her recent study of Western and hard-boiled genres, Cynthia S. Hamilton maintains that both formulas "are built around the testing and confirmation of key American values, especially individualism" and that the "theme which permeates every aspect of the master formula [supporting both Western and hard-boiled fictions] is the primacy of the individual; he is seen to be the key unit of society."[5]

Fortunately, several readers have refused to see Hammett's fiction as a glorification of this inherited frontier individualism. While it is true that Chandler, Spillane, Macdonald, and others influenced by Hammett have each embraced to some extent an ethos of rugged individualism, Hammett's fiction does not support such a doctrine. David Geherin justly asserts that "the conception of the private eye as a knight figure would be effectively developed by many later writers (notably Raymond Chandler) but it appears that Hammett wanted no part of it."[6] D. Glover concurs with Geherin's view that the individualism of Hammett's heroes is markedly different from that of his successors:

What is interesting in the Hammett novels is the way in which . . . individualism is tempered by a kind of job-consciousness; so that although their violence is sensationalized and given a sadistic attractiveness it is never pushed completely into the world of fantasy in

*Cover of comic-book version; David McKay, 1946
(Collection of Richard Layman)*

the way we find in, for example, the James Bond books. For the individualism of action and decision is not used to ground an illusion of total freedom—it is only relative to the job or work that the detective performs.[7]

In his seminal essay on the poetics of the private-eye, Robert Edenbaum proclaims that Hammett's novels not only temper individualism but also "present a 'critique' of the tough guy's freedom as well: the price he pays for his power is to be cut off behind his own self-imposed masks, in an isolation that no criminal, in a community of crime, has to face."[8] Sinda Gregory goes one step further in asserting Hammett's critique of individualism by insisting that a novel like *Red Harvest* "examines the failure of both the community and the individual to maintain justice, order, and human rights."[9] In a 1985 study, Robert Shulman offers a more complex understanding of Hammett's position on individualism when he suggests that in *Red Harvest*, *The Maltese Falcon,* and *The Glass Key,* rather than blindly promoting a frontier brand individualism, Hammett "brings alive the conflicting versions of individualism that society emphasizes."[10]

My focus on the problem of American individualism in Hammett's fiction is markedly different from those of previous critics because it depends on understanding the socio-cultural debates over the nature and direction of individualism that dominated the first three decades of this century. If Hammett's work "brings alive conflicting versions of individualism that society emphasizes" we had better take a closer look at what those conflicting versions of individualism were before we reevaluate Hammett's own critique of individualism. What will arise from this discussion is the concept of a "new individualism" that called for a complex submission and/or allegiance of the individual's desires to those of a larger, less traditionally individualistic collective body. Like his contemporaries, Hammett struggled to reconceive the nature of American individualism, to explore the possibility of redirecting the unsalubrious elements of an inherited frontier ethic into a more socially responsible new individualism. Hammett's two most important and influential novels, *Red Harvest* (1929) and *The Maltese Falcon* (1930), enact this exploration, for in them Hammett investigates the antagonistic relationship between residual nineteenth-century traditions of self-centered individualism and emerging twentieth- century calls for social collectivism.

## I

Perhaps the best place to begin our discussion of this new individualism in the twentieth century is with Herbert Croly's *The Promise of American Life* (1909). Rejecting the great tradition of American individualism proclaimed by Crèvecoeur, Jefferson, and Emerson, Croly expressed a central ethos of his time: "The Promise of American life is to be fulfilled—not merely by a maximum amount of economic freedom, but by a certain measure of discipline; not merely by the abundant satisfaction of individual desires, but by a large measure of individual subordination and self-denial."[11] Croly felt that "the traditional American system was breaking down" and that a twentieth-century faith in social planning needed to usurp a nineteenth-century faith in "chaotic individualism": "The experience of the last generation plainly shows that the American economic and social system cannot be allowed to take care of itself, and that the automatic harmony of the individual and the public interest, which is the essence of the Jeffersonian democratic creed, has proved to be an illusion."[12]

Croly's call for "individual subordination and self-denial" in shaping America's future continued to influence American social and political thought well into the 1910s and 1920s. Whereas in 1893 Frederick

Jackson Turner could assert that frontier individualism, though it had "from the beginning promoted democracy," had "its dangers as well as its benefits,"[13] by 1917 Van Wyck Brooks, influenced by his generation's perceptions of traditional American individualism, could highlight only the unsalubrious: "Our ancestral faith in the individual and what he is able to accomplish . . . as the measure of all things has despoiled us of the instinctive human reverence for those divine resources of collective experience, religion, science, art, philosophy, the self-subordinating service of which is almost the measure of the highest happiness. In consequence of this our natural capacities have been dissipated."[14] Though rejecting the "aberrant individualism" of such "preëminent cranks" as Henry David Thoreau and Henry George, Brooks did not reject outright the concept of individualism; instead he sought a redefinition of individualism "totally different in content from the individualism of the past." For Brooks, the "old spiritual individualism" was "essentially competitive" and "gave birth to the crank, the shrill, the high-strung propounder of strange religions, the self-important monopolist of truth." The new individualism, however, had "no desire to vaunt itself. . . . [I]t is not combative, it is coöperative, not opinionative but groping, not sectarian but filled with an intense, confused eagerness to identify itself with the life of the whole people."[15]

Croly, Brooks, and other political and social Progressives were seeking a balance between individual assertion and collective needs, and since the old individualism of the nineteenth century had created vast economic imbalances and had stratified social classes, a new type of individualism was sought, one which would be more amenable to collective change. Even such an "unashamed individualist" as Herbert Hoover tempered his nineteenth-century faith in individualism with a twentieth-century desire for collective social change. At the conclusion of his appropriately entitled *American Individualism* (1923), Hoover called for an adherence to individualism which seemed untouched by the Progressivist dialogue:

> Humanity has a long road to perfection, but we of America can make sure progress if we preserve our individualism, if we will preserve and stimulate the initiative of our people. . . . Progress will march if we hold an abiding faith in the intelligence, the initiative, the character, the courage, and the divine touch in the individual. . . . We can make a social system as perfect as our generation merits and one that will be received in gratitude by our children.[16]

All this seems a far cry from Croly's proclamation a decade earlier that reformers should "understand that there must be vigorous and conscious assertion of the public as opposed to private and special interests, and that the American people must to a greater extent than they have in the past subordinate the latter to the former."[17] Throughout Hoover's book, however, we sense, as we do with Croly and Brooks, that the individualism here championed is once again being redefined, that a "new individualism" is being offered in place of an old, outdated, and inherently destructive individualism: "Salvation will not come to us out of the wreckage of individualism. What we need is steady devotion to a better, brighter, broader individualism—an individualism that carries increasing responsibility and service to our fellows. Our need is not for a way out but a way forward."[18]

A way out of individualism is exactly what many political and social philosophers of the 1920s desired. Led by Communist thinkers such as Michael Gold, many intellectuals took the Progressivist call for a new individualism of subordination and discipline one step further and demanded that Americans reject all individualism, whether old or new. By the end of the decade, the nature and role of individualism in the collective effort to reshape society was at best precarious, and individualism, however it was defined, became the central focus of many texts. The calls for self-denial and discipline in reshaping American individualism seemed to have failed, and an emerging political and social radicalism increasingly threatened to throw individualism into violent conflict with the demands of social reform. In *Individualism Old and New* (1930), John Dewey noted "a submergence of the individual," proclaimed that "individuals are confused and bewildered," and, more than a decade after Brooks, offered his own ideas "Toward a New Individualism."[19] Horace M. Kallen, in *Individualism: An American Way of Life* (1933), lamented that "Individualism [not just 'rugged individualism'] is in eclipse."[20] In *The Conflict of the Individual and the Mass in the Modern World* (1932), Everett Dean Martin insisted that recent attempts to subordinate individual needs for the collective good had not created a new individual at all: "In practice the submergence of the individual in the mass, as the mass is organized to-day, divides the individual against himself. He is no longer a whole person, he counts only as he is part of some public. It is as producer, consumer, voter, subscriber—not as a person that he is of public interest."[21]

But these voices met with resistance. Many intellectuals still claimed that individualism, modified or not, continued to be a powerful and unhealthy influence in American culture. In *A Planned Society* (1932), George Soule urged that "Today more than ever we need synthesis, coördination, rational control. . . . [We are] thwarted by the dogma of absolute Liberty, by the chaos of indeterminateness, which is the natural accom-

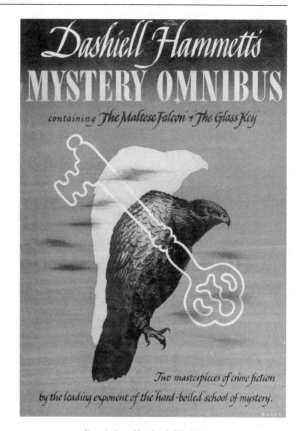

*Dust jacket; Cleveland: World, 1946*
*(Collection of Richard Layman)*

paniment of planless 'freedom.' We are concerned . . . with freedom from the blind compulsions of a disorganized and unreasoned society."[22] In a 1931 editorial, the *New Republic* warned its readership that "the old recipes of 'rugged individualism' and uncontrolled competition are seen on every hand to be insufficient. Our mechanized civilization has advanced to a point where it cries out for planning and control in the interests of all—a sort of planning and control which cannot possibly be executed without encroaching on vested [individual] interests."[23]

Amidst all of this dialogue on individualism in the late 1920s and early 1930s, perhaps Dewey best expressed the importance of the issue: "The problem of constructing a new individuality consonant with the objective conditions under which we live is the deepest problem of our time. . . . So regarded, the problem is seen to be essentially that of creation of a new individualism as significant for modern conditions as the old individualism at its best was for its day and place."[24]

*Red Harvest* and *The Maltese Falcon* can be understood as explorations of this call for a new individualism. Each novel examines the possibility of refashioning the inherited impulses of nineteenth-century individualism into a "better, brighter, broader individualism" which seeks, either through allegiance and/or willing submission, to promote collective rather than individual needs. In *Red Harvest,* Hammett's hero initially seems to have transcended the impulses of rugged individualism, and through allegiance to the Agency he appears to have submitted his own desires to those of a collective body. The novel enacts the Op's struggle to resist the impulses of aberrant individualism and to maintain his new individualism of collective identification. In *The Maltese Falcon,* Sam Spade begins as one immersed in competitive, self-centered individualism, for he is both unwilling and unable to act out of interests other than his own. His struggle is the reverse of the Op's: he must find a way out of a maddening and destructive individualism toward a new individualism which, through "control" and "self-sacrifice," will allow him allegiance to something beyond the self. Seen as such, *Red Harvest* and *The Maltese Falcon* embody what Dewey considered the "deepest problem" of Hammett's time, for the novels explore changing and competing conceptions of old and new individualism in American culture.

## II

Hammett locates his first novel in the aptly named town of Personville, Montana, a place victimized by nineteenth-century individualism run amok. As the name suggests, Personville is indeed a town of persons rather than a community, and each citizen seeks above all else to protect his or her own interests.[25] Dominating the politics and economics of Personville, old Elihu Willsson embodies the most unhealthy results of these unrestrained vested interests.

> For forty years old Elihu Willsson . . . had owned Personville, heart, soul, skin, and guts. He was president and majority stockholder of the Personville Mining Corporation, ditto of the First National Bank, owner of the *Morning Herald* and *Evening Herald,* the city's only newspapers, and at least part owner of nearly every other enterprise of any importance. Along with these pieces of property he owned a United States senator, a couple of representatives, the governor, the mayor, and most of the state legislature. Elihu Willsson was Personville, and he was almost the whole state.[26]

Eventually challenged by the labor advances of the I.W.W., old Elihu unmercifully squashes any threat of collective reforms: "Old Elihu hired gunmen, strike-breakers, national guardsmen and even parts of the regular army. . . . When the last skull had been cracked, the last rib kicked in, organized labor in Personville was a used firecracker" (7). In silencing this collective unrest, however, he surrenders most of his local control to the thugs he hired to protect his interests. As a result, Personville is ruled by four gangs that form a violent criminal network where, as critic Peter Wolfe suggests, "self-reliance knows no bounds."[27] The town's one voice of social reform, old Elihu's son Donald, is murdered before he appears in the text. A nightmare landscape of brutal self-interest, Personville is the twentieth-century apotheosis of nearly every evil associated with America's old, opportunistic individualism (note that Elihu's domination of Personville reaches back forty years, clearly identifying him and the town with the previous century). Perhaps Dinah Brand, Personville's beleaguered Siren, best articulates the town's attitude when she insists that "If a girl's got something that's worth something to somebody, she's a boob if she doesn't collect" (24).

It is down these mean streets that the Continental Op must go. Seeking the murderer of his would-be client, the Op demands that Personville "talk sense for a change" (12) and insists that "things have got to be explained" (17). As efficient as Hammett's hard-boiled prose, the Op moves about Personville with very little wasted effort, successfully pumping everyone he meets for information. Even before he solves Donald Willsson's murder, others note his skillful management and efficiency. Soon, old Elihu wants to hire him to "clean this pig-sty of Poisonville . . . to smoke out the rats, little and big" (29). When the Op asks for a ten thousand dollar retainer, old Elihu at first refuses to give so much money to a "man who's done nothing I know of but talk" (30). The Op's response, however, indicates how well he, unlike the citizens of Personville, has merged his own individuality with a larger collective body, suggesting that he has perhaps become what so many social and political philosophers of the times desired—a "new individual" seeking not self-assertion but loyalty to interests beyond his own: "When I say *me,* I mean the Continental" (30).[28] Only a short while later the Op will again assert this collective loyalty as he rejects a bribe: "The Continental's got rules against taking bonuses or rewards" (43).

Yet the Op's subordination to the rules of the Agency is not nearly as inviolate as the early sections of this novel would have us believe. When the chief of police betrays the Op and tries to have him killed, the Op loses his professional detachment. The self-denial he must maintain to perform effectively within the rules of the Agency gives way to vested self-interest. The efficient reformer can no longer subordinate his own desires and place them second to those of the Agency. After the attempt on his life, the Op no longer desires collective justice but personal revenge: "Your fat chief of police tried to assassinate me last night. I don't like that. I'm just mean enough to want to ruin him for it. Now I'm going to have my fun. I've got ten thousand dollars of your money to play with. I'm going to use it opening Poisonville up from Adam's apple to ankles" (43).[29] So much for reform.

The rest of the novel records the Op's "red harvest" of bloody revenge. The values of rational planning and cool efficiency asserted at the beginning of the novel collapse as the Op turns inward to fulfill his own violent form of frontier self-interest. We are witnessing a transformation in the Op's allegiances. The new individual who once equated his self with his Agency now reverts to the ethics of old individualism. Certainly, as Wolfe has suggested, "Responsibility to the Continental should have stopped [the Op] from playing the footloose justicer of cowboy fiction who cleans up a troubled town."[30] Unfortunately, the impulse to act from self-interest is too strong and the more independent the Op becomes from the regulations of the Agency, the more he begins to assume the guise of the cowboy justicer, except that unlike the heroic cowboy the Op "rejects his professionalism not to become the white knight who will liberate the countryside from evil and corruption but to get even."[31]

The Op's plans, once so effective, soon begin to go awry. Trying to antagonize the crime bosses, the Op "refixes" a fixed fight and, against plan, one of the fighters is murdered.[32] Soon, the Op confesses that "Plans are all right sometimes. . . . And sometimes just stirring things up is all right–if you're tough enough to survive, and keep your eyes open so you'll see what you want when it comes to the top" (57). His loyalties altered by his lust for personal revenge, the Op no longer desires to "clean" Personville. Pursuing his self-interests, he has turned Personville into a battleground, in the process losing his social consciousness:

> Off to the north some guns popped.
> A group of three men passed me, shifty-eyed, walking pigeon-toed.
> A little farther along, another man moved all the way over to the curb to give me plenty of room to pass. I didn't know him and didn't suppose he knew me.
> A lone shot sounded not far away.
> As I reached the hotel, a battered black touring car went down the street, hitting at least fifty, crammed to the curtains with men.
> I grinned after it. Poisonville was beginning to boil out under the lid, and I felt so much like a native that even the memory of my very un-nice part in the boiling

*Front cover for a Norwegian translation; Oslo: Gyldendals Flaggermusbøker, 1954 (Collection of Richard Layman)*

didn't keep me from getting twelve solid end-to-end hours of sleep. (77)

Finally, the Op rejects the demands of the Agency in favor of his own criteria: "It's right enough for the Agency to have rules and regulations, but when you're out on a job you've got to do it the best way you can" (78). When he tells two fellow operatives "don't kid yourselves that there's any law in Poisonville except what you make for yourself" (79), we can see the Op participating fully in Personville's powerful ideology of vested self-interests.[33]

Instead of being the town's efficient reformer, the Op admits that he has been "juggl[ing] death and destruction" (103). Rather than self-discipline, he must confess to having taken a less noble path: "[I could have played] legally. I could have done that. But it's easier to have them killed off, easier and surer, and, now that I'm feeling this way, more satisfying" (104). Unable to rationalize his actions, the Op confesses to Dinah that he is "going blood-simple" (104). Two surrealistic dreams preface the final movements of this otherwise intensely realistic narrative, further highlighting the irrationality which has slowly come to define the Op's experience. By the end of the novel, the reformer needs reforming. The "new individual" we saw at the beginning, the one who had merged his needs and allegiances with those of the Agency, we now find fixing up his reports "so that they would not read as if I had broken as many Agency rules, state laws and human bones as I had" (142).

The Op has become, as it were, a modern day Ahab, juggling death and destruction to satisfy the most irrational of self-centered desires—personal revenge. And, just as Ahab represented nineteenth-century individualism in destructive excess, so too does the Op represent the corruption of twentieth-century individualism, for as John Whitley proclaims, "Little in [the Op's] behavior suggests loyalty to ideals, human relations, or even abstract concepts of the law. He believes only in himself in the narrowest possible sense."[34] Fused momentarily to the reformative desires of a social agency, the Op succumbs to chaotic individualism and thus undermines the efficacy of collective action. In the end, Personville, the horrific landscape of American individualism, corrupts the Op, for "despite his code and despite being an indirect representative of law as an operative of the Continental Agency [he] becomes as lawless as the gangsters and crooked politicians."[35] As Dennis Dooley maintains, we, and perhaps the Op himself, have "glimpsed a frightful truth: that in the end evil springs not merely from greed or organized crime . . . [but] from the eternal willingness of human beings to compromise their ideals and betray their nobler impulses to satisfy their baser needs."[36]

### III

In *The Maltese Falcon* Hammett further explores the destructive pull of old individualism. In *Red Harvest* Hammett moves the Op from a stance of willing subordination to a posture of aberrant self-interest, and in doing so he undercuts the Op's position as the hero of the novel, a position the Op claims throughout the early chapters. The Op's failure to remain a "hero" is intimately related to his failure to resist an unhealthy individualism. The destructive threats of self-centered individualism are an even greater danger to Sam Spade. Whereas Hammett successfully suppressed two key elements of the Op's individuality—his name and specific physical description—he now positions these two elements at the very beginning of *The Maltese Falcon*:[37]

Samuel Spade's jaw was long and bony, his chin a jutting v under the more flexible v of his mouth. His nostrils curved back to make another, smaller, v. His yellow-grey eyes were horizontal. The v motif was picked up again by thickish brows rising outward from twin creases above a hooked nose, and his pale brown hair grew down—from high flat temples—in a point on his forehead. He looked rather pleasantly like a blond satan. (295)

Compare this opening paragraph to that of *Red Harvest:*

I first heard Personville called Poisonville by a red-haired mucker named Hickey Dewey in the Big Ship in Butte. He also called his shirt a shoit. I didn't think anything of what he had done to the city's name. Later I heard men who manage their r's give it the same pronunciation. I still didn't see anything in it but the meaningless sort of humor that used to make richardsnary the thieve's word for dictionary. A few years later I went to Personville and learned better. (3)

In *Red Harvest,* the focus rests on the community and we eventually see how this community of perverted self-interests manages to "poison" the reformative desires of the hero. In *The Maltese Falcon,* however, the focus begins with the individual and the "poison" exists within him, for he is "a blond satan." If the Op moves from hero to anti-hero as he succumbs to the poison of a selfish individualism, then Sam Spade, already poisoned, begins as an anti-hero.[38] Hammett's description of Spade in the introduction to the 1934 Modern Library edition of the novel attests to Spade's unhealthy self-focus: "he wants to be a hard and shifty fellow, able to take care of himself in any situation, able to get the best of anybody he comes in contact with, whether criminal, innocent by-stander or client."[39] The Op's challenge is to resist participating in the destructive individualism of Personville and to maintain his professional allegiance to the Agency. Certainly, the Op fails. Spade's challenge is to overcome his own destructive embracing of self-interest and to seek a greater collective identity.

The early chapters of *The Maltese Falcon* attest to Spade's anti-heroic posture of privileged individualism. Recall how in the opening chapters of *Red Harvest* the Op assumes an admirable stance, and, via his client Donald Willsson, is closely allied with social reform. The Op's early concerns for efficiency and justice position him well in our hearts. Not so for Spade. Whereas the Op has a client, someone he works for, Spade has a "customer" (295). Whereas the Op insists that Personville "talk sense for a change," Spade speaks "in a tone that was utterly meaningless" (304). Nearly all of Spade's early actions are self-centered, having less to do with advancing justice than with satisfying his own personal needs (recall his unwillingness to speak to Iva after Archer's murder). His secretary, Effie Perrine, warns him of the dangers of his ways, but in response Spade only reasserts his individualism:

> "You worry me," she said, seriousness returning to her face as he talked. "You always think you know what you're doing, but you're too slick for your own good, and some day you're going to find it out."
>
> He sighed mockingly and rubbed his cheek against her arm. "That's what Dundy says, but you keep Iva away from me, sweet, and I'll manage to survive the rest of my troubles." He stood up and put on his hat. "Have the *Spade & Archer* taken off the door and *Samuel Spade* put on. I'll be back in an hour, or phone you." (312–13).

Spade's individualism is explained in his often-cited story of Charles Flitcraft, whom Spade, at the time working in Seattle, was once hired to track down. Spade tells us that "Flitcraft had been a good citizen and a good husband and father, not by any outer compulsion, but simply because he was a man who was most comfortable in step with his surroundings" (335–36). One day, however, when a falling beam at a construction site nearly kills him, Flitcraft learns that he, "the good citizen-husband-father, could be wiped out between office and restaurant by the accident of a falling beam. He knew then that men died at haphazard like that, and lived only while blind chance spared them" (336). This experience gives Flitcraft a "new glimpse of life," one which leads him to the "discovery that in sensibly ordering his affairs he had gone out of step, and not into step, with life" (336). Flitcraft deserts his family and job in Tacoma, rejecting the social roles of citizen-father-husband, and, confronting absurdity for the first time, he embraces a meandering, uncommitted individualism: "He went to Seattle that afternoon . . . and from there by boat to San Francisco. For a couple of years he wandered around and then drifted by the Northwest" (336). The individualism Flitcraft embraces, however, does not endure, for soon after his drifting he settles down in Spokane and remarries. What fascinates Spade is Flitcraft's seemingly easy return to the "ordering of his affairs" after having rejected all such ordering as absurd. As Spade puts it, "He adjusted himself to beams falling, and then no more of them fell, and he adjusted himself to them not falling" (336).

Flitcraft's story serves to complement Spade's current position. Flitcraft's life before the beams begin falling is completely unlike Spade's present life: Flitcraft participated in society as citizen-father-husband, all roles that called for the subordination of self-interest to the larger collective interests of society and family.

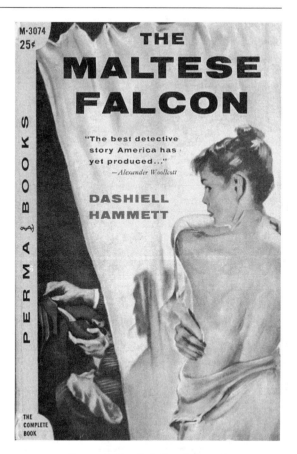

*Front cover; New York: Permabooks, 1957*
*(Collection of Richard Layman)*

Spade has rejected all such roles, and goes so far as to mock the role of husband by committing adultery. When the beams begin to fall, Flitcraft adjusts to his new glimpse of life. Convinced of "blind chance" and life's "haphazard" nature, Flitcraft makes a path for San Francisco via Seattle, a path symbolizing a rejection of his social roles in favor of a more self-centered individualism. Flitcraft, once so unlike Spade in his acceptance of social roles, is now very much like Spade. Note that Spade too moves to San Francisco via Seattle and that doing so suggests a rejection of a collective role for a more individual stance, for Spade tells Brigid that in 1927 he was "with one of those big detective agencies in Seattle" (335). He is now, of course, on his own, first with "Spade & Archer," and then with "Samuel Spade." Flitcraft's movement away from a collective identity to a purely individual one comes full circle when he repositions himself into his social role through remarriage.

Spade, however, has yet to make such a return; in fact, Spade seems to be moving farther and farther into pure individualism (i.e., "Spade & Archer" to "Samuel Spade"). Thus his fascination with Flitcraft's ability to "settle back naturally into the same groove he had jumped out of" (336) is in part a fascination with one man's ability to reassume social roles and obligations after experiencing a period of uncommitted individualism. Spade still feels what Flitcraft felt that day the beam fell. For Spade life is irrational, governed by blind chance, haphazard at best. Thus he believes in the one thing he can control and promote: his own self-interest. Faced with absurdity and chaos, Spade rejects social obligations and seeks stability by asserting his own desires and independence.

In pursuing the Maltese Falcon, Spade must confront the unhealthy effects of his rugged individualism when it is embraced by others. It is easy for Spade to promote his own self-interests while he is able to disassociate himself from others: it takes only a new paint job to remake the office door and simply a quick phone call to Effie to ward off the claims of Iva. Soon, however, Spade finds himself caught in a community where disassociation is not so easy and where self-interest is the supreme motivation of all involved. The world of Gutman, Brigid, Cairo and the ever-elusive falcon represents, as does Personville in *Red Harvest,* a community of aberrant individualists embracing an unhealthy doctrine of self-interests over the needs of others. When Gutman asks Spade whom he represents in this case and Spade indicates himself, Gutman articulates the philosophy of the micro-community to which Spade is now bound:

> "That's wonderful. I do like a man that tells you right out he's looking out for himself. Don't we all? I don't trust a man that says he's not. And the man that's telling the truth when he says he's not I distrust most of all, because he's an ass and an ass that's going contrary to the laws of nature." (365)

What Gutman here embraces, the social and economic reformers of the early twentieth century rejected outright, and the "new individual" of Croly, Brooks, Soule, and Dewey is in this world an "ass."

Supposed hero of the novel, Spade is as guilty as any in this circle of falcon-seekers. Gutman's exhortations could well be Spade's, for the detective has yet to act in any way which might indicate he thinks otherwise about "the laws of nature." At this point, the true "quest" of the novel emerges. Certainly Spade and the others seek the falcon, but, as the novel will soon bear out, that search proves to be an illusion. The real quest, the truly elusive (but not illusory) search, belongs to

Spade. Repeatedly immersed in his own self-centered desires, Spade must somehow differentiate himself from his criminal associates and become the "hero" of the text. To do this, he must reshape his desires according to the demands of some system or code greater than himself. In other words, Spade must make the first move toward a "new individualism," that is, begin to merge his own identity with a larger movement or collective body. Such a move calls for self-discipline and willing subordination, two traits Spade has heretofore lacked. Spade's final confrontation with Brigid enacts his struggle to overcome the insane individualism which has dominated this novel, an insanity in which he has fully participated.

When Spade tells Brigid that he knows she killed Archer, he also tells her that he will turn her over to the police. His motivations again appear to be fully shaped by self-interest: "You're taking the fall. One of us has got to take it, after the talking those birds [Gutman and Cairo] will do. They'd hang me sure. You're likely to get a better break" (436). Here, however, we can excuse Spade's "selfishness"—the self-centeredness here does not resemble his brush-offs of Iva or his willingness to auction off his services to the highest bidder—for Brigid does indeed deserve to be turned over. Brigid, citing what they once had "been to each other," demands to know why Spade must do this to her, for, as she tells him, "Surely Mr. Archer wasn't as much to you as [I was]" (438). Spade's litany of reasons, tripartite in structure, is quite telling and deserves careful reading.[40]

In his first attempt to explain his motivations, Spade calls on the code of the detective. The reasons are worth quoting in full:

> "When a man's partner is killed he's supposed to do something about it. It doesn't make any difference what you thought of him. He was your partner and you're supposed to do something about it. Then it happens we were in the detective business. Well, when one of your organization gets killed it's bad business to let the killer get away with it. It's bad all around—bad for that one organization, bad for every detective everywhere. Third, I'm a detective and expecting me to run criminals down and then let them go free is like asking a dog to catch a rabbit and let it go. It can be done, all right, and sometimes it is done, but it's not natural." (438)

Embracing the discipline of the detective code, Spade willingly subordinates his own needs to the needs of "every detective everywhere." What is "natural" here is not Gutman's insistence that all men look out for themselves; instead, professional demands and allegiances dominate any self-interests. Most critics consider these allegiances to be Spade's true motivation throughout the novel; they are thus able to excuse Spade's inexplicable moments of self-centeredness.

Should we believe, however, that Spade has been acting within this code all along?[41] If he has been, then Spade is indeed an heroic "new individual," acting always out of interests beyond his own in hopes of servicing justice. But, as Gregory notes of Spade's other actions throughout the novel, "Since the reader constantly sees Spade adopting whatever role seems most expedient, it becomes impossible for us to be certain of any of his intentions."[42] The same is true here. We would, I believe, like to think that Spade's actions have been intentionally serving a larger, collective good. Perhaps they have been, but then again, perhaps not. At best, we might be able to explain some, but not all, of Spade's actions as stemming from this collective code. The uncertainty confronting the reader here is not a fault in the novel. Instead, Hammett forces the reader to reconsider Spade's motivations and to reposition Spade's possible allegiances. We must listen further, for we feel at this moment as does Brigid: we do not fully believe that the code encompasses all of Spade's actions. His exhortation of the detective code may well be just another one of his well-devised deceptions.

Spade's second attempt to explain himself reveals a different set of motivations. Again, it is worth quoting in full:

> "Fourth, no matter what I wanted to do now it would be absolutely impossible for me to let you go without having myself dragged to the gallows with the others. Next, I've no reason in God's world to think I can trust you and if I did this and got away with it you'd have something on me that you could use whenever you happened to want to. That's five reasons. The sixth would be that since I've also got something on you, I couldn't be sure you wouldn't decide to shoot a hole in *me* some day. Seventh, I don't even like the idea of thinking that there might be one chance in a hundred that you'd played me for a sucker." (438)

Most critics privilege Spade's first three reasons (all having to do with loyalty to the code) and largely ignore reasons four through seven. We should consider, however, that both sets of motivations compel Spade (whether one or the other is *more* compelling is difficult to say at this point, though the novel would seem to bear out the primacy of individual desires over professional codes).[43] In this way, Spade enacts an important tension of his generation, for he desires affiliation with a collective body while still refusing to repress the importance of his own needs. His first three reasons submerge his own individual demands; the next four reasons assert them. Spade seems split

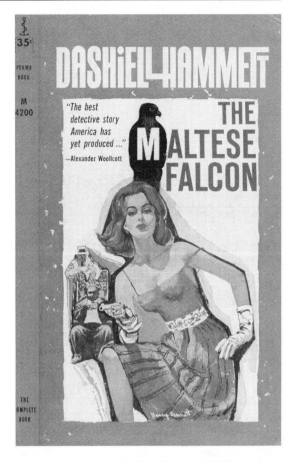

*Front cover; New York: Permabooks, 1961
(Collection of Richard Layman)*

between two allegiances: the collective good and individual self-interest.

Spade's third and final explanation receives little attention but it is perhaps the most important in his development:[44] "If [all of my reasons don't] mean anything to you forget it and we'll make it this: I won't [let you go] because all of me wants to—wants to say to hell with the consequences and do it—and because—God damn you—you've counted on that with me the same as you counted on that with the others" (439). Not wanting "to play the sap," Spade discovers a way out of the insane individualism of the Gutman-Cairo-Brigid trio: self-denial. Spade knows that Brigid has been counting on him to act in his own self-interests and to cover up for the lady he loves. Spade wants to let her go and a great deal in this final scene suggests that he may

*Front cover; London: Penguin, 1963*
*(Collection of Richard Layman)*

At the end of *The Maltese Falcon* we know that Spade is doing the right thing and that the right thing involves a curious calculation of allegiances to both personal and professional codes. Ultimately, however, the sum of these calculations adds up to self-denial. Via this self-denial Spade begins to reshape his individualism, recalling for us the words of Herbert Croly quoted earlier in this essay: "The Promise of American life is to be fulfilled—not merely by a maximum amount of economic freedom, but by a certain measure of discipline; not merely by the abundant satisfaction of individual desires, but by a large measure of individual subordination and self-denial." Spade's decision to surrender Brigid stands as a moment of discipline for a man repeatedly described in terms suggesting not discipline but bestial ("wolfish") need for satisfaction.[45] Spade's dilemma at the conclusion of the novel enacts a dilemma of his entire generation: in moments of crisis, where do we put our allegiances, how do we protect our own self-interests without violating the demands of a larger community, how do we fuse our own needs with the needs of society and still retain our inherent American desire for self-promoting individualism?

In *Red Harvest* and *The Maltese Falcon* we witness Hammett struggling with his generation's reconception of American individualism. Just as intellectuals were calling for the refashioning of nineteenth-century individualism through efficient planning, social control, and self-denial, Hammett was investigating the possibilities of achieving and maintaining this new individualism. These investigations, however, do not supply easy answers. In *Red Harvest* Hammett portrays the failure of new individualism, for the Op and all his allegiances to the Agency cannot withstand the pull of an old, self-seeking individualism. The lesson here seems to be that the inherited self-interest of the American landscape remains too powerful for the new allegiances to overcome. And yet in *The Maltese Falcon* Hammett reverses this movement and takes his hero from a self-indulgent individualism to a new individualism which seeks to wed collective and personal interests via self-denial. But, as John Patterson properly maintains, this movement toward a new individualism is far from triumphant: "Returned to his desk in the final scene of his career, [Spade] is in fact a bleak, lonely, and unhappy figure, without home, without love, without community, conscious perhaps that his victory is far from final and that it may have cost him far too much."[46]

The pull of old and new individualism is not resolved in these two novels, only highlighted. Hammett neither assures us of the possibility of achieving a new individualism nor does he maintain the necessary and

indeed love her. But he will not act upon his own desires exactly because they are his own desires.

If we recall Hammett's original description of Spade looking "rather pleasantly like a blond satan," then this moment of self-imposed self-denial astounds us. Certainly this initial image of Spade as a pleasant satan conjures up for us the image of another pleasant satan, that of Milton's in the early books of *Paradise Lost*. Like Milton's Satan, Spade and his defiant individualism initially attract our sympathies. But as their narratives mature, we readers perceive the divisive ramifications of such myopic stances. Spade finally sees the implications as well and thus embraces not self-assertion but self-denial as his final posture. He is, as it were, no longer shaking his defiant fist against the heavens and fate but against himself.

inevitable victory of the old individualism. It has been said of detective stories that they are "wish-fulfillment fantasies designed to produce certain agreeable sensations in the reader, to foist upon him illusions he wants to entertain and which he goes to this literature to find."[47] If so, then Hammett has successfully transcended the genre, for his novels offer us profound complexities in the place of wish-fulfillments, irreconcilable realities instead of entertaining illusions. If we approach *Red Harvest* and *The Maltese Falcon* as complementary explorations of a similar dilemma, then we must face the disagreeable sensations produced by these texts when read in tandem: that is, that the refashioning of American individualism toward a more collective identity, as desirable and as necessary as it may be for the promise of American life, has been, and will always be, a painful and a precarious process.

## Notes

1. William Curtis, "Some Recent Books," *Town and Country,* 15 February 1930, cited in Richard Layman, *Shadow Man: The Life of Dashiell Hammett* (New York: Harcourt, 1981), p. 113.
2. Leonard Moss, "Hammett's Heroic Operative," *New Republic,* 8 January 1968: 34.
3. Leslie Fiedler, *Love and Death in the American Novel* (New York: Criterion, 1960), p. 476.
4. H. H. Morris, "Dashiell Hammett in the Wasteland," *Midwest Quarterly,* 19 (Winter 1978): 200–201.
5. Cynthia S. Hamilton, *Western and Hard-Boiled Detective Fiction in America: From High Noon to Midnight* (Iowa City: University of Iowa Press, 1987), pp. 1–2. To her credit, Hamilton grants Hammett a high level of sophistication on the problem of individualism in his work. Of Hammett's novels, she writes, "Hammett appears to be caught in a philosophical 'Catch-22': competitive individualism is bad because it is divisive, but collective action is impossible because individuals are competitive. Hammett cannot get past the basic ideological assumption of the primacy of the individual, and can pose no alternative. In this respect, the later condemnation of Hammett's work as subversive must be considered wryly ironic" (32). Like Hamilton's, my focus is on Hammett's handling of complicated issues of individualism. But whereas Hamilton insists that Hammett "cannot get past the basic ideological assumption of the primacy of the individual" I would argue that Hammett is not trying to "get past" individualism but is exploring competing versions of individualism and their respective attractions and shortcomings. Any "alternative" which Hammett might pose would thus not be something outside of individualism but would be a different type of individualism. Hammett is not in the business of posing alternatives to individualism; he is, rather, interested in investigating irreconcilable and painful tensions.
6. David Geherin, *The American Private Eye: The Image in Fiction* (New York: Ungar, 1985), pp. 21–22.
7. D. Glover, "Sociology and the Thriller: The Case of Dashiell Hammett," *Sociological Review,* 27 (February 1979): 26.
8. Robert Edenbaum, "The Poetics of the Private-Eye: The Novels of Dashiell Hammett," in *Tough-Guy Writers of the 1930's,* ed. David Madden (Carbondale: Southern Illinois University Press, 1968), p. 81.
9. Sinda Gregory, *Private Investigations: The Novels of Dashiell Hammett* (Carbondale: Southern Illinois University Press, 1985), p. 29. Compare Gregory's statement to Hamilton's claim that in Hammett's novels the "need for self-reliance is emphasized. . . . The individual is shown to be the only source of positive social action" (31).
10. Robert Shulman, "Dashiell Hammett's Social Vision," *Centennial Review,* 29 (Fall 1985): 400. Shulman opposes the individualism of the Continental Op, Sam Spade, and Ned Beaumont (a type of individualism Shulman often refers to as merely "different") to the "competitive individualism" of those whom they must confront. Though I agree with Shulman's observation that a novel like *The Maltese Falcon* "brings to a suggestive focus [Hammett's] concern with American individualism," I would suggest that the conflicting versions of individualism in such novels as *Red Harvest* and *The Maltese Falcon* are most often played out within the hero rather than between the hero and his competitive society. Such a reading reveals not only Hammett's critique of an acquisitive capitalist culture, which most readings of his work manifest, but emphasizes Hammett's critique of his heroes as well.
11. Herbert Croly, *The Promise of American Life* (New York: Macmillan, 1909), p. 22.
12. Croly, pp. 25, 23, 152.
13. Frederick Jackson Turner cited in *Individualism and Conformity in the American Character,* ed. Richard Rapson (Boston: Heath, 1967), p. 26.
14. Van Wyck Brooks, "Toward a National Culture," in *Van Wyck Brooks: The Early Years,* ed. Claire Sprague (New York: Harper, 1968), p. 185.
15. Brooks, pp. 186, 190, 190, 190.
16. Herbert Hoover, *American Individualism* (Garden City, N.Y.: Doubleday, 1922), pp. 71–72.
17. Croly, p. 153.
18. Hoover, p. 66.
19. John Dewey, *Individualism Old and New* (New York: Capricorn, 1930), pp. 51–52. See also the chapter "Toward a New Individualism," pp. 74–100.
20. Horace M. Kallan, *Individualism: An American Way of Life* (New York: Liveright, 1933), p. 20.
21. Everett Dean Martin, *The Conflict of the Individual and the Mass in the Modern World* (New York: Holt, 1932), p. 33.
22. George Soule, *A Planned Society* (New York: Macmillan, 1932), pp. 91–92.
23. Cited in Richard H. Pells, *Radical Visions and American Dreams: Culture and Social Thought in the Depression Years* (Middletown, Conn.: Wesleyan University Press, 1984), p. 50.
24. Dewey, pp. 31–32.
25. The town's geographical location also holds symbolic resonance. Gregory writes that Personville's "pollution, in both a physical and spiritual sense, is even more dramatic because of its geographical position; by placing the city in the West, Hammett suggests a sort of ultimate corruption: the West–the promised land whose expanse offers freedom, escape, and the realization of America's promise of opportunity and unlimited possibility–has become as 'dirtied up' as the rest of the country" (31).

26. Dashiell Hammett, *The Complete Novels of Dashiell Hammett* (New York: Knopf, 1965), p. 7. All further references are to this edition and are cited in parenthesis.

27. Peter Wolfe, *Beams Falling: The Art of Dashiell Hammett* (Bowling Green, Ohio: Bowling Green University Popular Press, 1980), p. 90.

28. Gregory astutely observes the importance of the Op's allegiance to the Agency: "Unlike almost all of the hard-boiled detectives who work from a small one-man office and who pride themselves on their independence (Philip Marlowe, Mike Hammer, Race Williams), the Op is part of an organization. Thus he is not a renegade maverick at odds with the police. . . . The Continental Detective Agency is, in fact, a business that approaches crime and violence with no moralistic or evangelical zeal. The Op's anonymity is reinforced by his position in such an agency" (44). This description of the Op's unusual position in hard-boiled fiction will serve as an interesting contrast to Hammett's next creation, Sam Spade.

29. Discussing the importance of this moment, Glover observes: "It is this stubbornness which mitigates against seeing the Continental Op solely as the organization man he is and which limits the strong tendency for the detective to be reduced solely to his occupational function. Furthermore it is this irrepressible egoism which shifts the narrative towards the timeless realm of fantasy where the individual is totally superordinate and autonomous. The antinomies which the text invokes—between individual and occupation, realism and fantasy—are never ultimately resolved but provide for different modes of exposition and emphasis as the plot unfolds" (25–26).

30. Wolfe, p. 87.

31. Gregory, p. 50. George J. Thompson notes the Op's vengeful motives but argues differently: "The harvest of revenge promises to be red. Nowhere does the Op talk about law or justice in this vow; the matter is partly a personal one. The detective seems to represent himself more than his client, and yet his personal stand implies a social, even moral, perspective as well. The Op's emphasis is on a cleaning up, a harvesting of rottenness and corruption. The harvest image suggests a natural, if not moral, necessity for action" ("The Problem of Moral Vision in Dashiell Hammett's Detective Novels, Part II: *Red Harvest*, 'The Pragmatic and Moral Dilemma,'" *Armchair Detective*, 6 [1972]: 217).

32. Seeking to vindicate the Op's actions, Thompson insists the following: "Stirring things up and trying to stay tough enough to survive prove to be the Op's method throughout *Red Harvest*. In this initial case [of the fixed fight], his method is tried out: it's a pragmatic experiment, one which gets results even though a man is killed in the process. . . . we are not morally upset that Kid Cooper gets killed. He is not innocent, and his death is seen, though as non-legal, as poetic justice" ("The Problem of Moral Vision in Dashiell Hammett's Detective Novels, Part II: *Red Harvest*, 'The Pragmatic and Moral Dilemma,'" p. 218).

33. In his study of popular genres, John C. Cawelti insists that "to preserve his integrity [the hard-boiled hero] must reject the public ideals and values of the society and seek to create his own personal code of ethics and his own set of values" (*Adventure, Mystery, and Romance: Formula Stories as Art and Popular Culture* [Chicago: University of Chicago Press, 1976], p. 161). Certainly this is true of many hard-boiled

heroes, but in the case of the Op it is not so. When the Op chooses to begin his vendetta against Personville, he is embracing, not rejecting, the public ideals and values of the society. Also, when the Op seeks to fashion his own personal code and set of values (codes and values free of Agency constraints) we see the dissolution of integrity, not the preservation of it, as the Op descends into the ethics of revenge. Perhaps the harshest criticism of the Op's "personal code of ethics" comes from Christopher Bentley: "Apart from his narrow and sometimes questionable professionalism, it is hard to see that the Op has any ethical code, or that his violence is any more meaningful than that it serves to keep him alive and to kill people whom he wishes to see dead" ("Radical Anger: Dashiell Hammett's *Red Harvest*," in *America Crime Fiction: Studies in the Genre*, ed. Brian Docherty [New York: St. Martin's Press, 1988], p. 64).

34. John S. Whitley, "Stirring Things Up: Dashiell Hammett's Continental Op," *Journal of American Studies*, 14 (December 1980): 449.

35. Gregory, p. 57.

36. Dennis Dooley, *Dashiell Hammett* (New York: Ungar, 1984), p. 85.

37. Dooley writes: "How fitting, after six years of stories and novels featuring a nameless hero, that the first words of Hammett's new book should be the name of his detective" (99).

38. As William Ruehlman notes, "When Spade is compared to a 'blond satan' in the first paragraph, Hammett is deliberately setting him forth as a character who is a long way from being a hero" (*Saint With a Gun: The Unlawful American Private Eye* [New York: New York University Press, 1974], p. 73).

39. Cited in Layman, p. 106.

40. Thompson gives the most thorough reading of this confrontation, placing, as I do, great importance on all of Spade's reasons for surrendering Brigid ("The Problem of Moral Vision in Dashiell Hammett's Detectives Novels, Part IV: *The Maltese Falcon*, 'The Emergency of the Hero,'" *Armchair Detective*, 7 [1974]: 189). Though Thompson is not concerned as I am with Spade's struggle with competing versions of individualism, he recognizes, as many critics fail to do, that Spade's reasons "bridge moral and professional and personal concerns" (189). In contrast to most critics, William Kenney fails to discern the indispensable importance of the Spade-Brigid confrontation to the meaning of the novel. Kenney sees the confrontation as an "afterthought" because the main action of the novel, the quest for the falcon, ends with the discovery of the fake ("The Dashiell Hammett Tradition and the Modern Detective Novel," *Dissertation*, Michigan 1964, p. 110, cited in Thompson, "The Problem of Moral Vision in Dashiell Hammett's Detective Novels, Part IV: *The Maltese Falcon*, 'The Emergency of the Hero,'" p. 179).

41. Many critics do believe that Spade has been within the code all along. For instance, William F. Nolan believes that in this scene Spade "reveals the emotions of a man whose heart is with the woman, but whose code forbids his accepting her" (*Hammett: A Life at the Edge* [New York: Congdon, 1983], p. 61). Edward Margolies insists that Spade "can surrender Brigid to the police because, even though he loves her, his code comes first" (*Which Way Did He Go? The Private Eye in Dashiell Hammett, Raymond Chandler, Chester Himes, and Ross Macdonald* [New York:

Holmes, 1982], p. 30). William Marling asserts that Spade is "more perfectly than the Op a knight of the detective code" (*Dashiell Hammett* [Boston: Twayne, 1983], p. 76). Walter Blair concurs with the primacy of Spade's code in controlling his behavior throughout the novel: "Through his reading of much of the book the reader is kept in the dark as to what makes Spade tick. But as the story concludes, Spade's actions make clear that he is the only character who has integrity, who obeys a code" ("Dashiell Hammett: Themes and Techniques," in *Essays on American Literature in Honor of Jay Hubbell*, ed. Clarence Gohdes [Durham, N.C.: Duke University Press, 1967], p. 306). My inclinations are more in sympathy with Hamilton, who acknowledges that "we are never told [Spade's] thoughts, only given his words and actions. Spade may have involved himself with Brigid, Gutman, and Cairo in order to solve the murders, recover the falcon and prosecute the thieves; or he may be an opportunist who finds he must turn everything over to the police in order to save himself. Some understanding of Spade is possible because the vision underlying the book is his vision, but this does not help us to interpret his actions or to place moral value on them" (132). I feel it is not necessary to accept that Spade believes in a code; what is more important is that Spade desires to be affiliated with such a code, that he seeks, rather than believes in, allegiance to that code.

42. Gregory, p. 105. It is interesting to note here that although Gregory suggests the impossibility of discovering Spade's intentions, she is willing to believe in Spade's professionalism: "Despite all his personal complexities and idiosyncracies, Sam Spade is, above all, a very efficient private investigator, a man who has a shrewd business sense and loyalty to and respect for his profession" (94).

43. Perhaps John Patterson is correct in asserting "that when a man has so many reasons to advance he is not really sure of any of them" ("A Cosmic View of the Private Eye," *Saturday Review* [22 August 1953]: 32). Again, however, what remains important is not that we ascertain Spade's true allegiances but that we note Spade's struggle to articulate those allegiances.

44. I obviously disagree with Thompson, who feels that at this moment "Spade's diction—'If that doesn't mean anything to you forget it and we'll make it this'—certainly implies he is over-simplifying his complex reasons because he realizes all too well her inability to understand their meaning" ("The Problem of Moral Vision in Dashiell Hammett's Detective Novels, Part IV: *The Maltese Falcon*, 'The Emergency of the Hero,'" p. 189). Spade is not over-simplifying his motivations at this moment so that Brigid may understand him; instead, he is asserting, in a crystalized, but not an over-simplified form, his newly discovered virtue of renunciation.

45. Dooley writes: "As the novel nears its conclusion, we glimpse the animal in Spade again, looking 'hungrily from her hair to her feet and up to her eyes again.' But he denies his hunger, knowing that to satisfy it would be his undoing" (108).

46. Patterson, p. 32.

47. William Aydelotte, "The Detective Story as Historical Source," in *Dimensions of Detective Fiction*, ed. Larry Landrum (Bowling Green, Ohio: Popular Press, 1976), p. 69.

\* \* \*

*Front cover for a Spanish translation; Madrid: Revista literaria, Novelas y Cuentos, 1963 (Collection of Richard Layman)*

## Jameson, Genre, and Gumshoes: *The Maltese Falcon* as Inverted Romance
Jasmine Yong Hall
*The Cunning Craft: Original Essays on Detective Fiction* (Macomb: Western Illinois University, 1990), pp. 109–119

Of all detective stories, *The Maltese Falcon* (1930) has some of the most direct connections to the romance. Like the Grail Quest, it is a story of adventurers in search of a mystical object—"a glorious golden falcon encrusted from head to foot with the finest jewels" (Hammett 128) whose origins can be traced to a romantic period of knights, crusades, kings, and pirates. All detective stories, however, have a central, structural connection to the romance, for like the romance, the detective story highlights the division between word and world, matter and meaning. D. W. Robertson, Eugene Vinaver, and Northrop Frye have all described romance in terms of an external world of adventures, and a sacred truth which must be discovered in that external world. Tzvetan Todorov sees the structure of romance as composed of two different kinds of narrative:

> One unfolds on a horizontal line: we want to know what each event provokes, what it does. The other represents a series of variations which stack up along a vertical line: what we look for in each event is what it is. (*Poetics* 135)

Todorov goes on to point out that this opposition between actions in the world and their interpretation also lies at the heart of the detective story—where crime is the absent "real" event which must be represented by the investigation. Both the detective story and romance, then, are structurally divided into a narrative of action (the crime, the adventure), and the narrative which "reads" that action, giving it meaning and significance.

Frye does not make as concise a connection between the detective story and romance, but his frequent allusions to detective stories in *The Secular Scripture* make it clear that he considers the detective story a type of romance. Frye's description of romance, in fact, provides the best point of comparison with *The Maltese Falcon*, but before proceeding further let me point to a problem in this comparison which Frye does not articulate. Frye shows that movement between an external, material world, and a meaningful world form the structure of romance; he sees the ending of romance in an ascent to the meaningful—in which the word and world become one. But whether "the marriage of matter and meaning" (Vinaver 23) ever takes place in *The Maltese Falcon* is questionable. In *The Maltese Falcon*, there is a much stronger emphasis on the story as story, rather than on the story as revelation of truth.

The reason that this gap between sense and matter is harder to bridge in *The Maltese Falcon* lies in historical differences between the world of romance and the world of the detective story. Todorov points out that the passage from matter to meaning is made possible in the Grail Quest by the existence of a code, "a divine language" (*Poetics* 129); this code "is not the personal invention of the author of *The Quest for the Holy Grail*, it is common to all the works of the period" (125), but it is not a code available to the author of *The Maltese Falcon*. This text presents us with a secular world—a world in which religion does not provide a medium by which the material world can be translated into meaningful signs. If there is a transcendent power in *The Maltese Falcon*, it is the power of money, not of God. As Caspar Gutman's valuation of the Falcon suggests, it is money which defies description:

> The maximum? . . . I refuse to guess. You'd think me crazy. I don't know. There's no telling how high it

could go, sir, and that's the one and the only truth about it. (135)

If one ascends to a higher world here—a world in which one can finally get the "truth about it"—it is not heaven, but a world in which untold riches will finally be able to be told.

How can one analyze the implications of placing money rather than religion at the transcendent center of this novel? Frye's approach to genre criticism does not offer a methodology for dealing with this important difference between a medieval romance and the modern detective story; however, a more fruitful approach is developed by Fredric Jameson in his chapter on "Magical Narratives" in *The Political Unconscious*. Jameson shows that, by finding the same patterns in romance from the earliest myths to present day works of popular culture, Frye "aims at reinforcing our sense of the affinity between the cultural present of capitalism and the distant mythical past of tribal societies. . . ." Frye's approach is ahistorical—a "'positive hermeneutic,' which tends to filter out historical difference and the radical discontinuity of modes of production and of their cultural expressions." Jameson suggests instead the use of a "negative hermeneutic" which

> would on the contrary wish to use the narrative raw material shared by myth and "historical" literatures to sharpen our sense of historical difference, and to stimulate an increasingly vivid apprehension of what happens when plot falls into history, so to speak, and enters the force fields of the modern societies. (130)

The difference between the two approaches, then, is that Frye categorizes an individual text according to a generic definition, while Jameson examines the way in which an individual text deviates from its inherited generic structure. Following Jameson's lead, I will be looking at *The Maltese Falcon* through the filter of romance in order to highlight the historical differences between the romance structure which originates in a Christian, feudal society, and the novel which is produced in a capitalist, monied one.

Frye's definition of romance structure divides into two main subcategories: the quest romance, and the social romance. The quest romance centers on a hero whose purpose is to find a sacred object, while the social romance centers on a heroine whose purpose is to recover her social position/identity and to marry. The two types have a very similar structure: there is a break of consciousness at the beginning followed by a descent to a lower world. The lower world is a world in which external, physical reality is radically divorced from meaning. It is usually ruled over by a monstrous figure—a dragon, a giant, or in more displaced romances a

giant man, like Front de Boef in *Ivanhoe;* the protagonist's contact with this monstrous figure represents
over-involvement with the physical and abandonment
of the search for this world's truth. This over-involvement in the physical continues as the protagonist
becomes trapped—in prisons, labyrinths, and finally
within his/her own body. Through amnesia, loss of
consciousness, or the presence of doubles, the protagonist is confined within the body without a clear sense of
identity—of personal meaning. Underlying these stories
of imprisonment is the fear that one is trapped within
the body by death, the final loss of identity. The ending
of the romance serves to defuse this threat through the
protagonist's ascent to a higher, more meaningful
plane—either in heaven, or through marriage.

The movement of ascent from the lower world is
signalled by an escape, return of memory/conscious-
ness, and/or a discovery of the protagonist's real identity. Usually these events are associated with the
recovery of a talisman or precious object which comes
out of the sea, and with this recovery the romance
reaches its conclusion, one which serves to combine the
two worlds of matter and meaning. In the social
romance, the physical world is given social meaning
through marriage: physical desire becomes socially
sanctioned. In the quest romance, the recovery of the
precious object, by fulfilling the language of prophecy,
shows that there is a connection between language and
the world. With the recovery of the talisman the divine
language is shown to stand behind the events of the
world, and the hero can ascend to the source of that
language in heaven (Frye 65–157). In examining *The
Maltese Falcon,* I will make use of elements from both
quest romance and social romance; however, the critical question to be addressed is whether *The Maltese Falcon* ever achieves the successful combination of meaning
and matter which ends the romance.

At the outset, *The Maltese Falcon* looks very much
like a romance, with the same loss of identity and proliferation of doubles. There are two detectives, Spade and
Archer, and two damsels in distress, Miss Wonderly
and her sister, who has been seduced by Floyd
Thursby. The two detectives are reduced to one when
Archer is killed, but Spade's identity becomes confused
with the killer's: Did he kill Archer? Or did he kill
Thursby, who presumably killed Archer?

The two sisters resolve into one woman when we
discover that Miss Wonderly's sister was merely a fab-
rication of Miss Wonderly's, a lure to get the detective
to tail Thursby. However, Miss Wonderly herself also
disappears, resurfacing as "Miss LeBlanc," who then
tells Spade that her *real* name is Brigid O'Shaughnessy.
Her identities proliferate at a rapid rate at the beginning

*Front cover; New York: Vintage, 1964 (Collection
of Richard Layman)*

of the novel: as Spade remarks to Effie, his secretary,
"She's got too many names" (43).

In many ways, Brigid hearkens back to the romance
heroine who must constantly rely on disguises, tricks, and
lying. Like Rosalind in *As You Like It,* her motto might be
"I shall devise something, but I pray you commend my
counterfeiting to him" (IV.iii.181–182). An importance difference, though, is that unlike the romance heroine, Brigid
uses tricks and ploys to protect not her virginity, but her
identity as murderer. In fact, she uses her sexuality to protect that secret: she seduces Spade halfway through the
novel to end his interrogation of her, which is leading
closer and closer to revelation. I will discuss this difference
more thoroughly in describing the ending of the novel;
however, I want to point to the fact that Brigid, far from
preserving her virginity, uses her body to try to obscure

her connection with that other body—the corpse. In romance, the important body is the virgin's; the integrity of this body allows the revelation of the woman's identity at the end of the story. But in *The Maltese Falcon* the important body is a corpse, which is uncovered with the revelation of the woman's identity as murderer.

Brigid's most impressive skill, though, is not her sexual allure; her abilities as a story-teller are far more impressive. Caught in one lie by Spade, she will quickly manufacture a new one out of the threads of the old. Spade's habitual reply to her lies—"You're good, you're very good" (36, 58)—is both ironic and admiring, for Spade shares the ability to construct a story quickly. Spade's ability to switch from one interpretation of events to another is the source of his power over the other characters. This is especially evident in his dealings with Joel Cairo and Wilmer, neither of whom have the verbal dexterity of Spade or Brigid. Cairo, for example, complains after he, and not Spade, has had to spend the evening being interrogated by the police because of a rather unbelievable story Spade tells them. Spade comes up with yet another story to explain to Cairo why he told the police what he did. Cairo replies a bit "dubiously," "You have always, I must say, a smooth explanation ready," to which Spade answers: "What do you want me to do? Learn to stutter?" (100).

Wilmer, who does stutter, as well as grunt and whimper at various points in the novel, is disarmed by Spade both physically and verbally. Having stripped him of his weapons, Spade further humiliates him in front of his boss, Caspar Gutman, by telling Gutman that the guns were taken by "A crippled newsie, . . . but I made him give them back" (216). Wilmer is the most frequent object of Spade's verbal ridicule because he can't speak well. While often reduced to non-verbal communication, Wilmer also reveals his inability to use language through his use of clichéd expressions. He threatens Spade in phrases limited by the role he plays:

> "Keep on riding me and you're going to be picking iron out of your navel."
> Spade chuckled. "The cheaper the crook, the gaudier the patter," he said cheerfully. (125)

Spade triumphs over Wilmer not only (or even primarily) through physical force, but through superior verbal skills. He can beat Wilmer because he can "type" him according to the kind of language Wilmer uses. Spade also correctly identifies Brigid by her use of language. After hearing several versions of her involvement with the Falcon, he exclaims, "You *are* a liar" (192). This ability to name his opponents correctly is one that Spade shares, not with the hero of romance, but the romance's seer or sage figure. Like all detectives he

plays a double role: he is both the adventurer doing battle with the forces of evil in the lower world, and the sage who reads the truth of this lower world through his interpretation of clues, or his discovery of "real" identities. However, Spade's interest in the truth becomes less clear as he descends further into this lower world. When he talks to Cairo, for instance, he does not refer to the truth to justify his stories; instead he refers to his own verbal "smoothness," the fact that he doesn't stutter, as justification for being a story-teller.

The story which Cairo complains of, the story which sends him off with the police, even more clearly illustrates the continuing division between world and word in Spade's language. In the chapter entitled "Horse Feathers," first Brigid, then Cairo, and finally Spade tell the police different versions of the events that have just transpired. Spade's version is actually farthest removed from the truth, and draws the description of "Horse feathers" (82) from Lt. Dundy. The fantastic nature of this story leads not to belief, but to Spade's control of the situation. In Spade's version of events everything which has just taken place has been faked in order to play a joke on the police. Spade's story discounts "reality" in two ways: it is a lie, and it is a lie which claims that the real is a fraud, a fiction. The two policemen, Dundy and Polhaus, find themselves unable to cope with this story. Spade's control of the police and the two criminals in this scene shows that his power originates not in reconstructions of the real events, but in reconstructions which purposely maintain their distance from the real.

Dundy's final reaction, which is to hit Spade, does not represent the policeman's physical triumph but his verbal defeat—a defeat which leaves Spade free from police-questioning so that he can pursue the case on his own. However, the division between matter and meaning continues here, because Spade does not use his time to pursue the case, but to pursue Brigid and the Falcon. As he descends into the lower world he loses his identity as detective not only in being accused of the two murders, but also in seeming to lose interest in discovering Archer's murderer—in discovering the truth hidden by the corpse and by the seductive female body. The proliferation of stories, then, does not represent a search for truth, but the distance from truth; one story must quickly follow another, as Cairo's follows Brigid's, and Spade's follows Cairo's, because no transcendent true story ends the chain from signifier to signifier.

Spade's most important verbal confrontations in the lower world are with Caspar Gutman. Gutman embodies the two defining and divided aspects of that world: materiality, and the language which continually fails to explain that materiality. Like Brigid and Spade, he is an adept liar, and his gigantic size symbolizes his obsession with the material world. The narrator describes him as a man composed of a vast quantity of flesh and more body parts than are considered standard equipment:

> A fat man came to meet him. The fat man was flabbily fat with bulbous pink cheeks and lips and chins and neck with a great soft egg of a belly that was all his torso, and pendant cones for arms and legs. As he advanced to meet Spade all his bulbs rose and shook and fell separately with each step in the manner of clustered soap bubbles not yet released from the pipe through which they had been blown. His eyes made small by fat puffs around them, were dark and sleek. (108)

Like Front de Boef, Gutman is the monstrous figure which the hero must vanquish in order to escape the lower world. But unlike Front de Boef and Ivanhoe's, Gutman and Spade's battle is a battle of words. Gutman is a man who "likes talking to a man that likes to talk" (110). Gutman is therefore quite pleased when Spade tells him that he is a man who likes to talk; however, in their first two encounters Spade is not given much of a chance to exhibit his skills. In talking about the "Black Bird" (110), Gutman is able to overwhelm Spade with the story of "The Emperor's Gift" (title of Chapter 13). As Gutman gets closer and closer to revealing the value of the bird, a value which he emphasizes is impossible to name, Spade loses consciousness. He has been drugged by Gutman, but his loss of consciousness seems more directly related to the story Gutman is telling; it is when Spade tries to ask about the highest price the Falcon might bring that the drug begins to affect him: "'The—the minimum, huh? And the maximum?'" An unmistakable sh followed the x in maximum as he said it" (135).

The story which Spade is attempting to follow does not lead upward toward a revelation of truth; instead it sends Spade further into the lower physical world where he begins to lose the verbal skills necessary to complete the investigation. The hardboiled detective's "x's" become soft "sh's" as he loses consciousness, losing his identity and becoming only his physical body. Spade descends into this world because the story he listens to is not a sacred one, though it does have its roots in the crusades; it is, instead, a story of money. This story of money, as Gutman tells it, seems to embody world history. The Falcon originates as a tribute paid by the Knights of Rhodes to the Emperor Charles V. On its way to the Emperor it is stolen by the pirate, Khaired-Din, who takes it to Algiers where it stays for a hundred years. It is next recorded in the possession of Sir Francis Verney who takes it to Sicily, and

*Front cover; New York: Dell, 1966 (Collection of Richard Layman)*

there it becomes the possession of Victor Armadeus II. The story continues on like this for several pages, with remarkable details and references to obscure historical texts. It is interesting to note that it is much easier to give the history of the fetishized object than it is to discover the history of any of the characters in the novel. Just as the Falcon does not inherently belong to any of the people through whose hands it passes, it seems to rob those people of any inherent identity. They are merely ciphers who acquire value and meaning momentarily with the ownership of the precious object. But as there are no "right[s] of possession" (132) in this object, these characters have only a transitory identity as owners. The humanist ideal of individual rights breaks down in this story of money, as does the ideal of individual identity itself, and this breakdown of identity continues with Spade's loss of consciousness.

Gutman's story of money also secularizes the past, revealing that the crusades themselves were not religious quests, for as he tells Spade, "We all know that the Holy Wars . . . were largely a matter of loot" (128). In this secularization, the material world is not raised to the level of meaning; rather, meaning is constantly referred back to the material world–meaning equals price. And, as we have seen above, when meaning becomes price, and identity becomes ownership, meaning and identity no longer present themselves as unified, transcendent concepts.

Some remnants of the romantic tradition seem to remain in the Black Bird, however, for with its recovery from the ship *La Paloma,* Spade begins his ascent out of this meaningless world. The possession of the Falcon gives Spade power over Gutman in their final confrontation, a power which expresses itself in Spade's taking over again as story-teller. He demands that a plausible story be put together for the benefit of the police, a story that will involve pinning the murders on either Wilmer or Brigid (who are in fact the murderers). Even though Spade's identification of the murderers is couched in terms of coming up with a good story, this story does, in fact, reveal the truth. Here Spade begins to reassert his identity. He will not be the criminal: as he states to Effie at the end of the novel, "Your Sam's a detective" (229). And in the detective's role as sage, Spade finally gives the correct interpretation to the violent actions of the novel: Wilmer has killed Thursby and Captain Jacoby; Brigid killed Miles Archer.

Does the correct identification of the killers, and the return to the detective's role, lead to the marriage of meaning and matter in a rejuvenated world such as we find at the end of romance? Looking first through the filter of quest romance, we see that an important difference emerges. The Falcon turns out to be not the precious and meaningful object of a quest romance, but a fake–a black enamelled lead paper weight. When the Grail is found it fulfills God's word in a material object, but when the Falcon is found it fails to live up to the words Gutman used to describe it. From pricelessness it declines to worthlessness.

Even before the Falcon is revealed as a fake, its value takes a radical turn downward. Gutman has promised Spade half-a-million for his part in obtaining the bird, but once Spade fulfills his part of the bargain, he is given only ten thousand:

"We were talking about more money than this."

"Yes, sir, we were," Gutman agreed, "but we were talking then. This is actual money, genuine coin of the realm, sir. With a dollar of this you can buy more than ten dollars of talk." (183)

Actual value is contrasted here with the value of "talk." As in the expression "talk is cheap," language and the material world are divided, not connected. At this point, though, Gutman still anachronistically clings to a belief in the inherent value of money by describing it as "genuine coin of the realm." But "genuine coin of the realm," like "ten dollars of talk," is fictional money; in fact, it is a romance version of money. Gutman alludes to a feudal monetary system in which meaning and material were the same; gold both stands for value, and is in itself valuable, while the dollar only stands for value. Once the Falcon is in Gutman's possession, however, he finds that it has more in common with the dollar than with "genuine coin." Thus matter and meaning remain divided. Furthermore, the Falcon's worthlessness as a possession demonstrates what happens when value is abstracted into exchange value in a capitalist economy. Like money, the Falcon is only valuable as it passes from hand to hand; once possessed it is found to have no use value. The Falcon is an exemplum of the fetishized commodity.

Brigid O'Shaugnessy goes through a similar devaluation. In the opening of the novel she is Miss Wonderly, the romantic embodiment of femininity, "tall and pliantly slender, without angularity anywhere" (14). But by the end of the novel she is Brigid O'Shaugnessy, the murderer who is nothing *but* angles. Comparing the ending of Brigid's story with that of the heroine of social romance reveals other interesting reversals. When Gutman gives Spade the ten thousand dollars in the final confrontation scene, Spade discovers that one thousand dollars is missing, and Gutman implies that Brigid may have it. Throughout the novel, Spade has had the ability to "read" her correctly, to tell magically when she is lying. Here, however, Spade forces Brigid to undress in full sight of the others, and then searches her. Instead of ascending to a world where meaning becomes apparent, we are descending back to a world whose focus is on the physical. This accounts for Effie's reaction when Spade turns Brigid in. Even though Brigid killed one of her bosses, Effie is horrified that Spade has given Brigid over to the police, and she responds to his embrace with physical aversion. She has been expecting the more traditional social romance ending of marriage, but *The Maltese Falcon* ends with the lover's incarceration. In the traditional social romance, the revelation of the heroine's identity leads to a marriage which gives social meaning to physical desire. But *The Maltese Falcon* does not end on a higher, social plane. It descends back to the physical: the revelation of identity is pictured as a rape; and the heroine is decisively returned to a constricting physical world.

An earlier incident in the novel serves as a summary of this theme. When Rhea Gutman is drugged, she scratches her stomach with a pin to keep herself awake—she tries to avoid unconsciousness by writing on herself. Stories in *The Maltese Falcon,* like these scratch-marks, are ways to avoid entrapment in the physical body—to avoid death. But they are written over the body itself. Stories of adventure in a traditional romance end in a higher social or religious truth, but stories in *The Maltese Falcon* always return to the body—Rhea's body, Brigid's body, and finally Miles Archer's body. Stories, here, do not lead out of the lower world's threat of death, they return to it.

Perhaps the final place to look for meaningful conclusion to the novel would be in the punishment of Archer's killer, Brigid. Two of Spade's justifications for turning in Brigid should point to the significance of this final act in the novel: first, he won't behave as Miles Archer did—he won't "play the sap" (224, 225) for her; and second, he won't let her go because "all of me wants to" (227). I will deal with these justifications in reverse order. First, Spade says he must give Brigid up, just because he doesn't want to. *The Maltese Falcon* presents a world that is the very opposite of the wish-fulfillment world of romance; one can never have "Miss Wonderly." At the end of the traditional social romance the individual's desires and society's laws combine in marriage, but in *The Maltese Falcon,* Spade's public role as law-enforcer is directly at odds with his feelings. *The Maltese Falcon* ends not with the reintegration of the personal and the social, but with the alienation of the individual from the world at large.

Spade refuses to "play the sap" for Brigid; however, by the end of the novel he is turning into "the sap," Miles Archer. In the very last scene of the novel, Miles Archer's wife Iva is waiting for Spade in the outer office. Iva is an aging version of Brigid, and while Spade cannot have Miss Wonderly, or even Brigid, he can have Iva (whose very name suggests possession—"I've a"). She is, however, a possession that he has been trying to avoid since the beginning of the novel. At the time of Miles's death, it becomes clear that Spade had been having an affair with Iva. When Miles is killed, Iva wants Spade to become Miles's replacement—an assignment Spade does not seem to relish. Spade successfully avoids Iva as long as he is involved with the story of the Falcon, but at the end of the novel he directs Effie, with a "shiver" (229) in his voice, to send her in. He reacts to Iva with the same physical aversion that Effie displays to him.

Like the final possession of the Falcon, possession of the woman is presented in a strongly negative light.

*Front cover; London: Penguin, 1966*
*(Collection of Richard Layman)*

Iva is not romantically described, as is Miss Wonderly. Instead she is "sturdy," with a "facial prettiness [which] was perhaps five years past its best moment" (185). Iva's description allies her with the physical world: like Gutman, she is too fleshy, and like any other object in the physical world, she is subject to the forces of decay—her face has already passed its "best moment." She represents Spade's return to a decaying, material world. In embracing her, he also seems to be embracing Miles's fate (death).

Finally, it would seem that the detective story still finds its meaning in Spade's identification of Archer's killer. However, here too there is a problem. Spade says that he knew who the killer was as soon as he saw the body, an event which took place in Chapter 2. The size of the bullet hole showed that the killer had to stand close to Archer, and Brigid, Spade explains, is the only one who could have stood that close. Spade has known the identity of the killer virtually from the beginning of the novel. The whole plot, then, the detective story itself, is a meaningless delay between Archer's murder and Spade's exposure of Brigid as his killer.

The detective story—which in its conventional form promises both to reveal the truth about the world and return that world to order—becomes, in *The Maltese Falcon,* an arbitrary ellipsis framed by a corpse, a physical world devoid of meaning or order. In the middle of the novel, Spade tells Brigid a story which encapsulates this vision of the world, and demonstrates his knowledge that what he does as a detective is always meaningless. Spade had been hired to find a missing person named Flitcraft by Flitcraft's wife. Flitcraft is difficult to trace because there seems to be no motive for his disappearance; however, Spade eventually finds him and hears the story behind that disappearance. Flitcraft had led a very ordinary life: he was a real-estate agent with a wife and two kids who lived in a suburb of Tacoma. One day, though, he was almost hit by a beam falling off a construction site, and this near fatal accident revealed to him that people have no necessary or determined relationship with the material world. A falling beam could come out of the sky and hit you for no reason, not because you are good or evil, but just by chance. After this accident, Flitcraft abandoned his settled and ordered life and drifted from one place to another. He finally settled in Spokane, where Spade finds him leading pretty much the same life he had lived before the accident—now he is an automobile salesman, with a wife and baby living in a Spokane suburb. This is the part of the story which Spade enjoys the most: "He adjusted himself to beams falling, and then no more of them fell, and he adjusted himself to them not falling" (167). Flitcraft organized his life around a story in which he played the main role as father and breadwinner. The physical world intruded and showed him the meaninglessness of that organization. Yet he returns, in the end, to another version of that same story. Similarly Spade plays his role in the detective story only to confront the meaningless physical world represented by the Falcon, by Iva's presence, and by Archer's body. Yet he, too, returns to his role in the story; he continues to play the detective, an identity as meaningless as being the Falcon's owner.

Jameson notes that in studying the history of romance as a mode it is important to discover what takes the place of religion or magic in the modern work (113). In *The Maltese Falcon,* money takes the place of any other system of belief. As Spade says of Brigid's initial presentation, "We didn't exactly believe your story. . . . We believed your two hundred dollars" (133). But money does not present a transcendent value system as religion or magic do. It is inherently valueless. It must, itself, be connected to the material world in order to have meaning. This connection is not a necessary one, as people discovered in the 1929 Crash and the Depression that followed. If there is nothing behind these pieces of paper they are worthless; we can continue to exchange them but we cannot reach a stopping-point. Similarly *The Maltese Falcon,* initially published at the same time as the stock-market crash, offers no final resting place of meaning. In *The Maltese Falcon* people like Flitcraft move from one version of story to another; money as the arbiter of meaning causes endless exchange of stories—stories are passed back and forth like worthless stocks. There is no ascent to the upper world here, only the discovery of a radical division between meaning and the material world—a division revealed by the falling beam, or the corpse. The ending of stories is presented not as transcendence, but as alienation—alienation which can only be escaped by a return to story.

Jameson describes writers such as Kafka and Cortazar as "the last unrecognizable avatars of romance." In the works of these writers, the structure of romance is used to show the "absence at the heart of the secular world" (Jameson 135)—to show that there is nothing to take the place of religion or magic. *The Maltese Falcon,* I would suggest, goes one step further. Here, the structure of romance reveals that in a capitalist, monied society, money and exchange value take the place of religion and magic. The hardboiled detective novel, with its origins in Depression-era America, demystifies its romance background by showing that romantic tales are frauds—like the Falcon, like the histories of the Holy Wars, and even like the detective plot of the novel itself. Placing money at the heart of the romance inverts the structure of romance; as Philip Marlowe remarks in *The Big Sleep,* "Knights had no meaning in this game. It wasn't a game for knights" (Chandler 95). We end the social romance not with marriage, but with incarceration. We end the quest romance not with the precious talisman, but with the corpse. Finally we end not with transcendence and wish-fulfillment, but with the separation of private and public, of desire and possession, of matter and meaning, which is at the heart of the capitalist society.

### Works Cited

Chandler, Raymond. *The Big Sleep.* New York: Random House, 1988.

Frye, Northrop. *The Secular Scripture: A Study of the Structure of Romance.* Cambridge: Harvard University Press, 1976.

Hammett, Dashiell. *The Maltese Falcon*. New York: Random House, 1929.

Jameson, Fredric. *The Political Unconscious: Narrative as a Socially Symbolic Act*. Ithaca: Cornell University Press, 1981.

Todorov, Tzvetan. *The Poetics of Prose*. Trans. Richard Howard. Ithaca: Cornell University Press, 1977.

Vinaver, Eugene. *The Rise of Romance*. New York: Oxford University Press, 1977.

\* \* \*

## On Re-Reading *The Maltese Falcon*
Paul P. Abrahams
*Journal of American Culture*, 8 (Spring 1995): 97–107

Dashiell Hammett is commonly known by his third and most famous novel, *The Maltese Falcon*, uniquely featuring the detective hero, Sam Spade. A 1941 film version of the book, which had been published in 1929, was a box-office hit starring Humphrey Bogart. This partly accounts for the recognition Hammett and Spade continue to enjoy, but we measure the endurance of the author and his fictional creation by more than popularity, or the devotion of the Bogart cult. Together they established the fictional detective as a fully fledged social observer and critic. A close reading of the novel in the context of contemporary events shows that the author was working out the controversial 'lessons' of World War I, as they applied to the politics of peace and disarmament of the 1920s. To accomplish this, Hammett, an anarchist and an anti-fascist, created a character to mock bourgeois pretensions of law, order, and progress, which inspired the rhetoric of international relations during that decade.

How much did these motives account for Spade's original qualities and for his subsequent influence? To begin to answer these questions and to understand the vehicle Hammett fashioned for American detective fiction, a brief review of American politics and diplomacy during the 1920s and an exploration of their relation to certain features of political and literary thought is required.

Beginning in 1917, with the revelation of the secret European diplomacy that had preceded World War I, a stream of published documents and high-level memoirs refuted official versions of the war's origins and purposes (Fay 1–49 *passim*). For the horrendous expenditure of the war, which governments had justified in terms of 'freedom,' 'democracy,' and 'civilization,' society obtained little but death and disorder, it seemed. As facts demolished the idealistic picture painted by Allied wartime propaganda, Armistice Day ceremonies became solemn observations of needless

*Front cover for Dutch translation; Amsterdam & Antwerp: Archipel, 1972 (Collection of Richard Layman)*

sacrifices made to the failed god of nationalism. The doctrine of German war guilt enshrined in the Treaty of Versailles (1919) was also a casualty of revision, indicating the responsibility of Britain and France, states that had benefited from the Treaty's harsh peace terms to make appropriate adjustments in their relations with Germany.

This British, French, and German diplomats cautiously attempted with the Locarno Treaty (1925), which provided for the admission of Germany to the League of Nations, thus ending German isolation. The Treaty signaled the end of French predominance in Europe, giving Britain, France's ally, decisive influence over the continental balance of power. But it neither significantly altered the terms of the Treaty of Versailles nor eliminated Allied fears of German *revanchism*.

To insure against this eventuality, the French foreign minister Aristide Briand approached the American government with a non-aggression alliance in April 1927, the anniversary of the American declaration of war for the defense of France and Great Britain in World War I. Evading this politically risky entanglement, the Republicans in Washington offered the internationally minded a harmless revised version that appealed to the sovereign states of the world to take a rhetorical stand against aggression. This was known as the Kellogg-Briand Pact, a so-called Peace Pact history texts often describe as one of the diplomatic triumphs of President Calvin Coolidge's administration.

For Dashiell Hammett, working out his new novel based on the subject, glossing over *realpolitik* maneuvering with high sounding rhetoric was a characteristically insincere operation of the international state system. In fact, Britain and France together, contrary to disarmament agreements, planned to revise the standards of general military and naval forces in their favor. The French agreed the Admiralty could abandon the naval limitations of the Washington Conference (1922) pertaining to light cruisers.[1] In turn, the British government would approve a larger effective French army than allowed by the Treaty of Versailles. Though Briand played down these pending military aspects, together with the diplomacy pact (i.e., in its original form) would involve the U.S. in military arrangements reminiscent of the discredited pre-war alliance system that had brought on World War I. Though diplomats knew it was intended to guarantee France against German aggression, Briand had described his Pact as a measure to 'outlaw war,' a concept that had gained popular currency in preceding years as part of the American reaction to the Great War. Hammett incorporated these martial considerations into his plot, along with other sources of social disintegration he had probed in his previous novels. The prominence of history and diplomacy, which called forth Hammett's condemnation of the state system, also evoked the superior structural features that distinguished *The Maltese Falcon* from the author's previous novels.[2]

In both of those, written in 1927 and 1928, Hammett had attacked hypocrisy. His hero, the Continental 'Op,' traversed a sordid urban environment that mocked President Coolidge's credo: "The business of America is business." In *Red Harvest,* the Continental Operative, or 'Op,' battled prohibition, corrupt government, and gang rule. In *The Dain Curse,* he exposed predatory religious cults. Both episodes occurred in the purlieus of Hammett's adopted city of San Francisco, and suggest growing regional influence on American literature that opposed the increasingly felt centralizing tendencies of both government and business. The

nation and the international system and its wars of which it was a part appeared to him to share a common basis in capitalism. In *The Maltese Falcon,* for the first time, he was able to target its essential cultural feature as well: a specious literary moralism which, in describing the international system euphemistically, had laid the groundwork for the crusading propaganda of the war. This he criticized from the perspective of his indigenous radicalism, deploying the resources of his distinctive 'hardboiled' style in a more sophisticated and purposeful fashion as a result.

The 'working stiff' mentality of Hammett's short stories and novels contrasted with that of the cerebral British 'gentleman sleuths' and their American imitations, but the 'Op' lacked the established detective types developed by writers such as Arthur Conan Doyle, John Buchan, and Agatha Christie, and in America, S. S. Van Dine and E. Phillips Oppenheim. In turning to contemporary international events, Hammett accomplished a cosmic transformation of the 'Op' into a complete fictional personality whose proportions matched those of the classic detectives. Further exploration of the contemporary political and literary nexus of *The Maltese Falcon* will explain this catalytic effect, accounting for the novel's superior structure, and the more complex hero, who extended the range of the genre.

The response of the American public to Briand's initiative showed that revision had not established a consensus in the United States regarding the 'lessons' of the war. The nation remained divided between isolationism and internationalism. Briand, a Nobel Peace Prize–winner, played on this uneasy foundation of the Administration's isolationist policy with his offer of the pact, enlisting sanguine hopes of internationalists that a better world would come of guaranteeing French security and participation in a collective security arrangement in the spirit, if not the form, originally proposed by President Wilson. Wilson's 'crusade for democracy' had ended with the United States Senate rejection of this kind of arrangement. Separate peace treaties with Germany followed, launching America on an isolationist course.

This debacle strengthened the isolationists play on the public's belief that any participation in European alliances, even with the League of Nations, would entangle the United States in relationships hostile not only towards Germany, but colonial peoples around the world, especially where Britain was dominant. With the complicity of the League, the British, controlling an estimated one-third of the world's population, used force or the threat of it to suppress nationalist movements in Egypt, Ireland, and elsewhere in the Middle East and Asia. Contrary to understandings with the United States, Britain sought common cause with Japan to 'give direction' to events in China. In spite of this,

and real concerns about imperialism, American internationalists argued that American isolation jeopardized international stability and, consequently, progress toward a better world order. Further deterioration of world relationships as a result of isolation could be costly for the United States, even in the Orient where growing instability raised the stakes of the 'open door' policy.

The Administration could not ignore the persuasiveness of the internationalists' appeal. Six months after Briand's offer, Coolidge made a calculated gesture that appeared to build on Briand's proposal, but actually eliminated any obligations that would impair his party's policy of neutrality. Leaving aside the question of the threatened Anglo-French military buildup, Secretary of State Kellog [*sic*] counterproposed a less binding agreement for 'the outlawry of war' by all nations. The resulting Kellog-Briand Pact implied greater American involvement in European affairs, but was virtually an extension of the ineffective prewar arbitration agreements generated by Wilson's Secretary of State, William Jennings Bryan. Since each signatory power could exclude its vital interests from the Pact's jurisdiction, the Pact did not 'outlaw' war, as Secretary of State Kellog averred (12 November 1928 *New York Times*). Fascist Premier Benito Mussolini mocked it before the Italian Chamber of the Deputies: "I have called [the Kellogg Pact] sublime. It is in reality so sublime that it might be called transcendental. And if tomorrow other pacts are in view I shall hasten to sign them" ("Mussolini").[3] In contrast to the millennial expectations of the naive, the Kellog-Briand Pact, as Hammett foresaw, was destined to be one of those worthless paper deterrents torn up and discarded by the dictators who ultimately brought down the tottering Versailles System in World War II.

President Coolidge himself drove home the point that force, not law, constituted the basis of international relations. In November 1928, with the pact well on its way to Senate approval and his successor's election campaign successfully concluded, the President gave a saber-rattling Armistice Day speech (on November 11), threatening the Anglo-French militarists with a naval arms race if they persisted with their rearmament plans. The President added that it would be an error for European states to expect from Washington any initiative going beyond strictly American interests ( James 1). At home, the speech delighted isolationists, but deflated the expectations of the internationalists. The President's reassertion of American neutrality heightened the apparent hypocrisy of the entire 'peace' exercise, and extended the ambiguity that attached to its effects throughout the world. Underlying it was the militarism that haunted American foreign policy until December

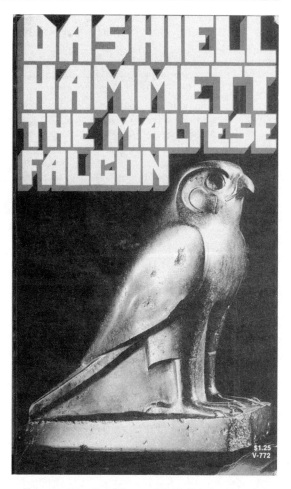

*Front cover; New York: Vintage, 1972. Published in May 1972, this edition is textually corrupt, having been reparagraphed throughout and in other instances flagrantly altered by Vintage editors. The Flitcraft episode, for example, is dated in the 1940s in this text, twenty years after the dates Hammett provided in the first edition (Collection of Richard Layman).*

1941. Hammett found in it a militaristic nationalism based on the love of power implied in nationalism and imperialism.

Hammett conceptualized this in terms of an interest he shared with contemporary intellectuals regarding the relationship between sex, sacrifice, and survival (Vickery 71–73).[4] Taking sexuality for the basic medium of social experience, Hammett assumed that, in its various corrupt forms, sexuality led to a will to power in individuals. This was magnified on the collective level into nationalism, and ultimately, into imperialism. Relationships, accordingly, fell into a motif of domination and submission. He combined archetypical characters representing social groups and nations involved in various ways in the state system, and dramatized the resulting individual, social, and international *strata* of his plot with their nihilistic struggle for power, a struggle that assumed its characteristic form because of its underlying sexual nature.

Developing this motivational and behavioral scheme, the author portrayed a drifting middle class society that sustains private ambition but except for the protagonist, Sam Spade, is deficient in the sense of justice required to discover the truth about the War. It is inured to the brutality in human relations that arises from the aberrations of its own acquisitive culture.

The story turns on a number of murders committed in connection with a mysterious *objet d'art,* a falcon of reputed great value. The detective, becoming personally involved through the murder of his partner, encounters the treachery of the gang of thieves who have stolen it, as well as the indifference, even hostility, with which the self-seeking society meets his efforts to bring the guilty to justice. The Americans are Effie Perine, Spade's secretary; Miles Archer, Spade's partner; his wife, Iva Archer; Polhaus and Dundy, policemen; and Bryan, the District Attorney. Except for Effie, who is simply naive, they manipulate legalisms in their own self-interest but are blind to the real forces driving events. Spade neutralizes their interference with his superior grasp of changing reality.

Miles Archer's male eagerness, idolizing females, misguides him into the kind of relationships with women which make him vulnerable. The author offers his murder at the beginning of the plot as representative of the many war deaths of American troops who were victimized because of the charms that intervention in a foreign war had for President Wilson in 1917. A second shooting, of the apparent gunman who killed Archer, follows. Iva Archer represents the women's movement, politically empowered by the 19th Amendment, which contributed to the 'peace' front in 1928 (Ferrell 155–157). Iva's indifference to her husband's murder shows that she is solipsistic, relating to events only out of her need for attention. She wants Spade to marry her and experiments with the belief that he killed his partner, Miles, the obstacle to their bliss. As this notion fades before Spade's scorn, she reveals the selfish nature of her love by threatening to put the detective in a bad light with the authorities investigating the murders. Spade frightens her by pointing out the weaknesses in her own alibi for the night of the murder and sends her to his lawyer for advice.

Spade's only comrade among the authorities is Sgt. Polhaus. They eat pigs' knuckles together but the cop's dog-like loyalty to the system strains their relationship. His superior, Lt. Dundy, inspired by District Attorney Bryan, hopes for a quick solution targeting Spade as the right suspect for one murder or another, which ever will fit. 'A politician with an orator's mouth,' the District Attorney is a parody, not only of former Secretary of State Bryan (one time leader, and 'Boy Orator' of the Democratic Party) but of all those American secretaries of state who exploited the political appeal of arbitration treaties, in a cynical effort to bend the arbitrary power of national sovereignty to some fictitious law of nations. The District Attorney wants the information to confirm a self-serving theory that places the murders in another, more sensational criminal case because it will bring an easy solution with a political payoff. Dundy's relentless pursuit of Spade is the result.

The other group of characters represents nations or nationalistic movements within the British Empire. Their deluded will to dominate makes them the active forces of world politics, drawn on by the steady, but false, allure of power symbolized by the Maltese falcon. The principal villain, Casper Gutman, also known as the Fat Man, is a caricature of the British Empire, which had achieved its greatest proportions as a result of World War I. The name Casper meant Keeper of the Treasure, in old Anglo-Saxon. In terms of sexuality, he seems potent enough, but is almost immobilized by size. He has sired a daughter, and exhibits paternal instincts toward a young man, but he exploits this American, Wilmer, in a homosexual fashion. Wilmer obeys Gutman's orders but the incestuous nature of the relationship, complicated by his interest in Gutman's daughter, leaves Wilmer (meaning Resolute Warrior) alternately sullen and bellicose.[5]

In Hammett's scheme of imperialist relationships, Wilmer represents American finance capitalism, headquartered in New York. Condemned after the war as 'Merchants of Death,' these capitalists, engaging in various schemes for profit and economic rehabilitation abroad during the 1920s, assumed they were heirs apparent to Britain's world financial power.[6] Wilmer begins tailing Spade soon after the detective learns that a missing black bird was involved in his partner's death.

The *femme fatale* first appears as Miss Wonderly, Hammett's reference to the real mysteries of sexual attraction and, incidentally, to her original, obviously phony, plea for help which made Spade and his partner wonder. After Archer's death she temporarily assumes the identity of Miss Le Blanc to avoid detection by the police. Securing Spade's continuing interest on her behalf, she admits to her real name, Brigid O'Shaughnessy, a synonym for Ireland, a nation experiencing a metamorphosis (of political form) between the end of the war and 1928. Hammett apparently believed that, because of the Irish boycott of the British draft in 1916, the United States had to enter the war the following year, a relationship rather peculiarly of the author's own vision and not generally acknowledged by American public opinion. Hammett develops Brigid's character around this perceived relationship (Carroll 192). Like Ireland, Brigid manipulates Americans for her own benefit. As Le Blanc, she fulfills the thinly veiled analogy to the maiden Blancheflor, from the legend of the Holy Grail ('Because of me, many worthy men are dead. . . . ' [de Troyes 46]).[7] Besides sending Archer to his doom, she betrays Floyd Thursby, an expatriate Detroit hoodlum, who is murdered in her defense; and she involves Spade and Captain Jacobi in the continuing friction with the Fat Man over the possession of the black bird, bringing about Jacobi's death.

Hammett also included the turbulent Middle East in the plot. There nationalist-imperialist struggles were rampant, especially over the strategic points, Constantinople and the Suez Canal. Hegemonic conflicts in the region had been responsible for the beginning of World War I. President Wilson had avoided involvement there after the war, declining the League of Nations offer of a mandate over Constantinople. Turkish nationalists were able to win back the city, but only after a prolonged military conflict with Greece and her British backers. The British stirred up another hornet's nest when they impeached Egyptian sovereignty by insisting on a British defense of the Suez Canal. Hammett introduced the homosexual, Joel Cairo, to characterize this seething drama of domination and submission. Cairo's behavior alternates between false charm and ineffective, petulant treachery. The name suggests Egypt and the Suez Canal, but the author describes the character more ambiguously as Levantine. In rifling his pockets, Spade finds a Greek passport, some French coins; altogether a Middle Eastern *pastiche* of nationalist rivalries. Spade first learns of the connection between the black bird and his partner's death from Cairo, who hires Spade to help locate 'a black bird' and return it to its 'true' owner, a Russian general in Constantinople.[8]

In developing the character Sam Spade, Hammett perfected the hard-boiled detective type. His *modus operandi* strikes a contrast with the sleuths of the genteel tradition by emphasizing autonomous action and experience rather than reason and principle. In the genteel tradition, the problem is 'Whodunit?' A sufficiency of clues leads to a solution. For Spade the problem is, 'What's real.' The detective finds out by purposely adapting to the changing environment. In this sense he creates himself and the solution in the same process. Where the Continental 'Op' was merely an employee of a large detective agency, accepting each assignment from an enigmatic, if sardonic, 'Old Man'—a metaphysical first cause, Spade is a partner in his own firm. He is autono-

*Front cover for German translation; Zurich: Diogenes, 1974 (Collection of Richard Layman)*

mous, incidentally assuming the privilege of social commentary himself, and achieving for the detective of this distinctive type a stature comparable to the detective heroes of the genteel tradition like Sherlock Holmes or Hercule Poirot.

Hammett establishes a universe for action in which experiential meaning is supreme, with a scenario Spade describes from one of his cases involving a missing person. An ordinary man, Flitcraft, after narrowly escaping death, suddenly understands that reality is flux, or chance, with the result that the familiar sentimental forms of his existence lose their meaning. He leaves his wife and family as a result. This individual, now calling himself Pierce, had re-discovered reality with all its possibilities for purposeful adaptation, but he fails to make much of this. Gradually habit asserts itself and Spade finds him living in another city, with a new family, leading a life much the same as the one he had left behind. Like most people, Pierce had concluded from his experience that change was an exceptional rather than a ruling condition of life. 'But that's the part of it I always liked,' remarks Spade, who takes sardonic pleasure in the contrast between reality and appearances (336). His ability to maintain the distinction is the basis of his heroic character. Because others are on fixed courses of habit, convenience, or ambition, he astounds them with his 'unpredictable' and 'wild' behavior, an advantage allowing him to outwit them by upsetting their expectations.

The autonomous, purposeful, and more skillful detective gains a third dimension through a commitment to certain values of love and work. Though at times he appears to be without scruple, he is neither immoral nor amoral. His is the morality of anarchist/syndicalist freedom espoused by the International Workers of the World (I.W.W.) and associated with the wandering life of the unattached male (Lasch 337).[9] The Continental 'Op,' who was middle-aged and avuncular, clearly would have been out of place in the sexual ontology of the new novel. Spade is a younger man whose pragmatic orientation to women is exclusively sexual, precluding extraneous corrupting influences. The hero's response to them is the same as to other features of the real environment, i.e., through necessity and opportunity. His encounters inevitably devalue the transcendental/superstitious qualities of repressed sex, expressed religiously as sacrifice, or politically as domination and submission. Outside the sensual sphere of life, comradely values of the work place provide a social environment that is meaningful and real within the universe of change. These are shown in the way Spade treats his secretary, Effie Perine, and other colleagues and in his speech at the end, when he emphasizes the importance of loyalty to one's job and fellow workers 'everywhere.' He accepts some handsome retainers during the case, but they don't compromise the integrity of his commitment to human, over market, values.

The detective is an icon of Hammett's syndicalist egalitarianism, the antithesis of the acquisitive individualism and predatory nationalism portrayed in the novel. Another feature is Spade's utopian disavowal of deadly force, or even the need for it, while the conventional world, especially the political world, relies on it. The plot turns on lies, threats, and sudden death, but the author keeps serious violence offstage. When the villains bring out their weapons, the detective dominates the scene with an amused contempt. The deliberateness of this departure from the author's previous slam-bang plots is illustrated by the obvious adaptation of a shootout scene with five dead, from his earlier Op story, into the skillfully negotiated denouement of *The Maltese Falcon*.[10] If the detective is 'tough' as is so frequently observed, it is because of a lack of sentimentality, and not because he readily resorts to violence.

To comprehend Hammett's indictment of the Anglo-American literary tradition that supported the bloody *realpolitik* of imperialism, we must turn to the influence of Sir James George Frazer's *The Golden Bough*. This influential survey of world mythology from an anthropological perspective had called attention to the apparently universal belief among ancient and primitive tribes that survival required the ritual murder of the king/god, an act insuring the continued fertility of the land and its people. The Cambridge University scholar's discoveries implied that religion and politics were basically a matter of superstitious fertility rites: plainly, murder and sex. In 1920, this same theme was found in the cult legends of the pagan King Arthur's Round Table, which had been Christianized into the myth of the Holy Grail during the Crusades.[11] The Grail was a cup from which Christ was said to have drunk at the Last Supper. Subsequently, it caught and preserved the savior's blood that flowed from a lance wound inflicted during the crucifixion. Resurrected by poet Alfred Tennyson ("Morte d'Arthur" 1842), and composer Richard Wagner (*Ring of the Niebelung* 1852), the myth had become popular and was used to justify a variety of political crusades up to and including World War I. When the sacred cup (and the lance!) acquired the sexual/political overtones of fertility rites, as scholar Jessie Weston suggested, it introduced ambiguities into the justifications traditionally advanced for the Crusader's quest, and all others. The implications captivated contemporary literary circles where the monumental failure of science and organization, dominant Western values epitomized by the War, excited much analysis and expression. T. S. Eliot's *The Waste Land* (1922) was a well-known example of one modernist's gloomy but successful effort to recapture the possibility of spiritual redemption from the threat of modern skepticism. F. Scott Fitzgerald's *The Great Gatsby* (1925) was another, narrowly romantic and completely disillusioned.

The analogy of the Crusades and their associated literary symbolism to World War I was obvious to Hammett. Reduced, or simplified, the Frazer/Weston framework would accommodate his anarchist critique of nationalism, social disintegration, and war brought about by the will to power, hidden in a literary/language tradition of repressed sex which could, and always would, justify sacrifice on the basis of some alleged 'higher' good. To make the comparison specific, he incorporated a parody of a representative literary work, *The Wings of the Dove* (1909) by Henry James into

*The Maltese Falcon.* James, an expatriate Bostonian, had frequently written about Anglo-American society. He had died during World War I, after showing his support for England's cause by becoming a British citizen, receiving His Majesty's Government's Order of Merit in return. James, as Harold Laski once observed, was 'a kind of a superbagman for European letters' (qtd. in Howe 721).[12] Secularized Protestantism, which gained sophistication from Ivan Turgenev's influence, inspired James's later work, including *The Wings of the Dove*. In common with many of his contemporary writers, Hammett had given the influential James a close reading. Later, he reported the influence of this book on *The Maltese Falcon*.[13]

In James' novel, Milly Thiel, a fabulously wealthy young American woman, has a fatal disease, and a limited but indeterminate period of time to live. She falls into the acquaintance of a genteel but impecunious and predatory English couple of her own age and develops a romantic interest in the young man, after the young Englishwoman, Kate, assures her that she has no particular attachment to him. The young man, Densher, who has been seduced by the much more clever Kate and is under her direction, develops a sublimated affection for Millie. The romance infuses new life into Millie, until she learns she has been the victim of deception. Though victimized for her wealth by Kate and Densher, she defeats the scheme of the British couple with a superior morality.

Dying of her condition, which has been aggravated by heartbreak, Millie shows her moral strength by forgiving Densher and leaving her estate to him. This outcome conforms to Kate's original intentions but ultimately it fails, even when Densher agrees to go through with the planned marriage to Kate, once she realizes his enduring love for Millie's memory. Kate concludes: "'I used to call her, in my stupidity—for want of better—a dove. Well she stretched out her wings and it was to that they reached. They cover us'" (James 404). It was this capability of the genteel tradition to effect a moral victory that Hammett wished to discredit, as a primitive notion because of its demand for sacrifice. In *The Maltese Falcon*, the highest stake is social survival that requires justice rather than a victim: plain truth rather than sentiment.

Hammett had dispensed with the charade of redemption and the inadequate emotion of sentiment in his previous novels and stories. In *The Maltese Falcon*, he attacks them. Since the dove was closely associated with the appearance of the Grail in the myth, as well as the innocence of James' heroine, Milly Thiel, and Christianity generally, it offered Hammett a most promising opening. In all probability it was behind his decision to base his Grail parody on a legendary predatory bird

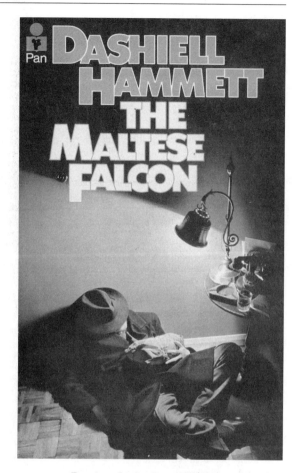

*Front cover; London: Pan, 1975 (Collection of Richard Layman)*

instead of some other object of value. Hammett used the literary form of the quest to traverse the distance from a tradition that placed a premium on ideals and sentimentalized inevitable human shortcomings, to a one-dimensional world of transience and adaptation. In a sardonic play on words, he has the falcon reach American shores on board the Pacific freighter, *La Paloma*, i.e., *The Dove*. Hammett's pragmatic ideal turned the metaphysical dualism of the 'higher good' upside down, by mocking the quest for the sacred Grail with one for an equally fabulous statuette of a falcon, exposing its ultimate hypocrisy. This reductionism could appeal to those disillusioned among a generation of many who found little improvement in a society which had endured a long period of Progressive 'reform' at home and abroad.

Of what, then, was the substance of the secular quest? The fabulous statuette was said to have originated with the Knights of the Hospital of St. John Crusaders. A military order, they had used the sacred quest as an excuse to loot the Middle-East during the 13th century. In the 16th century they fashioned a tribute, in the form of a jewel-encrusted golden falcon, in return for a lease on the island of Malta from the King of Spain. Stolen en route to the king, the illusive bird subsequently occasioned numerous thefts, betrayals, even murder, becoming so dangerous that, as rumor had it, one owner disguised its too-obvious attractions with a coating of black enamel. Hammett fashioned the falcon from the stuff of European history: '. . . Not Mr. Wells' history, [which would have been progressive, therefore duplicitous *ed.*], but history nevertheless,' he observed through his chief villain, Casper Gutman (Hammett, *Novels* 376). The author achieved synergy between the crusading Knights, World War I, and tawdry contemporary diplomacy surrounding the Kellogg-Briand Pact by associating all of them with Malta, the Royal Navy's huge base guarding the eastern Mediterranean, crux of empire ("Malta").[14] Identifying the elements of sacrifice, sex, and survival in a tangle of mythological and historical events, Hammett transposed them into a contemporary setting where the will to power, symbolized by the Maltese falcon, dominated an environment of deceit and violence.

The historical analogies begin after an association of villains pursues a defecting member, Brigid, who had temporary possession of the bird, to San Francisco. The story opens as she uses a ruse to get the detectives, Spade and Archer, to thwart her pursuers. The first day ends with a scene that recalls both the United States' entry into the war and the death of the companion knight at the opening of the Grail myth. Spade's partner Archer, symbolizing the American Expeditionary Force President Wilson sent to Europe in 1917, naively walks into a trap and is murdered. This sets the stage for Spade's quest for justice. To accomplish it he must avoid victimization by one or another of the villains and the lure of the Maltese falcon. As the characters race across a decade, from Archer's symbolic death to Armistice Day, 1928 in the five days of the plot, the author establishes World War I and the diplomacy of the 1920s as but another chapter in the history of the false quest for power, an illusion of dominance and submission that perverts the sense of justice in the conventional world.

As a means to his own ends, Spade had separately agreed to help Brigid and the Levantine get the bird. He brings them together to learn that they had acted earlier as Gutman's agents in obtaining the falcon from Kemidov, a Russian general, under suspicious circumstances in Constantinople. The pair had doublecrossed Gutman, then Brigid had absconded with Thursby and the falcon to Hong Kong, leaving Cairo behind. She sent the falcon to San Francisco with Captain Jacobi of the *Paloma*, before taking a faster ship with Thursby. In dread of the Fat Man, whose arrival in San Francisco she and Cairo agree was announced by the murders of Thursby and Archer, Brigid tantalizes Spade, believing she can persuade him to fend off her pursuers even if she does not tell him the truth about the bird. Because of the still vague connection of the falcon with Archer's murder, Spade's interest lies in Brigid. Their affair begins at the conclusion of the second day.

Before this, Spade had explained to her his pragmatic view of experience and adaptation, the story of Flitcraft/Pierce. This threatens Brigid's best weapon, emotional manipulation, which depends on men's persistent, and uncritical, sexual drive. When she casts her spell to be certain herself that it works on Spade, he demands more information about the falcon. After seducing him instead of telling, she whistles a few bars of the popular tango, *En Cuba* (popularly translated: *Cuba Is You*), evoking the imperial theme. Not wishing to discourage her illusions of domination, Spade leaves her asleep at his place while he goes to hers and searches it. Also at the end of the second day, Cairo has thrown in with Wilmer and the Fat Man, correctly anticipating Brigid will use Spade to doublecross him again.

The following day, Friday, the Maltese falcon reaches San Francisco on board the freighter. Brigid alone understands the connection between the Dove and the falcon. In the mistaken belief that he has placed her out of harm's way and out of action, Spade makes contact with the Fat Man through Wilmer, to learn more about the bird. There are two meetings. In the first, Gutman learns that Spade is pursuing his own interests in the case, which naturally appear to Gutman to be pecuniary. As they discuss the falcon's worth, he expresses astonishment at Spade's ignorance: "'You mean you don't know what it is?' Spade made a careless gesture with his cigar. 'Oh hell,' he said lightly, 'I know what it's supposed to look like. I know the value in life you people put on it. I don't know what it is'" (Hammett, *Novels* 365). The detective attempts to bluff Gutman by establishing the probability that he will get the falcon because of his closeness to Brigid. The bluff is unsuccessful.

There is a second meeting. The Fat Man tells the detective about the falcon and appears to accept Spade's terms for recovering it. Now made aware of the possible significance of the arrival of the freighter by Cairo, he decides to do without the detective's assistance. In a parody of the transcendental sleep of the Grail hero, the detective trustingly (unwisely, in a pragmatic world) accepts a drink that knocks him out until the following morning. Gutman, Wilmer, and Cairo leave for the harbor.

Spade awakens with the elements of the mystery within reach but finds he has been overtaken by events. It is Saturday, the fourth day. Grasping the significance of the *Paloma,* he arrives at the Embarcadero after Wilmer has set the ship ablaze and the Fat Man has taken Brigid, Captain Jacobi, and the falcon into custody. Wilmer shoots Captain Jacobi, who nevertheless escapes with the bird. We learn about these events after the fact, realizing that, during them, ironically, District Attorney Bryan and the detective were engaged in a futile negotiation about their mutual legal responsibilities in the case. The detective refuses to talk about the real criminals who, he feels, wouldn't interest a government lawyer anyway: "'You wouldn't want the kind of information I could give you, Bryan. You couldn't use it. It'd poop this gambler's–revenge–scenario for you'" (Hammett, *Novels* 393). The only way Spade can remove himself from the authorities' suspicion is to deliver the guilty parties to the police, all tied up, and he promises the District Attorney he will do that.

Following Brigid O'Shaughnessy's previous directions, the dying Captain Jacobi delivers the falcon to Spade's office where the detective has just returned. There is a bizarre moment when Spade, transfixed by the power that possession of the falcon has given him, tramples on the dead man's hand. Shocked that he too could climb over other men's bodies for greed, Spade breaks the spell, he checks the package at a luggage drop. After following a false lead to Brigid planted by Gutman, he returns to his apartment where the villains, including Brigid, are waiting in uneasy anticipation of a settlement.

In the final scene, which takes place on Armistice Day, Sunday, Hammett plays back the sacrifice metaphor against the perpetrators of Archer's murder, to destroy them and expose the illusory quest for the Maltese falcon. Spade confidently bets his life against the Fat Man's desire for the falcon, knowing the bird is instrumental to Gutman's notion of reality. Under the ineffective threat of Wilmer's guns, Spade renegotiates the terms of the original deal with Gutman, demanding a victim to take the blame for all the crimes. This will free the detective from suspicion. He suggests Wilmer. In the world of power relationships, Wilmer might as well be an innocent sacrifice since, as Hammett is careful to point out, the young man's actual guilt is incidental, a mere convenience that will make their story credible to the authorities. Actually, he *is* guilty of killing Jacobi. Reluctantly, Gutman yields, explaining to Wilmer: "'I couldn't be any fonder of you if you were

*Dust jacket; London: Book Club Associates, 1977*
*(Collection of Richard Layman)*

my own son; if you lose a son it's possible to get another–but there's only one Maltese falcon'" (*Novels* 424). The others, thieves without honor, concur. Wilmer will take the fall for them. So much for the state system, diplomacy, and the balance of power of a sacrificial system encompassing morality.

Gutman pays Spade $10,000. Whistling *En Cuba* (for he has totally dominated the scene), the detective sends Effie for the statuette, fulfilling his obligations to each of his clients. To their consternation, it proves to be made of worthless lead. The Fat Man accepts this development as a setback only, attributing it to some trick by the Russian he had not originally taken into account. Entirely corrupted by their illusion of power, Gutman and Cairo are unable to imagine life without it and enthusiastically agree to renew their quest. When Spade declines their invitation to come along, Gutman takes back the detective's payment at gunpoint. To convince the Fat Man he is too corrupt and that he will therefore not call the police, Spade retains $1,000.00. After they leave, Spade calls the police.

During the renegotiations that necessarily constitutes a review of the entire case, Gutman emphatically denies any knowledge of the murder of Spade's partner, Archer. Circumstantial evidence points to Brigid O'Shaughnessy, who confesses to Spade that she shot Archer to cheat her previous protector, Thursby, of his share in the falcon by implicating him in murder. Counting on Spade's sexual loyalty to lead him to self-sacrifice, she pulls his emotional strings with effect, but not success. He knows the police will charge him if he lets her off. Besides, his professional code demands that he do something about his partner's death. Hammett holds up the 'moral' resolution of self-sacrifice (as in *The Wings of the Dove*) before rejecting it for what it is: self-destructive hypocrisy. The tragic irony is that the right use of reason in penetrating and, in this instance, thwarting the misguided instincts of Gutman results in the loss of the hero's emotional fulfillment.

With Wilmer's arrest, and Spade's relinquishment to the police of the $1,000.00 in tainted money, along with Brigid, the detective exonerates himself. He promises Brigid he will wait for her, assuming she escapes the hangman. The police round up Cairo and Wilmer but not before the young man has shot Gutman to death. The symbolic father and the 'son' he sacrificed don't achieve the fulfillment of the Grail quest, but only what can be reasonably expected: murder of the father. So much for redemption, moral victories, and metaphysical dualism.

The author concludes the story of experience, adaptation, and survival in a universe of chance by exposing the dangers of hypocritical morality and the will to power. By re-experiencing the War as it was, rather than through the rhetorical veil of nationalist propaganda, Americans could take steps to avoid sacrifice to selfishness and greed. But conventional forms, which mask reality, have a way of returning. Impractical sentiment, with all its charms, still pertains. When Spade returns to the office, Effie rebukes him for his lack of chivalry. Iva is waiting.[15]

In *The Maltese Falcon*, Dashiell Hammett establishes action-based experience as the standard for the American detective novel. Through the third person voice, the reader follows Spade's experience through the maze of necessity and opportunity into the heart of the mystery. Hammett's *Falcon* was also distinguished from its predecessors in the 'hardboiled' tradition, which depended on the plain assumption of corruption or insanity to explain relationships between criminal society and the detective. That is why they often involved a degree of violence for its own sake. In the new novel, the outcome depends on conditions of pragmatic freedom, and the heroic possibilities of life. The detective's story is a matter of becoming rather than being, a distinction clearly made for the first time in a detective novel. The hero is inseparable from the problem and is of equal interest, at least. This completes the distinction of the type from the genteel detective hero, which stressed the availability of truths revealed by aloofness, rationality, and rigorous exercise of principle. The genteel hero's eccentricity followed from the same attributes. World politics produced the metaphysical and motivational reflections that matured Hammett's contrasting heroic vision, fashioning its structure for the occasion of *The Maltese Falcon*. It was a unique event for the author and an influential one for the genre.

With the Democrat President Franklin D. Roosevelt's New Deal (1933), the tone of political life avoided sentimentality in public discourse, conforming increasingly to a more pragmatic ideal. The empowerment of labor contributed a syndicalist note to the decade. With increasing frequency, novelists shifted their focus from the individual to dominating social forces. But following Spade, who had conquered such forces, the hardboiled detective remained one of the repositories of literary individualism. As the Depression lengthened and prohibition ended, Hammett himself stopped writing novels and became more politically active in left-wing front organizations. His last novel, *The Thin Man* (1934), about a man who disappeared, featured the reluctant detective Nick Charles who lived in hotels with his socialite wife, Nora, and drank too much. After that, Hammett became a script writer for MGM film studios.

Subsequent novelists in the genre benefited from Spade's commitment and purposefulness, which facilitated action writing and extended the range of social commentary available to them. Their protagonists responded to the polar conditions of necessity and freedom that changed according to the environment, and to the individual differences of the authors. The Depression dampened the literary libido, marking a return to sentiment in some respects. Raymond Chandler resurrected the knight of the holy Grail, developing his suffering and expressive protagonist, Philip Marlowe, in four superior novels, written between 1939 and 1943. Justice was sometimes difficult for Marlowe to achieve. It required discernment related to sensitivity and sentiment that Spade probably would have scorned. The unredeemed victims of the plot drive the hero to drink, blurring the perfection of the moral resolution, but it has definitely returned.

Sexual motives are powerful in Ross MacDonald's series (1949–1976) featuring Lew Archer, but no one

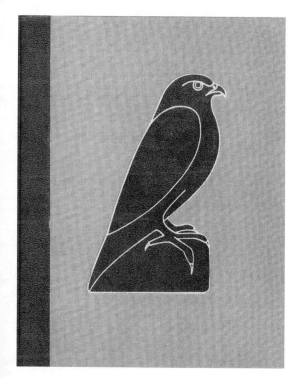

Advance Announcement

# THE MALTESE FALCON

The Arion Press will publish in early 1983 a deluxe limited edition of *The Maltese Falcon* by Dashiell Hammett. This classic of hard-boiled detective fiction was first published in 1930. A new intro-duction is being written by David Fechheimer, a private investi-gator who is an authority on Hammett. The style of the book will reflect its setting in San Francisco, late 1920s. The illustrations will be architectural photographs and street maps of the actual locations mentioned in the novel. The photographer, Edmund Shea, will supplement historic prints with new pictures of existing sites. These plates will be printed by duo-tone photo-lithography. The text will be printed by letterpress from 14 point Monotype Bodoni semi-bold and handset display types. The page format will be quarto, about 8 by 10 inches. The paper will be all rag content. An unusual binding is planned, with a leather spine and large, stylized falcons, cast in sculptural relief as mirror images, inset into the front and back covers. The edition will be limited to approximately 300 copies, and the price is expected to be $325. Reservations are now being accepted. Call or write:

## THE ARION PRESS

566 Commercial Street, San Francisco, California 94111
Telephone: (415) 981-8974

THE

# MALTESE

# FALCON

BY

DASHIELL HAMMETT

THE ARION PRESS : SAN FRANCISCO : 1983

*Announcement, front binding, and title page for the illustrated limited edition of* The Maltese Falcon *designed and printed under the direction of Andrew Hoyem in 1983 (Collection of Richard Layman)*

would mistake them for Spade's categories. The bias towards romantic love, even family values, is unmistakable. MacDonald is chiefly concerned with the failure of the older generation to provide appropriate guidance, i.e., examples, for youth. He has newer ideas than Hammett's about the psychology of frustrated sex and personality. As a result, the self-effacing Archer endures existential suffering like that of the psychiatric social worker. The domination/submission theme central to *The Maltese Falcon* remains prominent in Chandler and MacDonald. What they gain in psychological or emotional subtlety is at the expense of the powerful truths of Hammett's cosmology of materialism. Accordingly, World War II, often in the background of the Lew Archer stories, is not especially important; a backdrop suitable to MacDonald's real subject—the furies of interpersonal crimes of rejection, jealousy, and revenge.[16]

Published by Alfred Knopf, Inc. in 1930, *The Maltese Falcon* enjoyed an instant success, and the first film based on it appeared in 1931. The connection of the novel with the diplomatic controversies of Hammett's time was never commented on directly. John Huston, who directed the third, and only memorable motion picture version, released (November 1941) just before United States' entry into World War II, indirectly acknowledged the isolationist and anti-nationalist character of the story. In his autobiography, *An Open Book,* he mentioned his fidelity to Hammett's book by setting it in the pre-war mileau adding that a 'follow-up,' *Across the Pacific,* was required (87). This could have been a follow-up only in the sense that it featured the cast of the film (less Elisha Cook and Peter Lorre): Mary Astor, Sidney Greenstreet, and Humphrey Bogart. The story was entirely unrelated.

In the follow-up, required by the studio, Bogart, who according to *Variety,* had added 'immeasurable voltage to his marquee values' in his role as Sam Spade, portrayed a U.S. Army officer before the war. Under cover of a dishonorable discharge, he becomes a U.S. counterspy recruited by the Japanese to give them the details of the defenses of the Panama Canal. Turning the tables, he discovers their plan for a surprise attack on the Canal in time to defeat it. Made and released in September 1942, in a mobilization setting, it recapitulated the treachery of the Japanese at Pearl Harbor, rehearsing the appropriate next response. The battle for Guadalcanal was under way; American troops were about to land in North Africa. Obviously, propaganda was the reason for the sequel, which was intended to counteract the now unacceptable message hidden in *The Maltese Falcon.* The movie-going public followed Bogart through the war with *Casablanca* (January 1943); *Sahara* (1943); *To Have and Have Not*

(1944); and other stories of emerging commitment and international cooperation.

These sentiments supported Hammett's strong anti-fascist feelings, which went beyond words. In September 1942, in spite of frail health, he enlisted in the Army for the duration of the war. The left-front activities he continued after that got him into legal difficulties during the government's anti-communist crusade in the early 1950s. His books were banned for a while from government libraries; local public libraries followed suit in some instances. Hammett died on January 10, 1961 and, a veteran of two wars, was buried in Arlington National Cemetery.[17] In 1989, in accordance with the National Film Preservation Act, recognizing films deemed 'culturally, historically, or esthetically significant,' Huston's *The Maltese Falcon* was placed on the National Film Registry.

**Notes**

1. This disarmament conference had itself been opened by solemn observances at the Tomb of the Unknown Soldier in Arlington National Cemetery on Armistice Day, Nov. 11, 1921.
2. This is inference. Hammett's correspondence does not reflect this aspect of the novel.
3. The subject dominated the news during the election year of 1928.
4. I have substituted sacrifice here since this was the focus of Vickery's and Frazer's study of superstition.
5. Spade refers to Wilmer as Gutman's gunsel, slang for catamite, and as a 'punk,' i.e., one used for homosexual purposes.
6. Hammett used slang and innuendo to make these points in reference to Wilmer. E.g., 'Baumes rush' refers to the New York State Baumes' law which specified automatic life sentences for three-time offenders. Spade questions Wilmer's being 'on the gooseberry lay,' a reference to stealing (presumably women's undergarments) from backyard clotheslines.
7. William Marling, *Dashiell Hammett* (Boston: Twayne, 1983), p. 78, notes the connection.
8. The Russians had long-standing interests there and in obtaining access to the Mediterranean Sea.
9. For a good discussion of the 'Op' in this context see Stephen Marcus, Introduction to Dashiell Hammett, *The Continental Op* (New York: Random, 1974).
10. See "The Whosis Kid," in Dashiell Hammett, *The Continental Op*, Marcus (ed.), pp. 196–214.
11. Jessie L. Weston, *From Ritual to Romance* (Garden City, N.Y.: Doubleday, 1957 [reprint]), especially Ch. 9. T. S. Eliot expressed his debt to the book in the introduction to *The Waste Land*.
12. For Turgenev's influence see, James E. Miller (ed.) *Henry James: Theory of Fiction* (Lincoln: University of Nebraska, 1962), p. 291. For James' assumption of British nationality see Irene Willis Cooper, *England's Holy War: A Study of English Liberal Idealism During the Great War* (New York: Garland, 1972), p. 220.
13. I came across the connection first in the essay, "The Wings of Henry James," in James Thurber, *Lanterns and Lances* (New York: Harper, 1961), p. 90.

14. For an account of Wells as the self-appointed chief of the World War I crusaders see Cooper, p. 177.
15. Marling, p. 78, notes contemporary literary reservations towards discarding sentimentality altogether.
16. An excellent bibliography on the writers is Robert E. Skinner, *The Hard-Boiled Explicator: A Guide to the Study of Dashiell Hammett, Raymond Chandler and Ross MacDonald* (Metuchen, N.J.: Scarecrow, 1985).
17. I have used Diane Johnson, *Dashiell Hammett, A Life* (New York: Random House, 1983) for biographical details.

### Works Cited

Carroll, F. M. *American Opinion and the Irish Question, 1910–1923*. London: St. Martin's Press, 1978.

Cooper, Irene Willis. *England's Holy War: A Study of English Liberal Idealism During the Great War*. New York: Garland, 1972.

de Troyes, Chretien. *The Story of the Grail*. Trans. Robert White Linker. Chapel Hill: University of North Carolina Press, 1952.

Fay, Sidney. *The Origins of the World War*. New York: Macmillan, 1930.

Ferrell, Robert H. *Peace in Their Time*. New York: Norton, 1952.

Frazer, James George, Sir. *The Golden Bough: A Study in Magic and Religion*. 3rd ed. London: Macmillan, 1911–1915, 12 vols.

Hammett, Dashiell. *The Continental Op*. New York: Random House, 1974.

Hammett. *The Novels of Dashiell Hammett*. New York: Knopf, 1965.

Howe, DeWolfe. *Holmes-Laski Letters: The Correspondence of Mr. Justice Holmes and Harold L. Laski, 1916–1935*. Vol. 1. Cambridge: Harvard University Press, 1953.

Huston, John. *An Open Book*. New York: Knopf, 1980.

James, Henry. *Novels and Tales of Henry James*. Vols. 19, 20. New York: Scribners, 1937. 20 vols. 1907–1917.

Lasch, Christopher. *The True and Only Heaven: Progress and Its Critics*. New York: Norton, 1991.

"Malta Now Rivals Gibralter." *New York Times*, 25 November 1928, III 6.

"Mussolini Derides Pact." *New York Times*, 9 December 1928, p. 3.

"Text of President Coolidge's Armistice Day Speech." *New York Times*, 12 November 1928, p. 2.

"Text of Secretary Kellogg's Speech." *New York Times*, 12 November 1928, p. 12.

Vickery, John B. *The Literary Impact of the Golden Bough*. Princeton: Princeton University Press, 1973.

Weston, Jessie. *From Ritual to Romance*. Garden City, N.Y.: Doubleday, 1957.

\* \* \*

## The Emperor's Gift, or, What Did the Knights Give the Emperor?
R. H. Miller
*Studies in American Culture*, 21 (1998): 46–52

In his insightful piece, "The Metaphysical Falcon," Irving Malin describes Dashiell Hammett's famous Maltese falcon as "the deity of the mysterious world," argues that "the more we learn about it the more mysterious it becomes," and, further, that those who have died in its pursuit have died for an "untruth."[1] Malin holds that we are made to believe that "the original, if it can be found, is also fake" (106–107). He articulates what has been the prevailing attitude in much of the criticism of this novel that the falcon is bogus, a fraud.

While the symbolic, ineffable nature of this mysterious bird is crucial to the meaning of the novel, we ought not try to save the symbolic, or to use a somewhat unfashionable critical term, the allegorical, by weakening its literal base, although we cannot quarrel with the assertion that the statue that arrives in San Francisco is a fake. My argument is that the evidence of the novel shows that Hammett wants us to believe unreservedly in the palpability of the treasure and concomitantly in the fact that it is not within our power to possess it. The physical reality of the falcon relates directly to the parable of Flitcraft, in Chapter VII, who adapts his life to prevailing conditions. One pursues the goals that are within reach; one learns to accommodate, as did Flitcraft, who "adjusted himself to beams falling, and then no more of them fell, and he adjusted himself to them not falling" (336). Joel Cairo sums up Spade's ethic succinctly: "I . . . was assured that you were far too reasonable to allow other considerations to interfere with profitable business relations" (326). Calculatingly, Spade takes his meager fee rather than chase after the treasure, partly because he sees the futility of greed but also because he judges conditions to be adverse. So he spurns the statue, when he could have taken it. In Spade's calculus of values, the statue is not worth the sacrifice. While it is tempting to want to make this novel out to be solely a morality tale of greed, another Pardoner's Tale, Hammett's purposes are as much in the direction of speaking directly to the predicament of living in a world of randomness and relativism, as he does in the Flitcraft parable, as they are in preaching a sermon on avarice (Miller).

As a symbol the falcon belongs to the tradition of the grail of medieval romance, and, as many critics have shown, the American detective story is steeped in romance traditions. *The Maltese Falcon*, however, plays off those traditions in an ironic, inversive manner (Hall). The inverted romance of *The Maltese Falcon* gives us tar-

*Front covers; New York: Vintage Crime/Black Lizard, 1992, and a Chinese translation,* Taibei Shi:
Yuan liv chu ban shi ye gu fen you xiangonsi, *2000 (Collection of Richard Layman)*

nished knight Sam Spade, damsel in distress-whore Brigid O'Shaughnessy, and object of the quest the Black Bird, an enamel-encrusted, bejeweled treasure that stands symbolically in opposition to its romance counterpart, the grail. Like the medieval romance in its time the detective story in its own partakes strongly of allegory, not in a narrow formulaic sense, but in the broader sense articulated by Saint Augustine and the early allegorists, who understood that in allegory the literal and the spiritual are locked in a continuing narrative of significance where neither can be pried apart.[2] In the medieval romance the grail is a real grail, a specific object of great value, not just a convenient object that allows for treatment of more abstract matters. The falcon must be real not just in the minds of those who covet it, but real in an objective sense as well. Clearly, it represents ostentatious wealth. The Knights themselves could not accept the emperor's gift of Malta and the other islands without some ostentatious display of their

own in acknowledging the emperor's largesse. What more crass way to do so than to substitute a jeweled piece of artifice for a living piece of nature? This substitution of the jeweled bird for the live falcon is of course the ingenious creation of Hammett himself, who saw the symbolic possibilities in devising this fictional object to reflect the rapacity and fabulous wealth of the Knights.

As is necessary with any treasure if it is to have value, this falcon must have a history, a provenance. In his introduction to the Modern Library edition of the novel Hammett is vague as to the germination of the idea behind his story: "If this book had been written with the help of an outline or notes or even a clearly defined plot idea in my head I might now be able to say how it came to be written and why it took the shape it did, but all I can remember about its invention is that somewhere I had read of the peculiar rental agreement between Charles V and the Order of the Hospital of St. John of Jerusalem . . ." (vii). The story of the annual gift of a falcon by the Knights to the Emperor is a familiar one. It is described in the original agreement on display at the Armoury of Valletta, Malta. The document is called the "Exequatur" and constitutes ff. 4–19 of a volume of fifty folios (*Catalogue,* I, 204). An English translation of the Latin document appears in Porter, the relevant passage indicating that the Knights are to give into the hands of the Emperor's viceroy a hawk or falcon every year on All Saints' Day, in return for possession of Malta, Gozo, Comino, and Tripoli (II, 470). Hammett alters the history by having the Grand Master Villiers de l'Isle Adam order the making of the statue and then arrange its delivery to the Emperor himself. Immediately, however, on its initial journey to Spain to be presented to Charles V it is wrested from its deliverer, and thus it begins its movement from one owner to another (376).[3]

From there, in spite of his rather hazy recollection, Hammett set out deliberately to create a provenance for his created treasure. It is provided, appropriately, by the one person who has devoted more time than anyone to the falcon's pursuit, Casper Gutman, who for the past seventeen years has been obsessed with getting the treasure. In Chapter XIII, "The Emperor's Gift," Gutman traces its movement from its intended presentation to Charles V's viceroy down to its disappearance seventeen years ago. According to Gutman, the falcon is "not an insignificant live bird, but a glorious falcon encrusted from head to foot with the finest jewels in [the Knights'] coffers." Further, he cautions us, with relish, "These are facts, historical facts, not schoolbook history, not Mr. [H. G.] Wells's history, but history nevertheless" (376). Gutman then proceeds to recite a bibliography of printed sources and a series of historical events recounting the movement of the statue.

While Hammett's provenance is fanciful, his sources and the personages and events described are not, and he has provided an authentic history for the existence of this jeweled bird and its passage through time. The history of the knights, as Gutman recounts it, is well known. All the printed sources Gutman cites in that chapter are actual books, and as to the remaining historical information *per se,* Gutman again proves to be a reliable source.

•"J[oseph]. Delaville Le Roulx's *Les Archives de l'Ordre de Saint-Jean*" (376) is catalogued under its full title in the *National Union Catalog, Pre-1956 Imprints* (hereafter *NUC*) and the *British Museum General Catalogue of Printed Books,* (hereafter *BM*): *Les archives, la bibliothéque et le trésor de l'ordre de Saint-Jean de Jerusalem à Malte,* published at Paris by E. Thorin in 1883 (*NUC* 137:547; *BM* 50:518). It is a well known and often cited source of information about the order. Of course it contains only the traditional story of the gift of the falcon.

•"Paoli's *Dell' origine ed instituto del sacro militar ordine*" (377) is Sebastiano Paoli, *Codice diplomatico del sacro militare ordine Gerosolimitano oggi di Malta,* 2 vols. (Lucca, 1733–1737), a copy of which is in the British Library (*BM* 179:489).

•"Grand Master Villiers de l'Isle d'Adam [de l'Isle Adam]" (377), the famous early leader of the Knights at the time of the takeover of Malta and the Maltese Isles. He is documented in many sources.

•"A French knight named Cormier or Corvere" has proved to be the one elusive figure in Gutman's recitation, but it is likely that Hammett took his name from a printed source on the Knights.

•"Barbarossa, Redbeard, or Khair-ed-Din" (377) is the famed figure known also as Khizr from the family of Turkish pirates. He was born sometime after 1482 and died in 1547, and sailed out of Algiers, as Gutman says (*Encyclopedia Britannica,* 11th ed., s.v. Barbarossa; hereafter *EB*).

•"French historian Pierre Dan" (377): Born in Paris 1580, died 1649, was active in the captive exchange in Algiers in 1631. He was the author of several volumes, including *Histoire de Barbarie, et de ses corsaires . . . ,* published at Paris in 1637 (*BM* 48:129; *NUC* 132:154; *Dictionnaire de biographie française,* s.v. Dan, Pierre).

•"Sir Francis Verney, the English adventurer" (377): Noted seventeenth-century traveler, active in the Mediterranean, died, as Gutman states, in the hospital of St. Mary of Pity in Messina, September 6, 1615 (*Dictionary of National Biography,* s.v. Verney, Francis; hereafter *DNB*).

•"Lady Francis Verney's *Memoirs of the Verney Family during the Seventeenth Century*" (377) was published under that title at London by Longmans Green in a four-volume set in 1892–1899, and in a second edition, abridged, in a two-volume set in 1904 (*DNB,* s.v. Verney, Francis; *BM* 247:905; *NUC* 634:550).

•"Victor Amadeus [Amedeus] II" (377): Made King of Sicily in 1713, who married his second wife, the Contessa di San Sebastiano and then abdicated, and, as Gutman states, attempted to revoke his abdication (*EB,* s.v. Victor Amedeus II).

•"Carutti, the author of *Storia del Regno di Vittorio Amadeo II*" (377), is Domenico Carutti's history, correctly titled by Gutman, and published at Florence in 1863 (*BM* 34:783; *NUC* 97:334).

•The "father of Don José Monino [Moñino] y Redondo, Count of Floridablanco" (377): Little seems to be known of the famous count's father,

# Dashiell Hammett
## Le faucon de Malte

*Front cover for a French translation; Paris: Gallimard, 1999 (Collection of Richard Layman)*

other than that he was a retired military officer active in the Naples campaign, although his famous son is well documented. He was chief minister to Charles III of Spain (and of the Kingdom of Naples and Sicily) and died in 1808 (*EB*, s.v. Floridablanco, José Moñino y Redondo, count of; also *Enciclopedia italiana*, s.v. Florida Blanco; *Encyclopedia universal ilustrada*, s.v. Moñino).

Through the nineteenth and into the twentieth centuries Gutman's history becomes an oral one but nonetheless continues to retain its aura of historical authenticity. At some point the falcon receives its black enamel disguise and passes into the hands of the Greek dealer Charilaos Konstantinides in 1911 and thence into the hands of the Russian general Kemidov (378).[4]

In a world where no one is to be trusted, Spade trusts neither Gutman's motives nor his scholarship

and prevails upon Effie Perine, his loyal secretary, to contact her cousin Ted Christy, a history professor at Berkeley, to see if Gutman's sources check out. Effie returns later: "'Ted says it could be,' she reported, 'and he hopes it is. He says he's not a specialist in that field, but the names and dates are all right, and at least none of your authorities or their works are out-and-out fakes. He's all excited over it'" (387). As are we, we might add, because clearly the point made by the provenance of the statue is that it exists, or existed at some point in time, according to the evidence of the novel. It is documented in verifiable historical sources that are themselves vouched for by a history professor at Berkeley. Hammett seems to be having his wry little joke not only by giving his printed sources a kind of interior validity but by extending that validity beyond the confines of the novel to our own historical world, with a slight twist of the facts, to allow for the realness of the black bird. The evidence seems beyond doubt, Hammett is saying, given that a history professor at Berkeley is inclined to believe it.

Quite unlike its real presence the fake statue has a tortuous, difficult, and undocumented provenance. It comes into being through a gradual transformation reminiscent of the sinuous manner in which the thieves in Dante's *Inferno* manage to change identities with their fellow sinners, so that the moment of transformation from disguised treasure to manufactured fake is difficult to pinpoint. First it receives its coating of black enamel, sometime during the Carlist troubles in Spain (1820–1839). At this point the existence of the treasure becomes clouded, as we are not able to distinguish between real treasure, disguised treasure, and fake. From thence it passes into the hands of Konstantinides in 1911, who recognizes its value, in spite of its disguise, although all we have is Gutman's word that Konstantinides recognized the black bird as disguised treasure. He is killed in 1912, and the statue passes to Kemidov. Presumably it was he who had it copied in lead when he was tipped off to its value by Gutman, who makes him an overly generous offer for it. From thence the fake passes from the hands of Kemidov into those of Brigid O'Shaughnessy and Floyd Thursby, Brigid implying to Spade that she exchanged her sexual favors for it (352). They then take it to Hong Kong and there give it to Captain Jacobi of the ship *La Paloma* (ironically, the Dove), bound for San Francisco. The wounded and dying Jacobi delivers it into the hands of Spade, who puts it into the parcel room at the Pickwick Stage terminal and mails the claim check to one "M. F. Holland," a clear reference to "Maltese Falcon." Effie collects the statue and delivers it to Spade at his apartment, where Gutman pares away the enamel coating to expose its leaden composition and its real identity. When compared to the distinguished provenance of the original, the paternity of the fake is quite inelegant.

Consonant with the tradition of the hard-boiled novel, the falcon is also embedded securely in an environment of specificity and palpability, of empirical and positivistic values. The hard-boiled style is itself a style of particulars, honed to sharpen further their particularities. The characters of this novel are aberrations of their natural counterparts, displaying, as specifically and as "factually" as possible, their bizarre obsessions. And Spade himself is the supreme wizard of the empirical, an egoist, focused on self, on the job, and on the to-hand short-term goal, cash for services rendered. He is an avatar of the mythic Flitcraft, who, when faced with a world in which beams fell, adjusted to that fact, and when they no longer fell, he adjusted to that fact (334–336). Nothing is more fascinating than is the movement of money out of the hands of the characters and in and out of the hands of Sam Spade, culminating in his ending up only $800 to the good.[5] As many critics have noted, he turns in Brigid and keeps faith with the creed of the "job." Spade's rejection of the falcon is not the rejection of its material reality, but a rejection of it as an obtainable piece of wealth.

When we argue that the "statue" is bogus, we stand in danger of confusing the "dingus" with the real thing, *dingus* being defined as "something (as a gadget) whose proper name is unknown or forgotten" (*Webster's Third*), as Spade calls it twice, or the "damned thing," as he also calls it (380, 400–401). Both statues have palpable existences, but the fact that one is a fake does not negate the existence of the other. In truth, it can be argued that the making of a fake is itself testimony to the existence of the original. We might surmise that it has been destroyed, broken up and sold, but where is the ocular proof, as Othello says? We might surmise that it is still in the possession of Kemidov. We might surmise that it is "out there" somewhere still, wrested from the grasp of Kemidov, loose upon the world, waiting to entrap another Cairo, another Brigid, another Gutman in a death-dealing pursuit. The point of the novel is not that the pursuit of magnificent wealth is somehow pointless, but that it is very much to the point, no matter who we are or what the stakes happen to be. That point, however, is tempered by the lesson of Flitcraft: accommodate yourself to the realities, adopt a pragmatic, calculated view of life. As Steven Marcus pointed out some time ago, Flitcraft did not take on the pseudonym of Charles Pierce for no reason at all; he was acknowledging his philosophical mentor, Charles Sanders Peirce, the father of pragmatism (xix,

and Miller). Life is random; one must adjust one's existence to that fact. That there was and is a falcon whose value can be counted in the millions of dollars serves to drive the lesson home, so dearly learned by so many. The treasure's existence is real, its possession a precarious goal.

## Notes

1. I would like to acknowledge my indebtedness to the late E. R. Hagemann, colleague and friend, with whom I spent many hours discussing Hammett and aspects of this article.
2. Honig and others discuss this notion at length. See his book, particularly Chapter II and his closing discussion, pp. 179 ff.
3. William Nolan maintains that Hammett got the notion of grafting this account of the live falcon gift onto an account of a precious statue, from his ex-partner, a retired detective named Phil Haultain. In his possession Haultain had a jeweled skull, which itself had a gory history of death and theft attached to it, and according to Haultain, Hammett knew of it (89).
4. As to the question of Hammett's source(s), no single source has appeared that includes all Gutman's information, although a possibility is that Hammett was working from a history or travel book on Sicily and southern Italy, as almost all the information he provides has to do with personages and events in that area of the Mediterranean. Searches among books on Malta and the Knights have proved fruitless. Hammett's voracious reading habits and his extensive activities as a book reviewer are well documented (Hellman 292; Layman C68 ff.), and even he seems not to have been able to recall where he found his information, as I noted earlier.
5. Although Spade receives bribes, in money and sex, his earnings are small. He is offered $5,000 by Cairo, then $50,000 or 25% of the falcon's value by Gutman; none of this money materializes (322, 380). Initially he receives a retainer of $200 from Brigid, half of which he gives to Miles Archer (299–300). He gets another $500 from her (320). He takes a $200 retainer from Cairo, also (326). Of the $10,000 he receives from Gutman on turning over the statue he returns $9,000 when the falcon proves to be a fake, and he gives the remaining $1,000 to the police as evidence of a bribe (428, 431, 439). Total earnings: $800.

## Works Cited

*Catalogue of the Records of the Order of St. John of Jerusalem in the Royal Malta Library*. 2 vols. Comp. C. Gabaretta and J. Mizzi. Malta: Malta University Press, 1964.

Hall, Jasmin-Yong. "Jameson, Genre, and Gumshoes: *The Maltese Falcon* as Inverted Romance." In *Cunning Craft*. Ed. June M. Frazer. Macomb: Western Illinois University Press, 1990, pp. 109–119.

Hammett, Dashiell. Introduction to *The Maltese Falcon*. New York: Modern Library, 1934, i–ix.

Hammett. *The Maltese Falcon*. In *The Novels of Dashiell Hammett*. New York: Knopf, 1965, 293–440.

*Front cover for a Spanish translation; Madrid: Alianza Editorial, 2000 (Collection of Richard Layman)*

Hellman, Lillian. *Three*. Boston: Little, Brown, 1979.

Honig, Edwin. *Dark Conceit: The Making of Allegory*. Evanston, Il.: Northwestern University Press, 1959.

Layman, Richard. *Dashiell Hammett: A Descriptive Bibliography*. Pittsburgh: University of Pittsburgh Press, 1979.

Marcus, Steven. Introduction to *The Continental Op*. New York: Random House, 1974.

Miller, R. H. "Hammett's *Maltese Falcon*." *Explicator*, 54 (1996): 173–174.

Nolan, William. *Hammett: A Life at the Edge*. New York: Congdon & Weed, 1983.

Porter, Whitworth. *A History of the Knights of Malta of the Order of the Hospital of St. John of Jerusalem*. 2 vols. London: Longmans, et al., 1858.

* * *

## Hammettisms in *The Maltese Falcon*
Vince Emery

Scholars of Dashiell Hammett's work have identified elements that appear repeatedly throughout his writings. A useful term to label such a recurring item is a *Hammettism*.

Some Hammettisms are unique to Hammett. Others are techniques, themes, or motifs that are common to many good novels, but which are especially prominent in Hammett's fiction.

This list provides thirty-four Hammettisms that occur in several of Hammett's works and can be found in *The Maltese Falcon*, plus one Hammettism that appears in Hammett's other novels but is absent from the story of Sam Spade and the black bird.

**Third-person objective point of view** – In his essay "Perspective on Points of View" in *Writing Mysteries: A Handbook by the Mystery Writers of America*, second edition (Cincinnati: Writer's Digest Books, 2002; Sara Grafton, ed.), Loren D. Estleman observed: "The most restricting perspective, third-person objective calls for the writer who writes for the printed page to surrender his greatest advantage: the ability to get inside characters' heads. Shorn of his best mind-reading tools, he must define character entirely through action. . . . Dashiell Hammett achieved a powerful result by telling *The Maltese Falcon* completely from outside the skull of his protagonist, detective Sam Spade. It allowed Hammett to keep the reader guessing as to Spade's motives and character until the denouement." The technique enables Hammett to achieve other effects he could not accomplish with a more conventional narrative point of view, a topic requiring discussion too extensive to cover here. Third-person objective is not commonly employed because of the difficulties involved in writing with it. Few writers have been able to sustain it throughout a novel-length work. Hammett was one; Ernest Hemingway was another. Some literary historians have erroneously claimed that Hammett "borrowed" the third-person objective point of view from Hemingway. In fact, Hammett first used the technique in a Western story called "The Man Who Killed Dan Odams" he wrote in 1923, months before Hemingway's stories were available in the United States. After *The Maltese Falcon*, Hammett continued to develop his use of third-person objective point of view, employing it for short stories, his novel *The Glass Key*, and a never-completed version of *The Thin Man* substantially different from the one eventually published. For the published *The Thin Man*, Hammett resorted to first-person narration, much easier to write.

**Vivid, larger-than-life characters** – According to some critics, this was Hammett's preeminent strength. He was a master at creating memorable characters. *The Maltese Falcon* includes Sam Spade, the single most successful character Hammett ever created–in fact, one of the most famous characters any writer ever created. Spade's character has become a universal archetype. His imitations in literature, movies, and television number in the thousands. Even so, Spade is only one of many vivid characters in *The Maltese Falcon*. As in the best work of Charles Dickens or Mark Twain, even minor characters are enjoyable for their distinct personalities, appearances, and speech.

**Shifting relationships** – On his Web site "A Guide to Classic Mystery and Detection," Michael E. Grost describes the complex patterns of negotiations and interactions characteristic of Hammett's work, with stories "designed as an intricate dance, one in which the characters move in and move out in complex and beautiful ways." This quality was not typical in other mystery writers of Hammett's time, who presented characters in relationships that were static and who interested readers more by the cleverness of the mystery puzzles they unveiled.

**A whodunit puzzle** – Most of Hammett's fiction pieces are classical mysteries built around a formal whodunit puzzle. This is true of *The Maltese Falcon*, even though the existence of the puzzle (Who killed Miles Archer?) is hidden from the reader throughout most of the novel. Hammett also used this hide-the-puzzle technique in short stories: "Crooked Souls" (also known as "The Gatewood Caper") appears to be the case history of a kidnapping, but at its end the detective-narrator reveals that he first suspected the perpetrator halfway through the story; "The Gutting of Couffignal" appears to be a straight action yarn with no mystery at all until its conclusion surprises the reader by revealing that the story was in actuality a formal whodunit all along.

**A plot that foils romantic conventions** – Grost summarizes: "Hammett gets his major effects through his plotting. It is the plot that conveys the ever-growing complexity of the relationships among his principals, bizarre relationships that subvert all our notions of romantic bliss."

**A circular fable** – Hammett wrote several stories in which a character moves through dramatic events only to return to a life similar to that at the story's beginning. In *The Maltese Falcon*, Spade goes through danger, romance, and the promise of riches only to return to the same job he had and the same reluctant

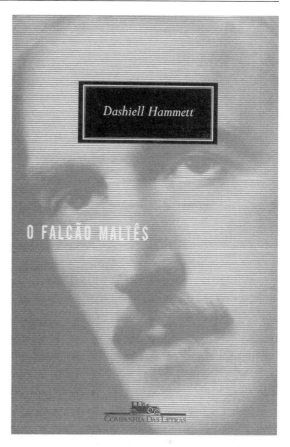

*Front cover for a Portuguese translation; São Paulo: Companhia Das Letras, 2001 (Collection of Richard Layman)*

relationship with Iva Archer. Similarly, in Chapter 7, when Spade tells the Flitcraft parable he provides a circular fable in miniature.

**Fresh scenes** – In a famous essay entitled "The Simple Art of Murder," Raymond Chandler wrote that Hammett's writing "was spare, frugal, hard-boiled, but he did over and over again what only the best writers can ever do at all. He wrote scenes that seemed never to have been written before." Even after being imitated again and again by hundreds of writers, many of the scenes in *The Maltese Falcon* are so well-constructed that they still pack enough punch to be unforgettable.

**Flavorful naturalistic dialogue** – Conversations from *The Maltese Falcon* work so smoothly they were dropped verbatim from Hammett's novel into the Humphrey Bogart movie's script. Hammett gave each character a different way of speaking–each with his or her own vocabulary, rhythm, and sentence structure. He kept his dialog crisp, made it sound like real people talking and

*Dust jacket; Thorndike, Me.: G. K. Hall / Bath: Chivers, 2001 (Collection of Richard Layman)*

not written prose, and made each conversation move the plot forward. Only the best writers accomplish all these tasks simultaneously. Hammett's ability to sustain many distinct voices—one for his narration, several others for his characters—is at its best in *The Maltese Falcon*.

**Tradecraft** – One reason Hammett's stories fascinate readers is that he lets readers see the tricks of the detective trade. Examples in *The Maltese Falcon* include remembering a conversation almost verbatim for later dictation, shaking a tail, and searching a room.

**Detective-style descriptions of people** – In his essay "The Decline and Fall of the Detective Story," Somerset Maugham pointed out that "Hammett and Raymond Chandler specify the appearance of their characters and the clothes they wear, though briefly, as exactly as do the police when they send to the papers a description of a wanted man." Throughout his works, Hammett describes people as a detective would: "Mr.

Joel Cairo was a small-boned dark man of medium height. His hair was black and smooth and very glossy. His features were Levantine. A square-cut ruby, its sides paralleled by four baguette diamonds [terminology that reflects Hammett's experience working for a jeweler], gleamed against the deep green of his cravat. His black coat, cut tight to narrow shoulders, flared a little over slightly plump hips. His trousers fitted his round legs more snugly than was the current fashion. The uppers of his patent-leather shoes were hidden by fawn spats. He held a black derby hat in a chamois-gloved hand and came towards Spade with short, mincing, bobbing steps. The fragrance of *chypre* came with him." A witness could give that description to a missing-persons detail: height, hair color, figure, clothing, how the person moves, even his perfume. Note how Hammett starts at the top of his subject's head and works his way down to the feet and hands.

**Superspecificity** – Author William Gibson invented this term. It refers to passages in which Hammett describes objects or events using extreme detail to draw us deeper into a scene. In an interview, Gibson described his excitement when he realized what Hammett was doing with superspecificity: "I remember being very excited about how he [Hammett] had pushed all this ordinary stuff until it was different—like American naturalism but cranked up very intense, almost surreal." One of the best-known examples of superspecificity in all of Hammett's writing occurs in Chapter 1: the sounds, sights, and smells in Spade's office as Brigid and Spade silently battle, both stalling to provoke the other to talk first. Raymond Chandler liked those three paragraphs so much that he imitated them in "Trouble Is My Business." The reader will find several additional instances of superspecificity in *The Maltese Falcon*.

**Biting humor** – As usual, Hammett's dry wit is present, often so understated that many readers miss it.

**Reworked elements from his own earlier works** – Hammett often refined and improved characters, situations, clues, and plot ideas that he had used before. Those who have read much of his fiction can identify his recyclings and trace them as they evolve over his career.

**A group standoff** – Hammett frequently included tense scenes of an extended standoff between a group of diverse characters, such as the one in Spade's apartment near the end of the book.

**Detective is surprised** – Sherlock Holmes was famed as being omniscient and rarely surprised.

Philo Vance and most other fictional detectives of the nineteen-twenties were similarly unflappable. Hammett countered this convention by ensuring that in every one of his stories that feature a detective, the detective is surprised at least once. This occurs in Chapter 5 of *The Maltese Falcon,* when Joel Cairo wakes up and says he really will pay Spade $5,000. Hammett explicitly describes Spade as genuinely surprised—one of the rare times in the book when the author tells us how a character feels. In Chapter 14, Spade is caught by surprise again when the fat man drugs him.

**Detective is beaten** – Hammett detectives are usually beaten up at least once. In Chapter 14, Spade suffers a kick in the head from Wilmer.

**Extra clues not explicitly pointed out** – According to a former policeman, Hammett often adds extra clues that an experienced investigator would recognize but that Hammett does not mention in his puzzle's concluding explanation. *The Maltese Falcon* presents two such clues. 1) A professional killer supposedly leaves his gun at the crime scene. A professional hitman does not casually abandon a traceable gun at a murder site; therefore all detectives on the case should suspect from the start that a professional did not commit this murder and that someone might be trying to frame the professional. 2) The second implied clue is one of Hammett's favorites, which he used before in the short stories "Who Killed Bob Teal?" and "The Gutting of Couffignal": a gunpowder burn on the coat. As soon as Spade hears about the powder burn, he knows the gun was fired at short range, implying that the killer was someone the victim recognized and trusted enough to approach closely. It is surprising that Spade does not mention the powder burn at the denouement.

**Main character is a loner**.

**Main character is working class** – Before Hammett, detectives were rich or at least upper class. Hammett had been a real detective; he knew better. Real detectives did hard work for low pay. They were not aristocratic. Sam Spade was a nail in the coffin of the tuxedo-clad detective.

**Main character does not drive** – Hammett had many fears. One was fear of driving. The result is that few of Hammett's central characters drive. Spade travels in taxis and streetcars. To go to Burlingame, instead of driving himself, he rents a car with a driver.

crime masterworks

Dashiell Hammett

The Maltese Falcon

'Possibly the best American detective novel ever written'
OTTO PENZLER

*Dust jacket; London: Orion, 2002*
*(Collection of Richard Layman)*

**A fat man**.

**Treacherous women**.

**Greeks** – Three appear in *The Maltese Falcon*.

**Russians** – Only one appears in the novel, but he holds the falcon.

**A movie theater and/or a movie theater owner** – In Chapter 12, Spade finds that Iva Archer went to a movie theater on Powell Street. In chapter 16, he takes on a movie theater owner as a new client.

**No children** – Surprisingly for a man who had two daughters and who loved children all his life, Hammett wrote stories that take place in a world without children. Although *The Maltese Falcon* has two seeming exceptions, they are actually adults. Gutman's so-called daughter Rhea is post-pubescent. Although described as a "boy," Wilmer Cook is in his twenties.

*Front cover for a Bulgarian translation; Plovdiv: Khermes, 2003 (Collection of Richard Layman)*

**Names based on people Hammett knew** – Polhaus was a boyhood chum. Hammett's own first name was Sam.

**Hard drinking** – Even though he wrote during Prohibition, few of his characters were teetotalers. For better or worse, Hammett popularized what is now a cliché: the hard-drinking detective.

***Celebrated Criminal Cases of America* by Thomas Duke** – This 1910 book appears twice in *The Maltese Falcon*. It is excerpted in *The Thin Man* and is referenced again in one of Hammett's nonfiction pieces.

**Slang** – Hammett loved colorful slang all his life, and used it to spice his writing. Note that in *The Maltese Falcon* his narration does not use slang, only the characters' spoken dialogs. To sharpen distinctions between the characters' personalities, each character's lines employ slang in a different way.

**The word "dingus"** – Hammett used the word "dingus" in many of his pieces. In *The Maltese Falcon*, Spade calls the bird "this dingus" at the end of Chapter 16.

**The phrase "all right."**

**A list without a connective before the final item**, such as "Every drawer, cupboard, cubbyhole, box, bag, trunk–locked or unlocked–was opened..." Most writers would have written "bag, *and* trunk." Hammett often deletes the "and."

**A numbered list** – Hammett was an advertising writer. Most classes and books that teach the techniques of writing advertisements instruct writers to add coherence and momentum to unstructured points by presenting them as a sequence of numbered items. Hammett included several numbered lists in his fiction. Perhaps the most well-known occurs in *The Maltese Falcon*, when Spade rattles off a numbered list during the most intense scene, giving Brigid seven reasons he cannot trust her. The astute reader will find other numbered lists in the novel as well.

**A lunger** – Finally, the exception–one Hammettism not present in *The Maltese Falcon*. Hammett nearly died of tuberculosis. His novels usually include a thin man who is a "lunger"–who suffers from Hammett's own lung disease: Dan Rolff in *Red Harvest*, Owen Fitzstephan (clearly a fictional version of Hammett himself) in *The Dain Curse*, Ned Beaumont in *The Glass Key*, Clyde Wynant–the title character–in *The Thin Man*. But no one has tuberculosis in *The Maltese Falcon*. (A case can be made that Captain Jacobi represents a lunger, but that is not realistic. Jacobi is thin, and he coughs up blood like a tuberculosis victim, but in Jacobi's case the blood comes not from disease but from six bullets in his chest.)

All the elements cataloged above recur in Hammett's fiction with a frequency sufficient to preclude argument as to their inclusion by accident or random chance.

There can be no doubt that some Hammettisms, such as the insertion of the word "dingus," were injected by the author deliberately. Others may have been included unconsciously, providing the reader with clues about the unseen forces that shaped Hammett's work. Whether selected consciously or reused unconsciously, these elements can help the reader comprehend Hammett's creative process. They also help scholars understand how his best work transcended the limits of genre fiction, and provide insight into why *The Maltese Falcon* and other works by Dashiell Hammett continue to provide fertile fields for general readers and scholars alike.

# Movies, Stage, and Radio:
## Hammett's Novel in Popular Culture

### Hammett after *The Maltese Falcon*

With the exception of a half decade during the 1950s when Hammett was blacklisted for his communist affiliations, The Maltese Falcon *has been continuously in print since its first publication on Valentine's Day, 1930. Few novels published in America have had such a successful publication history and such influence in their adaptations into other forms. The literary power of Hammett's novel was recognized immediately. Months after publication Warner Bros. bought performance rights and began production on the first of three movie versions, released under the novel's title in 1931.*

*Before the movie was released Hammett's agent, Leland Hayward of the American Play Company, contracted with playwright Benjamin Glazer for a stage production at Hammett's request, not realizing that stage rights had already been sold in the contract with Warner Bros. In the mid 1930s, Warner Bros. also saw the potential for a stage version of the novel and contracted with Laurence Stallings to write the script. He completed an unproduceable adaptation.*

*Four years later Hal Wallis decided that the 1931 movie adaptation could be improved, and he set to work on another version, a flop released in 1936 as* Satan Met a Lady. *Five years later, Warner Bros. tried again, this time with first-time director John Huston. The result was the classic movie starring Humphrey Bogart, Mary Astor, Sydney Greenstreet, and Peter Lorre. That movie has been released in more than fifteen countries in as many languages and appears on the American Film Institute list of Greatest Films of All Time.*

*In addition, there were at least two radio adaptations of the script during World War II, and two long-running radio serials based on characters from the novel. Sam Spade was used during Hammett's lifetime to advertise Wildroot Hair Cream and after his death in an ad featuring Humphrey Bogart for Gordon's Gin.*

*The proliferation of adaptations, the commercial appeal of Sam Spade and the faux falcon, and the enduring quality of the falcon story have a significance related directly to the literary value of Hammett's novel. His characters are strong enough to sparkle even in the form of caricatures. His dramatic sense has been strong enough to engage audiences for three-quarters of a century now. His ability to create a story that forcefully reverber-*

*Caricature Hammett gave his wife in the 1930s. The artist is unidentified (courtesy of Josephine Hammett).*

*ates basic truths about the human condition has allowed adaptations that draw their strength from the original.*

*The enduring quality of the 1941 movie is particularly notable because of the fidelity of John Huston's script to the novel. Much of the dialogue is verbatim from the book, and the plot changes are minimal—the least intrusive cuts necessary to fit the action into a very different medium. Hammett was an early movie fan, and by the time he wrote* The Maltese Falcon, *his work was clearly influenced by dramatic presentation. His dialogue is sharp and descriptive, independent of narrative exposition. The scenes are limited to main locations: Spade's office, his apartment, and Gutman's suite; scenes in other settings provide bridges to the main action. The camera provides a reliable substitute for the third-person narration of the book that focuses on Spade, seeing*

(4-3)

COPY

TO WHOM IT MAY CONCERN:

I, <u>JOSEPH T. SHAW</u>, do hereby certify, as follows: I am the Editor of Black Mask, which is published by Pro Distributors Publishing Co.Inc., a corporation organized and existing under the Laws of the State of New York, and have heretofore and prior to September 1929, as Editor of said Black Mask, acquired by purchase from Dashiell Hammett, the first serial publication rights to a story entitled "THE MALTESE FALCON", written by Dashiell Hammett; that I have paid the full consideration for the said publication to the said Dashiell Hammett; that the said story was published in the Black Mask Magazine, in the issues of September, October, November and December 1929, and the issue of January, 1930; that there was no written contract for the purchase of the said rights, but that the sale thereof was fully executed and completed; that the said story was copyrighted in the aforesaid issues of the said Magazine by Pro Distributors Publishing Co.Inc.; and I further certify that an assignment of the respective registrations of copyright with respect to the said story "THE MALTESE FALCON", was on the 30th day of December, 1929, assigned by Pro Distributors Publishing Co.Inc. to Alfred A. Knopf, Inc. I further state that the said publisher has no further or other interest in and to the said story.

WITNESS my hand and seal this 18th day of June, 1930.

JOSEPH T. SHAW     (L.S.)<br>
Editor .

*Affidavit of Joseph T. Shaw declaring the circumstances of his purchase of rights to* The Maltese Falcon *for* Black Mask *(courtesy of Warner Bros. Archive, University of Southern California)*

*the other characters as he would see them, moving through the action of the story along with him, without interpretation. The reader or viewer knows just what Spade knows. With the exception of brief fight scenes, violence occurs behind the scenes and is related in conversation. The success of the novel relies not on plot, but on character, on dramatic confrontation, and on the thrill of recognition well-told stories bring. John Huston's movie has a symbiotic relationship with the novel: the movie draws its strength from the story Hammett imagined, providing along the way a strong visual dimension to the novel. Never mind that the visual dimension sometimes detracts from the original—as in the pacing. There is enough strength to the symbiosis to overcome the weaknesses. Other adaptations are more parasitic in nature. They take their life from the cultural significance that* The Maltese Falcon *has achieved. Sam Spade, the Maltese Falcon, Caspar Gutman, and Brigid O'Shaughnessy have taken their place in our cultural vocabulary.*

## Dashiell Hammett, 1930–1960

Richard Layman

*Selected Letters of Dashiell Hammett*

(Washington, D.C.: Counterpoint, 2001)

### Celebrity

On 22 November 1930, the Saturday before Thanksgiving, Hammett attended a Hollywood party hosted by Darryl F. Zanuck, then supervisor of production at Warner Bros. In addition to *The Jazz Singer,* Zanuck had produced W. R. Burnett's 1929 novel *Little Caesar* (released January 1931) and *Public Enemy* (released April 1931), movies that initiated the gangster-film genre. He wanted Hammett on his payroll. Also at the party was Lillian Hellman, the wife of Hammett's colleague at Paramount, screenwriter Arthur Kober.

Hammett and Hellman left the party together that night, and they were companions for the rest of his life. The effect they had on each other was altogether remarkable. Though they were lovers, neither was ever faithful. Yet when together they were a formidable team, he providing the image of authority, and she its voice. Within a year of meeting Hellman, Hammett all but quit writing fiction for publication, though he entertained vague notions about a sixth novel and continued, as he had for at least five years, to mull over various ideas for plays. He concentrated instead on screenwriting and mentoring others, often young women. When Hellman and amorous writing partner Louis Kronenberger were unable to complete a satiric drama they were attempting and threatened to go away together to work on it, Hammett responded by giving her his idea for dramatizing a true crime story by William Roughead called "Closed Doors; or the Grand Drumsheugh Case" about a girls' school in Edinburgh, Scotland, forced to close in 1810 because its owners

were rumored to be lesbians. They worked on successive drafts together, and when it was produced under her authorship in 1934 as *The Children's Hour,* she was an overnight sensation. The play ran on Broadway for 691 performances, and by the year's close, Hellman was a name that could be uttered in literary circles in the same breath as Hammett.

He was serious about his writing, but he was also an opportunist—a man born poor who had lived through illness and who now wanted to wring all the benefits he could from success. Hammett was a literary man, but he was too much of a pragmatist to devote himself to literature. Like his characters the Continental Op and Sam Spade, he was contemptuous of images and the people who traded in them. When reviewers began to make too much of his work, he lost interest in their opinions; when editors or moviemakers or other writers began to take themselves too seriously, Hammett ridiculed them. Gradually the company he kept became too ludicrous in his eyes to abide sober. He opted for the solace of drunkenness.

His initial collapse came in stages, beginning in Hollywood. In spring 1931 he had a recurrence of venereal disease, which he had first contracted as a teenager. In winter 1931 he was charged with sexual assault against one of his girlfriends, Elise DeViane, and found guilty of civil charges the next summer. By mid 1934, his drunkenness was so alarming that his friends confided their concern about him to one another. In the winter of 1935, he sunk to suicidal despair. Another attack of venereal disease and alcoholic depression landed Hammett in Lenox Hill Hospital in New York. He was physically and psychologically broken, yet his celebrity remained untarnished. He recuperated at a rented house in Princeton, New Jersey, by attempting to drink himself well, and finally the parties became so raucous that he was evicted.

Hammett went back to Hollywood in spring 1937. The atmosphere there had changed and it had remained the same. So had he. On the one hand, Hollywood was still the nation's capital for crassness, ignorance, greed, arrogance, hypocrisy, licentiousness, and intemperance. On the other, the Hollywood image makers, attempting to avoid government regulation, had since July 1934 accepted the strictures their own Production Code Administration, known as the Hays Office, designed to rid movies of unwholesome content. The movie industry stood for values that Hammett despised, and some that he couldn't resist. He was contemptuous of Hollywood, and he reserved some of the contempt for himself because he gave in so easily to its temptations. Hammett found it easy to rationalize his work there when he was drunk. But during this, his last

*First pages in* American Magazine *(October 1932) of the second of three Sam Spade short stories Hammett wrote that year (Collection of Richard Layman)*

extended stay, he was mostly sober. He found a purpose in politics, and that work required a clear mind.

Hollywood developed a social consciousness of sorts in the last half of the 1930s. The Hollywood section of the Communist Party USA was newly formed, and Hammett was an active member. It was the time of the Popular Front, when, upon orders from the Comintern, the international policy-making body of the Communist Party, national parties worked to promote social change within established political structures. In 1937 Communist Party membership required a commitment to civil rights and to social equality, opposition to exploitation of workers and to fascism. It explicitly did not advocate subversion of the government or anti-Americanism. It was easy for a conscientious citizen with a liberal bent to be a communist sympathizer in the 1930s. But to be a card-carrying member required unqualified submission to Party discipline, which was strict and often severe. Hammett managed somehow to reconcile the demands of the Party with his anti-authoritarian convictions.

Communism provided a more or less formal expression of values that Hammett believed in well before he joined the Party in the mid-1930s. At the simplest level, communists championed the equality of all people. They opposed class systems that subordinated one person to another and supported their beliefs with a web of complex arguments that, in their public expression, focused more intently on social and economic theory than on practical solutions to the problems they identified. While Hammett held to a rigorous personal code of values, it seemed out of character for him to advocate a political party actively, however idealistic. Yet he was an unapologetic Marxist who found Communism the best political option available to him. Communism isn't perfect, he said, but it will do until something better comes along. He worked, when he worked at all, for the rights of the working man, and he enthusiastically studied the political situation around the world.

The Spanish Civil War was a major Communist cause in 1937. There, in the prequel to World War II,

*Hammett with his daughters, Josephine, left, Mary, right, at the Stork Club, New York City, circa 1941*
*(courtesy of Josephine Hammett)*

the Italians and the Germans supported a coalition of Fascist forces, ultimately led by Francisco Franco, that were attempting to overthrow the republican government. European communists, particularly Soviets, sent weapons and soldiers, in what were called International Brigades, to oppose the Fascist threat. Hammett believed in the cause fervently enough to attempt to join, at the age of forty-one, the Abraham Lincoln Battalion, the American volunteer group. Communist leaders told him he could do more good at home, and he followed their advice.

Hammett was an organizer. He attended meetings, took leadership roles in Communist organizations, and donated money to Party-sponsored causes. He also became involved in Hollywood union activities, fighting the corrupt International Alliance of Theatrical Stage Employees and Playwrights Guild, whose leadership had sold out to studio bosses. When the Screen Writers Guild reorganized in 1937 after a false start earlier in the decade, Hammett and Hellman were members of the board of directors. He worked diligently and effectively to gain formal recognition for the organization as an authorized agent for screenwriters, and he used the influence he garnered in his S.W.G. work to support other leftist causes.

On the whole, however, the late 1930s were depressing times for social libertarians. Hammett despaired as the republican cause in Spain went from doubtful to hopeless. To him the Fascist victory in the face of American neutrality signaled a threat to personal liberty in the United States, especially in those pre-war years when many Americans found much to admire in the strict order of Fascist states. Anti-Semitism and racial segregation, generally accepted as middle-class values during the Depression, were moral issues that Hammett reacted to sharply because of his basic belief in civil rights. His awareness of worldwide persecution of Jews was amplified by his relationship with Hellman and her circle of Jewish friends. There was little cause for optimism about worker's rights in the eighth and ninth years of the Great Depression, as long-term unemployment drained whatever sentiment people had for union-organized work disturbances.

Hammett's personal world was equally glum. The more independent Lillian Hellman became, the more flagrant she was with her sexual dalliances (and he with his), the more steadfast his love for her seemed to become. When she became pregnant in the fall of 1937 and pressed him to marry her, he took steps to oblige her by obtaining a mail-order Mexican divorce from Jose that was probably not valid in the United States. Hellman averted the crisis by getting an abortion, after which neither saw the point in legalizing their relationship. Having spent the spring and summer in Hollywood with Hammett, she left in the fall and began a romance with another lover.

*Hammett at work on* The Adakian *in the Aleutians during World War II*
*(courtesy of Josephine Hammett)*

In fall 1937 Hellman was gone, and he missed her. While he never lacked for girlfriends, he had discovered the gulf between sex and love. He was lonely and isolated. His paychecks came from M-G-M, where he labored over the third of the Thin Man movies. The work went slowly and without enthusiasm. He wrote three drafts of the screenplay for *Another Thin Man,* and while his work impressed his bosses at the studio, his work habits did not. For his own part, Hammett considered the results embarrassing. In 1933, when he wrote his novel *The Thin Man,* he was the charming drunk, Nick Charles, but not now. Hammett wrote Hellman in January 1938 that he had not had a drink in ten months. His political work gave him a reason to get up in the morning, but without her for support, he became overwhelmed by frustration and a sense of futility. He had to be drunk to face the world, especially the world in Hollywood those days; and when he began drinking again, he showed no restraint. The breakdown came in summer 1938. He had shrunk to 125 pounds, and he was helpless, both physically and emotionally. He felt he had nowhere to turn; he was in a state of collapse. Hellman took him in and nursed him out of the darkness of depression.

In New York, Hammett's health improved with his spirits as he worked out a new accommodation with Hell-man. They could love each other without being possessive. He had a permanent room at Hardscrabble Farm, which she purchased in her name in the summer of 1939 but which was a joint investment between them, and they entertained friends—and often lovers—independently there. They recommitted themselves to each other in a relationship as strong as marriage but with a different set of vows. Their lives took separate paths, which intersected at intervals. What they shared was a home base.

Hammett liked most of Hellman's lovers and treated them as friends. Arthur Kober, her former husband, was the first. Now, as Hellman's affairs more frequently blossomed into serious relationships, Hammett remained tolerant. In 1939, he worked closely with Ralph Ingersoll, though he rarely missed a chance to sneer at his idealistic naïveté. Broadway producer Herman Shumlin, *PM* Washington bureau chief Kenneth Crawford, and *New Yorker* editor St. Clair McKelway were others among Hellman's many lovers whose company Hammett tolerated if not enjoyed. Likewise, he had romantic entanglements with Laura Perelman, Jean Potter, and a bevy of actresses and hangers-on whom Hellman, in turn, endured. They could not make themselves invulnerable to jealousy, but they did resolve, more or less successfully, not to allow its destructive effects.

A sure sign that he was on the mend, Hammett announced late in 1939 that he was ready to begin work on his sixth novel. He resumed an active role in politics, backing up with action the principles he endorsed. He helped start a magazine, *Soviet Russia Today,* and he joined with Ralph Ingersoll in planning and organizing the communist-supported newspaper *PM.* He was president of the New York Civil Rights Congress, a Party-sponsored organization that mobilized support for Party causes. He was working with purpose again.

### Soldier

When the United States entered World War II, Hammett's convictions, which were based on unflagging patriotism, left him one course of action only. Though he was initially turned down by recruiters, he persisted and was inducted into the U.S. Army, despite being forty-eight years old and still on a disability pension from World War I. It was the start of the happiest time of his life.

With the exception of the few months in 1926 when he worked full time for Albert S. Samuels, Hammett's military service was the only time since he was a teenager that he had a daily schedule imposed by someone else. In the army he had assigned tasks each day, and he performed them, however mundane, with no more than a common amount of grumbling. He got up at a prescribed time in the morning and went to bed at an assigned time most nights. Because of his age and his celebrity, he enjoyed enough privileges to satisfy his need for freedom, but, for the most part, he lived by army rules. He drank in moderation, except for an occasional binge, and he ate regular meals. He maintained close contact with the people he loved and he seemed content with the terms of his separation from them. He read with pleasure and with boundless curiosity.

The isolation on Adak Island in the Aleutians, where Hammett spent most of the war, suited him. The weather was cold and the conditions were often brutal, but Hammett was robust. He gained weight and enjoyed good health and peace of mind. He had a job that mattered. He had progressed from his first assignment, rewriting training manuals, to the kind of creative project he enjoyed—launching a camp newspaper. *The Adakian,* his four-page daily, consumed him as he was planning it, gathering his news resources, organizing his staff, and acting as chief writer and editor. He enjoyed both the journalism and the teaching his job entailed. He liked being an authority, interpreting the news on his weekly radio show, and counseling soldiers less than half his age. He liked being respected and being in control of his project.

*The Adakian* was Hammett's creation, and it reveals much about him. It was a serious newspaper of fact, and it informed those soldiers on the island who cared about world events. As his letters reveal, Hammett was not content to rely on the traditional news sources available to him—Associated Press, Army News Service, Camp Newspaper Service, the Armed Services Radio Network, and the camp's short-wave radio. He insisted on supplementing his sources with a steady supply of publications otherwise unavailable to Alaskan soldiers, including such left-wing papers and periodicals as *PM,* the *Daily Worker,* and *New Masses.* He read British Communist Claud Cockburn's opinionated *The Week* regularly. He received reports of foreign short-wave radio broadcasts that provided information about war progress from perspectives different from the standard United States sources. Hammett digested this material into a paper, which he edited and partly wrote. *The Adakian* concentrated on international stories about the war and domestic news in the States. Camp news, sports, and entertainment appeared on page 4. Frequently a story relating the history of a military company or campaign was included. Soldiers were informed about post facilities, including the four post theaters and the library, which had over 8500 books in addition to free Armed Services Editions. There were typically two opinion cartoons per issue, often with captions by Hammett.

The purpose of *The Adakian* was to inform and to instruct—not to proselytize. Hammett provided gentle history and geography lessons along with his war news so soldiers could understand the war they were a part of. He took care to make the paper personally relevant to the soldiers on Adak. A remarkable fact, given the peacetime work record of its editor, is that *The Adakian* appeared with the regularity one expects of newspapers. In the Aleutians, Hammett did not miss deadlines.

He did get bored when the challenges faded, though. By late 1944, Hammett's newspaper was well organized, and his staff was trained. He was no longer needed, and he got restless. He eagerly accepted those assignments that took him off Adak to the Alaskan mainland, back where he had access to something like civilian life. The old temptations still held their power over him, but the effects were softened somewhat by his age. Hammett was past his fiftieth birthday by that time in an army that considered soldiers past the age of thirty-eight over the hill. The trips exhausted him; the bars sometimes bored him; the women were more appealing when they had something interesting to say.

As the war wore down, Hammett had visions of remaining in Alaska. He even bought a bar in Anchorage, but he gave it to the black woman who ran it for him. Attractive as life in Alaska may have seemed, it was not a real option. He had to go back to the States because the work he had committed himself to before the war remained to be done. The Allies had been victorious in the battle against Fascism, but the fight was not concluded. He planned a life as a politician, and speculated what offices he might seek so that he could continue to fight for the principles he believed in. His exile on Adak had allowed him to exorcise some personal devils, and now he had a winner's confidence. He looked to the future with eager anticipation of the important work that lay ahead. And, as always when he was feeling healthy, he resumed work on a novel.

### Activist

Hammett returned home after World War II to his room at Hardscrabble Farm in Pleasantville, which remained his permanent residence until Hellman sold the farm in 1952. He looked for an apartment in New York City where he could live during weekdays when he had business there. He found a temporary living quarters on East 66th St., but after six months, he moved to a studio apartment in Greenwich Village near the main office of the Civil Rights Congress and the Jefferson School where he taught. He kept an office on the ground floor and had a living room-bedroom with a fireplace that overlooked a small garden. He kept the apartment cold in the winter, because it reminded him of the Aleutians, he said.

The army gave Hammett a renewed sense of purpose. In the army he had served essentially as an educator, a role he liked, and he planned to enlarge upon it in civilian life. He wanted to be actively involved in politics, doing work he considered meaningful, making people aware of what he felt were abuses of power. The Civil Rights Congress, formed in April 1946 through the merger of three communist organizations, offered Hammett the opportunity to engage in the kind of activism he relished most: defending the rights of working people by involving himself in specific cases. He was named president of the Civil Rights Congress of New York, a job that required him to respond directly to events of the day— protesting against the lynching of blacks in Georgia; providing for the defense of those accused of violating the anti-Communist Smith Act; working to insure voters' rights; defending freedom of speech and political expression by actively opposing the House Committee on Un-American Activities. He organized, he spoke, he protested, and he educated. He built the CRC in New York into the most successful communist organization of its time, with a bail fund that had some $760,000 in cash by 1951. In the evenings, he taught mystery writing, among other courses, at the newly

formed Marxist college, the Jefferson School of Social Science.

In addition to his political commitment, but clearly secondary to it, Hammett had vague plans to resume his career as a writer. He had ideas for several novels, one of which he may have come close to completing, though no evidence survives except for the mention of it in his letters. He was at least thinking about short stories, and he took an active interest in Broadway theater, where his opinion was respected. But he put off the writing when there was a chance to do anything else instead. There were many distractions. Politics made heavy demands on his time, and so did his daughter Mary who suffered from mental illnesses that she sought haven from with drugs, alcohol, and sexual excess.

In 1946 Mary's condition was so bad that Jose felt she could no longer cope. Jose had shielded Hammett from the worst of Mary's transgressions but now, in desperation, she wrote him asking for help. He flew out immediately and, after discussion with Jose and Jo, decided—reluctantly—to take Mary east with him. He would take care of her, find her the very best of psychiatric help. It was a decision that had severe consequences for him.

For a while Mary shared his apartment, and then he got her one of her own. They drank together, each feeding the other's weakness. He had seen brief episodes of her erratic behavior before, but now he realized how deeply disturbed she was and the hopelessness of her condition. His own drinking worsened; by 1947 Hammett was in a downward alcoholic spiral that took him near the point of death.

His last prolonged bout of uncontrollable drinking ended with his collapse and hospitalization in December 1948. His doctor was blunt: he told Hammett that if he did not quit drinking immediately, he would die. He chose to live. Beginning in January 1949, Hammett quit drinking for good. His recovery was slow and incomplete. Mary returned to California in 1952 after her doctors admitted there was nothing more they could do for her, and Hammett gave up any hope of a relationship with his older daughter.

As Hammett's health improved, Hellman encouraged him to continue working in the theater and in Hollywood. She cautiously arranged for Kermit Bloomgarden, her producer, to hire him as a script doctor in late fall 1949. When she saw that Hammett was up to the job, she asked William Wyler at Paramount Pictures to hire him as a scriptwriter for an adaptation of Sidney Kingsley's novel and play *Detective Story*. In January 1950 Hammett moved to Los Angeles and found the movie industry as shallow as ever and the city even more offensive. He was disdainful of the project and must have been dismayed by the spectacle of his leftist friends feverishly denouncing their pasts. After three months' work he returned the money that had been advanced him and went home, never looking back.

The political atmosphere of the time was tense, especially in Hollywood. In October 1947 the House Committee on Un-American Activities launched a sensationalistic investigation of Communist activities in Hollywood, and the next month cited ten writers and directors for contempt of Congress when they refused to answer questions about their membership in the Communist Party. In May 1949, the Hollywood Ten, as they were called, unsuccessfully sued the studios for violating their constitutional rights by firing them, and in August 1950, their appeals of their contempt charge exhausted, all of them were sentenced to prison. At the same time, the Justice Department was attempting to force the party underground, using the Smith Act, which made it a crime to teach, advocate, or encourage the overthrow of the United States government, to jail more than a hundred accused communists. The blacklist, by which certain employers refused jobs to accused communists, was even more pernicious than legal assaults. Hundreds of people, especially those in movies, radio, and television, had their livelihood stripped from them.

The blacklist affected Hammett first; the courts followed soon afterward. In the late 1940s he received $1200 a week from the three radio shows based on his characters. By early 1950, two had been cancelled due to his political affiliations, and in 1951, the last was taken off the air. He was undeterred, continuing to serve in a highly public way as president of the Civil Rights Congress, an organization formally designated communist by the House Committee on Un-American activities. When eleven Communist leaders were found guilty of violating the Smith Act in November 1949, the bail fund committee of the Civil Rights Congress posted their bail of $260,000, so they could be free during the appeals process. In July 1951, after all appeals were exhausted, four of the men failed to surrender themselves, and the justice department launched an inquiry. As chairman of the bail fund committee, Hammett was subpoenaed to testify in federal court to aid in efforts to find men still at large. When he took the stand, he refused to give even his name. He and three other trustees of the bail fund were sentenced to federal prison for contempt of court. Hammett served five-and-a-half months.

His silence was predictable. A primary tenet of the Civil Rights Congress was that citizens had the right to their political beliefs without government interference, and that was a principle Hammett had embraced all his life. Now he did what he had to do without complaint. He went to jail and served his time as a model prisoner, without expecting or accepting sympathy. His letters from prison are unfailingly cheerful. Solitude never bothered him, and during his sober times he even sought it. Nonetheless, Hammett's confinement marked a turning point for him physically. His conviction was as resolute as ever, but after he was released from prison, he was a physically broken man with dwindling resources, and he acted the part.

## Survivor

Hammett was released from jail in December 1951, but his troubles had only begun. The blacklist was in full force, and it operated both in government and in the private sector. Hammett's radio programs had been canceled, his books went out of print, and his name lost the cachet it had held for twenty years. Now, in the public eye, he was a convicted communist, with no means or potential.

Hammett had considered taxes an annoyance since the 1930s, though his letters provide evidence that he did not ignore them entirely. Nonetheless the cost of his disdain for money finally came due. The Internal Revenue Service presented him with a bill for $111,008.60 in back taxes, an amount that grew to $140,795.96 by 13 December 1956, when the matter was settled in federal court by default judgment. New York State presented additional bills. Hammett never saved, except by buying war bonds, and these were liquidated and exhausted after the war. The interruption of his income had immediate effects.

Hellman, also beset with tax problems, sold Hardscrabble Farm, a terrible blow to Hammett. Although the farm was legally hers, Hammett had shared its expenses and it had been his refuge. When he could no longer afford to keep an apartment in the city, his friends came to his aid. Samuel and Helen Rosen, a socially active leftist physician and his wife, offered Hammett free use of a four-room cottage on their estate in Katonah, New York. Hammett insisted on paying $50 per month rent. He moved there in fall 1952 and stayed until his last illness, eight years later.

Senator Joseph McCarthy was at the peak of his demagoguery in the early years of the 1950s. Rather like the gossip columnists who had milked Hammett's name since *The Maltese Falcon* was published, McCarthy seized the opportunity to make a headline by questioning yet another celebrity. He subpoenaed Hammett to testify before his Senate committee on Government Operations on 26 March 1953 as part of an inquiry into the use of federal funds to purchase books by known communists for State Department

# DASHIELL HAMMETT JAILED IN CONTEMPT

## Mystery Writer Gets Six Months on Refusal to Tell Where Communists Get Bail Money

NEW YORK, July 9 (AP)—Mystery Writer Dashiell Hammett drew a six-month prison term today for refusing to tell where the Communist Party gets all its bail money.

A fellow bigwig in the Civil Rights Congress, W. Alphaeus Hunton, got a similar sentence.

U.S. Judge Sylvester J. Ryan sentenced both men for contempt, holding that their stubborn silence may aid the escape of four fugitive Communist leaders.

### Linked to Red Fronts

Hammett in the past has been linked in testimony before a Senate subcommittee with 40 to 50 so-called Communist-front groups.

The sentences were the heaviest handed out by Judge Ryan since he demanded that Civil Rights officials reveal where they got the money to post $80,000 bail for the runaway Red leaders.

Last Friday Judge Ryan sent Millionaire Leftist Frederick Vanderbilt Field to prison for 90 days on the same charge.

Field spent the week end in jail but finally got out today on $10,000 bond. He is appealing a 90-day contempt sentence from Judge Ryan.

### Large Bail Fund

The four fugitive Communists failed to show up for sentencing last week. A nationwide hunt is on for them. Their $80,000 bail—posted by the Civil Rights Congress—was ordered forfeited.

Judge Ryan insists the government might catch the four fugitives quicker if it knew who provided the Civil Rights Congress with the bail money.

The congress has a huge bail fund which it says comes from many contributors. The congress put up a total of $260,000 when all 11 Communist leaders first were released.

Hammett is chairman of the congress' bail fund.

*1951 clipping. Hammett's bail was refused when his secretary attempted to post $10,000 in cash and would not tell authorities where she got the money. He was sent to the Federal Correctional Institute, near Ashland, Kentucky, where he was incarcerated until 9 December 1951 (courtesy of Josephine Hammett).*

libraries abroad. Hammett surprised the senator and spectators alike by acknowledging that McCarthy's position was tenable given his goal. When asked whether he would favor the adoption of communism in the United States, Hammett answered no; it would be impractical if most people did not want it. When McCarthy asked Hammett whether he would buy books by communist authors to be distributed throughout the world if he were in charge of fighting communism, Hammett answered: "If I were fighting communism I don't think I would do it by giving people any books at all."

Hammett still felt the urge to write, and he struggled to shape his novelistic ideas. His theory of writing included the basic concept that each word had to matter. He struggled with every paragraph he wrote, and when he revised what he had written he edited most of it away. His last attempt at a novel is a 21,500-word fragment called "Tulip." The title character is an ex-soldier who had been stationed in the Aleutians during World War II with Pop, who is transparently Hammett himself. After the war, Tulip visits Pop, who is trying to write a novel, and they talk, often about literature. Pop says "if you're careful enough in not committing yourself you can persuade different readers to see all sorts of different meanings in what you have written, since in the end almost anything can be symbolic of anything else, and I've read a lot of stuff of that sort and liked it, but it's not my way of writing and there's no use pretending it is." A writer writes, Pop says, for "fame, fortune, and personal satisfaction. . . . That is and should be your goal. Anything less is kind of piddling."

Hammett's working draft for "Tulip" has not been located. Lillian Hellman had a fair copy typed, which served as setting copy for her collection of Hammett's stories published after his death, *The Big Knockover* (1966). The fragment ends, she says, with the words "If you are tired you ought to rest, I think, and not try to fool yourself and your customers with colored bubbles." By all evidence, with that thought Hammett ended his writing career in the summer of 1953.

The spirit of the McCarthy era lasted for the rest of the decade, though its figurehead self-destructed a year later. In 1955 Hammett was subpoenaed to testify before the New York State Joint Legislative Committee investigating philanthropic organizations. But by that time the threat of the communist hunters was blunted, and testifying was simply an annoyance to Hammett.

He was now very ill. Although he was only sixty-one in 1955, he had the appearance of a man much older. In August 1955 he suffered a heart attack,

*Hammett with his daughter Josephine and his grandchildren, Ann, Evan, and Julie in front*
*(courtesy of Josephine Hammett)*

and as he recovered, he mentioned with increasing frequency a pain he attributed to rheumatism in his shoulder. Hellman was less of a presence in his life after he got out of jail; she had other interests. He relied increasingly on Josephine and her growing family for gratification, but also withdrew more and more, preferring a quiet, solitary evening at home to anyone's company. After his heart attack, he no longer talked about finishing his novel.

In the summer of 1958 it was apparent that Hammett was unable to live alone, though he resisted pressure to move back in with Hellman. With collaboration from the Rosens, who said they needed the guest cottage Hammett was staying in for their daughter, Hellman arranged to have him move into her New York apartment. They spent summers in Martha's Vineyard, where she had a home. He grew steadily weaker, and after lung cancer was diagnosed late in 1960, the end came swiftly.

## Coda

Hammett died on 10 January 1961 in Lenox Hill Hospital. He was sixty-six. The cause of death was lung cancer complicated by emphysema and pneumonia, in addition to disease of the heart, liver, kidneys, spleen, and prostate gland. There was a memorial service at Frank E. Campbell's Funeral Home on Madison Avenue. Lillian Hellman delivered the eulogy.

Hammett's only income in the last years had been his veteran's pension of $131.10 per month. He died broke, with liens against his estate of more than $220,000, mostly for back taxes. His primary assets were his short stories and five novels, all written between 1922 and 1934—and a portion of at least one of the novels he had been promising since 1934.

As executor of the will, Lillian Hellman settled his income-tax debt and gained control of his literary estate. The blacklist was over by then, and she revived his literary reputation, arranging republication of his novels and editing *The Big Knockover,* a collection of his short stories which included "Tulip," a 21,500-word fragment of the last novel he attempted.

It is tempting for sympathetic observers to draw a melodramatic picture of Hammett's final decade, but to do so does him an immense disservice. He was not a man who tolerated pity, especially pity directed toward him. Following Benjamin Disraeli's dictum, he never explained and never complained. In that dark political age of the 1950s, Hammett avoided the acrimony and hatred and self-righteous indignity that consumed many of his colleagues and close friends. He was too proud, too self-sufficient to seek either approval or vindication from others. He believed in self-affirmation, and he held on to that basic principle to the moment of his death.

**1931**

*Clipping Hammett sent to his wife of a newspaper advertisement for the earliest movie adaptation of* The Maltese Falcon *released on 13 June 1931 (courtesy of Josephine Hammett)*

**THREE MOVIES**

**1936**

*Clipping of a movie ad, circa August 1936 (courtesy of Josephine Hammett)*

In the decade following their purchase of performance rights to The Maltese Falcon in 1930, Warner Bros. made three movies from the novel. The 1931 movie, directed by Roy Del Ruth, with a script by Brown Holmes and William Rees; the 1936 remake under the title Satan Met a Lady, directed by William Dieterle from another script by Brown Holmes; and finally the classic 1941 movie directed and written by John Huston. The first two movies take great liberties with the material from the novel. Huston's version adheres closely to the text. Hammett had no direct role in any of the movies. His reaction to the first two was negative. In 1941 he wrote his wife: "They made a pretty good picture of it this time, for a change"; and in 1953 he wrote his daughter Josephine: "Last week they ran the Humphrey Bogart version of The Maltese Falcon at the school and I sat through it again since I had promised to talk a little while afterwards. I liked it this time and wondered why I found it a little boring last time till I remembered that I'd seen it then at the Warner Bros.' studio in Burbank after looking at the two previous versions—both horrible jobs—during a lawsuit and while Maggie [Kober] was dying over at Cedars of Lebanon hospital, so I guess I would have found practically anything tiresome to sit through."

**1941**
*Poster for* The Maltese Falcon *(Christie's Auction Catalogue, lot 619 of 15 December 1996 sale). During the movie Bogart does not fire a gun.*

*Newspaper advertisement, 1941*

---

**MAKING THE FIRST MOVIE**

Dashiell Hammett's mystery novel, "The Maltese Falcon," was completed in film form last week at the Warner studios. It will be released under the title of "Woman of the World." Bebe Daniels and Ricardo Cortez have the principal rôles, with Dudley Digges, Una Merkel, Robert Elliott and Thelma Todd in the supporting cast.

*Clipping from the Hammett family collection, New York Times, 3 March 1931 (courtesy of Josephine Hammett)*

FORM 5 60M 3-31 SF41A

AND

FIRST NATIONAL PRODUCTIONS CORPORATION
BURBANK, CALIFORNIA

KOENIG INTER-OFFICE COMMUNICATION

VOIGHT

TO MR. ALL DEPARTMENT HEADS      DATE 4-2-31

McCORD

FROM MR. ZANUCK   VANCE      SUBJECT

The title of "WOMAN OF THE WORLD" has been definitely changed to- - -

"MALTESE FALCON"

On the main title, behind the lettering, we want the reproduction of the cover of the book "MALTESE FALCON". This cover has the image of the BLACK BIRD thereon, and Mr. Vance will make special note of this.

DARRYL ZANUCK

VERBAL MESSAGES CAUSE MISUNDERSTANDINGS AND DELAYS
(PLEASE PUT THEM IN WRITING)

*Memo from production supervisor Darryl F. Zanuck regarding the title for the 1931 movie adapted from Hammett's novel (courtesy of Warner Bros. Archive, University of Southern California)*

297. INT. AT CELL. CLOSE UP THRU BARS.

The Girl looking thru the bars after Spade. There is a tear in her eyes. For a long moment she looks after the only man she had ever seen that she couldn't beat. Then, slowly, she pulls herself together.

298 INT. AT CELL. CLOSE SHOT THRU BARS.

The Girl turns away from the bars. She sits on her bed and lights a cigarette. She crosses her legs. She blows a large cloud of smoke into the air.

FADE OUT.

THE END.

*Manuscript of revised ending for the 1931* Maltese Falcon *(courtesy of Warner Bros. Archive, University of Southern California)*

Note.----

I feel that not enough conflict, or suspicion on the part of
Archer, has been built up to warrant the belief in the minds
of any audience that Spade may have killed his pardner. as the
story continues after his death, --- if we can suggest that
point more strongly pxx that Archers wife is madly infatuated
with Spade and some kind of an affair has possibly been going on
behind his back, --- and possibly through a telephone conversation
that takes place in the office, which is accidently over heard
by Archer, --- I suggest the following manner to strengthen this
point, and really make us believe that over the wife angle we
might assume that Spade and Archer had words ~~over the wife~~ which
resulted in Spade shooting him that night in the alley.

While Spade in in the ~~midst~~ middle of conversation with Miss
Wonderly, in his private office which is shut off from the outer
office -- we cut directly to ~~the~~ Effie at her desk also in the
outer office, the phone rings, she picks up reciever. Saying Hello!

We cut to the other end of the wire and actually show Archers wife
in a very sexy pose in bed at her apt. she speaks.

        "Oh hello Effie, -- is Mr Spade
        there?"
                EFFIE.
        Yes - !
                IVA.
        Let me talk to him - tell him
        it's important.
              Miss.
                EFFIE.
        Hold the line -I'll switch the
        call to his office. (she puts
        reciever down and goes to Spades
        office, and tells him that Mrs
        Archer wants to talk to him, Spade excuses
        him self before Miss Wonderly and says Hello )

Cut back to outer office just as Effie is returning to her desk ,
the hall door opens and in comes Archer, x they exchange Hello's
and absently ~~mixxed~~ minded like and thing nothing in particular
about it she smiles and says.

        "Oh, Mr Archer- your wife just phoned
        - she's on the wire now - talking to
        Mr Spade"
Archer takes this - Effie thinking nothing picks up her letters
and etc and exits from the office - Archer watches her - glances
towrds Spades office - quickly picks up the phone and listens in
on conversation. (note the tone of conversation between Spade
and Archer's wife should be of rather an intimate nature, she
telling him she can't go on the way things are between them Spade
not saying much only trying to quiet her, saying have patience
things will work out - or don't leave him it'll cause ~~andxxxgiyx~~
trouble, this can worked out with few lines of dialogue -- the
conversation ends Spade hangs up - Archer quickly puts the reciever
down in the outerv office - shows plainly his reactions to the
situation - he looks at Spades office door, studies it a second
dangerous smile plays around his mouth he opens door enters.

*Note from director Roy Del Ruth requesting script revisions to the 1931* Maltese Falcon
*(courtesy of Warner Bros. Archive, University of Southern California)*

and continue on as is on page 5- Archer upon entering the office
comes face to face with Miss Wonderly who is faceing the door -
Spade swings around in his chair - a little suprised smiles
and says "come in Archer" - Archer is forced to pretend like
nothing has happened and the scene goes on with Miss Wonderly
telling her story To Archer, and the agreement between the ▆▆▆
three thats follows - ---- the sitaution possible could be built
with more tension  after the Girl leaves - Spade may sense a
coolness on Archers part - or possibly he may say "Oh - by the
way your wife called - wanted yto talk to you - seemed disappointed
when youb were'nt here - '

This added business I feel helps the whole thing very much - we
have now positively established  a mood between the two men -
Archer knows that there is somthing between Spade and his wife
this being so well planted in the minds of an audience that they
will surely believe  Spade could have killed him , --- and feeling
him guilty helps every other situation that followws follows in
the story.

     Del  Ruth.

230    SF3141

WARNER BROS. PICTURES, INC.
WEST COAST STUDIOS
**BUDGET**

Name___THE MALTESE FALCON_____Number___406.

Director___Roy Del Ruth_____Date___1-20-31.

| DESCRIPTION | BUDGET | |
|---|---|---|
| 1. Continuity and Treatment | 1 740.00 | |
| 2. Director | 21 500.00 | |
| 3. Assistant Director | 1 150.00 | |
| 4. Cameramen and Assistants | 4 752.00 | |
| 5. Cast | 68 475.00 | |
| 6. Extra Talent | 1 420.00 | |
| 7. Musicians | -0- | |
| 8. Property Labor | 3 000.00 | |
| 9. Construction of Sets | 15 000.00 | |
| 10. Operating Labor | 775.00 | |
| 11. Electrical Operating Labor | 3 475.00 | |
| 12. Striking | 750.00 | |
| 15. Property Rental and Expense | -0- | |
| 16. Electrical Rental and Expense | 450.00 | |
| 17. Location Expense | 1 865.00 | |
| 18. Trick Miniature, Glasses | 500.00 | |
| 19. Wardrobe Rental and Expense | 2 098.00 | |
| 20. Negative Film | 7 000.00 | 175 000 Ft. |
| 21. Positive Film | 2 225.00 | 150 000 Ft. |
| 22. Developing and Printing | 6 700.00 | |
| 23. Stills Materials | 500.00 | |
| 24. Stock Shots, etc. | -0- | |
| 25. Camera Rental and Expense | 75.00 | |
| 26. Meals | 500.00 | |
| 27. Transportation | 100.00 | |
| 28. Insurance and Taxes | 3 000.00 | |
| 29. Miscellaneous Expense | 850.00 | |
| 30. Vitaphone Expense | 4 000.00 | |
| 31. Retakes | -0- | |
| TOTAL DIRECT COST | 150 000.00 | |
| 35. General Studio Overhead | 60 000.00 | |
| 36. General Vitaphone Overhead | 20 000.00 | |
| TOTAL | 230 000.00 | |
| 40. Depreciation | 25 000.00 | |
| 41. Story Cost | 18 862.00 | |
| 45. Accumulation O.H. Prior to 10-127-30 | 13 600.00 | |
| GRAND TOTAL | 287 462.00 | |

Camera Work Started_____Finished_____

*Final budget for the 1931 version of* The Maltese Falcon *(courtesy of Warner Bros. Archive, University of Southern California)*

*Clippings Hammett sent to his wife at the time of the 1931 version of* The Maltese Falcon. *Una Merkel played Effie Perrine (courtesy of Josephine Hammett).*

**Mystery Grips Two Screens**

**Una Merkel**
Enacts an important supporting role in Dashiell Hammett's story, "The Maltese Falcon," which will be screened starting today at both Warner Brothers Hollywood and Downtown Theaters. Bebe Daniels and Ricardo Cortez are featured in the film.

Warner Bros. production and release. Directed by Roy Del Ruth. Based on mystery novel by Dashiell Hammett. Featuring Bebe Daniels and Ricardo Cortez. At the Winter Garden, New York, May 28, indef. on grind. Running time, 80 minutes.

Ruth Wonderly . . . . . . . . . . . . . . . Bebe Daniels
Sam Spade . . . . . . . . . . . . . . . . . Ricardo Cortez
Gutman . . . . . . . . . . . . . . . . . . . Dudley Digges
Effie . . . . . . . . . . . . . . . . . . . . . . .Una Merkel
Dundy . . . . . . . . . . . . . . . . . . . . Robert Elliott
Iva . . . . . . . . . . . . . . . . . . . . . . . Thelma Todd
Cairo . . . . . . . . . . . . . . . . . . . . . .Otto Matieson
District Attorney . . . . . . . . . . . . . . .Oscar Apfel
Archer . . . . . . . . . . . . . . . . . . . . . . Walter Long
Wilmer . . . . . . . . . . . . . . . . . . . . . Dwight Frye
Polhaus . . . . . . . . . . . . . . . J. Farrell McDonald
Captain Jacobi . . . . . . . . . . . . . . . . .A. Borgato

—*Variety*, 2 June 1931

*Mystery Galore.*

THE MALTESE FALCON, based on Dashiell Hammett's novel; directed by Roy Del Ruth; produced by Warner Brothers. At the Winter Garden.

| | |
|---|---|
| Ruth Wonderly | Bebe Daniels |
| Sam Spade | Ricardo Cortez |
| Guttman | Dudley Digges |
| Effie | Una Merkel |
| Dundy | Robert Elliott |
| Iva | Thelma Todd |
| Cairo | Otto Matieson |
| District Attorney | Oscar Apfel |
| Archer | Walter Long |
| Wilmer | Dwight Frye |
| Polhaus | J. Farrell MacDonald |
| Captain Jacobi | Agostino Borgato |

Into the spacious silences and shadows of the Winter Garden the Warners last night dropped a screen interpretation of Dashiell Hammet's "The Maltese Falcon" that brought back the reassuring hum which is the hallmark of contented audiences. An hour and ten minutes later, the inimitable Sam Spade having paid his last respects through prison bars to the inimitable Ruth Wonderly and brought the suave and almost gentle homicides of Mr. Hammett's story to a close, it appeared that Roy Del Ruth had done splendidly by an excellent mystery story and given wilted entertainment seekers a decent excuse for getting in out of the heat.

There also seemed no reasonable doubt that Mr. Del Ruth had really set a detective story moving on the screen without losing any of the suspenseful diversion it is reputed to have offered between book covers. The adventures of Sam Spade, private detective of the firm of Spade & Archer (that is, before Archer is waylaid in an alley and put out of the way), are here reported smoothly, fluidly, with cultivated humor and a keen intelligence, these qualities being manifest all the way along. Played with disarming ease and warmth by Ricardo Cortez, the character of Sam Spade is enormously unique and attractive.

The quest of the jewel-encrusted falcon, which is the excuse for at least four murders and various spectacular exits and entrances of any number of suave and lethal characters, does not reach its conclusion with the end of the film. The falcon tracked down by Sam Spade is proved a fake and most of the mysterious seekers exit at that point to continue the search elsewhere.

The refreshing surprise of the final fade-out is enough to commend "The Maltese Falcon" to cinema subscribers. There is a juicy hint that Sam Spade loves Ruth Wonderly, deadly creature that she is. He has ferreted out her connection with the murder of his partner. But there is the suspicion that Hollywood will somehow bring them together in holy union. Then Sam Spade turns over the woman to the police and the immanent gallows. A ruthless and selfish man, yet withal a man of light and whimsical humors, he leaves the looker-on with the feeling that he has spread his complex character out on the table for all to see and yet has shown nothing.

Bebe Daniels performs exceptionally well under Mr. Del Ruth's knowing hand, and there is no flaw in the miming of such players as Dudley Digges, Una Merkel, Robert Elliott, Otto Matieson and the others. But it is Mr. Cortez's film—and Mr. Del Ruth's. And probably Mr. Hammett's.

A. D. S.

*Clipping from* The New York Times, *29 May 1931*
*(courtesy of Josephine Hammett)*

# Reviews of the First *Maltese Falcon* Movie

### Review of *The Maltese Falcon*
*Variety,* 2 June 1931

Any type of audience will enjoy this picture. It can be booked with as much assurance by the deluxer at the 15¢ neighborhooder.

Bringing the "Maltese Falcon" to the screen as Warners have done was no easy job. Comedy, mystery, drama, burlesque, all the ingredients of the story pantry, rarely materialize in a box office pie. But director Roy Del Ruth skirted the omnipresent pancake possibilities by a definite margin. He let things take their course and with a naturally nonchalant, although extremely odd private detective in Ricardo Cortez, takes his audience out of the screen story rut for a series of surprise incidents and a totally different finis.

Although four men are murdered and two corpses revealed to the audience, the story treatment and the Cortez smile are such that a quick thrill sense is permitted, a laugh, and then, through the first 75% of the footage, additional interest to well sustained curiosity.

"Falcon" is essentially of that mystery weave which keeps the fans always concentrated. It can't be called naughty, even though Bebe Daniels, revealed in the last reel as an adventuress, as Ruth Wonderly spends the second night in the elaborate apartment of this unusual private detective.

The mystery element is so flung about that not until the last reel or so does the most studious fan follower know who did any of the killings.

Meantime a number of clever gags in disarming people, then apologizing; taking money and then having it taken from him; making love one minute and turning the girl over to the police the next—until, a few of these things happen through Sam Spade.

This bird, the Falcon, in the long run turns out to be just a lump of lead. The real crooks are handed over to the police after the final killing, that of Guttman, an excellent character role by Dudley Digges. Instead of jewels it's jail and reward for the police with special mention for the private detective, although the impression is general when he is in his office, well into the start of the picture is that the gentleman is a satyrist.
*Waly.*

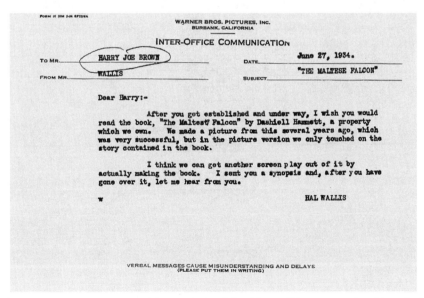

## Film Personalities
### By MARGUERITE TAZELAAR
### A Private Detective Does His Stuff in Hollywood

"I LIKED Hollywood. I went out for four months and stayed almost two years, and I'd go back again, for a time, if I had the chance."

Dashiell Hammett was speaking in a slow drawl, a glint of amusement in his eye, yet with a kind of shy, lazy seriousness, too. A tall, thin man with a pale, sensitive face and quiet voice, he is the last person in the world you would think of as a former Pinkerton detective or the creator of those sinister underworld types, so curiously alive, who peopled "The Glass Key" and "The Maltese Falcon."

The former mystery story is now in the hands of a picture company, pending production, and the latter was filmed last season. The criticism Hammett made of its screening was that he thought the producers had stuck too closely to his book. "You need to simplify a story as much as possible when you're going to make a picture of it," he said. "If you don't you'll have too many lines and so lose your full effect. No, I didn't work on the thing at all. I was doing originals most of the time. I believe it's better to have somebody else than the author do adaptations, because the story isn't so rigid in the mind of the man who hasn't written it."

For eight years Mr. Hammett was a Pinkerton detective. . . . "The first three or four years were fun. Then it got tedious. . . . For excitement the Anaconda strike, back in 1920–'21, tops the list. That was when they finally broke the I. W. W. The funniest case I ever worked on was the Arbuckle affair in San Francisco. In trying to convict him everybody framed everybody else."

Hammett is working on a book now and some short stories. His latest complete novel, "The Thin Man," will be published this winter. In his short pieces, he says, he has handled other than the mystery plots, and the novel he is working on now is not a mystery story. He says virtually every character he has written about he has known in person.

Detective stories can be done much better in books than on the screen, Mr. Hammett believes. The difficulty in filming them comes in handling the clews, for if you plant them so that the audience doesn't notice they have forgotten them by the time the big surprise unfolds, and if you point them up in the beginning, they catch on right away.

*Clipping of an interview article Hammett sent to his wife,* New York Herald Tribune, *12 November 1933 (courtesy of Josephine Hammett)*

FORM 16 10M 3-34 SF3336A

**WARNER BROS. PICTURES, INC.**
BURBANK, CALIFORNIA

## INTER-OFFICE COMMUNICATION

TO MR. ___HARRY JOE BROWN___   DATE___June 27, 1934.___

FROM MR. ___WALLIS___   SUBJECT___"THE MALTESE FALCON"___

Dear Harry:-

    After you get established and under way, I wish you would read the book, "The Maltese Falcon" by Dashiell Hammett, a property which we own. We made a picture from this several years ago, which was very successful, but in the picture version we only touched on the story contained in the book.

    I think we can get another screen play out of it by actually making the book. I sent you a synopsis and, after you have gone over it, let me hear from you.

                                  HAL WALLIS

VERBAL MESSAGES CAUSE MISUNDERSTANDING AND DELAYS
(PLEASE PUT THEM IN WRITING)

*Memo from Hal Wallis, executive producer of the 1936 version of* The Maltese Falcon, *to a member of the production team recommending a remake (courtesy of Warner Bros. Archive, University of Southern California)*

# MAKING *SATAN MET A LADY*

FORM 11 3M 10-33 SP41

WARNER BROS. PICTURES, INC.
BURBANK, CALIFORNIA

## INTER-OFFICE COMMUNICATION

TO MR. Wallis                                    DATE May 27, 1935

FROM MR. Blanke                                  SUBJECT

Dear Hal:

A few days ago we suggested a certain title for "MONEY MEN", and MacEwen wrote me a note saying that you didn't like it, and that we should try to find another title for this picture.

Here are the following suggestions:

From Blanke:

    1 - March On Crime
    2 - Women Handled
    3 - DIRT ROAD TO FAME

From Brown Holmes:

    3 - The Opportunist

From MacEwen:

    4 - The Hard Way
    5 - Dirty Money

From Anthony:

    6 - The Rough Way
    7 - Fire Away
    8 - The Fall Guy
    9 - Nice People
    10 - Special Investigator
    11 - Trouble Maker
    12 - Stop At Nothing
    13 - Some Call It Murder
    14 - Get Out Of Town
    15 - Rough Stuff
    16 - Watch Your Money
    17 - Pay Up
    18 - Stand and Deliver
    19 - When Cheaters Meet
    20 - Protection
    21 - Protection Money
    22 - Treasure Trap
    23 - Comedy Of Murder
    24 - A Tough Spot
    25 - Forgotten Gem
    26 - Jewel Chase

D                                                BLANKE

VERBAL MESSAGES CAUSE MISUNDERSTANDINGS AND DELAYS
(PLEASE PUT THEM IN WRITING)

*Memo to Hal Wallis from executive producer Henry Blanke with title suggestions for the 1936 version of* The Maltese Falcon *(courtesy of Warner Bros. Archive, University of Southern California)*

*money man*

June 4, 1935.

Mr. Jack L. Warner,
Warner Bros. Studios,
Burbank, California.

Dear Mr. Warner:

We have read with great care the second revised temporary script dated June 3, of your proposed production "MONEY MAN" and are sending you this letter so that you may have our reaction to it.

Calling your attention to our letter of January 31st, we still feel that the characterization of SHANE needs to be considerably cleaned up. Most important of all in the first piece of business is the scene in which he secures money from MRS. ARDEN by using as a "racket" the suggested idea that thugs are after her to do her possible bodily injury and that she should pay for protection. This is definitely a criminal act and must be changed before the picture is entirely acceptable.

Going through the script in detail, we wish to call your attention to other matters to be cleaned up.

The idea that SHANE is being much sought after by all of the women in your story - "kissed on the lips" by ASTRID - has MURGATROYD on his lap while dictating in the office - takes out the night club dancer and has scenes with VALERIE - might suggest a too sensual reaction and are likely to be deleted by political censor boards, as well as being objectionable from the standpoint of the Production Code.

Care should be used that none of the scenes in which the police appear make them seem to be negligent in their duty or too dumb to handle any situation. This is particularly dangerous from the censor standpoint.

In more detail: Scene 2 - where the blonde in satin negligee puts her hand on the shoulder of the timid little man and the speech "I might give you -- for the whole works" as he looks her over, has a very definite vulgar connotation.

Scene 26: The reference to the "body-guard racket they're falling for plenty out in Hollywood" should be eliminated.

*Memo from Joseph Breen, chief of the Production Code Administration, an enforcement body of the Motion Pictures Producers and Distributors of America, listing objectionable scenes and dialogue in the movie released in 1936 as* Satan Met a Lady. *The PCA was formed in 1934 to defend the industry against charges of immorality. Movies produced by members of the MPPDA had to be approved by the PCA prior to release (courtesy of Warner Bros. Archive, University of Southern California).*

281

Mr. J. L. Warner       -Two-       June 4, 1935.

Scene 27: We suggest a change in SHANE'S speech:
"What I meant was: It reminded me you took her over from me."
Also, the reference in AMES' speech in the same scene where
he says, "--all that went on then -- ." Both of these speeches
rather point to a previous sexual relation between SHANE and
ASTRID.

Scene 32: Be careful with the action of AMES patting
the knee of the girl in the office.

Scene 36: "You play <u>wet</u> nurse." The underlined word
should be omitted.

Scene 50: SHANE'S speech, "There's no place I'd
rather see a police detective than in a graveyard." comes under
our previous police warning. Also, in that same scene, care
must be used in shooting the scene of the chorus girls descending the fire escape while SHANE, POLLOCK, and DUNHILL, at the
foot of the fire escape are looking up eyeing them admiringly.

Scene 55: The speeches of ASTRID and SHANE regarding the death of her husband and how soon they can go out together, require careful handling.

Scene 59: Censor boards will certainly eliminate
the word "nerts."

Scene 70: English censor boards will delete the
word "gigolo."

Scene 80: The "strange noise" which MURGATROYD lets
out in this scene should not be suggestive of the Bronx cheer.

Scene 113: The speech of KENNETH, where he is bragging about the people he has killed, especially the speech -
"If I give it to you -- you won't be the first!" - will certainly be deleted by most of the censor boards.

Scene 162: We suggest the elimination of MADAME
BARABBAS' speech - "From what we've seen and heard of you -
you won't need our help in handling the law" - indicating
that SHANE has been "guilty of fixing cases." In this scene
the reference to the police as "you chumps" comes under the
head of our police warning.

Scene 171: We suggest the deleting of the business where MADAME BARABBAS "reaches down into the valley
that bisects her ample bosom, and seems to be scratching."

Mr. J. L. Warner          -Two-          June 4, 1935.


        Scene 177:  Under the head of suggested sexual re-
action, we are sending a caution to you on the kissing business between SHANE and VALERIE.  This also applies to the
kissing business in Scene 179.

        With all good wishes, I am

                        Sincerely yours,


                        Joseph I. Breen.


    &

    7/FS

COPY

November 27, 1935.

Mr. J. L. Warner,
Warner Brothers,
Burbank, Calif.

Dear Mr. Warner:

We have received and read your script THE MAN WITH THE BLACK
HAT, formerly submitted to us under the title MONEY MAN. While the
basic story is one which can, we believe, be done satisfactorily
under the provisions of the Production Code, the present script
contains a great deal of questionable sex emphasis which, in our
opinion, is not essential to your story in any sense, and if included
in your final picture, would, we believe, make it not acceptable.

More specifically, we believe it will be necessary to delete
all the action in which your leading character, Shane, is shown hugging
and kissing the various women in the script, and also do some rewriting
in order to clear up the present suggestive relationship between himself
and Mrs. Ames. We call your attention below to the individual items
which we believe you should delete; but we would again like to recommend
that in the shooting of the picture, you exercise great care to remove
this objectionable sex suggestiveness entirely from the finished product. Otherwise, we believe the picture will not be acceptable under
the provisions of the Production Code.

Page 15: It will, we believe, be necessary to modify this
suggestive relationship between Shane and Mrs. Ames. As now written,
the whole relationship is one of loose sex. Specifically, we call your
attention to the lines:

"Don't think you can come back after three years and take over
her, too".

"It reminded me you took her over from me".

"Just to show you that you - and all that went on then between
you - is completely forgotten".

It will, of course, be quite acceptable to suggest that both
Shane and Ames had once been in love with Mrs. Ames; this relationship
should be made plain, and cleaned up of any suggestiveness.

Page 17: Omit this action of Mrs. Ames hugging Shane.

*Memo from Breen (courtesy of Warner Bros. Archive, University of Southern California)*

Mr. Warner - page 2                                             Nov. 27, 1935.

Page 18:  Omit the action of Ames patting the knee of the girl.

Page 25:  Modify the line "You might have been with Astrid Ames tonight" to something less suggestive.

Page 32:  Care will be needed with this scene of the chorus girls coming down the steps, and the mens reaction as they watch them.

Page 39:  Omit this action of Shane hugging Mrs. Murgatroyd, and also omit the action of Shane pulling Mrs. Murgatroyd down onto his lap and hugging her to him.

Page 55:  Omit the line "A lady had a feeling she lost something there the other night".   *TAKE OUT THIS LINE*

Page 62:  Omit the line "For that much ... they can wreck me".

Page 71:  Omit the action of Shane kissing Valerie.

Page 75:  Omit the line "But you're a lot of woman" and the action of Shane moving to kiss Valerie.

Page 96:  Omit the action of Shane kissing Valerie.

Page 97:  Omit the action of Mrs. Murgatroyd sitting in Shane's lap.

Page 98:  Omit the action of Mrs. Ames putting her arms around Shane's neck.

Page 116:  Modify the expression "You won't need our help in handling the law". We suggest using the expression "satisfying".→

Page 125:  Omit the expression "I've often wondered what he'd look like with his hat off".

Page 133:  Omit the action of Valerie kissing Shane.

Page 140:  Omit the action of Valerie kissing Shane.

With every good wish, I am

                                             Cordially yours,


                                             Joseph I. Breen

"Roof Top"

WARNER BROS. PICTURES, INC.
BURBANK, CALIFORNIA

## INTER-OFFICE COMMUNICATION

TO MR. OBRINGER      DATE December 5th, 1935

FROM MR. WALLIS      SUBJECT "THE MAN WITH THE BLACK HAT"

Dear Roy:-

    Reminding you to look up the "MALTESE FALCON" contract and let me know if there are any specific restrictions as to the way we must bill the author, DASHIELL HAMMETT.   As you know, our picture "THE MAN WITH THE BLACK HAT" is a free adaptation of "THE MALTESE FALCON".

WALTER MacEWEN

Mr. MacEwen:
Our only obligation is that we agree to give Dashiell Hammet authorship credit on the main title of any photoplay or photoplays based on "Maltese Falcon."

R. J. OBRINGER

VERBAL MESSAGES CAUSE MISUNDERSTANDING AND DELAYS
(PLEASE PUT THEM IN WRITING)

*Memo in which Warner Bros.' obligation to Hammett is stipulated (courtesy of Warner Bros. Archive, University of Southern California)*

WARNER BROS. PICTURES, INC.
BURBANK, CALIFORNIA

## INTER-OFFICE COMMUNICATION

TO MR. WARNER      DATE July 9th, 1936

FROM MR. MacEWEN      SUBJECT "SATAN MET A LADY"

    I believe there is no doubt now that the title "SATAN MET A LADY" will be used on the picture, and I should like to have your okay to give $25 to the office boy who created this title.

    His name is HOWARD CLAUSEN, and he earns $20 a week. I know that you will agree he ought to get the bonus for such a clever title, after we had literally tried for months to get a good one, with no success.

WALTER MacEWEN

WM
P

VERBAL MESSAGES CAUSE MISUNDERSTANDING AND DELAYS
(PLEASE PUT THEM IN WRITING)

*Memo requesting bonus for an office boy. Walter MacEwen was a member of the production team (courtesy of Warner Bros. Archive, University of Southern California).*

July 1, 1936.

| | |
|---|---|
| Warner Bros. Pictures, Inc. | 25% |
| and the Vitaphone Corp. | |
| present | |
| SATAN MET A LADY | 100% |
| with | |
| Bette Davis - Warren William | 85% |
| and | |
| Alison Skipworth | 75% |
| Arthur Treacher - Winifred Shaw - Marie Wilson - Porter Hall | 60% |
| Olin Howland | 40% |
| Directed by William Dieterle | 20% |
| A Warner Bros. | 40% |
| Productions Corporation | 5% |
| Picture | 25% |

### CAST

| | | | |
|---|---|---|---|
| Valerie Purvis | Bette Davis | Ted Shane | Warren William |
| Miss Murgatroyd | Marie Wilson | Madame Barabbas | Alison Skipworth |
| Anthony Travers | Arthur Treacher | Ames | Porter Hall |
| Astrid Ames | Winifred Shaw | Pollock | Charles Wilson |
| Dunhill | Olin Howland | Babe | Barbara Blane |
| Kenneth | Maynard Holmes | | |

### SYNOPSIS

William, in the role of Ted Shane, a satanic private detective, experiences considerable difficulty keeping his sometimes questionable professional activities segregated from his affairs d'amour, a failing that is constantly getting him into trouble with various individuals including his secretary, Murgatroyd, Astrid, the wife of his partner, Ames, with the police and as the story opens, with Valerie Purvis, a young woman who seeks his aid in locating a man named Farrow, who she says, is her missing sweetheart.

Suspecting Valerie of some trick, Shane decides to kill two birds with one stone by having Ames shadow her, thus keeping her under surveillance and at the same time removing an obstruction in the form of a husband that is blocking his affair with Astrid.

Ames and Farrow are murdered within a few minutes of each other and Shane finds himself being shadowed by a round-faced, innocent looking beret-capped young man named Kenneth. He also finds himself being constantly harrassed by detectives who want to know what he knows about the murders, and by a tall Englishman named Anthony Travers, who wants to know whether Shane has the trumpet and if he will sell it.

Assuring Travers he has no trumpet, Shane learns from the Englishman that such an article actually does exist and that it was last known to have been in possession of Valerie Purvis, who Travers suspected had given it to Shane for safekeeping. Suspecting everyone, Shane becomes conscious of a connection between the so-called trumpet and the murders. Shortly he is taken by Kenneth to the apartment of Madame Barabbas, who is interested in the trumpet and offers $100.00 for it.

Shane, all this time busily engaged in simultaneous love affairs with Astrid, Murgatroyd and Valerie, receives a mysterious message inviting him to meet Eduardo Espinosa on the S.S. duParry. He finds the ship in flames, but sees a man, a duffle bag over his shoulder climbing a ladder at the pier. He is shot and killed and Shane is knocked unconscious. Shane claims the bag and finds the ivory trumpet inside. He mails it to himself. Kenneth, who hates Shane, tells that he killed Farrow and Espinosa but denies knowledge of the Ames killing. At this moment the mailman arrives with the trumpet and Shane at the point of Kenneth's guns, is forced to open the package. Out pours a stream of sand! Shane grabs Kenneth's weapons and turns the group over to the police with the exception of Valerie. With Valerie, he boards a train, first sending a wire instructing the authorities of the city of their destination to meet him.

On the train, professing his love for her, Shane draws from Valerie the confession that she shot Ames with Farrow's revolver, hoping the crime would be laid at Farrow's door and thereby eliminate him from sharing in the anticipated fortune contained in the trumpet. She later expected to kill Espinosa, after he had delivered the horn, which he was bringing from Greece, where it had been discovered by Barabbas and stolen by Valerie and Travers, her agents. She confesses it was she who, fearful of Barabbas, asked Shane to meet the latin on the arrival of the S.S. duBarry. At the depot Shane nonchalantly turns Valerie over to the police and gratefully renounces womankind forever. As he returns to his train, however, a pair of feminine arms are thrown around his neck. It is Astrid Ames.

"Oh well!" he groans with resignation.

\#\#\#\#\#\#\#\#

*Studio synopsis for the 1936 movie version of* The Maltese Falcon *(courtesy of Warner Bros. Archive, University of Southern California)*

Warner Bros. production and release. Features Bette Davis, Warren William. Directed by William Dieterle. Based on Dashiell Hammett's "The Maltese Falcon"; adaptation, Brown Holmes; dialog director, Gene Lewis: editor, Warren Low: camera, Arthur Edeson. At Strand, N. Y., week July 22, '36. Running time, 74 mins.

| | |
|---|---|
| Valerie Purvis | Bette Davis |
| Ted Shane | Warren William |
| Madame Barabbas | Alison Skipworth |
| Anthony Travers | Arthur Treacher |
| Astrid Ames | Winifred Shaw |
| Miss Murgatroyd | Marie Wilson |
| Ames | Porter Hall |
| Dunhill | Olin Howland |
| Pollock | Charles Wilson |
| Kenneth | Maynard Holmes |
| Babe | Barbara Blane |

*—Variety,* 29 July 1936

"SATAN MET A LADY"
Starring William Warren and Bette Davis is current at Warner Brothers Hollywood and Downtown theaters. William has possession of a trumpet which is reputed to contain a fortune in jewels. Bette, a notorious crook—in the picture of course—tries to get the horn.

*Clippings of a promotional photo and a movie ad Hammett sent to his wife, circa August 1936 (courtesy of Josephine Hammett)*

# Reviews of *Satan Met a Lady*

**At the Strand**
*The New York Times*, 23 July 1936

SATAN MET A LADY, from a story by Dashiell Hammett: screen play by Brown Holmes; directed by William Dieterie; a Warner Brothers production.

. . . . . . . . . .

Without taking sides in a controversy of such titanic proportions, it is no more than gallantry to observe that if Bette Davis had not effectually espoused her own cause against the Warners recently by quitting her job, the Federal Government eventually would have had to step in and do something about her. After viewing "Satan Met a Lady," at the Strand, all thinking people must acknowledge that a "Bette Davis Reclamation Project" (BDRP) to prevent the waste of this gifted lady's talents would not be a too-drastic addition to our various programs for the conservation of natural resources.

A cynical farce of elaborate and sustained cheapness, it causes still other intelligent actors and actresses—including Warren William, Arthur Treacher and Alison Skipworth—to behave like numskulls, and deserves to be quoted as a classic of dullness, in future press notices, as often as "The Thin Man"—also based on a Dashiell Hammett theme—has been quoted as a classic of scintillating wit. As Mr. William's blonde and nit-wit secretary remarks, about midway of the action :"I've got a cousin who specializes in brain diseases. Maybe we'd better turn the case over to him." The suggestion is tempting but probably wouldn't work for the good reason that this particular case would defy the diagnostic technique of a Crile.

So disconnected and lunatic are the picture's incidents, so irrelevant and monstrous its people, that one lives through it in constant expectation of seeing a group of uniformed individuals appear suddenly from behind the furniture and take the entire cast into protective custody. There is no story, merely a farrago of nonsense representing a series of practical studio compromises with an unworkable script. It is the kind of mistake over which the considerate and discreet thing is to draw the veil of silence, even it if takes three paragraphs.

B. R. C.

\* \* \*

**Review of *Satan Met a Lady***
*Variety*, 29 July 1936

This is an inferior remake of 'The Maltese Falcon,' which Warner Bros. produced back in 1931. Many changes have been made, in story structure as well as title, but none is an improvement. Chances are an outright revision might have worked out better. Publicity doesn't mention the 'Falcon' antecedents.

Bette Davis is dropped to featured billing rank in this one, on an equal basis with Warren William, and both under the title. But as for importance in the story, Miss Davis runs No. 2 most of the way and in actual footage has much less to do than at least one other femme member of the cast.

The fact that Dashiell Hammett wrote this detective story, plus the knowledge that Hammett turned out 'The Thin Man' and thereby started a vogue, obviously greatly impressed those concerned with the remake. Where the detective of 'Maltese Falcon' and his activities were natural and amusing, he and his satiric crime detection are now forced and unnatural, due to the unsuccessful effort at capturing the lackadaisical spirit of the better known Hammett story.

Among items subjected to change were the names of the characters as well as a few of the characters themselves. Sam Spade, played by Ricardo Cortez in the original, is now Ted Shane as played by Warren William. The plaster bird, supposedly bejewelled, which was the object of the crooks' affections in the original, is now a ram's horn. Whereas the mystery was sustained up to the finish in the original, there's hardly any mystery in this version. This endeavors to replace mystery with comedy, but the comedy isn't strong enough to fill the bill.

William tries hard to be gay as the eccentric private cop and his performance is all that keeps the picture moving in many lagging moments. Marie Wilson has a tendency to muff her best chances through overstressing, although she shows enough to indicate she can do a good comedy job with the right handling. Alison Skipworth and Arthur Treacher do the best they can with exaggerated crook parts.

Where 'Satan Met a Lady' comes in as the title isn't even hinted at. That's a deeper mystery than Hammett has ever concocted.

*Bige.*

# Making Huston's *Maltese Falcon*

DATE: May 19, 1941

TITLE: "MALTESE FALCON"

| SAM SPADE (Private Detective) | BRIBID O'SHAUG-Nessy Known as - (Miss Wonderly) | EFFIE PERINE (Sam's secretary) | IVA ARCHER (Mile's widow) | JOEL CAIRO (Greek) |
|---|---|---|---|---|
| George Raft ✗ | Ol. DeHavilland | Nancy Coleman | Claire Trevor | Peter Lorre |
| Humphrey Bogart | Loretta Young | Brenda Marshall | Gail Patrick | Martin Kosle |
| Ed. G. Robinson | Rita Hayworth | Jane Wyman | Lee Patrick ✗ | Sam Jaffe |
| Rich. Whorf | Ger. Fitzgerald | Julie Bishop | Eve Arden | Curt Bois |
| Franchot Tone | Mary Astor ✗ | Faye Emerson ✗ | | Eliz Kazan |
| Fred MacMurray | Paul. Goddard | Eliz. Fraser | Wendy Barrie | Porter Hall |
| Fred. March | Brenda Marshall | Mildred Coles | Leona Maricle | Gene Lockhar |
| Henry Fonda | Janet Gaynor | | Helen Vinson | Oscar Homoli |
| Brian Donlevy | Joan Bennett | Marg. Lindsey | Gladys George | Conrad Veid |
| Warner Baxter | Betty Field | Florence Rice | Glenda Farrell | Marc. Lawrenc |
| Paul Muni | Ingrid Bergman | Jane Wyatt | Binnie Barnes | J.Car. Naish |
| Robt. Montgomery | Frances Dee | Gale Page | Una Munsen | Geo. Tobias |
| Melvyn Douglas | Ruth Hussey | Gloria Holden | Muriel Hutchinson | Lee Cobb |
| Preston Foster | Lorraine Day | | Una Merkel | Akim Tamiro |
| Lloyd Nolan | Annabella | | Joyce Compton | Ed. Cianell |
| Tony Quinn | Illona Massey | | Barb. Pepper | J.Ed. Bromber |
| | Dorothy Lamour | | Joan Woodbury | Jos. Calleia |
| | | | | Rohman Bohne |
| | | | | Ab. Biberman |
| | | | | Noel Madiso |
| | | | | Don Costell |
| | | | | Vlad Sokolo |
| | | | | Licnel Royc |
| | | | | Turhan Bey |

| TOM POLHAUS (Detective) | DUNDY (Plice Lieut.) | THE BOY (Wilmer Cook) | KASPER GUTMAN (Fat Man) | MILES ARCH (Sam's Part Murdered) |
|---|---|---|---|---|
| Charles Wilson ✗ | Wm. Harrigan | Louis Adlon | Sid. Greenstreet | Don Costell |
| Don. McBride | Willard Robertson | Type. | Laird Cregar | Chas. Wilson |
| Ward Bond ✗ | Emory Parnell | Martin Koslick | Edw. Arnold | Joe. Sawyer |
| Cliff Clark | Ed. Dearing | Eliz Kazan | Geo. Barbier | Doug. Fowle |
| Barton MacLane | James Flavin | Elisha Cook Jr. | Lee Cobb | Harold Hube |
| Paul Kelly | Wade Boteler | Peter Lorre | Gene Lockhart | Bernard Nede |
| Alan Hale ✗ | Tommy Jackson | Alan Baxter | Gene Pallette | Ed. Pawley |
| Wm. Frawley | Add. Richards | Art. Kennedy | Akim Tamiroff | Ralph Harold |
| Robt. Homans | Joe Grehan | Nick Conte | J.Ed. Bromberg | Paul Guilfo |
| Wm. Gargan | Howard da Silva | Tom Neal | Sid Toler | Horace McMa |
| Ed. Chandler | Lee Phelps | Marvin Stephens | S.Z. Sakall | Ben Weldon ✗ |
| Doug. Fowley | Wm. Davidson | Billy Halop | Sig. Rumann | Barton MacL |
| | John Hamilton | Jas. McCallion | Guy Kibbee | LUKE (House Dect. |
| | Robt. Barrat | Frankie Darro | Alan Hale | Chas. Wilson |
| | Chas. Bickford | Bob Steele | Billy Gilbert | Jas. Burke |
| | | Joe Downing | Wm.B. Davison | Cy Kendall |
| | | | Ernest Cossart | Paul Hurst |
| | | | Albert Dekker | Wm. Davison |
| | | | Brod Crawford | Joe Sawyer |
| | | | | Cliff Clark |
| | | | | Bart. MacLa |

*List of possible cast choices for the 1941 version of* The Maltese Falcon *(courtesy of Warner Bros. Archive, University of Southern California)*

May 27, 1941

Mr. Jack L. Warner
Warner Bros. Pictures, Inc.
Burbank, California

Dear Mr. Warner:

We have read the final script, dated May 24, 1941, for your proposed production titled THE MALTESE FALCON, and regret to advise that while the basic story is acceptable, a picture based upon this script could not be approved under the provisions of the Code because of several important objectionable details, namely:

(1) it is indicated that Spade and Brigid have had an illicit sex affair and that the relationship between Spade and Iva has been illicit.

(2) Cairo seems to be characterized as a pansy.

(3) There is a great deal of unnecessary drinking.

It will be necessary to overcome these objections before the finished picture could be approved.

Going through the script in detail, we call your attention to the following points:

Page 13: Spade's line, "Damn her!" is unacceptable.

Page 14: In accordance with the Associations's policy re drinking, some other business besides drinking in Spade's apartment must be substituted on Pages 14 sqq. 19, 50 sqq. and 65 sqq.

*Memo from Breen listing objectionable scenes and dialogue in the 1941 version of* The Maltese Falcon
*(courtesy of Warner Bros. Archive, University of Southern California)*

Mr. Warner                              May 27, 1941

Page Two

Page 21:  Any flavor that Spade and
Iva have been illicitly intimate must be eliminated from this scene if it is to be approved
in the finished picture.  Accordingly, it is
essential that there be no physical contact
between Iva and Spade, other than that of decent
sympathy.  In this connection, see Page 80, where
the physical contact is unacceptable.  The entire
conversation between Iva and Spade will have to
be rewritten to get away from this flavor.

Page 35:  We cannot approve the characterization of Cairo as a pansy, as indicated by
the lavender perfume, high-pitched voice, and
other accouterments.  In this connection, we
refer you to Scenes 21, and 115, where Cairo
should not appear effeminate while rubbing the
boy's temple.

Page 54:  The action of Cairo slapping
Brigid should be indicated out of frame.  Otherwise, it will be deleted by some political censor boards.

Page 58:  Gruesomeness must be avoided
in this shot where Cairo is shown bleeding.

Page 67:  This fade-out of Spade and
Brigid is unacceptable because of the definite
indication of an illicit sex affair.  There must
be no indication that Brigid and Spade are spending the night together in Spade's apartment.
Otherwise it cannot be approved in the finished
picture.  In this connection, see Page 75.

Page 70:  The Boy's line, "--you!" and
his soundless repetition of the same words will
be unacceptable if curse words.

Page 81:  While the drinking in these
scenes is necessary as a story point, in order
to prepare for later scenes where Spade is drugged, we must insist that the actual drinking be
kept to the absolute minimum necessary to the
development of the plot.  It seems that audiences

Mr. Warner                          May 27, 1941
                    Page Three


are offended not so much by the presence of liquor
as by the actual drinking.

        Page 84:  Gutman's use of the inter-
jection, "by Gad", here and on Pages 92, 117, 121, 125,
126, and 128, seems to be offensive if only by the
number of times he uses it.  We suggest you use some
other interjection at times.

        There should be no gruesomeness in
Scenes 71, 81, 88 and 89.

        Pages 118 and 119:  Spade's speech
about the District Attorneys should be rewritten
to get away from characterizing most District
Attorneys as men who will do anything to further
their careers.  This is important.

        Page 141:  Brigid's line to Spade,
"Not after what we've been to each other ", is
unacceptable as pointing up the previous sex
affair.

        Page 143:  There must be nothing sex
suggestive in Spade's eyeing of Brigid.

        Page 144:  The underlined words in
Spade's speech are unacceptable, "I won't because all of me wants to -- wants to say to
hell with consequences and do it.."  Likewise,
in this conversation between Spade and Brigid,
there should be no flavor of a previous sex affair
underlying the conversation.

        Page 147:  The action of Spade putting
his hand on Effie's hips must not be offensive.

        You understand, of course, that our
final judgment will be based upon the finished
picture.


                        Cordially yours,



                        Joseph I. Breen

12:HF


                                    C O P Y

```
                    ~BUDGET~
              369  "THE MALTESE FALCON"                June 3, 1941.


     1a Continuity & Treatment:
         John Huston                            12 500
         Secretary                                 426
                                                                    12 926


     2 Director:
         John Huston                                                20 417


     2a Supervisor:
         Henry Blanke                                               25 888


     3 Assistant Director:
         to W/E May 24                              267
         Jack Sullivan   8 wks at 200             1 600
         Asst           6½ wks at  75               488
         Scriptclerk     7 wks at  70               490
         Al Alleborn     4 wks at 250             1 000
                                                                     3 845


     4 Cameramen & Assistants:
         Arthur Edeson  6½ wks at 500            3 250
         2nd           6 1/3 wks at 120            760
         Asst          6 1/3 wks at  66            418
         Stillman      6 1/3 wks at 102            646
         Tests, O.T. etc                           600
                                                                     5 674


     5 Star's Salary:
         Spade                                                      16 500

     5A Cast Salary:

         5b Contract Talent-
             Effie - Lee Patric                  2 667
             Polhaus - Alan Hale                 11 000
                                                            13 667

         5c Outside Talent-
             Brigid - Mary Astor  4 1/3 wks
                              @ 2 500            10 833
             Dundy - Barton MacLane 2 1/3 wks
                              @ 1 250             2 917
             Iva - part                           5 000
             Cairo - Peter Lorre                 10 000
             Wilmer - part 3 wks @ 1 000          3 000
             Gutman - S. Greenstreet 4 wks
                      (guar.) @ 1 000             4 000
             Archer - part 1½ wks at 750          1 125
                                              ─────────
                                                 36 875     50 542
```

*Final budget for the 1941* Maltese Falcon *(courtesy of Warner Bros. Archive,
University of Southern California)*

-BUDGET-
369 "THE MALTESE FALCON"                                    June 3, 1941.

6 TALENT:

   6a Extras                                                   6 231
   6b Bits (from casting)                1 018
      Additional bits-
      (6)  Capt Jacoby 1 day @150      150
      (7)  Mr.Freid  1 day @ 100      100
     (23) Luke      1 day @ 150      150
                            1 418
                                      7 649

7 MUSICIANS:

   7a Song Writers & Song Releases,etc    2 800
   7b Musicians                           8 000
                                     10 800

8 PROPERTY LABOR:

   8a Prop. Labor                           465
   8b Set Dressers                        1 375
   8d Prop. Oper. Labor                   3 025
                                     4 865

9 CONSTRUCTION OF SETS:

   9a Technical Cost                                         25 000

10 STANDBY LABOR:                                            6 950

11 ELECTRICIANS:

   11a Rigging                             2 000
   11b Operating                          8 975
   11c Striking                           1 075
                                     12 050

12 STRIKING:                                                 5 000

12A MAKEUP EXPENSE:

   12b Makeup Salaries                    1 381
   12c Hairdresser Salaries                 700
   12d Wigs Purchased and Rented             50
                                     2 131

13 ART DEPT SALARIES:                                        5 366

14 CUTTERS' SALARIES:                                        2 880

15 PROPERTY RENTAL AND EXPENSE:

   15a Outside Rentals                      250
   15b Outside Purchases                    305
   15d Studio Charges                       495
                                     1 050

16 ELECTRICAL RENTAL AND EXPENSE:

   16b Studio Charges                                          750

17 LOCATION EXPENSE:                                         1 758

-BUDGET-

369 "THE MALTESE FALCON"

June 3, 1941.

| 18 TRICK, MINIATURE, ETC: | | |
|---|---|---|
| 18a Set Construction | 1 375 | |
| 18b Cameramen | 935 | |
| 18c Operating Labor | 550 | |
| 18d Electricians | 700 | |
| | | 3 560 |
| 19 WARDROBE EXPENSE: | | |
| 19a Outside Rentals | 100 | |
| 19b Outside Purchases | 400 | |
| 19c Studio Charges | 1 562 | |
| 19d Wardrobe Labor | 4 695 | |
| | | 6 757 |
| 20 NEGATIVE FILM: | | 6 000 |
| 22 DEVELOPING AND PRINTING: | | 8 500 |
| 23 TECHNICOLOR: | | -o- |
| 25 CAMERA RENTAL AND EXPENSE: | | 200 |
| 26 MEALS: | | 300 |
| 27 AUTO RENTAL EXPENSE AND TRAVEL: | | 4 200 |
| 28 INSURANCE: | | 1 400 |
| 29 MISC'L EXPENSE: | | 2 000 |
| 30 SOUND EXPENSE: | | 1 750 |
| 31 TRAILER: | | 1 300 |
| 32 SOUND OPERATING SALARIES: | | 5 400 |
| 34 STILLS: | | 700 |
| 34A PUBLICITY: | | 2 500 |
| TOTAL DIRECT COST: | | 266 608 |
| 35 GENERAL STUDIO OVERHEAD 40% | | 106 394 |
| 40 DEPRECIATION 3% | | 7 998 |
| GRAND TOTAL COST: | | 381 000 |

WARNER BROS. PICTURES. INC.
BURBANK. CALIFORNIA

## INTER-OFFICE COMMUNICATION

To Mr. ___WALLIS___          Date ___June 13, 1941.___

From Mr. ___HUSTON___        Subject ___"THE MALTESE FALCON"___

Dear Hal;

    Regarding your note yesterday -- I am shrinking all
the pauses and speeding up all the action. You understand,
of course, that so far I have done only the slow scenes of
the picture. Unless that's kept in mind, a false impression
of monotony might easily arise. For instance: between the
telephone business in Spade's apartment and the scenes of
Spade and Iva, and Spade and Effie Perine in his office, there
are two scenes - those between Spade and the coppers - which
will go so fast they will make sparks.

    After the sequence I am doing at present - Brigid's
apartment - the story really begins to move. By the time we
reach the Cairo-Brigid-copper sequence in Spade's apartment,
it will be turning like a pinwheel.

    I mention these things only to reassure you that as
I am making each scene, I am keeping the whole picture in
mind. This picture should gain in velocity as it goes along.
Otherwise the very speed with which I intend playing the
coming sequences would become monotomous.

    Nevertheless, I am doing as you said in your note --
making Bogart quick and staccato and taking the deliberateness out of his action.

    I think if we had been shooting in sequence and you
had seen the Spade-copper scene in his apartment by this time,
all your anxiety regarding tempo would have been dispelled.
You may be sure that after I saw the first day's rushes, I
was well aware of the perils of slow timing.

*John*

VERBAL MESSAGES CAUSE MISUNDERSTANDING AND DELAYS
(PLEASE PUT THEM IN WRITING)

*Memo from director/screenwriter John Huston to executive producer Hal Wallis, who was concerned about the pacing of the
1941 version of* The Maltese Falcon *after viewing the scenes shot during the first week of production
(courtesy of Warner Bros. Archive, University of Southern California)*

WARNER BROS. PICTURES, INC.
BURBANK, CALIFORNIA

INTER-OFFICE COMMUNICATION

To Mr. T.C.WRIGHT

Date June 18, 1941

From Mr. AL ALLEBORN

Subject "THE MALTESE FALCON"

REPORT ON
"THE MALTESE FALCON" # 369 -aHUSTON
8TH SHOOTING DAY:

Report still showing "on time." This company is a
day and a half ahead of schedule. I will tell the Script
Girl to correct your report.

TUESDAY the company opened on the interior of SPADE'S
OFFICE on Stage #3, 9:00 call, first shot at 9:26, last
one at 5:50 P.M: Then the company rehearsed the following
shots which they were to shoot this morning. Company covered four minutes and four seconds, eight set-ups, four and
two-thirds pages of dialogue. Working in the cast: BOGART,
ASTOR, GLADYS GEORGE, LEE PATRICK. Holding WARD BOND and
BARTON MAC LANE.

PETER LORRE was in and put on his wardrobe for BLANKE
and HUSTON and was okayed. He starts in the picture this
morning.

BOB HAAS and MYSELF were up to see you this morning
with some plans on this picture. One in particular we are
anxious to get into work is the interior of GUTMAN'S APART-
MENT. This morning we were down on the back lot looking at
the exterior of the alley where we shoot on SATURDAY NIGHT
and we will go over to the PROVIDENCIA Ranch today to pick
the spot where they will shoot the balance of this sequence;
that is, the murder sequence.

As you know, on this story we have a Prop that works
the MALTESE FALCON which is a plastic model. BLANKE and
HUSTON have an outside modeller who is working on this
and the cost of it will be about $75.00 covering everything.
A requisition for this is coming in to you for an O.K. this
morning.

AA-WS

VERBAL MESSAGES CAUSE MISUNDERSTANDING AND DELAYS
(PLEASE PUT THEM IN WRITING)

*Memo from unit manager Al Alleborn on the eighth day of shooting the 1941* Maltese Falcon. *The lead-cast statuette weighed fifty pounds (courtesy of Warner Bros. Archive, University of Southern California).*

WARNER BROS. PICTURES, INC.
BURBANK, CALIFORNIA

INTER-OFFICE COMMUNICATION

TO MR.          T. C. WRIGHT                    DATE              July 19 1941

FROM MR.        AL ALLEBORN                     SUBJECT   #369 "THE MALTESE FALCON"

Report for 7-18-41:

34th shooting day.

Yesterday, FRIDAY, the Huston company had a 2:00PM shooting call (having worked until 2:30AM the night before) on Stage 19, INT. GUTMAN'S APARTMENT and INT. SPADE'S APT., also on Stage 19. After supper, the company moved to the back lot and shot the EXT. BURNING SHIP and the EXT. SUBURBAN STREET.

First shot 3:35PM, finished 2:00AM; camera set-ups 14; recording time 6'49"; pages of dialogue completed 7-1/6; script scenes shot 15.

Finished in the cast BOGART and GREEN-STREET.

The Huston company finished at 2:00AM shooting everything necessary to complete the picture.

I kept two Firemen on the boat all night, where we had the fire (these men were on duty anyway) to insure us against chances of having a fire break out from any unnoticed sparks.

The picture is finished, as stated above, but at Blanke's and Huston's request we eliminated the ending, as written in the script, which takes place on Stage 3 in SPADE'S OFFICE. These gentlemen feel they can cut the picture without this ending, and if necessary they can always get BOGART. Their feeling, however, is that the picture will not need the ending written for SPADE'S OFFICE.

I have notified Blanke the picture is finished, and have told the Crew to return to their respective departments as the picture is closed.

Costs as of THURSDAY'S work, July 17, stand at $327,182, or $54,000 under the Budget, which should see us through. No department has gone over its gross budget to any appreciable extent. This, in my opinion, is very gratifying. Production finished 2 days ahead of schedule.

AL ALLEBORN

AA-FS

VERBAL MESSAGES CAUSE MISUNDERSTANDING AND DELAYS
(PLEASE PUT THEM IN WRITING)

*Memo from the unit manager announcing completion of shooting for the 1941* Maltese Falcon
*(courtesy of Warner Bros. Archive, University of Southern California)*

## On the Set

*Mary Astor played Brigid O'Shaughnessy in the 1941 version of* The Maltese Falcon. *This excerpt from her memoir recalls the filming of the movie.*

### "Shall we talk about the Black Bird?"
Mary Astor
*Mary Astor: A Life on Film*
(New York: Delacorte, 1971), pp. 159–167

BEFORE THE LIGHTS WENT OUT, there was *The Maltese Falcon.* There is very little I can say about that one, because everything has been said. But anyway, "Shall we talk about the Black Bird?"

So often, I have been asked "What was it like?" to work in a picture that was so ahead of its time, such a departure in methods, point of view, etc. Of course you don't know you're making history while you're in there making it. We were, all of us, excited about a good story—one that had everyone confused! However, the "where was who when what happened" could be traced down. There wasn't a loophole in it. It helped a great deal that we shot the picture in sequence, except for some exterior night shots on the street set. But even so, John Huston often had to call time out to clear up matters. All of us had read the Dashiell Hammett book and studied the script, but it got so that when the "now just a minute" look came on to somebody's face, it became a joke to say, "When did Brigid shoot Thursby? On Friday!"

I had a lovely pot to boil for Brigid. It was quite a bitches' cauldron. First of all, she was a congenital liar ("I am a liar. I've always been a liar!"), and slightly psychopathic. And that kind of liar wears the face of truth, although they send out all sorts of signals that they are lying. There is an unstable quality to them like nitro. One of the tip-offs is they can't help breathing rather rapidly. So, I hyper-ventilated before going into most of the scenes. It gave me a heady feeling, of thinking at cross purposes. For there wasn't a single scene in the picture where what I said was even close to what I was thinking. In order not to cross myself up I had to keep it down to mostly one thought, "He's got to believe this." Brigid had to oversell so that when Sam Spade said, "You're good—you're very good!" the grateful smile had to be there, but the respiration rate would go automatically, because she was scared stiff.

It was Huston's picture, Huston's script. He'd had the wit to keep Hammett's book intact. His shooting script was a precise map of what went on. Every shot, camera move, entrance, exit was down on paper, leaving nothing to chance, inspiration or invention. Nobody improvised their way through this one! So let me hear the one about the "agony" of "limitation." It was highly limited, almost stylized. We never took our time with a scene. When

Johnnie said, "Action!" we were off and running. Even for the most deliberate scenes—Greenstreet's settling back to tell the history of the Black Bird—there was an exciting reason, not just dull exposition. For just when you thought he was being pretty damn long-winded about it all, you got it: He was waiting for the knockout drops to work on Spade.

Poor Sydney! He never did live down the Fat Man. I don't think he ever did a picture later in which that evil, hiccupy laugh wasn't exploited. He was a very fine, very versatile actor, within his physical limitations. The *Falcon* was his first picture and he was as nervous in his first scene—that same long-winded monologue—as though all his years in the theater counted for nothing. He said to me, "Mary dear, hold my hand, tell me I won't make an ass of meself!"

We had a more than adequate schedule for the picture. Because John's script was well prepared, and because he took time in rehearsal, the shooting went very quickly. Often there is much time lost in lack of preparation. There was and is too much of "Let's rehearse with film" in the hopes that something might happen that would be spontaneous and fresh, and wouldn't happen again. Sometimes it's true, sometimes it's good, but usually the director who does his homework not only comes in under the wire, but without any loss of quality. Of course, if you have actors who come unstuck, not because they are "artistic" and need "freedom to try something else" but because they lack any kind of professional firmness, or ability to get with it, to concentrate, then it all takes time. And something spontaneous and fresh may, in the finished picture, stand out in limbo. The *Falcon* was a jigsaw puzzle, and each scene related to what had happened before and what was to happen—precisely. In emotional levels, in tempos, in cadence of speech and movement. In passing, it is interesting perhaps to note that imitations of various scenes in the *Falcon,* and there have been many, just don't work. They don't have the chilling quality, because they are out of context.

John used his time to rehearse. He used his own personal intensity to excite us; we were never "back on our heels." And when he said "Let's make it—" we were ready. As a result there were never many takes to a scene and so we had lots of time to play.

And could that company play! If you recall, a tall burly figure staggers into Spade's office late one night, clutching a heavy package wrapped in torn newspapers. He is dressed in the clothes of a seaman, with his peaked cap pulled down over his eyes. He is the captain of the ship which burned in port late that afternoon. He mutters something about "the Falcon—the Bird—" and falls dead on the floor of the office with some bullet holes in him.

Just a bit—you never saw him before—and that's all he has to do, just stagger in and fall and drop the package. John thought it would be great fun to have his father, Walter Huston, come in one morning and do the part. And so did Walter—his son's first movie, etc. A bit of fun-sentiment.

John took hours to film it, and Walter got very grumpy: "Didn't expect to have to put in a day's *work*."

"Let's do it again. Sorry, Dad, you missed your mark."

"Take seven. Sorry, Dad. This time, try it without staggering so much."

"Take ten, please. Sorry, Dad. We've got to reload."

The next day, after they'd seen the rushes—they were fine, of course—John told me to call Walter's home and pretend to be his, John's, secretary. I called on the set phone and when Walter answered I told him that Mr. Huston was sorry, but that we'd have to retake the sequence that afternoon—something had happened to the film in the lab—and could he be ready to shoot at one o'clock?

I held the receiver from my ear and everybody could hear Walter yelling, "You tell my son to get another actor or go to hell! He made me take twenty falls, and I'm sore all over, and I'm not about to take twenty more. Or even *one!*"

There were other elaborate practical jokes, one of which was "Shock the Tourists." We didn't want people around watching us. We had an odd childlike territorial imperative about our set. It was hard work, and we didn't want anyone looking over our shoulder, so to speak. Also, we had a sneaky feeling that we were doing something different and exciting, and we didn't want to show it to anyone until it was finished. Hard to explain.

It all started one afternoon when we were lined up on a shot where I sit down and cross my knees elaborately—I think it was in Spade's office. I looked down and said, "Hold it a minute, I've got a goddam run in my stocking." I looked up and a little to the side of the camera was the publicity man with a half-dozen gentlemen of the cloth. They were ushered out politely by the publicity man who looked a little pale. When the big doors closed, everybody whooped and hollered and said, "That's our girl! That's the way to get 'em off the set!" After that John dreamed up an act for each one of us—designated by numbers. A stream of Helen Hokinson type club women would come in cooing like pigeons with the excitement of seeing Bogart, and John would sing out, "Number Five, kiddies. Number Five!" At which Bogie would go into the prepared act with Greenstreet. He'd start yelling at him, calling him a fat old fool, "Who the hell do you think you are? You upstaged me, and I'm telling you I'm not having any—" and John would be pleading with him to hold his temper. Very quickly, the uncomfortable and disillusioned ladies would exit and we could go back to work.

"Number Ten" was a bit more involved. I had to get into my portable with Peter Lorre before a group got over to where we were working. When they had been guided into position by the gracious John Huston, saying politely, "I think you'll see just fine right over here," in sight of the

WARNERS' "MALTESE FALCON" SET AT A GLANCE: Mary Astor "blowing" her lines when the assistant director informs her that hubby Manuel del Campo (now with the R.C.A.F.) is long-distancing . . . Gladys George: "Now I know what became of my favorite publicity man—I recognized his style today in a German war communique." . . . Five-foot Peter Lorre demonstrating jujitsu holds on six foot-two inch Barton MacLane . . . Tough-guy Humphrey Bogart and Writer Louis Bromfield heatedly arguing—about the proper methods of petunia culture! . . . Lee Patrick, staggering to a seat after lugging a 50-pound statue of the Falcon through a long scene: "If a role like this makes me an 'artist' — so's a hod-carrier!" . . . Director John Huston (son of Walter) ruefully accepting first aid after sitting on a fish-hook accidentally misplaced by Comedian Elisha Cook Jr., who makes trout flies as a hobby.

*Clipping of a gossip column regarding the 1941 version of*
The Maltese Falcon *Hammett sent to his wife*
*(courtesy of Josephine Hammett)*

door of my dressing room, he would then call out, "O.K., I think we're ready for Number Ten, now." Peter would open the door and come down the steps fastening his fly, and I would stick my head out the door, waving coy fingers as he said, "See you later, Mary."

Our long-suffering publicity man was not stupid. He finally came to John saying, "May I have your permission, *sir,* to bring over some rather important guests this afternoon? Without benefit of your goddam gags?" And John said, "You can try, my friend, you can try." Soon the *Falcon* company because a closed set and we could get our work done without people gaping at us.

The Lakeside Golf Club was just across the highway from Warner Brothers Studio and had a pleasant poolside dining area. Several of us were members and almost every day the company would gather there for a long hour and a half lunch period. People from other companies would eye us suspiciously because we weren't wolfing down sandwiches in a hurry to get back to work. We could boast smugly, "We're 'way ahead of schedule." I remember one sequence that we rehearsed late one afternoon. It would run about seven minutes. Johnnie had it planned to be shot with two cameras, both on tracks. We worked it out in detail in the afternoon and the next morning shot it in two takes and went over to Lakeside about eleven and played around the pool for the rest of the day. Seven minutes is a good day's work.

The combination of Huston, Bogart and Lorre was very fast company in the wit department; there was a kind of abrasive, high-powered kidding-on-the-level thing that went on, and you joined in at your own risk. Just to get into the act, one day at Lakeside I made the mistake of piping up with some kind of naïve smart crack and the ribbing was turned on to me unmercifully. I did the best I could for a while, but it was more than I could handle. I got sort of backed into a corner: "Then you *admit* you don't like pointillism, that the Fauves were a bunch of jerks?" "I didn't say that, I just said—" My eyes started to smart and I whimpered, "I just can't keep up with this!" Bogie laughed his head off, along with the rest and then got up and came around the table to my place. He wiped my tears away with elaborate care. "You're O.K., baby," he said. "So you're not very smart—but you know it and what the hell's the matter with that!" Although it still was on a kidding level, Bogie really meant what he said. "Be yourself. Be yourself and you're in."

Bogie just didn't have time to be anything but himself. He was a hardworking guy, a good craftsman. He would have hooted if anyone had called him an artist. (I would, but not to his face!) To him, "artist" meant someone unpredictable and fancy pants. He would have made a wisecrack if anybody had called him "Humphrey"—or even "Mr. Bogart."

He wasn't very tall; vocally he had a range from A to B; his eyes were like shiny coal nuggets pressed deep into his skull; and his smile was a mistake that he tried to keep from happening. He was no movie hero. He was no hero at all.

I have heard people say he wasn't *really* a good actor. I don't go along with that. It is true his personality dominated the character he was playing—but the character gained by it. His technical skill was quite brilliant. His precision timing was no accident. He kept other actors on their toes because he *listened* to them, he watched, he *looked* at them. He never had that vague stare of a person who waits for you to finish talking, who hasn't heard a word you have said. And he was never "upstage center" acting all by himself. He was there. With you.

As a person he looked at the world, his place in it, at movies and at life in general and he wore no rose-colored glasses. There was something about it all that made him contemptuous and bitter. He related to people as though they had no clothes on—and no skin, for that matter. If they grabbed at their various little hypocrisies for protective cover, his laugh was a particularly unpleasant chortle.

Bogie would have liked a world that was loyal and loving, truthful and generous. There was something in him that responded instantly to anyone or anything that was "for real." Not too closely. Not too deeply. He might get hooked. He was scared of "getting hooked with a dame." He hated the marriage trap, being used, being possessed, being made to buckle down as a provider. I think the remarkable Lauren Bacall knew who he was, let him be who he was and what he was, and in return, he was at last able to give something no other woman could grab from him—his total commitment.

Bogie had his troubles, his longing for a good world, his need to trust and believe in something. Like the rest of us. But he couldn't dismiss it with a philosophy, or stick his head in the sand. He was "aware" and he blew. Violently and often. And when he got drunk he was bitter and smilingly sarcastic and thoroughly unpleasant.

The Bogart cult that has emerged is very understandable. There he is, right there on the screen, saying what everyone is trying to say today, saying it loud and clear, "I hate hypocrisy. I don't believe in words or labels or much of anything else. I'm not a hero. I'm a human being. I'm not very pretty. Like me or don't like me." We who knew him well liked him. Bogie was for real.

I don't think there are many pictures which have had as many reruns as the *Falcon*. When it was first shown on TV it was just another rerun of an old movie, made to fit a time slot. It was a bad print and had been cut to pieces. Over the years it has gained respect. I don't know how they do such things, but they cleaned up the negative and the print is better, the sound has improved and today I'm sure there isn't a cut missing.

Of *course* I watch it! It's a wonderful, rich memory. Of people who were friends. There they all are, Sydney, Peter, Bogie:

> *Sydney:* "But Miss O'Shaughnessy had, by this time, obtained the Bird." [only he says, "Miss O–Shaughnessy."]
> *Peter:* "She shtruck me! She attacked me!"
> *Bogie:* "—and then you went down that dark alley, knowing he'd follow you—"

My dear ghosts.

The *Falcon* was eligible for Academy Awards the same year as *The Great Lie*. It got nothing. And if I'd had my druthers, I would have preferred getting my Oscar for Brigid rather than for Sandra.

302

## 'Maltese Falcon'

### CAST

| | |
|---|---|
| Samuel Spade | HUMPHREY BOGART |
| Brigid O'Shaughnessy | MARY ASTOR |
| Iva Archer | Gladys George |
| Joel Cairo | Peter Lorre |
| Lt. of Detectives Dundy | Barton MacLane |
| Effie Perine | Lee Patrick |
| Kasper Gutman | Sydney Greenstreet |
| Detective Tom Polhaus | Ward Bond |
| Miles Archer | Jerome Cowan |
| Wilmer Cook | Elisha Cook, Jr. |
| Luke | James Burke |
| Frank Richman | Murray Alper |
| Bryan | John Hamilton |

### PRODUCTION

**Directed by John Huston**

Screen Play by John Huston; Based Upon a Novel by Dashiell Hammett; Director of Photography, Arthur Edeson, A.S.C.; Film Editor, Thomas Richards; Sound by Oliver S. Garretson; Art Director, Robert Haas; Dialogue Director, Robert Foulk; Gowns by Orry-Kelly; Makeup Artist, Perc Westmore; Music by Adolph Deutsch; Musical Director, Leo F. Forbstein. (Running Time—100 Minutes)

### STORY

(Not for Publication): The private detective firm of Spade and Archer are retained by a Miss Wonderly (Mary Astor) to trail a man named Thursby. Archer is killed, and Spade (Humphrey Bogart) gets suspicious of his charming lady client when he learns, shortly after, that Thursby has also been murdered. Another stranger turns up in Spade's office, a slight, dainty foreigner named Cairo (Peter Lorre), offers him $5000 to find him a certain statuette, a black porcelain falcon. Miss Wonderly, Spade's newest romantic interest, now comes into the case in an active way, to help Spade find the falcon. Also involved are two other men, a Mr. Gutman (Sydney Greenstreet), and Wilmer (Elisha Cook, Jr.) his gun boy. Gutman offers $50,000 for the falcon if it is found. Spade learns that this mysterious bird was once a gift of the Knights of Malta to Charles of Spain, and that it is of fabulous worth, so fabulous, in fact, that the people who are after it are willing to commit murder to get possession of it. From here on, the chase gets fast and furious, with Spade keeping just one step ahead of his double-crossing clients, and winding up the case spectacularly.

*Pressbook copy for the 1941* Maltese Falcon *(Collection of Richard Layman)*

## Reviews of Huston's Movie

**Review of *The Maltese Falcon***
*Variety,* 1 October 1941

Hollywood, Sept. 30.
Warner Bros. release of Henry Blanks production. Features Humphrey Bogart, Mary Astor, Gladys George, Peter Lorre. Screenplay and direction by John Huston. Based on novel by Dashiell Hammett; camera, Arthur Edeson; editor, Thomas Richards; Ass't director, Jack Sullivan; dialog director, Robert Foulk. Tradeshown in L. A. Sept. 29, '41. Running time, 100 MINS.

. . . . . . . . . .

This is one of the best examples of actionful and suspenseful melodramatic story telling in cinematic form. Unfolding a most intriguing and entertaining murder mystery, picture displays outstanding excellence in writing, direction, acting and editing—combining in overall as a prize package of entertainment for widest audience appeal. Due for hefty grosses in all runs, it's textured with ingredients presaging numerous holdovers in the keys—and strong word-of-mouth will make the b.o. wickets spin.

John Huston, son of actor Walter Huston, makes his debut as a film director after several years as a film writer. His entrance into the directorial field is noteworthy, with display of keenest knowledge in tempo development and handling of the various players. Huston also wrote the script solo, endowing it with well-rounded episodes of suspense and surprise, but detouring from synthetic theatrics—and carrying along with consistently pithy dialog.

Of major importance is the standout performance of Humphrey Bogart, an attention-arresting portrayal that will add immeasurable voltage to his marquee values. Bogart not only dominates the proceedings throughout, but is the major motivation in all but a few minor scenes. Mary Astor skillfully etches the role of an adventuress whose double-crossing is not disclosed until the final scenes.

Critical and audience spotlight will be focused on Sydney Greenstreet, prominent member of the Lunt-Fontaine stage troupe, who scores heavily in his first screen appearance. Player displays consummate ability as an artist of high rank, and solidly holds attention through several extensive dialog passages that could easily fall apart in less competent hands. Advantageous support is provided by Lee Patrick, Peter Lorre, Ward Bond, Gladys George, Barton MacLane, Elisha Cook, Jr., Jerome Cowan and James Burke.

Picture is a remake of an original film turned out by Warners 10 years ago, with Bebe Daniels and Ricardo Cortez. Despite this fact, it's still a strongly melodramatic tale concocted in Dashiell Hammett's best style. Story details the experiences of private detective Bogart when called in to handle a case for Miss Astor—shortly finding himself in the middle of double-crossing intrigue and several murders perpetrated by strange characters bent on obtaining possession of the famed bejeweled Maltese Falcon. Keeping just within bounds of the law, and utilizing sparkling ingenuity in gathering up the loose ends and finally piecing them together, Bogart is able to solve the series of crimes for the benefit of the police.

An intriguing piece of melodramatic entertainment, 'Maltese Falcon' weaves swiftly through a series of attention-holding episodes to crack through to a most unsuspecting climax. To secure utmost in audience reaction, exhibs can take advantage of the surprise finish by publicizing starting times of the picture, and advising patrons to get maximum entertainment by seeing it from the start. Extra advance exploitation to obtain first day patronage will roll up hefty momentum in the key runs.

Picture is an A attraction in its class, and will hit biz of the same kind in all bookings.     *Walt.*

\* \* \*

**'The Maltese Falcon,' a Fast Mystery-Thriller
With Quality and Charm, at the Strand**
Bosley Crowther
*The New York Times,* 4 October 1941, p. 18

THE MALTESE FALCON, based on the novel by Dashiell Hammett, screen play by John Huston; directed by Mr. Huston; produced by Hal B. Wallis for Warner Bros. Pictures, Inc. At the Strand.

. . . . . . . . . .

The Warners have been strangely bashful about their new mystery film, "The Maltese Falcon," and about the young man, John Huston, whose first directorial job it is. Maybe they thought it best to bring both along under wraps, seeing as how the picture is a remake of an old Dashiell Hammett yarn done ten years ago, and Mr. Huston is a fledgling whose previous efforts have been devoted to writing scripts. And maybe—which is somehow more likely—they wanted to give every one a nice surprise. For "The Maltese Falcon," which swooped down onto the screen of the Strand yesterday, only turns out to be the best mystery thriller of the year, and young

Mr. Huston gives promise of becoming one of the smartest directors in the field.

For some reason, Hollywood has neglected the sophisticated crime film of late, and England, for reasons which are obvious, hasn't been sending her quota in recent months. In fact, we had almost forgotten how devilishly delightful such films can be when done with taste and understanding and a feeling for the fine line of suspense. But now, with "The Maltese Falcon," the Warners and Mr. Huston give us again something of the old thrill we got from Alfred Hitchcock's brilliant melodramas or from "The Thin Man" before he died of hunger.

This is not to imply, however, that Mr. Huston has imitated anyone. He has worked out his own style, which is brisk and supremely hardboiled. We didn't see the first "Falcon," which had Ricardo Cortez and Bebe Daniels in its cast. But we'll wager it wasn't half as tough nor half as flavored with idioms as is this present version, in which Humphrey Bogart hits his peak. For the trick which Mr. Huston has pulled is a combination of American ruggedness with the suavity of the English crime school—a blend of mind and muscle—plus a slight touch of pathos.

Perhaps you know the story (it was one of Mr. Hammett's best): of a private detective in San Francisco who becomes involved through a beautiful but evasive dame in a complicated plot to gain possession of a fabulous jeweled statuette. As Mr. Huston has adapted it, the mystery is as thick as a wall and the facts are completely obscure as the picture gets under way. But slowly the bits fall together, the complications draw out and a monstrous but logical intrigue of international proportions is revealed.

Much of the quality of the picture lies in its excellent revelation of character. Mr. Bogart is a shrewd, tough detective with a mind that cuts like a blade, a temperament that sometimes betrays him, and a code of morals which is coolly cynical. Mary Astor is well nigh perfect as the beautiful woman whose cupidity is forever to be suspect. Sidney Greenstreet, from the Theatre Guild's roster, is magnificent as a cultivated English crook, and Peter Lorre, Elisha Cook Jr., Lee Patrick, Barton MacLane all contribute stunning characters. (Also, if you look closely, you'll see Walter Huston, John's father, in a bit part.)

Don't miss "The Maltese Falcon" if your taste is for mystery fare. It's the slickest exercise in cerebration that has hit the screen in many months, and it is also one of the most compelling nervous-laughter provokers yet.

## 'Maltese Falcon' Rated Top 'Number' in New York

### · BY RICHARD GRIFFITH ·

NEW YORK, Oct. 13.—Three sizzling hits and one pleasant one mark this interesting fall week on Broadway. Warners' "The Maltese Falcon" is the surprise of the lot because the Dashiell Hammett novel has already been filmed twice, yet critics find it the freshest and most original film seen in New York since "Citizen Kane," at least.

This is no mean record to hang up, since the biting performances of Bebe Daniels and Ricardo Cortez made the 1931 version memorable and the Bette Davis-Warren William remake was no slouch, either.

The new version is the best because it is the most cynical, depraved and brilliantly melodramatic. There isn't an honest motive among the entire cast—which is why we accept the characters as real people such as are found against the background and participating in the incidents portrayed.

**DIRECTOR CREDITED**

This combination of realism and violent criminal action is intensely believable and appeals to the same public which acclaimed "Manpower" and other hit epics of low life.

Maximum credit for the breakneck pace and tension should go to novice John Huston, whose direction of this difficult piece marks him as the most imaginative new director we have had in some years. Besides imagination and novelty, he boasts expert filmcraft, for his veteran cast give finer performances under his newcomer's hand than more experienced direction.

Mary Astor, in particular, follows up her distinct hit in "The Great Lie" with a contribution which reveals her once more as one of the most knowing actresses in the business, as well as one of the best technicians. Reviewers are nuts about Miss Astor and they regard this role as one of her best opportunities in years.

Humphrey Bogart, Sydney Greenstreet, Gladys George and Elisha Cook Jr. are others who are said to be perfectly cast in one of the Strand Theater's most thrilling pictures.

**SENTIMENTAL VENTURE**

"It Started With Eve" really started with Cinderella, in the words of one reviewer, but wherever such pictures begin they always wind up at Radio City Music Hall. Which is to say that this gently humorous, generously sentimental story is precisely to the taste of Music Hall patrons.

It revolves around an eccentric millionaire, a character played for years on the screen by the late Walter Connolly, who concentrated his efforts on making the old codger human, natural and believable in spite of his foibles.

Charles Laughton attacks the role from the opposite direction. Every trick in his repertory is employed to make the millionaire a human being such as was never seen on land or sea.

Though some reviewers consider Mr. Connolly's method the more legitimate, all are forced to admit that Mr. Laughton knows all about the business of getting laughs, and that his appearance opposite Deanna Durbin gives each a picture that is a departure from their usual vehicles. It is the sort of picture which is known as "easy to take," any story will do as long as this expert actor and charming young girl are fooling around with it.

Robert Cummings again shows progress as Miss Durbin's young man, and Henry Koster's direction has the able smoothness we expect.

## PARAMOUNT TO HOLD PREVIEW

Paramount Theater will have a preview tonight of Paramount's newest comedy based on the romantic escapades of today's youth. Thursday brings the opening of Bob Hope's "Nothing But the Truth," with Paulette Goddard.

In "Nothing But the Truth" Bob Hope finds himself in a hilariously precarious situation. If he tells a lie he loses $10,000. If he tells the truth, he loses Paulette.

Edward Arnold, Lief Erickson, Helen Vinson, Catherine Doucet, Grant Mitchell, Rose Hobart and Willie Best are in the cast.

"Stump and Stumpy," New York entertainers, will top the array of talent in Paramount's "Floor Show."

## 'Virgin Bride' Cinema Farce

What Greek dramatists ar[...] Eugene O'Neill fashioned in[...] serious drama, the producers[...] "Mlle. Ma Mere," which p[...] sents Danielle Darrieux as "T[...] Virgin Bride," have turned i[...] rollicking farce, according to[...] ports preceding the film w[...] will screen Wednesday at[...] Grand Theater.

*Clippings Hammett sent to his wife (courtesy of Josephine Hammett)*

## Thrillers at Warners Rated Hits

BY PHILIP K. SCHEUER

"The Maltese Falcon" and "Target for Tonight," both at Warners Hollywood and Downtown theaters, are like the delayed-action bombs mentioned in the latter film. It may take them a while to get wound up, but when they do—fsssst, BOOM! they explode with the terrific force of solid hits. Both of them.

"The Maltese Falcon" is, I venture to say, the finest detective-mystery movie ever turned out by a Hollywood studio. Alongside it an earlier version pales into insignificance—and so do most thrillers of its type to date. John Huston, young writer and son of Walter Huston, the actor, has taken his own adaptation of Dashiell Hammett's hardboiled crime yarn and stretched it so taut that it fairly sings in your ears. Not only is his plot development critic-proof (in itself a phenomenon in Hollywood,) but he has imbued the players who interpret it with an erratic reality, a faithfulness and a fatefulness which makes them appear to have been caught completely off-guard by the camera.

### COMPELS RESPECT

You've never seen a detective like Sam Spade, for instance. In private practice, not above a shady deal or two, he nevertheless exhibits an honesty and directness in facing a situation which compel your admiration. Sam has what it takes; and Humphrey Bogart, who plays him, has what it takes, too.

The same is true of the others —as amazing an assortment of characters as ever came together for a film. Too alive, too detailed to be described at length here, they are portrayed—and how!—by Mary Astor, Sydney Greenstreet ("the fat man,") Peter Lorre, Lee Patrick, Gladys George, Elisha Cook Jr., Barton MacLane, Ward Bond, Jerome Cowan and James Burke. They'll all have to go some to top these roles.

The Maltese falcon is a statuette believed to have been shaped of gold and encrusted with gems —gift to a crusading king in 1539. The locale of the picture is modern San Francisco. If I were to satisfy your curiosity further, I would be giving something away, thus depriving you of the pleasure in store for you at the theater. And I wouldn't do that.

## Analyzing a Classic

*Of the three movies made from Hammett's novel, John Huston's version is the only one that has attracted substantial analysis. The following section provides a sampling of critical opinion.*

**Two Birds of a Feather:**
**Hammett's and Huston's *The Maltese Falcon***
Leslie H. Abramson
*Literature/Film Quarterly,* 16 (1988): 112–118

The Maltese Falcon of Dashiell Hammett's 1929 novel and John Huston's 1941 film is not only the object of ovewhelming desire, but the object of an immense amount of conversation as well. Its trail is less one of tangible clues and physical traces than an arsenal of narrative strategies and styles; truth, lies, confessions, history, recollections, gossip, testimony, and newspaper articles. Both on paper and celluloid, *The Maltese Falcon* is a highly self-conscious work of art which probes the methods and values of storytelling repeatedly. In these two hard-boiled fictive domains, facility as a storyteller is directly connected with power over the world. The characters employ various brands of narration to direct the action towards the fulfillment of their own aims. Sam's success as a detective is dependent upon his superior talents as a reader of plots and a storyteller, allowing him to gain control over the narrative and advance it to the conclusion he desires.

Much as the central concerns of the two works remain the same in Huston's near-literal transcription of the book, on screen Spade has a certain visual struggle which he escapes in print. As a man who must operate within the four walls of a film frame, Spade continually attempts to gain ascendancy over Gutman and his cronies by physically dominating the screen, and by bringing light—lamplight, streetlights, matchlight—into a dark underworld. Even more striking, though, is the way the visual world of Huston's film continually pays tribute to the print world from which it has sprung. The characters inhabit a city heavily populated with signs, numbers, and newsprint. Spade must feel his way through these disjointed sets of written characters, just as he must navigate among the verbal truths and lies of his adversaries, to sort out the crime.

In "Narration and Narrativity in Film"[1] Robert Scholes characterizes detective fiction as a genre heavily invested in exploring the strategies by which its plots are formulated.

The extraordinary popularity of detective fiction . . . is based upon the way in which this fictional form incorporates the principles of narrativity within the narration itself. We follow the detective moving through time from crime to solution, while he, in turn, is in the process of constructing a narration of the crime itself from a set of clues encountered without their temporal and causal situations having been clarified. From discrete clues, he constructs a criminal narrative. . . .[2]

Sam Spade and his adversaries, in both the book and the film, are well aware of this artistically strategic aspect of his role. Not only do Gutman and his gang continually try to throw Spade off the falcon's trail by using narrative methods against him—concocting false accounts of their motives for pursuing the bird, combining truth and lies to implicate others in the murders—they also engage in constant dialogues with Spade about the types of tales they use and how they are using them. Spade lives in a world of stories. Countless versions of every event in *The Maltese Falcon* are offered to him by Brigid, Cairo, Gutman, and the police, and from these he must construct the single, true chain of events that led to Miles's death.

Spade displays an overriding concern with establishing logical narratives from the outset. Practically his first words to the breathless Miss Wonderly, in both the book and the film are: "Suppose you tell me about it, from the beginning. . . ."[3] Despite his urging, she embarks on an anxious, scattershot account of her troubles, proceeding from her sister's youth to their unsuspecting parents vacationing in Europe, an unanswered telegram, her trip to San Francisco, and, finally, the shady instigator of these difficulties, Floyd Thursby. Miles Archer enters the office on the heels of this story, and Sam provides him with a quick introduction to their new client:

> Miss Wonderly's sister ran away from New York with a fellow named Floyd Thursby. They're here. Miss Wonderly has seen Thursby and has a date with him tonight. Maybe he'll bring the sister with him. The chances are he won't. Miss Wonderly wants us to find the sister and get her away from him and back home.[4]

Thus, Spade immediately establishes his expertise in rapidly piecing together a story from disjointed narrative elements.

Miles promptly offers an ending to the story—that Thursby marry Wonderly's sister. Yet the solution is inappropriate: Thursby is already married, according to Wonderly. Miles is clearly outclassed in this weight category. He displays a lack of insight and imagination as a plot reader and a storyteller by suggesting a simple, trite conclusion to a very complex tale. Sam will not make this mistake. Miles's lack of savvy as a detective soon leads to his death.

The initial motivation for the story is Brigid's lie, which leads to the inescapable fact of Miles's death, and thenceforth Sam moves through a murky middle ground of truths mixed with lies until he can return to the solid

footing of veracity again. His first sparring partner in this deadly game is Brigid. The two constantly banter about the strategies of lies as Sam engages in the process of trying to extract the real story from a litany of fake ones.

In their first conversation after Miles's death, in both the book and the film, Brigid admits that she told Sam a story." Sam responds, "We didn't exactly believe your story. . . . We believed your two hundred dollars. . . . I mean that you paid us more than if you'd been telling the truth. . . ."[5] Sam immediately establishes money as a measure of veracity. As a general principle, in both the book and the film, that which is printed on paper is authentic—whether it be hundred dollar bills or a shipping news column in the daily paper that lists the arrival time of some important cargo.

During Sam's second conversation with Brigid, after Cairo has turned a pistol on him in an attempt to acquire the falcon, Sam penetrates a little farther into her modus operandi.

> Sam: You, ah, you aren't exactly the sort of a person you pretend to be, are you?
> Brigid: Why, I'm not sure I know exactly what you mean.
> Sam: The schoolgirl manner—you know, blushing, stammering and all that.
> Brigid: I haven't lived a good life. I've been bad. Worse than you could know.
> Sam: That's good, because if you actually were as innocent as you pretend to be, we'd never get anywhere.

In this on-screen conversation, roughly equivalent to that in the book, Sam notes that Brigid's savvy is valuable, an asset that they can use to push the case forward.

Sam is willing to play along with Brigid, but only insofar as he knows there is a point to her dishonest discourse. Moments later in the same scene, he snaps,

> I don't care what your secrets are, but I can't go ahead without more confidence in you than I've got now. You've got to convince me that you know what this is all about, that you aren't just fiddling around, hoping it'll all come out right in the end.

Basically, he wants assurance that she's not just an amateur at this deadly serious game of plot formation.

At the end of the evening, when Brigid and Sam are alone in his apartment after meeting with Cairo and suffering the intrusion of Polhaus and Dundy, Brigid finally confesses to what she is made of.

> Sam: You *are* a liar.
> Brigid: I am. I've always been a liar. . . . Oh I'm so tired. I'm tired out lying and making lies, not knowing what is a lie and what is the truth.

*Lobby card (Collection of Richard Layman)*

In both the book and the film, what follows this admission is a kiss. Verbally, Brigid is a pathological liar, but physically, there is an honest attraction between her and Spade.

Sam encounters a whole different brand of stories, as well as a whole different standard of honesty, upon meeting Caspar Gutman. When Gutman welcomes Sam into his rooms for the first time, in both the book and the film, he immediately proposes a toast "to plain speaking and clear understanding." [6] Gutman is an unfailing truth-teller, and something more as well: a historian. During their second meeting, Gutman recounts the falcon's peregrinations from the Crusaders' time to the present day, including a chronicle of the past two decades which he has personally assembled while tracking the bird. Gutman tells Spade, "These are facts, historical facts. Not schoolbook history, not Mr. Wells's history, but history nonetheless." [7] Gutman, like Spade, is a man capable of assembling a single story from diverse sources. However, he proves a comically slow and dogged double of Spade. Gutman has been tracking the falcon for 17 years. Spade will capture his jailbird in three days.

When Gutman encounters Spade, historical facts meet that higher measure of truth against which Spade initially measured Brigid: money. Gutman bargains with Spade over the detective's cut for delivering the falcon, finally pronouncing, "There's no telling how high (the purchase price of the falcon) could go. That's the one and only truth about it." Gutman's ultimate truth is itself an uncertainty, suggesting how elusive actual knowledge really is. When Spade hears the "truth," he is literally knocked out; Gutman has slipped a mickey into his drink. The price of Sam's knowledge is a sort of temporary death.

Gutman proves himself a worthy adversary for Spade. Not only is he equally unafraid to tell the truth; he is clever enough to employ the act of narration creatively to thwart his opponent. Gutman's tale of the falcon lasts just long enough to allow the knock-out drops to take effect.

In the film, once Sam wakes from his forced slumber, he regains the falcon's trial by returning to the solid footing of the print world. He discovers a newspaper in Gutman's apartment which contains a circled column listing the arrival times of cargo ships. The printed schedule leads Spade to the boat on which the falcon has arrived in San Francisco. When the falcon is delivered to Spade, however, it is wrapped in *shredded* newspaper–not quite the genuine article.

Much as the practice impedes Sam's progress in his quest for the truth about Miles's murder, lying is not necessarily a negative act in either the book or the film. Rather, it is a skill to be used, as Gutman might say, "judiciously." Sam lies to the police in order to throw them off his trail: he lies to extricate himself from Iva's embraces when she hounds him in the office. For Hammett and Huston, lies are tools to be used in an aggravating world where police are quick to slap handcuffs on the nearest suspect, and former mistresses are unable to recognize when they're all washed up with a fellow.

Sam is the only character in *The Maltese Falcon* who can tell the truth and lie with equal dexterity. Brigid is a pathological liar; Gutman is a perpetual truth-teller. When Gutman ventures one lie at the story–accusing Brigid of stealing a one-thousand dollar bill that he has palmed–he is caught in the act. Gutman is thwarted by Brigid, who, at that moment, attempts one of her few stabs at the truth. In the film, when Gutman accuses Brigid of stealing the bill, Sam turns to her for a response and she shakes her head "no." Sam then immediately accuses Gutman of stealing the money himself. This is the first and perhaps the only time that Sam believes Brigid, and it is because she has communicated with her body, *not* her vocal chords. Her physical relationship with Spade is the one real and honest fact about her. In the book, the scene is played a bit differently, but the message is the same. Sam forces Brigid to remove her clothes on the premise that her body will not lie if, in fact, she has hidden the money on herself.

In this final scene at Sam's apartment, he concocts his own conclusion to the plot by successfully nominating Wilmer as the fall-guy for Gutman and his troop. Later on, by telling Brigid that the two of them are "on the gallows" and urging her to reveal the truth about the murders before the police arrive, Brigid at last acknowledges that it is she who killed Miles. Sam knows perfectly well that the police won't hang him for anyone's death, but by selling Brigid on this scenario, he stage-manages her confession. For Spade, these lies are in the service of an ultimate truth which is contained in the highest morality of rooting out evil, no matter what the cost, and avenging the death of one's "brother."

It is this ability both to piece together a narrative from disarraying plot points and half-truths, and concoct cunning stories of his own when necessary, that makes Sam so good at his job. For Spade the detective, just as for Hammett the writer and Huston the director, the unique, dual ability to read and write a plot is critical for professional success.

Much as the book and the film are spiritual allies, the view of the story from the typewriter and the lens is very different. In the book, Hammett dwells relentlessly on physical detail–Sam's facial expressions, his methodical way of rolling a cigarette, how he carefully fits a key into a lock. These particulars not only give the book a palpable feel; they also provide a clear, causal chain of events that anchors the reader in a world where few connections of this sort can be made. Just as Sam rolls together the separate materials of shredded tobacco and paper to make a cigarette, he assembles the scattered truths of the plot. Needless to say, in a story with as many complicated twists and turns as Hammett's, it is very satisfying to follow the simple, successful process of rolling a cigarette.

Yet, Spade's ponderousness is unsuited to the clip of a suspense film. In order to create a fast-paced movie from a methodical book, Huston cut 25 scenes from the text–mostly moments when Sam is meditating; eating; changing his clothes; tracking down fruitless leads; talking to the D.A., his lawyer, and policemen–in other words, leading the life of a somewhat average, law-abiding citizen. Huston's Spade thus becomes a quicker study, able to move more easily through his investigation.

By choosing the unintrusive third person point of view, Hammett necessarily limited himself to visual clues regarding Spade's thoughts. Consequently, in the book Spade is a visceral character who growls wolfishly or tends to show an eyetooth when rankled. The way he blinks his eyes or holds his jaw, what he looks at and what he ignores, are all closely scrutinized by Hammett. In this way, the author asks his readers to do double duty as detectives–to determine what Sam is thinking, and to sort out the mystery. In an attempt to mirror Hammett's point of view, Huston's camera follows Spade like a silent partner, often scanning the action from behind his back or peering over his shoulder. Yet, by using this technique, Huston forfeits the ability to record Sam's immediate reactions to what is taking place in the frame.

While Huston trims down the narrative girth of the story considerably, on a purely visual scale he adds a good deal of weight. Huston's version of *The Maltese Falcon* is a highly self-reflexive work, preoccupied with its origins in print. The film begins with a brief written

*Lobby card (Collection of Richard Layman)*

history of the falcon superimposed over a picture of the falcon itself.

> In 1539, the Knight Templars of Malta, paid tribute to Charles V of Spain, by sending him a Golden Falcon encrusted from beak to claw with rarest jewels—but pirates seized the galley carrying the priceless token and the fate of the Maltese Falcon remains a mystery to this day—

From the very outset, then, the audience is made aware of both the importance and the outcome of the story. We are allowed a glimpse of the much-prized falcon, and we are a told that its whereabouts still "remain a mystery." Thus the film locates itself in a broad narrative context from its opening frames as one episode in the falcon's colorful written history. From the beginning, the viewer is to be as jaded as Sam regarding the importance of the events contained in this brief chapter.

The film cuts from its initial explanation of the falcon's history to a shot of the Golden Gate Bridge, with the identification "San Francisco" superimposed on the image. The scene then dissolves to a view of the city skyline which contains a sign, "Golden Gate Bridge," and imme-

diately dissolves again to another shot of a bridge, the Oakland Bay Bridge. Finally, in this opening sequence, the film dissolves to a shot gazing out from behind a window on which the names "Spade and Archer" face outward. From this location, the camera pans directly downward to Humphrey Bogart as Spade, calmly rolling a cigarette. Words continually precede the pictures they represent in these first frames of the film as Huston refers again and again to the fact that the written story is the progenitor of his film images.

Hammett's book operates on the opposite principle—that the image precedes the word. The book begins not with an abbreviated history of the falcon, nor with a depiction of San Francisco, but with a description of Sam. He is the landscape Hammett means to ponder all through the case of the Maltese Falcon. The book begins,

> Samuel Spade's jaw was long and bony, his chin a jutting $v$ under the more flexible $v$ of his mouth. His nostrils curved back to make another, smaller $v$ . . . He said to Effie Perrine: "Yes, sweetheart?"[8]

There follows a detailed description of Effie as well, which ends with her response to his question: "There's a girl wants to see you. Her name's Wonderly."[9] After setting up an initial pattern of description followed by dialogue for the first two characters, Hammett introduces Wonderly not by her image, but by her voice, thanking Effie. In this way Hammett indicates that there is something not quite right about Wonderly. She has a certain uneasy ineffability. Wonderly's province is the verbal. In fact, she is all works with very little substance behind them. A physical description of Wonderly follows her verbal response to Effie.

Huston cautions the audience against Wonderly by formulating a scenario which illustrates her impact on the world of print. In his second shot of Brigid, the director stations the camera in front of Spade's desk, capturing Spade and Wonderly as they stand together before the picture windows. Huston frames the characters with half a window on either side. The signs on the windows are sliced in half in the following way:

Upon her entrance into the story, Wonderly splits the names "Spade and Archer" in two just as she will soon physically split up their partnership. Although she is a threatening, divisive force, the letters directly behind Spade, on the right half of the frame, urge him to "ADE (aid) HER."

As the scene progresses, and Wonderly begins to tell Sam about her sister, Huston cuts to a new shot of the two seated on either side of a picture window that reads, wholly, "Spade and Archer" again. Accordingly, Brigid will only split up the detectives' partnership momentarily. Throughout the exchange between Sam and Brigid, letters from Spade's and Archer's names are scattered all over the walls in shadow. As the scene ends, with a bit of banter between Sam and Miles, the camera pans down to the floor, on which the names "Spade and Archer" appear in an elongated, rectangular shadow, like a tombstone for their partnership.

In subsequent scenes, Sam moves through a world littered with street signs, signs on office doors and outside hotels, theater marquees, door numbers, and newsprint. These signs give a realistic and solid bearing to Sam's fictive and uncertain verbal world, but they also flood that world with disjointed words. Sam, the author of the single, unbroken chain of events in the film, will make it his business to reorder these jumbled signs into a rational, causal narrative.

Huston spells out the importance of this verbal linkage in a shot of a newspaper which appears after Polhaus's and Dundy's visit to Sam's apartment on the night of the murder. Slanted along the same line as the tombstone-like shadow at the end of the first scene, the headline reads, "THURSBY, ARCHER MURDERS LINKED!" and the camera zooms in to inspect the story. Archer now has a new partner, according to the headline–Thursby. Sam's project is now to determine the connection between their

murders and regain Archer as a partner by coming through for him one last time and sending his murderer to jail.

By displaying a newspaper headline, Huston employs the medium of print to convey the impact of Miles's murder on the city: it is front-page material. The broader social consequences of the case are of the utmost importance to Spade, who bases his decision to send Brigid to jail on the notion that:

> When a man's partner is killed he's supposed to do something about it . . . when one of your organization gets killed it's bad all around–bad for that one organization, bad for every detective everywhere. . .

In the book, the reverberations of the crime are felt in terms of Sam's frequent contact with the forces of law and order–the D.A., policemen, his attorney–who are working on various aspects of the case all over the city. What Hammett explains over the course of many pages, Huston communicates in a single shot.

While Huston's Spade is less deterred by figures of the establishment, he must engage in certain visual struggles which Hammett's Spade escapes. Throughout the film, Bogart vies on a purely visual level for ascendancy over every frame. Huston's scenes often function according to a pictorial "seesaw" principle whereby Spade and his adversaries tower over one another, sit head to head, or knock each other to the floor in the course of their power struggle over the plot.

In Sam's first meeting with Gutman, the two stand on an equal plane as they drink "to plain speaking and clear understanding." However, shortly thereafter, when Gutman begins to question Sam regarding whom the detective represents, the fat man is shot from a low angle, emphasizing the weight he carries in controlling the conversation. When Sam removes himself from Gutman's witness stand by insisting, "Now let's talk about the black bird," a two-shot of the men sitting in chairs opposite each other shows them on equal visual terms again. Yet, not for long. Once Gutman discovers that Sam knows virtually nothing about the falcon, he regains his authoritative weight, pictured again from a low angle.

At the point when Gutman seems to be hammering the final nail into Spade's coffin, remarking, ". . . I don't think we can do business," Sam takes decisive action to gain control of the plot and, simultaneously, the frame. He begins by standing up unexpectedly, towering over Gutman. "Well, think again and think fast. . . . I'm telling you now, you'll talk to me today or you are through. . . . You've got till 5:00. Then you're either in or out–for keeps!" At this point, Sam has managed to place Gutman in a position where the fat man must march to his drummer.

*Clippings of advertisements for a double feature of adaptations from Hammett's novels.* The Maltese Falcon *premiered in New York on 3 October 1941 and was released nationally on 18 October.* The Shadow of the Thin Man *was released on 21 November 1941 (courtesy of Josephine Hammett).*

The visual power that Huston and Bogart give Spade is critical to the film audience. In a plot littered with stories that are told and retold at every turn, where motives are manufactured nonstop in rapid-fire exchanges, it is the force of Bogart's presence that holds the plot together. This is a power that Hammett does not need to capture in print. The book's steady stream of complicated stories can easily be reread. But the film audience must somehow be able to grasp the action upon hearing the actors' speeches only once. Bogart does not operate alone. Huston augments his power by associating him with forces of light that penetrate the dark criminal world. Sam's head inevitably appears next to a lampshade, under a streetlight, or by a window. Bogart is constantly lighting matches.

The value of strong screen presences is evident in Huston's other choices of actors as well—Sydney Greenstreet, Peter Lorre, and Mary Astor. When Gutman tells Sam the complicated history of the falcon, the force of Greenstreet's intriguing characterization carries the viewer through the labyrinthine twists and turns of his account. Greenstreet even bears a certain resemblance to the falcon, with his comparatively small, hairless head, vaguely beakish nose, and puffed-out body. When he grasps the falcon in the last scene and turns it around on the table, his hands look like birds' talons. If not an actor of equal presence as Greenstreet, Bogart or Lorre, Mary Astor was no doubt aided in her portrayal of Brigid by the audience's knowledge of her off-screen history. Astor, who had begun making films in her teens, spent the early part of her career playing innocent young ladies. Yet, she was notorious for having an affair with John Barrymore at the age of 17 and a subsequent, steady stream of husbands and lovers.

Needless to say, according to Hollywood's moral standards in the 1940s, both Astor and Brigid get their due in the end. In the powerful closing moments of the film, the broken and disjunct shapes of words and letters re-emerge in the single, continuous pattern of the elevator cage which closes on Brigid like the prison bars behind which she will soon find herself.

The final sentence pronounced in the film is not a death sentence, but rather a life sentence for the creators of *The Maltese Falcon*. Detective Polhaus asks what the statue represents, and Spade responds, "The stuff that dreams are made of." At last, the disjointed assemblage of street signs and room numbers, the hotel names, printed theater tickets, marquees and newspaper articles collect in the falcon's single lump of lead–the metal from which type is fashioned. For the writer, the director, and the detective, the tale of the falcon returns to its origins, ready to be reshaped by another dream into new chains of type from which yet another story can be struck.

### Notes

1. Robert Scholes, "Narration and Narrativity in Film," *Film Theory and Criticism,* eds. Gerald Mast and Marshall Cohen (New York: Oxford University Press, 1979), pp. 417–433.
2. Scholes, p. 423.
3. Dashiell Hammett, *The Maltese Falcon* (New York: Vintgage Books, 1972), p. 5.
4. Hammett, p. 7.
5. Hammett, p. 33.
6. Hammett, p. 109.
7. Hammett, p. 128.
8. Hammett, p. 3.
9. Hammett, p. 3.

### Works Cited

Astor, Mary. *A Life on Film.* New York: Delacorte Press, 1971.

Hammett, Dashiell. *The Maltese Falcon.* New York: Vintage Books, 1972.

Huston, John. *The Maltese Falcon.* Warner Brothers, 1941.

Kaminsky, Stuart. *John Huston: Maker of Magic.* Boston: Houghton Mifflin Co., 1978.

Madsen, Axel. *John Huston.* New York: Doubleday & Co., 1978.

Mast, Gerald & Marshall Cohen, eds. *Film Theory and Criticism.* New York: Oxford University Press, 1979.

Nolan, William F. *John Huston: King Rebel.* Los Angeles: Sherbourne Press, Inc., 1965.

\* \* \*

### Tracking *The Maltese Falcon:* Classical Hollywood Narration and Sam Spade

William Luhr

*Close Viewings: An Anthology of New Film Criticism,* edited by Peter Lehman (Tallahassee: Florida State University Press, 1990), pp. 7–21

*The Maltese Falcon* is often cited as a milestone film. Its unexpected success not only solidly launched John Huston's career as a director and provided a major stepping stone in Humphrey Bogart's climb from contract player to major star but it also, with *Citizen Kane* in the same year (1941), became a progenitor of *film noir*. It is frequently shown in revival houses and on television but despite its popularity has seldom attracted detailed scholarly attention. As a partial corrective, this essay explores aspects of the film's narrative organization and indicates useful areas for further investigation.

*The Maltese Falcon* was made by Warner Brothers during the peak period of the production mode known as the studio system. That system used the narrative paradigm within which this film operates, and since that paradigm is the dominant one in fiction film production, it is useful here to outline some of its presumptions and techniques.

Classical Hollywood narration became regularized around the time of World War I, is still operative, and functions in distinctly different ways from other narrative modes, such as the international art cinema and many avant-garde cinemas. It focuses upon an individual or small group of individuals who early on encounter discrete and specific goals that are either clearly attained or clearly unattained by the film's end. The goals tend to exist in two spheres, and their pursuit is developed along parallel and often interdependent plot lines. One sphere is private, generally a heterosexual romance; the second is public–a career advance, the obliteration of an enemy, a mission, a discovery, and the like. In *The Maltese Falcon,* for example, Samuel Spade explores a romance with Brigid O'Shaughnessy as well as the case of the Maltese Falcon, and the two are interrelated. He resolves both in separate scenes at the film's end.

Causality provides the prime unifying principle in classical narration. Plot construction tends to be linear, one scene clearly leading to the next. The major hermeneutics raised near the beginning of the film (Will Shane, in *Shane,* bring peace to the valley? Will Marty, in *Marty,* find true love?) are developed, complicated, and then neatly resolved by the film's ending. This does not mean that classical narration requires a happy ending; a definitive failure to attain a goal is as clear a resolution as a success, but the spectator should know the outcome one way or the other.

*Poster for the 1941 French release of the movie (*Temps Noir:
La revue des Literatures Policieres, *no. 7;
Collection of Richard Layman)*

A distinction between the notions of story and plot is useful here. Plot is the sequence of events as presented in the film whereas story is the causal/chronological sequence of events as they theoretically would have occurred in actuality. The plot may begin near the end of the story sequence as a main character nears death and then backtrack to reveal the events that led up to this point, as in *Double Indemnity* or *Citizen Kane*. A story sequence for a film that runs 1-2-3-4-5 may be presented to the viewer as plot sequence 4-1-3-2-5, with the reshuffled event structure indicating part of the film's strategy for evoking spectator response. Classical narration often uses its plot to generate confusion, but it invariably clears up all such confusion by the end. It seldom allows for ambiguous presentation of story elements, something that commonly occurs in the international art cinema in films such as *Persona*.

The spatial, temporal, and sonic techniques of classical narration reinforce this story clarity. The spaces that are shown and the sounds that are heard are subordinated to the logic of the narrative. We seldom see space, for example, that we cannot situate in relation to the film's characters. A character may be

seen in the space or may be looking at it, and the linkage is generally quite clear. Objects are similarly subordinated to narrative causality. In differentiating the narrative strategies of Ozu from those of the classical paradigm, Kristin Thompson and David Bordwell use *The Maltese Falcon* to underline precisely this point: "John Huston wouldn't think of cutting away from Sam Spade and Brigid O'Shaughnessy to a shot of the coat-rack in the corner of the office unless the hats on it had some significance (e.g., in the unravelling of the enigma). Yet in *There Was a Father,* Ozu does cut to a coatrack to begin a sequence in a *go*-parlor, without ever drawing the hats or the space of the rack into the narrative action" (1976, 46).

In classical narration the camera pretends to be an invisible and ideal observer of preexistent events. We get the best views, cued by codes of lighting, framing, and movement, of the most significant actions necessary to further the plot. We see punches thrown and, from a different perspective, received; dialogue spoken and responded to; rockets fired and, miles away but seconds later, hitting their target. The events are presented as having their own integrity and not, as in some Godard films, as being developed with an intimate and formative relationship to the filmmaking apparatus. We do not see camera equipment in the rear of the shot or reflected in mirrors, and actors do not acknowledge the camera's presence. The process of production is concealed; the camera is omnipresent. The individual shots are stitched together according to the highly coded principles of classic continuity editing that emphasize clarity of action and story continuity according to realist norms.

Classical narration has not only changed over time but it also incorporates a wide range of options. It includes a number of genres whose norms of realism vary. A character in a comedy or musical may much more directly acknowledge the camera's presence or defy gravity than one in an historical epic; character options and motivations and actions may be much different in a western than in a detective film.

As a mystery, *The Maltese Falcon* works to confuse the viewer in ways that films in other genres, such as war films or romances, do not. Virtually all classical narrative tries to keep the viewer guessing as to what will happen next, but the mystery foregrounds this and also makes the viewer wonder what has happened in the past and even question the significance of what is happening right now. The project of the film's plot, as well as of the detective, is to uncover its story, and the plot reveals story information in often confusing and apparently contradictory ways. Little can be taken at face value when it appears, although all major story and plot elements become retrospectively consistent at the film's end.

The plot of *The Maltese Falcon* is linear and follows the involvement of the private detective Samuel Spade (Humphrey Bogart) with Brigid O'Shaughnessy (Mary Astor) and the case of the Maltese Falcon. It limits itself primarily to his point of view; with minor exceptions, new information appears as he learns it and events progress according to his participation in them. The film begins when O'Shaughnessy enters his office, moves chronologically forward as he becomes more deeply involved with her and with the complexities of the case, and ends when he turns her over to the police.

Spade must constantly process, question, and reformulate the often deceptive information he receives, and the sinister characters he encounters are developed with reference to deviations from cultural norms only hinted at in the dialogue. His triumph over mystery and danger lies at the center of the film. The ways in which the director, John Huston, organizes formal motifs, explores narrative alternatives and manipulations, and develops subtextual implications of foreignness and deviant sexuality to give that mystery and danger its specificity demonstrate the complexity and aesthetic value of *The Maltese Falcon*.

Early in the film we see a night shot of a half-open window with a slowly fluttering curtain before it. A telephone and a clock sit on a night table in the front of the frame. The phone rings. A hand reaches in from the right and pulls the telephone out of frame. The camera does not move. On the sound track, Spade's voice responds as he learns that his partner, Miles Archer (Jerome Cowan), has been killed. His hand returns the telephone into the frame. Only when the room light goes on do we see Spade's head, in silhouette, enter the frame as the camera moves slightly back. The curtain still flutters.

Spade leaves the apartment to view the scene of Archer's murder. When he returns, two police detectives arrive to tell him of another murder, that of Floyd Thursby, the man Archer had been following. When Detective Polhaus (Ward Bond) describes how Thursby was killed ("He was shot in the back four times with a .44 or .45 from across the street") Polhaus is framed by the same window, with the same fluttering curtain. That window and curtain become visual motifs increasingly associated with sinister events in and influences upon Spade's life.

Although Brigid O'Shaughnessy had first approached Spade concerning Thursby, Archer took the case because he was attracted to her. This leads to his death, which provides the film's first victim of O'Shaughnessy's relentless duplicity. She had originally given her name as "Wonderly" along with a false story

designed to get Spade to take the case. When she contacts him after the two killings, she is living under the name "Leblanc." Her names have changed, and her stories have changed, each change giving Spade a different perception of the situation. Although she has not told him the truth and repeatedly endangers him, she throws herself on his mercy, saying she has no one to turn to. She says she has no money and coyly asks, "What can I buy you with?" He kisses her.

When Spade first brings her to his apartment, she continues to deceive and coyly tantalize him. He catches her in her lies and she reclines on his sofa, saying she is tired of lying, of not knowing what is the truth and what is not. Clearly, part of Spade's attraction to her lies in the very blatancy of her evil, in the seductive danger she embodies. When she reclines, Spade's fluttering curtains are directly behind her, and he bends over to kiss her. Huston cuts to a close shot of her, then Spade's head descends into the frame. Suddenly he stops and looks at the curtains. The camera moves toward and into them, and we see through an opening at the center a sinister-looking man in the street below, watching.

This shot encapsulates major motifs in the film. The curtains have become associated with the dangers that surround Spade's involvement in the case; they evoke the often malignant world that so often intrudes upon him. He is in this scene physically closer to the curtains than at any other time in the film. The man outside is a murderer who has already killed at least one character and will kill more. At this point Spade does not know who this man is or why he is there, but he knows he is dangerous. Furthermore, at this point the danger comes not only from outside the curtains, as it did in the earlier instances, but also from inside them. O'Shaughnessy is within the apartment. She is sexually desirable and available to Spade. As with the man outside, Spade knows little about her, but he knows that she too is dangerous.

The narrative progression of this film is developed largely around befuddlement, around the trying out and discarding of one potential narrative linkage for another. Brigid O'Shaughnessy first came to Spade with a story about how Floyd Thursby ran off with her sister. She asked Archer to follow Thursby. Archer was killed and Thursby was killed and there was no sister. Spade had to return to square one. A bizarre, dandified foreigner, Joel Cairo (Peter Lorre), came to Spade's office and demanded the "black bird." Soon, both Cairo and O'Shaughnessy are terrified to learn that Gutman, "The Fat Man" (Sidney Greenstreet), is in town, and Spade learns that all seek the "bird," the fabled Maltese Falcon. From Brigid O'Shaughnessy's first story, apparent truths and continuities are replaced

*Lobby card for the Spanish version of* The Maltese Falcon, *released in 1941*
*(Collection of Richard Layman)*

by other apparent truths and continuities: nothing is certain.

At the center of all of this is Samuel Spade, who is particularly suited to function in such an environment. One of his basic characteristics is a remarkable analytical intelligence. When O'Shaughnessy first comes to him, she gives him a complicated story. He says little; he watches. When Archer arrives, however, Spade fires off an elaborate and detailed summary of what has been said, showing that he had missed nothing, retained everything, and plotted out a course of action. When he visits the scene of Archer's death he says little, simply looking around for a few moments; but then he quickly tells the police precisely how the murder took place. Many shots in the film simply show him watching, taking it all in, with little indication of his response. The film carefully develops in the viewer the sense that Spade understands virtually everything in complex ways.

A reinforcing instance occurs the day after the first two killings when Spade goes to O'Shaughnessy's rooms. She admits that her initial story was false. He shows neither surprise nor annoyance but tells her that neither he nor Archer believed her story; what they did believe was the two hundred dollars she paid them. He says that they knew the money was more than she would have given had she been telling the truth, and they considered it "enough more" to make her lie all right with them. In going over whether or not she bears responsibility for Archer's death, he tells her no—"Of course you lied to us about your sister and all that, but that didn't count. We didn't believe you." This gives a further insight into what he knew but did not reveal the day before and indicates very untraditional notions of truth, truthfulness, and moral responsibility.

She throws herself on his mercy. She admits that she has been "bad," says she is all alone and in danger, and begs to be allowed to rely on his strength. Utterly abject, she pleads, "Help me." She is appalled to find him not melting with compassion but smirking at her. He responds not to the abject situation she has described but rather critiques her performance in creating it. He says, "You won't need much of anybody's help. You're good. It's chiefly your eyes, I think, and that throb you get in your voice when you say things like, 'Be generous, Mr. Spade.'" In another scene in her room, after asking her a difficult question, he smiles and says, "You're not going to go around the room straightening things and poking the fire again, are you?", indicating his awareness of her ploys of nervous agitation, of diverting attention, of clever deception.

Spade is himself continually performing. In Gutman's rooms, dissatisfied at the slow pace of the negotiations, he loses control of himself, explodes, demands a deadline for a deal, and smashes a glass as he rages out of the room. Huston cuts to a long shot of him walking down a hallway toward the camera. He first appears to be storming, in a rage, but as he gets closer to the camera it is obvious that he is smiling. It has all been an act.

When summoned before the district attorney, he apparently becomes enraged at the infringement on his rights and launches into a seemingly deeply felt tirade against the D.A.'s methods. He suddenly stops, looks at the stenographer, and asks, "You getting all this right, son, or am I going too fast for you?" When the stenographer says he is getting it, Spade says, "Good work," switches back to his tone of outrage, and continues the tirade. Once more he shows himself to be in command of and carefully orchestrating what initially appears to be a spontaneous emotional outburst.

Much of the film's forward narrative drive revolves around Spade's aggressive search for the truth and his processing of and acting upon each new piece of information he receives. He shows a strong awareness of impediments in his way, of people's ability to lie, both in the information they give and in their manner. Not only can he see through many of the deceptions of others but he is also himself able to link and interpret information so as to give the appearance of truth. When he gathers O'Shaughnessy and Cairo in his apartment for the first time, the police arrive and demand entrance. Spade refuses. Suddenly they hear a scream and a crash, and they enter. Cairo's face is bloodied and O'Shaughnessy is holding a gun on him. As the police prepare to arrest them all, Spade smiles and says, "Oh don't be in a hurry, boys, everything can be explained." He then proceeds to concoct a story to "explain" the situation in a way that will divert the police from arresting them and also mollify the terrified Cairo. But no sooner has he finished with this story than he tells the police that both the violent incident and the story were jokes played upon them. He proceeds to tell an entirely different story using the same basic information but giving an

entirely different narrative interpretation to the events. At the end of the second story, he provokes one of the police into hitting him, making the detective vulnerable to brutality charges should the incident become public. Finally the police leave and no one is arrested. O'Shaughnessy looks at Spade in astonishment and admiration and says, "You're absolutely the wildest, most unpredictable person I've ever known." He has, reflecting the narrative tactics of the film, given two entirely different and reasonably logical versions, both false, of a simple event. The next day he encounters the exhausted and suspicious Cairo, who tries to break off contact with Spade after telling him that he always has a smooth explanation for everything. Spade defends himself by saying that it worked and arrogantly asks, "What do you want me to do, learn to stutter?"

When the Falcon is delivered to his office by a dying man, Spade leaves with the statuette and advises his secretary to tell the police everything as it happened, only to leave out the arrival of the statuette and to say that he, and not she, received a call from O'Shaughnessy. We see him making very slight alterations in the truth to create a new truth—not true, but coherent enough to convince. The film is comprised of dozens of these small narratives and narrative adjustments.

One of Spade's prime antagonists is Gutman, whose activities also point to the existence of different realms of truth. When he first appears, approximately halfway through the film, he does not lie about his goals. He quickly clears up a number of cryptic references to the "black bird" by telling Spade the history of the coveted Maltese Falcon. He tells Spade, "These are facts, historical facts. Not schoolbook history, not Mr. Wells's history, but history nevertheless." He then gives the story, largely one of piracy and murder, of the Falcon. Here he provides not a false reorganization of present information, but facts not recorded in traditional histories. He gives an alternate truth—not a false one as those presented by O'Shaughnessy and Spade—but a repressed one associated with evil. He has devoted his life to it.

The trail of evil that the film explores comes mainly from the search for the Maltese Falcon—originally gold and bedecked with jewels but later covered with black enamel for concealment. The one that ultimately appears turns out to be a copy—an enamel-coated, lead statuette. Like most of the "truths" in the film, this is also a chimera; it is constructed to convince but is not real.

It is important that the statue is Maltese—foreign—because the notion of foreignness is central to the presentation of evil in the film. The film is set

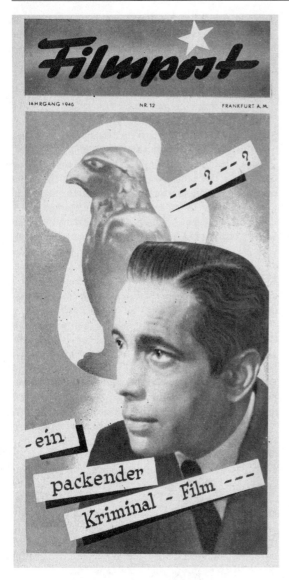

*Front cover of the German periodical with a feature on* The Maltese Falcon *in 1946, the year of its first German release (Collection of Richard Layman)*

Before we even see Joel Cairo, Effie (Spade's secretary, played by Lee Patrick) hands Spade Cairo's scented card and with a knowing smirk says, "Gardenia," implying effeminacy. This introduces another aspect of foreignness, that of deviant sexuality. Cairo is of unspecified origin, although he has at least three passports, and his name, if it is his, might suggest that he is Egyptian. But he is clearly coded as foreign, not American. The film also strongly implies that he is homosexual as perceived by codes of the 1940s: his effeminacy, dandification, "feminine" hysteria, at times mothering affection for Wilmer (Elisha Cook, Jr.), and apparent sexual rivalry with O'Shaughnessy over "that boy in Istanbul" all point to deviations from contemporary norms.

Associations of homosexuality are also given to Wilmer, Gutman's bodyguard and hired killer. While he shares none of Cairo's effeminate qualities and is in fact morosely pugnacious, he is constantly referred to as the "boy," and Spade refers to him as a "gunsel"–a term meaning gunman, but also meaning a boy used in pederasty. When Spade knocks him out near the end of the film, we see him unconscious on a sofa in a very curious shot that emphasizes his groin. Nothing is overt, but associations of homosexuality, of sexual otherness, are implied.

Gutman's nationality is not given, but he sounds and appears British. He shows a profound attraction to the Falcon, whose history is one of evil and betrayal in foreign places. His most recent encounter with it took place in Istanbul, where he also dealt with Cairo and O'Shaughnessy. When the false Falcon arrives, it has come from Hong Kong. When Gutman learns it is false, he prepares to return to Istanbul.

Gutman's sexuality is questionable. He shows no interest in women. Wilmer and Cairo seem fiercely devoted to him. But his real obsession appears to be a fetishistic one with the Maltese Falcon. When Spade demands he betray Wilmer in order to get the Falcon, Gutman does so. By way of apology he tells Wilmer, "I couldn't be fonder of you if you were my own son but, well, if you lose a son, it's possible to get another. There's only one Maltese Falcon. When you're young you simply don't understand these things." When what he thinks is the Falcon arrives, he unwraps it in an almost orgiastic ecstasy.

The film opens with a number of shots of San Francisco. It and Spade become established as norms against which all else is measured. Virtually all danger and evil come from "somewhere else." The most immoral thing we see Spade involved in is heterosexual excess: he has been sleeping with Archer's wife. And Archer is killed largely as a result of his heterosexual lust for O'Shaughnessy. The film ends as

entirely in San Francisco and carefully associates things evil with things different from the position that Spade occupies–that of an American, heterosexual, Anglo-Saxon male. The notion of foreignness is introduced early on. O'Shaughnessy first claims Thursby had a wife and three children "in England." Spade instantly recognizes the gun that killed Archer as British. O'Shaughnessy later admits that she met Thursby, a killer, in "the Orient," and her clothes come from Hong Kong.

Spade sends O'Shaughnessy off to jail for Archer's murder, a decision influenced by her sexual promiscuity. He knows she was Thursby's mistress and says, "I won't walk in Thursby's and I don't know how many other footsteps."

In many ways the film has two endings and two narratives cleverly blended. It seems to end after the Falcon is discovered to be false and Gutman and Cairo prepare to return to Istanbul to continue the hunt. Spade calls the police and reports them. All seems tied up. He has dealt definitively with the business of the Falcon, and he has saved O'Shaughnessy from the sinister crew, so the public and private spheres of the story seem resolved; but suddenly he turns on O'Shaughnessy and accuses her of Archer's murder. To this point it has seemed apparent that Thursby killed Archer, and all seem to accept this. Archer was following Thursby and was killed with Thursby's gun. Spade now shows O'Shaughnessy why this could not have happened, and she admits her guilt.

Now it is clear that what had first appeared to be the film's resolution was only a partial resolution. It is also apparent here that the story of O'Shaughnessy has very little to do with the story of the Maltese Falcon. It frames that story. The story really begins when Cairo enters Spade's office and ends when the statuette is found to be false. Within that story, O'Shaughnessy is little more than a pawn, an ally of Thursby, whom we never see. Even her intense sexual desirability serves her little in that story, since that is the story of deviant sexuality, of Gutman's fetishistic obsession and his possibly homosexual acolytes in exotic, foreign places.

In San Francisco, however, her sexuality serves her much better, and the framing story, the one opening and closing the film, is of her and Spade. It is also one of heterosexual excess in which Spade is complicit. Spade desires her; so does Archer. She kills Archer to implicate her lover, Thursby. Spade is implicated in the killing because the police know he has been sleeping with Archer's wife, who was also suspiciously absent from her home on the night her husband was killed. Archer's wife at times implicates Spade, perhaps because Spade has lost interest in her after he has met O'Shaughnessy.

When Spade tells O'Shaughnessy he is going to turn her in to the police, he sits in his apartment with a sickened, dazed look on his face. It is the only time in the film that he appears to be genuinely speaking from his heart. He explains his confusion and his vestigial morality and the reasons he must turn her in. It is part of the only daylight sequence in his apartment, and he

sits not in front of the curtains in the window but in front of their prominent shadow on the wall.

At this point, the Maltese Falcon has become irrelevant to the story, which now concerns only Spade, O'Shaughnessy, Archer, and Thursby. The curtains had earlier been significant in shots related to scenes of O'Shaughnessy's evil—when Spade learned of Archer's death, when Polhaus described Thursby's death, and when Spade was about to kiss O'Shaughnessy and paused as he spotted Wilmer through the curtains. At that point it appeared that Wilmer was the danger; we now know that in fact O'Shaughnessy was more dangerous. Her desirability masked her evil and almost entrapped Spade. It is likely that that kiss we never saw was only interrupted, not prevented by the sight through the curtains. The next time we see the two together they are much less formal, more affectionate; they call each other "Darling" and "Angel," and O'Shaughnessy tells Spade her apartment had been searched that morning, indicating that she may have spent the night with Spade. Given the censorship codes of the time, these subtextual hints provide a strong indication that the two have slept together, thus making Spade more vulnerable to her machinations.

From that point to the final scene in Spade's apartment the curtains do not serve a significant formal function. Then, suddenly, when the Falcon story is cleared away, they again become central. O'Shaughnessy sits more or less in front of them, but most important, their shadow now frames Spade in daylight. Now that Spade understands everything they no longer appear ominous, but they serve as a muted reference to the dangers Spade encountered and tamed.

### Works Cited

Thompson, Kristin, and David Bordwell "Space and Narrative in the Films of Ozu," *Screen,* 17 (Summer 1976): 46.

\* \* \*

**An Anomaly in *The Maltese Falcon***
Peter P. Gillis
*ANQ,* 8 (Summer 1995): 29–31

After acquiring the film rights to Dashiell Hammett's *The Maltese Falcon,* Warner Bros. had the good judgment not to vary Hammett's original story line. In fact, the film dialogue is largely taken verbatim from the novel, even though the credits list director John Huston as the author of the screenplay. This note addresses a small but significant dialogue difference between novel and film, found in an early exchange

*Lobby card for the Mexican release of* The Maltese Falcon, *released in 1948 (Collection of Richard Layman)*

between private detective Sam Spade (Humphrey Bogart) and police sergeant Tom Polhaus (Ward Bond).

The written version has Spade identify the weapon used to kill his partner, Miles Archer, as a "Webley Fosbery automatic revolver. That's it. Thirty-eight, eight shot" (14). The film version is almost identical except that "thirty-eight" is changed to "forty-five." Why change the caliber of the gun?

Before suggesting an answer, a brief description and explanation of the "Webley Fosbery automatic revolver" is in order. Near the beginning of the nineteenth century, Samuel Colt obtained patents for a firearm in which when the hammer was cocked, a cylinder rotated bringing a fresh charge into firing position behind a single, stationary barrel. At the close of the nineteenth century, arms manufacturers in Europe and America were making improvements to cartridge handguns that eliminated the traditional need to manually cock the hammer for each shot. Revolver lockwork was developed by which pulling the trigger cocked the hammer and rotated the cylinder. Semiautomatic (self-loading) pistols were developed that used a reciprocating, relative motion of one portion of the gun not only to recock its hammer but also to reload its firing chamber. In the vernacular, semiautomatic pistols are usually referred to as automatics.

The Webley Fosbery design applied the reciprocating motion of an automatic to an otherwise ordinary revolver. When it fired, the upper portion recoiled rearwards relative to the hand-held lower portion and returned to battery under impetus of a recoil spring. This relative motion recocked the hammer and rotated the cylinder.

The popularity of this unique firearm was minimal. When it appeared in 1900, it appealed largely to target shooters, who valued its feature of seemingly less recoil than other forty-five caliber handguns then available. To expand this initial market, the firm developed a model adapted to fire a thirty-eight caliber pistol cartridge used in the popular, contemporary, semiautomatic Colt pistols. These rimless cartridges required a special loading disc or clip to accommodate the revolver cylinder. This feature proved unpopular and the thirty-eight caliber Model 1902 consequently failed to sell. Although the manufacturer maintained an inventory and catalogued it until World War II, only a few hundred guns were sold. Knowledgeable recent estimates indicate clearly that the Model 1902, thirty-eight caliber, Webley Fosbery automatic revolver is, and always was, a very scarce item.[1]

Given its rarity, it was too valuable a piece to be toted in the overcoat pocket of a character the likes of Floyd Thursby (or to be casually loaned by him to the murderer who unceremoniously dumped it at the scene of the crime). Hammett wanted to provide singular weapons for Thursby, whose other gun, a Luger, was less exotic but not commonplace. No doubt when he wrote the novel, Hammett was unaware of the rarity of the Model 1902.

What prompted the change to a forty-five caliber, Webley Fosbery automatic revolver in the screen play? Any number of answers present themselves and all are conjectural. It may have been that a reader explained the situation to Hammett after the book was published. Perhaps during filming the prop department found it impossible to procure a thirty-eight. Possibly director Huston (or one of his assistants) was better informed about Webley Fosberys than Hammett.

However, in substituting a forty-five for the thirty-eight a new irony presents itself. The thirty-eight is an eight-shot model, as Spade says, but all forty-fives are six shooters. If Ward Bond had examined the specimen he showed to Humphrey Bogart in the film, he would have immediately noticed the inconsistency in the script. The prop man who loaded the single, blank cartridge for the scene in which Archer is shot must have known that either the capacity or the caliber was inconsistent with Bogart's lines. So even though the novel describes a gun that is extremely rare, the film dialogue describes a gun that is nonexistent.

**Note**

1. Bruce estimates the total Model 1902 production at about two to three hundred guns. He states that because there was no demand for thirty-eights, a hundred of these, in inventory at the factory, were disassembled so that parts could by reused in the manufacture of forty-five caliber models (25). In a Sales List dated October 21, 1991, for the Victoria Trading Company, RR 1, Box 1495, Newfane, VT 05345, J. R. Sinon, the so-called "Webley King," advertised a Model 1902 using this sales blurb: "FOSBERY, 1902, EXTREMELY RARE .38 Automatic, 6",
8-shot, 98% blue, perfect bore and grips, possibly finest specimen extant of this rarest of the Fosberys (only 40 manufactured, only 4 in private hands) . . . $20,000.00." The following month the final numbers were revised to read: "(est. prod. 100+, surviving specimens only 8–10, only 4 privately held) . . . sold."

\* \* \*

### *The Maltese Falcon:* Melodrama or Film Noir?
Steven H. Gale
*Literature/Film Quarterly,* 24 (1996): 145–147

Near the end of John Huston's classic film version of *The Maltese Falcon* the assembled cast of characters discovers that the statue which they have in their possession is not the solid gold, jewel-encrusted figure that they have been seeking. Realizing that "The Russian" has fooled them, Casper Gutman (played by Sidney Greenstreet) and Joel Cairo (Peter Lorre) determine to return to Istanbul to continue their quest. Sam Spade (Humphrey Bogart) and Brigid O'Shaughnessy (Mary Astor) elect to remain in San Francisco.

It would seem that this would be the end of the motion picture, yet the movie's conclusion is delayed for several minutes, until Spade turns O'Shaughnessy over to the police for having murdered his detective agency partner, Miles Archer (Barton MacLane). At first glance it seems that this final sequence is either anticlimactic or that it is not consistent with the rest of the action that takes place in the film. However, an examination of the opening minute and a half of the movie demonstrates not only that this extended ending is prepared for but that it is really what the film has been about all along.

Though Huston had been a writer in Hollywood for ten years, *The Maltese Falcon* was the first film that he directed. Still considered by many to be his best film (in an 18 September 1950 *Life* article, James Agee called this third cinematic adaptation of Dashiell Hammett's novel "the best private-eye melodrama ever made"), it contains some of the thematic approaches and cinematic techniques that characterize Huston's work throughout his extended and extraordinary directing career, including his final film, *The Dead.*

Scripted by Huston, the picture opens with the credits over a long take of the black falcon statue. It is a straight-on shot, a close-up, and the camera is stationary. Although not an establishing shot in the traditional sense of the term, this take prepares the audience for the importance of the figurine in the development of the plot. It also is a vital element to be taken into account in an assessment of the film, for it is one of the determining factors in whether *The Maltese Falcon* is deciding a melodrama or an example of *film noir,* a subject of critical debate when the film was released.

Melodrama as a genre has existed since the classical Greek theater, though in the early nineteenth century the definition began to focus on the

*Daybill for the Australian rerelease in the 1970s (Collection of Richard Layman)*

sensational actions and violent appeals to the emotions. According to various literary dictionaries, the characteristics that define a melodrama are that it intensifies sentiment, exaggerates emotion, and relates sensational and thrilling incidents in which all other elements are subordinated to extravagant sensational action and clearly virtuous characters are pitted against clearly vicious characters in sensational situations filled with suspense, with virtue triumphing over unlikely circumstances.[1] Traditionally, the social fabric has been incidental and not the fundamental focus of works in this genre.

*Film noir,* on the other hand, is a label that French film critics applied to certain American gangster films beginning in the 1940s. These movies are characterized by heavily low-key lighting and a bleak and literally black atmosphere in both the visual images and the themes conveyed. Typically, these motion pictures emphasize a fatalistic, despairing view of life in which dread and paranoia mold the characters' actions. There is a social component involved in *film noir* as the dark side of the psyches of the characters are examined, especially as they relate to social conventions.[2]

The falcon statue is what the major characters in Huston's *The Maltese Falcon* are seeking, and their search initiates the events that involve everyone else in the film. Still, the statue itself has no intrinsic value—its only worth is the symbolic value attached to gold and jewels. Part of the definition of a melodrama is that it is a conflict over an object that has no intrinsic value so, on a superficial level, *The Maltese Falcon* is a melodrama. This aspect of the film is underscored by the legend that is scrolled on the screen, purportedly to explain the origin and mystical history of the figure and, incidentally, to initiate a quest motif.

There follows an establishing shot of San Francisco, with the title "San Francisco" superimposed over the shot. If the next shot had been the start of the action in the Spade and Archer Detective Agency offices, the movie might well have unfolded as a mystery-action-adventure story. Instead, there is a pan of the bay panorama intercut with views of the Golden Gate Bridge and of Fisherman's Wharf. Although it is not clear at this point, the fact that there is a *series* of establishing shots transfers the emphasis of the film from the statue and involves humanity and contemporary 1941 American society.

The next shot is of a window in the detective agency office, seen from the inside. The painted words Spade and Archer appear on the window in reverse. The camera then pans down to reveal

Spade sitting at his desk. By this time the film's underlying thematic events have been exposed.

Hammett's 1930 novel contains the elements that director Huston develops to deliver a *film noir,* and these opening moments from the movie exemplify how well Huston exploits his cinematic medium in translating the novel to celluloid. In moving from the stationary shot of the statue to pans of the city, Huston directs his audience away from the melodramatic to a focus on the societal. By showing the lettering on the detective agency window, he clearly links the characters of Spade and Archer in their partnership. Because the names are seen in reverse, though, Huston is letting his audience know that everything is not exactly as it seems and that either the partnership or the characters are not pure and upstanding (the lettering reappears as shadows on the floor or walls in a number of subsequent scenes, reinforcing these motifs).

When Sam Spade is revealed, he is seen in a close-up, and the word Archer is seen on the window behind his head. Since he is the protagonist, it is fitting that Spade is the first character shown, that the shot is a close-up (the other characters are introduced in full shots), and that his face is brightly lit. The juxtaposition of his head and Archer's name, after the Spade/Archer partnership has been established by the window legend, prepares the audience for the final thematic strand. Spade may be presented as a somewhat dubious character involved in a somewhat dubious business, but ultimately he is found to be admirable because he adheres to an accepted societal code: partners are expected to look out for each other. If, as transpires in this tale, something happens to one partner, it is incumbent upon the other partner to set things right. Thus, when Spade rejects O'Shaughnessy at the end of *The Maltese Falcon,* he is exhibiting the highest order of integrity by refusing to let his personal desires overcome his societal responsibilities. All of this has been foreshadowed by the opening ninety seconds of the movie.

Interestingly, Huston's original script contains only the barest outline of what appears in the final cut of the movie. The working titles for the 1941 Warner Brothers release reflect how the film took on added significance during its transformation from scenario to celluloid. Neither *The Gent from Frisco* nor *The Knight of Malta* holds the symbolic values contained in *The Maltese Falcon,* and the first two shots in Huston's screenplay (a typescript version of which is in the John Huston Collection at the Margaret Herrick Library at the Academy of

*Poster advertising Gordon's Gin, 1983*
*(Collection of Richard Layman)*

Clearly, with the inclusion of the V motif and the allusion to Satan, Huston was consciously incorporating symbolic values in the film. Even the opening establishing shot through the agency window with the lettering seen in reverse must have been a conscious effort to begin the development of those thematic components discussed above. Still, the shots as described in the script do not allow for the manifestation of the full symbolic significance of the shadowy representation of Spade's world and ethics embodied in the filmed version of the scene—and it is the exploration of these aspects of the tale that transform it from a melodrama to *film noir*. Huston has successfully exploited his establishing shots, the use of shadow, and the concept of reversal to open what has become a major example of the genre and in doing so he has also demonstrated the effective kind of montage that will become characteristic of the genre.

Initially, the characters in *The Maltese Falcon* are clear representations of good and evil. As the movie proceeds, these impressions become blurred, only to be resolved at the picture's conclusion. The opening shots of the film, then, demonstrate how important the first moments of *The Maltese Falcon* are in establishing the tone, theme, and characterization that shape the rest of the movie. Even today, over fifty years later, the influence of this film is clearly evident in current movies. The definition of the *film noir* genre, with its dark emphasis on imperfect human characters confronted with the corrupting nature of greed, lust, and evil, yet salvaged by individual moral strength, can be traced to the very first images seen in *The Maltese Falcon*. Furthermore, these opening shots, compared to the written script, provide a nice example of how a cinematic artist such as John Huston truly develops his creative art only when he is working with the celluloid medium itself.

Motion Picture Arts and Sciences in Beverly Hills) are more in line with those tentative titles:

FADE IN.

1. CLOSE SHOT ON A WINDOW upon which the words—SPADE AND ARCHER—appear in reverse, in big black letters. Through the window we see in the left tall buildings that front San Francisco's Market Street, to the right, a section of the Bay Bridge.
CAMERA PULLS BACK TO:
2. INT. OFFICE CLOSE SHOT SAM SPADE behind his cheap office desk, back to the window. His jaw is long and bony, his chin a jutting V under the more flexible V of his mouth. The V motif is picked up again by thickish brows rising upward from twin creases above a hooked nose. His dark hair grows down to a point on his forehead. he looks rather pleasantly like Satan. Spade is rolling a cigarette. OVER SCENE the SOUND of the office door opening. He does not look up.
SPADE: Yes, sweetheart?

## Notes

1. See for instance *The Compact Edition of the Oxford English Dictionary* (Oxford: Oxford University Press, 1971); *The Companion to the Theatre* (Oxford University Press, 4th ed., 1983); Harry Shaw, *Concise Dictionary of Literary Terms* (New York: McGraw-Hill, 1972); and Sylvan Barnet, Morton Berman, and William Burto, *A Dictionary of Literary Terms* (Boston: Little, Brown, 1960).

2. See Frank E. Beaver, *Dictionary of Film Terms* (New York: McGraw-Hill, 1983), Louis Giannetti, *Understanding Movies* (Englewood Cliffs, N.J.: Prentice-Hall, 1996), and Gerald Mast, *A Short History of the Movies* (Indianapolis: Bobbs-Merrill, 1976), among others.

## Play Productions

There were two false starts on a stage version of The Maltese Falcon; the first terminated because rights could not be secured from Warner Bros.; the second terminated because it was not suitable for production. The idea for a play originated with Hammett, who wrote to Harry Block, his editor at Knopf, on 16

June 1929: "Though I hadn't anything of the sort in mind while doing it, I think now that it could very easily be turned into a play. Will you let me know if you agree with me? I wouldn't take a chance on trying to adapt it myself, but will try to get the help of somebody who knows the theater."

TELEPHONE:
LONGACRE 3301

MEMBER OF THE INCORPORATED SOCIETY OF AUTHORS' REPRESENTATIVES

CABLE ADDRESS:
AMPLACO

## AMERICAN PLAY COMPANY, INC.

REPRESENTING AMERICAN AND FOREIGN AUTHORS

33 WEST 42ND STREET      NEW YORK CITY

JOHN W. RUMSEY
PRESIDENT

LELAND HAYWARD
SECRETARY

HENRY A. HUBMAN
MANAGER MOTION PICTURE DEPARTMENT

EDWARD W. HART
MANAGER STOCK DEPARTMENT

MEMORANDUM OF AGREEMENT made this 1st day of August 1930, between Dashiell Hammett of New York City, N.Y., of the one part hereinafter called the Author and Benjamin F. Glazer of Hollywood, California, of the other part hereinafter called the Dramatist.

WHEREAS, the Author hereby warrants that he is possessed of the sole and exclusive right to dispose of all rights, excepting the serial publication rights, novel publication rights, and the world's talking motion picture rights of a novel entitled "THE MALTESE FALCON", and desires to have Glazer make a dramatization of the said novel; and

WHEREAS, Glazer desires to have the sole and exclusive right to make a dramatization of said novel.

1. The Author hereby grants to the Dramatist the sole and exclusive right to make a dramatization (to be performed by living actors on the spoken stage) of the said novel, and hereby states and guarantees to the Dramatist that he has not transferred, disposed of, or affected any of the right, of, in or to said novel, except serial publication rights, novel publication rights, and the world's talking motion picture rights, and that he has full right to enter into this agreement and to vest the Dramatist with the rights herein granted to him. The Author further hereby agrees that he will not during the term of this Agreement, give permission to, or authorize any other person, firm or corporation to make a dramatization of said novel and will not in any way, transfer, dispose of, or assign, or affect any rights in and to said novel, or incidental to or connected therewith.

2. The Dramatist agrees to make a dramatization of said novel in such a manner as he shall deem best, and shall exhibit same to the author on or before the 1st day of November 1930. In the event the Dramatist shall not so exhibit the dramatization of the said novel on or before the 1st day of November 1930, then, all rights granted hereunder shall terminate, and this agreement shall be considered at an end.

3. It is understood and agreed that upon the completion of such dramatization and its exhibiton to the Author, the Dramatist with the aid, help and advice of the Agents named in this agreement, shall use his best endeavors to obtain a contract for the production of the play by a first class management in the United States of America, or in Great Britain, on the best possible terms procurable. In the event that no

*First page of a contract between Hammett and Benjamin Glazer for stage dramatization of* The Maltese Falcon. *Because Warner Bros. had earlier bought all rights, including stage rights, the contract was terminated on 19 December 1930 (The Henry A. and Albert W. Berg Collection, New York Public Library).*

A Failed Play

HERE'S TO CRIME

By

LAURENCE STALLINGS

Adapted from
Dashiell Hammett's novel
"The Maltese Falcon"

Return to
Laurence Schwab
234 West 44th St.,
New York City.

HERE'S TO CRIME

NOTE:

   The suggested setting for this play consists of a
permanent front frame divided into three spaces.

   The centre space is about twenty feet wide. The
two spaces at the sides are each about seven feet wide.

   The centre space consists of a jack knife stage
holding two sets: SPADE'S APARTMENT AND SPADE'S OFFICE.
The centre space will also contain the prologue set of
CONSTANTINOPLE. This will be set, however, practically
in front of Spade's apartment, as it will consist of
a desk, a chair, a barred window and some drapes.

   One side stage will hold two sets: the BILLBOARD
scene firstly, and then MISS WONDERLEY'S apartment.
The other side will hold HOTEL LOBBY and, secondly,
a CHEAP BEDROOM. They will probably all be swung around
into set.

   Where scenes consist of telephone booths only,
these will also be fitted or moved into the side sets.
The sets never change, except for the drapes of the
Constantinople scene.

## "Maltese Falcon" Script Completed

Laurence Stallings has completed his dramatization of Dashiell Hammett's cold-blooded detective story, "The Maltese Falcon." The play will be one of Jed Harris's most ambitious enterprises of next fall, if all goes well. Mr. Stallings is through with work for the motion picture studios, he says, at least until silent pictures are once more a sizable item in film schedules.

*Announcement in the* New York Herald Tribune *(12 March 1931) along with the title page and a staging note for the 112-page stage dramatization by Laurence Stallings. The contract was finally terminated on 7 February 1946. The play was never produced (Mills Music Library, University of Wisconsin–Madison).*

## Radio Broadcasts and Serials

The Adventures of Sam Spade *(1946–1951) and* The Fat Man *(1946–1950) were among the most successful radio serials of the day. Though Hammett had nothing to do with either of them, except to license rights to his characters, he* *earned $400 a week for each. The idea for "The Fat Man" was originated by Hammett's agent Lawrence White, who based the character on Caspar Gutman. Both shows were canceled because of Hammett's political activities.*

EXECUTIVE OFFICES
321 WEST 44TH STREET
NEW YORK

TELEPHONE
EXCHANGE
HOLLY 1251

7. √

PICTURES, INC.
WEST COAST STUDIOS
BURBANK, CALIFORNIA

June 5, 1946

Famous Artists Corp.,
9441 Wilshire Blvd.,
Beverly Hills, Calif.

Gentlemen:

For and in consideration of the sum of One Thousand Dollars ($1,000) to be paid by you to us, as hereinafter set forth, we hereby grant to you, by way of license only, the right to use the screen play used by us as the basis of the motion picture heretofore produced and released by us under the title "MALTESE FALCON", for the purpose of presenting one (1) radio broadcasting program based upon said screen play, said radio program being known as the Academy Award Theatre, and to be broadcast over the Columbia Broadcasting System through its stations in the United States of America and its territories thereof and the Dominion of Canada on July 3, 1946, with the further right, if so desired by you, to broadcast once by short wave a de-commercialized transcription of your aforesaid radio program, which said transcription shall be broadcast only to the Armed Forces overseas.

It is, of course, understood and agreed that no property right of any nature whatsoever is hereby granted, conveyed or transferred to you in and to said screen play, but the privileges granted you hereunder are merely by way of license for the purpose aforesaid. We also agree that you may, and you are hereby authorized to, condense, modify and adapt the aforesaid screen play for the purpose of your said radio broadcasting program, and further agree that you and/or E. R. Squibb & Sons, sponsors of the aforesaid program, may use the name of the motion picture "MALTESE FALCON" in any proper way in connection with the advertising and/or giving of publicity to the said radio program.

You agree to submit to our Mr. Alex Evelove of our Publicity Department at our studio at Burbank, California for his approval, the script intended to be used as the basis of said radio program at least forty-eight (48) hours before the time set for said radio program. As a condition of our granting you the aforesaid license, you also agree, in connection with the presentation of said radio program, to make or cause to be made a statement or credit with respect to our motion pictures "The Big Sleep", "One More Tomorrow" and "The 20th Anniversary of Sound", and in this connection you agree to ascertain from Mr. Evelove the nature and extent of such statement.

You have represented to us that you have obtained, or will obtain, the consent of Columbia Pictures Corporation to the appearance

VITAPHONE

*First page of the contract granting radio rights for the broadcast of the screenplay of* The Maltese Falcon
*(courtesy of Warner Bros. Archive, University of Southern California)*

## The Case of *The Adventures of Sam Spade*

*On 28 May 1948 Warner Bros. sued the broadcaster, sponsor, producer, and director of the radio serial "The Adventures of Sam Spade" in U.S. District Court in California for copyright infringement and unfair competition, charging that the radio program had appropriated "among other things scenes, language, story, dialogue, plot, characters, and other materials" of* The Maltese Falcon, *to which Warner had bought all performance rights in 1930. On 9 June 1948 Hammett filed a successful complaint in U.S. District Court in New York seeking to be named as a party to the suit. On 28 December 1951, the California suit was decided in Hammett's favor, a decision upheld by the U.S. Court of Appeals on 9 November 1954, three years after the radio show had been canceled. This affidavit was filed in connection with that action.*

### Affidavit of Dashiell Hammett

UNITED STATES DISTRICT COURT,
SOUTHERN DISTRICT OF NEW YORK.
STATE OF NEW YORK,
COUNTY OF NEW YORK.

DASHIELL HAMMETT, being duly sworn, deposes and says:

I am the plaintiff above-named and submit this affidavit in support of the plaintiff's motion for summary judgment.

I was born in St. Mary County, Maryland on May 27, 1894 and am and have been a resident and citizen of the State of New York for well over the past ten years excepting only the period from September 13, 1942 to September 6, 1945 when I was in Military service with the U. S. Army. Following my honorable discharge on the latter date, I resided at 15 East 66th Street, New York City until about December, 1947 when I moved to my present address of 28 West 10th Street, New York City, where I have since resided. I have at no time resided in or been a citizen of the State of Delaware.

Professionally, I am and have been an author for about the past 25 years. My writings have consisted mainly of fiction in the mystery or detective story field. I have lectured on and have also been a critic and reviewer of literature in those fields. During the year 1926 as well as during the years of 1930 and 1931 I was engaged and served in the latter capacities for the *Saturday Review of Literature* and the New York *Evening Post* respectively. Prior to 1929 when I wrote the mystery detective story entitled "The Maltese Falcon" I had written a number of detective stories and two novels entitled "Red Harvest" and "The Dain Curse." These writings were published and well received.

*Clipping of an advertisement for the radio adaptation of*
The Maltese Falcon, *broadcast in 1943*
*(courtesy of Josephine Hammett)*

"The Maltese Falcon" was first published serially under that title about the latter part of 1929 in the periodical known as the *Black Mask* magazine. This work brought favorable response and as a consequence was published in book or novel form in early 1930 by the publisher, Alfred A. Knopf, Inc. The latter had received copyright assignments covering the work from the periodical publisher and had registered its own copyright on the book at about the time of its publication. The book successfully impressed critics and public alike.

This volume was translated and published in Denmark, Spain, France, England, Germany, Hungary, Sweden and Portugal, as well as in English on the Continent. Other American editions besides Knopf's were put out by Grosset and Dunlap, McClure, the Modern Library, and Pocket Books. It was included in "The Hammett Omnibus" which has been published by Grosset and Dunlop, the World Publishing Company, and Pocket Books. Serializations have appeared in foreign newspapers and American magazines.

The following comments have been made about "The Maltese Falcon":

SAM SPADE                                  (REVISED)        -2-
7-9-46

ANNCR:     Dashiell Hammett, America's leading detective fiction

           writer and creator of Sam Spade, the hard-boiled private

           eye, and William Spier, radio's outstanding producer-

           director of mystery and crime drama, join their talents

           to make your hair stand on end with the Adventures of Sam

           Spade...(MUSIC ACCENT)...presented each week by Wildroot

           Cream Oil, the non-alcoholic hair tonic that will put

           your hair back in place again...grooming it neatly,

           naturally the way you want it. Wildroot Cream Oil....

           the non-alcoholic hair tonic that contains LANOLIN.

           Everyday life is full of mysteries...and one of them, men,

           is how to make a hit with a girl. So give a listen while

           I give you a clue in the form of a recent survey. 97

           out of 100 girls said they turn thumbs down on a man

           whose hair is either unkempt or too slicked down. So don't

           look that way! Spruce up with Wildroot Cream Oil. It

           grooms your hair neatly and naturally. And as our

           survey shows, that's exactly how girls like to see it.

           Besides, non-alcoholic Wildroot Cream Oil relieves dryness

           and removes loose dandruff. It contains LANOLIN. So ask

           for Wildroot Cream Oil. (MUSIC: SNEAK UNDER) And now,

           Wildroot brings to the air for the first time, the

           greatest private detective of 'em all...in....the

           Adventures of Sam Spade!

MUSIC:     UP TO SHOW

*First page of a radio script for* The Adventures of Sam Spade. *The weekly radio serial was broadcast on CBS from 12 July 1946 to 1949 and on NBC from 1949 to 1951 (Collection of Richard Layman).*

"The story has plenty of action, a good plot, excellent characterization, and a startling denouement * * *. This is not only probably the best detective story we have ever read, it is an exceedingly well written novel."

W. R. BROOKS,
*The Outlook,* 2/26/30

"Mr. Hammett has written a fascinating story, thrilling from cover to cover, and amazing in its developments * * * Grand literature it is, a racy American sort of writing * * *."

*Detroit News,* 2/23/30

" * * * combine the traditional elements of detective fiction with quick humor, hard, real characters and effective writing."

*New York Post,* 3/27/30

"Dashiell Hammett's 'The Maltese Falcon' is an excellent and thrilling mystery story."

STANLEY WALKER
*New York Herald-Tribune*
7/27/30

About this time, too, Warner Brothers Pictures, Inc., one of the major motion picture companies, became interested in making a motion picture of or based upon "The Maltese Falcon." Negotiations with

said defendant company (hereinafter also referred to as "Warner's") took place in New York City, where I resided. After a price of $8,500. was fixed, Warner's sent over to the publisher Alfred A. Knopf, Inc. in New York City its proposed agreement (Exhibit "A" to Complaint) for execution by the publisher and myself. It was signed by the publisher and myself at the former's offices in New York City on June 30, 1930 and countersigned by Warner's also in New York City the day following.

In this work I for the first time employed the fictional private detective whom I named "Sam Spade." He is a leading character in the book. He was a figure originated and created from my imagination as well as my personal experience with private detectives garnered during the period from 1915 to 1922, when I was myself a Pinkerton (private) detective. In making his debut, "Sam Spade" too was well received in the select circle of fictional detectives. Ellery Queen, one of my colleagues in this field of literature refers to him as "the great Sam Spade" (introduction to "The Return of the Continental Op" published by Jonathan Press Inc., 1945) and comments at length about this character in his Introduction to the collection entitled "The Adventures of Sam Spade" hereinafter referred to. I subsequently employed Sam Spade as the central character in three later stories written by me from about 1932 to 1934 and first published in *Collier's* and the *American Magazine.* These stories were thereafter published in a collection of stories entitled "The Adventures of Sam

*Comic-strip advertisement published in newspapers. Wildroot was the sponsor for* The Adventures of Sam Spade *(Collection of Richard Layman).*

# John Crosby
# Sam Spade's style stirs up new crime detection angle

The curtain had just risen on the Sam Spade program (KNX, 8 p.m. Sundays), when Mr. Spade's secretary got a phone call from the boss, who, it appears, was in jail charged with murder.

"Bring a pencil and $20,000 down to the jail at once," he commanded.

"Sam," she protested, "where will I find a pencil at this hour? What are you doing in jail, anyway?"

"My apartment's being redecorated, toots."

That is not the sort of badinage you and I would employ in a fairly serious situation but it's hardly surprising to find Mr. Spade behaving that way. Dashiell Hammett, who still writes the Spade series, started this offhand sort of talk back in 1934 when he hit the big time with "The Thin Man." He is now the most widely imitated detective story writer on earth and the casual attitude toward homicide has become established as good manners among all plain-clothed cops.

Mr. Hammett has always taken a detached and rather cold view of human life. His great detective stories, "The Thin Man," "The Maltese Falcon" and "The Glass Key," rang with authenticity because of it. Now, however, the imitators have so crowded the field that Mr. Hammett is beginning to sound like one of them. The great virtue of the Sam Spade series is that it is still written by the old master, and once in awhile, even sounds like it.

The effectiveness of his dialogue (and the above is a rather bad sample) is heightened by his trick of playing against one another a widely divergent crew of characters.

Besides Mr. Spade, who can still break a man's thumb without effort or remorse, Mr. Hammett recently resuscitated Casper Gutman. Mr. Gutman, you will recall, was the elegant and unscrupulous hunk of blubber who chased the Maltese Falcon halfway around the world in 1931. At the end of that book he was dumped into San Francisco Bay and we were all under the impression that he didn't survive the experience. Well, he did and he's back, still talking his curious 19th century prose. ("And now, sir, if you are so disposed, shall we talk?")

Wilmer, the baby-faced murderer, was not revived for the occasion but Gutman has brought along his brother, an equally furious youngster. There is also a

strange young man who says at one point to Mr. Spade: "At my hotel there is a mildewed character who accuses me of acting without charm."

Says Mr. Spade in return: "You better get out of California before Walt Disney sees you," a decidedly arresting remark to hear on the air.

These odd people were all taken from life, surprising as that may seem. Mr. Hammett in his days as a private detective with the Pinkerton agency mixed with a lot of people whom you and I are not likely to encounter in a lifetime. In his books they had great individual flavor. You never quite knew what they were going to do next. By now, however, they've been re-used as often as a paper clip and are getting a little bent and rusty.

Just the same, if you like detective stories of the hard-boiled school, Sam Spade is your best bet. Mr. Hammett, incidentally, is still interested in ancient art. The Maltese Falcon has disappeared forever, I guess, but this time Gutman and crew are after the Kandy Tooth, which is right out of Buddha's mouth and is presumably even more valuable than the Falcon. When I last listened, they were still looking.

*Clipping from the* New York Herald Tribune *Hammett sent to his wife. Mr. Crosby was mistaken about Hammett's authorship of "The Adventures of Sam Spade" (courtesy of Josephine Hammett).*

Spade and other stories by Dashiell Hammett", two of these editions being published under the 1944 copyright of The American Mercury, Inc. Copies of these two editions will be handed up to the Court as Plaintiff's Exhibits "1" and "1a" hereto.

In utilizing Sam Spade as the central and leading character in these later stories after his successful debut in "The Maltese Falcon" I have been following a custom in detective story writing which is virtually as old as this form of literature itself. This branch of literature is generally regarded as dating from the emergence of the classic Sherlock Holmes stories over a half century ago. "A Study in Scarlet," the first of these stories by the late British author, Sir Arthur Conan Doyle, which recounted the exploits of the fictional detective, Sherlock Holmes, was published in England in 1887.

Some of the better known fictional sleuths who have followed Sherlock Holmes in a career of solving crime as recounted in different stories featuring new adventures of the same sleuth are:

| | |
|---|---|
| Philo Vance | by S. S. Van Dine |
| Perry Mason | by Erle Stanley Gardner |
| Nero Wolfe | by Rex Stout |
| Father Brown | by G. K. Chesterton |
| Hercule Poirot | by Agatha Christie |
| Hanaud | by A. E. W. Mason |
| Ellery Queen | by "Ellery Queen" |
| The Saint | by Leslie Charteris |
| Philip Trent | by E. C. Dentley |
| Max Carrados | by Ernest Bramah |
| Craig Kennedy | by Arthur B. Reeve |
| Charlie Chan | by Earl Der Biggers |

Indeed, I have followed this custom of using the same sleuth or sleuths as the central figure of successive different adventures in other instances besides Sam Spade. The Thin Man characters of "Nora and Nicky Charles" and the "Continental Op" are some of my well known characters who are such examples. They each appear in a number of different adventure stories which have been widely exploited through publications or motion pictures.

My four "Sam Spade" stories have been successful. Apart from republication, readers have inquired and have asked for more. Warner's has already produced three different motion pictures of or based on "The Maltese Falcon," the first and third under that

# HERO
## By Hammett
CBS Now Airs the Adventures of America's Favorite Fiction Detective, Dashiell Hammett's "Sam Spade"

### By
### Delle Hunter

Sunday, 9 p.m.
CBS-KNX

SAM SPADE calls everybody 'sweetheart.' Because it's an old-fashioned word, when it comes from him it becomes just about the most hard-boiled thing he could say.

"Sam frankly does a job for the money he's going to make. He says to a client, 'How much you got on you? Okay—I'll take that, and you pay me the rest when the job is done.'

"Spade is thrifty. He takes the trolley instead of a cab. And he'll put the dime he spends on his expense account for his client to pay.

"Sam Spade doesn't let anybody stick a gun in his ribs and get away with it. He'll smile and talk easy up to that point, but when a gun is pulled on him, he gets tough and the guy with the gun finds a fight on his hands.

"Sam is no superman, not by a long shot. Just because they've hired him as a private eye, his clients aren't necessarily safe. Sam's clients get killed as many times as not.

"The police never like private eyes, and they like Sam Spade least
*(Please Turn to Page 15)*

"SAM SPADE" IS NO SUPERMAN.
His clients get killed as many times as not. The Dashiell Hammett detective hero is ether-acted by Howard Duff.
CBS Photo

*Clippings Hammett sent to his wife. Howard Duff was Sam Spade's radio voice. Like Hammett, Duff was blacklisted for suspected membership in the Communist Party in 1951, causing the radio show to be canceled (courtesy of Josephine Hammett).*

THE 1946 EDGAR ALLAN POE AWARD went to bearded producer William Spier for his work on the "Sam Spade" series. Here star Duff (center) receives praise from Ken Crossen, Regional VP of the Mystery Writers of America, Inc., who awarded Bill Spier. (CBS-KNX photos.)

SAM SPADE is not only one of his listeners' favorites . . . he is the favorite role his portrayer, Howard Duff, plays.

# The Duff Caper

*The Man Who Does "Sam Spade" Has No Hobbies; He Hates Exercise as Such, but Forgets to Be Lazy When He's Doing Something to Help the Other Guy*

## By Jane Pelgram

*Sunday, 9 p.m.*
*CBS-KNX-KSDJ*

THE RUGGED-looking actor who portrays the hard-hitting "Detective Sam Spade" in CBS' Sunday night mystery series is too lazy to be very tough . . . unless he's on one of his crusades.

When Howard Duff isn't sleeping, he's reading. He digs into old and new books and magazines until the early hours, then sleeps as late as he can, cheerfully admitting he'd stay in bed all day if he could get away with it.

A casual meeting with Howard does nothing to create an impression of great energy. He wears very good clothes, but they are donned so casually as to make a regular reader of Esquire squirm. Quiet in speech and manner, Howard usually lounges on the edge of a group, smoking cigarettes and doodling on the nearest tablecloth as he listens to people chatter. But let the conversation turn to actors and things get less casual. Right now Howard has the banners way up for fellow actors.

Young Mr. Duff's own background explains the battleground of his latest crusade. He knows what being an unrecognized radio actor means.

Shortly after graduation from Roosevelt High School in Seattle, Washington, Howard joined the Seattle Repertory Playhouse. There was no salary attached, so Duff worked days as assistant window trimmer at a department store until he was fired for refusing to work nights. His low, poised speaking voice won him a job immediately as staff announcer

THERE'S TROUBLE brewing for some crook when these three key figures, Lurene Tuttle, Bill Spier, and Duff, get their heads together. Lurene plays Secretary Effie Perrine.

Cover for the pressbook and poster for the 1951 movie loosely based on Hammett's character Caspar Gutman. The Fat Man in 1951 weighed 120 pounds less than Sidney Greenstreet did when he made the role of Gutman famous a decade earlier (Collection of Richard Layman).

Advertisement, circa 1948

title in about 1931 and 1941 and the second under the title of "Satan Met a Lady" in about 1936. Also, according to Warner's admission (Freston & Files letter to Regis Radio Corporation, May 13, 1948, Exhibit "2" hereto), a number of broadcasts have been made of dramatizations of "The Maltese Falcon" under the guise of a Warner's license. In fact, as late as December of 1947 the Columbia Broadcasting System, Inc. requested of Warner's a license for broadcasting "The Maltese Falcon", which proposed license Warner's refused to grant.

On May 15, 1946, there being an apparent demand for a radio series featuring further adventures of "Sam Spade," I granted the authorization to E. J. Rosenberg and Larry White for the use in radio and other media of the character "Sam Spade" and of the title "The Adventures of Sam Spade," as per copy of agreement with said parties hereto annexed as Exhibit "3". I have known said E. J. Rosenberg and Larry White for a number of years and know them to be residents of New York City, New York and Huntington, Long Island, New York respectively.

As will be noted the authorization and rights granted under said agreement relate solely and merely to the character "Sam Spade" and to the title containing such name. There is no grant or obligation with respect to any script or story content in which the character "Sam Spade" may be used or to which such title may be applied. In fact, my warranties therein are expressly made inapplicable to the "scripts or substance" of any Sam Spade productions (Par. 6). I have never written, collaborated in the writing of, made suggestions for, approved or disapproved of, nor have I been consulted nor have I requested consultation concerning, the scripts or substance which have been the subject of weekly broadcasts for over two years under the title of "The Adventures of Sam Spade." These scripts and material have been prepared and written by others. Nor have I had any connection with any other phase of the presentation and production of this program other than that I have been referred to by name on each week's program at least twice as the creator of the character "Sam Spade".

Save for one or two possible interruptions, the aforementioned "Adventures of Sam Spade" radio series has been broadcast weekly on Sunday, 8:00 p.m., New York time, since July 12, 1946 over transcontinental radio networks embracing approximately 160 radio stations in various localities including every important city in the nation. It has been regularly originated and broadcast from a radio station in Hollywood, California. Throughout it has been commercially sponsored by Wildroot Company, Inc., a major national advertiser. Since about September 29, 1946 such

weekly broadcasts have been over the Columbia Broadcasting System, Inc. network. Such weekly programs have been produced for such radio presentation by the Regis Radio Corporation.

The latter corporation organized and controlled by the aforementioned E. J. Rosenberg and Larry White, uses the Spade character and title for the above radio series pursuant to the aforementioned agreement for such use. That corporation has regularly paid me the stipulated royalty of $400.00 per broadcast (weekly) pursuant to that agreement.

Each of the weekly broadcasts in the "Adventures of Sam Spade" series is of a half-hour duration and involves with but a few exceptions a dramatization of a new, different and complete adventure or case of Sam Spade. The few exceptions are those programs which have presented a repeat of the same adventure which appeared in a prior week of the series or which have presented the same adventure spread over two successive weekly half-hour installments.

As shown in the accompanying affidavit of E. J. Rosenberg, President of Regis Radio Corporation, the program has been extensively and regularly advertised and promoted since its inception over two years ago. It is one of the most popular mystery programs on the air. In slightly over two years of regular broadcasting it has reached a total audience aggregating tens, if not hundreds of millions of listeners. Obviously such wide exploitation has made the name and character Sam Spade even better known to many millions of people. It can safely be said that there is scarcely a man, woman or child regularly listening to radio who has not thereby become familiar or better acquainted with the name and character Sam Spade. Indeed (as further shown in the above affidavit), when Howard Duff recently made his appearance as an actor in motion pictures, the press and even the defendant's own theatre ads referred to him typically as "radio's Sam Spade" or "Sam Spade of radio."

Until this year the defendant had made no complaint concerning the Sam Spade program. It was not until after the refusal of the defendant late in December of last year to grant a radio license to Columbia Broadcasting System, Inc. for "The Maltese Falcon" and the use instead by Columbia Broadcasting System, Inc. on a "Suspense" program of January 10, 1948 of "The Kandy Tooth," another Sam Spade adventure story previously broadcast in the above Sam Spade series, that the defendant first began to make claims. Defendant's first claim letter to Columbia Broadcasting System, Inc. of January 29, 1948 (Exhibit "4" hereto) shows the defendant's particular pique over the use of the "Kandy Tooth", claiming

*Album covers for sound tracks related to* The Maltese Falcon *(Collection of Richard Layman)*

that to be a *plagiarism* of "The Maltese Falcon" and its film version, and then further expands its claims to include all past Spade character and title uses.

In the later initial letter of May 13, 1948 to Regis Radio Corporation (Exhibit "2" hereto) defendant's attorneys set forth demands solely with reference to the name and character of Sam Spade. On June 1, 1948 I was notified by Regis Radio Corporation of Warner's claims for the use of the character "Sam Spade" and the title "The Adventures of Sam Spade" and advised that pursuant to the warranties in our agreement of May 15, 1946 (Exhibit "3" hereto), Regis would look to me for their prompt elimination.

\* \* \* \* \*

It is evident from the above facts that the present or continuing assertion of defendant's claims to the character Sam Spade and any title featuring that name is and will be highly damaging to me.

Unless this Court declares that I as author am privileged to use such name and character free from let or hindrance on the defendant's part, I will be prevented from engaging in or authorizing similar independent dealings for new Sam Spade stories in the radio, television and motion picture fields. How costly this controversy can be to me and how valuable name and character rights such as those in question are is illustrated by the following typical facts: On January 15, 1934 I executed a contract with Metro-Goldwyn-Mayer Corporation for my story "The Thin Man" (Exhibit "8" hereto). This contract is similar to my instant Warner's contract of June 23, 1930 (Exhibit "A" to Complaint) except that it contains grants even possibly broader in favor of the motion picture purchaser. I received a consideration of $21,000 therefor. Subsequently, on October 23, 1934, I executed another motion picture agreement with the same producer for a sequel to the "Thin Man" story featuring the same central characters (Exhibit "9" hereto). For the latter story I received a consideration of $20,000. Notwithstanding, I later entered into the agreement of February 11, 1937 (Exhibit "10" hereto) with Metro-Goldwyn-Mayer wherein I expressly and specifically sold the right to the use of the "Thin Man" characters and name or title in connection with motion pictures for a consideration of $40,000.

Thus, aside from the loss of royalties and revenue with which I am threatened by the defendant's claims, I will be subjected to the further annoyance and expense of defending against such claims pursuant to the warranties that I would be obliged to give in connection with any of my such dealings for the name or character Sam Spade.

Although aware of the broadcast, the claims, and the litigation between Warner's and myself, the publisher of "The Maltese Falcon," Alfred A. Knopf, Inc., has made no claim with respect to the character Sam Spade or any title containing that name. As shown by the pleadings, the publisher has been named by Warner's as a formal party plaintiff in Warner's California action by reason of Warner's having invoked a clause in our 1930 agreement (Exhibit "A" to Complaint). Thus, insofar as the controversy concerns the rights to the character Sam Spade or any title containing that name, it relates solely to my rights therein *vis-a-vis* Warner's.

I have fully and fairly stated the above facts herein to Leonard Zissu, Esq., my attorney, and as I am informed and verily believe: there is no genuine issue as to any material fact; I as plaintiff am entitled to judgment as a matter of law; there is no merit in the answer of the defendant but on the contrary such answer was interposed merely for the purpose of delaying this action to which there is no defense.

I hereby certify that all papers or parts thereof referred to in my affidavit or attached as exhibits thereto are true copies of such original papers or parts thereof.

Wherefore I respectfully pray that an order be made striking out defendant's answer and granting judgment in my favor for the relief sought in the complaint.

DASHIELL HAMMETT.

(Sworn to by Dashiell Hammett, September 20th, 1948.)

# Selected Publications of *The Maltese Falcon*

*There is no more telling evidence of the enduring influence of a book than its publication history, and the bibliography of* The Maltese Falcon *is impressive. Since its serialization in* Black Mask *magazine began in September 1929, the novel has been continuously in print, except for a brief period in the 1950s when Hammett faced public scrutiny for his political activities. It has been published as a newspaper supplement (in both the United States and Great Britain), as a giveaway to soldiers during World War II, as a cheap paperback, as a collectible book in fancy binding, and as a fine-printing limited edition. It has become as valuable to collectors as it is popular with readers. The trade edition in the earliest dust jacket has been offered for as much as $150,000, though the normal price in 2003 for a fine copy is between $50,000 and $65,000.*

*The* Maltese Falcon *has enjoyed even greater respect in Europe, particularly in France, than in the United States. It has been translated widely and often. Because of the difficulty in searching foreign publications, only a checklist is available here, but this survey identifies seventy-six foreign editions published in thirty countries. These numbers do not include numerous piracies.*

*The worldwide reputation of* The Maltese Falcon *is solid evidence of the novel's literary power. For nearly three quarters of a century it has provided readers all over the world with the complex enjoyment that the best fiction provides. Hammett set out to make literature out of the detective novel. The list that follows suggests the magnitude of his success.*

## Publications in the United States

*The Maltese Falcon* (New York: Knopf, 1930);

*The Maltese Falcon* (New York: Grosset & Dunlap, 1930);

*The Maltese Falcon,* with a new introduction by the author (New York: Modern Library, 1934);

*Dashiell Hammett Omnibus: Red Harvest, The Dain Curse, The Maltese Falcon* (New York: Knopf, 1935);

*Dashiell Hammett Omnibus: Red Harvest, The Dain Curse, The Maltese Falcon* (New York: Grosset & Dunlap, 1937);

*The Maltese Falcon,* abridged version as newspaper supplement, *Philadelphia Record,* 9 October 1938;

*The Complete Dashiell Hammett* (New York: Knopf, 1942)—includes *Red Harvest, The Dain Curse, The Maltese Falcon, The Glass Key,* and *The Thin Man;*

*The Maltese Falcon* (New York: Grosset & Dunlap, 1943);

*Dashiell Hammett's Mystery Omnibus* (Cleveland & New York: World, 1944)—includes *The Maltese Falcon* and *The Glass Key;*

*The Maltese Falcon* (New York: Pocket Books, 1944)—#268;

*The Maltese Falcon* (New York: Knopf, 1945)—"A Black Widow Thriller";

*The Maltese Falcon* (New York: Readers League of America, 1945);

*The Maltese Falcon* (New York: Knopf, 1957);

*The Maltese Falcon* (New York: Permabooks, 1957);

*The Maltese Falcon* (New York: Vintage, 1957);

*The Maltese Falcon* (South Yarmouth, Mass.: J. Curley, 1957)—large-print edition;

*The Maltese Falcon* (San Francisco: National Association for Visually Handicapped, 1959)—large-print edition;

*The Maltese Falcon & The Thin Man* (New York: Vintage, 1964);

*The Novels of Dashiell Hammett* (Garden City, N.Y.: International Collectors Library, 1965)–includes *Red Harvest, The Dain Curse, The Maltese Falcon, The Glass Key,* and *The Thin Man;*

*The Maltese Falcon* (New York: Dell, 1966);

*The Maltese Falcon* (New York: Vintage, 1972);

*The Maltese Falcon* (New York: Amereon, circa 1972);

*Dashiell Hammett: Five Complete Novels* (New York: Wings, 1980)–includes *Red Harvest, The Dain Curse, The Maltese Falcon, The Glass Key,* and *The Thin Man;*

*Dashiell Hammett: Five Complete Novels* (New York: Avenal, 1980)–includes *Red Harvest, The Dain Curse, The Maltese Falcon,* and *The Glass Key;*

*The Maltese Falcon* (Manchester, Mich.: Heron Books, 1982);

*The Maltese Falcon* (South Yarmouth, Mass.: J. Curley, 1982)–large-print edition;

*The Maltese Falcon* (San Francisco: Arion Press, 1983)–limited to 400 copies, printed under the direction of Andrew Hoyem;

*The Maltese Falcon* (San Francisco: North Point, 1984);

*The Maltese Falcon* (Toronto & New York: Bantam, 1985);

*The Maltese Falcon* (New York: Chatham River Press, 1986);

*The Maltese Falcon* (Franklin Center, Pa.: Franklin Library, 1987);

*The Maltese Falcon* (New York: Vintage Crime/Black Lizard, 1992);

*The Maltese Falcon* (New York: Knopf/Otto Penzler Books, 1993)–facsimile of first edition;

*The Maltese Falcon* (Shelton, Conn.: First Edition Library, 1997)–facsimile of first edition;

*The Maltese Falcon,* foreword by Robert Crais (New York: Mystery Guild, 1999);

*The Maltese Falcon, The Thin Man, Red Harvest* (New York: Knopf, 2000);

*The Maltese Falcon* (Pleasantville, N.Y.: ImPress, 2001);

*The Maltese Falcon* (Thorndike, Me.: G. K. Hall / Bath: Chivers, 2001)–large-print edition.

**Comic-Book Adaptation:** *The Maltese Falcon,* illustrated by Rodlow Willard (Philadelphia: David McKay, 1946).

## Translations and Foreign Editions of *The Maltese Falcon*

**Argentina**

*El halcon maltes,* translated by Eduardo Warshawer (Buenos Aires: Ediciones Siglo Veinte, 1946);

*El halcón maltés,* translated by E. F. Lavalle (Buenos Aires: Cía. General Fabril Editora, 1960).

**Basque Provinces**

*Maltako belatza,* translated by Xabier Olarra (Iruñea: Igela, 1997).

**Brazil**

*O falção maltês,* translated by Candida Villalva (Pôrto Alegre: Globo, 1963);

*O falção maltês,* translated by Rubens Figueiredo (São Paulo, S.P.: Companhia das Letras, 2001).

## Bulgaria

*Prokălnata krăv i dr.,* translated by Žečka Georgieva (Sofia: Narodna kultura, 1985)–includes *The Dain Curse, The Maltese Falcon,* and *The Thin Man;*

*Maltüsküart sokol,* translated by Georgieva (Plovdiv: Khermes, 2003).

## Canada

*The Maltese Falcon* (Toronto: Dell, 1966);

*The Maltese Falcon* (Toronto: Bantam, 1985).

## China

*Ma'erta zhi ying,* translated by Lin Shuqin (Taibei Shi: Mai tian chu ban gu fen you xian gong si, 1998);

*Hei yu chao xiao,* translated by Chen Qiumei (Taibei Shi: Yuan liu chu ban shi ye gu fen you xian gong si, 2000).

## Colombia

*El halcón maltes,* translated by Fernando Calleja (Bogotá: Ediciones Nacionales, 1979).

## Croatia

*Malteški sokol,* translated by Mate Maras (Koprivinica: Šarini dućan, 2003).

## Czechoslovakia

*A máltai sólyom,* translated by Edna Lénárt (Bratislava: Tatran, 1967);

*Maltézsky sokol,* translated by Šarlota Barániková (Bratislava: Obzor, 1971).

## Denmark

*Den maltesiske falk* (Copenhagen: Hudibras Forlag, 1946);

*Malteserfalken,* translated by Kurt Kreutzfeld (Copenhagen: Fremad, 1966);

*Ridderfalken,* translated by Kreutzfeld ([Viborg?]: Fremad, 1984).

## Finland

*Maltan haukka,* translated by Jouko Linturi (Helsinki: Tammi, 1955);

*Maltan haukka,* translated by Kalevi Nyytäjä (Porvoo: Werner Söderström, 1974).

## France

*Le Faucon de Malte* (Paris: Gallimard/Le Scarabee d'Or, 1936);

*Le Faucon de Malte,* translated by Henri Robillot (Paris: Gallimard, 1950)–Série noir 58;

*Le faucon maltais,* translated by Janine Hérisson and Robillot (Paris: Gallimard, 1980).

## Germany

*The Maltese Falcon* (Hamburg, Paris, and Bologna: Albatross, 1932);

*Der Malteser Falke,* translated by Peter Fischer (Nürnberg: Nest-Verl., 1952);

*Der Malteser Falke,* translated by Peter Naujack (Stuttgart: Europ. Bildungsgemeinschaft / Gütersloh: Bertelsmann / Berlin & Darmstadt: Dt. Buch-Gemeinschaft, 1976).

## Great Britain

*The Maltese Falcon* (London: Knopf, 1930);

*The Maltese Falcon,* newspaper serialization, *The London Evening Standard,* serialization beginning 3 January 1931;

*The Dashiell Hammett Omnibus: The Thin Man, The Maltese Falcon, The Glass Key, The Dain Curse, Red Harvest & Four Short Stories* (London, Toronto, Melbourne, Sydney & Wellington: Cassell, 1950);

*The Maltese Falcon* (London: Pan, 1951);

*The Maltese Falcon* (London: Hamilton, 1958);

*The Maltese Falcon* (Harmondsworth: Penguin, 1963);

*The Maltese Falcon* (London: Cassell, 1974);

*The Four Great Novels: Red Harvest; The Dain Curse; The Maltese Falcon; The Glass Key* (London: Pan, Picador, 1975);

*The Maltese Falcon* (Bath: Lythway Press, 1977);

*The Maltese Falcon* (London: Book Club Associates, 1977);

*The Maltese Falcon* (London: Inner Circle, 1985);

*The Maltese Falcon* (London: Bison, 1991);

*The Maltese Falcon, The Thin Man, Red Harvest* (London: Everyman, 2000);

*The Maltese Falcon* (London: Folio Society, 2000);

*The Maltese Falcon* (Bath: Camden, 2002)–large-print edition;

*The Maltese Falcon* (London: Orion, 2002).

### Greece
*To geraki tës maltas,* translated by Eleni Kekropoulos (Athens: Nea synora, 1989).

### Hungary
*A máltai sólyom,* translated by Edna Lénárt (Budapest: Európa Kiadó, 1967).

### Israel
*Ha-Nez mi-Malta,* translated by B. Rahel (Tel Aviv: Schocken, 1967).

### Italy
*Il falcone maltese,* translated by Marcella Hannau (Milan: Longanesi, 1953).

### Japan
*Malte no taka,* translated by Ichirô Kinuta (Tokyo: Hayakawa shobô, 1954);

*Malta no taka,* translated by Seijirô Tanaka (Tokyo: Shinchô-sha, 1956);

*Malta no Taka,* translated by Hiroo Murakami (Tokyo: Sogen-sha, 1959);

*Malta no taka,* translated by Ichirô Ishi (Tokyo: Kadokawa shoten, 1963);

*Maruta no taka,* translated by Narumi Shirô (Tokyo: Chikuma shobô, 1970);

*Maruta no taka,* translated by Kameyama Tatsuo (Tokyo: Akane Shobô, 1973);

*Malta no taka,* translated by Fukushima Masami (Tokyo: Bunken shuppan, 1977);

*Malta no taka,* translated by Kodaka Nobumitsu (Tokyo: Kawade shobô shinsha, 1985);

*Ogon no tori renzoku satsujin jiken: Maruta no taka,* translated by Michio Ochi (Tokyo: Popurasha, 1990).

### The Netherlands
*De Maltezer valk,* translated by Thomas Nicolaas (Amsterdam & Antwerp: Archipel, 1972).

**Norway**

*Malteserfalken,* translated by Leif Kristiansen (Oslo: Gyldendals Flaggermusloøker, 1954);

*Malteserfalken,* translated by Olav Angell (Stabekk: Den Norske Bokklubben, 1979).

**Poland**

*Sokól maltański,* translated by Waclaw Niepokólczycki (Warsaw: Iskry, 1963).

**Portugal**

*O falçao de Malta,* translated by Helena Domingos (Lisbon: A Regra do Jogo, 1979).

**Romania**

*Şoimul maltez,* translated by Constantin Popescu (Bucharest: Minerva, 1970).

**Russia**

*Mal'tiiskü sokol,* translated by Iu. Zdorovov (Riga: Poliaris, 1996);

*Mal'tiiskü sokol* (Moscow: AST, 2000);

*Mal'tiiskü sokol* (Moscow: Vagrius, 2001).

**South Korea**

*Malt'a ui mae,* translated by Kim Un-jong (Seoul: Itsin Sojok Kongsa, 1988).

**Spain**

*El halcón del rey,* translated by F. de Casas Gancedo (Madrid: Dédalo, 1933);

*El halcón maltés,* translated by Antonio Rubio (Barcelona: Planeta, 1953);

*El falcó Maltés,* translated by Marga Garcia de Miró (Barcelona: Edicions 62, 1966);

*El halcón maltés,* translated by Fernando Calleja (Madrid: Alianza Editorial, 1969);

*El halcón maltés,* translated by Francisco Páez de la Cadena (Madrid: Editorial Debate, 1992).

**Sweden**

*The Maltese Falcon* (Stockholm: Continental Books / Zephyr, 1943);

*Riddarfalken från Malta,* translated by Olov Jonason (Stockholm: Norsted, 1958).

**Switzerland**

*Le faucon de Malte,* translated by Henri Robillot (Lausanne: Ed. Rencontre, 1965);

*Der Malteser Falke,* translated by Peter Fischer (Wollerau: Krimi Verl, 1967);

*Der Malteser Falke,* translated by Peter Naujack (Zurich: Diogenes-Verlag, 1974).

**Turkey**

*Malta sahini,* translated by Selim Yildirim (Istanbul: Parantez, 1995).

**Ukraine**

*Mal'tijs'kyj sokil,* translated by Nadija Kuznetsovoï-Borovyk (Kiev: Molod', 1972).

**Yugoslavia**

*Malteški sokol,* translated by Anton Mejač (Ljubljana: Državna založba Slovenije, 1983).

# For Further Reading

**Bibliography:**
Layman, Richard. *Dashiell Hammett: A Descriptive Bibliography*. Pittsburgh: University of Pittsburgh Press, 1979.

**Biographies:**
Hammett, Jo. *Dashiell Hammett: A Daughter Remembers*. New York: Carroll & Graf, 2001.

Johnson, Diane. *Dashiell Hammett: A Life*. New York: Random House, 1983.

Layman, Richard. *Shadow Man: The Life of Dashiell Hammett*. New York: Harcourt Brace Jovanovich, 1981.

Mellen, Joan. *Hellman and Hammett: The Legendary Passion of Lillian Hellman and Dashiell Hammett*. New York: HarperCollins, 1996.

Nolan, William F. *Hammett: A Life at the Edge*. New York: Cogdon & Weed, 1983.

Symons, Julian. *Dashiell Hammett*. New York & San Diego: Harcourt Brace Jovanovich, 1985.

**Letters:**
*Selected Letters of Dashiell Hammett*, edited by Richard Layman with Julie Rivett. Washington, D.C.: Counterpoint, 2000.

**References:**
Abrahams, Paul P. "On Re-Reading *The Maltese Falcon*," *Journal of American Culture*, 18, no. 1 (Spring 1995): 97–107.

Abramson, Leslie H. "Two Birds of a Feather: Hammett's and Huston's *The Maltese Falcon*," *Literature/Film Quarterly*, 16, no. 2 (1988): 112–118.

Anobile, Richard J. *The Maltese Falcon*. New York: Universe, 1974.

Babener, Liahna K. "California Babylon: The World of American Detective Fiction," *Clues: A Journal of Detection*, 1, no. 2 (Fall/Winter 1980): 77–89.

Balter, Leon, Stephen F. Bauer, and Winslow Hunt. "The Detective as Myth: *The Maltese Falcon* and Sam Spade," *American Imago: A Psychoanalytic Journal for Culture, Science, and the Arts*, 35 (1978): 275–296.

Bazelon, David T. "Dashiell Hammett's Private Eye," in *The Scene before You: A New Approach to American Culture*, edited by Chandler Brossard. New York & Toronto: Rinehart, 1955, pp. 180–190.

Bentley, Christopher. "Radical Anger: Dashiell Hammett's *Red Harvest*," in *American Crime Fiction: Studies in the Genre*, edited by Brian Docherty. New York: St. Martin's Press, 1998, pp. 54–70.

Blake, Richard A. "The Detective Story: *The Maltese Falcon*," in *Screening America: Reflections on Five Classic Films*. New York: Paulist Press, 1991, pp. 205–239.

Bonfantini, Massimo. "Impare semiotica dal *Falcone Maltese*," in *Letteratura: Percorsi possibili*, edited by Franca Mariani. Ravenna: Longo, 1983, pp. 123–127.

Boon, Kevin. "In Debt to Dashiell: John Huston's Adaptation of *The Maltese Falcon,*" *Creative Screenwriting,* 4, no. 2 (Summer 1997): 99–117.

Bottiggi, William D. "The Importance of 'C-ing' in Earnest: A Comparison of *The Maltese Falcon* and *Chinatown,*" *Armchair Detective: A Quarterly Journal Devoted to the Appreciation of Mystery, Detective, and Suspense Fiction,* 14, no. 1 (Winter 1981): 86–87.

Broich, Ulrich. "Dashiell Hammett's *The Maltese Falcon* und die 'Flitcraft Story,'" in *Exempla: Studien zur Bedeutung und Funktion exemplarischen Erzählens: Schriften zur Literaturwissenschaft,* edited by Bernd Engler and Kurt Müller (Berlin: Duncker & Humblot, 1995).

Burelbach, Frederick M. "Symbolic Naming in *The Maltese Falcon,*" *Literary Onomastics Studies,* 6 (1979): 226–245.

Cahill, Marie. *Hollywood Classics: The Maltese Falcon.* New York: Smithmark, 1991.

Chandler, Raymond. "The Simple Art of Murder," *Atlantic Monthly* (December 1944): 53–59.

Chastain, Thomas. "The Case for the Private Eye," in *The Murder Mystique: Crime Writers on Their Art,* edited by Lucy Freeman. New York: Ungar, 1982, pp. 27–32.

Constantino, Julia. "Sir P. I. and the Hard-Boiled Knight," *Anuario de Letras Modernas,* 6 (1993/1994): 11–27.

Day, Gary. "Investigating the Investigator: Hammett's Continental Op," in *American Crime Fiction: Studies in the Genre,* edited by Docherty. New York: St. Martin's Press, 1998, pp. 39–53.

Delaney, Bill. "Hammett's *The Maltese Falcon,*" *Explicator,* 57, no. 2 (Winter 1999): 103–106.

Delaney. "Hammett's *The Maltese Falcon,*" *Explicator,* 58, no. 4 (Summer 2000): 216–218.

Dooley, Dennis. *Dashiell Hammett.* New York: Ungar, 1984.

Edelman, Lee. "Plasticity, Paternity, Perversity: Freud's Falcon, Huston's Freud," *American Imago: Studies in Psychoanalysis and Culture,* 51, no. 1 (Spring 1994): 69–104.

Edenbaum, Robert I. "The Poetics of the Private-Eye: The Novels of Dashiell Hammett," in *Tough Guy Writers of the Thirties,* edited by David Madden. Carbondale: Southern Illinois University Press, 1968, pp. 80–103.

Fanning, Michael. "*The Maltese Falcon* and *My Alligator,* Academically Considered," *Clues: A Journal of Detection,* 5, no. 1 (Spring/Summer 1984): 147–156.

Fechheimer, David, ed. *City of San Francisco,* special issue (4 November 1975).

Gale, Steven H. "The Maltese Falcon: Melodrama or Film Noir?" *Literature/Film Quarterly,* 24, no. 2 (1996): 145–147.

Gillis, Peter P. "An Anomaly in *The Maltese Falcon,*" *ANQ: A Quarterly Journal of Short Articles, Notes, and Reviews,* 8, no. 3 (Summer 1995): 29–30.

Gores, Joe. *Hammett: A Novel.* New York: Putnam, 1975.

Gould, Karen. "Copies conformes: La Réécriture québecoise d'un polar américain," *Etudes Françaises,* 29, no. 1 (Spring 1993): 25–35.

Greenberg, Harvey R. "*The Maltese Falcon*–Even Paranoids Have Enemies," in *The Movies on Your Mind.* New York: Saturday Review Press/E. P. Dutton, 1975, pp. 53–78.

Gregory, Sinda. *Private Investigations: The Novels of Dashiell Hammett.* Carbondale & Edwardsville: Southern Illinois University Press, 1985.

Grost, Michael E. *A Guide to Classic Mystery and Detection* <http://members.aol.com/mg4273/classics.htm>.

Hagemann, E. R. *A Comprehensive Index to Black Mask, 1920–1951.* Bowling Green, Ohio: Bowling Green State University Popular Press, 1982.

Hall, Jasmine Yong. "Jameson, Genre, and Gumshoes: *The Maltese Falcon* as Inverted Romance," in *The Cunning Craft: Original Essays on Detective Fiction and Contemporary Literary Theory,* edited by June M. Frazer and Ronald G. Walker. Macomb: Western Illinois University Press, 1990, pp. 109–119.

Hall, Ken. "American Hard-Boiled Fiction and *La cabeza de la hidra* by Carlos Fuentes," *University of Dayton Review,* 24, no. 1 (Fall 1996): 83–95.

Hamilton, Cynthia S. *Western and Hard-Boiled Detective Fiction in America: From High Noon to Midnight.* Iowa City: University of Iowa Press, 1987.

Hare, William. "A Noir Morality Play" and "A Detective and His Partner" in *Early Film Noir: Greed, Lust, and Murder Hollywood Style.* Jefferson, N.C., and London: McFarland, 2003, pp. 15–18 and pp. 18–21.

Herron, Don. *The Dashiell Hammett Tour,* Herron's Literary Walks in San Francisco. San Francisco: City Lights Books, 1991.

Huston, John; Luhr, William, ed. *Rutgers Films in Print Series: The Maltese Falcon: John Huston, Director.* Piscataway, N.J.: Rutgers University Press, 1995.

Irwin, John T. "Unless the Threat of Death is Behind Them: Hammett's *The Maltese Falcon,*" *Literary Imagination: The Review of the Association of Literary Scholars and Critics,* 2, no. 3 (Fall 2000): 341–374.

Joly, André. "Pour une analyse systématique des modalités non verbales de la communication," in *Communiquer et traduire: Hommages à Jean Dierickx/ Communicating and Translating: Essays in Honour of Jean Dierickx,* edited by Jean-Pierre van Noppen. Brussels: Eds. de l'Univ. De Bruxelles, 1985, pp. 131–141.

Krajewski, Bruce. "Play Hermeneutics Again, Sam," *Iowa Journal of Literary Studies,* 6 (1985): 22–31.

Krutnik, Frank. *In a Lonely Street, Film Noir, Genre, Masculinity.* London: Routledge, 1991.

Layman, Richard. "Dashiell Hammett," in *Dictionary of Literary Biography: Documentary Series,* volume 6: *Hardboiled Writers,* edited by Matthew J. Bruccoli and Layman. Detroit: Gale Research, 1989.

Layman. *Literary Masterpieces: The Maltese Falcon.* Detroit: Manly/Gale, 2000.

Layman. *Literary Masters: Dashiell Hammett.* Detroit: Manly/Gale, 2000.

Linder, Daniel. "Hammett's *The Maltese Falcon,*" *Explicator,* 60, no. 3 (Spring 2002): 154–157.

Linder. "Hammett's *The Maltese Falcon* and Chandler's *The Big Sleep,*" *Explicator,* 60, no. 1 (Fall 2001): 35–37.

Luhr, William. "Tracking *The Maltese Falcon:* Classical Hollywood Narration and Sam Spade," in *Close Viewings: An Anthology of New Film Criticism,* edited by Peter Lehman. Tallahassee: Florida State University Press, 1990, pp. 7–23.

Macdonald, Ross. "Homage to Dashiell Hammett," in *Self-Portrait: Ceaselessly in the Past.* Santa Barbara: Capra Press, 1981, pp. 109–112.

Mahan, Jeffrey H. "The Hard-Boiled Detective in the Fallen World," *Clues: A Journal of Detection,* 1, no. 2 (Fall/Winter 1980): 90–99.

Malin, Irving. "Focus on *The Maltese Falcon:* The Metaphysical Falcon," in *Tough Guy Writers of the Thirties,* edited by Madden. Carbondale: Southern Illinois University Press, 1968, pp. 104–109.

Maxfield, James F. "La Belle Dame sans merci and the Neurotic Knight: Characterization in *The Maltese Falcon,*" *Literature/Film Quarterly,* 17, no. 4 (1989): 253–260.

McGurl, Mark. "Making 'Literature' of It: Hammett and High Culture," *American Literary History,* 9, no. 4 (Winter 1997): 702–717.

Metress, Christopher. "Dashiell Hammett and the Challenge of New Individualism: Rereading *Red Harvest* and *The Maltese Falcon,*" *Essays in Literature,* 17, no. 2 (Fall 1990): 242–260.

Metress. ed. *The Critical Response to Dashiell Hammett.* Westport, Conn.: Greenwood Press, 1994.

Michaëlis, Bo Tao. "Fra Sam Spade til Sigmund Freud: To film af John Huston," *Litteratur og Samfund,* 41 (May 1986): 102–112.

Miller, R. H. "Hammett's *The Maltese Falcon,*" *Explicator,* 54, no. 3 (Spring 1996): 173–174.

Naremore, James. "John Huston and *The Maltese Falcon,*" *Literature / Film Quarterly,* 1 (1973): 239–249.

Nolan, William F. *The Black Mask Boys: Masters in the Hard-Boiled School of Detective Fiction.* New York: Morrow, 1985.

Nolan. *Dashiell Hammett: A Casebook.* Santa Barbara, Cal.: McNally & Loftin, 1969.

Pattow, Donald J. "Order and Disorder in *Maltese Falcon,*" *Armchair Detective: A Quarterly Journal Devoted to the Appreciation of Mystery, Detective, and Suspense Fiction,* 11 (1978): 171.

Rabinowitz, Peter J. "'How Did You Know He Licked His Lips?': Second Person Knowledge and First Person Power in *The Maltese Falcon,*" in *Understanding Narrative,* edited by James Phelan and Rabinowitz. Columbus: Ohio State University Press, 1994.

Raubicheck, Walter. "Stirring It Up: Dashiell Hammett and the Tradition of the Detective Story," *Armchair Detective,* 20 (Winter 1987): 20–25.

Reeves, W. J. "The Mutation of *The Maltese Falcon,*" *American Notes and Queries,* 18 (1979): 21–24.

Reilly, John M. "Sam Spade Talking," *Clues: A Journal of Detection,* 1, no. 2 (Fall/Winter 1980): 119–125.

Richardson, Carl. "Film Noir in the Studio: The Maltese Falcon," in *Autopsy: An Element of Realism in Film Noir.* Methuen, N.J.: Scarecrow, 1992, pp. 37–75.

Seals, Marc. "Thin Man, Fat Man, Union Man, Thief: Constructions of Depression-Era Masculinities in *Red Harvest* and *The Maltese Falcon,*" *Storytelling: A Critical Journal of Popular Narrative,* 2, no. 1 (2002): 67–79.

Shokoff, James. "The Feminine Ideal in the Masculine Private Eye," *Clues: A Journal of Detection,* 14, no. 2 (Fall/Winter 1993): 51–62.

Shulman, Robert. "Dashiell Hammett's Social Vision," *Centennial Review,* 29, no. 4 (Fall 1985): 400–419.

Smith, Marcus. "*V.* and *The Maltese Falcon:* A Connection," *Pynchon Notes,* 2 (1980): 6.

Thompson, George J. "The Problem of Moral Vision in Dashiell Hammett's Detective Novels: Part IV: *The Maltese Falcon: The Emergence of the Hero,*" 6 (May 1973): 153–156; 6 (August 1973): 213–225; 7 (November 1973): 32–40; 7 (May 1974): 178–192; 7 (August 1974): 270–280; 8 (November 1974): 27–35; 8 (February 1975): 124–130.

Tomasulo, Frank P. "The Maltese Phallcon: The Oedipal Trajectory of Classical Hollywood Cinema," in *Authority and Transgression in Literature and Film,* edited by Bonnie Braendlin and Hans Braendlin. Gainesville: University Press of Florida, 1996.

Wolfe, Peter. *Beams Falling: The Art of Dashiell Hammett.* Bowling Green, Ohio: Bowling Green University Popular Press, 1980.

# Index

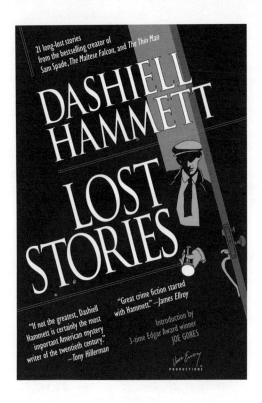

# 21 long-lost stories by the creator of Sam Spade, *The Maltese Falcon,* and *The Thin Man*

A Featured Alternate Selection
of the Book-of-the-Month Club

♠

A Featured Alternate Selection
of the Mystery Guild

Many of Dashiell Hammett's stories—including some of his best—have been out of the reach of anyone but a handful of scholars and collectors—until now.

*Lost Stories* rescues 21 long-lost Hammett stories, all either never published in an anthology or unavailable for decades. Stories range from the first fiction Hammett ever wrote to his last. All stories have been restored to their original versions, replacing often-wholesale cuts with the original text for the first time.

For each story, Hammett researcher Vince Emery tells how Hammett's life shaped the story and how the story affected his life. Emery's comments reveal surprises about Hammett's life not covered in any other book.

To round out this celebration of Hammett, three-time Edgar Award winner Joe Gores has written an introduction describing how Hammett influenced literature, movies, television, and Gores' own life.

"A hugely important book. The volume belongs on the shelf of every detective fiction reader and collector." —Otto Penzler, *New York Sun*

Edited by Vince Emery. 8 illustrations, 38 photographs; 352 pages. Trade hardcover edition, $24.95. ISBN 0-9725898-1-3.

## Deluxe collector's edition

Limited to 195 hand-numbered copies, signed by Joe Gores and Vince Emery, housed in a decorative slipcase, with spine of Saderra leather. Spine and front cover are stamped with genuine gold. Page edges are gilt with genuine gold, $149.95. ISBN 0-9725898-0-5.

www.emerybooks.com

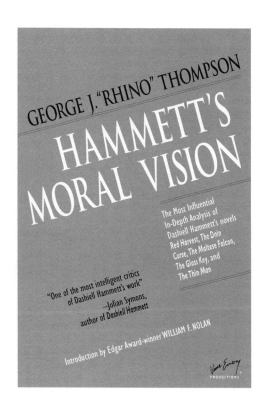

"If you haven't read Thompson, you don't know Hammett."

—*Vince Emery*

*H*ammett's Moral Vision is the single most influential full-length investigation of Dashiell Hammett's novels, even though it has never been available in book form—until now.

First serialized in seven issues of *Armchair Detective* magazine, *Hammett's Moral Vision* has affected almost all subsequent analyses of Hammett's work. But people could read *Hammett's Moral Vision* only by digging up all seven tough-to-find issues of *Armchair Detective*, and only for collector's prices of more than $100 per set.

Now *Hammett's Moral Vision* is available as an affordable book, updated, and with a new introduction by William F. Nolan, the Edgar Award winning author of *Hammett: A Life at the Edge* and *Logan's Run*. In addition, a new chapter by George J. "Rhino" Thompson explains how reading Hammett changed his life, and what he did after writing *Hammett's Moral Vision*.

The heart of the book is Thompson's analysis of five Hammett novels: *Red Harvest*, *The Dain Curse*, *The Maltese Falcon*, *The Glass Key*, and *The Thin Man*. He examines each one in detail, and compares what others have written about the novels with his own insights.

William F. Nolan says *Hammett's Moral Vision* is "incredibly well done, beautifully researched, and displaying tremendous insight into what made Hammett tick as a writer. ... [Thompson's] vision is timeless."

*About the author:* Reading Hammett led George J. "Rhino" Thompson to change careers from university English teacher to police officer. He later became the best-selling author of *Verbal Judo: The Gentle Art of Persuasion*. As president of the Verbal Judo Institute, "Rhino" has trained thousands of police officers in crisis control skills.

Trade hardcover publication date 21 November 2005. $24.95. ISBN 0-9725898-3-X.

# Huston's Black Bird
## by Richard Layman

The statuette used in the 1941 movie of *The Maltese Falcon* is a most curious bird. In *Black Dahlia Avenger* (2003), Steve Hodel claims that the falcon was designed by Jack Warner's friend Fred Sexton, a sculptor who was an accomplice of the Black Dahlia murderer and who was the likely killer of author James Ellroy's mother. Moreover, the identity of the four verifiable copies of the falcon is a matter that would have attracted Caspar Gutman's attention in and of itself. In the novel, Gutman estimates that the Maltese Falcon may be worth $2 million. That is the present insured value of the lead falcon that seems to have been used as a prop in Huston's movie.

Christie's auction house claims the world auction record for a piece of movie memorabilia—the lead statuette of the Maltese Falcon used in Huston's movie (inside front cover). The statuette, given by studio head Jack Warner to actor William Conrad, was sold in New York in December 1994, nine months after Conrad's death, for $398,500 to Ronald Winston, president of jeweler Harry Winston, Inc. The 11½-inch-high statuette is made of lead and weighs 45 pounds. It is marked with the Warner Bros. inventory number WB90066 engraved both on the underside of the base and at the back of the tail feathers.

The Conrad falcon is one of two known-to-be-authentic lead statuettes related to the movie. The other, acquired by the respected collector Dr. Gary Milan in about 1986 and marked with the inventory number WB90065, is on loan to the Warner Bros. Museum (inside back cover). Dr. Milan argues convincingly that his falcon is the one used in the movie. It differs from the Conrad specimen in that the tail feathers are slightly bent. Dr. Milan suspects that a limited number of falcons were cast after the movie was made and given as special mementos to friends of Jack Warner. But only the Milan and the Conrad copies have been located.